THE RISE AND DEMISE OF PAPER MONEY IN IMPERIAL CHINA

The invention of paper currency marked a watershed in global financial history. In this deeply researched study, Richard von Glahn explains why paper money first arose in China rather than any other part of the world – and why it ultimately failed. Although paper money achieved notable success during the Song and Yuan dynasties, it collapsed under the very different principles of political economy adopted by the Ming. In the first English-language examination of the rise and demise of paper money, von Glahn argues that the answer lies in China's unique monetary system and political economy, introducing readers to the eleventh-century origins of paper money in China, the principles of Chinese monetary theory, and China's bronze coin monetary standard and specific forms of fiscal governance. This is not only an essential introduction to Chinese monetary history but a major contribution to global economic history.

RICHARD VON GLAHN is Distinguished Research Professor of History at the University of California, Los Angeles. He is the author of *The Economic History of China from Antiquity to the Nineteenth Century* and co-editor of *The Cambridge Economic History of China.*

THE RISE AND DEMISE OF PAPER MONEY IN IMPERIAL CHINA

Fiscal Innovation, Market Growth, and Monetary Transitions, c. 1000–1500

RICHARD VON GLAHN
University of California, Los Angeles

CAMBRIDGE
UNIVERSITY PRESS

CAMBRIDGE
UNIVERSITY PRESS

Shaftesbury Road, Cambridge CB2 8EA, United Kingdom

One Liberty Plaza, 20th Floor, New York, NY 10006, USA

477 Williamstown Road, Port Melbourne, VIC 3207, Australia

314–321, 3rd Floor, Plot 3, Splendor Forum, Jasola District Centre, New Delhi – 110025, India

Cambridge University Press is part of Cambridge University Press & Assessment, a department of the University of Cambridge.

We share the University's mission to contribute to society through the pursuit of education, learning and research at the highest international levels of excellence.

www.cambridge.org

Information on this title: www.cambridge.org/9781009699488
DOI: 10.1017/9781009699440

When citing this work, please include a reference to the DOI 10.1017/9781009699440

First published 2026

Cover image: Old Folded Paper White Background / pierredesvarre / iStock/ Getty Images

Cover image: Grunge paper, vintage background / All rights belong to Dmitri Smoljannikov / iStock / Getty Images

A catalogue record for this publication is available from the British Library

A Cataloging-in-Publication data record for this book is available from the Library of Congress

ISBN 978-1-009-69948-8 Hardback
ISBN 978-1-009-69945-7 Paperback

CONTENTS

FIGURES

MAPS

TABLES

ACKNOWLEDGMENTS

This book has had an unusually long gestation that has lasted more than twenty years, and I've received advice, criticism, and encouragement from many scholars and students over this time. In the interest of brevity, I will simply single out those who have been especially helpful in the final writing process. I owe special gratitude to Christian Lamouroux, with whom I have collaborated in our work on Song fiscal history. Christian's invitation to be a visiting scholar at the École des Hautes Études en Sciences Sociales (EHESS) in 2017 provided the occasion for many long conversations on Song fiscal and monetary history and the opportunity to present my work at a series of lectures at EHESS and the Paris School of Economics. I am similarly indebted to Nuno Palma and Meng Wu, who arranged for me to join them at the University of Manchester in 2022 as the Hallsworth Visiting Professor, which also afforded opportunities to discuss our mutual interests in Chinese monetary history and to present lectures at Manchester and the University of Oxford (kindly arranged by another of my collaborators, Debin Ma). I also wish to thank Professor He Ping for the invitation to present some of my research at his panel on the history of paper money in China at the XIX World Economic History Congress in Paris in 2022.

Nuno Palma read the entire book manuscript and offered perceptive queries and advice, although I haven't been able to incorporate all of his suggestions. Justin Rietz read the first half of the book draft, likewise from the perspective of an economist, and his critique was very helpful to my thinking, even if we do not always agree. Paul Smith and Charles Hartman, fellow Song historians, read the Song chapters, which are much improved thanks to their suggestions and corrections. I owe all of the above, and two anonymous readers for the press, much gratitude for their time, energy, and expertise. And I am grateful once again to Dr. Lucy Rhymer of Cambridge University Press and her colleagues for deftly shepherding this project into print.

An earlier version of Chapter 7 originally appeared as "Re-examining the Authenticity of Song Paper Money Specimens" in the *Journal of Song–Yuan Studies* 36 (2006): 79–106. Major portions of Chapter 8 were published in my article "Monies of Account and Monetary Transition in China, Twelfth to Fourteenth Centuries" in the *Journal of the Economic and Social History of the Orient* 53.3 (2010): 463–505. I am grateful to the journal editors for permission to republish these materials.

Introduction

It was Marco Polo who, after having resided in China during the final two decades of the reign of Khubilai Khan (r. 1260–1294), first reported to an incredulous European audience that the subjects of the Mongol ruler conducted trade exclusively using money made of tree bark:

> This paper currency is circulated in every part of the Great Khan's dominions; nor dares any person, at the peril of his life, refuse to accept it in payment. All of his subjects receive it without hesitation, because, wherever their business may call them, they can dispose of it again in the purchase of merchandise they may require; such as pearls, jewels, gold, or silver. With it, in short, every article may be procured. . . . All his Majesty's armies are paid with this currency, which is to them of the same value as if it were gold or silver. Upon these grounds, it may certainly be affirmed that the Great Khan has a more extensive command of treasure than any other sovereign in the universe.[1]

Polo's testimony about the ubiquity of paper money (*monoie de charte*) in the Mongol Empire was one of the main reasons why many contemporary European readers dismissed him as an outlandish fabulist (Figure I.1). Polo's audience also was offended by his repeated boasts, including here, that the heathen khan was the greatest monarch in the world, superior to any Christian king. Polo's account of Khubilai's "art of producing money," which he likened to "the secret of the alchemists," revealed that paper currency was as much an instrument of royal self-aggrandizement as a convenience for the benefit of the people.

Polo's depiction of the Great Khan's paper money deviated markedly from the conception of money in early modern Europe as concisely distilled by Bernardo Davanzati in his oration "A Discourse upon Coins," delivered to the Florentine Academy in 1588. Davanzati, a rich merchant whose fortune allowed him to pursue a life of scholarship, set forth the proposition that

[1] Marco Polo, *The Travels of Marco Polo [The Venetian]* (New York: Liveright, 1926), pp. 160–61.

Figure I.1 The Great Khan's money exchange. Merchants exchange coin for paper money (in boxes) under the watchful eye of the Mongol ruler Khubilai Khan.
Source: *Livre des merveilles du monde* (Paris, 1410 ms.; Bibliothèque nationale de France, Ms. fr. 2810, fol. 45).

"*Money* therefore is Gold, Silver, or Copper coin'd by publick Authority at pleasure, and by the Consent of Nations made the Price and Measure of things, to contract them the more easily."[2] Davanzati firmly hewed to the principle that money derives its value from its metallic content (what became known as the *metallist* doctrine); only coins made from gold and silver (and to a limited degree copper) could serve as money. While the prince through coinage performs a necessary role in establishing a consistent standard, Davanzati, following in the footsteps of the 14th-century scholastic philosopher Nicole Oresme, denied the ruler's right to alter the substance of his money.[3] The purpose of money is to serve the needs of commerce within

[2] Bernardo Davanzati, *A Discourse upon Coins*, (trans.) John Toland (London: Awnsham and John Churchil, 1696), p. 12.

[3] André Lapidus, "Metal, Money, and the Prince: John Buridan and Nicholas Oresme After Thomas Aquinas," *History of Political Economy* 29.1 (1997): 21–53; Adam Woodhouse, "'Who Owns the Money?' Currency, Property, and Popular Sovereignty in Nicole Oresme's *De moneta*," *Speculum* 92.1 (2017): 85–116. For Oresme's influence on subsequent monetary thought, see Jotham Parsons, "Money and Sovereignty in Early Modern France," *Journal of the History of Ideas* 62.1 (2001): 59–79. On the triumph of metallism in European discourse about money in the 16th–17th centuries, see Jérôme Blanc and Ludovic Desmedt, "Debating Sound Money in Early Modern Europe: From Dualist to Metallic Monetary Systems," in Renate Pieper, Claudia de Lozanne Jefferies, and Markus

and beyond the polity, not to enrich the ruler. The form of coin is incidental to its value, but the prince must faithfully abide by the true substantive value of its metal and not debase his coin or alter its value by fiat:

> The Law requires Money to be coin'd, yet whether this or that way, that is, round or square, broad or narrow, more or less pure, with this or that Stamp, under one Denomination or another, these are all Accidents, and left entirely to the Magistrate's Discretion. It suffices that he touch not the Substance of it, which he has no Power to do: that is, he may coin no Money but of the three known Metals, nor set a false Price upon the Pieces.[4]

Only precious metals whose value is universally recognized can serve the needs of trade beyond the ruler's realm, and the ultimate purpose of money is to enable trade (what Joseph Schumpeter dubbed the *catallactic* theory of money, from the Greek word for "exchange").[5] After likening money to blood that nourishes the body (a "second blood"), Davanzati asserts that:

> Money . . . does, by circulating out of the richer Purses into the poorer, furnish all the Nation, being laid out upon those things whereof there is a continual Consumption for the Necessities of Life. From the poorer it returns again into the richer Purses; and thus circulating without Intermission, it preserves alive the *Civil Body* of the Common-wealth.[6]

Polo's declaration that Khubilai Khan utilized his paper money to amass the greatest treasure in the world would be anathema to Davanzati, and to European economic philosophy as a whole.[7]

The Mongols were not the first Chinese regime to use paper money. Government-issued paper money was inaugurated by the Song dynasty (960–1276) in the early 11th century. Initially restricted to the western region of Sichuan, a distinct economic and monetary circuit, paper currencies eventually were enacted in most of the rest of the empire in the 12th–13th centuries and also adopted by the rival Jurchen Jin regime that occupied North China for a century (1127–1234) before the onset of the Mongol conquests. Thus,

Denzel (eds.), *Mining, Money and Markets in the Early Modern Atlantic: Digital Approaches and New Perspectives* (Cham, Switzerland: Springer Nature, 2019), pp. 29–61.

4 Davanzati, *Discourse upon Coins*, p. 14.

5 Joseph A. Schumpeter, *History of Economic Analysis* (New York: Oxford University Press, 1954), p. 63. These neo-Aristotelian principles also informed the genesis of political economy and monetary theory in early-17th-century England. See Carl Wennerlind, *Casualties of Credit: The English Financial Revolution, 1620–1720* (Cambridge, MA: Harvard University Press, 2011), pp. 17–43.

6 Davanzati, *Discourse upon Coins*, p. 18.

7 Ironically, Davanzati invoked the case of China not to refer to paper money, which had fallen into disuse nearly two centuries before, but rather to applaud its current money, silver bullion, which by virtue of being uncoined was free from the kind of manipulation by rulers that he deeply deplored. Davanzati, *Discourse upon Coins*, p. 26.

paper money had become the monetary standard of the Chinese ecumene well before Khubilai Khan founded his Yuan dynasty (1271–1368). The Song period witnessed dramatic growth in the market economy, and paper money has long been perceived as emblematic of the precocity of the Chinese economy during the Song "medieval economic revolution."[8] Yet the precise role of paper money and its effects on economic activity in the Song have not received attention commensurate with its significance as the first viable paper currency system in world history.[9] The invention and evolution of paper money in China must be explained in terms of the unique features of the Chinese monetary system, and ultimately in the context of the distinctive institutional foundations of Chinese political economy.

Metallic coinage first arose virtually simultaneously – yet independently – in the 7th–6th centuries BCE in the Mediterranean and China, and perhaps in India as well.[10] From the founding of the first unified empire of Qin in 221

[8] The idea of a Song "economic revolution" was popularized by Mark Elvin, *The Pattern of the Chinese Past* (Stanford, CA: Stanford University Press, 1973), which has had enormous impact on global economic history scholarship in the West. Elvin discusses paper money on pp. 155–61.

[9] For a concise overview of the forms and evolution of paper money in the Song–Yuan period, see Richard von Glahn, "The Origins of Paper Money in China," in William N. Goetzmann and K. Geert Rouwenhorst (eds.), *Origins of Value: The Financial Innovations That Created Modern Capital Markets* (New York: Oxford University Press, 2005), pp. 65–89. The pioneering research on Song paper money was conducted by Japanese scholars, notably Katō Shigeshi, Hino Kaisaburō, and Sogabe Shizuo, in the 1930–1940s. Recent comprehensive studies in Japanese include Takahashi Hiroomi 高橋弘臣, *Genchō kahei seisaku seiritsu katei no kenkyū* 元朝貨幣政策成立過程の研究 (Tokyo: Tōyō shoin, 2000) – which, despite its title, devotes considerable attention to the paper currency systems of the Song and Jin – and, on Chinese monetary history generally, Miyazawa Tomoyuki 宮澤知之, *Chūgoku zenkindai no kahei to zaisei* 中国前近代の貨幣と財政 (Kyoto: Kyoto daigaku gakujutsu shuppankai, 2023). The most important Chinese studies of Song monetary history, including the role of paper money, are Gao Congming 高聡明, *Songdai huobi yu huobi liutong yanjiu* 宋代货币与货币流通研究 (Baoding: Hebei daxue chubanshe, 1999); Wang Shengduo 汪圣铎, *Liang Song huobi shi* 两宋货币史 (Beijing: Shehui kexue wenxian chubanshe, 2003); and Wang Wencheng 王文成, Zhao Xiaoping 赵小平, Liu Xin 刘欣, and Ding Qiong 丁琼, *Song Jin Yuan Ming shiqi de shichang fazhan yu huobi liutong yanjiu* 宋金元明时期的市场发展与货币流通研究 (Beijing: Zhongguo shehui kexue chubanshe, 2021). See also Liu Sen 刘森, *Song Jin zhibi shi* 宋金纸币史 (Beijing: Zhongguo jinrong chubanshe, 1993), which is primarily an institutional history and offers little in the way of economic analysis. Indispensable for any study of Chinese monetary history is Peng Xinwei's seminal work: Peng Xinwei 彭信威, *Zhongguo huobi shi* 中國貨幣史. 2nd ed. (Shanghai: Shanghai renmin chubanshe, 1965). Peng's work has been translated by Edward H. Kaplan: Peng Xinwei, *A Monetary History of China*, (trans.) Edward H. Kaplan (Bellingham: Western Washington State University Press, 1994).

[10] Most Indian numismatists argue for the early advent of coinage in India in the 7th–6th centuries BCE, but definitive archaeological evidence is lacking. See Deme Raja Reddy, "The Emergence and Spread of Coins in Ancient India," in Peter Bernholz and Roland

BCE, "money" in China invariably referred to state-issued, low-value bronze coin (both rendered as *qian* 錢). Before the Qin unification, from the 6th to the 3rd centuries BCE, a great variety of bronze currencies (mostly in the shape of miniature knives and two-pronged spades rather than round coins) had proliferated. Many of these currencies were issued by royal governments, but many more were issued by local cities and clearly intended to serve as a means of market exchange. In the 4th century BCE, the Qin state created a unique round bronze coin designated as Banliang (or "half-ounce," nominally 8 g). The Banliang coin was perforated by a square hole, which made it convenient to string the low-value coins together into larger units. During its brief existence, however, the Qin Empire (221–206 BCE) was unable to establish its Banliang coin as a uniform currency standard. Despite its reputation for severe and uncompromising laws, the Qin state tolerated deviations from its monetary standard and instructed its officials to accept heterogeneous coins in payment. In the early years of the Han dynasty (202 BCE–220 CE), a wide variety of bronze currencies remained in circulation. Although the Han, like the Qin, issued coins in a single denomination designated by weight, the actual weights varied over time. The early Han rulers repeatedly adjusted the weight of their coins, but from 112 BCE the government established a uniform weight (*wuzhu* 五銖, or 3.35 g) for the issue of a new eponymous Wuzhu coin that remained the official standard for the Han and its successor regimes down to the 7th century.

Under the empires, bronze coin became a principal instrument of revenue collection. The Han government collected capitation taxes as well as a variety of commercial and consumption taxes in coin, which constituted nearly half of total state income (the rest mostly paid in grain and fodder) in the 1st century BCE. Although it remains unclear whether the Qin state imposed taxes in coin, it assessed legal fines to be paid in coin and also made loans in coin to its subjects (private lending was forbidden under Qin law).

Ample evidence exists for the use of coin in market transactions before and after the establishment of the unified empire. Still, according to Walter Scheidel's calculation, the Han economy remained considerably less monetized than the Roman Empire. The per capita money supply of Han China in the 1st century BCE was roughly half the level of the Roman Empire in its heyday. Money figured more significantly as a means of state payment in Han China, whereas a larger portion of the money stock remained available for trade and private savings in the Roman world. State payments consumed 30 percent or more of the total amount of coin in circulation in

Vaubel (eds.), *Explaining Monetary and Financial Innovation: A Historical Analysis* (Cham, Switzerland: Springer International Publishing, 2014), pp. 53–77.

Han China, in contrast to probably less than 10 percent in the case of Rome.[11] Of course, the composition of the Han money supply wholly differed from that of Rome. Coin in circulation in the Roman Empire c. 160 CE consisted (in value) of approximately 60 percent gold coins, 30–35 percent silver coins, and 5–10 percent bronze coins, while the Han money supply was comprised almost entirely of low-value bronze coins.[12]

In contrast to Rome, where only the oligarchic senatorial elite and affluent citizens could afford to accumulate gold coins, the circulation of money penetrated more deeply into the lower strata of Han society.[13] Prices, wages, and debts were all calculated in coin, and it was routine practice to describe great family fortunes in terms of tens (or hundreds) of millions of coins. But, already in the late Han period (1st–2nd centuries CE), the mounting costs of coinage sharply curtailed mint output. The late Han state largely substituted silk cloth in lieu of coin in tax collection and disbursements. After the fall of the Han Empire in 220 CE and its division into rival regional regimes, coin largely ceased to circulate in the heartland of North China. From 317, a relatively stable division of the Chinese ecumene into foreign-ruled northern regimes and a series of short-lived Chinese dynasties in the south emerged. The revenue systems devised by northern rulers assessed taxes in grain, cloth, labor, and military service, entirely omitting coin. The principal features of this tax system were retained by the Sui (581–618) dynasty, which reestablished a unified empire in 589, and its successor, Tang (618–907). Despite the political instability and military weakness of the southern dynasties, during the period of disunion, South China – especially the capital region in the Yangzi Delta (conventionally designated Jiangnan) – experienced dynamic economic growth. Jiangnan remained highly monetized, but the short-lived southern dynasties were unable to maintain a durable monetary standard. Instead, a heterogeneous array of coins – including Han Wuzhu coins, newly minted (but lighter) coins issued by the current ruling houses, and a plethora of private coins – circulated concurrently.

Following the Sui–Tang reunification, the market economy underwent steady growth, especially in the south. Although the Tang supplanted the

[11] Walter Scheidel, "The Monetary Systems of the Han and Roman Empires," in Walter Scheidel (ed.), *Rome and China: Comparative Perspectives on Ancient Empires* (New York: Oxford University Press, 2009), p. 204.

[12] For the Roman data, see Scheidel, "Monetary Systems," pp. 177–78.

[13] Gold coins remained almost entirely in the hands of the wealthy elites of the Roman Empire. Silver coins achieved wide distribution (geographic and social) through trade and army payments, but the production and circulation of bronze currencies were highly localized. See Sitta von Reden, *Money in Classical Antiquity* (Cambridge: Cambridge University Press, 2010), pp. 86–91; Constantina Katsari, *The Roman Monetary System: The Eastern Provinces from the First to the Third Century AD* (Cambridge: Cambridge University Press, 2011), pp. 167–78, 207–8.

Wuzhu coinage with a new standard currency (the Kaiyuan tongbao coin, first issued in 621), demand for coin greatly exceeded the limited supply Tang mints could provide. Silk continued to prevail over coin in the Tang fiscal system. The Tang government created a new revenue system in 780 that, for the first time since the Han dynasty, levied substantial taxes in coin, but chronic shortages compelled the state to commute most of the coin assessments to payments in silk and other cloths.

At this same time, from the 9th century onward the market economy in China experienced dramatic growth, which as mentioned above has often been described as a "medieval economic revolution." Rapid expansion of wet-rice farming (and food surpluses), the development of commercial agriculture (tea, fiber crops, oil seeds, sugar, and timber), technological innovations in iron metallurgy, porcelain manufacture, shipbuilding, silk-weaving, and printing, and the growth of maritime foreign trade spurred the formation of market networks on local, regional, and international levels. After the Tang dynasty fell in 907 and the Chinese ecumene was divided into roughly ten regional kingdoms, rulers waged monetary warfare by issuing debased currencies (using iron and lead coins as well as bronze alloy coins) to discourage the export of coin. Upon restoring a unified empire in 960, the founders of the Song dynasty made concerted efforts to restore a unified monetary system and increase the money supply. Mint output during the Northern Song era (960–1127) rose to the highest levels in Chinese imperial history. Yet demand continued to outstrip supply, and the Song was repeatedly plagued by shortages, dubbed "coin famines" by contemporary observers. Nor was the Song able to fully reunify its monetary system. The Song retained the iron currency system established in the 10th century by a regional regime in the western region of Sichuan and often resorted to issuing iron coin currencies in the northern frontier provinces, which bordered the hostile steppe kingdoms of Liao and Xia. At the same time, the Song exacerbated the strain on the money supply by steadily increasing the proportion of revenues levied on trade and consumption and paid in money, which rose from 48 percent of total revenues in 977 to a peak level of 81 percent in 1077. The state's difficulty in supplying sufficient coin to satisfy the growing public and private demand intensified in the Southern Song period (1127–1276), by which time the main copper mines had been exhausted and mint output fell to only a small fraction of the levels achieved in the 11th century. Demand for media of exchange as well as means of state payment compelled the Song state to experiment with alternative currencies, including the creation of paper money. By the end of the 12th century, state-issued paper currencies circulated in nearly all parts of the Song Empire.

As we can see even from this brief survey, the Chinese monetary system diverged markedly from other parts of the world. The spread of coinage in the western half of Eurasia was closely linked to Greek institutions and culture, and Greek silver coins were imitated in Achaemenid Persia, Carthage, Egypt, and later by the Roman and Islamic empires. Alexander the Great's conquests disseminated his gold and silver currencies throughout a vast territory from the Mediterranean to the farthest reaches of the Persian ecumene. Alexander's gold stater became the international currency of the Hellenistic empires, inaugurating a pattern in which international trade was conducted in gold coin while silver coins were reserved for domestic circulation.[14] Although Alexandrine currencies lost their privileged status in the 2nd century BCE, gold regained ascendancy under the Roman Empire, especially after Constantine introduced the gold solidus in the early 4th century CE. Following the fall of Rome, coinage, notably royal coinage, atrophied in the empire's western provinces for several centuries. But the gold solidus coin minted by the Byzantine emperors (colloquially known as bezants) prevailed as the common currency of international trade ("the dollar of the middle ages," as Robert Lopez put it) in Western Europe as well as the Mediterranean world.[15] Coinage in the form of silver pennies was revived by local rulers in Western Europe in the 7th century and subsequently by the Carolingian monarchs. Islamic coinage, which derived from Roman and Sasanid precedents, likewise combined gold coins (dinars) that were largely reserved for elite consumption and international trade with silver coins (dirhams) that circulated as the main form of market money throughout the Muslim domains and beyond.[16]

In imperial China, however, rulers never issued gold or silver coins (the first official silver coins, modeled after Mexican Republican dollars, were introduced only in 1889). Precious metals were too scarce to be amenable to the sovereign control of money on which Chinese monetary theory was premised, as we will see. Instead, bronze coin remained the staple currency of the Chinese empire. Bronze coin was an encumbrance to long-distance trade, given the inconvenience of transporting large quantities of bulky, low-value coins. The high transaction costs entailed by China's standard coins, iron as

14 Alain Bresson, *The Making of the Ancient Greek Economy: Institutions, Markets, and Growth in the City States* (Princeton, NJ: Princeton University Press, 2016), p. 273.

15 Robert S. Lopez, "The Dollar of the Middle Ages," *Journal of Economic History* 11.3 (1951): 209–34.

16 This brief summary necessarily simplifies far more complicated stories. For the complex terrain of coinage and money use in medieval Western Europe, see Rory Naismith, *Making Money in the Early Middle Ages* (Princeton, NJ: Princeton University Press, 2023); Peter Spufford, *Money and Its Use in Medieval Europe* (Cambridge: Cambridge University Press, 1988). Unfortunately, there are no comparably comprehensive studies of money in the age of the Islamic empires. For a brief synopsis, see Stefan Heidemann, "Numismatics," in Chase F. Robinson (ed.), *The New Cambridge History of Islam*, vol. 1: *The Formation of the Islamic World, Sixth to Eleventh Centuries* (Cambridge: Cambridge University Press, 2010), pp. 648–63.

well as bronze, were one causal factor that spurred the adoption of paper currency. Yet, given their low value, bronze coins generally were deemed fungible and accepted without discriminating among coins of greater or lesser metallic content.[17] Thus the value of bronze coins was measured by count (tale), in contrast to gold and silver coins that typically were treated as bullion and valued according to their specific weight and fineness, as Davanzati insisted they should be.

Since bronze coins circulated by tale, they acquired a fiduciary value independent of their intrinsic metallic content. In the Tang–Song period, the fiduciary nature of Chinese coin was reinforced by the prevalence of "short string" (*duanmo* 短陌) accounting units in both public payments and private transactions. At this time, coins generally circulated in "strings" (i.e., coins strung together in units) known as *mo* 陌, which denoted 100 coins. But the *mo* string often contained fewer than 100 coins. In the late Tang, market exchange chiefly was conducted based on an 80-coin *mo* unit, and in 977 the Song government established an "official *mo*" (*shengmo* 省陌) standard of 77 coins per string for fiscal payments and expenditures. Market rates generally were lower: in the capital of Kaifeng, a 75-coin *mo* standard was most common, although the rates varied among different groups of tradesmen: 74 coins for gold- and silversmiths, 72 coins for meat, fish, and vegetable sellers, and as low as 56 coins for scribes.[18] The proliferation of "short string" units of account not only reflected the scarcity of coin relative to demand but also attested to the nominal value of coins used in monetary transactions. The fiduciary character of Chinese bronze coin also facilitated acceptance of fiat paper currency, whose value derived solely from the ruler's decree.[19]

Chinese rulers enjoyed a unique degree of monetary sovereignty. Throughout its long history the Chinese empire continually confronted formidable military challenges from steppe nomad polities, and at times the Chinese succumbed to foreign conquest. But the steppe polities lacked the infrastructural capacity and technical resources to sustain coinage except on the most limited scale. The supply of coined money in China was wholly

[17] This was the general rule, but at times – especially when counterfeiting proliferated – bronze coins too were subject to discrimination and rejection.

[18] On the practice of "short strings," see Miyazawa Tomoyuki 宮澤知之, *Sōdai Chūgoku no kokka to keizai* 宋代中國の国家と経済 (Tokyo: Sōbunsha, 1998), pp. 281–324; He Ping 何平 and Lin Lin 林琳, "Zhongguo gudai tongzhubi liutong lingyu 'duanmo' xianxiang de qiyuan jiqi xingzhi yanjiu" 中国古代铜铸币流通领域'短陌'现象的起源及其性质研究, *Zhongguo jingji shi yanjiu* 中国经济史研究 2013.1: 10–22.

[19] Throughout this book, I distinguish between fiduciary money, whose value is commonly accepted by money users, and fiat money, whose value is imposed by the ruling authority's decree. Fiduciary money is based on trust, fiat money on coercion.

endogenous.[20] Although gold and silver bullion flowed across political borders, Chinese bronze coin had no rival as a monetary medium. Amid the massive increase in mint output during the Northern Song period, Chinese coin became the international currency of eastern Eurasia and was adopted as current money by its steppe adversaries, Japan, and across maritime Southeast Asia.[21] In contrast, the political fragmentation of medieval Europe constrained monetary sovereignty. Although European rulers could exercise considerable power over domestic money (mostly silver pennies), debasing their metallic content or crying up their nominal value as they saw fit, they could not tamper with gold coin: any diminution of the weight or purity of gold coins would unleash an outflow of gold to other regions that abided by the prevailing standard. To be sure, there were limits to Chinese rulers' arbitrary authority over money; radical debasement or revaluation of bronze coin would encourage counterfeiting, which in most cases effectively checked monetary manipulation. In addition, the higher value of Chinese coin abroad induced a drain of coin overseas beginning in the early Southern Song period.[22]

Another key feature – although by no means a unique one – of the Chinese monetary system beginning with the commercial expansion of the Song dynasty was the presence of multiple currencies, including bronze and iron coins, paper currencies, and for some purposes silver, in concurrent circulation. Akinobu Kuroda has drawn attention to the "asymmetry" of monetary media in the premodern world, that is to say, "the difficulty of harmonizing heterogeneous demands for money and uneven supplies of currency."[23] Examining the variation in the spatial range of money use in late imperial

20 Silver drachm coins minted by the Persian Sasanid Empire (224–651) served (along with bolts of silk) as the common trading currency along the Silk Road as far east as Turfan, where Sasanid coins remained the principal commercial money even after the establishment of Tang suzerainty over Turfan in 640, although they disappeared c. 700. See Helen Wang, *Money on the Silk Road: The Evidence from Eastern Central Asia to c. AD 800* (London: British Museum Press, 2004), pp. 34–36, 78–85, 88–91. Yet even during the Tang period, when the presence of foreign merchants in China reached its zenith, no foreign currencies were allowed in domestic exchange.

21 Inoue Masao 井上正夫, *Higashi Ajia kokusai tsūka to chūsei Nihon: Sōsen to kawase kara mita keizai shi* 東アジア国際通貨と中世日本：宋銭と為替からみた経済史 (Nagoya: Nagoya daigaku shuppankai, 2022).

22 Richard von Glahn, "The Ningbo–Hakata Merchant Network and the Reorientation of East Asian Maritime Trade, 1150–1300," *Harvard Journal of Asiatic Studies* 74.2 (2014): 251–81; Richard von Glahn, "Chinese Coin and Changes in Monetary Preferences in Maritime East Asia in the 15th–16th Centuries," *Journal of the Economic and Social History of the Orient* 57.5 (2014): 629–68.

23 Akinobu Kuroda, "Concurrent but Non-Integrable Currency Circuits: Complementary Relationships Among Monies in Modern China and Other Regions," *Financial History Review* 15.1 (2008): 18. See also Kuroda Akinobu 黒田明伸, *Kahei shisutemu no sekaishi: "Hitaishōsei" o yomu* 貨幣システムの世界史:《非対称性》をよむ (Tokyo: Iwanami shoten, 2003).

China, Kuroda contrasts the monetary needs of local markets – driven by highly seasonal demand for currency at harvest and tax collection times – with long-distance merchants' needs for much more liquid monetary media. Bronze coin tended to disperse and settle in pools in local markets, remaining idle ("stagnant" is Kuroda's term) most of the time. Silver instead was mobile, flowing through higher-level currency circuits, and rarely settling in local markets. Yet silver too was subject to strong regional preferences, as can be seen in the dozens of distinct regional and local silver standards that existed in 18th-century China. This asymmetry in money use was broadly true across the premodern world. The difficulty of establishing a single monetary standard proceeded from the imperfect fit between bottom-up demand, which generated endogenous means of exchange, and the state's fiscal needs, which required enforcement of officially mandated means of payment. Despite its sovereign powers, it was not easy for the state to establish a universally accepted means of exchange. Consequently, the divergent needs of proximate and distant transactions as well as the fiscal priorities of the state fostered a plurality of monies in concurrent circulation.[24] In the case of the Song, the imperial state adapted to this reality by collecting revenues in a variety of monetary media. As we shall see, the tax regime also was a powerful tool for enhancing popular confidence in the value of paper currency.

In recent years, the study of monetary history has undergone a fundamental transformation that has brought money to the center of scholarship on economic history. Underlying the recent developments in monetary history are significant changes in the understanding of how money, monetary policy, and fiscal institutions have shaped the course of economic development from antiquity to modern times. The question of the nature of money itself has been subject to profound rethinking. No longer relegated to the margins of economic analysis, how money is made, by whom, and for what purposes now are recognized as vitally important elements in the construction and governance of human societies. Throughout China's long imperial history, statesmen and scholars recognized the crucial link between sovereign authority and the power to make money. But this link has been obscured in mainstream economic theory.

In orthodox neoclassical economic theory, money serves merely as a *numéraire*, a unit of account, to facilitate transactions in "the real economy," the production and exchange of goods and services. Orthodox theory, in a tradition dating back to Aristotle, focuses on money as a medium of exchange. In the standard narrative, espoused by Adam Smith and canonized in mainstream economics, money originated as a more efficient means to exchange

[24] Akinobu Kuroda, *A Global History of Money* (London: Routledge, 2020).

goods than cumbersome barter.[25] Following in the footsteps of John Locke, Smith argued for the ontological priority of property as the foundation of human society. Not only property, but markets and media of exchange also existed prior to the rise of government. In the opening pages of *The Wealth of Nations*, Smith famously defined human nature in terms of "the propensity to truck, barter and exchange one thing for another," which "is common to all men, and to be found in no other race of animals."[26] This predilection for exchange was driven by the self-interest of individuals. No one invented money; it emerged spontaneously from private transactions. Money itself was a commodity (possessing some intrinsic value) mutually agreed upon to serve as a measure to calculate the value of all other commodities (expressed as prices). For much of human history, money took the form of coins, and in more recent times symbolic representations of coin in the form of bills, and in the present day bits of electronic data disembodied from any material form. The history of money typically has been framed within the evolution of financial institutions. Economists commonly depict the progression from commodity monies to metallic coins to paper bills as part of the march of technological innovations in finance – from accounting systems and contracts to codified laws, business corporations, and banks – that reduced transaction costs, facilitated the accumulation of wealth, and allocated capital for investment in trade and production.[27]

But anthropologists, historians, and even some dissident economists have come to question the validity of this narrative, instead arguing that money is an independent economic force whose creation, circulation, and consumption have significant effects on the operations of the rest of the economy. An alternative explanation of the nature of money locates its origins not in barter or market exchange but rather in accounting systems for expressing debts, especially debts owed to political authorities. David Graeber has argued that the "standard account of monetary history is precisely backwards. We did not begin with barter, discover money, and then eventually develop credit systems. It happened precisely the other way around."[28] There now is a substantial body of archaeological and historical evidence to sustain the proposition that money should be understood as "a political institution enacted by

25 Adam Smith, *The Wealth of Nations* (New York: Modern Library, 1937), bk. 1, ch. 4, pp. 22–29. Smith's barter theory of the origins of money was widely adopted in economic history as well. For a prominent example, see John Hicks, *A Theory of Economic History* (Oxford: Clarendon Press, 1969), pp. 63–65.

26 Smith, *Wealth of Nations*, bk. 1, ch. 2, p. 13.

27 Exemplary of this approach to money and finance as a story of technological innovation is William N. Goetzmann, *Money Changes Everything: How Finance Made Civilization Possible* (Princeton, NJ: Princeton University Press, 2016).

28 David Graeber, *Debt: The First 5,000 Years*. Revised ed. (Brooklyn, NY: Melville House, 2014), p. 40.

governments to mobilize the resources that underwrite the political economies of complex societies."[29] Money thus has a far more ancient history than coin, dating back to Mesopotamia in the third millennium BCE. Rather than markets giving rise to money, as orthodox theory holds, the reverse is true: markets presuppose the existence of money, which was created by the ruling authority.

This approach to understanding money is by no means new; it informed the monetary theories developed by early-20th-century economists such as Georg F. Knapp, Alfred Mitchell-Innes, and John Maynard Keynes. In *The State Theory of Money* (published in German in 1905), Knapp coined the term *chartalism* to express the idea that money is an arbitrary "token" (*charta*) created by the state rather than a commodity with intrinsic value independent of the will of any sovereign (as the notion of the gold standard, ascendant in Knapp's day, affirmed).[30] In his 1914 essay "The Credit Theory of Money" Mitchell-Innes proposed that money was in the first instance a standard of deferred payment, a debt owed to the government that could be reclaimed through taxation. In addition, Mitchell-Innes argued that rather than emerging spontaneously from exchanges among individuals, markets relied on the legislative framework and enforcement systems of the state to bring them into existence.[31] In more recent times, the "credit theory of money" has led to the development of what has become known as Modern Monetary Theory (MMT), a radical and controversial challenge to the tenets of mainstream theory.[32]

The basic principle enunciated in the credit theory of money distinguishes money from currency (that is to say, the material embodiments of money) and posits that money is an abstract measure of value established by an authority for the purpose of assessing debts. In Geoffrey Ingham's formulation, "money is a claim or credit that is constituted by social relations that exist independently of the production and exchange of commodities."[33] Far from being a neutral intermediary in economic exchange, money is employed by powerholders to acquire resources and to organize and regulate social relationships. Political authorities create money as a unit of account for settling debts owed to them in the form of tribute and taxation. The validity of money is established not by trust, but by coercion. By extension, the value of money does not

[29] Robert M. Rosenswig, "Money, Currency, and Heterodox Economics for Archaeology," *Current Anthropology* 65.2 (2024), p. 4 [online pagination].

[30] George Friedrich Knapp, *The State Theory of Money* (London: Macmillan, 1924), p. 32. On Knapp's chartalist theory, see Schumpeter, *History of Economic Analysis*, pp. 807–11; Geoffrey Ingham, *The Nature of Money* (Cambridge: Polity Press, 2004), pp. 47–49.

[31] A. Mitchell-Innes, "The Credit Theory of Money," *Banking Law Journal* 31 (1914): 151–68.

[32] For the theoretical formation of MMT by its foremost exponent, see L. Randall Wray, *Modern Money Theory: A Primer on Macroeconomics for Sovereign Monetary Systems*. 2nd ed. (Houndmills, UK: Palgrave Macmillan, 2015).

[33] Ingham, *Nature of Money*, p. 12.

derive from the commodity value of the stuff employed as money (whether coins, shells, brass bracelets, cacao beans, wampum belts, or stone disks, to cite just some of the substances historically used as money); all monetary instruments are tokens of abstract values. At the same time, the political authority's guarantee of the acceptability of money in discharging debts owed to it creates a general validity that enables money to be utilized in market transactions. Money makes possible anonymous exchange among parties who have no personal relations of trust with one another.[34]

Christine Desan's landmark study of money in medieval and early modern England likewise underscores the idea that money, rather than having natural or intrinsic value, was a deliberate contrivance of the political community. "Making money," Desan asserts, was a crucial part of governance, a "constitutional project" designed to collect and distribute resources, at the same time creating and validating sovereign authority.[35] Desan echoes the credit theorists' critique of the orthodox mythology of money and its origins, but she also emphasizes that however important the conception of the unit of account is to making money, money must also assume tangible material forms that pass among users. Moreover, once created, money can be manipulated by private actors to pursue their own interests. Coinage marked a crucial watershed in the history of money, enhancing both the power of the state over money and the potential for private appropriation. On one hand, rulers controlled minting and set standards for acceptable coin, established legal tender, and mandated the use of its coin to pay debts. Rulers gained the capacity to tax and spend this money, strengthening their dominion over the polity. By setting tax rates and paying for goods and services in the coin deemed acceptable for tax payments, the ruler exercised powerful influence over his subjects' economic activities. Debt obligations had to be settled in particular coins whose value was defined by the unit of account, excluding other forms of payment and fortifying the ruler's monopoly over the making of money. On the other hand, coined wealth also could be more readily exploited as a means of evading control by the political authority. Legitimate coin could be deployed for uses other than paying taxes. The ruler had to sanction the use of coin in private exchange in order to reinforce its utility as a means of tax payment. Furthermore, the ruler had to maintain the quality and quantity of coin to ensure sufficient liquidity in the money supply and stability in the value of the unit of account – by no means easy tasks. Private possession of liquid

[34] This capsule summary of the credit theory of money is based on Ingham, *Nature of Money*, but broadly reflects the position adopted by other theorists. See Graeber, *Debt*; Michel Aglietta, *Money: 5,000 Years of Debt and Power* (London: Verso Press, 2016).

[35] Christine Desan, *Making Money: Coin, Currency, and the Coming of Capitalism* (New York: Oxford University Press, 2014), p. 1.

economic power in the form of coin empowered individuals to pursue economic goals beyond the reach of the state's control.

In medieval Europe, coinage was one of the few truly sovereign powers exercised by monarchs. The right to coin money derived from the monarchal constitutional order (found in England, France, the Spanish kingdoms, and the Holy Roman Empire) defined as the *domain state*: the king was entitled to the resources necessary for the upkeep of his household and the court, but these resources were restricted largely to his own seigneurial domain.[36] In addition, income from customs duties and the seigniorage yielded by coinage were deemed to belong properly to the king. However, extraordinary levies for the defense of realm (external, internal, and spiritual) required the consent of the nobility, to whom most land and persons were subject. Direct taxation of land or persons was frowned upon as an encroachment on private property and lawful only under very strict conditions. The right to levy general taxes – invariably for the purpose of waging war – advanced unevenly, assuming different forms in different states and rising and falling with the exigencies of warfare, not becoming a general sovereign right until the "fiscal revolution" of the 17th century.[37] Still, the power to coin money and above all to establish the unit of account for payment of debts and public obligations entailed significant control over economic life. The money of account that rulers employed in public payments (and which they used to pay their own creditors) fixed the exchange values among current coins in the marketplace. (England's monarchs were mostly successful in excluding foreign coin, but the continental monetary world was characterized by a bewildering heterogeneity of coins – a French edict of 1577 counted 180 kinds of coin in circulation, from twenty different sovereign territories.[38]) Yet monetary standards were notoriously unstable and required constant renegotiation and adjustment. Even if full control over money was elusive, in making money the sovereign authority constituted a political community.

36 W. M. Ormrod and Janos Barta, "The Feudal Structure and the Beginnings of State Finance," in Richard Bonney (ed.), *Economic Systems and State Finance* (Oxford: Oxford University Press, 1995), pp. 53–79. The distinction between the medieval domain state and the modern tax state was first articulated in Joseph A. Schumpeter, "The Crisis of the Tax State" (1918), rpt. in Joseph A. Schumpeter, *The Economics and Sociology of Capitalism* (Princeton, NJ: Princeton University Press, 1991), pp. 99–140.

37 Richard Bonney and W. M. Ormrod, "Introduction: Crises, Revolutions and Self-Sustained Growth: Towards a Conceptual Model of Change in Fiscal History," in W. M. Ormrod, Margaret Bonney, and Richard Bonney (eds.), *Crises, Revolutions, and Self-Sustained Growth: Essays in European Fiscal History* (Stamford, UK: Shaun Tyas, 1999), pp. 1–21.

38 *Ordonnance du Roy, sur le faict & Reglement de ses Monnoyes* (Paris: Veufve Jehan Dallier, 1578).

Under the Chinese empires, not only monetary authority but fiscal power was fundamental to governance and the sovereignty of the state, to a far greater degree than in medieval Europe or the Islamic world. Implicit in Chinese conceptions of political economy since antiquity was a faith in the capacity of the state and its agents to serve as positive forces for the creation and equitable distribution of wealth. In contrast to the domain states of medieval Europe, the institutional apparatus of the *fiscal state* – which I define as centralized planning of taxation and expenditure to satisfy the state's commitments to good governance, including defense of the realm and the economic welfare of its subjects – already was a defining feature of Chinese governance from the outset of the imperial era.[39] For example, the Qin and Han empires imposed direct taxation on their subjects and awarded landholdings to individual households. The Han state instituted uniform capitation taxes in coin and labor service on all adults, male and female (children aged 6–14 were also liable for a reduced head tax in coin). Universal conscription of adult men for military service required two year-long tours of duty. State finances were institutionally separate from those of the imperial household, which received dedicated revenues from a variety of sources, including (like medieval European rulers) seigniorage, customs duties, and commercial excises, but only trifling amounts from seigneurial estates. Money was crucial to implantation of the fiscal state. In the early Han, the state's monopoly over coinage was disputed and even rescinded for a period of thirty years. But by the reign of Emperor Wu (r. 141–87 BCE), that debate was firmly decided in favor of imperial monopoly. Even the harshest critics of Emperor Wu's fiscal policies upheld the sovereign's sole authority to mint coin, even if they insisted that he should not debase the coin or issue purely fiat money. Monopoly over making money remained an abiding feature of imperial governance.

As we have already observed, Chinese bronze coin had a strongly fiduciary character – the monetary value of the coin was not strictly tied to its metallic content. Yet during periods of strong imperial rule (most notably in the Song

[39] Richard von Glahn, "Modalities of the Fiscal State in Imperial China," *Journal of Chinese History* 4.1 (2020): 1–29. There is an enormous scholarship on the fiscal state in the context of European history, which I briefly summarize in this article. European historians have focused on a "fiscal revolution" in the early modern era that transformed the medieval domain states into "tax states" which acquired vastly greater fiscal capacity. The taxonomy developed by Richard Bonney and W. M. Ormrod charts an evolution from *tribute state* (the Roman Empire as archetype) to *domain state* (medieval European polities), *tax state* (early modern European nation-states), and the modern *fiscal state* (first appearing in Britain at the advent of the 19th century). At the same time, Bonney and Ormrod trace the origin of the "rise of the fiscal state" in Europe to c. 1200, with the temporary emergence of a "tax state" in Britain that subsequently reverted to a domain state. See Bonney and Ormrod, "Introduction: Crises, Revolutions, and Self-Sustained Growth."

period), imperial coinage displayed remarkable stability in weight and copper content, largely inhibiting counterfeiting.[40] The classical tradition of Chinese monetary theory that coalesced during the Han period (which we will examine in Chapter 1) diverged markedly from the mainstream of Western monetary thought. In contrast to the catallactic and metallist precepts enunciated by Aristotle – and later reprised, one way or another, by Oresme, Davanzati, Locke, and Smith – Chinese monetary theory rested on the chartalist principle that money is an arbitrary creation of the state. Although money possesses no intrinsic value and cannot itself satisfy utilitarian needs for food, clothing, and shelter, through his monetary and fiscal policies – increasing or decreasing the money supply and intensifying or relaxing taxation – the sovereign can manipulate the exchange value of money and by extension commodity prices. This leverage over exchange values enables the state to dictate the terms of trade and thus manage economic activity within the domestic realm as well as maintaining a favorable balance in international trade. Such leverage can be obtained only if the ruler possesses a monopoly over making money. Chinese monetary theory thus not only recognized the fiduciary character of money but also provided the logical foundation for the state to issue fiat currency. This logic undergirded the creation of state-issued paper money, the fiat currency par excellence, in the Song dynasty and after.

To be sure, the fiscal constitution of the Chinese Empire underwent repeated metamorphosis throughout the long imperial era. For example, as mentioned earlier, during the Song period the fiscal base of the state shifted dramatically from direct taxation of people and land to indirect taxation of commerce and consumption. But the state's monopoly over making money remained the bedrock of monetary and fiscal policy. Paper money originated with privately issued bills, but in intervening to impose a state monopoly over the issuance of bills the Song government reaffirmed its mission to make money serve public interests.

[40] Sheng Qian and Lemin Wu, "Who Defended Monetary Stability in a Specie Regime? Evidence from Chinese History," *Frontiers of Economics in China* 13.3 (2018): 397–435.

PART I

Theoretical and Institutional Antecedents

1

Classical Chinese Monetary Theory and the Foundations of Fiat Currency

As in the Mediterranean world, coinage of metallic money in China dates back to the 7th–6th centuries BCE. In contrast to the silver coinages that quickly spread throughout the Hellenic city-states, however, the earliest currencies in China were made of bronze – a noble metal in the Sinitic ecumene, where bronze had been used chiefly to manufacture ritual vessels that embodied sacred power, sovereign authority, and exalted status. From the inception of the first empires in the 3rd century BCE, Chinese governments would continue to rely on low-value copper alloy coins (mostly bronze, but brass coins after 1600) as their monetary standard down to the 19th century. Precious metals were never coined before the late 19th century, when Chinese authorities began to strike their own imitations of the Mexican Republican silver dollar. Not surprisingly, given the differences in the physical forms of money, the philosophy of money in China diverged radically from Western traditions rooted in the writings of ancient Greek philosophers.

Beginning with Hesiod's famous articulation of history as the ignominious descent from the noble ages of gold and silver to the degenerate present day of bronze races, the Greeks spoke of metals in the language of moral and social values.[1] Gold was associated with divine purity, rightful sovereignty, and the eternal moral standards upheld by the aristocratic elite. By contrast, in Herodotus silver coinage appears as an instrument of tyrannic power, and silver coins were aligned with the hubris and venality of the Persian kings, whom Herodotus derogated as petty-minded shopkeepers. Yet historically speaking, within the Greek world silver coinage was a powerful force for the creation of the city-state (*polis*) – conceived as an autonomous community of citizens – as a political institution. In the Greek *poleis*, coin initially figured chiefly in payments to or from the state, such as military and officeholding stipends, fines, payments for services to the *polis*, taxes, and tribute. Civic law

[1] This paragraph draws on the analyses of Leslie Kurke, *Coins, Bodies, Games, and Gold: The Politics of Meaning in Archaic Greece* (Princeton, NJ: Princeton University Press, 1999), and David M. Schaps, *The Invention of Coinage and the Monetization of Ancient Greece* (Ann Arbor: University of Michigan Press, 2003).

was construed as founded on a "silver standard" of natural and unchanging justice. The resort to issuing "wretched" bronze currency amid Athens' political and military misfortunes in the late 5th century BCE likewise was seen as evidence of the debasement of the citizenry itself following the enfranchisement of slave soldiers with citizen's rights.[2]

Aristotle's conflicting statements concerning the origins of coinage reflected the shifting discourse on money as a symbol of value.[3] Within the space of a few lines in *Politics*, Aristotle suggests on one hand that silver coin prevailed as money in market exchange because its inherent metallic value (that is to say, its commodity value) was universally recognized, while on the other hand he ascribes the use of coin to arbitrary convention. In either case, Aristotle postulates that money emerged from the needs of members of different communities seeking to exchange goods with one another (more specifically, he locates the origins of money in transcultural trade among foreign peoples). Money is first and foremost a medium of exchange. Aristotle thus subscribes to what was described in the Introduction as a *catallactic* theory of money, premised on the priority of money as a means of exchange. But Aristotle also distinguishes between the noble "art of exchange," which "exists for the replenishment of self-sufficiency," and the iniquitous "art of wealth-getting," in which commerce becomes a means to the end of acquiring wealth and power. Here Aristotle counterposes the satisfaction of needs within the household economy, which is good and natural, and the merchant's (or tyrant's) insatiable pursuit of riches, an end that respects no natural limit, subverting the common good.[4] In *Nicomachean Ethics*, Aristotle proposes an alternative theory of money as a standard of value. By enabling comparison of the values of different goods, money – "the measure of all things" – makes possible fair trade, and thus comports with social justice.[5] But in the hands of "the sort of people who exceed in respect of getting, taking from every source and all they can; such are those who follow degrading trades, brothel-keepers and all people of that sort, and petty usurers who lend money in small sums at a high rate of interest," money and market values pervert justice.[6] It is the use value of a thing, not its exchange value, that denotes its true value. Still,

[2] The association of "wretched bronzes" with alien slave soldiers appears in Aristophanes' *The Frogs*. See Thomas Figueira, *The Power of Money: Coinage and Politics in the Athenian Empire* (Philadelphia: University of Pennsylvania Press, 1998), pp. 501–2.

[3] For analyses of Aristotle's writings on money and trade, see Josef Soudek, "Aristotle's Theory of Exchange: An Inquiry into the Origins of Economic Analysis," *Proceedings of the American Philosophical Society* 96.1 (1952): 45–75; Scott Meikle, *Aristotle's Economic Thought* (Oxford: Clarendon Press, 1995); Kurke, *Coins, Bodies*, pp. 45–47, 76–77, 85–86, 318–19; Schaps, *Invention of Coinage*, pp. 5–13, 27–29, 175–78, 206–9.

[4] Aristotle, *Politics*, bk. 1, pp. 1257a–b.

[5] Aristotle, *Ethics*, bk. 5, p. 1133a.

[6] Aristotle, *Ethics*, bk. 4, p. 1121b.

Aristotle equates true value with fine silver, as when he states that "the judge is like an assayer of silver, whose duty is to distinguish spurious from genuine justice."[7]

The virtues of coins minted from precious metals – rarity, durability, partibility, fungibility, and portability – recommended them as ideal choices for a means of exchange. The value of precious metal currencies, for which there was universal demand and the costs of minting or melting coins were relatively low, remained closely linked to the commodity value of the metals they contained. Consequently, the *metallist* conception of money articulated by Aristotle prevailed in Western thought prior to modern times.[8] The value of China's bronze coin, by contrast, often varied from its intrinsic metallic value; bronze coin typically circulated as a fiduciary currency whose value was determined by the demand for it in market exchange and state payments. In contrast to the catallactic and metallist theories of money stemming from Aristotle, Chinese monetary philosophy hewed to the principles of *theoretical chartalism*: money is an arbitrary creation of the community or state whose value is fixed by convention or legislation rather than its intrinsic commodity value. The tenets of chartalism established the conceptual foundations for the precocious emergence of paper money in China. Western theorists eventually arrived at an endorsement of paper money (more specifically bank money) as fiat currency by an entirely different route.[9]

At the time that bronze currencies first appeared in the Chinese world, the once-powerful Zhou kingdom (1045–256 BCE) had fragmented into scores of smaller polities, conventionally deemed city-states. The emergence of money – along with private merchants and market exchange – coincided with the rise of militarized autocratic states that conquered and absorbed many of the city-states beginning in the late Spring and Autumn period (770–453 BCE). During the Warring States era (453–221 BCE), two distinct patterns of state formation

[7] Aristotle, *Rhetoric*, bk. 1, p. 1375a.

[8] Meikle (*Aristotle's Economic Thought*) contends that later writers, especially 19th-century economists who perceived in Aristotle the germ of the theory of marginal utility that became the foundation of neoclassical economics, fundamentally misconstrued Aristotle's statements. But misapprehension as such did not diminish the indisputable impact of Aristotle's writings. The pervasive influence of Aristotle on the ideas of medieval scholastics about money and exchange is extensively documented in Joel Kaye, *Economy and Nature in the Fourteenth Century: Money, Market Exchange, and the Emergence of Scientific Thought* (Cambridge: Cambridge University Press, 1998). One historian has observed that Aristotle's "authority remained unparalleled among those involved in monetary policy" in 16th-century France: Jotham Parsons, *Making Money in Sixteenth-Century France: Currency, Culture, and the State* (Ithaca, NY: Cornell University Press, 2014), p. 68. For the preeminence of Aristotelian views on money among English political economists in the early 17th century, see Wennerlind, *Casualties of Credit*, pp. 30–43.

[9] Roy Green, *Classical Theories of Money, Output, and Inflation: A Study in "Historical Economics"* (Houndmills, UK: Macmillan Press, 1992), pp. 105–60.

took shape. In the Zhou heartland of the Central Plain (the lower Yellow River basin), where commercial and industrial growth was concentrated, mercantile cities enjoyed some degree of autonomy. In the less economically developed peripheral states, autocratic rulers created strong bureaucracies that controlled much production and trade. By 300 BCE, the Zhou ecumene had been partitioned among the centralized monarchies of the peripheral states (Qin, Qi, Yan, and Chu) and the Central Plain states of Wei, Zhao, and Hann, in which a looser form of monarchal rule prevailed. During the 3rd century BCE, the kings of Qin progressively vanquished their rivals and, in 221 BCE, created the first unified empire. Although the Qin Empire (221–206 BCE) endured for a mere fifteen years, its political and fiscal institutions were largely retained by its successor, the long-lived Han dynasty (202 BCE–220 CE), during which the basic features of China's imperial form of government were established. What became the classical tradition of Chinese monetary thought took shape during the Han period.

1.1 The Invention of Metallic Currency

The precise beginnings of coinage in China remain obscure, but the recent excavation of a mint located at the site of Guanzhuang, a city in the state of Zheng, has pushed back the inauguration of coinage to c. 640–550 BCE.[10] The earliest bronze currencies consist of two basic types, in the shapes of miniature spades and knives, with distinct spheres of circulation. Spade-shaped currencies (known as *bu* 布), such as those cast at the Guanzhuang mint, proliferated in various states – including Royal Zhou, Wey, Song, and Jin – clustered around Zheng in the Zhou heartland of the western Central Plain (Figure 1.1a). The heterogenous *bu* currencies comprise dozens of subtypes, further subdivided into large and small sizes, bearing hundreds of different inscriptions, mostly city names. *Bu* currencies circulated widely, well beyond the territories of their home jurisdictions. It seems likely that they were issued by a multitude of agents, either private merchants or moneyers working on behalf of city authorities or royal patrons. In the Warring States era, when the ruling houses of Wei, Hann, and Zhao consolidated control over the western portion of the Central Plain, they began to mint substantial quantities of currency – probably for payments to soldiers – but their local cities continued to issue coins in their own names.[11]

[10] Hao Zhao et al., "Radio-Carbon Dating an Early Minting Site: The Emergence of Standardised Coinage in China," *Antiquity* 383 (2021): 1161–78. Two other mint sites, at the capital cities of Jin and Zheng, have been dated to the early 6th century BCE, but the dating of these sites is more tenuous.

[11] Emura Haruki 江村治樹, *Shunshū Sengoku jidai seidō kahei no seisei to tenkai* 春秋戦国時代青銅貨幣の生成と展開 (Tokyo: Kyūko shoin, 2011), pp. 136–42.

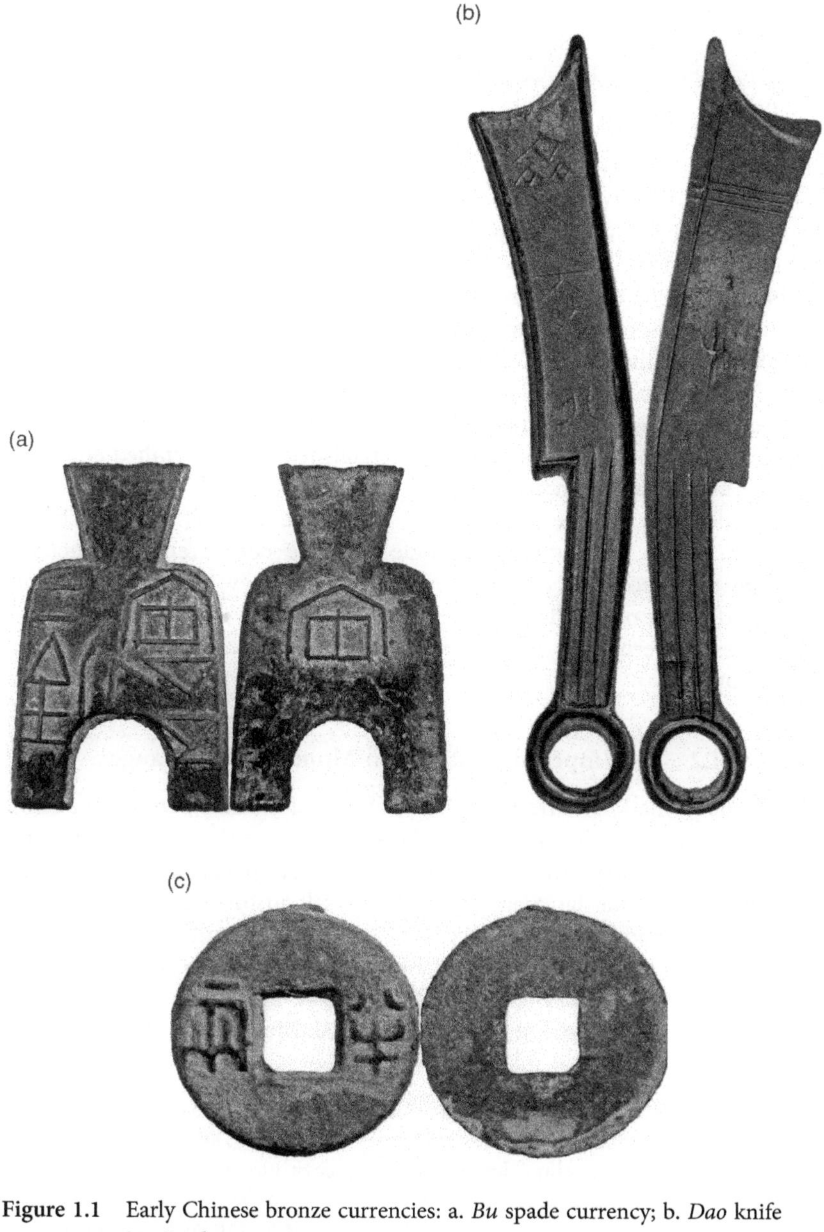

Figure 1.1 Early Chinese bronze currencies: a. *Bu* spade currency; b. *Dao* knife currency; c. Qin Banliang coin.

Source: Thierry, *Monnaies*, p. 49, fig. 22; p. 35, fig. 8, p. 70, fig. 25.

Knife-shaped currencies (known as *dao* 刀) emerged in the northeast, in the general area of the peripheral state of Yan, a region of few cities and sparse commerce (Figure 1.1b). Consensus opinion maintains that the early *dao* currencies – consistent in size but varying widely in alloy and inscriptions believed to be moneyers' marks – were created to facilitate trade between Yan subjects and the non-Chinese Di peoples inhabiting this region.[12] Initially, then, minting of *dao* currencies was dispersed, but as Yan and even more so its southern neighbor Qi developed into powerful kingdoms in the 5th–4th centuries BCE their coinage was brought under control of the central state and became highly standardized.

Round coins developed relatively late in China, in the 4th century BCE. The state of Qin in the far west issued its Banliang 半两 (half-ounce) coins – perforated with a square hole – beginning in 336 BCE, the culmination of a sweeping program of institutional reforms that transformed Qin into a military juggernaut (Figure 1.1c). After Qin established the first unified empire in 221 BCE, its Banliang coin became the standard model for Chinese state-issued currency down to the late 19th century. In the late imperial era, the Chinese monetary system expanded to include multiple concurrent currencies – including the precocious development of paper money in the 11th century and the adoption of a bullion silver monetary standard in the 15th century – but Chinese governments never coined precious metals until the end of the 19th century.

1.2 Pre-Imperial Writings on Money and Exchange

As was true in the Mediterranean, the invention of metallic currency in China was scarcely noted by historians or philosophers at the time of its birth. Only in the late 5th century BCE do references to money appear in surviving texts, in regrettably laconic language – but that itself insinuates that the use of money was already commonplace. The earliest substantive discussion of money appears in the *Discourses of Zhou*, probably composed c. 400 BCE. In 524 BCE, we are told, King Jing of Zhou (r. 544–520 BCE) was preparing to issue large bronze coins, but his minister Lord Mu of Dan objected in the following words:

> In antiquity, when floods and disasters unleashed by Heaven occurred, the ruler would measure goods and money (*liang zibi* 量資幣) and adjust their relative values (lit., "the light and the heavy") to aid and succor the people. When the people suffer from the currency being too light, the ruler makes it heavier. When the people suffer from the currency being

[12] Huang Xiquan 黄锡全, *Xian Qin huobi tonglun* 先秦货币通论 (Beijing: Zijincheng chubanshe, 2001), pp. 200–216; Emura, *Seidō kahei*, pp. 28–29, 105–11.

> too heavy, he makes light currency and circulates it. Thus the "mother" balances the "child," and the people obtain all they need. If the currency is excessively heavy, then the ruler circulates lighter currency without withdrawing the heavy currency. In this way the "child" balances the "mother" in circulation and great and small alike benefit.
>
> If now your majesty withdraws the light currency and only mints heavy coins, the people will lose their means of livelihood (*zi* 資). Can any of them avoid destitution? If the people are destitute, the king will lack sufficient revenues for his needs, and he then resorts to increasing his impositions on the people. Unable to satisfy his demands, they will think only of fleeing to other states. In this way the ruler alienates his people.[13]

Crucial as this passage figures in the history of Chinese monetary thought, it poses many problems. It is highly doubtful that it represents the monetary situation of King Jing's time; indeed, we have no corroboration that King Jing issued any currency. Leaving aside this issue, two points made by Lord Mu became staple axioms of Chinese monetary thought.

First, Lord Mu attributes the origins of money not to the need to ensure equity in exchange but rather to the magnanimity of benevolent rulers who provide for their people in times of dearth. An abiding tradition depicted the sage-kings of yore as demiurges who invented useful technologies to advance the progress of civilization. For example, Shun was acclaimed by the philosopher Mozi (fl. c. late 5th century BCE) for teaching farming, pottery, and fishing to his subjects.[14] The canonical *Book of Documents* attributed the origins of trade to Yu the Great (legendary founder of the Xia dynasty), who upon resettling the people after catastrophic floods "strove to induce them to exchange what they had for what they lacked."[15] According to the "Great Tradition" commentary on the *Book of Changes* (dating to no later than the 2nd century BCE), markets and exchange were the creation of the most ancient of the sage-kings, the Divine Husbandman, who "held the market at noon and bade the people of the Subcelestial Realm to come hither, thus gathering all the

13 "Zhouyu (xia)" 周語(下), "Dan Mugong jian Jingwang zhu daqian" 單穆公諫景王鑄大錢, in Lai Kehong 来可泓 (ed.), *Guoyu zhijie* 国语直解, ([hereafter *GY*]; Shanghai: Fudan daxue chubanshe, 2000), pp. 158–59. The quotation of this passage in the "Food and Money" chapters in the *History of the Former Han Dynasty* made it a canonical statement of wise monetary policy. See Ban Gu 班固, *Han shu* 漢書 ([hereafter *HS*]; Beijing: Zhonghua shuju ed.), 24B.1151.

14 Chs. 9 and 10, "Shangxian 賞賢 (中), (下)," in Wu Yujiang 吳毓江 (ed.), *Mo Zi jiaozhu* 墨子校注 (Beijing: Zhonghua shuju, 1993), 1, pp. 77, 97. This claim is frequently repeated in Warring States and Han texts. In *Mencius* (3.A.4), Shun was credited with introducing the use of fire to render the land suitable for cultivation by burning forests and driving off wild beasts.

15 Ch. 5, "Yiji" 益稷, in *Shang shu* 尚書 [hereafter *ShS*], in Ruan Yuan 阮元 (ed.), *Shisanjing zhushu* 十三經注疏 ([hereafter *SSJZS*]; rpt., Beijing, Zhonghua shuju, 1980), 1, p. 141a.

products of his realm. Each exchanged what they possessed for what they desired, and then retired."[16]

But such descriptions suggest little more than barter exchange. Advocates of an assertive state presence in economic life went farther, claiming that the sage-kings not only invented markets to facilitate the exchange of goods but also created money for the express purpose of rescuing the people from poverty in times of distress. The *Guan Zi* traces the origins of coinage to the sage-kings Yu the Great and Tang (legendary founder of the Shang dynasty): during times of flood and drought, when the starving multitude resorted to selling their children into slavery, "Tang availed himself of the metal of Mount Zhuang, and Yu took the metal of Mount Li, to cast money, which they used to redeem the children from bondage."[17] A clearly apocryphal but widely disseminated tradition relates that King Wu of Zhou, upon completing his conquest of Shang (c. 1045 BCE), released the stores of coin and grain accumulated by the tyrannical last Shang ruler to bring relief to the poor.[18]

Second, the *Discourses of Zhou* passage introduces the concept of the "mutual balance between child and mother" (*zimu xiangquan* 子母相權), which became a cardinal axiom of Chinese monetary thought. A similar idea appears in the "Great Relief" chapter of the *Lost Documents of Zhou*, a probably contemporary text but even more certainly apocryphal as actual history. This account relates that at the time of a great famine the progenitor of the Zhou royal house, King Wen, declared:

> Let itinerant traders enjoy extensive travels in circulating their goods. Let them have access to water transport and lodgings on their way, let them be welcome wherever they arrive. If money (*bizu* 幣租) is light, then create (*zuo* 作) a "mother" [currency] to enable the "child" to circulate, which will facilitate exchange of goods dear and cheap and ensure that itinerant merchants can venture forth unimpeded. so that there will be no obstruction to trade.[19]

16 "Xici" 繫辭, in *Zhou yi* 周易, in *SSJZS*, 1, p. 86c.

17 Ch. 75, "Shanquanshu" 山權數, in Li Xiangfeng 黎翔鳳 (ed.), *Guan Zi jiaozhu* 管子校注 ([hereafter *GZ*]; Beijing: Zhonghua shuju, 2004), 3, p. 1300.

18 The account of this act that appears in the *Book of Documents* – in a chapter now regarded as apocryphal – refers to releasing stores of "wealth" (*cai* 財). See "Wucheng" 武成, in *ShS*, in *SSJZS*, 1, p. 185b. Other Warring States–Han versions of this event substitute "coin" (*qian* 錢) for "wealth." See ch. 66, "Banfajie" 版法解, in *GZ*, 3, p. 1205; bk. 15, ch. 1, "Shenda" 慎大, in Chen Qiyou 陳奇猷 (ed.), *Lüshi chunqiu jiaoshi* 呂氏春秋校釋 (Shanghai: Xuelin chubanshe, 1994), 1, p. 844; ch. 9, "Zhushuxun" 主術訓, and ch. 12, "Daoyingxun" 道應訓, in Liu Wendian 劉文典 (ed.), *Huainan honglie jishi* 淮南鴻烈集釋 (Beijing: Zhonghua shuju, 1989), 1, pp. 311, 412; Sima Qian 司馬遷, *Shi ji* 史記 ([hereafter *SJ*]; Zhonghua shuju ed.), 3.108; 32.1480.

19 Ch. 11, "Dakuang" 大匡, in Huang Huaixin 黃懷信et al. (eds.), *Yi Zhou shu huijiao jizhu* 逸周書彙校集注, ([hereafter *YZS*]; Shanghai: Shanghai guji chubanshe, 2007), 1, pp. 157–58.

In this text, too, the purpose of coinage is to relieve the people's distress in times of dearth, but here it is more explicitly linked to the intermediation of merchants. The implication of these evocations of the mother-and-child metaphor is that rulers issued coins of different values that circulated concurrently in the marketplace.[20] In the 4th century BCE, the rulers of some states, notably Wei and Qi, began to inscribe currencies with units of weight that denominated their exchange value. For example, some Wei *bu* currencies have three weight values (one-half, one, and two *jin*), while others specify a fixed exchange rate with gold. Opinion on the significance of these values diverges, however. Some scholars believe that currencies denominated in weight measures were intended for international exchange. Others, observing that rulers had little leverage to enforce fixed exchange rates in international trade, have concluded that they were instead intended for purely domestic circulation.

These passages affirm a moral transactional order in which the ruler creates money and markets to relieve the distress of the people, thus binding them to the ruler's patriarchal authority.[21] We find here the germ of the Chinese doctrine of theoretical chartalism whereby rulers choose the media of exchange and determine their nominal values. Yet these passages also concede some measure of autonomy to the market, and regular intervention of the ruler is required to maintain stable relationships of value between different types of currency as well as between money and goods (i.e., prices). Despite the marking of Banliang coins and other bronze currencies with units of weight, the weights of surviving specimens vary widely and invariably diverge from these nominal standards, with a general trend of becoming smaller and lighter over time. From the outset, then, Chinese currencies were conceived as fiduciary monies whose exchange value was determined not by their intrinsic material substance but rather by tacit social contract.[22]

By the late Warring States period, as the autocratic model of state-making achieved ascendance, coinage became increasingly consolidated not only in the peripheral states but in the more commercialized Central Plain states as well. Gold currency also emerged as a principal form of money. Gold

[20] In this respect, the episode differs from one recorded by the Han historian Sima Qian concerning King Zhuang of Chu (r. 613–591 BCE) in which the king tried to enhance the value of his coin. Having determined that his coin was too light, King Zhuang "made the small large" (i.e., raised the value of his coin), but the resulting uproar in the marketplaces forced him to rescind the order three days later. See *SJ* 119.3100. Since the Chu state only began to issue bronze currencies much later than King Zhuang's time, this account is clearly apocryphal.

[21] Tamara Chin, *Savage Exchange: Han Imperialism, Chinese Literary Style, and the Economic Imagination* (Cambridge, MA: Harvard University Asia Center, 2014), pp. 263–67.

[22] This is a principal theme of François Thierry, *Les Monnaies de la Chine ancienne: des origines à la fin de l'empire* (Paris: Belles Lettres, 2017).

currency originated in the southern state of Chu, which developed a distinctive multiple-currency system based on sheets of gold-leaf and bronze imitations of cowries decidedly unlike the currency systems of North China. The Chu gold-leaf currency (which was stamped with squares that could be torn into fractional units) became an important medium of international trade, especially in Qin and Wei. The Qin state incorporated gold and units of hemp cloth along with its Banliang coins into a tripartite currency system. Writings on money from the 3rd to 2nd centuries BCE typically refer to a dual monetary system based on gold and bronze currencies.

1.3 Monetary Doctrines in the *Guan Zi*

None of the major philosophers of the Warring States period – an "axial age" of philosophical writing in China, as in the contemporary Mediterranean world – devoted attention to the theory of money. But the subject of money emerged as a central theme in the sundry discourses on political economy gathered together in the work known as the *Guan Zi*. The *Guan Zi* purports to be a series of Socratic dialogues between two salient figures heralded (or reviled) as precursors to the rise of the autocratic state, Lord Huan of Qi (r. 685–643 BCE) and his prime minister Guan Zhong (c. 710–645 BCE). But the book was compiled much later. The older portions of the *Guan Zi* probably were composed at the Jixia Academy at the court of Qi during the 4th–3rd centuries BCE. These essays are eclectic in theme and spirit, representing a wide spectrum of philosophical principles, in some cases diametrically opposed ones. A more coherent set of economic doctrines – decidedly dirigiste in outlook – appears in the "Ratios of Exchange" (lit., "Light and Heavy") chapters, which most likely date from the first century of the Han dynasty. Although surely the work of several hands, the ideas in the "Ratios of Exchange" chapters are sufficiently consistent to consider them the product of a single author, who for the sake of convenience I will refer to as "Pseudo-Guanzi."[23]

The vision of political economy found in the older chapters, whose authors (again for heuristic purposes) I will refer to collectively as "Proto-Guanzi," rests on the cardinal principle that the ruler – as "shepherd of the people," to quote the title of the book's first chapter – must accumulate stores of grain and goods to provide for his subjects in times of dearth. Proto-Guanzi recognized the tensions and conflicts engendered by the simultaneous rise of the autocratic state and the market economy, as expressed in this terse formulation: "private families compete with public storehouses for goods, while gold

[23] This distinction between the economic philosophy of the "Ratios of Exchange" chapters and the eclectic perspectives voiced in the older chapters is based on Kanaya Osamu 金谷治, *Kanshi no kenkyū* 管子の研究 (Tokyo: Iwanami shoten, 1987).

competes with grain for value."[24] Production and exchange are both essential to the welfare of the state and the people, but the ruler must act to maintain the delicate balance between the two: if the profits of commerce exceed the returns from agriculture, farmers will abandon their lands; if the ruler demands exorbitant revenues, the people will have no reserves in times of hardship. Seasonal and annual variations in the supply and demand for grain can cause ruinous gyrations in the price of foodstuffs, with potentially devastating consequences: cheap grain impoverishes farmers, while dear grain imperils consumers.

Despite the vagaries of nature and harvests, the wise ruler ensures the welfare and prosperity of his people by balancing supply and demand for goods and money. "If goods are plentiful and productive tasks properly regulated, there will be little need to seek blessings from Heaven," writes Proto-Guanzi in a chapter devoted to fiscal management. Although Proto-Guanzi repeatedly warns that extravagant and frivolous expenditures on the part of the ruler will impoverish the people and ultimately undermine the state, he advocates restraint, not austerity. The ruler must strike a balance between thrift and indulgence:

> Gold is the standard of expenditures. The prince who discerns the fundamental laws of gold will understand the dangers of parsimony and prodigality. Knowing this, he will exercise moderation in his expenditures.
>
> Now, parsimony in expenditure harms husbandry, while prodigality in expenditure harms trade. Parsimony causes the value of gold to fall, and when gold is cheap productive tasks remain uncompleted. For this reason, then, parsimony is harmful to husbandry. Prodigality in expenditure, by contrast, causes the value of gold to rise, and when gold is dear, the value of goods declines. For this reason, prodigality harms trade.
>
> Thus goods remain unsold and the people suffer privation: such a state of affairs results from ignorance of the standard of expenditures. Production halts and yet the surfeit of goods grows: such a state of affairs results from ignorance of the need to moderate expenditures.[25]

Proto-Guanzi here denies that goods or money have value in themselves. It is the ruler, through his fiscal policies, who establishes their relative values. Meager revenue extraction and spending will reduce the demand for gold, and the resulting surplus of money in the market causes prices to rise. Conversely, excessive taxation and expenditure, by increasing the demand for gold, induces deflation and discourages production. Thus, the inordinately frugal ruler is just as harmful as the extravagantly profligate one.

[24] 家與府爭貨，金與粟爭貴. Ch. 3, "Quanxiu" 權修, in *GZ*, 1, p. 52.
[25] Ch. 5, "Chengma" 乘馬, in *GZ*, 1, pp. 88–89.

The Proto-Guanzi chapters generally focus on fiscal policies, not money. But in the early Han dynasty, the problem of monetary policy surged to the forefront of political economy. After the creation of the unified empire in 221 BCE, the Qin government sought to establish its Banliang coin as a universal currency, to little effect. The early Han rulers introduced their own Banliang coins but struggled to produce sufficient supplies to displace the multitude of current currencies or to establish a consistent monetary standard. The empire was soon deluged with debased and underweight coins that triggered price inflation. With the ascension of Emperor Wen (r. 180–157 BCE), the Han state pivoted toward more liberal economic policies inspired by the Huang-Lao philosophy of government, in which the ruler ensures the well-being of his subjects through personal frugality, minimal taxation, and refraining from disrupting their livelihood.[26] The most controversial of Emperor Wen's policies was his abrogation, in 175 BCE, of the state monopoly on coinage. Wen's action was intended to restore a sound currency by stipulating a new standard for the size and weight of coins (known as Sizhu 四銖 or "four *zhu*," half the nominal weight of Banliang coins) but allowing private minting. The emperor's leading advisers condemned free coinage for further debasing the money supply, encouraging commerce at the expense of agriculture, and worsening inequality. The counselor Jia Yi upheld the chartalist principle of sovereign monetary authority as the key to economic management in language that echoed the "Ratios of Exchange" chapters of the *Guan Zi* (see below):

> If copper is not dispersed among the people below, it will all revert to the ruler above. The sovereign manipulates his stores of copper to yoke the exchange values of money and goods. If coin is light [i.e., undervalued], he employs strategies to gather it; if coin is heavy, he employs strategies to disseminate it. In so doing, his money surely will be well-ordered.[27]

Emperor Wen remained undeterred. In 144 BCE, these critics persuaded Wen's successor to repeal free coinage, but the government was unable to maintain a uniform Sizhu coin standard. However, in 118 BCE, Emperor Wu (r. 141–87 BCE) began minting a new Wuzhu 五銖 ("five *zhu*") coin that quickly found favor and supplanted the heterogeneous coins then in

[26] For an introduction to the Huang-Lao philosophy of government, see R. P. Peerenboom, *Law and Morality in Ancient China: The Silk Manuscripts of Huang-Lao* (Albany: State University of New York Press, 1993).

[27] 銅不布下，畢歸於上，挾銅積以御輕重，錢輕則以術斂之，錢重則以術散之，則錢必治矣. Jia Yi 賈誼, "Tongbu" 銅布, in Yan Zhenyi 閻振益 and Zhong Xia 鐘夏 (eds.), *Xinshu jiaozhu* 新書校注 ([hereafter *XS*]; Beijing: Zhonghua shuju, 2000), 3, p. 111. See also Elisa Levi Sabattini, "To Ban or Not to Ban: Jia Yi on Copper Distribution and Minting Coins," in Elisa Levi Sabattini and Christian Schwermann (eds.), *Between Command and Market: Economic Thought and Practice in Early China* (Leiden: Brill, 2022), pp. 318–57.

circulation. The Wuzhu coin would remain the nominal standard for Chinese coin for centuries, even after the demise of the Han dynasty in 220 CE.

The Wuzhu coinage was part of a far-reaching program of fiscal reform implemented by Emperor Wu that broke with his predecessors' laissez-faire policies toward money and commerce. Needing to amass revenues to pay for costly campaigns of conquest and colonization in Central Asia, Korea, southern China, and Vietnam, Emperor Wu's regime placed the lucrative salt and iron industries under state monopoly, imposed onerous taxes on merchant income and capital assets, and created government agencies to stockpile commodities and intervene in markets to smooth out price fluctuations. Emperor Wu's fiscal system relied heavily on indirect taxation in coin, which comprised most of the central government's income and nearly half of total revenue. The strongly interventionist philosophy of political economy espoused in the "Ratios of Exchange" chapters of the *Guan Zi* most likely took shape amid the debates over the economic role of the state during the first century of the Han dynasty, and they found concrete expression in the policies adopted by Emperor Wu.

The commanding role of the state in managing the economy to redress inequality, satisfy the subsistence needs of the people, and enhance the state's power against its rivals advocated by Pseudo-Guanzi can be regarded as a type of mercantilism.[28] As in early modern Europe, Chinese mercantilism was premised on a world of multiple competing states, profitable long-distance trade, and the asymmetries of comparative advantage. Amid the constant clash of economic forces, it is the ruler alone who can create the balance (*heng* 衡) and stability (*zhun* 准) – two of Pseudo-Guanzi's favorite watchwords – necessary to enrich the people and the state. In many respects, Pseudo-Guanzi's principles of political economy – maximizing exploitation of agricultural, mining, and manufacturing resources; maintaining a favorable balance of trade; and amassing reserves of gold and bronze coin that enable the state to control prices and consumption – parallel the mercantilist strategies of early modern European states. Unlike European mercantilism, however, Chinese mercantilism sought not to strengthen the domestic merchant class but rather to replace it.[29]

Money was central to Pseudo-Guanzi's mercantilist strategies. In contrast to Proto-Guanzi's focus on agriculture, Pseudo-Guanzi urged the ruler to

28 On the application (with important qualifications) of "mercantilism" to Pseudo-Guanzi's economic philosophy and Emperor Wu's fiscal policies, see von Glahn, "Modalities of the Fiscal State," pp. 14–17.

29 On the economic philosophy of the "Ratios of Exchange" chapters of the *Guan Zi*, see Hu Jichuang 胡寄窗, *Zhongguo jingji sixiang shi* 中國經濟思想史 (Shanghai: Shanghai renmin chubanshe, 1962), vol. 1, pp. 238–377; Kanaya, *Kanshi*, pp. 152–75; Chin, *Savage Exchange*, pp. 32–68.

manipulate the terms of trade and especially the money supply to induce an inflow of wealth and prevent dissipation of his own resources. Control of the money supply enabled the ruler to adjust prices, ensure a favorable balance of trade, and maintain an equilibrium between domestic producers and consumers. Pseudo-Guanzi expresses little interest in the question of the morality of exchange, the fundamental problem that preoccupied the Greek philosophers and later Christian scholastics. Instead, he asserts that the value of a commodity is determined by the laws of supply and demand. Drawing, no doubt, on empirical observations of price fluctuations, Pseudo-Guanzi enunciates an equation of exchange that became the keystone of Chinese monetary thought: the values of money and commodities were related in inverse proportion to each other. This equation can be seen as a quantity theory of money since it holds that the value of money (measured by purchasing power) and the value of goods (measured by prices) are functions of the relative quantities of each. By manipulating the supplies of money and goods the ruler can adjust the ratios of exchange and thereby control market prices. This idea was an extension of the mother-and-child metaphor which we have seen applied to the relative values of small and large currencies.

The role of money as a measure of value, which Aristotle deemed its principal function, received scant attention from Pseudo-Guanzi. In addition, Pseudo-Guanzi denies that money has any use value: "The three forms of money [pearls and jade; gold; and *bu* and *dao* bronze currencies] offer no warmth to the naked, nor can they fill the bellies of the hungry. The former kings used money to preserve wealth and goods and thereby regulate the productive activities of the people, whereupon they brought peace and order to the Subcelestial Realm."[30] The crucial quality of money was its utility, not as a measure of value but as a store of value. Just as the ruler must store up reserves of grain to feed his subjects during famine years, so too should he maintain stockpiles of money to purchase grain and other staples when natural disasters strike. Psuedo-Guanzi affirms that money serves as a source of wealth in lieu of grain, the true source of wealth in an agrarian society; far from being merely a symbolic representation of goods, money itself was a form of wealth. A state requires a stock of money proportional to its size, population, and productive capacity.[31]

The question to which the "Ratios of Exchange" chapters – and indeed Chinese thinking about money generally – is addressed is not how to equilibrate the values of commodities exchanged through market transactions (i.e., to establish "just" prices) but rather how the ruler can overcome the vicissitudes of dearth and plenty and satisfy the material needs of the people. Grain,

[30] Ch. 73, "Guoxu" 國蓄, in *GZ*, 3, p. 1279.

[31] Ch. 73, "Guoxu," in *GZ*, 3, pp. 1264, 1275; ch. 75, "Shanquanshu," in *GZ*, 3, p. 1306.

the supreme form of wealth, determined the value of all other commodities. If the supply of grain diminished, causing its price to rise, the value of all other goods fell. Wealthy merchants exploited their market advantage by hoarding grain and other commodities to control prices. In one of his most famous passages, Pseudo-Guanzi warns of the disastrous consequences of diluting the ruler's control over the wealth of society:

> If wealth issues from a single source, the state will be invincible. If wealth issues from two sources, the state's military strength will suffice to defend its borders. If wealth issues from three sources, the ruler will find it impossible to raise an army. If wealth issues from four sources, his state is doomed. The former kings, knowing this to be true, therefore prevented the people from accumulating excess wealth and sealed off the paths to profit. Supply and demand (lit., "giving and taking") remained the prerogative of the ruler, and wealth and poverty were subject to the ruler's will. Thus the people worshipped the ruler like the sun and the moon, and cherished the ruler as they would their fathers and mothers.[32]

Of course, the ruler is incapable of exercising direct control over the supply of grain, a commodity produced and consumed by nearly every household and subject to the vicissitudes of nature. Instead, the ruler utilizes his leverage over the supply of money to obtain ample supplies of staple goods. Unlike grain, "gold and copper know no years of dearth."[33] Through adroit manipulation of the exchange ratios between money and grain, the ruler acquires godlike power over human society: "The five grains are the Sovereign of Destiny (Siming 司命) to the people. Gold and bronze currency serve as the universal medium (*tongshi* 通施). Therefore the prescient ruler grasps the reins of the universal medium in order to bridle the Sovereign of Destiny."[34] The overriding goal of the ruler is to arrogate to himself sole authority over the ratios of exchange.

The theorem of exchange ratios, perhaps the most noteworthy contribution of Pseudo-Guanzi to Chinese economic thought, was predicated on the belief that money cannot be produced by the people themselves. Consequently, by exercising a monopoly over the issue of money, the ruler can regulate its quantity (and thus its value):

32 Ch. 73, "Guoxu," in *GZ*, 3, pp. 1262–63.

33 From the commentary of the Han scholastic Zheng Xuan (130–200 CE) on a passage in the *Rituals of Zhou*, quoted by the Ming statecraft scholar Qiu Jun 邱濬 in his *Daxue yanyi bu* 大學衍義補 ([hereafter *DXYYB*]; SKQS ed.), 26.3b.

34 Ch. 73, "Guoxu," in *GZ*, 3, p. 1259. The metaphors of grain as Sovereign of Destiny (a deity believed to have the power to determine the length of an individual's lifespan) and money as the universal medium also appear in two other places in the "Ratios of Exchange" chapters: ch. 78, "Kuidu" 揆度; ch. 81, "Qingzhong (yi)" 輕重 (乙), in *GZ*, 3, pp. 1382, 1451, respectively.

> Jade originates in the mountain frontiers of Yuezhi [in central Asia]; gold originates beyond the banks of the Ru and Han Rivers [in the Chu realm, renowned for its gold]; pearls originate from the Crimson Barrens [i.e., the southern littoral of present-day China]. All of these places lie 700 or 800 leagues from the Zhou realm, accessible only by difficult and perilous roads. Therefore, the former kings availed themselves of these valuable and rare goods and made pearls and jade their superior currency and gold their secondary currency, while knife-shaped and spade-shaped bronzes were relegated to the position of inferior currencies. When the ruler demanded gold, its value would rise; when his demand for gold eased, the value of gold fell. The former kings issued decrees as they saw fit to raise or lower the value of gold and thereby exercise control over commodities and consumption.[35]

It is the scarcity of jade, pearls, and gold, then, that endows them with the capacity to serve as money. By taking advantage of his exclusive access to their sources of supply, the ruler can adjust the quantity of money in circulation and thereby manipulate its exchange value.

The "Ratios of Exchange" chapters in the *Guan Zi* gave birth to the fundamental axiom of Chinese monetary theory: "the purchasing power of the medium of exchange was solely a result of its quantity, in the form of money, in relationship to the supply of all other commodities."[36] The state buys or sells goods – or, conversely, disburses or withdraws money – to achieve a desired price level: "If nine-tenths of the kingdom's currency remains in the hands of the ruler and only one-tenth circulates among the people, the value of money will rise and the prices of the myriad goods will fall. The ruler acquires goods using money as a medium of exchange. He thereby transfers money to the public domain, while accumulating goods in his own realm, thus causing the prices of the myriad goods to increase tenfold."[37] Failure to intervene in the market and maintain an appropriate balance between the respective values of money and commodities opens the door for private merchants to dominate commerce and extract excessive profits. This

[35] This passage appears, in slightly different wording, four times in the "Ratios of Exchange" chapters. This translation is based on ch. 77, "Dishu" 地數, in *GZ*, 3, p. 1360. See also ch. 73, "Guoxu"; ch. 78, "Kuidu"; and ch. 81, "Qingzhong (yi)" in *GZ*, 3, pp. 1279, 1383, 1446, respectively. Despite the suggestion that pearls and jades served as the "superior currency," the author invoked these precious gems merely to illustrate his larger claims about the nature of money; there is no evidence that pearls or jades were ever used as currency in ancient China.

[36] Robert M. Hartwell, "Classical Chinese Monetary Analysis and Economic Policy in T'ang-Northern Sung China," *Transactions of the International Conference of Orientalists in Japan* 13 (1968): 71.

[37] Ch. 74, "Shanguogui" 山國軌, in *GZ*, 3, p. 1284.

concern was expressed in the following admonition spoken by Guan Zhong to Lord Huan:

> At present, the *dao* and *bu* currencies remain secreted in the state treasuries, while the merchants exploit monetary stratagems to manipulate the price of commodities. They raise the value of currency to force prices down or lower the value of currency to cause prices to rise... The prince who can balance (*heng* 衡) the exchange values of grain, bronze currency, and gold is capable of restoring order to the empire. This is the key calculus (*shu* 數) for preserving the empire.[38]

Given the crucial role of money not just in determining the price level but also in fostering production, it is no wonder that Pseudo-Guanzi insisted that the ruler's monopoly on coinage must not be compromised.

In practice, however, the theoretical chartalism of Pseudo-Guanzi had its limits. Fiscal policymakers typically counterbalanced the heady illusions of imperial omnipotence found in the "Ratios of Exchange" chapters with sober pragmatism. If the state significantly debased its coin by reducing its weight or adulterating it with cheaper metals, the disparity between intrinsic value and market value would invite counterfeiting. Thus the principle of full-bodied coin, though not grounded in a metallist theory, became a hallmark of prudent monetary policy. This tendency to accept metallism in practice though not in theory is known as *practical metallism*.[39]

1.4 Han Debates over Money and the Morality of Exchange

As suggested earlier, the mercantilist principles expressed by Pseudo-Guanzi corresponded in many respects to the model of political economy inaugurated in the late 2nd century BCE by Emperor Wu and his advisers, notably Sang Hongyang, the son of a merchant whom Wu appointed as his exchequer. Although Emperor Wu and Sang Hongyang did not explicitly invoke the *Guan Zi* – they were statesmen, not philosophers – their policies echoed Pseudo-Guanzi's prescriptions. The most controversial of Emperor Wu's policies, his imposition of state monopolies on the production and sale of iron and salt in 119 BCE, had been explicitly endorsed by Pseudo-Guanzi, who advocated indirect taxation of commerce and consumption in lieu of direct

[38] Ch. 76, "Shanzhishu" 山至數, in *GZ*, 3, p. 1342. The word *shu* ("calculation") appears hundreds of times in the *Guan Zi*, and the "Light and Heavy" chapters make repeated reference to "calculation of exchange values" (*qingzhong zhi shu* 輕重之數). In the passage cited here, the word refers more abstractly as "method." On the central importance of calculation and quantification in the *Guan Zi*, see Chin, *Savage Exchange*, pp. 20, 40–51.

[39] Schumpeter, *History of Economic Analysis*, pp. 288–93.

taxation of agricultural production.[40] The "equitable delivery" (*junshu* 均輸) and "balanced standard" (*pingzhun* 平準) policies implemented by Emperor Wu marked an even deeper intrusion of the state into commerce. Under the equitable delivery system, local officials used their money revenues to purchase goods (especially textiles) to supply the capital and the frontier armies. In 110 BCE, the equitable delivery system was merged with the salt and iron monopolies and rechristened the balanced standard policy. Government agents throughout the empire used public funds, including monopoly revenues, to smooth out regional variations in price fluctuations by buying up goods where prices were low and selling them where prices were high. The issue of the new Wuzhu coin by state mints consolidated in the Han capital of Chang'an likewise reflected Pseudo-Guanzi's preeminent principle of maintaining control of the money supply.

The most notable critique of Emperor Wu's fiscal policies appears in the "Treatise on the Balanced Standard" included by the contemporary historian Sima Qian in his *Historical Records* (c. 90 BCE).[41] Much of Sima's jeremiad against Wu's fiscal agenda focused on the venality of a bloated government bureaucracy, the folly of the emperor's military adventures, and the confiscation of wealth that failed to redress the plight of the poor. Sima summed up Emperor Wu's rule in these words: "there once was a time when the entire wealth and resources of the empire were exhausted to provide for the ruler, and yet he found them insufficient."[42]

More broadly, Sima Qian's denunciation of state control of commerce was rooted in his admiration of the entrepreneurial skills of merchants and peddlers, who relied on the virtues of intelligence, industry, and thrift to earn a living in contrast to those who inherit wealth or use the perquisites of political office to acquire it.[43] He also was fascinated by the operation of the market as a spontaneous and autonomous force:

> Society must have farmers to provide food; woodsmen, fishers, and miners to supply the products of nature; artisans to transform them into the necessities of life; and merchants to distribute them. What need, then, is there for government decrees, requisitions and allocations, or periodic summons to labor? *Let each man exercise his own abilities and apply his own effort to obtain what he desires.* [my emphasis] . . . When each person pursues his own occupation and delights in his work, like water running

[40] Ch. 74, "Shanguogui," ch. 78, "Kuidu," in *GZ*, 3, pp. 1297, 1379.

[41] For an English translation of this chapter, see Sima Qian, *Records of the Grand Historian: Han Dynasty II*, trans. Burton Watson (New York: Columbia University Press, 1993), pp. 61–85.

[42] *SJ* 30.1443.

[43] Sima's views on merchants and commerce are expressed in his chapter "Biographies of the Moneymakers." For a translation, see Sima, *Records: Han Dynasty II*, pp. 433–54.

> downhill goods will flow ceaselessly night and day without being summoned; the people will produce them without being asked.[44]

It was in this dynamic interplay of ability, effort, and desire that Sima located the special genius of the entrepreneur.

Even more radically, Sima Qian dissented from the prevailing view that money and markets were the handiwork of the sage-kings. Money, Sima asserted, was a spontaneous product of exchange among the people rather than a deliberate intervention by sage-rulers to relieve economic distress: "When farmers, artisans, and merchants first began to exchange with each other, money in the forms of tortoise shells and cowries, gold and bronze coins, and knife and spade-shaped currencies arose among them. Thus the origin of money is very remote; it existed even before [the sage-king] Gao Xin."[45] In erasing the sage-kings from economic life and livelihood, he implicitly challenged the assumption among Confucian critics of Emperor Wu that money and exchange were instruments of a moral transactional order. Yet Sima – parallel at least in this respect to Pseudo-Guanzi – acknowledged that it was necessary for the state to monopolize coinage in order to establish a reliable monetary standard. Private power over money not only fostered the concentration of wealth in the hands of aggrandizers but also encouraged challenges to sovereign authority. Sima was unsparing in his condemnation of Emperor Wen – whom he otherwise depicted as a model ruler for his restraint in not interfering in the private economy – for yielding the right to coin money to princes and merchants, most notoriously the Prince of Wu, who rose up in insurrection in 154 BCE. At the same time, he condemned Emperor Wu's various attempts to create fiat currencies – including a deerskin "bill" valued at 400,000 coins and silver/tin coins in several arbitrary denominations – before instituting the Wuzhu coinage.

Sima's views on merchants are remarkably free of the moralistic judgments in which both Emperor Wu's advisers and his Confucian critics couched their arguments. Yet his writings are suffused with a profound ambivalence about the power of money.[46] For individuals, the calling of the merchant offered the opportunity to raise themselves up to honorable station in society. Yet the rich inevitably exploit their power; free enterprise was no salve to economic inequality. The triumph of market values reduced all goods, even human beings, to mere commodities; the unfortunate, impoverished by debt, were

[44] *SJ* 129.3254.

[45] *SJ* 30.1442. Elsewhere Sima writes: "Money circulates to connect farmers and merchants" 維幣之行以通農商; *SJ* 129.3306.

[46] Michael Nylan, "Assets Accumulating: Sima Qian's Perspectives on Moneymaking, Virtue, and History," in Hans van Ess, Olga Lomová, and Dorothee Schaab-Hanke (eds.), *Views from Within, Views from Beyond: Approaches to the* Shiji *as an Early Work of Historiography* (Wiesbaden: Harrassowitz, 2015), pp. 131–68.

reduced to slavery. While condoning the private pursuit of gain, Sima – no less than the Confucian critics – harshly condemned the intrusion of the values of the marketplace into the conduct of government. The individual properly should focus on enriching his family, but the ruler must pursue the very different agenda of enriching society and preventing exploitation of the poor by the rich. In the eyes of other philosophers and statesmen, however, Sima's formulation of different sets of values for the individual and the state was logically flawed, and his radical views attracted few adherents.

The unprecedented intrusion of the autocratic state into economic life during Emperor Wu's reign provoked sharp conservative reaction, especially among Confucian officials. Overt challenges to Wu's fiscal policies were rare during the emperor's lifetime; Sima Qian's *Historical Records* circulated only posthumously. But soon after Wu's death in 87 BCE, dissident officials sharply questioned the morality of state control over commerce and industry. In 81 BCE, the legacy of Wu's fiscal policies became the subject of a formal debate convened by Wu's successor, Emperor Zhao (r. 87–74 BCE). Sang Hongyang – still a senior statesman at the Han court – was called upon to defend policies such as the salt and iron monopolies against an array of "Learned Men" summoned to the capital to present their grievances. A digest of the debate between Sang and his Confucian detractors has been preserved in dialogue form in the work entitled the *Salt and Iron Debates*.[47]

In the *Debates*, Sang Hongyang insists on the ruler's responsibility to manage the economy for the benefit of the commonwealth in language reminiscent of Pseudo-Guanzi:

> The true king should monopolize natural resources, regulate custom barriers and marketplaces, ensure that the tasks appropriate to each season are fulfilled in a timely manner, and govern the people by controlling the ratios of exchange. In good years of bountiful harvests, the ruler stores up goods to provide for times of scarcity and want. In bad years of meager yields, the ruler disburses money and goods, circulating his accumulated surplus in order to make up for shortfalls.[48]

Beyond this affirmation of mercantilist principles, Sang justifies his policies by pointing to their achievements: rationalization of imperial finances; establishment of a sound, unified currency; strengthening the agricultural base of the empire through irrigation and flood-control projects and diffusion of advanced farming technologies; and equalization of the tax burden among

[47] For a translation of the *Salt and Iron Debates*, see Jean Levi (trans.), *La Dispute sur le sel et le fer* (Paris: Belles Lettres, 2010). Anthony Barbieri-Low is preparing an English translation.

[48] Ch. 2, "Ligeng" 力耕, in Huan Kuan 桓寬, *Yantie lun jiaozhu* 鹽鐵論校注, Wang Liqi 王利器 (ed.) ([hereafter *YTL*]; Beijing: Zhonghua shuju, 1992), 1, p. 28.

different regions. He also upholds the managerial role of the state by extolling the virtues of systematic, long-range planning in contrast to the short-term, survival-oriented decision-making of individual households.

Moreover, Sang Hongyang underscores the crucial role of the state in achieving economic justice. He repeatedly urges the ruler to take decisive action to "place a yoke on the noble princes," "expel the rich and great merchants," and prevent "untitled powermongers" from dominating the trade in vital goods such as salt and iron for their personal profit.[49] If the ruler relinquishes the "levers of profit" (*quanli* 權利) – the power to coin money, the wealth generated by trade in salt and iron – private self-interest will overwhelm the public good, and aggrandizers will impoverish the people. But if the government acts to create "balance" (*heng*) and ensure "stability" (*zhun*) – invoking here the keywords of Pseudo-Guanzi's political economy – then "even if you send a knee-high child to the market, none would be able to deceive him."[50]

Sang Hongyang also describes the invention of money in language echoing Pseudo-Guanzi:

> In antiquity, during the flood in the time of Yu the Great and the drought in the time of Tang, the distress of the common folk drove them to sell their children to obtain the necessities of food and clothing. Yu coined money from the gold of Mount Li and Tang coined money from the copper of Mount Zhuang so that the people could redeem their children from bondage. All under Heaven praised them for their benevolence.[51]

Sang goes on to say that institutions must change with historical circumstances. Ancient dynasties used cowries as money, but such a cumbersome form of currency could not suit the needs for exchange in the present. Invoking the disastrous results of Emperor Wen's free coinage, he reaffirms the need for the ruler to monopolize coinage as well as crucial sources of wealth such as salt and iron:

> If the ruler does not impose a levy on the natural resources of the mountains and marshes [i.e., iron and salt], he must share their bounty with his vassals. If the ruler does not monopolize the manufacture of currency, then counterfeit coin will circulate with the genuine. If the vassals attain great wealth, they will seek to exceed each other in their display of opulence. If ordinary subjects monopolize the sources of wealth, they will seek to undermine one another.[52]

[49] Ch. 2, "Ligeng"; ch. 14, "Qingzhong" 輕重; and ch. 5, "Jingeng" 禁耕; in *YTL*, 1, pp. 27, 179, 67, respectively.

[50] Ch. 5, "Jingeng," in *YTL*, 1, p. 68.

[51] Ch. 2, "Ligeng," in *YTL*, 1, p. 28.

[52] Ch. 4, "Cuobi" 錯幣, *YTL*, 1, p. 57.

In contrast to Sima Qian's contention that the division of labor among farmers, artisans, and merchants occurred naturally, Sang asserts that the operation of the economy requires the ruler's intervention:

> If artisans do not produce, farmers will lack tools; and if merchants do not produce, the media of exchange [*baohuo* 寶貨] will not circulate. When farmers lack tools, grain is not planted, and when the media of exchange do not circulate, the treasury will be impoverished. Now, the salt and iron monopolies and the equitable marketing system are the means by which the ruler circulates accumulated wealth and adjusts the supply of and demand for goods. Surely it would be unwise to abolish them."[53]

The artisans and merchants in this passage are not private agents. Instead, under Emperor Wu's monopolies on strategic sectors of production and exchange, they have become agents of the state and extensions of the ruler's managerial role in the economy.

In response, the Learned Men conjoin the assertion that agriculture is the true source of all wealth with Confucian moral dicta concerning the iniquity of the profit motive, the nobility of frugality, and the dignity of poverty. The Learned Men interpreted *quanli* not only as the instruments for amassing wealth and power but also as a psychological disposition, a "calculus of profit," in which self-interest and material gain eroded all consideration of ethical conduct. Restoration of the pristine agrarian order of antiquity must be reinforced by a rededication of government to the moral regeneration of society:

> The task at the present moment lies in eradicating the miseries of cold and hunger by abolishing the salt and iron monopolies, repudiating the calculus of profit, dividing and allocating arable lands, urging dedication to the primary occupation [i.e., agriculture], fostering cultivation of mulberries and hemp, and maximizing the productivity of the land. If the ruler restrains his ambitions and curbs his expenditures, the people will enrich themselves.[54]

Rebuffing mercantilist doctrines, the Learned Men espouse a vision of society founded on self-sufficient farming families shielded from the economic uncertainties and moral depravity of the marketplace. In their view, not only was the imperial state profiting at the expense of its subjects, but the emphasis on increasing revenues distracted officials from their proper duties as guardians of both the spiritual and material welfare of the people.

[53] Ch. 1, "Benyi" 本議, in *YTL*, 1, p. 3. In translating *baohuo* as "media of exchange" (i.e., money), I diverge from the standard translation of the word as "luxury goods" (cf., for example, Levi, *Le sel et le fer*, p. I.7).

[54] Ch. 36, "Shuihan" 水旱, in *YTL*, 1, p. 429.

Beyond condemning the state's expropriation of commercial and industrial enterprises, the Learned Men at times repudiate the market economy itself as corrupting. They assert that in antiquity the minimal exchange necessary for meeting subsistence needs was conducted through barter. The introduction of money inevitably promoted dishonesty, conflict, and the breakdown of social solidarity:

> The ancients had marketplaces but no coinage. Everyone exchanged what they had for what they lacked, such as the weaver who brought finished cloth to trade for yarn. In later ages, tortoise shells, cowries, and metallic money emerged as the media of exchange. Each time the currency system changed, the people became more and more dishonest. Now, dishonesty can be rectified by returning to native simplicity; errors can be prevented by reverting to codes of ritual duty.[55]

Elsewhere, however, the Learned Men champion private enterprise in place of state monopoly:

> When the people paid excises to forge iron and extract salt, salt was no more dear than grain, and tools were sharp-edged and of fine quality. Now, with government officials in charge of manufacturing iron tools, most are poorly made, at exorbitant cost; the convict laborers in state workshops resent the work and do not exert themselves. When family members work together, fathers and sons applying all their effort, each is devoted to crafting fine tools; poorly made ones are rejected. During the peak seasons of agricultural work, they load the tools onto carts and bring them to the countryside. The people freely buy and sell, exchanging goods and grain to obtain new tools to replace worn-out ones. Sometimes goods are bought on credit so that no one will neglect their tasks.[56]

The Learned Men go on to extol the division of labor among rural communities that included potters, carpenters, and other artisans as well as farmers but required no intervention on the part of the ruler.

The court debate of 81 BCE did not fundamentally alter the Han state's fiscal regime; Emperor Zhao was persuaded to retain the salt and iron monopolies. But in the following decades the conservative reaction against Wu's fiscal strategies swelled. The anti-statist ideology and physiocratic principles enunciated by Sang Hongyang's critics were widely shared among the rising class of Confucian statesmen that came to dominate the Han government after Emperor Wu's time. In their view, the monarch should serve as a paragon of moral excellence whose activities are largely confined to ritual duties. They rejected not only Emperor Wu's mercantilist fiscal regime but also the market

55 Ch. 4, "Cuobi," *YTL*, 1, p. 57.

56 Ch. 36, "Shuihan," in *YTL*, 1, p. 430. I am indebted to Anthony Barbieri-Low for correcting a crucial error in this passage in the *YTL* version of the text.

economy itself. During the reign of Emperor Yuan (r. 49–33 BCE) the political ideology of this group became deeply insinuated in government policy and institutions. In 44 BCE, the minister Gong Yu went so far as to propose abolishing metallic money altogether. Gong's proposal was deemed impractical, but Han statesmen fully retreated from Emperor Wu's state activism. Consequently, this ascendant class of Confucian officials fashioned themselves into an oligarchic elite of magnate clans who dominated public office and private wealth. The rise of the magnate clans also set in motion important economic changes, most notably a reorientation of wealth and investment from commerce to landed estates and a further widening of the gulf between rich and poor.

The growing power of the magnate clans provided the catalyst for the ambitious attempt at radical reform of state and society launched by Wang Mang in the early years of the 1st century CE. Upon becoming regent to a child-emperor in 1 BCE, Wang sought to reinvigorate strong imperial rule through a wholesale reorganization of Han social and political institutions inspired by the *Rituals of Zhou*, a canonical text purporting to be a detailed blueprint of the administrative organization of the ancient Zhou kingdom. After the child-emperor died in 6 CE, Wang declared himself emperor of his own Xin ("New") dynasty and launched a draconian program of reform. Invoking the ancient doctrine that all land and wealth is the property of the ruler, he confiscated the landholdings of many estate owners and redistributed them to the poor. Wang Mang was equally assertive in expanding state control of commerce and money. While still regent, he had introduced two new forms of bronze currency with purely nominal values that circulated concurrently with the existing Wuzhu coin. In keeping with Wang's atavistic ideology, the key-shaped design of some of these coins grafted the form of the ancient *dao* currency onto the standard round coin. As emperor, Wang proscribed the use of Wuzhu coin and created a bewildering array of new currencies by recoining old Wuzhu coins.[57] Other measures adopted by Wang Mang broadened the reach of the state monopolies on commodities, subjected trade and moneylending to strict regulation, and nationalized gold stocks. Such policies drove sound coin and gold out of circulation, unleashing rampant inflation and severely disrupting commerce and industrial production.

Wang Mang's ambitious agenda directly challenged the political and economic power of the magnate families, provoking fierce opposition. Government officials resisted implementing policies that threatened the vested interests of their kinfolk. Political chaos bred economic distress, antagonizing all ranks of society. In the end, popular insurrections toppled Wang's

[57] For surveys of Wang Mang's monetary reforms and new currencies, see Thierry, *Monnaies*, pp. 119–29; Yamada Katsuyoshi 山田勝芳, *Kahei no Chūgoku kodaishi* 貨幣の中国古代史 (Tokyo: Asahi shinbunsha, 2000), pp. 143–86.

government. In 23 CE, Wang was deposed and put to death, and the Han dynasty was reestablished two years later.

1.5 The New Consensus

The demise of the usurper Wang Mang was hailed as a moment of profound moral renewal. Restoration of the Han dynasty further entrenched Confucian political ideology and the social and economic dominance of the magnate families. Among the projects undertaken to glorify Han rule was the writing of an imperially endorsed history of the dynasty down to Wang Mang's usurpation, to replace Sima Qian's monumental work, which was deemed iconoclastic in its deviations from Confucian orthodoxy. Ban Biao (3–54 CE), a prominent scholar, had begun such a project as a private undertaking but died before completing it. In 66 CE, his son Ban Gu (32–92 CE) received an imperial appointment to complete his father's work, which ultimately was finished after his death by his sister Ban Zhao. The Ban family's *History of the Former Han Dynasty* displaced Sima's *Historical Records* as the authoritative history of the first half of the Han dynasty and inaugurated a tradition of official dynastic histories that became the cornerstone of Chinese historical writing throughout the imperial period.

In his chapters on "Food and Money" and "Biographies of the Moneymakers," Ban Gu rewrote the economic history of the early Han as recorded in Sima Qian's *Historical Records*, erasing Sima's positive evaluation of commercial entrepreneurship and reasserting the primacy of agriculture as the foundation of a ritually ordered moral community.[58] Ban reiterated the Confucian maxim that the moral transformation of the people proceeds from satisfying their subsistence needs: "once the people are well-fed and goods circulate unhindered, the state can be sustained, the people enriched, and moral renovation brought to completion."[59] In sharp contrast to Sima's depiction of the spontaneous emergence of markets and money among the people, Ban re-centered economic life on the benevolent handiwork of the sage-kings, who fashioned tools, built cities, opened marketplaces, invented money, and founded schools to level the disparities between rich and poor.

Ban Gu fused the principle of agriculture as the primary occupation to his vision of a strong and benevolent monarchy. With the chronic warfare and economic competition of the Warring States era now past, the emperor need not amass great wealth. But the ruler must take an active role in shaping the social hierarchy, establishing a division of labor among the four occupational

[58] For a translation – dated, but serviceable – of the "Food and Money" chapters, see Nancy Lee Swann, *Food and Money in Ancient China: The Earliest Economic History of China to A.D. 25* (Princeton, NJ: Princeton University Press, 1950), pp. 109–359.

[59] *HS* 24A.1117.

categories of governors (the learned elite), farmers, artisans, and merchants by assigning tasks according to the abilities of each individual. Ban shared the widespread apprehension about the incompatibility of the family farm economy and the values of the marketplace. In his rewriting – an inversion, really – of Sima Qian's chapter on the moneymakers, Ban repudiated Sima's celebration of the entrepreneurial genius of merchants and instead upheld the traditional status order, depicting merchants as avaricious thieves who impoverish the state and the people alike.[60] Yet he did not join Gong Yu and others in repudiating the use of money altogether. Instead, Ban sought to subordinate market exchange to a tributary economy focused on the satisfaction of needs rather than an acquisitive economy motivated by wants. The vision of the providential state expressed in Ban's "Food and Money" chapters would become the canonical paradigm of political economy for centuries to come.[61]

In the introduction to the "Food and Money" chapters, Ban Gu defines money (*huo* 貨) as "bast and silk fabrics that can be worn as well as gold, bronze currencies, tortoise shells, and cowries, by means of which wealth can be apportioned, utility disseminated, and places of surplus and scarcity joined together."[62] In his narration of the evolution of money, Ban states that no records concerning money prior to the Zhou survive, but the early Zhou rulers created a tripartite monetary system consisting of gold pieces, round coins, and bolts of cloth – which describes the monetary system of the Qin Empire, not the early Zhou. According to Ban, the three types of money served different economic functions: "money drew its precious value from gold and its utility from bronze currencies; coin flowed like water from a spring; bast fabrics were widely disseminated; and silks were stored in bundles."[63] Putting Ban's language into modern analytical terms, gold served as the measure of value, bronze currencies (ultimately coins) and cloth made from bast fibers (hemp and ramie) as means of exchange, and silk as a store of value. In describing this monetary system as the deliberate invention of the Zhou founders, Ban reaffirmed the role of the sage-kings in creating money and denied Sima Qian's vision of an autonomous market.

By Ban Gu's day, gold had ceased to serve as money apart from imperial gifts and largesse. Bronze coin had eclipsed other forms of money as the medium of market exchange, although the scarcity of sound coin – the revived Han government produced only limited quantities of Wuzhu coin, often of poor quality – compelled the government to resort to converting money taxes

60 *HS* 91.3679–94; Chin, *Savage Exchange*, pp. 185–87. For a translation of Ban's "Biographies of the Moneymakers," see Swann, *Food and Money*, pp. 413–53.

61 On the "providential state" as a mode of Chinese political economy, see von Glahn, "Modalities of the Fiscal State," pp. 22–27.

62 *HS* 24A.1117.

63 *HS* 24B.1149.

into payments of hemp, ramie, and silk cloth. After the dissolution of the Han Empire into competing regimes in the early 3rd century, coinage mostly ceased altogether, and the coin in circulation became highly degraded. Not surprisingly, monetary theory shifted in the direction of metallism. In 482, advisers at the court of the short-lived Qi dynasty (479–501) called for a debasement to boost the supply of coin in circulation. In response, an otherwise obscure official named Kong Yi delivered a sharp rebuttal that eventually attained renown as the classic defense of the metallist doctrine of full-bodied coin. It was Kong Yi who enunciated the principle of "hold not copper too dear, nor begrudge the expense of labor" (*buxi tong bu'ai gong* 不惜銅不愛工) that became the watchwords of monetary prudence:

> The reason why people engage in counterfeiting despite stringent laws outlawing the practice is that the ruler, in coining money, cherishes copper and begrudges the expenditure of labor [i.e., reduces the cost of coinage by relaxing standards of purity and workmanship]. Cherishing copper and begrudging the expenditure of labor, the ruler claims that coin is a tool which can be used to facilitate the exchange of goods irrespective of its intrinsic value. Seeking to ensure that coin is cheap and plentiful, the ruler economizes on the labor invested in coinage in order to reduce the cost of minting coin without giving careful thought to the consequences of this course of action. During the more than 500 years between the initial issue of the Wuzhu coin in the Han dynasty and the reign of Emperor Wen of Song (r. 424–452), dynastic institutions changed repeatedly, yet none altered the standards for minting Wuzhu coin. This shows that the weight and quality of the Wuzhu coin was in proper proportion to the requirements of a medium of exchange, and thus the Wuzhu coin stands as a model deserving emulation.[64]

Although Kong recognized that shortages of coin hindered commerce, he considered counterfeiting and depreciation of coin more iniquitous threats to economic welfare. Full-bodied coin, Kong argued, will deter counterfeiting because it is too expensive to imitate. The problem of currency shortages could be resolved by withdrawing all substandard coin from circulation and recoining it. Kong's belief that the Han Wuzhu coin – still a nominal standard – should be honored as a timeless standard for the size and weight of bronze currency became an article of faith among proponents of full-bodied coin.

Kong's metallist argument ignored the reality that copper had use value independent of coin and that full-bodied coin quickly disappeared into the melting pot. Chinese theorists had given little thought to the commodity value of copper; in their mind, "copper" meant coin. The rapid spread of Buddhism

[64] Xiao Zixian 蕭子顯et al., *Nan Qi shu* 南齊書 (Zhonghua shuju ed.), 37.652. See also Du You 杜佑, *Tongdian* 通典 ([hereafter *TD*]; Shitong ed.), 8.45a.

during the post-Han period created a competing source of demand for copper. The countless religious icons and other devotional objects manufactured from bronze offended both the secular sensibilities of Confucian statesmen and their conception of economic utility, since they deemed lavish expenditure on religious worship extravagant and wasteful.

Chronic shortages of money became especially acute under the Tang dynasty (618–907), when state mints failed to generate sufficient coin to meet rising market demand. Still, chartalist principles remained unshaken. When the minister Zhang Jiuling in 734 drafted a plan to restore private coinage, his proposal encountered fierce opposition at the court. Critics contended that private coinage would only exacerbate the problem by increasing the demand for copper. In an oft-cited critique, Liu Zhi, a low-ranking official, returned to the idea that copper had no natural use value; it was inferior to iron in making weapons and inferior to lacquer in making tableware. If the state outlawed frivolous uses of copper (i.e., Buddhist icons and other religious paraphernalia), the demand for copper would abate, thus ensuring an adequate supply and lowering the cost of coinage. In essence, Liu maintained that the state could legislate the use value of copper out of existence.[65] Later commentators conflated Liu's suggestion that the state could eradicate the use value of copper with the view that coin lacked intrinsic value to argue that bronze coinage entailed no real cost because it did not diminish the supply of useful goods.

In the aftermath of this debate, the canon of monetary analysis centered on the chartalist principles of Pseudo-Guanzi assumed definitive form. The *Comprehensive Statutes*, the encyclopedic survey of Chinese political institutions published by the historian Du You in 801, enshrined the *Guan Zi* as the paramount authority on monetary matters. The arguments of proponents of theoretical chartalism such as Jia Yi and Liu Zhi were prominently featured in the *Comprehensive Statutes*, but so too was the practical metallism of Kong Yi. Despite his allegiance to chartalist principles, Du You also incorporated the essentially metallist doctrine that bronze coin was uniquely suited to the needs of currency as a means of exchange and a measure of value:

> Gold and silver are worked into utensils and articles of adornment, which inhibits their circulation. Grain is too bulky, and silk too fragile, to transport over considerable distances. Bronze coin alone meets the needs of commerce. It pours forth and flows freely like a fountain. Not only are grain and silk bulky and fragile, but they also cannot be easily divided into

65 For discussions of the debate and translation of key documents, see Penelope Herbert, "A Debate in T'ang China on the State Monopoly on Casting Coin," *T'oung Pao* 62.4–5 (1977): 254–92; Mei Ah Tan, "Monetary Policy as the Key to State Authority and Income in Tang China," *Journal of Chinese Studies* 64 (2017): 85–90.

> fractional units. Of all monetary instruments, the Wuzhu coin alone has served as the only practical currency throughout successive dynasties.[66]

Invoking the simile of an eternally flowing fountain, Du asserted that bronze coin was a superior form of money because of its liquidity, that is to say, its convenience as a means of exchange. Du You's synthesis of theoretical chartalism and practical metallism would become the touchstone for later writings on monetary theory.[67] In reformulating Du's argument for the superiority of coin as a means of exchange, the 15th-century statecraft scholar Qiu Jun added a chartalist codicil borrowed from Pseudo-Guanzi's quantity theorem:

> Considerable waste results from dividing gold and silver into fractional units, while cloth is completely ruined by doing so. Only by casting copper into coin can the ruler obtain a suitable currency. If there is a surfeit of goods, a greater quantity of coin can be issued to raise prices; conversely, if there is a dearth of goods, then less coin is issued and prices will fall. Gold and silver are produced by Heaven, while coins are fashioned by man. Bronze currency requires the joint efforts of Heaven and man to be rendered into a useful substance.[68]

Qiu alludes to the signal drawback of precious metals: the natural scarcity of gold and silver negated their utility as currency. Coin, in contrast, was deemed an inexhaustible resource and thus amenable to the ruler's will. Qiu's treatise was intended as a defense of the utility of coin at a time when silver had begun to displace coin as a means of exchange. Like many political economists of the late imperial era, Qiu drew on the precepts of both theoretical chartalism and practical metallism to affirm the superiority of bronze currency over precious metals.

Rejecting the premise that the purpose behind the invention of money was to facilitate trade, Qiu reiterated the proposition that the sage-kings created money to relieve the suffering of the people in times of distress.[69] Chinese monetary thought remained anchored to the idea that money was a tool used by the ruler to promote economic welfare by ensuring an equitable distribution of goods and income. The basic axioms of classical monetary analysis formulated in the Han dynasty and codified in institutional histories such as Du You's *Comprehensive Statutes* required modifications as new forms of currency – paper money and silver – displaced bronze coin as the monetary standard, as we shall see. But the vital role of the state in managing the supply of money to balance the exchange ratios between money and commodities and to satisfy the needs of both producers and consumers remained beyond dispute.

66 *TD* 8.45a.

67 Among the most important examples, see Ma Duanlin's 馬端臨 *Wenxian tongkao* 文獻通考 (1324) and Qiu Jun's *Daxue yanyi bu* (1487).

68 *DXYYB* 26.11b.

69 *DXYYB* 26.1a–b.

2

Debt, Contracts, and Financial Transactions

Debt created money, not vice versa. Contrary to the prevailing orthodoxy in economics, there is persuasive historical and archaeological evidence that the origin of money is to be found not in the exchange of commodities but rather in promises of payment. In the words of Geoffrey Ingham, the nature of money consists in "social relations of credit and debt denominated in a money of account."[1] The essential quality of money inheres in its utility as an abstract measure of value, not (pace Aristotle) in the intrinsic worth of a material substance. Most importantly, the value of money derived from the public authority's declaration of its acceptability in payment of debts or taxes. The earliest evidence for the origin of money, from Mesopotamia c. 2400 BCE, consists of records of debts measured in a silver unit of account (shekel). The shekel was not an actual physical money but rather a weight of silver (240 barley grains, or 8 g) linked to the *gur*, the monthly ration of barley for a family (120 liters).[2] Debts measured in shekels overwhelmingly consisted of obligations owed to public authorities (temples and palaces), even if some of these debts may have been incurred through loans from private individuals. Although denominated in silver, these debts were usually redeemed through labor service or goods, almost never in actual silver.[3] By the time of the Third Dynasty of Ur (21st century BCE), a sophisticated accounting system was used to assess taxes that allowed the conversion of virtually any kind of commodity into units of silver, barley, and labor time.[4]

1 Ingham, *Nature of Money*, p. 12. On this point see also Graeber, *Debt*.

2 Ingham, *Nature of Money*, p. 94; Michael Hudson, "The Archaeology of Money: Debt Versus Barter Theories of Money's Origins," in L. Randall Wray (ed.), *Credit and State Theories of Money: The Contribution of A. Mitchell Innes* (Cheltenham, UK: Edward Elgar, 2004), pp. 109–13.

3 Marc Van De Mieroop, "The Invention of Interest: Sumerian Loans," in Goetzmann and Rouwenhorst, *Origins of Value*, pp. 20–23, 27–28.

4 Michael Jura and Juan Carlos Moreno Garcia, "Ancient Near East and Egypt," in Andrew Monson and Walter Scheidel (eds.), *Fiscal Regimes and the Political Economy of Premodern States* (Cambridge: Cambridge University Press, 2015), p. 125.

The essential point here is that the origin of money reposed in its use as a fixed measure of value for debts to public authorities.[5] An alternative theory for the origin of money, espoused most notably by Philip Grierson, traces it to the legal practice of *wergild*: recompense for personal injury initially stipulated as a fine denominated in commodities – especially living commodities, such as cattle and slaves – and subsequently converted to silver equivalents.[6] The antiquity of such practices is uncertain; the best-known historical cases, the Germanic and Celtic law codes of the first millennium CE, date from well after the common use of silver coin. The laws attributed to the Athenian statesman Solon stipulated penalties for injuries expressed in drachmas of silver, although coinage had not yet appeared in Greece at that time (early 6th century BCE).[7] But in this theory, too, the value of money inheres in its utility as a measure of value fixed by law or custom, not in market exchange. The value of compensation in *wergild*, Grierson argues, reflected social distinctions of wealth and honor, not the exchange value of the goods themselves. Generalized application of monetary values to commodities could scarcely have come about before the appearance of market economies.

Credit money thus long preceded coinage. In ancient Mesopotamia, early exchange was conducted by running up debts for future repayment rather than spot settlement of transactions. As early as 2400 BCE, officials and merchants advanced loans to farmers, recording on clay tablets the sums of money owed (plus interest) after the harvest. Such loans required collateral – ranging from sheep and goats to houses, fields, and household members – that was subject to seizure in the event of default. Harvest failures precipitated debt crises, which threatened to reduce debtors to peonage (involuntary service to repay debts). The social disruption caused by debt crises in turn prompted Sumerian and Babylonian rulers to issue amnesties. Babylonian rulers routinely annulled debts, especially at the outset of their reign, and also in the event of catastrophic harvest failure.[8] The issue of Solon's law code was

[5] Of course, once created, money was adapted for the purposes of exchange, notably interregional trade. The earliest evidence for commercial networks and the use of silver as a unit of account in exchange (and also commercial loans), dating from the beginning of the second millennium BCE, comes from the city of Kanesh in central Anatolia, which housed a flourishing colony of Assyrian traders dealing in silver, copper, tin, and wool. Klaas R. Veenhoff, "Assur: The City, Its Traders, and Its Commercial Network," *Journal of the Economic and Social History of the Orient* 53.1 (2010): 39–82.

[6] Philip Grierson, "The Origins of Money," *Research in Economic Anthropology* 1 (1978): 1–35. See also Ingham, *Nature of Money*, pp. 91–93.

[7] Von Reden, *Money in Classical Antiquity*, p. 21.

[8] Hudson, "Archaeology of Money"; Michael Hudson, "Reconstructing the Origins of Interest-Bearing Debt and the Logic of Clean Slates," in Michael Hudson and Marc Van de Mieroop (eds.), *Debt and Economic Renewal in the Ancient Near East* (Bethesda, MD: CDL Press, 2002), pp. 7–58. See also Graeber, *Debt*, pp. 64–65, 214–17. Chinese emperors,

precipitated by debt crisis as well, and one of its principal features was the abolition of debt peonage. David Graeber observes that in Greece and Rome coinage seems to have been instituted as a solution to debt crises.[9] Coinage was integral to the articulation of the emerging *polis* city-state as a civic community as well as new and subversive notions of social value and economic worth.[10] By extension, cancellation of debts was crucial to the maintenance of social peace within the city-states from Solon's time onward.[11]

In China as well, debt was a crucial feature of market exchange within the context of state formation. Before the rise of markets and money in the 7th–6th centuries BCE, economic exchange in the Chinese ecumene was dominated by gift exchange rooted in personal and moral obligations based on principles of hierarchical reciprocity to recompense favor, awards, gifts, and service. Reciprocity here did not imply equality; on the contrary, exchange served the purpose of reaffirming the unequal political and social status of superiors and inferiors. The transformation of gifts into debts required a system of accounting to specify debt in quantitative terms. Quantification also rendered debt impersonal; by extension, debts can be transferred to others. Debt in this specific sense was simultaneously a product of markets that measured the value of goods in terms of money and of bureaucratic institutions used to record, extract, and transfer rents, fees, fines, and loans. Commercial exchange is premised on equalities of value in the goods exchanged and of the legal equality of the parties who engage in exchange. Debt, however, creates inequality; a debt contract is an agreement that establishes an unequal relationship between debtor and creditor for the duration of the debt. Thus the creation of debts generated tension between the state, which assumed the paternalist duties of rulers in the premarket world, and the market, which denied any such obligations. Both state and market claimed moral foundations, but from the perspective of the market, justice consisted in always paying one's debts. During the process of state formation in the Warring States period, the state embodied society's obligations to popular welfare, while the market epitomized the pursuit of individual profit as the means of creating wealth.

Philosophers of the Warring States period devoted little attention to the question of debt and its moral implications. Mozi borrowed the notion of "profit" to define a concept of social utility that denied the values of the marketplace and deplored private accumulation. Confucian philosophers

too, routinely issued amnesties including forgiveness of debts in the first year of their reign.

9 Graeber, *Debt*, pp. 228–32.

10 Kurke, *Coins, Bodies*; Schaps, *Invention of Coinage*.

11 Von Reden, *Money in Classical Antiquity*, p. 96; Bresson, *Making of the Ancient Greek Economy*, p. 228.

enunciated concepts of social well-being that completely rejected profit-seeking calculation. But the realignment of the ruler–subject relationship under the autocratic state reframed the logic of debt: no longer an opportunity for the ruler to display his magnanimity, debt, like taxation, became a means for fixing the obligations owed to the state in quantitative terms expressed in units of commodities, money, and above all labor time. Ironically, it was under the autocratic state that the market conception of debt as moral obligation achieved ascendancy. Yet the moral ambiguity of debt remained unresolved.

The demise of the patrimonial political order of the Spring and Autumn era amid the rise of autocratic states was evinced by a transition away from blood covenants (*meng* 盟) and oaths (*shi* 誓) as the foundations of interpersonal relationships, political loyalties, and diplomatic order. Instead, a new and more steeply hierarchical set of political and social ties emerged that rested on bonds (*yue* 約), written pledges that subsequently became the basis for codified law.[12] Private bonds in the sense of binding obligations also served as the basis for commercial contracts. At this time it was common practice to use split tallies to validate accords among sovereign rulers. Tallies made of wood, bamboo, bronze, or even jade were divided equally along the vertical axis into two halves, and each party took possession of one half.[13] Matching the tallies together verified their authenticity, and thus became a metaphor for trust, as we see in the words of the 3rd-century BCE Confucian philosopher Xunzi: "matching tallies and verifying contracts are the means by which trust is established."[14] Two-part tallies gradually were replaced by impressed seals as a mode of verification and fell into disuse in the early imperial period, but the term "matched tallies" (*hetong* 合同) – which often was inscribed on the reverse of contracts as a witnessing mark – was preserved, and it continues to denote business contracts even today.

Early commercial contracts appear to have derived from such tallies. The oldest extant contracts, dating from the 2nd century BCE, were written on wooden slips.[15] Following the widespread adoption of paper to document administrative records from the 2nd century CE, it is likely that contracts too were inscribed on paper, although no early written contracts on paper have survived in China itself. The use of contracts written on paper in turn made

12 Mark Edward Lewis, *Sanctioned Violence in Early China* (Albany: State University of New York Press, 1990), pp. 43–80.

13 Lao Kan, "The Early Use of the Tally in China," in David T. Roy and Tsuen-hsuin Tsien (eds.), *Ancient China: Studies in Early Civilization* (Hong Kong: Chinese University of Hong Kong Press, 1978), pp. 91–98; Zhang Chuanxi 张传玺, "Zhongguo gudai qiyue xingshi de yuan he liu" 中国古代契约形式的源和流, in Zhang, *Qin Han wenti yanjiu* 秦汉问题研究 (rev. ed., Beijing: Beijing daxue chubanshe, 1995), pp. 167–86.

14 合符節別契券者，所以為信也. Ch. 12, "Jundao" 君道, in Li Disheng 李滌生 (ed.), *Xun Zi jishi* 荀子集釋 ([hereafter *XZ*]; Taipei: Xuesheng shuju, 1979), p. 265.

15 For a survey of these documents, see H. Wang, *Money on the Silk Road*, pp. 47–64.

possible the invention of paper fiduciary instruments, such as the remittance bills first introduced by the Tang government in the 8th century CE (see Chapter 3). These remittance bills in turn provided the technical as well as conceptual foundations for the issue of paper money by the Song government in the early 11th century.

2.1 Origins of Debt in China

The earliest references to debt in the Chinese documentary record coincide with the emergence of money and markets in the 7th–6th centuries BCE. Yet these records link debt not to the market economy or contractual obligations between equals but rather to the hierarchal norms of political and social institutions. They conspicuously portray instances of lending (grain, not money) by rulers and ministers in times of dearth as virtuous acts of noblesse oblige rather than a means of aggrandizement. Through such displays of magnanimity, the leaders of society affirmed their dedication to the public interest and hence reinforced their legitimacy. This trope repeatedly recurs in the *Chronicles of Zuo*, compiled c. 400 BCE. Examples include Gongzi Bao, younger brother of the ruler of Song, who in 611 BCE lent out his stores of grain to provide sufficient food for all of Song's citizens; the general Wei Jiang, who in 564 BCE persuaded Lord Zhuo of Jin to compel all who held stocks of grain to make loans to citizens in need, earning Jin a reputation as a land where both want and avarice were absent; and Zipi, chief minister in Zheng, who at a time of famine in 544 BCE allocated grain rations from public stores to the citizenry.[16] Zipi's contemporary, Sicheng of Song, imitated his example, requiring that all state officers lend grain in years of dearth. The author of the *Chronicles of Zuo* praised Zipi and Sicheng as examples of "generosity without expectation of gratitude" (*shi er bude* 施而不德) whose actions won them the allegiance of the citizenry and ensured the longevity of their states amid the devastating internecine warfare of the age.[17] Although these figures all were said to have issued loans (*dai* 貸), it is likely that there was no expectation that such loans would be repaid. Indeed, the chronicler specifically declared that Sicheng kept no records of the debts. Notably, these loans were directed at the citizenry of the capital, a potent political force in the city-states of the Spring and Autumn era. Thus, these dispensations were more than magnanimous benefactions; the borrowers incurred debts of honor to be repaid with political loyalty.

[16] Okada Isao 岡田功, "Shunshū sengoku Shin Kan jidai no taishaku kankei o meguru ichikōsatsu" 春秋戦国秦漢時代の貸借関係をめぐる一考察, *Sundai shigaku* 駿台史学 78 (1990): 69–73.

[17] *Zuozhuan* 左傳 (hereafter *ZZ*), Xianggong 29.7, in *SSJZS*, 2, p. 2005b.

Violations of this moral economy of debt also became the subject of admonitory lessons. Luan Hengzi (d. 556 BCE), who inherited the chief ministership of Jin from his virtuous father, betrayed his father's legacy through his venal conduct, notably by engaging in usury (*jiadai juhui* 假貸居賄). Nonetheless, Luan was shielded from recrimination by his father's reputation. But his son, despite trying to rectify his father's abuses and redeem his grandfather's good name, was banished by the citizens of Jin.[18] The *Chronicles of Zuo* relates the case of Tian Chang, a noble in Qi, who when lending grain used a large measure but substituted a smaller one when he collected repayment, in essence discounting the loan rather than collecting interest. Tian's generosity as a creditor – and the fair prices he charged for timber, fish, and salt (i.e., products of the "mountains and marshes" that in the past had been common resources available to all) – earned him the lasting goodwill of the Qi people. The minister Yan Ying, rebuking the Qi ruler for levying inordinate taxes and imposing monopolies on the "wealth of the mountains and marshes," invoked the example of Tian Chang as a proper model of leadership – and a premonition of the later usurpation of the rulership of Qi by the Tian house.[19]

The language used for these benefactions, *dai*, could simply mean providing aid in times of need, but the word had already acquired the meaning of "loan." Despite the absence of references to private loans or payment of interest, surely such practices existed; the anecdotes cited above implicitly contrasted the generosity of these virtuous figures with the cupidity of those who, like Luan Hengzi, enriched themselves through usury. The prevailing view of how the wealthy should behave was summed up by Yan Ying, esteemed by later historians as a paragon of probity: "Take stock of your wealth, whether great or little, and use it prudently; when rich, hoard no gold, and when poor, make no recourse to debt; this is what is called 'frugality.'"[20]

As mentioned above, the transformation of gifts into debts required a system of accounting to specify debt in quantitative terms. Accounting practices typically arose from the actions of states in levying taxes, fees, tariffs, and fines. We lack documentation that would shed light on how such accounting came to be created in China, and we can see it in operation only during the formation of the Qin Empire in the late 3rd century BCE. But the existence of such accounting systems was implicit in the wave of initiatives to register

[18] "Jinyu" 晉語 8, "Shu Xiang lun youde buyoupin" 叔向論憂德不憂貧, in *GY*, p. 692.

[19] *ZZ*, Zhaogong 3.3, in *SSJZS*, 2, p. 2031a–b. This story was widely retold; see "Jin Shu Xiang wen Qi guo ruohe Yan Zi dui yi Qi de shuai min gui Tian shi" 晉叔向問齊國若何晏子對以齊德衰民歸田氏, in Zhang Jingxian 张景贤 (ed.), *Yan Zi chunqiu* 晏子春秋 ([hereafter *YZCQ*]; Zhengzhou: Zhongzhou guji chubanshe, 2010), p. 194; *SJ* 46.1883.

[20] "Shu Xiang wen se lin ai zhiyu xing heru Yan Zi dui yi linzhe junzi zhi dao" 叔向問嗇吝愛之于行何如晏子對以嗇者君子之道, *YZCQ*, p. 205.

arable lands and populations for the purpose of taxation throughout the 6th century BCE – concurrent with, not coincidentally, the issue of the first metallic currencies. Chu pioneered the development of bureaucratic tools to mobilize the state's resources, conducting the first universal registration of able-bodied men for military service in 589 BCE and compiling a comprehensive survey of land, forest, mineral, and livestock resources in 548 BCE. The first record of registering land for taxation dates to 594 BCE, but by 500 BCE most states had implemented some form of land taxation.[21] The imposition of regular taxation and the steady expansion of money use and the market economy exposed the population to greater economic risks. At the same time, the growing autocratic power of monarchal states inevitably eroded patron–client ties among the ruling elites. After 500 BCE, mention of debt amnesties directed toward the citizenry disappear from the *Chronicles of Zuo*.

From this time too, we can glimpse a transition in the logic of debt that shifted focus away from bolstering support for the ruler among the capital's citizenry and toward improving the economic welfare of the farming population. As we saw in Chapter 1, the "Great Relief" chapter of the *Lost Documents of Zhou* includes the issue of coin in its enumeration of the means by which the ruler can relieve the people's distress in times of dearth. The same chapter also urges the ruler to disseminate loans in the form of money to the people, although local officials were obliged to certify that the beneficiaries of such largesse were trustworthy and sincere. Rather than requiring recipients to repay the loan following the next harvest, however, the loan was deemed a strategic investment "to enable them to augment their wealth" (*yi fu zhicai* 以輔殖財). Only when "their wealth is augmented, and they have sufficient food for their subsistence" should the officials seek repayment of the debt.[22] On one hand, this passage enunciates the idea that local officials must act as guarantors for such loans, a principle that reappears in 3rd-century BCE texts such as the *Rituals of Zhou* and the corpus of administrative laws of the Qin state excavated from the Shuihudi tomb. On the other hand, the length of the loan is determined not by a fixed period of time but rather the recipient's ability to repay, with the further implication that the loan is intended not merely for immediate famine relief but also to enhance the future economic welfare of farm families.[23] Recently excavated documents from the region of the Chu state dating 322–316 BCE provide firsthand evidence of government loans as investments in economic security. This set of documents records loans (*dai*) in

[21] For an overview of the political economy of this period, see Richard von Glahn, *The Economic History of China from Antiquity to the Nineteenth Century* (Cambridge: Cambridge University Press, 2016), pp. 52–60.

[22] Ch. 11, "Dakuang," in *YZS*, 1, pp. 157–58.

[23] Wang Lianlong 王连龙, *Yi Zhou shu yanjiu* 逸周书研究 (Beijing: Shehui kexue wenxian chubanshe, 2010), pp. 209–12.

gold (Chu was unique among the Warring States polities in issuing a gold currency) made by local officials to enable the local populace to purchase seed in the spring planting season. In most cases these loans were not repaid, suggesting that the earlier practice of forgiving debts continued to some degree.[24]

These texts make no reference to interest, probably because righteous leaders not only refrained from assessing interest payments but even forgave the principal of the loans. What becomes the common word for denoting interest on debts, *xi* 息, derived from the offspring of livestock, as was true of many ancient languages.[25] Although such usage does not appear before the Han, Warring States texts increasingly underscore the plight of farm families who incur debts to meet their subsistence needs. Mencius, writing in the mid 4th century BCE, bemoaned the practice of calculating land taxes based on the average harvest over a number of years because it made no exceptions for poor harvests. In times of dearth, Mencius lamented, the people "cannot support their elderly parents, no matter how hard they work throughout the year, even as they resort to borrowing and pile on debts."[26] The implication here is that the ruler's subjects must resort to private borrowing in order to satisfy fixed demands for tax payments and thus are plunged into a vicious cycle of indebtedness.

A similar concern that rulers contributed to the impoverishment of their subjects by saddling them with debts appears in a famous anecdote recorded by the Han historian Sima Qian concerning Tian Wen (d. 279 BCE), best known as Lord Mengchang of the royal house of Qi and at one time chancellor of the Qi state. Tian Wen won renown (and reproach) for the generosity he lavished on his retainers, whose numbers swelled to 3,000 when he was serving as chancellor. Hard pressed to provide the upkeep for this extravagant entourage, Tian relied on interest payments from the loans he extended to farming families in his personal domain of Xue. In a year when Xue suffered a poor harvest, however, the debtors failed to repay their loans. Tian sent one of his retainers – Feng Huan, an avatar of austerity – to dun those in arrears. Feng gathered together all of the debtors: from those who could make restitution he collected interest payments totaling 100,000 coins, but from the indigent he simply "gathered their loan contracts" (取錢之券書) and burned them. Feng's

[24] Wang Ying 王颖, "Cong Baoshan Chujian kan Zhanguo zhongwanqi Chuguo de shehui jingji" 从包山楚简看战国中晚期楚国的社会经济, *Zhongguo shehui jingji shi* 中国社会经济史 2004.3: 14–17.

[25] Graeber, *Debt*, p. 215.

[26] 終歲勤動,不得以養其父母,又稱貸而益之; *Mencius* 3A.3. Mencius here was referring to the *gong* 貢 system, which he ascribed to the venerable Shang dynasty, even though he deemed it the "worst method" of land taxation. There is no evidence for such a tax system in the Shang period, but it is likely that such a method was employed by rulers of Mencius' day.

actions outraged Tian Wen, who summoned Feng and demanded explanation. Feng replied, "the reason my lord has lent money is to provide a stable livelihood (*benye* 本業) to those with no means of support; the reason you require interest payments is because you lack sufficient means to maintain your retainers." Yet the poor will only grow more indebted as interest charges mount, Feng pointed out, and ultimately they will be forced to flee. "By burning the worthless debt contracts and writing off debts that can never be repaid," Feng declared, "I have induced the people of Xue to revere their prince and burnished the good reputation of my lord." Tian, Sima Qian tells us, instantly recognized the wisdom of Feng's actions.[27] Another, earlier, version of this event, included in *Stratagems of the Warring States*, differs in this respect. In this rendition, Feng chided Tian for not cherishing his subjects but rather "extracting profit from them as would a merchant." By burning the loan contracts Feng had "purchased righteousness" (*shiyi* 市義). But Tian remained displeased and dismissed Feng. It was only years later, when Tian returned to Xue after suffering political disgrace and was welcomed by throngs of people hailing his virtue, that he understood the logic of Feng's actions.[28]

These authors portray Tian Wen as an aloof and vainglorious ruler who measured his majesty by the number of his retainers rather than the welfare of his subjects. Like earlier writers, they consider debt not a mark of shame but an essential tool for survival, the means by which the people can secure a "stable livelihood." The ruler has a moral obligation to provide loans to the indigent, but collecting interest on these debts constituted pernicious exploitation of his most vulnerable subjects – behaving like a profit-scheming merchant rather than an honorable sovereign. It is striking that the *Stratagems of the Warring States* describes Feng's burning of the loan contracts as "purchasing" righteousness, telling testimony of the pervasiveness of the language of the marketplace even while repudiating the goal of personal enrichment.

The principle of abjuring profit from debts is echoed in other late Warring States accounts. Fan Li, once a leading statesman in Yue, turned to a career as a merchant after retiring from political life and achieved renown for his business acumen. Sima Qian described Fan's business strategy as "finding the right time to make a profit and not demanding restitution of debts from others."[29] Even

[27] *SJ* 75.2359–61.

[28] "Qiren you Feng Huan zhe" 齊人有馮諼者, in Cheng Zhuchang 程朱昌 and Cheng Yuquan 程育全 (eds.), *Zhanguo ce jizhu* 戰國策集注 (Shanghai: Shanghai guji chubanshe, 2013), pp. 103–4. See also Andrew Meyer, "Feng Buys Rightness, Gongyi Xiu Expels His Wife: Economic Exemplars in the Warring States and Early Han," in Sabattini and Schwermann, *Between Command and Market*, pp. 145–61.

[29] 與時逐而不責於人; *SJ* 129.3257. My gloss of *buze* 不責as *buzhai* 不債 ("not demanding restitution of debts") diverges from standard commentaries, which render *buze* as "not making demands on/not reproaching others." My reading draws support from the excavated Qin administrative documents from Shuihudi and Liye, which frequently use

the *Dao De Jing*, the ultimate negation of striving for worldly success, employed the language of debt to evoke the idea of an exemplary ruler who sustains the trust and confidence of his people by not exploiting their economic vulnerability: "the sage holds the left tally, yet seeks no restitution / The virtuous safeguard the tallies; the ruthless ordain levies."[30] This passage alludes to the use of split tallies as contracts for certifying debts, but like the paragons of rulership in the *Chronicles of Zuo* the Daoist ruler refrains from demanding repayment.

Such sentiments found little purchase in the political economy of the ascendant autocratic state, however. Instead, debt became a crucial instrument of bureaucratic control. The triumph of bureaucratic state power during the Warring States era was made possible above all by the state's command of labor through military conscription and statutory labor service. The rulers of Qin utilized public loans to enhance their control over the labor power of their subjects. As a result, the Qin population was ensnared in perpetual indebtedness that bound them ever more tightly to the command economy.[31]

Qin administrative documents reveal the state's keen interest in mobilizing labor through the instrument of public debt. The Qin regulations delineate the procedures whereby state debtors repaid loans received from the government by performing labor service. Documents preserved in the Liye archive, dating from the first decade of the Qin Empire, record loans of grain to individuals who were fulfilling military service obligations there, serving sentences for criminal offences, or working off debts to the state. These records make no mention of deadlines for repayment, collateral held as surety, guarantors, or interest. Instead, debtors worked off their debt according to a fixed daily rate measured in coin (eight coins per day, or six if food rations were provided).[32] Subsistence loans in grain thus were measured in a bronze currency unit of

ze as a loanword for *zhai* in references to "persons obliged to work off fines and debts owed to the state" (*juzi shuze (zhai) zhe* 居貲贖責者) and "indebted to the state" (*youze (zhai) yu gong* 有責於公). See Maxim Korolkov, "Between Command and Market: Credit, Labour, and Accounting in the Qin Empire (221–207 BCE)," in Sabattini and Schwermann, *Between Command and Market*, pp. 162–243. Consider also the oft-repeated story of the young Liu Bang, future founder of the Han dynasty, who in his spendthrift youth regularly borrowed money for wine. His creditors, seeing the aura of kingliness around Liu Bang, "tore up the debt notes and cast aside any restitution" 折券棄責. See *SJ* 8.343; *HS* 1A.2. See also my translations of *Dao De Jing* and *Garden of Eloquence* below.

30 以聖人執左契, 不責於人; 有德司契, 無德司徹. Ch. 79 in Zhu Qianzhi 朱謙之 (ed.), *Lao Zi jiaoshi* 老子校釋 (Beijing: Zhonghua shuju, 1984), pp. 304–5.

31 The following discussion of Qin debt and labor service is based on Korolkov, "Between Command and Market."

32 Robin D. S. Yates, "The Economic Activities of a Qin Local Administration: Qianling County, Modern Liye, Hunan Province, 222–209 BCE," in Sabattini and Schwermann, *Between Command and* Market, pp. 247–317.

account but redeemed through labor time. Public debt under the Qin was grounded in an accounting system that established fungible equivalences among commodities, money, and legally commodified labor.[33] Moreover, the sophisticated bureaucratic communication system of the Qin state enabled local officials to transfer this labor power to different jurisdictions, enhancing the flexibility of the state to deploy its most crucial resource. Qin officials were actively encouraged to extend loans but also punished for failing to collect on these debts. The Qin "Statutes on Currency" itemize regulations concerning government lending, including loans of state-owned tools, carts, and oxen as well as grain, and stipulate penalties for losses, breakage, or failure to make restitution.

The administration of public debt under Qin rule placed debtors within a continuum of coerced labor including slaves, hard-labor convicts, indentured servants, and wage labor. Debtors, like criminals, were assessed monetary fines that were commuted to labor time. At that time, wage labor itself was a mark of menial status, expressed in contemporary idiom as "wage slave" (*yongnu* 庸奴). Given the prevalence of state land allocations based on award of merit ranks that defined "good subjects" (*liangmin* 良民), the pool of hired laborers consisted mostly of landless vagrants who emigrated from their home territories in search of work.[34] Private employment of wage labor thus bore an uncomfortable resemblance to debt indenture; both could be deemed acts of lèse-majesté, infringing on the supreme power the state wielded over its subjects. The Qin government outlawed private debt indenture, but as Maxim Korolkov observes, the repeated prohibitions against forced debt indenture (*qiangzhi* 強質) – that is to say, peonage – in Qin and early Han legal statutes probably can be taken as evidence that it was a well-established practice.[35] The word employed here for "indenture," *zhi* 質, typically is translated as "pledge," and has the general meaning of pledging something of value in return for a loan – in essence, collateral.[36] But this meaning is

[33] The merit ranks awarded by the Qin government for military service also served as fungible instruments of debt redemption. Debts of less than 10,000 coins could be expunged by forfeiting one degree of rank. Korolkov, "Between Command and Market," p. 204.

[34] Shi Yang 石洋, "Liang Han Sanguo shiqi 'yong' qunti de lishi yanbian: yi minjian guyong wei zhongxin" 两汉三国时期'佣'群体的历史演变: 以民间雇佣為中心, *Zhongguo shi yanjiu* 中国史研究 2014.3: 53.

[35] Korolkov, "Between Command and Market," p. 211.

[36] The *Shuowen* lexicon glosses *zhi* as such: "to pledge goods in return for a loan" 以物相贅. See Duan Yucai 段玉裁 (ed.), *Shuowen jiezi zhu* 說文解字注 ([hereafter *SW*]; Shanghai: Shanghai guji chubanshe, 1981), p. 281b. In the *Rituals of Zhou*, compiled around this time, *zhi* is used to denote "major" contracts, those used in transactions involving the exchange of slaves or livestock (i.e., living beings), which required additional scrutiny and endorsement by market officials. See "Zhiren" 質人, in *Zhouli zhushu* 周禮注疏 (hereafter *ZL*), 2, "Diguan situ" 地官司徒, in *SSJZS*, vol. 1, p. 737b.

derived from its frequent use since the Spring and Autumn era to denote "hostages" – politically valuable persons, such as the son of a ruler, who were offered as security to ensure that treaties and truces would be honored.[37] Debtors in essence were hostages to creditors, and the private debt indenture deprived the state of its most indispensable resource – labor.

The discourse concerning debt shifts in the Han period to this problem of private debts – not, however, as a threat to state power but as an affliction suffered by the people. In 178 BCE, the minister Chao Cuo warned Emperor Wen that natural disasters, heavy taxes, and above all the growth of the market economy were impoverishing the populace. The burden of debt had forced a multitude of subjects to sell off their lands, dwellings, and even their children, while the great merchants accumulated fortunes by charging interest equal to the amount of the debt.[38] The "Light and Heavy" chapters of the *Guan Zi* express ambivalence about private debt: although the people suffered from the crushing burden of debt, Pseudo-Guanzi acknowledged that the people depended on borrowing for survival. In one chapter, Lord Huan seeks Guan Zhong's advice on how to remedy the problem of "rich merchants, aggrandizing tradesmen, and usurious moneylenders" (*fushang xugu chengdaijia* 富商、蓄賈、稱貸家) who profit at the expense of the poor masses, causing the farming folk to lose their means of livelihood (i.e., their landholdings). Yet, in this same passage, Lord Huan expresses gratitude to the moneylenders for "making it possible for my subjects to plow in the spring and weed in the summer." In this instance, Lord Huan himself makes restitution for private debts.[39] One crucial remedy, according to Pseudo-Guanzi, is to curb private

37 Ogura Yoshihiko 小倉芳彥, "Chūgoku kodai no shichi: sono kinō no henka o chūshin to shite" 中国古代の質: その機能の変化を中心として, *Rekishigaku kenkyū* 歴史学研究 266 (1962): 1–15.

38 *HS* 22A.1132. Chao Cuo's reference to selling one's children probably should be understood as debt peonage. Here and in other Han texts interest charges are expressed as "double repayment" (*beicheng* 倍稱, *beixi* 倍息). Although we lack information regarding legal rates of interest in the Han, later imperial law codes capped total interest payments at 100 percent of the principal, and most likely that was standard practice in the Han as well. Han-era mathematical treatises contain problems that specify a monthly interest rate of 3 percent (36 percent per annum) for short-term loans (less than one month in duration). See Christopher Cullen, *The Suàn shù shū* 筭數書 *'Writings on Reckoning': A Translation of a Chinese Mathematical Collection of the Second Century BC, with Explanatory Commentary* (Cambridge: Needham Research Institute, Cambridge University, 2004), pp. 58–59. The *Guan Zi* suggests that interest rates varied by region from 20 to 100 percent; see ch. 83, "Qingzhong (ding)" 輕重丁, in *GZ*, 3, p. 1475.

39 Ch. 83, "Qingzhong (ding)," in *GZ*, 3, pp. 1474–75. This dependence on private debt is underscored later in the same chapter, which presents an improbable scenario in which the moneylenders voluntarily annul the debts owed to them. Dismayed that his demands for revenue obliged the people of Qi to assume debts that saddled them with onerous interest payments, Lord Huan sought Guan Zhong's counsel. Guan Zhong advised Lord Huan to lavish honors on the moneylenders (*daicheng zhi jia* 貸稱之家) and acclaim

debts through state loans of grain and seed during times of dearth, thus ensuring that "there will be no merchants who reap a tenfold profit, and no subjects who must make double repayment."[40] Confucians likewise bewailed the burden of debt on farming families, but they were more likely to blame their predicament on the government. The Confucian savants summoned to the court in 81 BCE to debate the mercantilist policies of Emperor Wu asserted that onerous taxation reduced farmers to penury, compelling them (quoting the passage from *Mencius* cited above) "to resort to borrowing and pile on debts."[41] Even when observing that wealthy households were oblivious of the suffering that debt inflicted on the poor, they singled out private loans received from local officials as the main cause of their affliction.[42] Although the burden of debt was uniquely born by the poor, the rich also suffered from government maladministration.[43]

Even as they bemoaned the deleterious effects of the pursuit of profit on public morality, Confucian critics of the autocratic state depicted the private market as a positive force that augmented the wealth of the local community. As we have seen in Chapter 1, in the "Flood and Drought" chapter of the *Salt and Iron Debates* the Confucian literati offer a remarkable encomium to the operation of the market economy unshackled from the suffocating grip of state officials. Confucian literati also revived the idea that lordly virtue resides in forgiving debts. This sentiment recurs in the *Garden of Eloquence*, a collection of historical anecdotes compiled by Liu Xiang, custodian of the imperial library, which Liu presented to the throne in 17 BCE. Liu records that when Zhuang Xin, a minister in Chu in the early 3rd century BCE, was asked by the king of Chu, "In what consists the wealth of the gentleman (*junzi*)?" Zhuang replied:

> The wealth of the gentleman resides in not collecting debts when he lends money to others even though they do not express gratitude, and in not imposing bondage on those whom he bestows food and drink even though they offer him no service. His kinfolk cherish him, the populace esteems him, and the unworthy serve his will. All wish that he will live a long and happy life without suffering misfortune.[44]

their contributions to public welfare, which induced the latter not only to "tear up their contracts and erase their ledgers" (折其券而削其書) but also to distribute their stores of wealth to the poor. See ch. 83, "Qingzhong (ding)," in *GZ*, 3, p. 1492.

40 Ch. 78, "Kuidu" 揆度, in *GZ*, 3, p. 1388. Elsewhere the *Guan Zi* advocates government lending of tools and clothing to the people to enable them to complete their seasonal tasks; when these goods are returned to the state storehouses the officials should "tear up the loan contracts." See ch. 74, "Shanguogui," in *GZ*, 3, p. 1291.

41 Ch. 15, "Weitong" 未通, in *YTL*, 1, p. 191.

42 Ch. 41, "Quxia" 取下, in *YTL*, 2, pp. 466–67.

43 Ch. 28, "Guochi" 國疾, in *YTL*, 1, p. 235.

44 君子之富,假貸人不德也,不責也; 其食飲人不使也,不役也; 親戚愛之,衆人喜之,不肖者事之,皆欲其壽樂而不傷於患. Ch. 5, "Guide" 貴德, in Liu Xiang 劉向, *Shuoyuan* 說苑

Still, in this passage – which surely reflects the intellectual temper of Liu Xiang's own day – debt is entirely impersonal: the creditor seeks no gratitude, nor does he enslave the debtors. One figure lauded for exemplifying this ideal of magnanimity was Fan Zhong, maternal grandfather of the first emperor of the Later Han dynasty, Liu Xiu. According to his biographer, Fan "wasted nothing in the management of his properties and ensured that each of his slaves was employed at a task suited to his skills . . . whereby he doubled his fortune every year, bringing more than 300 *qing* of land under cultivation." As death approached, Fan forgave the debts owed to him by burning the contracts for outstanding loans totaling several million coins.[45]

Yet Fan Zhong's story also implies that the formation of such great estates was achieved through the loss of smallholdings due to debt forfeitures. The widening gulf between rich and poor catalyzed the ambitious attempt to curb the economic power of magnate landowners launched by Wang Mang, who deposed the Han emperor in 6 CE and subsequently declared his own Xin dynasty (9–23 CE). In addition to confiscating the manorial estates of the great landowners, banning the sale of land and slaves, and subjecting trade to strict regulation, Wang Mang's program of popular relief included setting the interest rate for public loans at 3 percent.[46] The restoration of Han rule by Liu Xiu in 25 CE reversed Wang's initiatives, reinforcing the concentration of land and wealth in the hands of magnate estate owners. In a tomb inscription dated to 108 CE detailing the division of a modest estate of a dozen or so farms among the deceased's heirs, nearly all of the land was assessed in terms of a debenture (*zhi* 質) or sale (*gu* 賈) value.[47] These notations suggest that the estate was built up either through purchase or possessory loans, in which the creditor assumed control of real property in lieu of interest payments.

As private moneylending and debt seizures became commonplace in the Han, creditors no longer were tainted by the moral stigma of usury, while indebtedness increasingly was viewed as a mark of dishonor.[48] Han texts often

(Taipei: Guoli Taiwan shifan daxue chuban zhongxin, 2012), p. 41. Compare the early Han stateman Jia Yi's corresponding pronouncement on "the wealth of the gentleman": "The wealth of the gentleman consists in sharing his riches with the people; thus the officials and people delight in him" 故君子之富也,與民以財,故士民樂之. See ch. 9, "Dazheng" 大政, in *XS*, p. 340.

45 *Hou Han shu* 後漢書 ([hereafter *HHS*; Beijing: Zhonghua shuju ed.), 32.1119. On Fan Zhong, see also Inaba Ichirō 稲葉一郎, "Kandai no kazoku keitai to keizai hendō" 漢代の家族形態と経済変動, *Tōyōshi kenkyū* 東洋史研究 43.1 (1984): 95–98, 105–7.

46 On Wang Mang's fiscal policies, see Yamada Katsuyoshi 山田勝芳, "Ō Mō dai no zaisei" 王莽代の財政, *Tōyōshi kenkyū* 東洋史研究 33.1 (1975): 63–85. Wang's monetary policies were discussed in Chapter 1.

47 See von Glahn, *Economic History of China*, pp. 138–39.

48 To be sure, Confucians continued to vilify merchants who enriched themselves through moneylending and debt indentures, as we see in Ban Gu's revision (*HS* 91) of Sima Qian's

refer to debt indentures in which the debtor pledges his son or wife (that is to say, their labor) in return for a loan as *zhui* 贅, a word that implied self-debasement in pursuit of material gain.[49] The same word was applied to uxorilocal marriage (*zhuixu* 贅婿), an arrangement in which the husband renounced his own patriline and became part of the wife's family, considered a shamefully unfilial act of avarice. In the early Han, at least, uxorilocal husbands were lumped together with merchants under a legal prohibition barring them from holding office. During the early Han period, the growth of the market economy and rising demand for labor improved the social standing of hired laborers; although still indelibly associated with poverty, wage labor no longer implied mean social status. But the rise of the manorial economy in the early centuries CE reversed the urban and commercial growth of the early Han, reducing market demand for labor as well. The great magnate landowners acquired large numbers of bondservants for both domestic and field labor. Although hired laborers were not subject to the legal subservience imposed on bondservants, in the eyes of the public there was little difference between the two.[50] In the third decade of the 1st century CE, the philosopher Huan Tan wrote that "in the present day rich merchants often dole out money and goods to engage the menfolk of middling families as indentured laborers (*baoyi* 保役), compelling them to do their bidding as menials just like slaves or bondservants."[51] In the post-Han period, wage labor was eclipsed by bond-servitude. Debt, too, once again connoted servility. The frequent practice of debt indenture, deemed akin to enslavement, revived the old meaning of *zhi* as "hostage."[52]

However much it resembled personal servitude, debt indenture – as the term implies – required a written contract, as was true for most economic transactions. The Qin–Han "Statutes on Finance" required that officials draw up contracts for sales of goods, collection of rents, and pledges to secure debts.[53] In the elaborate bureaucratic apparatus delineated in the *Rituals of Zhou*, market supervisors were required to endorse contracts for a wide range

"Biographies of the Moneymakers," but their opprobrium did not extend to the great magnate families.

49 The *Shuowen* lexicon (*SW*, p. 281b) glosses *zhui* as "to pledge goods for a loan of money" 以物質錢, and the word was closely linked to the idea of debenture (see note 36, this chapter). But it retained an unsavory whiff.

50 Shi Yang, "'Yong' qunti."

51 *HHS* 28A.958.

52 Niida Noboru 仁井田陞, "Kan Gi Rikuchō no shichi seido" 漢魏六朝の質制度, in Niida, *Chūgoku hōsei shi kenkyū: tochi hō, torihiki hō* 中國法制史研究:土地法,取引法 (Tokyo: Tokyo daigaku shuppankai, 1960), pp. 477–89.

53 Anthony Barbieri-Low and Robin D. S. Yates, *Law, State, and Society in Early Imperial China: A Study with Critical Edition and Translation of the Zhangjiashan Legal Texts from Zhangjiashan Tomb no. 247* (Leiden: Brill, 2015), vol. 2, p. 925.

of private market transactions, especially slaves, livestock, weapons, and "rare and exotic goods." Disputes over transactions and debts were to be settled according to imperial law, which stipulated criminal penalties for violations.[54] To be sure, the omnipresent state portrayed in the *Rituals of Zhou* was scarcely realized in practice. But the corpus of excavated Han documents from Juyan and Dunhuang, which concern the activities of soldiers stationed at frontier garrisons, include numerous sales contracts for quotidian goods such as clothing. These contracts specify the names of the buyer and seller, the goods and their cash value, the names of witnesses, and the deadline for payment. Contracts for consignments of goods for sale (*shimai* 貰賣) include the names of guarantors, although they did not specify a deadline for repayment. Land sales contracts required government endorsement and registration. Loan documents required not only guarantors (typically countrymen of the debtor) but also collateral – for example, a pledge of monthly salary, which would be paid directly to the creditor. The Juyan documents also attest to the widespread practice of hiring substitutes (again, from the individual's home county) to perform military and labor services in exchange for cash payments.[55]

Debt thus was an omnipresent feature of economic life in the early empires. But debt was not constructed as a form of impersonal exchange between equals within a market institution premised on the right to free disposition of property. In principle the assumption of debt was a voluntary action, but economic circumstances often compelled individuals to resort to public or private debt for survival. Although by law the terms of the debt must be spelled out and agreed upon by contract, failure to repay debts entailed severe consequences beyond the stipulations of the contract, often resulting in the surrender of personal liberty. In this respect, public loans were preferable to private ones: at least the loss of freedom and compulsory labor service was governed by the fixed terms of imperial law. Private debts often resulted in loss of lands pledged as collateral as well as peonage imposed on the debtor or, in many cases, their son. In the post-Han Period of Disunion, debtors often pledged family members, slaves, or lands as collateral for debts, and debt contracts typically asserted the creditor's right to seize the land of the debtor if the loan remained unpaid after a specified time.[56] Debt indenture remained a common practice in Tang and Song times, even if prohibited by imperial law. The Song

54 "Zhiren" 質人, in *ZL* 2, "Diguan situ" 地官司徒, and "Chaoshi" 朝士, in *ZL* 5, "Qiuguan sikou" 秋官司寇, in *SSJZS*, 1, pp. 737b and 878a–b, respectively.

55 Feng Zhuohui 冯卓慧, *Handai minshi jingji falü zhidu yanjiu: Hanjian ji wenxian suojian* 汉代民事经济法律制度研究: 汉简及文献所见 (Beijing: Shangwu yinshuguan, 2014), pp. 52–100. See also Hugh Scogin, "Between Heaven and Man: Contract and the State in Han Dynasty China," *Southern California Law Review* 63.5 (1990): 1325–1404.

56 Niida, "Shichi seido."

founder issued a decree banning debt indenture in 971, yet the practice not only continued but often was certified by contract.[57]

With the expansion of the market economy in Tang–Song times, contracts became an indispensable feature of market exchange, and by extension the use of contracts entered into every nook and cranny of social life. Property and labor became freely disposable commodities, and their exchange – not only in sales, tenancy, labor, and loan agreements but also through marriage, property division, and inheritance – was governed by contracts. The use of contracts in commercial transactions was facilitated by the invention and spread of woodblock printing from the 8th century onward, which in turn fostered standardization of the forms and language of contracts. Market growth resulted in greater recourse to debt, both in subsistence loans and as a source of investment capital. The widespread use of contracts also necessitated new forms of financial intermediation in the persons of brokers and guarantors. The earliest mention of brokers' involvement in land sale negotiations dates to the mid 10th century.[58] Contracts also became crucially important in the resolution of legal disputes. In the words of a Southern Song jurist, "as a general principle, in settling disputes over property and marriage, it is the written contract that takes precedence."[59]

2.2 Contracts, Debt, and Commercial Transactions in the Tang–Song Era

The use of contracts to specify the terms of market transactions and debt agreements has an ancient history in China, as in other societies. More unusually, from Song times onward, contracts also performed a crucial role in securing ownership rights to property, notably arable land. In the early imperial era, governments strove to update registers of population and land on an annual basis. Such records were essential to state allocation of lands, notably in the Qin–early Han era and again under the equal-field system of land allocations introduced by the Northern Wei in 486 and maintained in altered forms under subsequent dynasties down to the An Lushan rebellion of 755–763. Even before the rebellion, however, the Tang state found it increasingly difficult to track the movement of people and land transfers.

57 Guo Dongxu 郭东旭, "Songdai maimai qiyue zhidu de fazhan" 宋代买卖契约制度的发展, *Hebei daxue xuebao (zhexue shehui kexue ban)* 河北大学学报 (哲学社会科学版) 1997.3: 28–29.

58 Chen Mingguang 陈明光 and Mao Lei 毛蕾, "Tang Song yilai de yaren yu tianzhai diandang maimai" 唐宋以来的牙人与田宅典当买卖, *Zhongguo shi yanjiu* 中国史研究 2000.4: 64.

59 "Zheng tianye" 爭田業, in *Minggong shupan Qingming ji* 名公書判清明集 ([hereafter *QMJ*]; Beijing: Zhonghua shuju, 1987), 1, p. 179.

The post-rebellion fiscal reforms abandoned the equal-field system and accepted the principle of de facto private landownership. Consequently, the state invested less effort in maintaining thorough records of landownership and exchanges.[60] In Song legal practice, sales contracts, whether or not endorsed by local officials, were regarded as the most authoritative testamentary evidence for landownership rights.

In contrast to the prevailing practice in the Qin–Han period, in the Tang–Song era contracts, including land sale contracts, were essentially private documents. The *Tang Code* required market supervisors to draw up a "market contract" (*shiquan* 市券) in the specific cases of sales of livestock and female slaves to verify ownership.[61] Tang law distinguished between private contracts (*siqi* 私契) and "market contracts," but public authorities did not set standards for the composition or execution of the former. The *Penal Code of the Song*, the digest of laws largely based on Tang precedents promulgated by the Song court in 963, stipulated state intervention in debt transactions only in cases where the interest rate exceeded the legal maximum (6 percent per month or a maximum of 100 percent over the life of the loan, the rates established in Tang law in 737), the repayment was greater than authorized by the contract, or when the creditor demanded repayment in a different form than the original loan.[62]

Surviving contracts from the central Asian oasis towns of Turfan and Dunhuang dating from the 4th to the 10th centuries provide concrete evidence for the forms and language of debt contracts. Although Turfan and Dunhuang were remote from the Chinese metropole and often subject to non-Chinese rulers, the extant contracts – for purchases of land, houses, and slaves; loans of grain, cloth, and money; tenancies; and hiring labor – largely adhere to Chinese laws and practices.[63] After Turfan came under Chinese rule in 640, all subsequent contracts from there were designated *qi* (契), as was the case for the later Dunhuang contracts from the 9th to the 10th centuries.

[60] Richard von Glahn, "Household Registration, Property Rights, and Social Obligations in Imperial China: Principles and Practices," in Keith Breckenridge and Simon Szreter (eds.), *Registration and Recognition: Documenting the Person in World History* (Oxford: Oxford University Press, 2012), pp. 39–66.

[61] Such contracts attested that these kinds of property were lawfully acquired and were intended to forestall disputes if the animals or slaves proved to be sickly or otherwise defective. See Valerie Hansen, *Negotiating Daily Life in Traditional China: How Ordinary People Used Contracts, 600–1400* (New Haven, CT: Yale University Press, 1995), pp. 39–42.

[62] *Song xing tong* 宋刑統 (Beijing: Zhonghua shuju, 1984), 26.412.

[63] Hansen, *Negotiating Daily Life*, pp. 20–73. One routine deviation from Chinese law found in these contracts was to not allow the annulment of debts by periodic imperial amnesties.

The Dunhuang contracts, with a few exceptions, concern loans of goods rather than sales.[64] Most Dunhuang loan contracts involved borrowing grain (for food or seed), and thus were consumption loans. Loans of grain typically were made by Buddhist religious institutions to their clerical and lay members and levied no interest, although the contracts might specify forfeitures of property or a doubling of the amount due as penalties for failure to pay the debt by the specified deadline. By the 10th century, temples as well as private lenders charged interest. Seizure of goods for unpaid debts disappears in 10th-century loan contracts and instead was replaced by pledges of guarantorship (typically by a wife or son) or collateral. Some contracts specified that the debt was to be repaid through the indentured labor of the debtor's son for a fixed period of time. These contracts denoted loans of grain as "conveyance" (*ji* 寄), "convenience" (*bian* 便), or "convenient conveyance" (*bianji* 便寄).[65] "Convenience" (*bian*) in this context denoted a credit exchange. This nomenclature is quite striking because of the importance of the terms *ji* and *bian* in remittance bills, as we shall see in Chapter 3.

A total of forty-seven 10th-century Dunhuang contracts involved loans of textiles – mostly silk, some in wool, a few in cotton or hemp cloth. In some 40 percent of these cases, the contracts specify that the loan was made for a commercial venture to other towns, but in the rest the purpose of the loan is unclear. Coin had ceased to be used in market exchange at this time (Dunhuang fell under the rule of the Tibetan kingdom and local dynasts after 781), and pongee silk (*juan* 絹) had superseded Chinese coin as the monetary standard in the local economy. Loans of cloth generally specified a longer term of debt – one year in most cases – and interest payments in grain. Loans of cloth for trading journeys fell due upon the return of the debtor to Dunhuang and were "assessed interest payment according to local custom" (*xiangyuanli shengxi* 鄉原例生息), as was often stipulated in Song economic transactions as well.

Loans of cloth charged substantial interest, but they did not require collateral. For loans of grain, however, collateral often was demanded, perhaps indicating the heightened risk of lending to borrowers motivated by subsistence needs rather than commercial entrepreneurship. Collateralized debt took two forms: in the first, the debtor pledged forfeiture of the collateral goods to the creditor in the event of default but did not relinquish possession; in the second, the debtor surrendered the pledged goods, which the creditor would

64 The following paragraphs on Dunhuang loan contracts are based on Éric Trombert, *Le Crédit à Dunhuang: vie matérielle et société en Chine medieval* (Paris: Collège de France Institut des Hautes Études Chinoises, 1995).

65 Trombert, *Crédit à Dunhuang*, pp. 138–40. The term *bian* was used exclusively in contracts for loans in grain. Loans in cloth were designated as *dai* 貸; see Trombert, pp. 186–87.

have use of until the debt was repaid. At Dunhuang, both types of collateralized loans were designated as *dian* (典) or *zhidian* (只 [= 質] 典). Pledged collateral took the form of movable goods – tools, carts, livestock, clothing, jade, silver cups – but almost never land, and the value of the collateral goods was markedly greater than that of the loan. Still, not all such loans required collateral, and the amount of the collateral varied, probably in tandem with the creditworthiness of the debtors, who presumably were personally known to the creditors. Dunhuang's inhabitants in the 10th century were generally poorer and less commercially oriented than during the heyday of the Silk Road trade, and none of the extant loan contracts from Dunhuang were executed by pawnbrokers or professional financial institutions.

Although the use of land as collateral is rare in Dunhuang contracts, mortgaging of land became a common feature of the credit market under the Song. Both imperial law and common sentiment militated against the alienation of land, which was regarded as the material foundation of the family and the crucial means of ensuring the continuity of the family line (patriline) across generations. Sale of arable land was sanctioned only as a last resort, when penury afforded no other options. Even then Song law sought to protect the property rights of the original owner (and his descendants). Consequently, land transfers largely were conducted in the form of the kind of collateralized loans (*dian*) that appear in Dunhuang loan contracts.

In the Song, the most common type of land transfer was the conditional sale (*dianmai* 典賣), in which the seller relinquished the use of the land to the buyer but retained the right to redeem the land upon repayment of the original sale price within twenty years. Alternatively, in an irrevocable sale (*juemai* 絕賣) the owner would foreswear all claims to the land. Since a conditional sale conveyed only provisional ownership (in effect, usufruct rights), the prices for conditional sales were far lower than irrevocable sales. In the early Song, parties to conditional sales of real property made two copies of the contract (known as *hetongqi* 合同契), one that was retained by the buyer/creditor (*qianzhu* 錢主, i.e., "the financier") and the other submitted to the local commercial tax collection agency. A ruling in 1022 required making four copies of the sales contract, one each for the buyer and seller, one for the local commercial tax agency, and the fourth for the county government. But this requirement does not seem to have been widely observed. In the Southern Song, the standard practice was for both buyer and seller to hold one copy of the land transfer contract, but government agencies did not receive copies.[66]

[66] Aoki Atsushi 青木敦, "Sōdai teitōhō no suii to 'nōdenchoku': yōso shijō ni okeru shihō to shūkan" 宋代抵当法の推移と「農田勅」：要素市場における司法と習慣, in Furuta Kazuko 古田和子 (ed.), *Chūgoku no shijō chitsujo: jūnana seiki kara nijū seiki zenhan o chūshin ni* 中国の市場秩序：十七世紀から二十世紀前半を中心に (Tokyo: Keio daigaku shuppankai, 2013), p. 38.

A third type of land transaction, known as *didang* 抵當 (or *yidang* 倚當), should be understood as a type of securitized loan. Under the *didang* arrangement, the seller retained possession and use of the land but forfeited ownership rights if the principal and interest on the loan were not repaid (nominally as "rent") by the specified deadline. The fact that the *didang* arrangement really was a loan rather than a sale is reflected in the language employed to identify the parties: the "seller" (debtor) is referred to as the "property owner" (*yezhu* 業主), the one who issues a pledge (*zhichuren* 質出人), while the "buyer" (creditor) is identified as the "financier" (*qianzhu* 錢主) who assumes the pledge (*zhiquzhu* 質取主). To protect against debt seizures of arable land, the mainstay of farm families' social survival, in 1027 the Song state outlawed the practice of *didang* as well as repayment of cash debts by transfer of landownership rights. The edict mandated that sellers quit the land, surrender usufruct to the buyer, and foreswear any interest payments. But the deeply engrained customary practice of *didang* collateralized loans persisted in defiance of the strict letter of the law.[67]

Rising land prices encouraged the original owner (or their heirs) to seek redemption of lands relinquished through conditional sales years or decades before and to challenge the validity of irrevocable sales. The sharp increase in land prices in the 13th century – in large part due to the depreciation of paper money – spawned numerous lawsuits over redemption rights. In adjudicating such disputes, magistrates assigned principal weight to sales contracts and secondarily considered who actually cultivated the land and paid the taxes assessed on it. Official land registers – principally dating from the comprehensive cadastral survey conducted by the Southern Song government in 1142, after the Song–Jin truce was declared – were regarded as obsolete compared to contracts. But contracts that violated dynastic law were deemed void. In contrast to later Ming–Qing jurisprudence, Song magistrates commonly invoked legal statutes and precedents in adjudicating land disputes. At the same time, they also gave consideration to "the body of local customary precedents" (*xiangyuan tili* 鄉原體例) in matters such as what was deemed a fair price in land sales. Regarding debts and land sales, then, the state chiefly intervened when laws were broken, to maintain public order, and to protect the integrity of family assets. Otherwise, officials largely delegated such

67 On property transfers in Song law and social practice, see Dai Jianguo 戴建国, "Songdai de tianzhai jiaoyi toushui pingyou he guanyin tianzhai qishu" 宋代的田宅交易投税凭由和官印田宅契书, *Zhongguo shi yanjiu* 中国史研究 2001.3: 97–111; Dai Jianguo, "Songdai de mintian dianmai yu 'yitian liangzhu zhi'" 宋代的民田典卖与「一田两主制」, *Lishi yanjiu* 历史研究 2011.6: 99–117; Aoki Atsushi 青木敦, "Kaihatsu, chika, minjiteki hōki: 'Seimeishū' ni mieru jakkan tochi tenbai kankeihō o megutte" 開発, 地価, 民事的法規：「清明集」に見える若干土地典売関係法をめぐって, *Machikaneyama ronshū (shigaku hen)* 待兼山論集 (史学篇) 40 (2006): 1–47; Aoki, "Sōdai teitōhō."

matters, and economic transactions in general, to market institutions and private actors.

Already in the Tang, major commercial centers boasted an array of specialists in financial and credit services, including goldsmiths and silversmiths, moneychangers, pawnbrokers, and deposit and consignment shops. Deposit houses (*guifang* 櫃坊) accepted deposits of coin, silk, and silver for safekeeping. Tang accounts of deposit houses typically locate them in the West Market of the imperial capital of Chang'an, the terminus of the Silk Road and the hub of international trade. Clients could use deposit affidavits as negotiable bills for major purchases such as real estate and also to make loans, and the deposit shops themselves – which typically paid interest on the deposits they received – used the assets they held to issue loans, thus operating as pawnshops. Consignment shops (*jifupu* 寄附鋪) accepted deposits as well, but more distinctively they received consignments of commercial goods or household property for sale. The consignment shop contracted with the consignor to dispose of the goods by a fixed date, although we have no information on how the profit was shared between the two parties.[68] In 782, when the central government was desperate to raise funds for war against renegade provincial governors, fiscal officers proposed imposing compulsory loans on rich merchants in Chang'an with assets of 10,000 *guan* or more. They predicted that some 1,000–2,000 merchants, chiefly operators of pawnshops and deposit shops, would be liable for this levy, which required merchants to surrender one-fourth of their assets.[69] Although the plan was shelved, the proposal gives some sense of the scale of these financial institutions in the Tang capital. They presumably operated in other major commercial centers such as Yangzhou, Chengdu, Guangzhou, and Jiangling as well.

Consignment loans of merchandise (*shemai* 賒買) for future payment appear in only a few late Tang records, chiefly concerning government consignments of salt and tea.[70] An imperial amnesty dating from c. 846 granted forgiveness to a consortium of tea merchants who had fallen deeply in arrears on loans they received from the central government's finance departments.[71] This document describes these loans as "consignment sales" (*shemai* 賒賣),

[68] Hino Kaisaburō 日野開三郎, "Tōdai no kifuho to kibō: Tōto Chōan no kin'yūgyōsha" 唐代の寄附鋪と櫃坊: 唐都長安の金融業者, in *Hino Kaisaburō Tōyō shigaku ronshū* 日野開三郎東洋史学論集, vol. 5, *Tō Godai no kahei to kin'yū* 唐五代の貨幣と金融 (Tokyo: San'ichi shobō, 1982), pp. 159–202.

[69] Sima Guang 司馬光, *Zizhi tongjian* 資治通鑑 ([hereafter *ZZTJ*]; Beijing: Zhonghua shuju, 1956), 227.7325–26; Wang Pu 王溥, *Tang hui yao* 唐會要 ([hereafter *THY*]; Shanghai: Shanghai guji chubanshe, 1981), 84.1585–86.

[70] For examples of private consignment of commercial goods, see Hino, "Kifuho to kibō," pp. 168–69.

[71] "Shou zunhao chiwen" 受尊號赦文, in *Quan Tang wen* 全唐文 (Beijing: Zhonghua shuju, 1983), 82.18a.

but it clearly indicates that these were debts with explicit contractual terms. By Song times, merchants commonly settled accounts through assignment transfers on deposits and negotiated consignment contracts (*she* 賒) to obtain merchandise on credit.[72] In 1092, when serving as the prefect of Hangzhou, the renowned poet Su Shi asserted that "as a rule, cash is scarcely used in private trade in recent times. Instead, retail shops rely on guarantees provided by trustworthy and wealthy individuals to make purchases on consignment from traveling merchants. Year after year they redeem the old debts and make new purchases."[73] An edict issued in 1022 sought to codify the practice of consignment. Although stipulating that ordinarily commercial transactions must be settled immediately in cash, the government allowed merchants with substantial amounts of merchandise to consign goods for future sale. In such cases, the recipient had to obtain at least three guarantors among reputable men of means and draw up a contract specifying the time of settlement. If the recipient failed to repay on time, then reimbursement was made either through forfeiture of collateral (if collateral was used) or else by the guarantors.[74] A mid-12th-century anecdote provides a cogent digest of the operation of consignment sales. It refers to a cloth merchant who arrived at the city of Xingzhou (Hebei) with a stock of 5,000 bolts of cloth and informed the chief local broker that he was seeking "a reputable shopkeeper to whom I can consign these goods. He should draw up a contract to give to me, and upon my return to this town I will come to collect from him the coin earned from the sale of cloth." In the end, the traveling merchant left his consignment with a man – also described as a broker, but one of modest means – who had done him a good turn ten years before.[75]

This anecdote underscores the importance of trust in such transactions, which relied on contracts but even more so on personal reputation, as well as the pivotal role of brokers (*yaren* 牙人, *yabao* 牙保, *zangkuai* 駔儈) in business dealings. Government-licensed brokers (*guanya* 官牙) provided a wide range of services such as negotiating sales of goods and real property, acting as guarantors, operating inns and warehouses, arranging shipping, handling consignments, hiring laborers and servants, notarizing contracts,

72 On *she* consignment sales – which required the intermediation of a broker – see Katō Shigeshi 加藤繁, "Sōdai no shōshūkan 'sha' ni tsuite" 宋代の商習慣'賒'に就いて, in Katō, *Shina keizai shi kōshō* 支那経済史考證 (Tokyo: Tōyō bunko, 1952), vol. 1, pp. 222–34; Miu Kunhe 繆坤和, *Songdai xinyong piaoju yanjiu* 宋代信用票據研究 (Kunming: Yunnan daxue chubanshe, 2002), pp. 35–38.

73 "Jiao jin yingzhao suolun sishi zhuang" 繳進應詔所論四事狀, in Su Shi 蘇軾, *Su Dongpo quanji* 蘇東坡全集 (Taipei: Shijie shuju, 1982), 2, p. 503.

74 Xu Song 徐松 (ed.), *Song huiyao jigao* 宋會要輯稿 ([hereafter *SHY*]; rpt. Taipei: Xinwenfeng chuban gongsi, 1976), shihuo 食貨, 37.9a–b.

75 Hong Mai 洪邁, *Yijian zhi*夷堅志 ([hereafter *YJZ*]; Beijing: Zhonghua shuju, 1981), yizhi 乙志, 7.242–43.

registering deeds, and making tax payments. Unlicensed brokers, working in the shadows of legality, offered many of the same services. Rural inhabitants often marketed their produce through urban brokers. In 926, the Later Tang government decreed that brokers should be prohibited from meddling in the trade of goods such as grain, cloth, and firewood, but their intermediation was required in sales of real property, human beings, or livestock.[76] This ruling was prompted by complaints that brokers bought up goods cheaply from rural producers and sold them at inflated prices to urban consumers, but at the same time it was tempered by the need for proper certification of transactions in which ownership must be beyond dispute (as we saw in the case of "market contracts" in the Tang). In Song law, too, licensed brokers were prohibited from trading on their own account, but deterring this practice proved difficult, and by Southern Song times the government appears to have abandoned its efforts to enforce the prohibition. Licensed brokers also acted as commission agents for the state, for example in managing the tea monopoly in Sichuan, procuring rice through the "harmonious purchase" system of compulsory sales, and determining the value of cargoes of imported goods for the purpose of assessing customs duties.[77]

The Song state also relied heavily on licensed brokers to negotiate private sales and debt contracts. Brokers also were responsible for collecting stamp fees for official endorsements of contracts; avoiding payment of stamp fees – initially set at 4 percent but rising to as much as 15–16 percent in the mid 12th century – was a major reason why most contracts lacked such official validation. Still, the influential role of brokers in mediating such transactions contributed to the highly standardized formulas used to compose contracts.[78] The necessity of using brokers to negotiate major private transactions such as land sales, including drawing up and certifying contracts, is fully attested in *Enlightened Judgments*, a casebook of exemplary legal rulings in civil disputes from the late Song period.[79] A magistrate's manual from the late Song era further underscores the crucial role of brokers in land sale transactions:

76 Wang Pu 王溥, *Wudai huiyao* 五代會要 (Shanghai: Shanghai guji chubanshe, 1978), 26.415.

77 On brokers in the Song, see Shiba Yoshinobu 斯波義信, *Sōdai shōgyō shi kenkyū* 宋代商業史研究 (Tokyo: Kazama shobō, 1968), pp. 391–407 (for an abbreviated translation, see Shiba, *Commerce and Society in Sung China* (Ann Arbor: University of Michigan Center for Chinese Studies, 1970), pp. 165–73); Miyazawa, *Kokka to keizai*, pp. 205–78; Li Weiguo 李伟国, "Songdai jingji shenghuo zhong de shikuai" 宋代经济生活中的市侩," in Li, *Songdai caizheng he wenxian kaolun* 宋代财政和文献考论 (Shanghai: Shanghai guji chubanshe, 2007), pp. 123–47; Dai Jianguo 戴建国, *Tang Song biange shiqi de falü yu shehui* 唐宋变革时期的法律与社会 (Shanghai: Shanghai guji chubanshe, 2010), pp. 407–50.

78 Hansen, *Negotiating Daily Life*, p. 82.

79 For a partial translation of this work, see Brian E. McKnight and James T. C. Liu (eds.), *Enlightened Judgments, Ch'ing-ming Chi: The Sung Dynasty Collection* (Albany: State University of New York Press, 1998). From 1022 the Song government required copies of

> In property transactions, what requires the utmost precaution is to prevent youths and menials or orphans and widows who make overlapping claims out of selfish interest from causing miscarriage or obstruction. In addition, the magistrate must ensure that in matters such as transfers of money and property and contracts drawn up by brokers all terms and conditions are clearly specified. Documenting consultations with relatives and neighbors, submitting and certifying contracts according to legal requirements, timely transfer of property and payment of taxes, and ensuring no hindrance due to outstanding debts are all necessary to ensure the smooth completion of transactions.[80]

Brokers assumed some legal liability for the contracts they prepared, and they were harshly punished for knowingly abetting fraudulent actions. The indispensable role of brokers in mediating business transactions also fomented much opprobrium. In his judgment of a lawsuit involving a broker who defrauded a merchant client, the magistrate Hu Ying contrasted the parasitic broker with the merchant who risks much to earn an honorable living:

> Generally speaking, the pursuit of profit is hardest for merchants and easiest for brokers. Traveling near and far, constantly exposed to the dangers of winds and waves, such is the hardship of the merchant. Yet the broker sits comfortably in his office and rakes in his earnings. The merchant must put up severalfold capital for the thinnest margin of profit; if his calculations are off the mark, or his timing isn't right, then eight or nine times out of ten he will lose all his investment; this, too, is the hard life faced by merchants. Yet the broker need not concern himself about the profits or losses of his clients because his commission is fixed and he will be paid in full.[81]

In the case over which Hu presided, a merchant was swindled out of money he had deposited with a broker with whom he had long done business. As we shall see in the next chapter, Hu's opinion of the perfidy of brokers echoed the views of merchants and officials alike toward the financiers whose strategic importance in the market for negotiable bills gave them enormous leverage. The market power attributed to brokers likewise derived from the salient importance of contracts in commercial exchange, and in social life in general.

contracts for conditional land sales to be submitted to local government offices, and in 1085 it promulgated a template to be used in composing such contracts. See Dai Jianguo, *Tang Song falü*, pp. 435–36.

80 "Jin hutian" 謹戶田, in Ying Jun 應俊, *Qintang yusu bian* 琴堂諭俗編 (SKQS ed.), *xia* 下, 12a. Since relatives and neighbors had rights of first refusal in sales of arable land, the law required that brokers provide written quit claims to allow sales to other parties. See Dai Jianguo, *Tang Song falü*, pp. 422–24.

81 "Zhi yakuai fuzi qipian zhi zui" 治牙儈父子欺騙之罪, in *QMJ*, 2, p. 409. See McKnight and Liu, *Enlightened Judgments*, pp. 398–99.

In Song times, then, private contracts rather than public records provided the legal foundations for ownership of assets, settlement of debts, and adjudication of disputes. Contracts also were the basis of credit transactions such as moneylending. Given the near universal distribution of landownership rights during the Song – and the frequent recourse to debt, at least for subsistence purposes – written contracts were familiar features of economic life for virtually all households. The Song economy was very much a paper economy. The quotidian use of contracts in economic life also facilitated the development of bills of exchange for commercial and financial transactions.

3

Paper Bills and State Finance in Tang and Northern Song China

The immediate precursors for the issue of paper money in the Song were various types of public and private remittance bills and bills of exchange that had come into common use before the Song issued its own paper money in the early 11th century.[1] These bills – which served to transfer funds over long distances, especially between the provinces and the capital – became an integral part of state finance in the early years of the Song dynasty. Under constant military threats from steppe-based polities, the Song state's survival hinged on sustaining a "perpetual wartime fiscal regime."[2] This relentless military crisis induced the Song state to adopt institutional innovations for raising revenues and mobilizing resources, building on late Tang initiatives such as the salt monopoly and the monetization of taxation under the twice-a-year taxation system as well as the mercantilist interventions in the

[1] A note on nomenclature is necessary here. I use the term "remittance bill" to designate instruments for transferring sums of money from one location to another. These were known in the Tang as *bianhuan wenqian* 便換文錢, or colloquially as "flying cash" (*feiqian* 飛錢), and as "convenient cash" (*bianqian* 便錢) in the Song. "Bill of exchange" here refers to bills that involved an exchange transaction over time and distance; for example, payment of grain or money in one place in return for payment in money or state monopoly goods in another. These instruments were known in the Song as *jiaoyin* 交引 or *chaoyin* 鈔引. The Song bill of exchange was similar to the bill of exchange in medieval Europe in that they involved monetary transactions at a distance whereby one form of value was exchanged for another. But it also was fundamentally different from the European bill of exchange, which invariably involved exchange between two different sovereign zones (with different sovereign monies) using a common money of account. In Europe, issuance of bills of exchange was restricted to a small club of exchange bankers, and the bills were not transferable before the late 16th century. In Song China, the state issued bills of exchange which were transferable, and therefore a secondary market of private (but government-authorized) dealers in exchange bills emerged. On the European bill of exchange, see Raymond de Roover, *L'Évolution de la lettre de change, XIVe–XVIIIe siècles* (Paris: Libraire Armond Colin, 1953); Marie-Thérèse Boyer-Xambeu, Ghislain Deleplace, and Lucien Gillard, *Private Money and Public Currencies: The Sixteenth Century Challenge* (London: Taylor & Francis, 1994).

[2] Sogabe Shizuo 曽我部静雄, "Sōdai no zaisei ippan" 宋代の財政一般, in Sogabe, *Sōdai zaisei shi* 宋代財政史 (Tokyo: Seikatsusha, 1941), p. 3.

commercial economy pioneered by the post-Tang regimes in South China. Song fiscal planners incorporated bills of exchange as the mainstay of the state's financing of frontier defense and the wars fought against its enemies along the northern frontier. At the same time, these bills became negotiable financial instruments widely used in private transactions, and speculative investments as well. The vital importance of bills of exchange both in the fiscal operations of the Song state and in private long-distance trade also contributed to the rise of powerful groups of merchants who came to exercise oligarchic domination over key sectors of the Song commercial economy.[3]

3.1 Origins of Remittance Bills: Tang "Flying Cash"

The earliest form of state-issued paper bills, which acquired the sobriquet of "flying cash" (*feiqian* 飛錢), were issued by the Tang government in the aftermath of the devastating An Lushan rebellion in the mid 8th century. From its outset, the Tang had been plagued by shortages of bronze coin, a continuation of the endemic scarcity of coin China had suffered since the beginning of the imperial era. The Tang state succeeded in issuing a high-value bronze coin (Kaiyuan tongbao 開元通寶, literally "inauguration of a new age") beginning in 621, creating a new monetary standard that replaced the long defunct Wuzhu coins of the Han, which were finally demonetized.[4] The Tang government's primary source of revenue, the *zu-yong-diao* 租庸調 capitation taxes, were collected in kind (grain and cloth) and labor services, not money. Only minor revenues – the household (*hushui* 戶稅) and land (*dishui* 地稅) taxes levied in the less-populated southern regions – were assessed in coin. Nonetheless, demand for money quickly exceeded the modest amounts of Kaiyuan coins issued by state mints. Already in the 660s, debased coins with markedly inferior copper content were in wide circulation, prompting vain efforts to prohibit their circulation, to accept them in state payments at steep discounts, or – least successfully and short-lived – to issue a new, larger, but highly overvalued official coin (nominally equivalent to ten Kaiyuan coins, but with nearly the same copper content as a single Kaiyuan coin). As economic growth accelerated during the long period of domestic peace before the An Lushan rebellion, the demand for means of exchange grew, as did the circulation of debased private coin.

[3] For general surveys of paper fiduciary instruments employed in the Song, see Kusano Yasushi草野靖, "Sōdai de yōirareta tegata no meishō to sono keishiki" 宋代で用いられた手形の名称とその形式, in *Nakajima Satoshi sensei koki kinen ronshū* 中嶋敏先生古稀記念論集 (Tokyo: Kyūko shoin, 1981), pp. 351–83; Miu, *Songdai xinyong piaoju.*

[4] On Tang coinage, see Thierry, *Monnaies*, pp. 205–53. For the evolution of Tang monetary policy, see Tan, "Monetary Policy."

The devastation wrought by the An Lushan rebellion of 755–763 compelled desperate measures to shore up state finances and to meet the urgent need to pay mercenary armies, both domestic and foreign. Another effort to introduce large-denomination coins (worth ten and fifty Kaiyuan coins) was initiated in 758 but discontinued after Liu Yan was appointed salt commissioner (Yantieshi 鹽鐵使) – with responsibility for coinage as well – in 760. During his twenty-year tenure as salt commissioner, Liu Yan transformed the foundation of Tang public finance by creating a state monopoly over the production and sale of salt. All salt producers were made state employees and required to deliver their salt to government directorates, which sold salt to wholesale merchants at a substantial markup. Liu's substitution of indirect taxation of consumption (including liquor as well as salt) and commerce (through new commercial and real estate taxes) in place of the traditional reliance on direct taxation on land and population proved a stunning fiscal success. By 779, salt revenues had risen tenfold and provided more than half of the government's annual income.[5]

Although the An Lushan rebellion was finally suppressed in 763, its political and economic aftershocks reverberated for the rest of the 8th century and beyond. The rebellion left the Central Plain heartland in ruin, and warlord regimes supplanted the imperial bureaucracy in the worst-hit regions of Hebei and Shandong. The court's most pressing priority was to reassert its authority over the provinces and fiscal resources. Much of the Central Plain remained outside direct central control and yielded little revenue. The virtually unchecked power wielded by Liu Yan over state revenues provoked deep dismay among other officials. In 779, a bitter rival of Liu, Yang Yan, took office as chief minister determined to wrest control of the state's fiscal powers from the Salt Commission and return it to the Ministry of Revenue (Hubu 戶部). Yang also undertook a sweeping fiscal reform aimed at restoring direct taxation as the main source of state revenue. Although Yang's attempt to abolish the salt commission was aborted, the new tax system he created would endure throughout the rest of the imperial era.

Yang Yan's reform acknowledged that the *zu-yong-diao* taxes that had been the cornerstone of the Tang state finances were defunct. Yang's plan formally abolished the *zu-yong-diao* assessments while merging the household (*hushui*) and land (*dishui*) levies into a new tax structure, known as the twice-a-year taxes (*liangshui* 兩稅), that was applied in all regions of the empire. In keeping with the procedures for the existing *hushui* levy, households were ranked into nine property grades and assessed a tax measured in coin. The land tax, as before, was assessed in grain. The household tax was collected in late summer

[5] Denis Twitchett, "The Salt Commissioners After An Lu-shan's Rebellion," *Asia Major*, new series, 4.1 (1954): 60–89; Denis Twitchett, *Financial Administration under the T'ang Dynasty* (Cambridge: Cambridge University Press, 1963), pp. 49–54.

and the land tax after the autumn harvest; hence the name twice-a-year tax. In contrast to the uniform allocation of taxation assessed on adult males under the *zu-yong-diao* system, however, the twice-a-year tax transferred the basis of direct taxation from people to property, the household's actual assets.[6]

The combination of Liu Yan's consumption taxes and Yang Yan's twice-a-year tax dramatically increased the money revenues of the Tang central government, from 2 million *guan* in 749 to 10–12 million *guan* annually by the end of the 8th century. By the same token, they exacerbated the shortage of bronze coin and the demand for copper. By 793, the price of copper had risen to a level that raised the bullion value of full-bodied Kaiyuan coin to more than three times its nominal value, precipitating widespread meltage of state-issued coin.[7] Counterfeiting surged, as did the use of "short strings" (*duanmo* 短陌) of fewer coins to represent the token value of a full string of coin.[8] Coercive measures to halt counterfeiting or prevent the melting of coin predictably failed, leaving the government no choice but to countenance the circulation of debased coins. Compounding the scarcity of coin, mint output fell to roughly one-third of the peak output in the 740s.

Lack of coin precipitated a deflationary spiral that began in the 780s and lasted until the middle of the 9th century. Deflation in effect increased the real cost of taxes denominated in coin. To relieve the demand for coin in state payments, the court accepted conversion of the coin portion of the twice-a-year tax to payments in textiles; by 821, much of the coin assessment had been commuted to payments in silk and hemp cloth.

Nonetheless, the scourge of deflation impelled the government to take forceful measures to boost the amount of coin in circulation. In addition to reiterating the prohibition against hoarding coin issued three years before, in 811 the Tang court also attempted to make compulsory the substitution of silk in lieu of coin as means of payment in purchases of livestock and houses as well as commercial transactions of more than ten *guan*. Among the measures adopted by the court in 811 was a ban on the use of "flying cash." "Flying cash" referred to remittance bills, perhaps first issued privately, for money transfers over long distances. Although best known now by the rubric "flying cash," at the time these bills were usually called "convenient exchange cash" (*bianhuan*

6 On Yang Yan's reforms and their consequences, see Li Zhixian 李志贤, *Yang Yan jiqi liangshuifa yanjiu* 杨炎及其两税法研究 (Beijing: Zhongguo shehui kexue chubanshe, 2002). The voluminous Chinese and Japanese scholarship on the twice-a-year tax reform is critically reviewed in Funakoshi Taiji 舟越泰次, *Tōdai ryōzeihō kenkyū* 唐代兩稅法研究 (Tokyo: Kyūko shoin, 1996).

7 Miyazawa, *Kokka to keizai*, pp. 335–36.

8 Tan, "Monetary Policy," pp. 73–90; Thierry, *Monnaies*, pp. 215–34. On "short strings," see Introduction.

wenqian 便換文錢).[9] The earliest mention of such bills dates from c. 785, but they seem to have been in common use by 800. Merchants in outlying provinces deposited cash with various government agencies – notably local branches of the Memorial Forwarding Bureau (Jinzouyuan 進奏院), which was in charge of sending and receiving official communications – or private parties in return for a remittance bill (*quan* 券, *die* 牒). Upon presentation of the remittance bill at the corresponding government office or private agent at the capital, the bearer would receive the sum deposited in the provinces. The few references to these bills emphasize their convenience compared to bulky low-value coins for transferring large sums over long distances. The most enthusiastic users of "flying cash" were tea merchants engaged in trade between the capital and the distant tea-producing regions of Huainan and Sichuan.

The 811 interdiction appears to have been motivated by concerns that redeeming remittance bills depleted the coin reserves held in central government treasuries. Local officials often prohibited the export of coin outside their jurisdiction to conserve local stocks, and the ban on the use of remittance bills was requested by the metropolitan prefect of Chang'an, the imperial capital, where the scarcity of coin was felt most acutely. But the prohibition only further encouraged hoarding of coin, aggravating the shortage of currency and driving prices down further. In the following year, the court reversed itself at the instigation of the Ministry of Revenue, which began to issue its own remittance bills while charging drawees a fee of 10 percent. Merchants proved unwilling to accept this tithe, however. The ministry soon relented and began to issue bills that could be redeemed at par. Subsequently the common use of remittance bills resumed. The author of an anthology of anecdotes composed c. 850 mentions the practice of depositing cash in public treasuries (*gongcang* 公藏) in return for remittance bills, which "are what the world refers to as 'convenient exchange' (*bianhuan* 便換)."[10] A memorial from 867 reported that merchants routinely obtained remittance bills issued at the capital by the Ministry of Revenue (*shengsi bianhuan wendie* 省司便換文牒), but following the recent outbreak of war with the Nanzhao kingdom in the southwest provincial officials had refused to redeem them, claiming that all their funds had been commandeered for the military campaigns. Consequently, merchants no longer were willing to draw bills at the capital, causing disruption to state finances. Local officials were ordered to redeem the bills promptly,

9 The 811 edict refers to *bianhuan xianqian* 便換見錢: see *Jiu Tang shu* 舊唐書 ([hereafter *JTS*]; Beijing: Zhonghua shuju ed.), 48.2102; *THY* 89.1934. Elsewhere in the *JTS*, these bills are described as "'flying cash,' which is referred to as 'convenient exchange' (*bianhuan*)": *JTS* 49.2121.

10 Zhao Lin 趙璘, *Yinhua lu* 因話錄 (SKQS ed.), 6.2b.

using funds belonging to the Ministry of Revenue held in local treasuries, such as twice-a-year tax revenues and liquor excises.[11]

The renewal in 812 of remittance bills issued by the Ministry of Revenue was linked to its efforts to exert control over the money supply; but in contrast to later Song practice, Tang officials did not seek to integrate these bills into the fiscal system.[12] The proliferation of state-issued remittance bills in the late Tang attests to how growing long-distance trade in goods such as salt and tea promoted interregional transfers of wealth. The fragmentation of the empire into numerous regional states following the fall of the Tang dynasty in 907 fractured the institutional foundations of the empire. Yet continuing economic growth, especially in the south, and intense political and military competition among the regional states fostered new fiscal institutions aimed at exploiting commercial wealth to bolster state power.

3.2 Political Fragmentation, Regional Economic Development, and Mercantilist Fiscal Policies in the Post-Tang Era

The preeminence of military rule that prevailed during the late Tang continued after its fall. In the north, a series of five successive dynasties claiming the mantle of the Tang Empire rose and fell before the establishment of the Song dynasty in 960 (hence this period from 907 to 960 is generally known as the Five Dynasties era). Actual power devolved to dozens of local warlord regimes. In the south, however, a relatively stable multistate system of seven regional kingdoms arose, the last of which submitted to Song rule only in 978. Rulers in both the north and south intensified the efforts undertaken by Tang statesmen in the wake of the An Lushan rebellion to amass the economic resources needed to sustain their military power and political survival. In so doing they embraced mercantilist strategies designed not only to maximize public revenues and invigorate domestic commercial development but also to inhibit the kind of interregional transfers of wealth facilitated by the use of remittance bills.

Constant warfare and frequent changes in ruling houses drove rulers to increase existing taxes and implement new ones, especially indirect taxes on commerce and consumption. These taxes, such as levies on urban real estate and retail sales, tolls at bridges and fords, wine brewing excises, and salt consumption levies, were intended as emergency measures but often became

[11] *THY* 59.1195–96; Wang Qinruo 王欽若 et al., *Cefu yuangui* 冊府元龜 (rpt. Beijing: Zhonghua shuju, 1960), 484.20a–b.

[12] Wu Liyu 吴丽娱, "Shiyan de huobi zuoyong yu zhebozhi de fazhan: jian lun chaoyin zhidu de qiyuan" 食鹽的貨幣作用與折博制的發展: 兼论钞引制度的起源, *Zhongguo jingji shi yanjiu* 中国经济史研究1994.4: 94–102.

permanent.[13] As in the late Tang, salt revenues were a crucial source of revenue. The northern regimes occupying the Central Plain heartland adopted a profusion of salt excises, including forced sales and loans of salt. One notorious example was the compulsory loan program known as "silkworm salt" (*canyan* 蠶鹽) enacted by the Later Tang (923–936) regime.[14] Under this program, often described as a form of advance payment or consignment (*she*), the government distributed salt as loans to sericulture households in early spring, when households were short of cash, that would later be repaid in woven silk textiles. These advance payments purportedly were intended to spare households from resorting to usurious borrowing for their capital needs, but in practice they became compulsory loans based on property rank, and thus a confiscatory tax on wealth. The high rates of repayment demanded by officials – typically in coin rather than cloth – merely redirected usurious profits into state coffers. "Silkworm salt" loans became a precedent for the Song state's practice of making consignment loans to silk-producing households.

The war-torn north witnessed little prosperity during the Five Dynasties period. But the emergence of independent and more stable regional states in South China stimulated robust economic growth. Regional specialization in the production of tea, salt, timber, paper, copper, silver, and textiles burgeoned. Although political fragmentation and hostile relations posed obstacles to interregional trade, the rulers of these states also depended on commerce to obtain vital strategic supplies – notably iron, salt, sulfur, and alum – as well as now-indispensable consumer staples such as tea.[15] The southern states developed cordial trading relations with the remote foreign states on the northern frontier, the Tanguts and the Khitan Liao, principally based on the exchange of tea for warhorses. The coastal kingdoms of Wu–Yue, Min, and Southern Han actively promoted overseas trade with the Khitan, the Koryŏ kingdom in Korea, and Japan, as well as Southeast Asia.

13 For a synopsis of the fiscal policies of the Five Dynasties' regimes, see Hino Kaisaburō 日野開三郎, "Godai shi gaisetsu" 五代史概説, in *Hino Kaisaburō Tōyō shigaku ronshū* 日野開三郎東洋史学論集, vol. 2: *Godai shi no kichō* 五代史の基調 (Tokyo: San'ichi shobō, 1982), pp. 87–124.

14 Guo Zhengzhong 郭正忠, *Songdai yanye jingji shi* 宋代盐业经济史 (Beijing: Renmin chubanshe, 1990), pp. 568–78. Guo suggests that silkworm salt loans existed in the final years of the Later Liang (907–923) as well.

15 Miyazaki Ichisada 宮崎市定, *Godai Sōsho no tsūka mondai* 五代宋初の通貨問題 (Kyoto: Hoshino shoten, 1943), pp. 83–117. For a synopsis of the southern regimes' economic policies, see Hugh D. Clark, "The Southern Kingdoms Between the T'ang and the Sung, 907–979," in Denis Twitchett and Paul Jakov Smith (eds.), *The Cambridge History of China*, vol. 5, pt 1: *The Sung Dynasty and Its Precursors, 907–1279* (Cambridge: Cambridge University Press, 2009), pp. 171–88.

The rulers of the South China states adopted explicitly mercantilist policies intended to strengthen their national economies, seeking to capitalize on their comparative advantages in resources.[16] In this respect, the Southern Tang kingdom (937–975), occupying the lower reaches of the Yangzi River valley (spanning most of the modern provinces of Jiangsu, Anhui, and Jiangxi), held a substantial edge. The Southern Tang established a tea monopoly in the Huainan region that became a crucial source of government revenue.[17] Most remunerative of all was the government's control of the Huainan salterns. The salt monopoly enabled the Southern Tang rulers to extract substantial revenues from their own subjects and also gave them enormous leverage in trade with the inland kingdoms of Chu and Jingnan, which depended entirely on imports of salt.[18] For its part, Chu (907–951) fell back on its greatest asset, tea. After declaring his independence from the defunct Tang dynasty, the Chu ruler Ma Yin aggressively promoted tea exports, recruiting brokers and merchants to procure tea from producers and to coordinate convoys of traders to sell tea in Henan and Hebei, where they would purchase silk and warhorses in return. In the judgment of the 11th-century historian Sima Guang, "Chu became wealthy and prosperous because of this trade."[19] In contrast to the monopolies created by the Southern Tang, Ma Yin relied on market incentives, including suspending tariffs and commercial excises on merchants from other states, who were said to have flocked to his realm.[20]

Ma Yin and other rulers also pursued bullionist policies to prevent the drain of high-value monies – bronze coin, silver, and gold – to neighboring rivals. Lacking domestic supplies of copper, Ma soon abandoned issue of bronze coins in favor of minting cheaper lead and iron coins. According to Sima Guang, because the lead and iron coins were unacceptable beyond Chu borders, foreign merchants had no choice but to take payment in Chu goods, stimulating Chu exports.[21] Yet officials in the north regularly complained that local markets were flooded with debased lead coins brought by the merchant convoys from Chu, triggering repeated edicts prohibiting their use in trade. Archaeological evidence suggests that both lead and iron coins circulated as

16 Miyazaki, *Tsūka mondai*, pp. 8–82. See also Miyazawa Tomoyuki 宮澤知之, "Godai Jūkoku jidai no tsūka jōkyō" 五代十国時代の通貨状況, *Ōryō shigaku* 鷹陵史学 34 (2008): 1–35.

17 Zhang Zexian 张泽咸, *Tang Wudai fuyi zhidu shicao* 唐五代赋役制度史草 (Beijing: Zhonghua shuju, 1986), p. 206.

18 Miyazaki, *Tsūka mondai*, pp. 39–42; Guo Zhengzhong, *Songdai yanye*, pp. 711–13.

19 *ZZTJ* 266.8702.

20 Hino Kaisaburō, "So no Ba In no tsūka seisaku to Godai jidai no kin'yūgyōsha" 楚の馬殷の通貨政策と五代時代の金融業者, in *Hino Kaisaburō ronshū*, vol. 5: *Tō Godai no kahei to kin'yū* 唐五代の貨幣と金融, pp. 417–84.

21 *ZZTJ* 274.8953.

domestic currencies within Chu.[22] Another contemporary historian wrote that because Chu's iron currency had very low unit value (said to be worth only one-hundredth of bronze coin at the official exchange of exchange), "in the shops and marketplaces transactions were conducted using deposit bills of exchange."[23] The use of such bills in lieu of cumbersome, low-value iron coins in Chu anticipated the invention of *jiaozi* bills in Sichuan, likewise an iron coin region, in the late 10th century.

Even states with ample copper supplies such as Wu–Yue and Southern Tang ultimately resorted to minting iron coins to forestall the drain of bronze coin beyond their borders. These monetary policies contributed to a pattern of regional monetary autarky that persisted after the Song reunification. The Song succeeded in withdrawing lead and iron coins from most regions soon after its conquest of the last independent southern regime in 978. Although the bronze coin standard prevailed throughout most of the Song empire, currency stocks were unevenly distributed, and the western region of Sichuan remained an outlier. When the Later Tang vanquished the Former Shu state in Sichuan in 925, the victors had brought back great quantities of gold and silver as well as six billion copper coins to Luoyang.[24] After the Later Shu kingdom (934–965) reestablished an independent Sichuan regime, it began to mint iron currency to replace the depleted stocks of bronze coin. The Song annexed Later Shu in 965, but repeated efforts to reintroduce a bronze coin standard in the Sichuan region failed. The persistence of the iron coin monetary standard in Sichuan figured significantly in the emergence of paper currencies in this region later in the 10th century.

3.3 Bills of Exchange and Commodity Licenses in Northern Song State Finance

Song fiscal and monetary policies were molded by the distinctive economic regions that enjoyed considerable autarky during the Five Dynasties era. At the same time, the task of reunifying these disparate regions required both

[22] Hino ("Ba In no tsūka seisaku," pp. 457–75) argued that the lead coins were produced mainly for export, while the iron coins served as Chu's domestic currency. But archaeological evidence indicates the prevalence of lead coins over iron coins within the Chu territory. See Thierry, *Monnaies*, pp. 274–76; Miyazawa Tomoyuki 宮澤知之, *Chūgoku dōsen no sekai* 中國銅銭の世界 (Kyoto: Shibunkaku shuppan, 2007), pp. 185–86.

[23] Liu Shu 劉恕, *Shiguo jinian* 十國紀年, cited in *Quanzhi* 泉志, a numismatic treatise composed in the mid-twelfth century by Hong Zun 洪遵, rpt. in Ren Renren 任仁仁 (ed.), *Quanzhi wai sanzhong* 泉志外三種 (Shanghai: Shanghai shudian chubanshe, 2018), p. 82. The language Liu employed (*quanqi zhiduo jiaoyi* 券契指垛交易) seems to indicate bills drawn on local deposit banks engaged in giro transactions between depositors, although we have no knowledge of how such institutions operated.

[24] Hino, "Godai shi gaisetsu," pp. 46–47.

centralization of power and territorial reorganization to reintegrate the administrative and economic orders.[25] The founding rulers of Song, Zhao Kuangyin (Emperor Taizu, r. 960–976) and his brother Zhao Kuangyi (Emperor Taizong, r. 976–997), concentrated military and fiscal authority in two institutions placed under direct imperial control: the Bureau of Military Affairs (Shumiyuan 樞密院) and the Finance Commission (Sansi 三司). Both institutions had antecedents in the late Tang and Five Dynasties regimes, but they acquired unprecedented powers during the Song. The disparate regions of the empire, divided into twenty-odd circuits (*lu* 路), were linked to the center through circuit intendants with discrete authority over fiscal, military, judicial, and educational affairs.

The new fiscal regime that emerged during the Tang–Song transition accelerated the shift away from taxing people to taxing wealth, at the same time eliminating military conscription and most labor services, thus liberating land, labor, and capital for more efficient uses. State initiatives to capture the wealth generated by the market economy reached their apogee with the deeply interventionist New Policies inaugurated by the prime minister Wang Anshi in the late 11th century. Although many of the specific regulations enunciated in Wang's New Policies were dismantled in the Southern Song period, public finance still relied on taxation of commerce and consumption. Fiduciary instruments, notably bills of exchange and paper currency, occupied a prominent place in Song state finance from the outset and grew in importance over time.

The central place of finance in the constitution of the Song state stemmed from the dire military predicament that beset the regime from its founding. During the 10th century period of disunion, the non-Chinese Khitan kingdom, based in modern Manchuria and Mongolia, arose as the most potent military power within the Chinese ecumene. After declaring himself emperor of the Liao dynasty in 916, the Khitan ruler Abaoji expanded his realm into neighboring territories. Abaoji's successor seized parts of the former Tang Empire in northern Hebei and Shanxi, known as the "Sixteen Prefectures," in 937, and briefly captured Kaifeng, the future capital of the Song dynasty, in 947. The annexation of the Sixteen Prefectures, including the region around modern Beijing, gave the Liao strategic supremacy over the Five Dynasties

[25] Christian Lamouroux, "Organisation territorial et monopole du thé dans la Chine des Song (960–1059)," *Annales: Économies, Sociétés, Civilisations* 46.5 (1991): 977–1008. On the efforts of the early Song emperors to create a "standardized imperial geography" by dismantling the military infrastructure of the warlord regimes of the Five Dynasties era, establishing new defensive perimeters along the empire's frontiers, and mobilizing the economic resources of the wealthy regions of the Yangzi Delta and southeastern China to defray military costs, see Ruth Mostern, *"Dividing the Realm in Order to Govern": The Spatial Organization of the Song State (960–1276 CE)* (Cambridge, MA: Harvard University Asia Center, 2011).

regimes based in the Central Plain. The Liao's geopolitical advantages would persist after the reunification of the rest of the Chinese ecumene by the Song dynasty after 960.

On its northwestern frontier, the Song faced another rival steppe regime, the Tangut confederacy, located in the Ordos region encircled by the great bend of the Yellow River. The Tanguts became a tributary vassal of the Tang in the late 9th century; and in the post-Tang era, relations between the Tangut rulers and the north China regimes remained cordial. The Tanguts lent assistance to the Song in its efforts to subdue the state of Northern Han in central Shanxi, which it finally accomplished in 979. But a succession crisis in the same year caused a schism among the Tangut leadership, with one faction, under the leadership of Li Jiqian, seeking to establish an independent Ordos kingdom in defiance of Song authority. Tense relations between Li Jiqian and the Song ensued. In 1002, Li Jiqian succeeded in imposing his rule over the whole of the Ordos region, and the Song begrudgingly conceded to his de facto suzerainty over this territory.

The campaign launched in 979 by Emperor Taizong to conquer the Northern Han followed immediately upon the Song conquest of the last of the independent southern regimes the year before. Taizong not only annexed the Northern Han territory but also inflicted a major defeat on the Liao army sent to repel the Song forces. Emboldened by this triumph, Taizong pushed on, seeking to recover the Sixteen Prefectures from the Liao as well. But the Song army, wearied by battle and short on supplies, was routed by the Liao forces, and the wounded emperor himself barely escaped capture. Stung by his ignominious defeat, Taizong redoubled his efforts to wrest back the Sixteen Prefectures. However, a renewed Song offensive in 986 once again resulted in resounding defeat and heavy losses of troops and materiel. Subsequently the Song was thrown on the defensive. In the 990s, the number of troops mustered into the Song armies doubled to 660,000 men, and substantial forces were stationed along the Liao frontier to defend Song cities. These preemptive measures incited the Liao to launch an all-out offensive in 1004. Although the Liao forces quickly pierced the Song border defenses, eventually their advance into Hebei stalled at Chanyuan, on the northern bank of the Yellow River. Still, the Liao held the upper hand in truce negotiations. In the Treaty of Chanyuan (1005), the Song conceded suzerainty over the Sixteen Prefectures and agreed to make annual tribute payments of silver and silk to the Liao, while withdrawing their troops to a more circumscribed defensive perimeter.[26]

Confronted by these dire geopolitical straits, the Song adapted the existing system of remittance bills to finance the delivery of provisions to the armies

[26] On the military struggles of the Song leading up to the Treaty of Chanyuan, see Peter Lorge, *The Reunification of China: Peace Through War Under the Song Dynasty* (Cambridge: Cambridge University Press, 2015).

stationed along its northern borders. From the outset, the Song government had continued the Tang "convenient exchange" remittances, establishing a Convenient Cash Agency (Bianqianwu 便錢務) in the capital in 970. Merchants paid a sum of coin to the Left Treasury (Zuocangku 左藏庫), the main depository for the government's operating funds, plus a 2 percent fee for notes that were payable on demand at the Broad Exchange Agencies (Zhebowu 折博務) in local prefectures. In 997, the state fixed the quota for "convenient cash" notes at a total of 1.7 million *guan*, which was raised to 2.83 million *guan* in 1021. As in the Tang, local prefectures were hard pressed to redeem the remittance bills with ready cash. Therefore they were obliged to substitute other goods, including silk and silver, in lieu of coin.[27]

But the Song went much farther than the Tang in integrating paper bills into its fiscal system as a means of payment. The Song was said to have employed three types of market procurement (*shidi* 市糴): (1) "harmonious purchases" (*hedi* 和糴), for which the state paid in coin; (2) "broad purchases" (*bodi* 博糴), which were compensated in goods, specifically goods controlled by the state under the regulated monopoly system; and (3) "convenient purchases" (*biandi* 便糴), in which merchants received negotiable bills of exchange (*chaoyin* 鈔引).[28] Shen Gua, who headed the Finance Commission in 1076–1077, described the market procurement system in somewhat different terms. According to Shen, "broad purchases" and "convenient purchases" both referred to procedures whereby the Finance Commission held reserves of cash and tea licenses at the capital to reimburse merchants who delivered supplies of grain and fodder to armies stationed along the northern frontiers; they differed chiefly in terms of where the supplies were delivered and where the tea could be procured. Shen also refers to "direct purchases" (*zhidi* 直糴) whereby merchants paid coin to the military units at the frontier and were reimbursed in coin at the capital. In all three cases, the merchants received "exchange licenses" (*jiaoyin* 交引) which they brought to the capital for redemption in cash or licenses to engage in trade in tea, a regulated commodity in most regions of the empire in the early Song.[29] Shen Gua's conflation of "broad purchases" and "convenient purchases" reflected the merger of frontier military procurement and state-issued bills of exchange in his day.

27 Li Tao 李燾, *Xu zizhi tongjian changbian* 續資治通鑒長編 ([hereafter *XCB*]; Beijing: Zhonghua shuju, 2004), 85.1936–37.

28 *SHY* shihuo 食貨, 41.1a. Unfortunately, this statement is not dated, nor is it attributed to any person or office.

29 Shen Gua 沈括 in Hu Daojing 胡道靜 (ed.), [*Xin jiaozheng*] *Mengxi bitan* [新校正]夢溪筆談 ([hereafter *MXBT*], Beijing: Zhonghua shuju, 1957), 11.120–21. See also Christian Lamouroux, "Endettement public, trésor impérial, et monnaie dans la Chine des xᵉ et xɪᵉ siècles," in Jean Andréau, Gérard Béaur, and Jean-Yves Garnier (eds.), *La Dette publique dans l'histoire* (Paris: Institut de la gestion publique et du développement economique, 2006), pp. 129–74.

The issue of *jiaoyin* bills of exchange to merchants who delivered grain and other military supplies to the frontier army camps, what became known as *ruzhong* 入中 procurement, was a cardinal feature of Song fiscal and military strategy.[30] By entrusting provisioning of the frontier armies to merchants, the Song leaders hoped to reduce the costs and logistical inefficiencies of state-managed procurement.

As mentioned above, the Southern Tang regime had created a government monopoly on the production and sale of tea in the Huainan region in Central China. At that time, Huainan constituted the frontier between the Southern Tang and the northern regimes based at Kaifeng. Tea production made Huainan a rich economic prize. The Northern Zhou seized Huainan from the Southern Tang in 956; and after his overthrow of Zhou, the Song founder established his own monopoly in the Huainan region in 962 to wrest control of the tea trade and its revenues from the Southern Tang, still engaged in a protracted struggle against the Song. Huainan tea became a crucial source of revenue for the fledgling Song regime, which in 964 set up a Regulated Commodity Bureau (Quehuowu 榷貨務) at Kaifeng to manage the tea monopoly. Fourteen purchasing depots were created across the Huainan region to ensure government control of tea supplies. Merchants exchanged coin, gold, silver, and silk at the capital's Quehuowu for exchange licenses (*jiaoyin*) that entitled them to obtain tea from the Huainan purchasing depots. By 977, the state monopoly on tea sales was extended throughout all tea-growing regions with the exceptions of Sichuan and the far southern circuits of Guangdong and Guangxi, but Huainan tea figured most importantly in Song fiscal administration.[31]

The Huainan tea farmers were essentially wards of the state. Tea farmers received advanced payments as seed capital, for which some portion of their

30 According to the Yuan institutional historian Ma Duanlin, citing the Southern scholar Chen Fuliang, the *ruzhong* system was initiated in 985. See Ma Duanlin 馬端臨, *Wenxian tongkao* 文獻通考 ([hereafter *WXTK*]; ST ed.), 15.155c. But no contemporary records confirm this dating. An 11th-century biography of the official Liu Shi credits Liu with proposing the *ruzhong* idea to Emperor Taizong. Liu then was serving as superintendent of the Lifengjian salt depot in the Huainan region (in Tongzhou prefecture) and previously had been prefect of the tea-producing prefecture of Tanzhou (Changsha) in Hunan. The biography states that Taizong was so pleased with Liu's suggestion that he summoned Liu for a personal audience and subsequently appointed him as supervising auditor of the Finance Commission (Pan Sansi dumokan si 判三司都磨勘司), an office created in 989. See Dai Yixuan 戴裔煊, *Songdai chaoyan zhidu yanjiu* 宋代鈔鹽制度研究 (rev. ed., Taipei: Huashi chubanshe, 1982), pp. 232–33. Most likely Liu made his proposal in the aftermath of the ignominious defeat of the Song forces at the hands of the Liao in 986.

31 For overviews of the operation of the tea monopoly in the early Northern Song, see Lamouroux, "Monopole du thé"; Zhu Zhongsheng 朱重聖, *Bei Song cha zhi shengchan yu jingying* 北宋茶之生產與經營 (Taipei: Xuesheng shuju, 1985), pp. 281–331.

crop was remitted to the government as "rent" (in lieu of taxes); the remainder was sold to the state purchasing depots. The tea licensing system transferred the costs of delivery, storage, and sale to merchants. But mediating among the conflicting interests of the state, tea producers, and tea merchants proved difficult, especially as tea production and sales became tightly yoked to military procurement for frontier defense.

In its struggle to maintain a balance between its needs for revenue and provisioning the frontier armies on one hand with providing fair compensation to producers and merchants on the other, the government repeatedly tinkered with the formulas for remuneration. In 995, officials sought to make the frontier procurement system more appealing to merchants by basing compensation on the remoteness of the frontier bases. In 1002, the procurement system was expanded to include redemption in licenses for other government-controlled commodities, namely salt and exotic imports such as frankincense, medicines, and ivory, which the government had accumulated in substantial quantities through its regulation of maritime trade.[32] The use of tea licenses to finance military procurement succeeded in inducing merchants to deliver provisions to frontier armies but not in constraining the costs of frontier supply. At moments of crisis, merchants demanded substantial price markups (*xugu* 虛估) for the provisions they delivered, and desperate officials had little choice but to comply. During the 1004 Khitan war, the finance commissioner Ding Wei reported, officials had disbursed tea licenses amounting to 3.6 million *guan* in return for grain deliveries worth only 500,000 *guan*.[33] Yet the cessation of hostilities after the Treaty of Chanyuan left merchants holding more licenses than could be redeemed with the available supply of Huainan tea, which drove down the licenses' market value and forced merchants to wait years to redeem them. In 1005, the government revised the *ruzhong* procurement system to enhance its attractiveness to merchants by setting the value of tea licenses at more than twice the value of the goods or money they delivered to frontier garrisons. In the opinion of many officials, the *ruzhong* system became too favorable to the great tea merchants at the expense of both the state and tea planters.[34] Ultimately the government sought to stabilize the frontier provisioning system by shifting its focus from tea to salt.

32 Under the Song maritime customs regulations, foreign merchants were obliged to sell these exotic imports to the government, giving the state monopoly control over domestic supplies.

33 *Song shi* 宋史 ([hereafter *SS*]; Beijing: Zhonghua shuju ed.), 183.4483.

34 In addition to the Lamouroux and Zhu studies cited in n31 above, see the seminal essays by Saeki Tomi: "Sōdai Rin Toku no chahō kaikaku ni tsuite" 宋代林特の茶法改革について and "Sōdai Ninsōchō ni okeru chahō ni tsuite" 宋代仁宗朝における茶法について, reprinted in Saeki Tomi 佐伯富, *Chūgoku shi kenkyū* 中国史研究 (Kyoto: Kyoto daigaku bungakubu Tōyōshi kenkyūkai, 1971), vol. 2, pp. 105–30 and 131–69, respectively.

At the time the *ruzhong* procurement system was created in the late 980s, the salt licenses issued to merchants, like the tea licenses, were focused on the Huainan production region. As in the case of tea, the Song government divided the empire into distinct salt production and consumption zones. The main sources of salt were (1) sea salt, including four separate coastal regions; (2) the Xiezhou salt lake in Shanxi; and (3) the underground brine extracted by wells in inland Sichuan, which as in other respects remained a separate zone of production and distribution. The Huainan salterns were the largest production region for salt (known as *moyan* 末鹽), followed by the Xiezhou salt lake; between them they accounted for two-thirds of the total annual production quota of the salt monopoly. The Huainan *moyan* sales region encompassed both the Yangzi River valley and the Hebei/Hedong regions along the Liao frontier, and thus the Huainan salt licenses were a natural complement to the provisioning of the armies along the northeastern border. In 996, however, the government reinstituted a full state monopoly on the sale of Huainan salt, and the sale of licenses to merchants was suspended. The use of salt licenses to obtain Xiezhou salt for sale in Jingxi circuit (including parts of modern Shaanxi, Hubei, and Henan provinces) continued.

At the turn of the 11th century, as the Tangut menace along the northwestern border grew, the importance of Xiezhou salt revenues to military logistics rose correspondingly. Unlike the Hebei frontier, which was readily reached by canal transport across the Central Plain, the military camps along the Shaanxi frontier were located far from the main grain-producing regions and largely inaccessible by water transport. Salt also was a flashpoint in the Song–Tangut conflict. Eager to develop transborder trade, the Tangut chief Li Jiqian brought salt from Wubai salt lake (Yanchi in modern Ningxia) within his domain to sell to Chinese settlers in Shaanxi. In its efforts to unseat Li, the Song government sought to interdict this trade and instead supply Shaanxi with Xiezhou salt. Merchants purchased salt licenses at the capital that could be exchanged at Xiezhou to obtain the salt they would bring to Shaanxi. However, because of the high transport costs, few merchants were interested in this trade, and ultimately the Song repealed its ban on transborder salt purchases. Instead, the Song offered Xiezhou salt licenses for the centrally located Jingxi circuit consumption region to merchants who would deliver provisions to the Shaanxi armies. In 1004, the government allowed merchants to receive the salt licenses in the frontier zones where they delivered military supplies, eliminating the need to travel to Kaifeng. Still, as in the case with tea, the search for balance between government costs and merchant profits continually vexed state policymakers. Officials' complaints that merchants demanded excessive prices (*xugu*) for delivery of provisions were legion, as were merchants' gripes about supplementary surcharges on license purchases (*tiena* 貼納) and insufficient supplies of goods to redeem their licenses (*xuyin* 虛引).

Table 3.1 *Military expenditures for northern frontier armies, 1038 and 1043*

	1038 expenditures (figures in millions)	1038 expenditures	1043 expenditures (figures in millions)	1043 expenditures
Shaanxi	15.51	37%	33.62	47%
Hebei	18.23	43%	25.52	35%
Hedong	8.59	20%	11.76	18%
Total	42.33	—	72.17	—

Note: Figures give the total sums of units of coin, cloth, grain, fodder, and grain rations without separating out individual amounts; it is unclear whether the proportions among these items remained constant.
Source: *XCB* 140.3366.

The fiscal demands on the Song state soared after war with the Tanguts erupted in 1040. In 1038, the Tangut leader Weiming Yuanhao disavowed the Tanguts' nominal subordination to Song suzerainty and proclaimed himself emperor of the Great Xia state, precipitating a suspension of cross-border trade and violent reprisals, culminating in a fierce Xia offensive in the first month of 1040. The Tanguts dominated the Song forces on the battlefield but suffered enormous strain on their own resources, leading to a peace treaty in 1044 in which Yuanhao declared himself "subject" to the Song emperor in return for annual tribute payments in silk and silver like those paid to Liao.

Although Song policymakers remained chiefly concerned with the Liao menace on the northeastern frontier, the Song–Xia war of 1040–1044 (known as the Qingli War, after the reign-era of these years) marked a dramatic shift in the costs of war. According to the finance commissioner Wang Yaochen, by 1043 outlays for frontier defense had risen 70 percent compared to 1038, and spending on frontier defense had pivoted from the Hebei and Hedong garrisons on the Liao frontier to Shaanxi on the Xia frontier, a pattern that would persist throughout the rest of the Northern Song (Table 3.1). Despite the truce enacted in 1044, the burden of military expenditures did not abate. The Song was obliged to station large standing armies on the Shaanxi frontier and to maintain much longer supply lines. The number of troops mobilized for defense of the northern frontier doubled from 400,000 to 800,000, further straining the fiscal capacity of the Song state.[35] In 1064, the finance commissioner Cai Xiang calculated that more than three-fourths of state expenditures

[35] The total number of troops in the Song armies rose from 912,000 in the early 1020s to 1,162,000 in the mid 1060s; 54 percent of military units were stationed on the northern frontier, 36 percent in or around the capital, and only 10 percent in other regions. Tseng-yu Wang, "A History of the Song Military," in John W. Chafee and Denis Twitchett

Table 3.2 *State revenues and military expenditures, 1064*

	Total income	Total expenditures	Military expenditures	Percentage military expenditures
Coin (strings)	36,822,541	33,170,630	9,940,147	30
Silk cloth (bolts)	8,745,535	7,255,640	7,422,768	102
Grain (piculs)	26,943,575	30,472,708	23,170,223	76
Fodder (sheaves)	29,396,113	29,520,469	24,980,464	84

Sources: Cai Xiang, "Lun bing shishi" 論兵十事, *Song Duanmingdian xueshi Cai Zhonghui gong wenji*, 18.16b–18a; viz. Wang Shengduo, *Liang Song caizheng shi*, vol. 2, p. 691.

of cloth, grain, and fodder, as well as 30 percent of its money outlays, were dedicated to the military (Table 3.2). Cai estimated total state income, if converted into coin as the unit of account, at 60 million *guan*, of which 50 million *guan* was spent on the military.[36]

Despite a litany of memorials from Song officials and scholars urging the government to economize on its expenditures, it became fully apparent that the deficits incurred by maintaining the frontier garrisons could only be redressed by tapping new sources of state revenue. Two major actions were taken: (1) integrating Shaanxi more directly into the fiscal regime and far richer regional economy of Sichuan; and (2) creating a new salt licensing system. Linking the Shaanxi border region to the Sichuan economy involved the formation of a common currency zone, including the *jiaozi* paper money first issued as a state currency in 1024, which we will discuss in Chapter 4. Here we will consider the reform of the salt monopoly, which decoupled the salt licenses from the *ruzhong* procurement system and further enhanced their value as negotiable bills.

The new salt license system ratified by the court in 1048 had been proposed by Fan Xiang, an official with long experience in Shaanxi fiscal affairs. Instead of requiring that merchants deliver grain and other supplies to frontier garrisons, they could pay bronze coin at the frontier branches of the Quehuowu in exchange for Xiezhou salt licenses. The value of the licenses varied depending on the remoteness of the frontier base. Also, merchants could bring the licenses directly to Xiezhou rather than having to make the

(eds.), *The Cambridge History of China*, vol. 5, pt. 2: *Sung China (960–1279)* (Cambridge: Cambridge University Press, 2015), pp. 220, 224–25.

36 Cai Xiang 蔡襄, "Guolun yaomu" 國論要目, *Song Duanmingdian xueshi Cai Zhonghui gong wenji* 宋端明殿學士蔡忠惠公文集 (1740 Xunminzhai ed.), 18.7a.

journey to Kaifeng. In addition to Xiezhou salt licenses, merchants could also purchase (at a premium) licenses for the *moyan* salt regions in Huainan and the southeast. In 1058, the system was amended to allow merchants to make payments in coin at the capital, eliminating the need to travel to the frontier prefectures. Fan's plan reduced transaction costs for the government (which purchased provisions directly through the market, rather than having to offer the salt licenses at inflated rates of compensation) and for merchants (who no longer had to deliver supplies to the frontier). Fan also established fixed purchasing prices for salt licenses and annual maximum quotas on the number of licenses issued to avoid the recurring problem of imbalances in the supply of licenses and market demand for salt. The Salt Supervisory Office (Duyanyuan 都鹽院) at the capital was charged with maintaining an equilibrium in the supply and demand of salt licenses to keep retail prices within a relatively narrow range (35–40 *wen* per *jin* in Kaifeng). When prices rose above this range, the Salt Supervisory Office was authorized to sell additional licenses; when retail prices fell below the minimum target, the government would buy up licenses to reduce the supply. Finally, Fan's policy allowed merchants to ship salt from Xiezhou to the northwestern frontier, for which they would be amply compensated with salt licenses of greater value.[37]

Although officials reported that merchants initially opposed Fan Xiang's salt license system, it proved to be a resounding success for state finances. In 1052, it generated 2.15 million *guan* in revenues, an increase of nearly 50 percent over 1046. Moreover, it reduced state expenditures on military provisions while eliminating the problem of excess salt licenses in the hands of merchants (*xuyin*). A year after Fan's plan was implemented, Bao Zheng, a veteran fiscal official sent to Shaanxi to evaluate the effects of the reform, confidently predicted that it would erase the Quehuowu's cumulative deficit of 5–7 million *guan* within one or two years.[38] Xue Xiang, who served as the Xiezhou salt commissioner from 1061 to 1069, was celebrated for expanding on Fan Xiang's program by eliminating local excises on salt purveyors and lowering the price of salt in frontier areas.[39] Shen Gua, writing in the 1070s, enthused: "[Fan's salt license system] has been implemented for several decades, and down to the present it has been regarded as beneficial."[40] The operation of the salt monopoly indeed remained stable until Shen Gua's time, when a new military crisis and the fiscal exigencies it engendered propelled the Song leadership into massive new spending.

[37] For details, see Dai Yixuan, *Chaoyan zhidu*, pp. 270–86.
[38] *XCB* 167.4018.
[39] Dai Yixuan, *Chaoyan zhidu*, pp. 287–89.
[40] *MXBT* 11.130. See also the encomium on the five virtues of Fan Xiang's policy voiced by the chief councilor Lü Dafang in 1092: *XCB* 471.11237.

Although still designed to meet the state's urgent need to supply its frontier armies, Fan Xiang's salt licensing system severed the bills of exchange from the actual delivery of military provisions. Instead, the salt licenses became more flexible financial instruments, serving as negotiable bills and speculative investments. Implementation of the *ruzhong* policy had tied military procurement to the market, enabling the emergence of powerful groups of merchants and financiers. The dominance of these merchant blocs over key sectors of the commercial economy persisted even after Fan Xiang's reform of the salt monopoly.

3.4 Negotiable Bills and Merchant Power

Smooth operation of the Song state's military procurement and logistics depended on the participation and intermediation of merchants. But different merchant constituencies had divergent, and in some cases competing, interests.[41] For example, tea merchants and salt merchants promoted policies that would enhance the values of their respective commodity licenses, often pitting them against each other. Government agents – fiscal planners in the Finance Commission, the Quehuowu at the capital, military and civil officials in frontier regions, and provincial officials responsible for the management of the tea and salt monopolies – had separate and conflicting interests as well. Fiscal planners seeking to adjust policies regarding military procurement and the operation of commodity monopolies routinely convened meetings with representatives of relevant merchant communities to negotiate solutions. An especially powerful constituency was the exchange bill shops (*jiaoyinpu* 交引鋪) in Kaifeng, which comprised a vital link in the market for bills of exchange and commodity licenses.[42]

The secondary market for these financial instruments existed from the inception of the *ruzhong* system. Few of the frontier merchants who delivered supplies to the garrisons and were compensated with *jiaoyin* bills had any interest in traveling to the capital to redeem them. Instead, they would sell the bills at major commercial towns in the vicinity to long-distance merchants, who in turn would bring them to the *jiaoyinpu* in Kaifeng. Merchants redeeming the bills also were required to obtain guarantees from *jiaoyinpu*

[41] On this point, see especially Lamouroux, "Endettement public."

[42] The most comprehensive study of *jiaoyinpu* is Hino Kaisaburō, "Hoku-Sō jidai no enshō ni tsuite – fu: kōinho" 北宋時代の塩鈔について—附：交引鋪, in *Hino Kaisaburō ronshū*, vol. 6, pt. 1: *Sōdai no kahei to kin'yū* 宋代の貨幣と金融 (Tokyo: San'ichi shobō, 1983), pp. 19–244 (for *jiaoyinpu*, see pp. 144–244). See also Gotō Hisakatsu 後藤久勝, "Hoku-Sō jidai Kahoku ryōsō no ryūtsū to kōinho no honin ni tsuite" 北宋時代河北糧草の流通と交引鋪の保任について, *Kyūshū daigaku tōyōshi ronshū* 九州大学東洋史論集26 (1998): 29–48.

registered with the Quehuowu in Kaifeng, which provided the *jiaoyinpu* with ledgers of the bills it issued (known as *hetong haobu* 合同號簿).[43] After the *jiaoyinpu* verified the bills, the merchants brought them to the Quehuowu and redeemed them for cash or commodity licenses. The *jiaoyinpu* also bought tea and salt licenses directly from long-distance merchants for resale to merchants based in the salt- and tea-producing regions.[44] These financial houses thus were the interface between the state and market that made it possible for the frontier provisioning system to function. The circulation of *jiaoyin* bills and commodity licenses among different merchant groups, with the *jiaoyinpu* occupying a central place in the matrix of exchange, is illustrated schematically in Figure 3.1. *Jiaoyin* bills obtained in frontier regions typically passed through the hands of at least two or three merchant firms before being redeemed by government agents.

Jiaoyinpu occupied a central place – literally and figuratively – in the business districts of the Song capitals and were reputed to be immensely wealthy. A memoir of Kaifeng informs us that "Nantong Street is the place where trade in gold, silver, brocade, and silks is conducted. The shops are splendid and imposing edifices with broad and spacious entrances. They carry on businesses involving vast sums of money in the thousands and ten thousands of *guan*, truly astonishing to anyone who sees it."[45] Although this passage does not explicitly mention *jiaoyinpu*, it is likely that the reference to the gold and silver trades implies not just dealers in gold and silver but financiers such as *jiaoyinpu* as well (most likely, firms that combined trading in bills and bullion exchange).[46] When Kaifeng was under siege by the Jurchen invaders in 1126, government officials dispatched agents to all of the capital's "exchange bill, moneylending, gold and silver, and brocade and silk shops" (*jiaoyin zhiku jinyin caibo zhupu* 交引質庫金銀采帛諸鋪) to confiscate their stocks of currency, "amounting to a thousand or ten thousand ounces of silver for a single shop."[47]

43 These merchants were referred to as 行商, which is open to two readings: *xingshang*, "traveling merchants"; and *hangshang*, "guild merchants." Many scholars, beginning with Katō Shigeshi, have interpreted the term in the latter sense, but there is no firm evidence that trade guilds existed at this time. Recent scholarship instead interprets the term as referring to merchants engaged in long-distance trade, not a trade guild. See Miyazawa, *Kokka to keizai*, pp. 144–46; Gotō, "Kōinho no honin," pp. 30–32; Nakajima Satoshi 中嶋敏 (ed.), *Sōshi shokkashi yakuchū* 宋史食貨志譯註 (Tokyo: Tokyo bunko, 2004), vol. 5, p. 255n130.

44 *XCB* 60.1335–36, 100.2313–14; *SHY* shihuo 55.23b.

45 Meng Yuanlao 孟元老, *Dongjing menghua lu* 東京夢華錄 2, in *Dongjing menghua lu wai sizhong* 東京夢華錄外四種 ([hereafter *DJMHL*]; Beijing: Zhonghua shuju, 1962), p. 14. The phrase "splendid and imposing edifices" typically was used to describe grand Buddhist temples.

46 Wang Shengduo, *Liang Song huobi shi*, vol. 2, p. 905.

47 Xu Mengxin 徐夢莘, *Sanchao beimeng huibian* 三朝北盟會編 ([hereafter *SCBM*]; 1939 ed.; rpt. Taipei: Dahua shuju, 1977), vol. 2, p. 153 (Jingkang zhongzhi 靖康中帙 juan 卷 47).

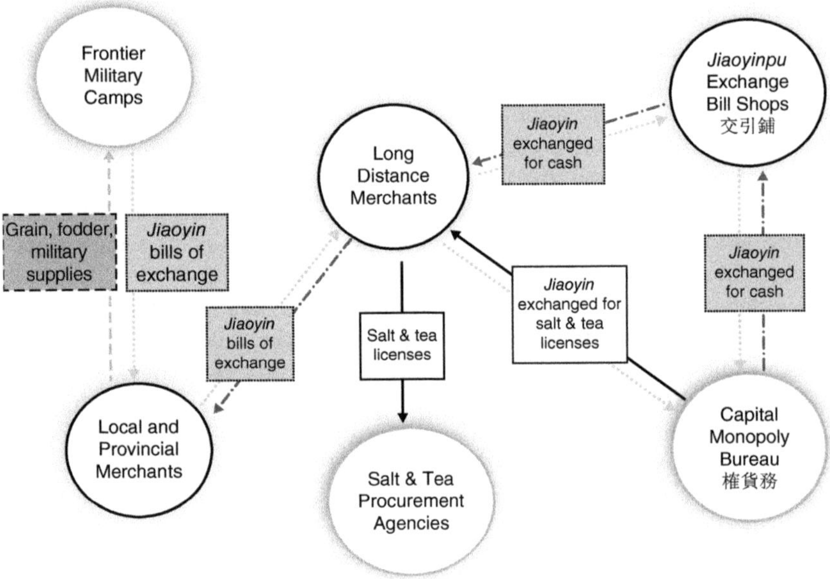

Figure 3.1 Circulation of *jiaoyin* bills of exchange and commodity licenses under the *ruzhong* military procurement system.
<key>
<black circle>Merchant groups
<grey circle>Government agencies
<dashed line>Movement of frontier supplies
<dotted line>Movement of *jiaoyin* bills
<solid black line>Movement of tea and salt licenses
<dash-dotted line>Movement of coin

Jiaoyinpu firms were an equally prominent fixture of the urban landscape in the Southern Song capital of Hangzhou. A gazetteer of Hangzhou published in 1235 describes the "Five Flowers" quarter in Hangzhou's central business district, where "the two streets are lined with top-drawer shops that trade in gold, silver, and negotiable bills (*jinyin chaoyin jiaoyi pu* 金銀鈔引交易鋪), numbering over a hundred altogether."[48] This passage is repeated in a 1272 gazetteer, which adds that these shops held reserves of coin for redeeming salt licenses issued by the Quehuowu. It also singles out as particularly renowned the Shen Family and Zhang Family Gold/Silver/*Jiaoyin* shops, explicitly

[48] "Puxi" 鋪席, in *Ducheng jisheng* 都城記勝, in *DJMHL*, p. 100.

linking together individual dealers in gold and silver with the trade in bills of exchange.[49] The concentration of *jiaoyinpu* in the heart of the Five Flowers commercial district in Southern Song Hangzhou can readily be seen in Map 3.1, which shows the locations of shops named in the inscriptions on extant silver ingots.[50] Nearly all of these shops were tightly clustered together just north of the Wujian Tower, a renowned wineshop that symbolized the city center, and perhaps not coincidentally adjacent to the Commercial Tax Office (Dushangshuiwu 都商稅務). (The *Huizi* Depository (Huiziku 會子庫) was located directly south of the Five Flowers district, together with the Quehuowu and other tax agencies.)[51] *Jiaoyinpu* also were found – in more modest numbers – in provincial commercial centers. Commercial tax records from a Ningbo gazetteer indicate that in 1225 there were six *jiaoyinpu* firms in the city, a flourishing hub of maritime trade.[52]

One major advantage the *jiaoyinpu* had in the circulation of bills derived from information asymmetry. A constant refrain voiced by fiscal planners was that the frontier merchants earned little from trading bills of exchange; instead, it was the *jiaoyinpu* who reaped the major profits.[53] The frontier merchants, pressed for time to dispose of the bills, were unaware of the fluctuations in their market value in the capital. Government officials struggled to maintain a balance between the supply and demand for commodity licenses while extracting the share of revenues needed for frontier defense. As mentioned earlier, during military crises such as the 1004 Liao war, urgent demand for supplies drove up premiums (*xugu*) – denominated in tea licenses – offered to merchants; but the resulting glut in tea licenses caused their value to plummet. Nonetheless, the frontier merchants, who needed to convert the licenses they held to cash, were obliged to sell, further depressing the market value of licenses. The excess volume of tea licenses, far greater than the amount of tea available for purchase, forced tea merchants to wait years before they could exercise their purchase options. *Jiaoyinpu*, in contrast, had

49 "Puxi" 鋪席, in Wu Zimu 吳自牧, *Meng liang lu* 夢粱錄 [hereafter *MLL*] 16, in *DJMHL*, pp. 239–40.

50 The ingots were stamped with inscriptions that identified the name of the shop and its street location within Hangzhou. The ingots also attest to the overlap between the shops' dealings in silver bullion as well as exchange bills. Li Xiaoping 李小萍, "Nan Song jinyin yanchao jiaoyinpu yanjiu" 南宋金银盐钞交引铺研究, *Zhongguo qianbi* 中国钱币 2010.2: 24–30.

51 Nearly all of Hangzhou's most famous retail shops, restaurants, and female entertainment quarters (known as *wazi* 瓦子) were also located in the Five Flowers district. See the maps in Shiba Yoshinobu 斯波義信, "Sōto Kōshū no toshi seitai" 宋都杭州の都市生態, in Shiba, *Sōdai Kōnan keizai shi no kenkyū* 宋代江南経済史の研究 (Tokyo: Tokyo daigaku shuppankai, 1988), pp. 340–63.

52 [*Baoqing*] *Siming zhi* [寶慶] 四明志 (SYDFZ ed.), 5.17a–b.

53 *XCB* 100.2313; *SS* 183.4483.

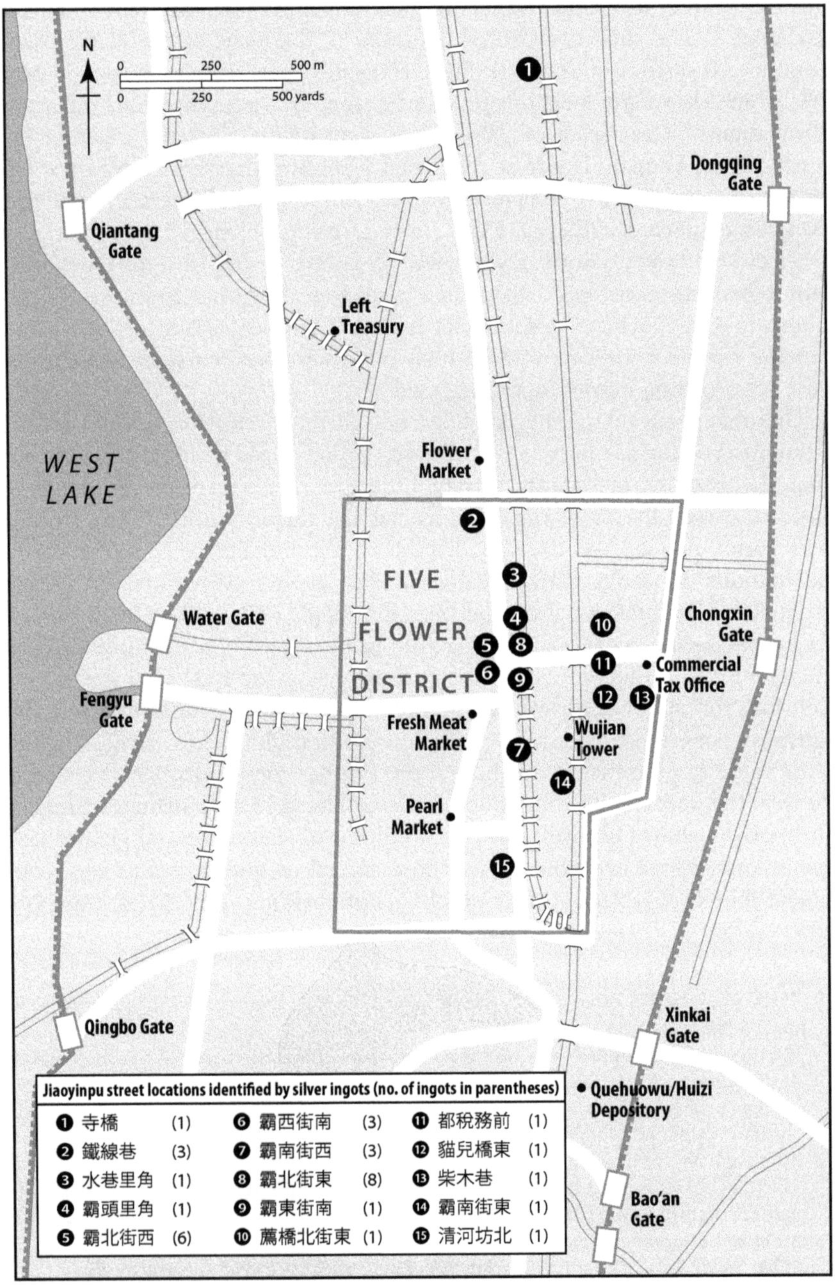

Map 3.1 *Jiaoyinpu* shops in Southern Song Hangzhou.
Source: Adapted from Li Xiaoping李小萍, "Nan Song jinyin yanchao jiaoyinpu yanjiu" 南宋金银盐钞交引铺研究, *Zhongguo qianbi* 中国钱币 2010.2: 24-30

substantial capital reserves and could afford to hold onto commodity licenses and wait until their market price improved.[54] Already as early as 1006, the capital *jiaoyinpu* were described as wielding a "stranglehold over bills of exchange" (*jiaoyinlian* 交引鏈).[55]

Another advantage exploited by the *jiaoyinpu* was the requirement that merchants seeking to redeem bills of exchange obtain guarantorship from a *jiaoyinpu* firm.[56] Merchants bitterly railed against the guarantorship requirement and lobbied for its elimination. In 1014 and again in 1015, the Finance Commission, alleging that *jiaoyinpu* manipulated this device to control access to commodity licenses and to compel merchants to accept discounts in remuneration, sided with the proponents of repeal.[57] Nonetheless, the guarantorship requirement remained in place until 1036 – testimony, it seems, to the powerful political influence exerted by the *jiaoyinpu* firms.[58] Although the policy adopted in 1036 allowed merchants to proceed directly to the Quehuowu to obtain tea licenses, *jiaoyinpu* continued to dominate the secondary market for bills of exchange.

In 1005, the assistant commissioner for salt and iron, Lin Te, implemented a dual price structure for tea licenses to compensate merchants for falling prices: the Quehouwu in the capital sold licenses in exchange for coin, silver, or silks at a 100 percent markup in value, while frontier officials issued licenses to *ruzhong* merchants at further premiums of 10–30 percent, depending on the remoteness of frontier garrisons. These substantial premiums reduced government revenues from license sales, but Lin Te declared the policy a success, because expenditures on military procurement declined even more, yielding a net gain.[59] Still, the glut of licenses persisted, leading to long delays for

54 Hino, "Kōinho," pp. 147–55.

55 *SHY* shihuo 36.8b.

56 Hino argued that initially guarantorship was needed because the issue of *jiaoyin* bills in frontier regions was unsystematic; local authorities issued their own notes, creating ample opportunity for forgery. The Quehuowu relied on *jiaoyinpu* to validate the bills. By 1015, more formal procedures were adopted whereby frontier authorities delivered affidavits of authenticity (*kantong didie* 勘同遞牒) to the capital to verify bills brought by merchants, which should have obviated the need for guarantorship, but the two systems continued to be used together down to 1036. Gotō, in contrast, argues that guarantorship initially was created to protect merchants from bureaucratic malfeasance. Both scholars agree that *jiaoyinpu* themselves abused their power over the process. See Hino, "Kōinho," pp. 181–82; Gotō, "Kōinho no honin," pp. 39–42.

57 *SHY* shihuo 36.11a–b.

58 Hino, "Kōinho," p. 163.

59 Government officials offered contrasting views regarding merchant reaction (Lin claimed they favored the new policy). By 1015, however, most agreed that the new policy was not working well. See Saeki, "Chahō kaikaku"; Zhu, *Bei Song cha*, pp. 298–305.

merchants to redeem them.[60] Tea merchants in Kaifeng – well-connected with the *jiaoyinpu* and influential officials – had the advantage over small provincial merchants in securing early redemption of their licenses. From this time, government officials routinely noted the conflict of interests between the "magnate merchants" (*haoshang* 豪商) and "petty merchants" (*xiaoshang* 小商) among tea traders.[61] In order to shore up the position of the latter, the government continually raised the nominal value of tea licenses, which further diminished its own revenues.[62]

The enthronement of the twelve-year-old Emperor Renzong (r. 1022–1063), inaugurating the regency of Empress Dowager Liu, provided an opportunity for the finance commissioner Li Zi to propose a thorough reconsideration of the fiscal state of empire, leading to the institution of a new Fiscal Planning Bureau (Jizhisi 計置司) in early 1023.[63] Li immediately took the initiative to decouple military procurement from the tea monopoly by introducing a new arrangement under which frontier officials purchased provisions on a cash basis, compensating merchants with "ready-cash bills of exchange" (*xianqian jiaoyin* 見錢交引) that they could redeem in the capital for coin. Tea merchants also could purchase licenses at the capital through cash payments.[64] Li's "ready-cash" policy was intended to streamline costs in both military provisioning and operation of the tea monopoly as well as to raise revenues. But it also aimed to diminish the power of powerful merchant blocs to arbitrage profits from tea licenses and bills of exchange while broadening access to the tea trade for smaller merchants. However, the new policy adversely affected provisioning merchants, who still needed to redeem the ready-cash bills of exchange on the secondary market. An investigation by the fiscal planning bureau the following year determined that revenues had doubled while deliveries of supplies to frontier garrisons also increased.[65] Yet opposition within the government as well as from merchants swiftly mounted, and by the end of

60 According to Shen Gua, the government was also forced to intervene and buy up excess notes. See *MXBT* 12.134.

61 E.g., *XCB* 85.1936; *SHY* shihuo 36.11b–12a. See Zhu, *Bei Song cha*, pp. 298–305.

62 Hino, "Kōinho," pp. 171–72.

63 *XCB* 100.2310–15. During the regency of Empress Liu (1022–1033) revenue enhancement became a chief priority of government and commercial interests gained unprecedented influence in the halls of power. See Charles Hartman, *Structures of Governance in Song Dynasty China, 960–1270 CE* (Cambridge: Cambridge University Press, 2023), p. 9.

64 Under the new policy of "direct sales" (*tieshe* 貼射), the government no longer provided seed capital to tea planters, who now could sell directly to merchants at a "median" market price. To prevent contraband sales, tea merchants still were required to bring the tea they purchased to the state monopoly bureau for weighing and paying a license fee (*xiqian* 息錢), whereupon they received a verification certificate. Zhu, *Bei Song cha*, pp. 306–8.

65 *XCB* 102.2360–61.

1025 Li's ready-cash initiative had been rescinded and Li himself dismissed from office.

Complaints that the Kaifeng *jiaoyinpu* manipulated the market for bills of exchange and commodity licenses persisted.[66] In 1036, the Finance Commission, concerned over the exorbitant costs of tea license premiums, invited Li Zi, then commissioner of military affairs, and others to consult with the tea merchants about reforming the tea monopoly under the aegis of a new Tea Policy Inquiry Commission (Xiangding chafa suo 詳定茶法所).[67] The result of these deliberations was to revive the ready-cash bills of exchange Li had introduced in 1023.[68] The new iteration of the ready-cash policy also voided the requirement that merchants seeking to redeem bills of exchange must obtain guarantees from *jiaoyinpu*, allowing them to go directly to the Finance Commission for certification. Once again, however, the reform incited strong opposition, and the *ruzhong* policy was reinstated in 1038, on the eve of the outbreak of war with the Xia that would end in humiliating defeat for the Song armies. The failure of Li Zi's repeated efforts to decouple frontier provisioning from the tea monopoly has been attributed to the influence wielded by powerful merchant blocs, above all the *jiaoyinpu* and the "magnate merchants" who dominated the tea trade.[69]

Abandonment of the ready-cash policy also was prompted by the government's fiscal straits and its dwindling cash reserves. In the face of soaring military expenditures during the Qingli War, attention was intently focused on exploiting every means to raise revenues, culminating with the implementation of Fan Xiang's salt license system in 1048. In 1043, the state councilor Fan Zhongyan responded to criticisms of the operation of the tea monopoly by frankly acknowledging the state's dependence on the income it generated: if the government did not extract revenues from commerce, it would be forced to tax farmers.[70] But Fan defended the tea monopoly on grounds of expedience, not principle. After the truce with Xia was concluded in 1044, Fan abruptly reversed his position, declaring that the monopolies harmed

[66] E.g., *XCB* 110.2569, from 1031.

[67] Zhu (*Bei Song cha*, p. 153) claims that this body was instituted in 1016, but that is not attested by the sources he cites, and *XCB* and *SHY* both state that it was created in 1036.

[68] *XCB* 118.2773, 2781–82; *SHY* shihuo 30.9a; Zhu, *Bei Song cha*, pp. 313–14.

[69] Hino, "Kōinho," p. 184; Lamouroux, "Monopole du thé," pp. 998–1002. According to Fan Zhongyan, there were roughly 100 long-distance merchants engaged in the tea trade in 1043 (see *XCB* 141.3390). The high degree of consolidation persisted even after the abolition of the tea monopoly in 1059. In 1072, Wang Anshi claimed that control of the tea trade rested in the hands of a cartel of only a dozen great merchants in the capital. See *XCB* 236.5738.

[70] *XCB* 141.3387–88; *MXBT* 12.132.

commerce and advocating their abolition.[71] Yet the cessation of hostilities did little to constrain military costs.

The Qingli War also had significant repercussions for the management of state finances. During the first century of the Song, the Finance Commission, headed by veteran officials with long experience in fiscal matters, exercised firm control over the central government's fiscal operations. Most government revenues, including the twice-a-year tax income, were deposited in the Left Treasury, under the authority of the Finance Commission. At the same time, a host of nonagricultural revenues – domestic and foreign tribute, customs duties, mining excises, mint seigniorage, and various commercial levies – were diverted to the Inner Palace Treasury (Neicangku 內藏庫), created in 978 for the upkeep of the palace and the imperial clan and managed by palace eunuchs. Buoyant income in the Left Treasury generated surpluses, which were regularly transferred to the Inner Palace Treasury. But from the mid 1030s, soaring military expenses left the Finance Commission in chronic deficit, necessitating frequent transfers of revenue from the Inner Palace Treasury to the Left Treasury.[72] Eunuch administrators of the Inner Palace Treasury – many of whom, as Charles Hartman has shown, had technocratic expertise in fiscal matters – began to eclipse the Finance Commission in fiscal policymaking.[73]

In 1047, the finance commissioner Zhang Fangping lamented that the Song military had swelled from 500,000 troops in the 1030s to a million men in the present day; the *ruzhong* payments for maintaining the armies on the northern frontiers had reached an unsustainable level of 10 million *guan* per year, necessitating annual transfers of 3 million *guan* from the Inner Palace Treasury to relieve the deficits incurred by the Finance Commission. The only way to hold down costs, Zhang concluded, was to reduce the size of border forces.[74] But none were willing to risk shrinking military manpower. The *ruzhong* formula for reimbursing delivery of frontier supplies adopted in 1048 – 40 percent in the form of tea licenses, 30 percent "cash" (10 percent in the form of *jiaoyin* bills), 15 percent salt licenses, and 15 percent licenses for exotic imports (aromatics, medicines, etc.) – still left provisioning merchants in the situation of needing to dispose of bills in the secondary market, and

71 *XCB* 151.3670–73; Zhu, *Bei Song cha*, p. 320.

72 Umehara Kaoru 梅原郁, "Sōdai no naizō to sazō: kunshu dokusaisei no zaiko" 宋代の内蔵と左蔵: 君主独裁制の財庫, *Tōhō gakuhō* 東方学報 41.1 (1971): 127–75; Robert M. Hartwell, "The Imperial Treasuries: Finance and Power in Song China," *Bulletin of Sung-Yuan Studies* 20 (1988): 18–89.

73 Hartman, *Structures of Governance*, pp. 121–29.

74 *XCB* 161.3895–98; Zhang Fangping 張方平, "Lun guoji chuna shi" 論國計出納事, in *Zhang Fangping ji* 張方平集 ([hereafter *ZFPJ*]; Zhengzhou: Zhongzhou guji chubanshe, 1992), 23.334–35.

hence strengthened the position of the *jiaoyinpu* and tea merchants, who drove down the market value of tea licenses.[75]

The mounting costs of propping up tea licenses gave impetus to the long-stalled campaign to abolish the tea monopoly altogether. In place of *jiaoyin* bills and commodity licenses, the government would simply purchase supplies on the market in frontier regions.[76] In 1056, Xue Xiang, the intendant for grain and fodder purchases in Hebei, proposed that most of the *ruzhong* remittances be converted to purchases in silk and coin, but few merchants expressed interest.[77] Opposition to the tea monopoly among fiscal officials had reached a tipping point, however. In 1058, when two low-ranking officials again submitted a memorial requesting abolition of the tea monopoly, their proposal was quickly endorsed by the council of state, which convened a committee headed by Zhang Fangping – then serving his second term as finance commissioner – to consider it.[78] Zhang reported that the tea monopoly in 1057 had brought in only 1.28 million *guan* of revenue, 1 million short of the quota, and when the inflated value of the tea licenses and the subsidies for tea planters were taken into account the net return was a mere 469,000 *guan*, not including administrative costs. Zhang proposed that the government cease subsidies to producers, who then should be allowed to sell tea freely on the open market. To make up for the loss in monopoly revenue the planters would pay an excise fee; moreover, the government would collect commercial taxes on market sales of tea.[79] In early 1059, the emperor approved the repeal of the tea monopoly, ushering in a new era for both the domestic market and military procurement.

3.5 *Tongshang*: Market-Based Solutions for Military Procurement

The abolition of the tea monopoly in 1059 was portrayed as a triumph of *tongshang* 通商, or what we might loosely translate as a "market-based" fiscal policy. The term *tongshang* would seem to lend itself to interpretation as "free trade" or "laissez-faire," but such readings would be misleading. Indeed, in the case of the salt monopoly, *tongshang* was invoked not as a call to abolish the state monopoly but rather to designate the salt licensing system introduced by Fan Xiang in 1048 (i.e., a form of indirect monopsony). *Tongshang* encompassed not only the free trade in tea allowed after the 1059 repeal of the tea

75 Hino, "Kōinho," pp. 162–67; Saeki, "Ninsōchō chahō," pp. 153–56.
76 As proposed in Zhang Fangping, "Lun jingshi junchu shi" 論京師軍儲事, *ZFPJ* 24.345–52.
77 *XCB* 184.4450, 188.4526.
78 *XCB* 188.4527.
79 *XCB* 189.4549; Zhang Fangping, "Qi shi chajin shu" 乞弛茶禁疏, in Yang Shiqi 楊士奇 (ed.), *Lidai mingchen zouyi* 歷代名臣奏議 ([hereafter *MCZY*]; 1416 ed.), 264.7a–b.

monopoly but also the monopsonies adopted under Fan's salt licensing system and the franchise (*maipu* 買撲) arrangements used at times in salt production and trade but especially in the wine brewing industry.[80] In Song political economy discourse, *tongshang* reflected an accommodation to market forces that I have defined as the "synergistic" mode of the Chinese fiscal state.[81]

As early as 989, a bureau chief in the Ministry of Revenue, Zhang Ji, had vociferously opposed the tea monopoly, arguing that *tongshang* would both "be a blessing to the planters" and increase state revenues.[82] But such appeals largely vanished once the tea monopoly was linked to the *ruzhong* procurement system. In 1001, Sun Mian floated the idea of adopting *tongshang* in the empire-wide operation of the salt monopoly, but his proposal was tabled because of concerns that local governments would lose the revenues they derived from the monopoly. In this case, what Sun meant by *tongshang* was to adopt the bill of exchange system used in the tea monopoly to provision frontier armies.[83] In 1023, the Fiscal Planning Bureau established by Li Zi recommended linking Xiezhou salt allocations for sale in the capital region to the *ruzhong* frontier provisioning policy, but this initiative was reversed shortly afterward. In 1030, however, the rising burden of frontier military expenditures persuaded the Finance Commission to adopt the *tongshang* approach for the marketing of Xiezhou salt. Strikingly, one of the virtues cited by the proponents of *tongshang* was that it would promote liquidity in the money supply by encouraging merchants to participate more extensively in market exchange.[84] This reform of the salt monopoly essentially adopted Li Zi's program of ready-cash bills of exchange for the Huainan tea monopoly, which at this time had already been suspended.

In 1036, at the same time that Li Zi's ready-cash bill of exchange system was reinstated for tea purchases in Huainan, a Ministry of Revenue official, Ye Qingchen, proposed the more radical reform of abolishing the tea monopoly altogether and forgoing the revenues it generated (which, according to Ye, were meager).[85] Ye argued that the various changes in the operation of the tea monopoly since the founding of the dynasty had been orchestrated by the cartel of tea merchants to serve their own interests. The frequent inclusion of tea merchants in policy deliberations, Ye declared, had resulted in an "inversion of control over the levers of profit (*quanli* 權利)" – an allusion to the Han

[80] Dai Yixuan, *Chaoyan zhidu*, pp. 56–57, 67–70.

[81] von Glahn, "Modalities of the Fiscal State."

[82] Zhang Ji 張洎, "Qi ba queshan xingfang fa" 乞罷榷山行放法, in *MCZY* 263.9b–13b.

[83] *XCB* 50.1084–85. For the ongoing debates about the implementation of *tongshang* policies in the salt monopoly before the adoption of Fan Xiang's salt license system, see Guo Zhengzhong, *Songdai yanye*, pp. 904–20.

[84] *XCB* 109.2545.

[85] *XCB* 118.2279–81; *MCZY* 263.16b–17a.

statesman Sang Hongyang's use of this term to denote the state's monopoly over coinage and the salt and iron industries (see Chapter 1). Ye argued that a genuine *tongshang* policy – namely, a fully free market in tea – would break the power of the cartel, enabling smaller merchants to enter the tea trade and benefiting both tea planters and consumers.

This endorsement of free trade was reiterated by the scholar Li Gou, widely admired for his acumen on matters of political economy although he never passed the civil service exams or held bureaucratic office. In 1039, Li Gou wrote a set of ten essays entitled "Strategies for Enriching the State" that he circulated among influential statesmen, especially the coterie gathered around Fan Zhongyan and Ouyang Xiu. In his voluminous writings on statecraft, Li displays a strong affinity, based on the vision of an all-encompassing state expressed in the *Rituals of Zhou*, for activist state intervention to rectify the shortcomings of the market economy.[86] In "Strategies for Enriching the State," Li decries the negative effects of commercialization, such as worsening inequality and frivolous production and consumption of luxury goods, and advocates state intervention to control grain prices and curb the concentration of landownership.[87] Yet in his final two essays, on the salt and tea monopolies, Li paradoxically comes to the conclusion that "at the present moment, nothing is more imperative than *tongshang*."[88] In these essays, Li extols the advantages of market trade: by abolishing the monopolies, markets become competitive (numerous merchants will seek to buy these commodities, for which demand is universal) and extensive (reaching all consumers). Under the monopoly, consumers must purchase from a limited number of sellers who wield excessive power over markets and prices. Free trade will foster an environment in which wholesalers compete to establish connections with local retailers, thus ensuring good quality and competitive prices for consumers. Li Gou echoed the prevailing discourse among critics of the state monopolies that abolishing them would curb the power of merchant cartels and create genuine free trade.

Nonetheless, the need to raise funds for the war effort impelled the government to restore the monopoly on Xiezhou salt in early 1040. A year later, Ouyang Xiu submitted an appeal to abolish the commodity monopolies. More

[86] In 1042, Li composed a lengthy work entitled *On the Rituals of Zhou as the Road to Grand Peace* that proposed using the *Rituals* as the template for radical reformation of Song political institutions – an idea later taken up by Wang Anshi. See Jaeyoon Song, *Traces of Grand Peace: Classics and State Activism in Imperial China* (Cambridge, MA: Harvard University Asia Center, 2015), pp. 52–77.

[87] For a digest of Li's "Strategies for Enriching the State," see Étienne Balazs, "A Forerunner of Wang An-shih," in Balazs, *Chinese Civilization and Bureaucracy* (New Haven, CT: Yale University Press, 1964), pp. 277–89.

[88] This statement (今日之宜,莫如通商) is repeated in both essays: "Fuguo ce (jiu) (shi)" 富國策 (九) (十), in Li Gou 李覯, *Li Gou ji* 李覯集 (Beijing: Zhonghua shuju, 2011), 16.154, 16.155.

broadly, Ouyang articulated a vision of political economy that favored cooperation rather than competition between the state and the private market:

> The reason why these two commodities of salt and tea are regarded as precious is that they generate money revenues to finance the state's fiscal needs. Yet accumulating stockpiles that surely will rot away serves no purpose. The great merchants who can discern the value of goods have no desire to sell them in piecemeal fashion in the marketplace for a few coins. There must be petty shopkeepers and small peddlers who will acquire and distribute such goods, but they will not do so unless they can obtain some profit. Hence the great merchants do not begrudge sharing profit with the peddlers but rather depend on them to spread their goods broadly. Even if the peddlers earn only a slim profit, goods will circulate freely to distant regions; stockpiles will be reduced and amply put to use . . . The truly astute statesman does not covet profit but rather enlists the great merchants and shares the profits with traders and shopkeepers. This is the strategy for taking less and achieving more.[89]

Ouyang described his strategy as one of "leveraging merchants" (*quan shanggu* 權商賈).[90] Yet unlike other proponents of *tongshang*, Ouyang sought cooperation with both the merchants who dominated long-distance wholesale trade and the local retailers catering to ordinary consumers. Although Ouyang's arguments failed to persuade the court at the time, the adoption of Fan Xiang's salt license system in 1048 – with the blessing of Ye Qingchen, then acting finance commissioner – was hailed as a triumph of *tongshang* principles.[91]

This evenhandedness toward both great and small merchants explains why Ouyang Xiu himself would decry the full abolition of the tea monopoly after it was enacted in 1059. A year later, Ouyang submitted a memorial detailing the drawbacks of the new policy, including the higher costs absorbed by tea planters, reduced revenues for the state, and the inconvenience incurred by both the state and merchants in having to make cash purchases of military provisions in the frontier regions instead of using bills of exchange. But Ouyang's chief objection was that the new measures were intended to "suppress the magnate merchants" (*yi haoshang* 抑豪商) in the name of broadening participation by petty merchants in the tea trade. However, Ouyang observed, petty merchants lacked the capital resources and network

[89] *XCB* 129.3069–70; Ouyang Xiu 歐陽脩, "Tong jinsi shang shu" 通進司上書, in *Jushi ji* 居士集 45, in *Ouyang Xiu quanji* 歐陽脩全集 ([hereafter *OXQ*]; Taipei: Shijie shuju, 1971), 2, pp. 306–11.

[90] This is the wording in *OXQ*; *XCB* instead reads *que shanggu* 榷商賈, which surely is incorrect.

[91] See, for example, the reports of Bao Zheng, who Ye dispatched to Shaanxi to evaluate the effects of Fan's policy, which were fully endorsed by the Finance Commission: *XCB* 167.4016–19, 171.4111; Bao Zheng 包拯, "Yan Shaanxi yanfa" (yi) (er)" 言陝西鹽法 (一) (二), in *Bao Xiaosu zouyi ji*包孝肅奏議集 (SKQS ed.), 8.3a–8b.

connections of the great merchants and could hardly replace the latter in long-distance trade. As a result, the tea industry as a whole was suffering. Consistent with the emphasis in his 1041 memorandum on the indispensable roles of both long-distance wholesalers and retail shopkeepers, Ouyang chastised the current leadership for their hostility toward the former, reiterating the hoary maxim that "even in the age of impeccable governance during the Three Dynasties, the sages divided the people into the four occupations so that they would nurture and benefit each other."[92]

Ouyang's dissent from the new tea policy exposed the undercurrent of tension among the proponents of *tongshang*. Rather than envisioning a synergistic relationship between merchants and the state as Ouyang did, many policymakers were becoming increasingly alarmed at the wealth and power exerted by the "magnate merchants." This concern was most evident in the views of Wang Anshi, who after his appointment as state councilor in 1069 undertook the most dramatic institutional reformation of fiscal administration in Chinese imperial history. At the time of the abolition of the tea monopoly in 1059, Wang wrote an essay in favor of the repeal in which he focused his derision on "fiscalists" at the court determined to extract the maximum amount of revenue, making no mention of the role of merchants.[93] In a later essay, however, Wang delivered an acerbic jeremiad precisely calling for the "suppression of the great merchants" (*yi jushang* 抑巨商) deplored by Ouyang Xiu.[94] In a court discussion about the defects of the tea policy held in 1072, after he had been elevated to chief state councilor, Wang again observed that under the *ruzhong* policy only merchants with large capital reserves could enter the tea trade, giving the cartel of a dozen or so "great merchants" (*dagu* 大賈) complete power over the market.[95] Wang's outrage over the tea oligopoly was a major motivation behind his creation a year later of the State Trade Agency, whose agents were empowered to seize control of wholesale commerce in the Kaifeng metropolitan region (see Chapter 4).

3.6 Conclusion

Remittance bills initially served – as their original name, "convenient exchange bills," suggests – to facilitate transfers of funds by private merchants between the capital and the provinces, serving as a substitute for cumbersome bronze coin. Early in the Song period, however, government officials seeking to

[92] "Lun chafa zouzhuang" 論茶法奏狀, in *OXQ*, 2, pp. 883–84. An abbreviated version – omitting the passage quoted here – is included in *XCB* 191.4618–19.
[93] Wang Anshi 王安石, "Yi chafa" 議茶法, in *Wang Linchuan quanji* 王臨川全集 ([hereafter *WLQ*]; Taipei: Shijie shuju, 1966), 70.443–44.
[94] Wang Anshi, "Chashang shiershuo" 茶商十二說, in *WLQ* 70.444–45.
[95] *XCB* 220.5348–49.

achieve fiscal goals through recourse to market institutions made *jiaoyin* bills of exchange an integral part of state finance. Under the *ruzhong* policy enacted in the late 980s, the state compensated merchants who delivered provisions to garrisons along the northern frontier with licenses to obtain goods – initially tea, and later salt and exotic imports – whose distribution and sale was regulated by the state monopoly bureau. Bills of exchange and commodity licenses subsequently became negotiable financial instruments. The state came to rely on dealers in bills of exchange (*jiaoyinpu*) as clearinghouses for verification and exchange of these bills. Our knowledge of *jiaoyinpu* comes almost exclusively from official reports, which depict them as a powerful cartel controlling the market for bills to the detriment of both state finances and commodity merchants. Yet, as Christian Lamouroux observes, the *jiaoyinpu* were a vital part of the system of financial mediation that enabled massive growth of means of payment in remote frontier regions where money was scarce.[96] The limited cash reserves in state treasuries also compelled the government to rely on commodity licenses and bills of exchange to sustain military logistics. In this respect the commodity licenses acted as cash substitutes.

Fiscal officials perpetually tinkered with the *ruzhong* policy and the operations of the tea and salt monopolies, creating ad hoc commissions and eventually standing councils to evaluate the benefits and drawbacks of current policy. Government officials also routinely invited leading merchants to join their deliberations. Critics considered this decision-making process too favorable to powerful merchants who sought to exploit the *ruzhong* compensation rates to their own advantage at the expense of other stakeholders – tea planters, retail merchants, and the state itself. Lamouroux has argued that government officials generally favored concentration of commercial power in the hands of great merchants, which reduced the risk of fraud or financial failure.[97] In fact, Song officials were far from unanimous in their views toward merchants, or the nature of the market economy in general. The fiscal state established in the early decades of the Song dynasty, while still premised on a fundamentally agrarian economy, acquiesced to the autonomy of the market and sought to harness rather than arrest market forces to meet the state's fiscal and economic goals. The operation of the commodity license system reflected this new reorientation toward a cooperative rather than antagonistic relationship with the merchant class. Yet this pivot toward a more "synergistic" engagement with the market also was complicated by the diverse and competing interests among different groups of merchants. As Song officials repeatedly noted, the interests of tea magnates, retail traders, and tea planters often clashed. We could also say the same about the interests of merchants who

96 Lamouroux, "Monopole du thé," p. 998.
97 Lamouroux, "Monopole du thé," p. 994.

delivered provisions to the frontier garrison, *jiaoyinpu* at the capital, and the long-distance traders in tea, salt, and grain.

The almost exclusive focus of this review of Song bills of exchange on their place in the fiscal system reflects the bias of our sources. Anecdotal evidence for the private use of remittance bills is exceedingly scarce, but one example deserves mention. The official Zhang Shunmin, writing in the early 12th century, applauded Fan Xiang's salt licenses, saying that they are "not exclusively used to obtain salt, but equally serve as 'flying cash.' Nowadays, if you transport a hundred strings of coin to another prefecture, it would indeed be a heavy load; but if you exchange the coin for salt licenses, it would amount to only a few sheets of paper."[98] The version of this passage preserved in Zhang's own writings suggests that Zhang was referring to his personal experience in transferring funds when he was dispatched to serve as a local prefect in the south.[99] Regrettably, how commonplace such a practice was beyond the rarefied circles of officialdom is impossible to verify.

As we shall see in the next chapter, *jiaozi* bills originated in the private market and initially functioned as bills of exchange. The state takeover of the issue of *jiaozi* bills was prompted by a desire to stabilize the monetary system in the Sichuan region. Still, like *jiaoyin* bills, the *jiaozi* paper money also would become a crucial part of the Song fiscal system as a means of facilitating provisioning of the frontier armies. More significantly, *jiaozi* bills would displace iron coin as Sichuan's monetary standard.

98 *XCB* 471.11237.

99 Zhang Shunmin 張舜民, *Huaman lu* 畫墁錄, in Tao Zongyi 陶宗儀 (ed.), *Shuofu* 說郛 (1646 ed.), 18b.

PART II

Invention of Paper Money in Song China

4

Northern Song Monetary Policy and the Invention of Paper Currency in Sichuan

From the inception of coinage in pre-imperial times down to the Tang dynasty, bronze currencies prevailed as the monetary standard of the Chinese ecumene. During the Five Dynasties interregnum, the bronze coin standard began to falter as rival regimes pursued monetary autarky and issued iron and lead coins. Despite the efforts of the Song leaders to reestablish bronze currency throughout their domains, monetary unification proved elusive. The creation of *jiaozi* paper money in the Sichuan region in the 11th century was directly related to Sichuan's distinct status as an iron currency zone, which persisted throughout the dynasty. The loss of northern China to Jurchen invaders in 1127 radically reshaped the empire and its resource base, necessitating a wholesale reordering of Song fiscal administration and its monetary policies. During the Southern Song, the court created four separate monetary zones, each with its own distinctive paper currency linked to different regional metallic currencies.

A striking feature of the Song monetary system, then, was the existence of multiple currencies – including bronze and iron coins, paper money, and uncoined silver – in concurrent circulation. Different monies occupied separate niches within the Song monetary system. Silver, for example, assumed importance in state finances, interregional transfers, and savings, but it was rarely used in market exchange. Yet the absence of a unified monetary system scarcely hindered the growth of the money economy during Song times. The invention of paper money coincided with prodigious growth in mint output of bronze coin (to the highest levels in Chinese history), whose use permeated most regions of China down to the level of ordinary villagers. Moreover, the pervasive impact of "fiscal circulation" – monetization of taxation, interregional transfers of revenues, and state procurement and expenditure – facilitated the integration of these diverse currencies into a coherent monetary order. The crucial importance of fiscal circulation – on a scale far greater than what we witness in Europe and the Islamic world at that time – explains why the Song government (and its Mongol-ruled successor, the Yuan dynasty) succeeded in maintaining a viable paper currency. At the same time, paper currencies also became indispensable to market trade. Although bronze coin remained the unit of account throughout the Song period and the lifeblood of everyday commerce, during the 12th and 13th centuries paper currencies in many respects superseded coin in public and private finance.

4.1 The Early Northern Song Monetary System

The regional economic autarky that emerged in the wake of the Tang Empire's collapse was most evident in the heterogeneity of coins employed in different parts of the Chinese ecumene. The Tang Kaiyuan bronze coins remained in circulation, especially in the Central Plain, where the successor regimes to Tang minted only negligible quantities of new coin. Still, each regime sought to establish its legitimacy by minting some coin of its own. The practice of inscribing coins with reign-titles – another token of sovereignty – became generalized, although not universal, during this era. As we saw in Chapter 3, rulers of the southern kingdoms were keen to foster commercial growth and exploited their domestic mineral resources to mint coin, leading to a profusion of iron, lead, and even tin coins.[1] The Southern Tang (937–975) government, with prolific copper mines at its disposal, strove to maintain a high-value bronze coin. But the proliferation of debased currencies and mounting military expenses compelled the Southern Tang to mint its own iron coin; beginning in 959, its coinage consisted of 60 percent iron coins and only 40 percent bronze coins. The historical records also assert that from this time market exchange in the Southern Tang was conducted exclusively in iron coins, although few specimens of iron coins survive in the archaeological record. Despite the inconsistencies between the documentary and numismatic evidence, it appears that even in the Southern Tang territories widespread counterfeiting compelled steady debasement and depreciation of state-issued currencies.[2]

In 962, two years after the founding of the Song dynasty, Emperor Taizu prohibited the circulation of the bronze, iron, and lead currencies issued by the former southern regimes, requiring that holders of these coins exchange them for his new Songyuan tongbao 宋元通寶 coins.[3] Although this mandate likely was unenforceable, coins issued by the Five Dynasties regimes quickly

[1] For the documentary evidence of Five Dynasties coinages, see Miyazaki, *Tsūka mondai*, pp. 8–82; Miyazawa, "Jūkoku tsūka."

[2] The numismatic and archaeological evidence for Five Dynasties coinages is surveyed in Thierry, *Monnaies*, pp. 255–91. Thierry examines the inconsistencies between documentary and numismatic evidence for Southern Tang coinage in some detail; see *Monnaies*, pp. 280–91.

[3] The name of these coins should be read as "Current Treasure Inaugurated by the Song." It reprised the language of the coin issued by the Song's immediate predecessor, the Later Zhou (951–960), which was designated Zhouyuan tongbao 周元通寶. See Thierry, *Monnaies*, p. 299.

Table 4.1 *Temporal distribution of coins from Northern Song hoards*

Period	Percentage of total
Pre-Tang	0.3
Tang	8.0
Five Dynasties	0.6
Song 960–1000	5.7
Song 1000–1015	7.3
Song 1016–1048	19.0
Song 1049–1067	12.5
Song 1068–1093	36.1
Song 1094–1125	20.0

Source: Miyake, *Chūgoku no uzumerareta senka*, p. 89, table 15.

disappeared from circulation. The number of Five Dynasties coins recovered from forty-five Northern Song hoards analyzed by Miyake Toshihiko – nearly all of which were buried at the time of the conquest of North China by the Jurchen in 1127 – is negligible, scarcely greater than the number of pre-Tang coins (Table 4.1). Annexation of the Southern Tang territories and their rich mines in 975 enabled the Song court to increase its annual output of bronze coin fivefold to 300,000 strings by 983, in addition to the iron coins that continued to be minted in Fujian and Sichuan.[4] From this time forward, the Song routinely inscribed coins with the current reign-title (which changed regularly, even within the reign of an individual ruler). Designating coins by reign-titles became conventional practice throughout the rest of the imperial era.[5]

In 997, Song mints cast 800,000 strings of bronze coin, two-and-a-half times the peak Tang output of Kaiyuan coin in 732. During the first decade of the 11th century, mint output doubled again, to an average of 1.5 million strings annually, although in 1021 the annual quota was reduced to 1.025 million strings, a level that was maintained until the 1040s (Table 4.2). By 983, iron currencies had been withdrawn from circulation in all regions except Fujian and Sichuan, and the demonetization of iron coins was completed in Fujian by

4 Government mint output was calculated in "strings" (*guan* 貫) of 1,000 coins. The same word (*guan*) was used as the unit of account in Song fiscal records, so to distinguish physical coins from the *guan* unit of account I will denote the former in numbers of strings.

5 In addition to its standard practice of reign-title issues, the Song at times minted generic "Song" coins, such as the Huang Song tongbao 皇宋通寶 coins, issued in prodigious quantities from 1039 to 1054 during the Qingli War and its aftermath, and the Sheng Song yuanbao 聖宋元寶 coins minted during 1101–1106, the early years of Emperor Huizong (r. 1100–1125).

Table 4.2 *Estimated issue of bronze currency in Northern Song*

Period	Average annual coinage (millions)	Total output for period (millions)	Accumulated output (millions)	Percentage of accumulated output
976–982	70	490	490	0.2
983–996	300	4,200	4,690	1.6
997–999	800	2,400	7,090	0.9
1000–1015	1,250	18,750	25,840	7.2
1016–1048	1,000	33,000	58,840	12.6
1049–1073	1,600	40,000	98,840	15.3
1074–1085	4,500	54,000	152,840	20.6
1086–1125	2,800	109,200	262,040	41.7

Source: Gao, *Huobi liutong*, p. 103.

1012.[6] Only Sichuan remained an iron currency zone. Bronze coinage soared along with the fiscal activism of Wang Anshi's New Policies from the 1070s. Data from coin hoards and mint output indicate that more than 60 percent of Northern Song coinage was emitted under the aegis of the New Policies regimes from 1069 to 1125.

The explosive growth of the money supply over the course of the Northern Song abetted the expansion of the market economy and the monetization of state finances. From the outset, the Song state retained many of the fiscal innovations of the late Tang dynasty and the Five Dynasties interregnum. The rising costs of national defense following the military defeats inflicted by the Khitans and Tanguts intensified the need to extract greater revenues. After the Qingli War of 1040–1044, military expenditures consumed 60–80 percent of central government expenditures. Loath to raise direct taxes on land, Song leaders instead doubled down on taxation of consumption and commerce. At the same time, the focus of indirect taxation underwent important changes (Table 4.3). Salt and tea revenues were roughly equal during the first half century of the Song but diverged dramatically afterwards. During the New Policies era that commenced in 1069, tea revenues dwindled to a negligible level, while the salt monopoly became the single most important source of the state's cash income. The new fiscal organs created as part of the New Policies, such as the State Trade Bureau and ever-normal granary intendants, also generated substantial money revenues. Consequently, under Wang Anshi's regime, money revenues constituted more than four-fifths of total state income.

[6] Robert Hartwell, "The Evolution of the Early Northern Sung Monetary System, A.D. 960–1025," *Journal of the American Oriental Society* 87.3 (1967): 280–89.

Table 4.3 *Coin revenues in the Northern Song (millions of* guan*)*

	997	1007	1021	c. 1044	1064	c. 1077[a]
Salt	3.00	3.55	3.00	7.15	11.23	22.30
Tea	2.86	2.80	3.30	1.50[b]	1.18	0.77
Liquor	3.26	4.28	11.59	17.10	12.86	12.93
Subtotal for state monopolies	9.12	10.63	17.89	25.75	25.27	34.70
Commercial taxes	4.00	4.50	12.04	19.75	8.46	8.05
Coinage seigniorage	?	?	?	?	?	5.95
Twice-a-year tax (coin portion)	?	?	?	?	4.93	5.59
New policies	—	—	—	—	—	18.12[c]
Total coin revenues[d]	16.93	?	29.93	45.50	36.82	72.41
Total revenues (coin equivalent)	35.59	?	57.23	?	60.00	89.33
Percentage of total revenues in coin	48%	?	52%	—	61%	81%

Notes: [a] Figures variously from 1076, 1077, and 1078; does not include revenues from green sprouts loans and maritime customs (because revenue data for these categories is not divided into coin and non-coin portions).

[b] Figure from 1034; 1054 figure was 1.28 million.

[c] This figure is incomplete, because we do not have data on all sources of New Policies revenues. Included in this figure are money income from the hired service (*mianyi* 免役) levy (10.17 m *guan*); commercial tax franchises (*fangchang hedu* 坊場河渡) excises (0.387 m *guan*); the State Trade Agency (1.41 m *guan*); ever-normal granary interest income (0.2 m *guan*); and seigniorage (5.95 m *guan*).

[d] Total revenues also included additional revenues apart from the above categories.

Sources: Wang Shengduo, *Liang Song caizheng*, vol. 2, p. 691, appendix table 1.6; p. 705, appendix table 4; pp. 709–13, appendix table 7; pp. 748–49, appendix table 22; Guo Zhengzhong, *Songdai yanye*, pp. 676–77, table 44; Jia Daquan, "Songdai fushui jiegou chutan," 53–54; Miyazawa, *Kokka to keizai*, p. 43, table 1; p. 56, table 4; Zhang Fangping, "Lun guoji shi" 論國計事, in *ZFPJ* 24.354.

The massive increase in mint output during the 11th century appears to have had negligible inflationary effects. Although grain prices doubled in the 1030s and escalated dramatically during the Qingli War, they fell in the 1050s and remained stable for the remainder of the 11th century (Figure 4.1). Indeed, beginning in the 1060s, officials frequently complained that shortages of coin – described as "coin famines" (*qianhuang* 錢荒) – had resulted in

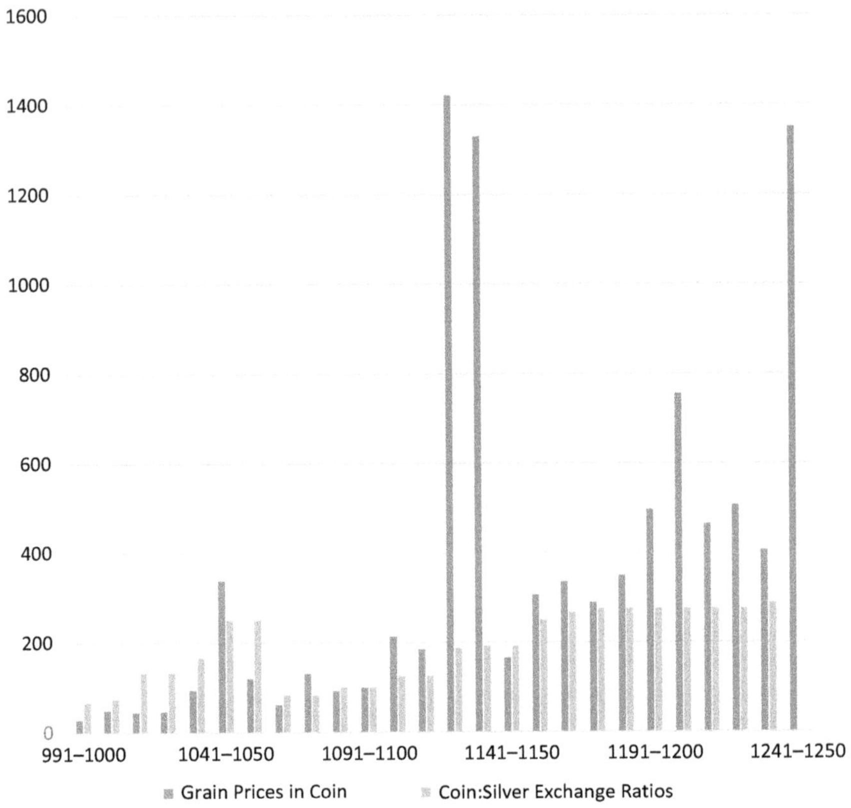

Figure 4.1 Grain prices and bronze coin:silver exchange ratios, 990–1250 (expressed as indices; 1091–1100 = 100).
Source: Peng, *Zhongguo huobi shi*, pp. 487, 505.

falling grain prices, to the detriment of farmers. The abrupt upsurge in the state's fiscal demands in the New Policies era intensified the pressure on the money supply. The "coin famine" problem persisted despite the unprecedented increase in mint output, which in the 1080s reached the highest recorded level in Chinese imperial history. Only after 1100, when Cai Jing's fiscal administration debased bronze coinage, did grain prices again surge, followed by the catastrophic inflation triggered by the Jurchen invasion and conquest of North China after 1125. The trend in the silver:bronze exchange ratio – which fell sharply after the Qingli War and remained relatively low throughout the rest of the Northern Song – also confirms that the growth of the money supply did not induce a depreciation of bronze currency. Rising demand for money in both state payments and private commercial exchange diluted the inflationary effects of coin output.

4.2 Sichuan's Iron Currency Zone and the Introduction of Jiaozi Paper Currency

Under the rule of the Former and Later Shu kingdoms, the western region of Sichuan typified the monetary autarky of the Five Dynasties era. The heart of Sichuan is a large basin, once an ancient inland sea, encircled by mountain ranges that walled off the region from the rest of the empire. Insulated from the civil wars and political strife that beset the Tang Empire after the mid 8th century, Sichuan underwent an economic boom during the 9th and 10th centuries, boosted especially by the region's fine silk cloths and burgeoning tea industry. Although the Former Shu kingdom (907–925) was conquered by the Later Tang regime in 925, the viceroy sent to assume command in Sichuan, Meng Zhixiang, soon asserted his independence from his Later Tang overlords. In 934, Meng declared himself emperor of (Later) Shu, only to die months later. Under his son and successor, Meng Chang (r. 934–965), Sichuan regained its former prosperity and enjoyed relative monetary stability compared to its rivals until the mid 950s, when Shu again faced the threat of invasion by the Central Plain regimes, first Northern Zhou and then Song. In 955, rising defense costs forced Meng Chang to mint iron currency to supplement Sichuan's limited supply of bronze coin, creating a dual currency system using both iron and bronze coins. Like the Shu bronze coinage, the iron coins were minted with the same size and weight as the Tang Kaiyuan coins, but the official tariff set their value at 0.4 *qian*, or 40 percent of the value of bronze currency.

After annexing Later Shu in 965, the Song retained the dual currency system inaugurated by Meng Chang.[7] According to the Southern Song historian Li Tao, the Song armies seized Shu's treasures – mostly fine silks, but also its stocks of bronze coin – and delivered them to the Inner Palace Treasury in the capital.[8] In 970, the Song declared Sichuan an exclusive iron currency zone and established iron coin mints in the region. Bronze coin remained the money of account, with the iron coins tariffed at a rate of 0.1 *qian* (i.e., one-tenth of the value of bronze coin). In 979, as part of its effort to reestablish a uniform monetary system throughout its empire, the Song sought to restore bronze currency to Sichuan by requiring that 10 percent of taxes be paid in bronze coin, with further increases of 10 percent each year over the next ten years, at which time iron coin would be discarded. Because of the scarcity of bronze coin in the region, however, this policy sparked a panic among

7 On early Song monetary policies in Sichuan, see Hartwell, "Northern Sung Monetary System," 285–89; Christoph Schifferli, "Le Système monétaire au Sichuan vers la fin du xe siècle," *T'oung Pao* 72.2 (1986): 269–90.

8 Yang Zhongliang 楊仲良 (comp), *Zizhi tongjian changbian jishi benmo* 資治通鑑長編紀事本末 ([hereafter *CBBM*]; rpt. Guangya shuju, 1893), 11.1a, 13.1a–b.

taxpayers desperate to obtain bronze coins for tax payments. Within a year, the value of iron coins plunged by 40 percent. Three years later, the government conceded that the plan was failing and abandoned it. Instead, fiscal policymakers resigned themselves to the practical necessity of maintaining a separate iron currency zone in Sichuan. Merchants from other regions had to exchange their bronze currency for iron coins upon arriving in Sichuan, and vice versa for Sichuan merchants engaged in interregional trade. Sichuan's mints exclusively manufactured iron coins based on the old Shu kingdom standard.

Sichuan's iron currency suffered from serious drawbacks. The low intrinsic value of iron coins, worth a mere tenth of the equivalent amount of bronze coin, imposed a great burden on merchants who needed to convey their purchasing capital from one place to another and on ordinary consumers as well. A housewife would have to bring a pound and a half (680 g) of iron coin to the marketplace to buy a pound (453 g) of salt, and a merchant from the capital would receive ninety-one pounds (41.2 kg) of iron coin in exchange for an ounce (28 g) of silver.[9] In 991, the imperial chamberlain Zhao Anyi, returning to the court from a mission in Sichuan, reported that the iron coins circulating in Sichuan were extremely low in value; it took 10,000 of these coins to purchase one bolt of silk gauze. Zhao proposed replacing the current iron currency with large iron coins valued at ten small iron coins. Although the emperor authorized Zhao to return to Sichuan and commence minting large iron coins, the proposal was opposed by many fiscal officials as well as the general public in Sichuan. After producing a mere 3,000 strings of large coins, Zhao's initiative was aborted.[10]

Sichuan's unique status as an iron currency zone presented serious problems for interregional transfers of money for the public authorities as well as private merchants. Since neither iron coin nor bronze coin could perform this function, silver became the preferred means of interregional payments.[11] In part because of this demand for silver in interregional transfers, the price of silver in Sichuan was consistently higher than elsewhere, and merchants readily brought silver there to reap arbitrage profits. Initially, officials in Sichuan converted salt, liquor, and commercial revenues to silver, silk, or even gold before they were forwarded to the capital.[12] From 1006, the formula for

9 Calculations from Hartwell, "Northern Sung Monetary System," 288.

10 *CBBM* 11.2a–b; *SS* 180.4378.

11 There is no evidence that "convenient cash" remittance bills (see Chapter 3) were used extensively for interregional transfers of money beyond Sichuan. Miyazaki Ichisada (*Tsūka mondai*, pp. 299–300) noted the coincidence that the "convenient cash" bills were created in the same year (970) that bronze coin was demonetized in Sichuan, but since the bills were denominated in bronze coin he doubted that they had much utility in the Sichuan economy.

12 *SHY* shihuo 36.4b.

remitting commercial revenues from Sichuan was set at half in silk and half in silver, and later they were transmitted entirely in silver, as was the case in other remote regions such as Fujian and Guangdong.[13] Salt imported from Xiezhou also was paid for in silver.[14] In 1027, the prefect of Chengdu observed that since Sichuan lacked silver mines, merchants who traded silk goods at the capital returned to Sichuan with silver. Yet in recent years, a sharp rise in the price of silver in Sichuan relative to small iron coins had caused a threefold increase in the real burden of taxation and brought distress to interregional trade.[15]

In the mid 990s, Sichuan's economy suffered a severe shock. An insurrection against Song rule broke out in Sichuan in 993. Contemporaries blamed the uprising on the confiscatory despoliation of Sichuan's commercial wealth, especially its renowned silk and tea industries, by the Song regime, but the unrest also was fueled by the relentless depreciation of iron currency. The rebels succeeded in capturing Chengdu, the capital of Sichuan, and held the city until June of 994. Most of the rebel forces were defeated by 996, but the tremors of economic dislocation lingered into the early 11th century.[16]

The rebellion forced the closure of Sichuan's mints, which remained shut even after the imperial government regained control of the region. The ensuing shortage of coin, in combination with the inconvenience of transporting bulky iron coin, prompted some merchants to begin issuing their own paper bills of exchange. The few documents concerning these private bills at our disposal do not reveal their exact nature, but it seems likely that they were issued in exchange for deposits of cash or other assets (gold, silver, and silk), much like the government-issued "convenient cash" bills, and circulated through market trade.[17]

13 *XCB* 63.1406; Zhang Fangping, "Zou caiji weibianhe shangliang tiaojian" 奏財計未便合商量條件, in *ZFPJ* 23.342.

14 *SS* 183.4473.

15 *SHY* shihuo 37.10b–11a.

16 On the Wang Xiaobo–Li Shun rebellion, see Paul J. Smith, *Taxing Heaven's Storehouse: Horses, Bureaucrats, and the Destruction of the Sichuan Tea Industry, 1074–1224* (Cambridge, MA: Harvard University Council on East Asian Studies, 1992), pp. 93–99.

17 The most important sources for the origins of *jiaozi* as private bills of exchange are *XCB* 101.2342–43; Li You 李攸, *Songchao shishi* 宋朝事實 ([hereafter *SCSS*]; Wuyingdian zhenban ed., rpt. Taipei: Wenhai chubanshe, 1967), 15.5a–7b; and *Chubi pu* 楮幣譜 [hereafter *CBP*], cited in Cao Xuequan 曹學佺 (ed.), *Shuzhong guangji* 蜀中廣記 ([hereafter *SZGJ*]; Shanghai: Shanghai guji chubanshe, 2020), 67.710–11. Although Cao ascribed authorship of *CBP* to the late Yuan official Fei Zhu 費著, Xie Yuanlu has demonstrated the implausibility of this attribution and persuasively argues that the text was originally compiled for inclusion in a now-lost gazetteer of Chengdu published in 1199. See Xie Yuanlu 谢元鲁, "Dui 'Chubi pu' he 'Qianbi pu' zuozhe ji xiezuo shidai de zairenshi" 对 «楮币谱» 和 «钱币谱» 作者及写作时代的再认识, *Zhongguo qianbi* 中国钱币 1996.1: 3–6.

Over the next ten years, these privately issued "bills of exchange" (*jiaozi* 交子) achieved a significant place in Sichuan's intraregional trade. Yet the proliferation of numerous sundry private bills, some issued by unscrupulous entrepreneurs, also resulted in widespread abuse and a surge of lawsuits. In 1005, the prefect of Chengdu, Zhang Yong, undertook a series of reforms aimed at stabilizing Sichuan's monetary situation.[18] First, Zhang secured the court's permission to reopen Sichuan's mints and at the same time introduce a large iron coin tariffed as equivalent to ten small iron coins or one small bronze coin. Second, he subjected the *jiaozi* paper bills to government regulation. Zhang restricted the right to issue *jiaozi* to a consortium of sixteen merchant houses in Chengdu deemed to have sufficient financial resources. In addition, he mandated that the merchants issue *jiaozi* in standardized size, color, and format, though each merchant also marked their bills with their own seals and "hidden" insignia (perhaps something like a watermark). The actual printing of the bills was done using labor and materials supplied by the prefectural government. As before, the *jiaozi* had no standard denomination. The issuer inscribed the value of the bill in ink on the bill itself. The bills circulated freely as exchange media, and when a bearer wished to cash a bill he was required to pay a commission fee of 3 percent. The government imposed no limits on the amount of *jiaozi* the designated merchants could issue. The quantity of bills in circulation followed the rhythms of seasonal demand, as financiers typically doubled their issue of bills in early summer, when new silk yarn reached the market, and at the time of the rice harvest in the autumn. *Jiaozi* also were widely used in large-scale transactions such as sales of lands, dwellings, shops, and luxury goods.[19]

Though greatly celebrated by his contemporaries, Zhang Yong's initiatives failed to resolve Sichuan's monetary troubles. The large iron coins, undervalued by the official tariff, quickly disappeared from circulation. Consequently, in 1014 the weight of the iron coins was reduced by half to bring their intrinsic value in line with their nominal value.[20] The lighter large iron coins quickly gained favor, and not surprisingly the small iron coins soon vanished.

18 *XCB* 59.1315. Although this source states that the problems with private *jiaozi* – namely nefarious behavior by the firms that issued them, leading to a proliferation of lawsuits – instigated the decision to emit large iron coins, it makes no mention of Zhang's regulation of *jiaozi* bills (for which see the texts cited in the previous footnote). Several Song writers wrongly dated Zhang's intervention to 1011, but by then he had long left the post of Chengdu prefect. For the misdating of Zhang's measures to 1011, see Wen Ying 文瑩, *Xiangshan yelu* 湘山野錄 (Xuehai leibian ed.), shang上, 5a–b; *CBP*, in *SZGJ* 67.710. For clarification of this issue, see Li Shan 李埏 and Lin Wenxun 林文勛, *Song Jin chubi shi xinian* 宋金楮幣史系年 (Kunming: Yunnan minzu chubanshe, 1996), pp. 9–13.

19 *SCSS* 15.5b.

20 *XCB* 82.1865–66.

Henceforth the mints exclusively issued large iron coins, which became the new monetary standard in Sichuan.

Zhang Yong's effort to regulate paper currency also encountered problems. The merchant houses authorized to issue *jiaozi* bills invested their cash deposits in commercial real estate, arable lands, and luxury commodities, leaving many of them without sufficient liquidity to redeem the bills they issued. Counterfeiting also mushroomed, resulting in incessant legal squabbles, and some of the issuers shut their doors. In 1016, the fiscal intendant stationed in Chengdu, Xue Tian, proposed a government takeover of paper currency in Sichuan, but his recommendation went unheeded. Five years later, in 1021, *jiaozi* were being discounted by 20 or 30 percent, and the newly appointed prefect of Chengdu, Kou Jian, ordered a halt to the issue of new bills, although current *jiaozi* remained in circulation.

After Kou Jian completed his tenure as prefect in 1023, however, he was succeeded by Xue Tian, who declared that the suspension of *jiaozi* issues had had a harmful effect on private trade and once again pushed for the government to assume direct authority over paper currency. This time Xue's proposal was accepted. The court authorized the establishment of the Chengdu Jiaozi Currency Bureau (Yizhou Jiaoziwu 益州交子務), which was given exclusive authority to issue *jiaozi*. The format of the new bills was modeled on the earlier private issues but restricted to two fixed denominations (1 and 10 *guan*). The government also set terms of expiry for the new bills, which could circulate for two years before they had to be redeemed (at the cost of the 30 percent service fee). The idea of limiting the time during which a bill remained in circulation served several purposes. It ensured that bills would be removed from circulation and destroyed before they became worn and tattered, and thus reduced the risk of tampering or counterfeiting. In addition, the terms of expiry allowed the state to maintain firm control over the amount of paper money in circulation. The biennial quota for each issue of *jiaozi* was fixed at 1,256,340 *guan*.[21] The state-issued *jiaozi* currency, inaugurated in 1024, proved highly popular, especially with Sichuan tea merchants engaged in interregional and international commerce, and often traded at a premium over its nominal value.[22]

The invention of paper money was propelled not only by these economic conditions and fiscal initiatives but also by technological innovations in papermaking and printing. Hemp fiber had been the chief raw material for paper in China until the Tang dynasty, but the invention of printing sometime in the early Tang imposed new technical requirements. By the early Song

[21] *XCB* 101.2342–43; *SCSS* 15.5b-7a; Tang Shichi 唐士耻, "Yizhou Jiaoziwu ji" 益州交子務記, *Lingyan ji* 靈巖集 (SKQS ed.), 4.20b–23a; *CBP*, in *SZGJ* 67.710. See also Wang Shengduo, *Liang Song huobi*, vol. 2, pp. 610–20.

[22] Memorial of 1086 by Su Che cited in *XCB* 366.8805.

period, tree bark, especially mulberry bark, displaced hemp fiber as the pre-eminent raw material for paper used in printing both books and ephemera such as calendars and almanacs. Mulberry paper was prized for its superior durability and whiteness, and also because it was relatively inexpensive to manufacture. Already by the 9th century, Sichuan had emerged as a center of printing and mulberry-paper manufacture (mulberry leaves are the favorite food of silkworms, and Sichuan, famous for the high quality of its silk goods, had abundant supplies of mulberry bark). Thus, by the beginning of the Song period, the technology and raw materials developed for printing books were readily available in Sichuan for adaptation to use in printing currency. The major innovations in printing currency were the use of metal printing plates (in contrast to carved woodblocks used for printing books down to the 19th century) and overlapping impressions in multiple colors (see Chapter 7). The large quantities involved in printing currency necessitated substituting metal printing plates for woodblocks, which wore out relatively quickly. After the government took over the issue of *jiaozi* in 1024, both the manufacture of paper stock and the printing of the bills were entrusted to the Jiaozi Currency Bureau in Chengdu, though from the 1070s the paper was manufactured at a separate government workshop in the city's suburbs.[23]

4.3 *Jiaozi* and Frontier Military Procurement

In addition to providing a convenient currency for merchants, *jiaozi* soon were incorporated into the *ruzhong* military provisioning system. As we saw in Chapter 3, the government compensated merchants who delivered supplies to frontier military bases with *jiaoyin* bills of exchange, which could be exchanged at the capital for cash or monopoly commodity licenses. Sichuan merchants who delivered supplies – principally silk clothing – to the Shaanxi border camps also had received *jiaoyin* bills, which they usually redeemed in silver before returning to Sichuan. In 1026, the government acceded to the request of Shaanxi authorities to use the new Sichuan paper money to attract Sichuan merchants to supply the frontier armies. The Sichuan merchants would be compensated with "ready-cash bills of exchange" (*xianqian jiaoyin* 見錢交引) redeemable in Sichuan either for iron coin or *jiaozi* bills.[24] The exchange of *jiaoyin* for *jiaozi* is expressed schematically in Figure 4.2.

[23] Xie Yuanlu 谢元鲁, "Songdai Sichuan zaozhi yinshua jishu de fazhan yu jiaozi de chansheng" 宋代四川造纸印刷技术的发展与交子的产生, *Zhongguo qianbi* 中国钱币 1996.3: 21–25.

[24] *SHY* shihuo 36.18b–20b. This entry concludes with an addendum stating that six months later the use of Shaanxi bills of exchange (*jiaochao* 交鈔) was "temporarily suspended." However, there is evidence that the use of these bills subsequently was revived. See Li Shan and Lin, *Chubi shi xinian*, p. 28. Although these "ready-cash bills of exchange"

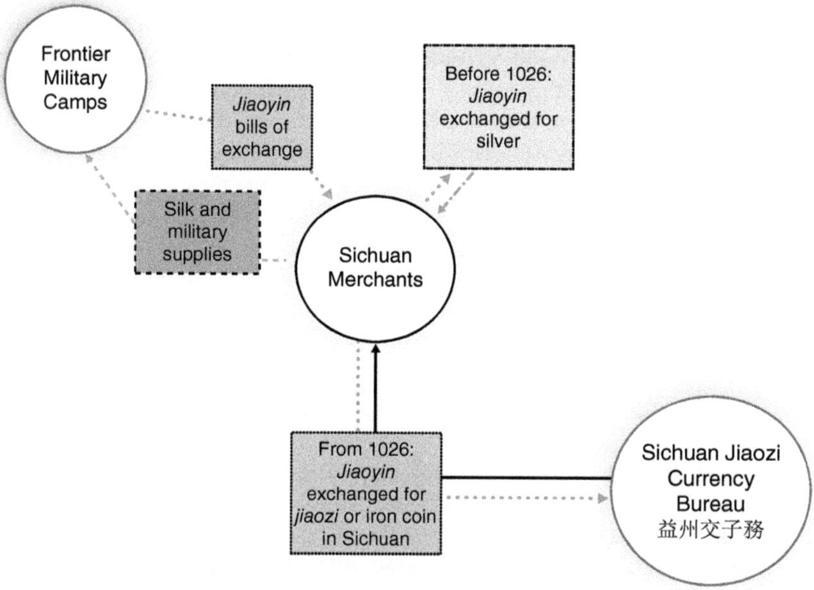

Figure 4.2 Exchange of *jiaoyin* for *jiaozi.*
<key>
<black circle>Merchant groups
<grey circle>Government agencies
<dashed line>Movement of frontier supplies
<dotted line>Movement of *jiaoyin* bills
<dash-dotted line>Movement of silver
<solid black line>Movement of *jiaozi* bills

In 1040, the government also began to issue salt licenses to Sichuan merchants who deposited silver either with the Shaanxi military procurement offices or the Quehuowu in the capital. These licenses could be used to obtain salt in Sichuan or to pay the excise levies collected from salt and liquor dealers.[25] On the eve of the Qingli War with Xia in 1040, then, silver, *jiaozi*, and salt licenses all were employed to facilitate the delivery of provisions from Sichuan to the Shaanxi frontier garrisons.

bore the same name as the *xianqian jiaoyin* bills that Li Zi had introduced during his tenure as finance commissioner in 1023–1025 (see Chapter 3), the Sichuan bills remained linked to the *ruzhong* frontier procurement system.

25 *SS* 183.4473.

As we have seen, military expenditures in the Shaanxi frontier soared following the outbreak of the Qingli War, prompting government officials to redouble their efforts to tap Sichuan's rich commercial economy to provision the frontier military camps. To augment the means of payment in frontier regions, in 1040 the government established mints in Shaanxi and Hedong that began to cast large 10-*wen* bronze coins as well as small and large iron coins, in addition to minting iron coins in the main mints in the south that were shipped to the frontier zones.[26] These initiatives accompanied a broad increase in the mint output of bronze coin, which more than doubled during the war years.[27] The large coins – including the 10-*wen* Qingli zhongbao 慶曆重寶 bronze coin, issued in the rest of the empire during 1041–1048 – were highly overvalued, which triggered rampant counterfeiting and price inflation. The iron coins were soon withdrawn from Hedong, but Shaanxi came to rely largely on iron currency.[28] As such, it became an extension of the Sichuan iron currency zone.

Frontier officials sought to capitalize on the monetary integration of Sichuan and Shaanxi by introducing *jiaozi* bills to Shaanxi. In 1045 and again in 1047, the Chengdu Jiaozi Currency Bureau delivered 300,000 *guan* of *jiaozi* bills to Shaanxi, where they were used to compensate *ruzhong* merchants directly, obviating the need for *jiaoyin* bills of exchange. Wen Yanbo, the prefect at Chengdu before his elevation to the Council of State in the spring of 1047, applauded the convenience of using *jiaozi* to facilitate exchange. But Wen was concerned that the Jiaozi Currency Bureau had insufficient reserves of coin for redeeming the bills and requested that 3 million *guan* from excise levies and commercial taxes be earmarked for this purpose.[29] There is no evidence that the court acted on Wen's petition. In 1051, the finance commissioner Tian Kuang reported that *jiaozi* bills were widely used in private trade in Shaanxi. But because only limited cash reserves had been set aside, Tian urged that the Shaanxi authorities cease disbursing *jiaozi* bills. His proposal was adopted, but *jiaozi* continued to circulate in the region, as a later report of 1074 confirms.[30]

26 The sources give contradictory accounts as to whether iron or bronze coins were issued first. Both were in circulation by the end of 1041. See Wang Shengduo, *Liang Song huobi*, vol. 2, pp. 531–35.

27 *MXBT* 12.133. This increase in coinage is confirmed by archaeological data. The Huang Song tongbao 皇宋通寶 coins, first cast in 1039 (and continued until 1054), comprise more than 10 percent of the total number of coins in Song hoards. See Thierry, *Monnaies*, pp. 308–9.

28 Gao, *Huobi liutong*, pp. 128–31.

29 Wen Yanbo 文彥博, "Qi zhuzhou gongqian bochong jiaoziwu" 乞諸州供錢撥充交子務, *Wen Lugong ji* 文潞公集 (SKQS ed.), 14.10b–11a.

30 *SCSS* 15.7a–b; *XCB* 249.6072.

As we saw in Chapter 3, in 1048, after the cessation of war with the Xia, the government opted for a new system of military procurement that raised revenues from Xiezhou salt licenses instead of *ruzhong* deliveries of military supplies. It also adjusted the monetary system in Shaanxi. The exchange ratio of large iron coins to small bronze coins was reduced from 1:10 to 1:2, which blunted the incentive for counterfeiting. Small bronze coins largely disappeared from the region, leaving large coins, both iron and bronze (which traded at par), in market circulation.[31] Fan Xiang's salt license system enabled merchants to purchase licenses in the frontier with iron coin and redeem the licenses in the capital in bronze coin, thus integrating the two monetary zones and sustaining the viability of Shaanxi's iron currency.[32]

The relative stability of Shaanxi's iron currency from the 1050s to the 1070s was paralleled in Sichuan as well. Between 1056 and 1059, the Sichuan mints sharply curtailed their production, reducing the annual output of large iron coins from 270,000 to 30,000 strings. The reason given for this cutback was the depreciation of coin, suggesting a fall in demand for iron coin as a means of exchange.[33] During the Qingli War, the price of grain in Sichuan skyrocketed, as was true of other regions (see Figure 4.1). Although the price shock abated after the cessation of hostilities, grain prices in Sichuan from the 1050s to the 1070s remained substantially elevated compared to the first quarter of the 11th century.[34] But this pattern, too, held generally true for other regions. With the introduction of Wang Anshi's New Policies in the 1070s, however, rising demand for money in state payments triggered deflation. In 1073, shortages of coin prompted the Chengdu fiscal intendant to request that mint output be raised to half of the old quota "to maintain equilibrium with *jiaozi* bills."[35] In 1078, the mint output quota was raised further to 230,000 strings per year, but prices remained stubbornly low.

Within Sichuan, *jiaozi* became a staple of trade finance. The falling demand for iron coin no doubt was caused in part by the growing preference for *jiaozi* bills in market exchange generally. Strict limits on the volume of *jiaozi* in circulation maintained their value in the private sector, where the bills traded at par (and at times at a premium) with coin. Beginning with Wang Anshi's

31 This compromise was achieved after a drawn-out process of tinkering that lasted into the mid 1050s. See Wang Shengduo, *Liang Song huobi*, vol. 2, pp. 535–42.

32 Gao, *Huobi liutong*, pp. 142–45; Christian Lamouroux, "Bureaucratie et monnaie dans la Chine du XIe siècle: les désordres monétaires au Shaanxi," in Bruno Théret (ed.), *La Monnaie dévoilée par ses crises* (Paris: Éditions de l'École des Hautes Études en Sciences Sociales, 2007), vol. 1, pp. 178–87.

33 Wang Shengduo, *Liang Song huobi*, vol. 2, pp. 500–501.

34 To be sure, this broad depiction is based on only a few price reports. For Sichuan rice prices in the 11th century, see Cheng Mingsheng 程民生, *Songdai wujia yanjiu* 宋代物价研究 (rev. ed., Nanchang: Jiangxi renmin chubanshe, 2021), pp. 129–30.

35 *XCB* 245.5961.

administration, however, the state once again sought to exploit the convenience and minimal cost of paper bills to fulfill its fiscal goals, with some adverse effects on the market value of *jiaozi*. In the early 12th century, when Wang Anshi's self-anointed successor Cai Jing dominated the court, profligate issue of *jiaozi* to meet exorbitant state expenditures fatally compromised their viability as financial instruments, and the government was obliged to replace the *jiaozi* with a new form of state-issued paper currency.

4.4 State Finance and Monetary Trends in the New Policies Era

Following humiliating defeat in the Qingli War, Emperor Renzong retreated to a posture of forbearance in military affairs and tamped down criticism that his reticence constituted appeasement to the Tanguts' ambitions for territorial expansion. After Renzong's death in 1063, however, his successor Yingzong (r. 1063–1067) deferred to senior statesmen such as Han Qi and Ouyang Xiu, who in their youth had been ardent supporters of Fan Zhongyan's reform agenda in the 1040s, including his aggressive military stance toward the Xia. Belligerent maneuvers on both sides triggered violent reprisals, tilting Yingzong toward a pro-war stance. After Yingzong's premature death in 1067, he was succeeded by his nineteen-year-old son, who reigned as Emperor Shenzong (r. 1067–1085). Unlike his vacillating predecessors, Shenzong was ardently committed to the irredentist aspirations of the dynastic founders, including the recovery of the Sixteen Prefectures from the Liao. Renewed hostilities with the Tanguts provided the pretext for Shenzong to pursue his revanchist dreams and his ambitions for a more muscular monarchy.[36] Within months of his enthronement, Shenzong issued an appeal for men of intellect and imagination who could rise to the challenge of "meeting the urgent priorities of governing the realm" and devising "secret strategies for repulsing the enemy."[37] He would soon find his paladin in an ambitious and brilliant statesman, Wang Anshi, whose bold vision of a renascent empire deeply impressed the fledgling monarch.

Under Wang Anshi's leadership, fiscal management – literally, "regulating wealth" (*licai* 理財) – displaced personal ethics, ritual propriety, and literary mastery as the defining feature of the art of government. Wang shared Shenzong's worry that the military threats posed by the Tanguts and the Khitans imperiled the survival of the dynasty, but he was equally dedicated

[36] Paul Jakov Smith, "Shen-Tsung's Reign and the New Policies of Wang An-shih," in Twitchett and Smith, *Cambridge History of China*, vol. 5, pt. 1, pp. 347–57; Paul Jakov Smith, "The Fragility of Peace: Song China's Northwestern Frontier and Erosion of the Chanyuan Paradigm in the Mid-Eleventh Century," *Journal of Chinese History* 9.1 (2023): 1–29.

[37] *SHY* zhiguan 職官 60.3a.

to relieving what he perceived as the economic misery engendered by the unchecked expansion of the market economy. Above all, Wang was determined to reform the operations of the government by purging the sclerotic bureaucracy and recruiting a cadre of upstart officials who shared his vision of transformative political reform. Despite strenuous opposition by senior advisers, Shenzong appointed Wang to the Council of State in early 1069, where he swiftly elbowed aside its other members and succeeded in creating a new body, the Finance Planning Commission (Zhizhi Sansi tiaoli si 制置三司條例司), the brain trust that became the incubator for his sweeping institutional reforms, collectively known as the "New Policies" (*xinfa* 新法). The establishment of the Finance Planning Commission was prompted by Shenzong's questioning of his newly appointed state councilor about how to enhance the value of iron currency in Shaanxi. In his response, Wang sidestepped the practical problems of currency policy and instead invoked the ancient institutions described in the *Rituals of Zhou* "whereby the former kings thwarted personal aggrandizement (*jianbing* 兼併) and brought relief to the poor and weak … In the present day, if you wish to manage wealth (*licai*), then you must restore the institution of the Public Treasury (Quanfu 泉府, i.e., the royal treasury of the *Rituals of Zhou*) to recover the 'levers of profit' (*liquan* 利權)."[38] Wang's formal request to create the Finance Planning Commission likewise was replete with references to the mercantilist principles enunciated in the *Rituals of Zhou* and the "Light and Heavy" chapters of the *Guan Zi*.[39]

Wang persuaded Shenzong that fulfilling the emperor's revanchist objectives required far-reaching changes in the organization of the bureaucracy, in the administration of government, and above all in fiscal policy. Bypassing the Finance Commission, which staunchly opposed his fiscal innovations, Wang delegated the drafting of the New Policies to the Finance Planning Commission and an obscure office, the Exchequer of Imperial Lands (Sinongsi 司農寺), which superseded the Finance Planning Commission in 1070. Implementation of the New Policies was entrusted to a new corps of provincial officials such as the intendants for ever-normal granaries, husbandry, and water works (*tiju changping nongtian shuili shi* 提舉常平農田水利使) and to ad hoc institutions such as the State Trade Bureau (Shiyiwu 市易務) in Kaifeng and the Tea

[38] This dialogue is recorded in multiple sources, with slightly different wording. My translation is based on Chen Jun 陳均, *Huangchao biannian gangmu beiyao* 皇朝編年綱目備要 ([hereafter *HCBY*]; rpt. Taipei: Chengwen chubanshe, 1966), 18.5a; see also *CBBM* 66.1a–b; Peng Baichuan 彭百川, *Taiping zhiji tonglei* 太平治蹟統類 (SKQS ed.), 13.8a–b. On the Quanfu institution in the *Rituals of Zhou*, see *ZL*, ch. 2, "Diguan situ" 地官司徒, in *SSJZS*, p. 738b–c. As we saw in Chapter 1, the Han statesman Sang Hongyang coined the term "levers of profit" (*liquan*) to refer to state monopolies and coinage.

[39] "Qi Zhizhi Sansi tiaoli si" 乞制置三司條例司, in *WLQ* 70.445.

Marketing Agency (Chachangsi 茶場司) in Sichuan and Shaanxi. The new fiscal institutions devised by these agencies were intended to increase the state's income from monopoly commodities and foreign trade; streamline taxation by reducing or eliminating in-kind payments and labor services in favor of money taxes; and revitalize the agrarian base of society through state investments in irrigation and flood control projects, making low-cost loans to farmers, and expanding the reach of public relief in rural areas.[40] Above all, Wang saw himself as the defender of family farms and small shopkeepers against rapacious rentier landowners and the great merchant houses, whom he castigated as "aggrandizers." Wang feared that unbridled market exchange created imbalances in the distribution in wealth and was vulnerable to manipulation by merchant cartels, epitomized by the powerful bloc of tea merchants. To forestall such inequities, he advocated state intervention in commerce and moneylending. Wang created new state agencies to manage wholesale trade at the capital and provide credit for retail businesses, turned private brokers into government agents, tightened the state's control of foreign trade, and created a new monopoly on tea cultivation in Sichuan.

The New Policies were consistent with the trends toward monetization of fiscal administration and growing state intervention in the marketplace that had been underway since the An Lushan rebellion. Wang Anshi's regime abandoned the synergistic model of fiscal practices, however, and instead revived mercantilist principles of fiscal governance unseen since the time of Emperor Wu of the Han. Conventional economic thinking regarded wealth as a static quantity, a simple function of the labor power invested in agriculture. In contrast, Wang – inspired by the ways in which money multiplied itself through market exchange and interest on debt – conceived of the commercial economy as a dynamic force that increased the stock of wealth.[41] But the intervention of the state was necessary to ensure that the fruits of market growth would be liberally shared with the entire populace and not merely hoarded by aggrandizers for their private advantage. As Wang had stated – invoking the language of the *Guan Zi* – to Emperor Shenzong in the dialogue cited above, the sage-kings of yore had "transformed and circulated the wealth of the Subcelestial Realm and ensured that its benefits would issue from a single source."[42]

40 For a digest of the New Policies and their implementation, see P. J. Smith, "Shen-Tsung's Reign," pp. 392–406. For comprehensive surveys, see Higashi Ichio東一夫, *Ō Anseki shinpō no kenkyū* 王安石新法の研究 (Tokyo: Kazama shobō, 1970); Qi Xia 漆侠, *Wang Anshi bianfa* 王安石变法 (Shanghai: Shanghai renmin chubanshe, 1979).

41 P. J. Smith, "Shen Tsung's Reign," p. 388.

42 *CBBM* 66.1a–b; Qin Xiangye 秦緗業 and Huang Yizhou 黃以周 (eds.), *Xu zizhi tongjian changbian shibu* 續資治通鑑長編拾補 ([hereafter *XCBSB*]; 1882 ed., rpt. Shanghai:

In the monetary realm, Wang sought to free up productive energies in an economy undergoing rapid monetization by converting labor services to cash payments and pumping vast amounts of currency into the economy. Mint output surged to the highest levels recorded in Chinese imperial history (see Table 4.2). Renewed hostilities with the Xia kingdom became the catalyst for efforts to increase the monetary resources available to frontier commanders in the northwest, and *jiaozi* bills once again became crucial tools of state finance.

In 1068, a brash young official named Wang Shao responded to the emperor's call for advice on handling foreign relations with a multipronged plan to take the offensive against Xia through alliance with Tibetan chiefs, colonization of the border regions, and raising new revenues to support military operations. Impressed, Shenzong appointed Wang Shao as a military intendant in the remote Shaanxi frontier, where he began planning an offensive against the Tibetan Qingtang polity (in modern Qinghai), which had recently allied with the Tanguts against the Song.[43] In early 1070, Wang – bemoaning that "all of the profit from cross-border commerce accrues to private merchants" – proposed creating a new State Trade Agency (Shiyisi 市易司) to assume control over the exchange of Sichuan tea for Tibetan horses. The emperor quickly approved, allocating Sichuan *jiaozi* to serve as the capital for the new venture.[44] Wang Anshi at first had urged restraint in dealing with the Xia, but Wang Shao's initial battlefield successes against the Qingtang convinced him to endorse Wang Shao's military colonization plan. Shenzong, eager to take the offensive, supported his generals' provocative actions to seize and fortify bases on the fringe of the Xia territories. But a resounding defeat at the hands of the Tanguts early in 1071 forced the Song forces into a hasty retreat.

Following this setback, the Song leaders turned their attention to amassing a formidable war chest before reprising any further military offensives. The "Green Sprouts" (*qingmiao* 青苗) rural credit system, conceived primarily as a means of breaking the dominance of usurious aggrandizers over loans to farmers, mutated into the chief source of revenues for disaster relief, public works, and defense expenditures. Service exemption fees (*muyiqian* 募役錢), which replaced the obligations of affluent households to perform routine administrative services with money payments, also became a notorious form

Shanghai guji chubanshe, 2006), 4.5b. For the antecedents of these statements, see ch. 23, "Bayan" 霸言, and ch. 73, "Guoxu" 國蓄, in *GZ*, 1, pp. 465–66, 3, p. 1262, respectively.

43 On Wang Shao's campaigns against the Qingtang, see Paul Jakov Smith, "Irredentism as Political Capital: The New Policies and the Annexation of Tibetan Domains in Hehuang (the Qinghai–Gansu Highlands) under Shenzong and His Sons, 1068–1126," in Patricia B. Ebrey and Maggie Bickford (eds.), *Emperor Huizong and Late Northern Song China: The Politics of Culture and the Culture of Politics* (Cambridge. MA: Harvard University Asia Center, 2006), pp. 78–130.

44 *SHY* zhiguan 27.38a.

of predatory extraction when the fees were imposed on the poor in addition to the well-to-do.[45] In 1072, building on Wang Shao's pioneering precedent in the northwest, Wang Anshi's administration created the State Trade Bureau (Shiyiwu; hereafter STB) at Kaifeng. Initially, the STB issued loans to merchants to purchase surplus commodities that had not attracted buyers, generating revenue from the interest collected on these loans. Inevitably, the government itself stepped in to purchase and sell these goods. Although Wang Anshi's critics vehemently protested against the state's intrusion into private commerce, Shenzong was entranced by the power of interest to create wealth. The emperor himself contributed 3 million *guan* from the Inner Palace Treasury to expand the STB's operations. The STB also absorbed the Quehuowu, giving it control over commodity licenses; the Central Commercial Tax Bureau (Du shangshui yuan 都商稅院) and its commercial tax revenues; and the capital's Collateralized Loan Office (Didangsuo 抵當所), which issued cash loans. In 1073, the STB was elevated to the status of an empire-wide institution with branch offices in nearly every province. The STB proved to be highly lucrative for the state. In 1077, it earned 1.41 million *guan*, a net return of 28 percent on its operating capital of 5 million *guan*.[46]

The court also sought to expand the use of paper money to facilitate military logistics. At the beginning of 1070, *jiaozi* currency bureaus were established in Hedong and Shaanxi.[47] In the case of Shaanxi, the fiscal intendant Shen Qi proposed that, given the shortage of currency in the frontier region amid the renewal of hostilities, the government should issue *jiaozi* to obtain bronze coin from the populace; in the future, once peace was restored, the government would buy back the bills with coin. But the introduction of *jiaozi* currency into these regions adversely affected the salt licenses that had become the mainstays of military procurement. Merchants preferred to receive *jiaozi* rather than commodity licenses, causing the market value of the latter to fall. Moreover, Shen Qi's plan apparently involved compulsory exchanges of coin for *jiaozi*, which raised objections from local prefects that this measure would disrupt the livelihood of their constituents. Consequently, the new currency bureaus were abolished, in Hedong in late 1070 and in Shaanxi in mid 1071.[48] But the government also tapped the current *jiaozi* in circulation to fund not only Wang Shao's State Trade Agency in the northwest frontier but also New

45 On the "Green Sprouts" loans and service exemption levies, see P. J. Smith, "Shen-Tsung's Reign," pp. 394–403, 414–29.

46 On the State Trade Agency, see P. J. Smith, "Shen-Tsung's Reign," pp. 403–7, 429–35; Liang Gengyao 梁庚堯, "Shiyifa shu" 市易法述, in Liang, *Songdai shehui jingji shi lunji* 宋代社會經濟史論集 (Taipei: Yunchen wenhua shiye gongsi, 1997), pp. 104–260; Higashi, *Ō Anseki shinpō*, pp. 620–90.

47 *XCBSB* 6.12b; *CBBM* 66.6a–b.

48 *XCB* 213.5170, 222.5402.

Policies programs, such as the "Green Sprouts" rural credit operation and ever-normal granary grain purchases, in Sichuan itself.[49] To accommodate these new functions, in 1072 the court authorized a doubling of the volume of *jiaozi* by allowing two issues of 1.25 million *guan* each to circulate concurrently.[50]

Border officials in the northwest, in their zeal to bolster military preparedness under the looming threat of renewed war with Xia, sharply increased the number of salt licenses they issued to provisioning merchants. In the summer of 1074, the secretariat reported that during the previous year Shaanxi had taken in 5.23 million *guan* in coin payments earmarked for military provisions, but only 42 percent of the salt licenses it issued in return (worth 2.2 million *guan*) could actually be redeemed with salt. Since merchants had become leery of accepting salt licenses, officials had to offer them at a steep discount. The secretariat decided to reintroduce *jiaozi* to Shaanxi in quantities proportional to available cash reserves "so that *jiaozi* can circulate in the market no differently than coin."[51] Several months later the emperor authorized a disbursement of 3 million *guan* (2 million according to another source) in coin from the Inner Palace Treasury to repurchase excess salt licenses, and the Finance Commission imposed a cap of 1.8 million *guan* on the annual amount of salt licenses to be issued in the northwest.[52] In early 1075, minting of "two-cash" (*zhe'er* 折二) iron coins (large iron coins with the value of two small bronze coins) recommenced in order to provide a cash reserve for *jiaozi* bills.[53]

Despite these efforts to shore up the value of salt licenses, the chronic problem of provisioning expenses in the range of 5 million *guan* annually remained unresolved. In late 1074, the court established the Tea Marketing Agency (TMA) to coordinate the delivery of Sichuan tea to frontier markets for horse purchases.[54] Initially, the TMA bought tea in the private market, but its intendants soon began to push for exclusive tea procurement zones, culminating with the creation of a full state monopoly on tea production and sale in Sichuan in 1076.[55] The co-intendant of the TMA, Pu Zongmin, immediately proposed a plan to use tea sales not only to finance horse

49 *XCB* 219.5330, 220.5348.

50 *SS* 181.4404.

51 *XCB* 254.6214–15.

52 *XCB* 254.6290–91. According to *SS* 183.4420, the Inner Palace Treasury disbursed 2 million *guan* as a loan to the Finance Commission, which was delivered to the regional office of the State Trade Bureau in the northwest for repurchasing salt licenses.

53 *XCB* 258.6300, 260.6330–31.

54 In 1086, the horse procurement operations were formally merged with the TMA, which was renamed the Superintendency for Tea and Horses (Duda tiju chama si 都大提舉茶馬司).

55 On the operation of the Sichuan tea monopoly, see P. J. Smith, *Taxing Heaven's Storehouse*.

purchases but also to underwrite tea production in Sichuan. Observing that merchants could obtain *jiaozi* cheaply in Shaanxi and sell them at a premium (100 percent markup) in Sichuan, Pu recommended that the TMA obtain silver, *jiaozi*, and salt licenses from tea sales in Shaanxi which it would bring to the Jiaozi Currency Bureau in Chengdu to exchange for cash that in turn would supply the TMA's working capital. Pu also noted that the Jiaozi Currency Bureau (operated by the Chengdu fiscal intendancy) had already begun to make annual transfers of 100,000 *guan* of *jiaozi* to Shaanxi in addition to the new issue of Shaanxi *jiaozi* bills.[56] Although the details are unclear, it appears that Pu sought to wrest control of the Sichuan *jiaozi* sent to Shaanxi from the Chengdu fiscal intendancy and commandeer them for the TMA's own purposes. In 1076, the TMA succeeded in obtaining a full monopoly over Sichuan tea production, and it gradually extended its monopsony over tea sales in Shaanxi. Under the monopoly, tea production in Sichuan surged, and TMA revenues increased fivefold within a decade.[57] But the creation of the TMA monopoly had adversely affected the value of *jiaozi*. In 1086, Su Che, a Sichuan native and staunch opponent of the New Policies, observed that the value of *jiaozi* had fallen because tea merchants, who had been the most avid users of *jiaozi* for long-distance transfers of funds, had lost their business. Whereas in the past the demand for *jiaozi* was so strong that they circulated at a premium (10 percent above their nominal value), now they were discounted by as much as 10 percent.[58]

In addition, the value of salt licenses continued to sink. Early in 1076, the court was persuaded to suspend the issue of *jiaozi* in Shaanxi. In his diary, the state councilor Lü Huiqing recorded a conversation between the emperor, Wang Anshi, and himself in the autumn of 1075 in which Wang strongly opposed the use of *jiaozi* in Shaanxi because they undermined the value of salt licenses. Shenzong was skeptical of Wang's argument, declaring that "*jiaozi* are backed by coin, while salt licenses are backed by salt; the two cause no harm to each other."[59] But some months later – after Lü had been forced out of the Council of State – fiscal officials in Shaanxi prevailed in persuading the emperor to suspend the issue of *jiaozi*, claiming that the depreciated value of salt licenses made procurement of military provisions more expensive and played into the hands of "aggrandizers" – in this case, speculators who bought

[56] *XCB* 258.6306–7.

[57] P. J. Smith, *Taxing Heaven's Storehouse*, p. 139. As Smith observes (*Taxing Heaven's Storehouse*, p. 149), since the tea monopoly in Huainan had been annulled in 1059, the TMA did not compete with other agencies for tea revenues, and thus it was allowed to expand its range of monopoly territory.

[58] *XCB* 366.8805–6; Su Che 蘇轍, "Lun Shucha wuhai zhuang" 論蜀茶五害狀, *Luancheng ji*欒城集 (SBCK ed.), 36.6b–13a.

[59] Lü's diary entries are quoted at length in *XCB* 272.6668–70.

up salt licenses at discounted prices. Yet criticism against Shaanxi officials for continuing to issue an excessive volume of salt licenses persisted. A crucial reason for the weakening demand for salt licenses was the narrowing of the sales regions in which merchants could operate after the STB imposed a government monopsony on large swaths of the Xiezhou salt merchandising zone, in effect dismantling Fan Xiang's *tongshang* policy.[60] But from 1077, with Wang Anshi again forced into retirement, support for the New Policies agenda began to wane. The finance commissioner Shen Gua, who previously had supported Wang's intention to expand the salt monopoly, reversed himself and pushed for a return to the *tongshang* policy in Shaanxi and the metropolitan region.

The monetization of taxation – and by extension the economy in general – under the New Policies placed severe strain on the money supply. Ironically, despite the unprecedented output of new bronze coin (Table 4.2), with the onset of the Wang Anshi's fiscal program complaints of "coin famines" became even more vociferous. Contemporaries often blamed "coin famines" on wealthy elites and merchant cartels, who were roundly denounced for manipulating money and markets to induce artificial shortages that increased the value of the fortunes they hoarded. But Wang Anshi's critics were even more strident in blaming the monetization of taxation for raising the demand for coin. In their view, the vast quantities of coin held in government treasuries – which the minister of revenue Li Chang in 1086 estimated at nearly 100 million *guan* – reduced the money supply in circulation, causing commodity prices to fall, to the detriment of farmers and silk producers.[61] Although grain prices on average declined from the 1070s to the 1080s, the exchange value of coin relative to silver remained stable, and there seems to be little evidence of pronounced deflation (Figure 4.1). Gao Congming has concluded that the supply of coin was adequate but unevenly distributed. Shenzong's wars, the New Policies fiscal programs, and growing monetization of taxes caused coin to flow to the capital and frontier garrisons, thus triggering "coin famines" in regions, such as the Yangzi Delta, where commercial growth and demand for money was booming.[62]

In 1077, the Hebei fiscal intendant proposed to remedy the problem of "coin famine" in the region by initiating minting of iron coin. Shen Gua, the finance commissioner, axed the proposal, citing the failure of iron coin to circulate in neighboring Hedong in the 1040s. At the same time, Shen appended a lengthy disquisition on the "coin famine" problem.[63] Shen reiterated some of the common explanations for the shortage of coin adduced by other officials,

60 Guo Zhengzhong, *Songdai yanye*, pp. 940–46.
61 *XCB* 384.9352–53, 407.9904.
62 Gao, *Huobi liutong*, pp. 333–44.
63 *XCB* 283.6928–29.

including Wang Anshi's lifting of the ban on nonmonetary uses of copper (allowing the metal to be diverted into manufacture of Buddhist devotional icons and ritual paraphernalia), the drain of coin beyond the Song borders, and excess stocks of coin in state treasuries. More intriguingly, Shen went on to say that in the past rich households had often held savings in the form of salt licenses, but the repeated changes in salt monopoly policies had undermined confidence in the value of the licenses, which the wealthy now disposed of in favor of hoarding coin. The government needed to restore faith in the long-term value of the salt licenses. Even more strikingly, Shen proposed that the stock of money could be substantially increased by monetizing precious metals, especially silver, which was abundantly available. Although Shen did not specify coining silver, his analysis attests to the ways in which paper instruments like salt licenses as well as silver had achieved social utility as monetary instruments that augmented the stock of money beyond the supply of bronze coin.[64] Shen's thinking was a harbinger of the ways in which paper money and silver would be recognized as vital components of the monetary system in the Southern Song, when the output of bronze coinage abruptly decreased.

The New Policies remained in place after Wang's departure from the halls of power, and they proved successful in their chief objective: replenishing the imperial treasuries. The cash revenues of the central government rose dramatically (Table 4.3). The STB's capital resources rose from 5 million *guan* in 1077 to 12.3 million *guan* in 1085, although the return on its investments apparently had begun to decline.[65] The Yuanfeng Treasury (Yuanfengku 元豐庫), created in 1080 as a depository for the proceeds of the New Policies programs, also became a new source for funding military procurement.[66] After

[64] Shen also observed that in the northwestern frontier region the problem was a surfeit of money rather than a shortage, which resulted in a fourfold rise in grain prices. He encouraged the idea of exporting iron coin to the Tibetans in exchange for warhorses, in essence killing two birds with one stone.

[65] P. J. Smith, "Shen-Tsung's Reign," p. 433.

[66] Beginning in 1083, the Ministry of Revenue began to compensate provisioning merchants in Shaanxi with bills of exchange known as *xianqian gongju* 見錢公據 that could be redeemed at the Yuanfeng Treasury, flush with revenues generated by the New Policies. Some 2 million *guan* of *xianqian gongju* bills, in denominations of 5- and 10-*guan*, were issued for this purpose annually. See *XCB* 341.8201–2. The court suspended the issue of *xianqian gongju* in 1086 because they competed with salt licenses (*XCB* 389.9452–54), although there is some evidence that they continued to circulate in Shaanxi after this date. See Hino Kaisaburō, "Nan-Sō no shihei 'Gensen kōkyo' oyobi 'Gensen kanshi' no kigen ni tsuite" 南宋の紙幣'見銭公據'及び'見銭關子'の起源について, in *Hino Kaisaburō ronshū*, vol. 7, pt. 2: *Sōdai no kahei to kin'yū* 宋代の貨幣と金融 (Tokyo, 1983), pp. 25–51. In 1092, Su Che, then executive of the chancellery, observed that the excess of *zhe'er* iron coins in Shaanxi had resulted in steep depreciation, price inflation, and high costs for military procurement, yet the region's commercial economy remained buoyant because of the widespread use of "flying bills" (*feichao* 飛鈔). It is not entirely clear what

Li Chang – a staunch critic of Wang Anshi's fiscal reforms – was appointed minister of revenue in 1086, he reported that the surpluses generated by the New Policies had amounted to 56 million *guan*, even after the Song had conducted another ill-conceived and costly war against the Tanguts in 1081–1083.[67]

The Song offensive launched in the winter of 1081 caught the Tanguts off guard, but after initial setbacks the Xia army regrouped for a counterattack that annihilated the Song forces. Shenzong, stunned by this decisive defeat, was forced to rethink his military strategy, and he began to sour on the New Policies fiscal agenda as well. A full retreat from Wang Anshi's reforms and Shenzong's feckless quest to recover the northern borderlands commenced after Shenzong fell ill and died at the age of thirty-seven in 1085. His mother, the dowager empress Xuanren, became regent presiding over the court on behalf of her eight-year-old grandson, who would reign as Emperor Zhezong (r. 1085–1100). Xuanren replaced Wang Anshi's acolytes with conservative opponents of the New Policies long held at bay during Shenzong's reign. Within a year of Shenzong's death, many of the fiscal policies and institutions instituted by Wang Anshi, notably the STB, had been abolished. However, the ascendant anti-reform coalition itself soon fractured into rival factions, and partisan conflict paralyzed the government for the remainder of Xuanren's regency, which ended with her death in 1093. Once Zhezong assumed personal rule, he revived the institutional legacy of his father, including the STB. More ominously for the Song state, Zhezong also embraced his father's irredentist hopes of vanquishing the Xia.

4.5 The Demise of *Jiaozi* and the Creation of *Qianyin* Paper Currency in Sichuan

During the personal rule of Zhezong after Empress Xuanren's death (1093–1100) and throughout the reign of his half-brother and successor, Emperor Huizong (r. 1100–1125), the Song court revived the New Policies agenda. Zhezong and Huizong also reverted to the bellicose stance taken by their father, Emperor Shenzong, toward the Xia. From 1096 to 1117, the Song repeatedly encroached on Xia territories, provoking swift reprisals. Both sides suffered substantial casualties without either gaining definitive victory until the Xia routed a Song offensive in 1116–1117. The two decades of nearly

Su meant by "flying bills," but he specified that they were redeemed at the Yuanfeng Treasury, which would suggest *xiangqian gongju* rather than salt licenses (which were redeemed by the Quehuowu). Most likely Su was referring to both *xianqian gongju* and salt licenses, whose fiscal functions essentially overlapped. See Su Che 蘇徹, *Longquan lüezhi* 龍川略志 (Beijing: Zhonghua shuju, 1982), 8.49.

67 *XCB* 407.9904.

incessant warfare took an enormous toll on Song state finances. Zhezong and Huizong both supported ministers keen to restore the New Policies fiscal institutions to cope with the growing costs of warfare. Later historians universally castigated Cai Jing, who served three tenures as chief state councilor between 1102 and 1124 (nineteen years altogether), as the epitome of a "treacherous minister," one whose rapacious fiscal policies and inept leadership impoverished the populace and culminated in the debacle of the loss of the northern half of the empire, including the capital of Kaifeng, to the Jurchen in 1126–1127.[68] Of the many calamities attributed to Cai's fiscal policies, among the most reviled were his efforts to manipulate monetary policy and the salt and tea monopolies to maximize state revenues.

Shortly after his elevation to the Council of State in 1102, Cai Jing established the Advisory Council (Jiangyisi 講議司), an ad hoc agency similar to Wang Anshi's Finance Planning Commission, to draft the agenda for his fiscal measures, which for the most part revived the New Policies institutions but also added new state spending on schools, poor relief, and maintenance of the imperial clan.[69] Under the new iterations of these policies, one historian has written, "resource extraction reached astronomical heights" as the government "bled the private sector to enrich the state, and the monarch and his courtiers."[70] This was especially true of the salt monopoly, which reportedly generated annual revenues of 40 million *guan* by 1117, or more than double the level achieved under the New Policies.[71]

The resumption of warfare against the Xia once again depleted the state's fiscal resources. In 1096 and again in 1097, the Yuanfeng Treasury disbursed 4 million *guan* to fund military procurement in Shaanxi; in 1099, the Inner

[68] On the historical narratives of Cai Jing's rule, see Charles Hartman, "A Textual History of Cai Jing's Biography in the *Song shi*," in Ebrey and Bickford, *Emperor Huizong*, pp. 517–64.

[69] John W. Chaffee, "Huizong, Cai Jing, and the Politics of Reform," in Ebrey and Bickford, *Emperor Huizong*, pp. 35–40; Hartman, *Structures of Governance*, pp. 207–9.

[70] Ari Daniel Levine, "The Reigns of Hui-tsung (1100–1126) and Ch'in-tsung (1126–1127) and the Fall of the Northern Sung," in Twitchett and Smith, *Cambridge History of China*, vol. 5, pt. 1, p. 590. The Southern Song statesman Ye Shi claimed that under Cai Jing government revenue doubled compared to the Wang Anshi regime: Ye Shi 葉適, "Cai zonglun (er)" 財總論(二), *Shuixin bieji* 水心別集11, in *Ye Shi ji* 葉適集 ([hereafter *YSJ*]; Beijing: Zhonghua shuju, 1961), 3, p. 773.

[71] The 40 million *guan* figure comes from *SS* 182.4452–53 (repeated in *WXTK* 16.162a, which probably derives from the same source), but it is not corroborated by extant Song records. The Quehuowu reported income of 16 million *guan* for a nine-month period in 1116–1117; see *SHY* shihuo 25.9a–b. Dai Yixuan (*Chaoyan zhidu*, p. 328) accepts the *SS*/*WXTK* figure of 40 million *guan*. Guo Zhengzhong's tables on salt revenues give figures of 4 million *guan* for Xiezhou and 25 million *guan* for Huainan for 1119, but Guo provides no citations for these figures. See Guo Zhengzhong, *Songdai yanye*, p. 652, table 18; pp. 676–77, table 44.

Palace Treasury likewise transferred 2 million *guan* in silver and silk to Shaanxi.[72] The Xiezhou salt monopsony had become the crucial revenue source for maintaining the Song military forces in Shaanxi, but in 1098 this system was upended when a dike breach inundated the Xie salt lake with fresh water, forcing a halt to salt production at Xiezhou that lasted for seven years. For lack of coin, in late 1102 Cai Jing was obliged to scour government storehouses for goods such as silks, lacquer, ivory, aromatics, and medicines to redeem 3.7 million *guan* of procurement licenses accumulated by a mere six or seven merchants (most likely *jiaoyinpu* financiers, telling evidence of the scale of their operations) over the previous seven years.[73] In the aftermath of the catastrophic loss of Xiezhou salt income – 4 million *guan* per year on average – Cai was compelled to raise revenues from other sectors of the salt monopoly and to transfer Sichuan *jiaozi* to Shaanxi to augment the money stock there.

The main features of Cai Jing's reorganization of the salt monopoly, inaugurated in 1102, involved (1) replacing government sales of *moyan* salt produced in the Huainan monopoly region with the Xiezhou salt licensing system (i.e., adopting the *tongshang* system); (2) extending the monopsony zone for *moyan* salt into areas previously reserved for Xiezhou salt, including the Kaifeng metropolitan region, Henan, Shaanxi, and western Sichuan; (3) charging merchants a steep surcharge (from 30 to 50 percent) to exchange Xiezhou salt licenses (now worthless, since Xiezhou produced no salt) for *moyan* licenses; and (4) establishing an Exchange Bill Purchasing Bureau (Maichaosuo 買鈔所) at Kaifeng to wrest control of the secondary market in salt licenses from the private *jiaoyinpu* merchant houses.[74] The new salt licensing policies doubled the income of the Huainan *moyan* monopoly, from 5–6 million to more than 11 million *guan*.[75] Moreover, in contrast to previous practice in which *moyan* revenues were mostly reserved for local administrative expenses, the proceeds from the new license system accrued to the Quehuowu in the capital. Yet critics of Cai's policies claimed that the Kaifeng Quehuowu had no coin reserves with which to reimburse merchants for delivering supplies to the frontier garrisons. According to a memorial submitted by the censor Mao Zhu in 1110, since the 1070s the standard practice had been to compensate delivery of military provisions to Hebei in coin (using *jiaoyin* bills as the intermediary), Hedong procurement half in coin and half in

[72] Dai Yixuan, *Chaoyan zhidu*, p. 259.

[73] *HCBY* 26.12b. A year later, the advisory council reported that the Xiezhou salt licenses were still in circulation, but merchants were forced to sell them to the *jiaoyinpu* in the capital at a steep discount. *SHY* zhiguan 27.17b–18a.

[74] Guo Zhengzhong, *Songdai yanye*, pp. 815–23, 962–65.

[75] *WXTK* 15.156a, citing an untitled memorial by Chen Fuliang (1137–1203) not included in Chen's collected works.

silver and silk, and Shaanxi procurement in Xiezhou salt licenses. "The long-distance merchants were delighted," wrote Mao, "and they competed to deliver fodder and grain to the frontiers; merchandise flowed freely, and prices remained stable." But now the Quehuowu had no cash reserves and merchants refused to accept government bills, which not only rendered the bills worthless but also forced frontier officials to purchase supplies locally at exorbitant prices.[76] The implication of Mao's report was that the real concern of Cai Jing's government was not to ensure provision of supplies for the frontier armies but rather to divert the enormous revenues generated by the salt monopoly to other purposes, especially the ostentatious spending for which Emperor Huizong became infamous.[77]

The collapse of the Xiezhou salt licensing system following the inundation of the salt lake in 1098 dealt a massive blow not only to military procurement but to the Shaanxi economy as a whole. As the vice-minister of revenue Sun Lan observed in 1095, "Since iron coin does not circulate on its own, its utility depends on salt licenses. If the authorities are able to raise and lower the price of licenses to equilibrate the value of iron currency, then iron coin can circulate. It is the combination of licenses and coin that enables them to function as viable currencies."[78] In 1098, with the Xiezhou salt licenses steeply discounted, the value of iron coin in Shaanxi fell to a mere one-fourth (relative to bronze coin) of the level of 1080.[79] In 1103, Cai Jing, ostensibly acting to prevent the drain of bronze coin into the hands of the Tanguts and Khitan, approved a proposal to mint a large "tin-alloy" (*jiaxi* 夾錫) coin in Shaanxi and Hedong. The government set the official tariff for the tin-alloy coins, which consisted of one-third tin and two-thirds iron, at two small bronze coins, but they quickly encountered resistance in the marketplace and spiraled into steep depreciation. The tin-alloy coins, which remained in circulation until 1116, only exacerbated the monetary chaos in the frontier regions.[80]

76 *SS* 182.4445–48; *MCZY* 270.2b–5a. Nor was Cai able to curb the power of the *jiaoyinpu* over the secondary market for bills of exchange. In 1119, the Quehuowu, lacking cash to redeem bills of exchange for frontier procurement amounting to several million *guan*, proposed a deferred payment schedule for eventual redemption of the bills. Many merchants were unable to wait, however, and were forced to sell the bills at a steep discount to *jiaoyinpu*. See *HCBY* 28.20b.

77 Dai Yixuan, *Chaoyan zhidu*, p. 308. Cai Jing had been forced to resign temporarily as state councilor in 1109, opening the door to harsh criticisms such as Mao Zhu's memorial. But Cai regained control of the central government in 1112.

78 *XCBSB* 12.18a. For the attribution of this statement to Sun Lan (rather than to his then deceased brother Sun Jue, as recorded in the original text), see Lamouroux, "Bureaucratie et monnaie," p. 184n34.

79 Gao, *Huobi liutong*, pp. 149–50.

80 Gao, *Huobi liutong*, pp. 160–63. For a metallurgical analysis of *jiaxi* coins, see Dai Zhiqiang 戴志强 et al., "'Jiaxiqian' wenti zaiyanjiu" '夹锡钱'问题再研究, *Zhongguo qianbi* 中国钱币 1991.1: 6.

Table 4.4 *Emission of Sichuan* jiaozi *bills*

	Biennial quota (in *guan*)
1023	1,256,340
1072	2,512,680
1094	2,812,680
1098	3,772,680
1102	6,772,680
1103	11,430,000
1105	17,130,000
1107	24,300,000

Source: Miyazawa, "Hoku-Sō kōshi ron," p. 16.

Fiscal planners turned to Sichuan *jiaozi*, which continued to circulate in the private market in the northwest after the court suspended emission of the Shaanxi *jiaozi* bills in 1076, to replace the salt licenses as monetary instruments in Shaanxi. In 1098, the authorities increased the emission of Sichuan *jiaozi* by one-third, to a total volume of 3.77 million guan.[81] In 1102, Cai Jing instructed the Jiaozi Currency Bureau to raise the volume of Sichuan *jiaozi* in circulation to a total of 6.77 million *guan* to enable "*jiaozi* to circulate in Shaanxi along with coin and salt licenses."[82] Over the next few years, the emission of *jiaozi* soared to stratospheric heights, a nearly tenfold increase since Wang Anshi's time (Table 4.4). In addition, in 1104 the court authorized the creation of a new bill of exchange to replace the Xiezhou salt licenses. These bills were printed with the legend "Official Seal of the Capital Supervisor of Jiaozi" (*Zaijing tiju jiaozi guanyin* 在京提舉交子官印), apparently to encourage their use not only to remit funds to the capital but as a general means of market exchange like the Sichuan *jiaozi*. The circulation zone for these new *jiaozi* extended beyond the capital to Shanxi, Henan, and Huainan, but they failed to win popular acceptance. In 1105, the bills were renamed *qianyin* 錢引 (a contraction of *xianqian jiaoyin*, not to be confused with the *qianyin* bills introduced in Sichuan in 1107 [see below]), but with no greater success in the marketplace. In 1106, the *qianyin* bills were withdrawn, and with the resumption of salt production at the Xiezhou salt lake the government once again began to issue Xiezhou salt licenses.[83]

81 *CBP*, in *SZGJ* 67.710.

82 *HCBY* 26.21a.

83 *SS* 181.4404; *SHY* zhiguan 27.18b; Hino Kaisaburō, "Hoku-Sō jidai no tegata 'Gensen kōin' o ronjite shihei 'Sen'in' no kigen ni oyobu" 北宋時代の手形 '見銭交引' を論じて紙幣 '銭引' の起源に及ぶ, in *Hino Kaisaburō ronshū*, vol. 7: *Sōdai no kahei to kin'yū (II)*, pp. 120–27.

Not surprisingly, given the enormous quantity of *jiaozi* bills pumped into circulation within Sichuan, their value cratered, prompting the government to undertake a radical devaluation. In the summer of 1107, the government announced the inauguration of a new paper money, designated as *qianyin* 錢引, to replace the Sichuan *jiaozi* bills.[84] *Jiaozi* bills still in circulation could be redeemed with *qianyin* bills at a steep discount of 75 percent of face value. The government also decreed that large payments (more than 10 *guan*) had to be made half in coin and half in *qianyin*, while 80–90 percent of disbursements for official salaries would be made in *qianyin*.[85]

Since old *jiaozi* bills remained in circulation, and no coin reserve was set aside to redeem the new bills, the introduction of *qianyin* bills created enormous disruption and confusion. In the eighth month of 1108, a prefect in Shaanxi, Zhang Chi, reported that the market value of *qianyin* bills (perhaps referring to the old *jiaozi*?) in his jurisdiction was a mere one-tenth of their face value.[86] Zhang proposed that to enhance their acceptance at least 80–90 percent of state payments should be made in bills rather than coin. His proposal was approved, and Zhang was promoted to assistant fiscal intendant in Chengdu to take charge of managing *qianyin* bills. But the value of the bills continued to erode, and Zhang took it upon himself to mark the bills issued as official salaries with a special seal (to deter counterfeiting?), declaring bills without the seal void. But in the first month of 1110, Zhang was dismissed from office on the grounds of "making unauthorized changes in *qianyin*," presumably a reference to the special seal.[87] In 1109, while Zhang was in office, the court issued an edict declaring that the old *jiaozi* issues no longer would be redeemed with new bills and setting the annual quota for the emission of *qianyin* at the original 1023 level of 1.25 million *guan*.[88] After Zhang's departure, a reserve fund for *qianyin* was established, which reportedly gave a significant boost to popular confidence in them. Moreover, the government discontinued the practice of emitting two issues of bills simultaneously while allowing the populace greater flexibility in using *qianyin* in payments to the state (up to this point taxpayers were required to pay 70 percent in coin).[89] These reforms were attributed to the administration of Zhang Shangying, who briefly replaced Cai Jing as chief state councilor in mid 1110. But even after Cai's return

[84] The sources describing the replacement of *jiaozi* by *qianyin* are by no means fully clear or consistent. My digest is based on Wang Shengduo, *Liang Song huobi*, vol. 2, pp. 632–36; Li Shan and Lin, *Chubi shi xinian*, pp. 58–63; Miyazawa Tomoyuki 宮沢知之, "Hoku-Sō kōshi ron" 北宋交子論, in Miki Satoshi 三木聰 (ed.), *Sō-Shindai no seiji to shakai* 宋-清代の政治と社会 (Tokyo: Kyūko shoin, 2017), pp. 17–19.

[85] Like *jiaozi*, the new *qianyin* bills were issued in denominations of 500 *wen* and 1 *guan*.

[86] This memorial is recorded in *SS* 181.4405 and (more coherently) in *WXTK* 9.97b.

[87] *SHY* zhiguan 68.20a.

[88] *SS* 181.4405; *CBP*, in *SZGJ* 67.711.

[89] *SS* 181.4405.

to power in the spring of 1112, fiscal prudence appears to have prevailed in the management of Sichuan's *qianyin* paper currency, and by all accounts its value remained stable prior to the onset of the Song–Jurchen wars in 1125.

4.6 Conclusion

Since the pioneering studies of Katō Shigeshi, Hino Kaisaburō, and Sogabe Shizuo, published in the 1930s, most scholars have regarded the state-issued *jiaozi* bills as genuine paper money, the world's first viable paper currency, a product of the growth of the market economy in Song times. But in recent years, skepticism has been voiced challenging this consensus. Among the first to do so was Bao Weimin, who contended that the *jiaozi* was not a form of fiduciary money for market exchange but rather a token substitute for coin whose circulation was driven by the "extra-economic powers" of the state. Bao emphasized that coin remained the standard of value throughout the Song and beyond, down to the late Ming era. But Bao's analysis was strongly inflected by what he regards as the normative historical experience of Europe, where a "natural" evolution from precious metal monies to "symbolic" paper monies occurred.[90] Miyazawa Tomoyuki even more emphatically has challenged the fundamental premise of the Song economy as a market economy. Miyazawa postulates that paper bills in the Song were a form of administrative money operating within a sphere of "fiscal circulation" wherein the state retains large quantities of money in its treasuries and directly or indirectly organizes the circulation of goods on a national scale through its procurement policies, especially military expenditures. Miyazawa contends that "market circulation" only achieved prominence during the 16th and 17th centuries, when massive imports of foreign silver led to the establishment of uncoined silver as the monetary standard for both public and private transactions.[91]

Miyazawa extends this argument in his study of *jiaozi*, in which he argues that the primary purpose behind the state's issue of *jiaozi* was to facilitate military procurement, not to promote market exchange.[92] In his view, three institutional features of *jiaozi* hindered their utility as money. First, the bills were issued in large denominations that would have been impractical in petty trade. Although the 1023 edict authorizing the issue of *jiaozi* specified that

[90] Bao Weimin 包伟民, "Shilun Songdai zhibi de xingzhi jiqi lishi diwei" 试论宋代纸币的性质及其历史地位, in Qi Xia 漆侠 and Hu Zhaoxi 胡昭曦 (eds.), *Songdai yanjiu lunwenji* 宋代研究论文集 (Baoding: Hebei daxue chubanshe, 1994), pp. 135–52. Bao's main argument has been endorsed and amplified more recently by Wang Shen 王申, "Zhidu, liutong yu guojia caizheng: Nan Song zhibi shi yanjiu shuping" 制度，流通与国家财政：南宋纸币史研究述评, *Tang Song lishi pinglun* 唐宋历史评论 5.1 (2019): 203–21.

[91] Miyazawa, *Kokka to keizai*; Miyazawa, *Kahei to zaisei*.

[92] Miyazawa, "Hoku-Sō kōshi."

they would be printed in ten denominations ranging between 1 *guan* and 10 *guan*, in 1039 a new formula was enacted whereby 80 percent of *jiaozi* would be issued as 10-*guan* bills, and the remainder in 5-*guan* bills; the other denominations no longer would be issued.[93] Second, the *jiaozi* bills could be redeemed for coin only at one place, the Chengdu Jiaozi Currency Bureau, which would have been a severe inconvenience for merchants located elsewhere. Third, the two-year term of expiry mandating regular exchange of old *jiaozi* bills for new ones would have exacerbated this problem. Miyazawa maintains that the incorporation of *jiaozi* into the Song state's system of "fiscal circulation" – the mobilization of resources through market mechanisms to meet its urgent military and logistical needs – in the 1040s marked the first step toward their transformation into a genuine means of exchange. But it was only when *jiaozi* were adopted as a means of state payments in the early 12th century that this transformation finally occurred.

Jiaozi bills did indeed occupy an important place in the Song state's fiscal circulation. Yet we should not overlook the significance of the *jiaozi* bills in Sichuan's private economy – especially given the bias of our sources, which overwhelmingly reflect the concerns of fiscal officials rather than the private sector. To begin with, the problem that impelled the state to take over issue of *jiaozi* – the inability of private financiers to redeem the bills they issued – indicates that the bills were not merely certificates of deposit but rather that the financiers issued *jiaozi* based on fractional currency reserves. The regulations established by Zhang Yong in 1005 were intended to ensure the solvency and credibility of the private financiers – to no avail, as it turned out. In the words of the early 12th-century encyclopedist and Sichuan native Li You, when the private issuers of *jiaozi* shut their gates because they were unable to redeem the bills, "crowds milled around their shops, bursting into protest and clamor, and the magistrates had to send their constables to restrain them. Holders of 1-*guan* bills in the end received only 700–800 *wen*, tantamount to defrauding the poor folk (*qinqi pinmin* 侵欺貧民)."[94] We should not take Li You's reference to "poor folk" too literally, but his account suggests that *jiaozi* bills were broadly disseminated among the populace and not restricted just to merchants engaged in interregional trade. Moreover, Kou Jian's suspension of new private *jiaozi* in 1021 caused havoc in commercial markets to the extent that the court authorized the state takeover of issuing *jiaozi* two years later, further testimony to their use in commercial transactions.

Jiaozi, along with silver, performed unique roles as means of interregional payment between the Sichuan iron currency monetary zone and other parts of

[93] *CBP*, in *SZGJ* 67.710.
[94] *SCSS*, 15.5b.

the Song Empire where the bronze currency standard prevailed.[95] Miyazawa is entirely correct to underscore the ways in which Song fiscal planners sought to utilize *jiaozi* to facilitate military procurement in the Shaanxi frontier, especially given the troubles they encountered in using tea licenses for this purpose. Once *jiaozi* were introduced into Shaanxi in the 1040s, however, they quickly found favor in local markets. Although the finance commissioner Tian Kuang ordered Shaanxi officials to cease disbursing *jiaozi* in 1051 because the government had insufficient reserves to redeem the bills, he ruefully acknowledged that it was impossible to curb their use in private exchange.[96]

After the military crisis of the 1040s passed (and with the success of the new salt license system instituted by Fan Xiang), *jiaozi* no longer played a salient role in frontier military procurement. But *jiaozi* became increasingly more prominent in the Sichuan commercial economy. The steep reduction of Sichuan's iron coinage output in the 1050s most likely reflected a shift in demand away from coin to paper bills in market exchange. In 1068, the government recalibrated the denominations for *jiaozi* bills. In place of the 10-*guan* and 5-*guan* bills that had been issued since 1039, new bills would be issued in much smaller denominations of 1-*guan* and 500-*wen* "to facilitate their circulation."[97] These bills certainly were too large for daily market transactions – to put them in perspective, at this time 500 *wen* could purchase 25–35 liters of rice (enough to feed a family of five for 7–10 days) in Sichuan, and daily wages at Sichuan tea plantations were 60 *wen*, plus a food supplement probably worth 10–20 *wen*.[98] But the 90 percent reduction in the denominations of *jiaozi* bills surely attested to growing demand in retail trade rather than interregional commerce.

Finally, the two-year term of expiry does not seem to have interfered with the utility of *jiaozi* bills in the commercial economy. Miyazawa acknowledges that in the early 12th century Sichuan's state-issued bills – particularly the new *qianyin* bills – functioned as genuine paper money and became the monetary standard for the region. But the bills were still subject to the same two-year term of expiry throughout the remainder of the Song dynasty. In the Southern Song period, *qianyin* bills prevailed as the monetary standard in Sichuan, which remained a separate monetary zone, even more geographically isolated from the new national capital of Hangzhou and the dynamic commercial economy of the Yangzi Delta. Government fiscal records and price reports

95 The parallels between *jiaozi* and silver as means of interregional settlements have been emphasized in Inoue Masao 井上正夫, "Hoku-Sō Shisen ni okeru kōshi no hassei katei ni tsuite" 北宋四川における交子の発生過程について, *Matsuyama daigaku ronshū* 松山大学論集 32 (*kinengo* 記念号) (2020): 5–32.

96 *SCSS* 15.7a–b.

97 *SCSS* 15.7b.

98 Cheng, *Songdai wujia*, pp. 129, 272.

from Southern Song Sichuan invariably use the *qianyin* unit of account (*dao* 道), positive proof that it had superseded coin as the monetary standard in the region.[99] The volume of *qianyin* in circulation soared during the first decade of the Southern Song, to over 40 million *dao*, before stabilizing at that level following the truce concluded with the Jin in 1142. Although the quantity of paper money in Sichuan far exceeded the level of the Northern Song, there is no evidence that this increase resulted in social unrest or severe depreciation of their value before new military crises arose in the 13th century. Instead, the Southern Song court was emboldened to create new paper monies that ultimately became integral features of the monetary system and market exchange throughout its realm.

[99] Miyazawa, "Hoku-Sō kōshi," p. 19; Cheng, *Songdai wujia*, pp. 130–31.

5

Formation of Multiple Currency Regions in the Song Ecumene

Despite the endemic hostility between the Song and the Xia and Liao states, the existential challenge to the Song dynasty would come from an entirely new and unanticipated direction: the Jurchen Jin confederation. The Jurchen, semi-nomadic peoples inhabiting the northern reaches of modern-day Manchuria, had long been vassals of the Liao kingdom. In 1114, a Jurchen chief, Wanyan Aguda, united the Jurchen tribes and revolted against the Liao. In the following year, Aguda declared himself an emperor, inaugurating his Jin ("Golden") dynasty (1115–1234), and subsequently forged an alliance with the Song against the Liao. From 1120, the Jin forces swiftly overwhelmed the Liao, seizing all of the Liao territories by early 1123. Emboldened by this success, the Jin renounced the alliance with the Song and launched an invasion of the Song domains, culminating in the sack of the capital, Kaifeng, in 1127. Emperor Huizong was taken prisoner, but remnants of the court fled to the south, where the Song government was reconstituted at Hangzhou, which was designated the "temporary residence" of the new emperor, Gaozong (r. 1127–1162). But as the prospects of retaking the northern territories receded, Hangzhou in effect became the capital of the Southern Song (1127–1276) regime.[1] The threat of foreign invasion, first by the Jin and later by the Mongols, would continue to menace the dynasty throughout the remainder of its existence, which ended with the Mongol capture of Hangzhou in 1276. Military exigencies likewise exerted unrelenting pressure on the government's fiscal and monetary systems.

Despite the loss of the northern half of the empire to the Jin after 1127, the Chinese economy underwent unprecedented growth during the Southern Song period. The relocation of the Song capital to Hangzhou gave further impetus to the Jiangnan region (largely equivalent to Liangzhe circuit, encompassing modern Zhejiang and southern Jiangsu provinces) in the lower Yangzi River basin as the dynamic engine of agricultural and commercial expansion.

[1] On war and diplomacy between Song and Jin, see Jing-shen Tao, "The Move to the South and the Reign of Kao-tsung (1127–1162)," in Twitchett and Smith, *Cambridge History of China*, vol. 5, pt. 1, pp. 672–94.

Jiangnan had already become the empire's most prolific grain-producing region in the Northern Song, and the rapid advance of rice paddy polders to transform the delta's lowland swamps into productive farmland during the 12th and 13th centuries enhanced its dominant place within the Song economy. Jiangnan's population increased by 50 percent between 1102 and 1223, in contrast to 9 percent for the Southern Song territories as a whole.[2] Bountiful agricultural surpluses and the construction of elaborate canal networks linking rural producers to urban consumers fostered the impressive efflorescence of towns and cities, above all Hangzhou, whose population surpassed 1 million residents. Urbanization also stimulated long-distance trade and regional specialization. Southern industries such as silk, tea, porcelain, timber, papermaking, printing, shipbuilding, oil pressing, and sugar refining flourished, and overseas trade with Japan and Southeast Asia boomed. Commercial development naturally increased the demand for money as well as for financial intermediaries such as brokers, pawnshops, and money changers.[3]

At the same time, the military predicament of the Song court was no less precarious than in the Northern Song. Before an armistice with the Jin was negotiated in 1142, the very survival of the dynasty remained in question. The creation of a new frontier severing the Central Plain from the Yangzi River basin radically reshaped the empire's geography and resource base, necessitating a wholesale reordering of Song fiscal administration and its monetary policies. The military crisis forced the Song to adopt emergency measures to raise revenues, resulting in a proliferation of new capitation and consumption taxes. Still, the burden of fiscal extraction did not stunt the flourishing commercial economy, and the supposedly provisional taxes were retained even after the armistice was ratified. The cessation of hostilities granted the Song court a respite to turn to the task of reconsolidating control over its shrunken domain. The government launched empire-wide cadastral surveys to shore up its tax base, while building a wholly new infrastructure of regional military and fiscal institutions to funnel resources to the main armies stationed along the southern bank of the Yangzi River and the forward military bases near the Huai and Han Rivers, which demarcated the Song–Jin frontier.

A new military crisis arose in 1161 when the Jin ruler Digunai (best known as Prince of Hailing; r. 1050–1161) unleashed a campaign to seize the territories lying between the Huai and Yangzi Rivers, part of a broader plan to move the Jin court to the former Song capital at Kaifeng. After rebuffing the initial Jin assaults, the Song launched a counterattack to recover its lost territories in

[2] Wu Songdi 吴松弟, *Nan Song renkou shi* 南宋人口史 (Shanghai: Shanghai guji chubanshe, 2008), pp. 183–84, tables 5-1, 5-2. In 1223, Liangzhe circuit comprised 22 percent of the total Southern Song population.

[3] For a synopsis of the Southern Song economy, see von Glahn, *Economic History of China*, pp. 255–78.

Map 5.1 Song–Jin frontier in 1165.

the north. But the Song offensive stalled, and in early 1165 a new treaty was signed that reaffirmed the 1142 boundary between the two rival states (Map 5.1). Nonetheless, the revanchist ambitions of the Song leadership continued to simmer, and additional resources were invested in the military in preparation for a future war of reconquest.

Among the chief fiscal problems facing the Song regime was an acute shortage of coin. Not only was the central government shorn of its hard currency reserves (as many as 100 million strings of bronze coin may have been left behind when the court fled Kaifeng), but the output of state mints plummeted to a mere one-tenth of the annual average of the Northern Song. The government was forced to debase its bronze coin, which in turn invited widespread counterfeiting. Northern Song issues of full-bodied bronze coin vanished from circulation, compounding the monetary crisis. During the Song–Jin war of 1161–1165, the court created a new paper money, known as *huizi* 會子, to finance the upsurge in military expenditures. Initially intended as a wartime expedient, the *huizi* currency soon became a pillar of the state's fiscal and monetary systems, and the court subsequently introduced additional paper currencies in other regions. By the 1190s, the empire had become divided into four different monetary zones, each with its own separate paper currency. The Jin state, too, came to rely on paper currency for the operation of its fiscal system.

5.1 Reorganization of State Finances

Following the sack of Kaifeng, the Song government was in utter disarray, even after Hangzhou was chosen to serve as the provisional capital in 1129. Emperor Gaozong, hastily enthroned after the Jurchen captured his father and elder brother, had little choice but to concede broad military and fiscal discretion to the roughly thirty military commanders charged with maintaining defensive lines across the Huai and Yangzi River valleys. In 1134, the Song armies were consolidated under the command of four pacification commissioners (Xuanfusi宣撫司), who also exercised broad authority over tax collection and expenditures. The State Council tried to restore the fiscal authority of the Ministry of Revenue, but with limited success, especially in far-off Sichuan. Tensions arose between the pacification commissioners Yue Fei and Han Shizhong, who favored aggressive action to recapture the territories lost to the Jurchen, and Gaozong, who by 1138 had abandoned the revanchist cause and desperately desired a peace settlement. Gaozong was crucially supported by the state councilor Qin Gui, to whom Gaozong delegated full control over the civil administration. In the summer of 1141, Gaozong summoned three of the pacification commissioners (excepting Sichuan) to Hangzhou and stripped them of their commands. Qin Gui sought to quell resistance to peace negotiations by accusing Yue Fei, who had become a national hero for his battlefield victories, of treason. The imprisonment and execution of Yue Fei in late 1141 followed on the heels of the armistice settlement (formally adopted in the spring of 1142) that fixed the Song–Jin border along the Huai River and obliged the Song to submit tribute of silver and silks to the Jin as earlier Song emperors had done to secure peace with Liao and Xia.

With the pacification commissioners removed, the court undertook a fundamental reorganization of its fiscal administration by creating three general commands (Zonglingsuo 總領所) – Huaidong, headquartered at Zhenjiang; Huaixi, at Jiankang (modern Nanjing); and Huguang, at Ezhou (modern Wuhan) – that would supersede the pacification commissioners as supreme regional authorities and assume control of military procurement and logistics (Map 5.2). A fourth general command was established in Sichuan in 1145. The general commands received a portion of the twice-a-year tax income in their respective regions and revenues from the salt, tea, and liquor monopolies, as well as a variety of new money revenues instituted during the military emergency of the 1120s designated as "frontier supply and defense funds" (*jingzong zhiqian* 經總制錢), and "monthly sequestration funds" (*yuezhuangqian* 月椿錢). The case of the Huaidong General Command, based at Zhenjiang, succinctly illustrates the new paradigm for financing the military. In the 1160s, the Huaidong General Command supplied provisions for 68,000 troops, 50,000 of whom were stationed at forward bases around Chuzhou. Most of its grain supplies derived from twice-a-year tax revenues in Jiangdong and Jiangxi circuits, but at least 20 percent was procured through the market – through "harmonious purchases" (*hedi* 和糴) – in Jiangxi. The general command's cash income, in contrast, largely came from Liangzhe circuit, primarily from salt monopoly revenues (60 percent of the total). At current rice prices, cash revenues comprised 75–87 percent of the Huaidong General Command's total income in the second half of the 12th century.[4]

Scholars remain divided on the question of whether the creation of the general commands resulted in a devolution of fiscal authority or conversely a recentralization of fiscal power in the hands of the Ministry of Revenue. Robert Hartwell concluded that the general commands fostered greater regional independence in revenue collection and expenditure.[5] Recent scholarship, in contrast, argues that the Ministry of Revenue exercised effective control over the general commands and the new system enhanced the capacity of the central fiscal administration to mobilize a greater share of locally collected revenues.[6] The general command system also strictly segregated fiscal operations from the

[4] Nagai Chiaki 長井千秋, "Waitō Sōryōjo no zaisei un'ei" 淮東総領所の財政運営, *Shigaku zasshi* 史学雑誌 101.7 (1992): 1235–66.

[5] Hartwell, "Imperial Treasuries," 75.

[6] Christian Lamouroux, "Fragmentation and Financial Recentralization: The Emergence of the Four General Commands (1127–1165)," in Franz-Julius Morche and Hilde de Weerdt (eds.), *Political Communication in Chinese and European History, 800–1600* (Amsterdam: Amsterdam University Press, 2021), pp. 105–41; Lei Jiasheng 雷家聖, *Julian mouguo: Nan Song Zonglingsuo yanjiu* 聚斂謀國: 南宋總領所研究 (Taipei: Wanjuanlou tushu gongsi, 2013). Charles Hartman has shown that during the 1160s–1180s there was a high degree of overlap between the key personnel in the general commands and the Ministry of Revenue. See Hartman, *Structures of Governance*, pp. 266–67, fig. 9.1.

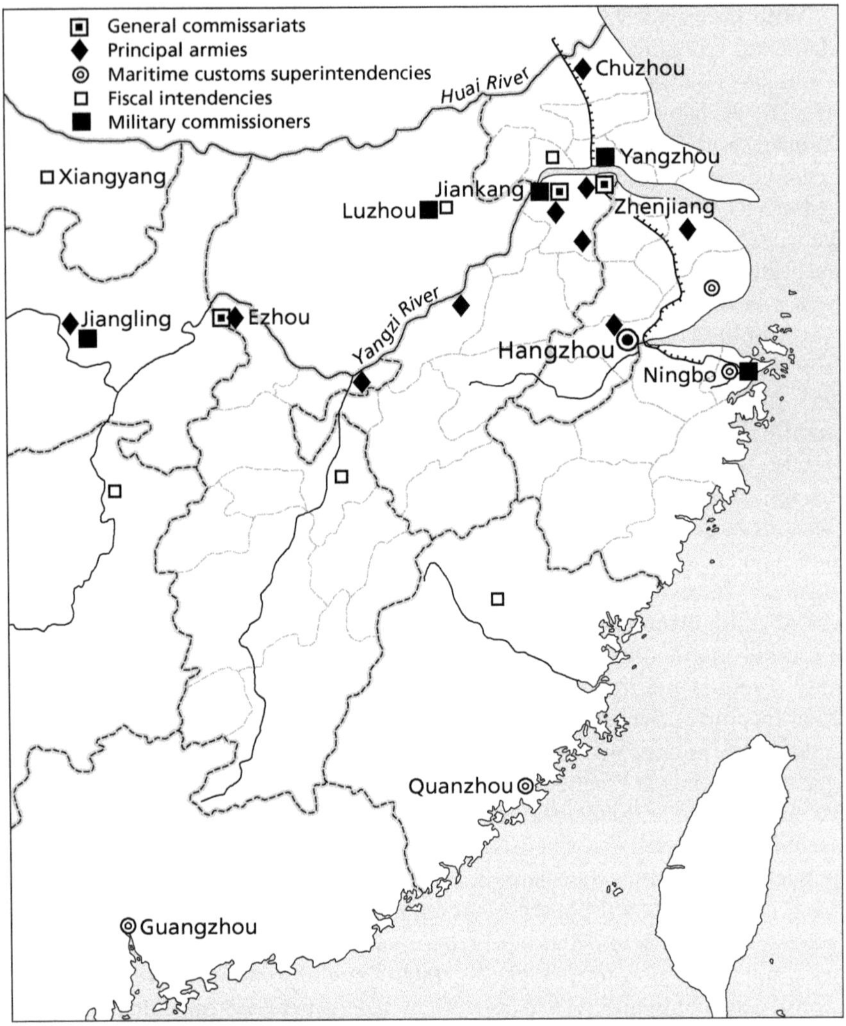

Map 5.2 Military procurement in southeastern China in the Southern Song.
Source: Adapted from Nagai 1992, "Waitō Sōryōjo," p. 1249, map 3. Reproduced from von Glahn, *Economic History of China*, p. 258, map 7.1.

military commanders, except in Sichuan, where Wu Lin was able to establish a de facto military satrapy after being appointed pacification commissioner in 1161. The Sichuan General Command – far removed from the capital – was largely under the purview of Wu Lin and his successors.

The progressive monetization of state finances that developed during the Northern Song further accelerated in the Southern Song. The frontier supply

Table 5.1 *Twice-a-year tax* shanggong *grain quotas*

Circuit	Northern Song quota (millions of *shi*)	Southern Song initial quota (millions of *shi*)	1159 new quota (millions of *shi*)
Huaidong and Huaixi	1.50	0	0
Jiangdong	0.99	0.93	0.85
Jiangxi	1.21	1.26	0.97
Hunan	0.65	0.65	0.55
Hubei	0.35	0.35	0.10
Liangzhe	1.50	1.50	0.85
Total	6.20	4.69	3.32

Source: Shimasue, *Sōdai zeisei shi kenkyū*, p. 447.

and defense funds and monthly sequestration funds diverted salt and liquor revenues formerly retained at the local level to the treasuries controlled by the Ministry of Revenue and the general commands. Grain revenues generated by the twice-a-year tax fell sharply during the Song–Jin wars of 1126–1141. Huainan, formerly one of the central government's principal sources of grain, had become the new defensive perimeter of the Southern Song and no longer delivered any tax grain to the central government (Table 5.1). Twice-a-year tax revenues (mostly derived from land taxes) generated only three-quarters of the grain quotas that local jurisdictions owed to the center (designated *shanggong* 上供); the remainder had to be obtained through "harmonious purchases," mostly in Liangzhe circuit. After the war with the Jin ended in 1142, the agrarian economy – especially in Jiangnan and Jiangxi – prospered, ensuring sufficient revenues for the state and ample supplies of grain in the private market. In 1159, the government formally reduced the *shanggong* grain quotas borne by localities to half the level of the Northern Song. Government agencies continued to make "harmonious purchases" through the market in the range of roughly 1.25 million *shi* per year, 40 percent of which was delivered to the general commands and the remainder stored at the capital for the upkeep of the imperial family, stipends for troops stationed at the capital, and famine relief reserves.[7]

The diminished importance of *shanggong* revenues further accelerated the shift from direct taxation on agricultural production to indirect taxes on

[7] Shimasue Kazuyasu 島居一康, *Sōdai zeisei shi kenkyū* 宋代税政史研究 (Tokyo: Kyūko shoin, 1993), pp. 445–81.

Table 5.2 *Revenues and expenditures of the general commands*

General command	Revenues from Quehuowu (1167) (millions of *guan*)	Expenditures (c. 1164–1173): Money (millions of *guan*)	Expenditures (c. 1164–1173): Grain (millions of *shi*)
Huaidong	4.0	7.0	0.7
Huaixi	12.0	12.0	0.7
Huguang	8.0	9.6	0.9
Total	24.0	28.6	2.3

Note: The Quehuowu was not the only source of revenues for the general commands, but we lack data on other income
Source: *CYZJ* jiaji, 17.388–91.

commerce and consumption that already had been a distinctive feature of the Song fiscal state. The income of the Quehuowu from monopoly licenses rose from 6.09 million *guan* in 1131 to 13 million in 1136 and continued to rise even after the armistice of 1142. By 1162, annual Quehuowu revenues totaled 21.65 million *guan*. In 1167, the revenue quota of the Quehuowu was fixed at 24 million *guan*, all of which would be apportioned to the general commands – except Sichuan, where the general command independently raised its revenues from local sources (Table 5.2).

Although we do not have complete figures for state revenues for the Southern Song period, the available data suggests that in the second half of the 12th century total cash revenues amounted to approximately 75 million *guan*, not much less than the peak total of 88 million *guan* attained in the New Policies era, when the empire's population probably was 40 percent larger (Tables 5.3, 5.4).[8] The general commands garnered the lion's share of revenues, chiefly in cash, which were expended on the armies defending the Jin frontier. A large portion of the receipts of the palace treasuries and the Ministry of Revenue also were dedicated to military expenses supporting the armies stationed in and around Hangzhou. The total number of soldiers mustered by the Southern Song state – 318,000 in 1160 – was significantly fewer than in the Northern Song, but costs per soldier rose. Still, the evidence suggests that from the 1140s to the end of the 12th century the general commands had adequate resources to meet their obligations.[9] The exception was the impoverished Huguang region, which required annual subventions from Sichuan and the palace treasuries.

[8] Wu Songdi has calculated the population in the 1180s (which he regards as the peak of the Southern Song period) as 12.9 million households, in contrast to the total Song population of 18.1 million households in 1102. Wu Songdi, *Nan Song renkou shi*, pp. 65, 196.

[9] Nagai, "Waitō Sōryōjo," pp. 1256–58.

Table 5.3 *Cash revenues in the Southern Song*

	Sichuan* (c. 1164–1173) (millions of *guan*)	Southeast circuits (c. 1185) (millions of *guan*)	Southeast circuits (variable dates) (millions of *guan*)
Shanggong portion of twice-a-year tax	2.0+	2.0	—
Liquor excise	2.78	—	6.3 (c. 1160)
Salt monopoly	1.87	—	27.0 (1169)
Tea monopoly	0.52	—	4.2 (c. 1175)
Total monopoly revenues and *hedi* income	—	44.9	—
Frontier supply and defense funds (*jingzong zhiqian*)	1.16	14.4	—
Monthly sequestration funds (*yuezhuangqian*)	NA	4.0	—
Paper money service fees	0.45	NA	—
Miscellaneous	0.17	NA	—
Total	8.95	65.3	—

Note: *Sichuan figures have been deflated by 50 percent because Sichuan revenues were calculated in *qianyin* paper money, which was worth roughly half of the bronze coin/*huizi* paper money in circulation in the southeast circuits.
Sources: *CYZJ* jiaji, 17.391; Guo Zhengzhong, "Nan Song zhongyang caizheng huobi suishou kaobian," p. 179, table 6; p. 181, table 8; Wang Shengduo, *Liang Song caizheng shi*, 2, p. 703, appendix table 4; 2, p. 706, appendix table 6; 2, p. 716, appendix table 7.

Although the demand for monetary revenues increased, minting of bronze coin fell sharply. The Southern Song retained control of the principal copper mines, but their ore deposits had been mostly exhausted, and the rising costs of coinage compelled the government to debase the coinage. In 1135, it was reported that coinage incurred substantial losses given that it cost 2.4 *guan* to mint 1,000 coins nominally worth 1 *guan*. Mint output continually lagged behind its target quota, set in the 1130s, of 500,000 *guan* per year, even though

Table 5.4 *Cash revenues of government agencies, 1190*

Southeastern circuits	Revenues (millions of *guan*)
Palace treasuries	9.65
Ministry of Revenue	18.72
General commands	29.01
Other military units	10.62
Total	68.0
Sichuan General Command*	8.05
Total	76.15

Note: *Sichuan figures have been deflated by 50 percent because Sichuan revenues were calculated in *qianyin* paper money.
Source: *SHY* shihuo 56.65a–68b.

Table 5.5 *Coin alloy standards in the Song period*

	1021 1-cash coin (*xiaoping*) mint standard	c. 1160 1-cash coin (*xiaoping*) mint standard	c. 1160 2-cash coin (*zhe'er* mint standard	Excavated specimens of Shaoxing (1130–1162) coins
Copper	56%	56%	39%	41–71%
Lead	37%	40%	30%	19–50%
Tin	7%	4%	31%	1–23%

Sources: Mint standards: Gao, *Huobi liutong*, pp. 168–69; Excavated specimens: Thierry, *Monnaies*, p. 340.

the mints mostly produced 2-*wen* (*zhe'er* 折二) coins. The *zhe'er* coins had twice the nominal value of the 1-*wen* (*xiaoping* 小平) coin but actually contained less copper (Table 5.5). In 1157, the Ministry of Revenue, while acknowledging that the mints normally produced only 140,000 *guan* of coin, requested an increase in the annual quota to 500,000 *guan*. Yet in 1161 mint output had fallen even further to only 101,000 *guan*. The annual quota was reduced to 150,000 *guan*, consisting of 18,000 strings of *xiaoping* coins and 66,000 strings of *zhe'er* coins. The debasement of the coinage unsurprisingly induced counterfeiting, especially of the overvalued *zhe'er* coins.[10]

To compensate for the diminished output of bronze coin, the role of silver in the Song fiscal administration expanded greatly over the course of the 12th

[10] Gao, *Huobi liutong*, pp. 165–70.

Table 5.6 *Annual state disbursements for military and official salaries, c. 1174–1189*

	Expenditures	Equivalent in coin[a]
Cash[b]	15,580,000 *guan*	15,580,000 *guan*
Silver	2,930,000 *liang*	9,670,000 *guan*
Gold	8,400 *liang*	333,640 *guan*
Silk yarn (絲綿)	1,180,000 *liang*	141,600 *guan*
Silk cloth (絹帛)	1,260,000 *pi*	3,780,000 *guan*
Sum of above	—	29,502,0000 *guan*
Total	—	30,000,000+ *guan*[c]

Notes: [a] Calculations based on current price data.
[b] The source does not indicate the proportions of bronze coin and *huizi* bills in this category; most likely the ratio was two-thirds *huizi* and one-third coin.
[c] Figure given in source.
Source: *CYZJ jiaji*, 17.381.

century. Both merchants and government officials commonly used silver as a means of remitting money across long distances. The Song government routinely converted various types of income to "light goods" (*qingji* 輕齎) for interregional transfers. While in the early Song period "light goods" referred almost exclusively to silk fabrics, by the end of the Northern Song the term had come to denote precious metals, especially silver, and paper instruments such as commodity licenses. By the early Southern Song, silk fabrics – long a staple of imperial China's fiscal system – no longer functioned as a form of money. Instead, silk goods received as tax payments were treated as articles of consumption and forwarded to the imperial household and army depots to be made into clothing.[11]

The government also turned to silver as a substitute for coin in tax collection and state disbursements. The supplementary consumption and capitation taxes (*jingzong zhiqian*), although denominated in coin, often were collected in silver. In 1161, owing to the shortage of coin, the state began to pay half of soldiers' salaries (and 60 percent of officials' stipends) in silver. In 1172, the formula for soldier's pay was set at 20 percent bronze coin, 30 percent silver, and 50 percent *huizi* bills.[12] A report dating from the Chunxi reign period (1174–1189) indicates that about 30 percent of actual expenditures for military and official salaries were indeed paid in silver (Table 5.6).

[11] Wang Wencheng 王文成, *Songdai baiyin huobihua yanjiu* 宋代白银货币化研究 (Kunming: Yunnan daxue chubanshe, 2001), pp. 126–39, 164–68.
[12] Gao, *Huobi liutong*, pp. 74–76.

Table 5.7 *Holdings of the Reserve Depository of the Left Treasury, 1186*

	Holdings	Equivalent in coin
Gold	800,000 *liang*	31,680,000 *guan*
Silver	1,860,000 *liang*	6,140,000 *guan*
Coin	5–6,000,000 *guan*	5–6,000,000 *guan*
Total	—	42–43,820,000 *guan*

Source: *CYZJ jiaji*, 17.383.

The new importance of precious metals in the Southern Song fiscal administration also is reflected in the substantial quantities of silver and gold held in state treasuries. An 1186 inventory of the holdings of the Reserve Depository of the Left Treasury (Zuocang fengzhuangku 左藏封樁庫), the government's principal emergency fund, shows that its holdings of precious metals greatly exceeded those in coin (Table 5.7). Although complete figures are lacking, one scholar has estimated that the state's average annual revenues in silver during the Southern Song amounted to at least 3 million *liang* (112,500 kg) per year (a figure equivalent to total annual silver disbursements for official salaries and military stipends, as we see in Table 5.6).[13] Still, silver remained a finite resource. To meet escalating military costs, the Southern Song government resorted to issuing paper currency – initially as an expediency, and ultimately as a necessity. In addition, silver came to perform a new and crucial function as the monetary reserve that backed the paper currencies issued by the Song state.

5.2 The Invention of *Huizi* Paper Money

In the midst of the wars against the Jin, the Song court readily resorted to paper bills to facilitate military procurement. In 1131, the court revived the practice of using *xianqian guanzi* 見錢關子 remittance bills to compensate merchants for "harmonious purchases" of grain to supply the army camps. The bills were to be redeemed at Quehuowu offices in Hangzhou or Shaoxing with a 10 percent premium.[14] But by 1135, the Quehuowu lacked sufficient cash reserves to redeem these *guanzi* bills. Merchants refused to accept them, and this practice was halted.[15] Early in 1136, a fiscal official, Zhang Cheng,

13 Wang Lingling 王菱菱, *Songdai kuangyeye yanjiu* 宋代矿冶业研究 (Baoding: Hebei daxue chubanshe, 2005), p. 137.

14 Li Xinchuan 李心傳, *Jianyan yilai xinian yaolu* 建炎以來繫年要錄 ([hereafter *XNYL*]; Beijing: Zhonghua shuju, 1988), 48.865.

15 *XNYL* 85.1391. See also Wang Shen 王申, "Cong bianqian dao zhibi: lun Shaoxing shiqi xianqian guanzi zhi dongnan huizi de yanjin guocheng" 从便钱到纸币：论绍兴时期见

proposed the creation – in imitation of the Sichuan precedent – of a *jiaozi* currency bureau at Hangzhou to issue *jiaozi* bills for circulation in Liangzhe and Jiangnan East and West circuits.[16] These *jiaozi* bills were intended both to finance "harmonious purchases" of grain supplies for the military and to circulate as paper currency in private market exchange. But this initiative immediately encountered a fierce storm of criticism, and three months later the project was canceled. Numerous reasons were cited for this swift reversal. Opponents claimed that although the Ministry of Revenue had ordered that 1.5 million *guan* in coin be set aside to redeem these bills, in fact there was no such reserve. Others voiced concerns that the bills could not be used in state payments; they would invite counterfeiting and fraud; the large (1-*guan*) denomination of the bills rendered them inconvenient for most market transactions; and they would incite price inflation and hoarding of bronze coin.[17] It appears that there were also private bills in circulation in the capital region at this time. These bills, variously referred to as "convenient cash checks" (*bianqian huizi* 便錢會子) or "consignment checks serving as convenient cash" (*jifu chong bianqian huizi* 寄付充便錢會子), were said to have been issued by "wealthy magnates" (*haoyou* 豪右), presumably consignment shops or deposit banks, perhaps even the *jiaoyinpu* exchange bill shops.[18] In 1135, the state banned the circulation of private *huizi* beyond the walls of Hangzhou, but the resulting hue and cry forced officials to rescind the ban the next day.[19] To what extent the government's attempt to introduce *jiaozi* into market exchange conflicted with the use of such private bills can only be guessed.

As the output of bronze coin by state mints slowed to a trickle, shortages of currency (once again referred to as "coin famines") began to cause acute distress. Scarcity of coin throttled trade, grain prices fell, and farmers found themselves trapped between deflation and mounting burdens of taxes and debts. In 1159, fiscal officials seized upon reports that private individuals were hoarding as much as a million strings of bronze coin to persuade the court to impose severe restrictions on savings of coin. Henceforth, private citizens were allowed to hold a maximum of 10,000 strings of coin (families of officials were allowed 20,000 strings). Any excess stocks of coin beyond these limits had to be surrendered to the government in exchange for commodity licenses or

钱关子至东南会子的演进过程, *Zhongguo shehui jingji shi yanjiu* 中国社会经济史研究 2019.3: 11–19. Hino asserted that the *xianqian guanzi* continued to be used for military procurement, but there is no evidence to confirm this, at least not before 1159 (see below). See Hino, "Gensen kōkyo," pp. 60–64.

16 *XNYL* 98.1611.

17 *XNYL* 101.1656–59. See also Wang Shengduo, *Liang Song huobi shi*, vol. 2, pp. 657–60.

18 Li Xinchuan 李心傳, *Jianyan yilai chaoye zaji*建炎以來朝野雜記 ([hereafter *CYZJ*]; Beijing: Zhonghua shuju, 2006), jiaji 甲集, 16.361. Li Shan and Lin Wenxun (*Chubi shi xinian*, p. 133) propose that "wealthy magnates" specifically referred to *jiaoyinpu*.

19 *XNYL* 93.1547–48.

silver.[20] The 1159 anti-hoarding law, though it probably had little effect on hoarding of coin, may have dealt a sharp blow to the private *huizi* by compromising the liquidity of money changers who issued such bills.

In the same year, the Ministry of Revenue proposed that the Quehuowu issue 2 million *guan* of bills of exchange to be dispatched to the general commands (800,000 *guan* of *xianqian gongju* 見錢公據 each to Huaixi and Huguang, and 400,000 *guan* of *xianqian guanzi* 見錢關子 to Huaidong) for "harmonious purchases" of military provisions. These bills were to be issued in five denominations ranging from 10 to 100 *guan* with terms of expiry (three years for *guanzi* and two years for *gongju*).[21] Issuing these bills in fixed denominations (albeit large ones) with terms of expiry suggests that the government expected that they would be exchanged in secondary markets, and perhaps even in commercial transactions. These *guanzi* and *gongju* bills were designated as "triple endorsement" (*san hetong* 三合同) bills, meaning that they could be redeemed – half in silver and half in coin – at the general commands at Ezhou, Jiankang, and Zhenjiang, which saved merchants the trouble of having to convey them to the capital for redemption.[22]

The following year, in early 1160, the newly appointed prefect at Hangzhou, Qian Duanli, began to issue *huizi* bills in the name of the prefectural government to augment its scarce cash reserves and to repay debts to merchants it had accumulated over a number of years. The bills issued by the prefectural government were deemed legal tender within the capital, but private bills continued to circulate without restriction.[23] Later in 1160, Qian was promoted to a major post in the Ministry of Revenue, where he began to campaign for the central government to take over the issue of *huizi*, emphasizing their utility as a means of financing the military.[24] With renewed war with the Jin looming, the court readily agreed. In early 1161, the government established a Capital

20 *XNYL* 182.3025.

21 *XNYL* 182.3021.

22 On these "triple endorsement" bills, see Kaneko Yasuharu 金子泰晴, "Nan-Sō shoki no Kokō Sōryōjo to sangōdō kanshi" 南宋初期の湖廣総領所と三合同関子, *Shikan* 史観 123 (1990): 34–46.

23 *XNYL* 187.3129; *CYZJ* jiaji, 16.361. These sources do not specifically date the inauguration of Qian's *huizi* policy, but it surely must have begun between the time of his appointment as prefect in the second month of 1160 and his promotion to acting vice-minister of revenue four months later. See Li and Lin, *Chubi xinian*, p. 134.

24 In his new post, Qian instructed the Quehuowu to issue 3 million *guan* of *gongju* and *guanzi* to the general commands to stockpile grain supplies. See *XNYL* 185.3102. Qian Duanli enjoyed high repute as a fiscal expert, and his promotion of *huizi* clearly was aimed at strengthening the fiscal capacity of the Song state in anticipation of a new outbreak of hostilities with Jin. But Qian himself was skeptical that the Song could marshal sufficient fiscal resources to sustain prolonged warfare against the Jin, and he played a key role in the peace negotiations of 1165. See Hartman, *Structures of Governance*, pp. 296–97, 347.

Huizi Bureau (Xingzai huiziwu 行在會子務; later placed under the aegis of the tea agency of the Quehuowu) to commence issuing the new bills. The *huizi* bills, issued in three denominations of 1, 2, and 3 *guan* (smaller denominations of 200, 300, and 500 *wen* were added from 1164), were to be accepted in state payments and expenditures as well as private transactions. At first the actual printing was assigned to Huizhou prefecture, a major papermaking center, but soon this responsibility was transferred to Chengdu, which had long experience in printing the *qianyin* bills used in Sichuan.[25]

As noted above, private exchange bills had circulated in the capital region since at least the beginning of the Southern Song period. It is difficult to say how extensively these bills were used. Hong Kuo, while serving as prefect in Huizhou during 1159–1161, informed the Ministry of Revenue that because of the region's rugged terrain and poor transport little coin was available in local markets, and instead commercial transactions were conducted using *huizi* bills.[26] Whether Hong was referring to the *huizi* bills circulating in Hangzhou or a purely local contrivance is unclear, but Huizhou in fact had relatively good waterway connections to Hangzhou. It appears that during his tenure as prefect at Hangzhou Qian Duanli deliberately sought to usurp the place of private bills in the marketplace. According to one contemporary observer, the state-issued *huizi* bills were modeled after private bills such as *jifu huizi*.[27] The historian Li Xinchuan, writing several decades later, described Qian as "seizing the profit [yielded by *huizi*] and restoring it to the government."[28] In any event, the state-issued *huizi* bills were warmly greeted by the public and soon drove the private bills out of circulation.[29]

The government apparently did not set a fixed quota for the volume of *huizi* to be issued. Hong Mai, a contemporary, wrote that initially 500,000 *guan* were printed at Huizhou, but subsequently larger quantities were issued. Dai Zhi, writing in the 1230s, asserted that the volume of *huizi* "in total did not

25 *XNYL* 188.3150. In 1168, when *huizi* were made permanent, the printing of bills was moved to Hangzhou.

26 Hong Kuo 洪适, "Hubu qi mian fa xianqian zhazi" 戶部乞免發見錢劄子, in *Panzhou wenji* 盤洲文集 (SBCK ed.), *Panzhou shiyi* 盤洲拾遺, 27a.

27 Wei Jing 衛涇, "Zhi Fuzhou ri shang miaotang lun chubi lihai zhazi" 知福州日上廟堂論楮幣利害劄子, *Houle ji*後樂集 ([hereafter *HLJ*]; SKQS ed.), 15.9a.

28 奪其利而歸於官, *CYZJ* jiaji, 16.361.

29 Hino Kaisaburō, "Nan-Sō Rin'anfu no shika kaishi ni tsuite" 南宋臨安府の私下會子について, in *Hino Kaisaburō ronshū*, vol. 7: *Sōdai no kahei to kin'yū* (II) (Tokyo, 1983), p. 209. Several sources reported that *huizi* initially circulated at a premium above their face value: Hong Mai 洪邁, *Rongzhai suibi* 容齋隨筆 ([hereafter *RZSB*]; Shanghai: Shanghai guji chubanshe, 1978), sanbi 三筆, 14.584–85; Dai Zhi 戴埴, "Shuquan yuanliu" 楮券源流, *Shupu* 鼠璞 ([hereafter *SP*]; SKQS ed.), shang 上, 36b.

exceed 4 million *guan*."[30] Dai presumably was referring to the amount issued per year. In the first month of 1167, vice-minister of revenue Tang Zhuan reported that from 1161 to mid 1166, 28 million *guan* of *huizi* were issued (i.e., 5 million per year), of which 15.6 million had been redeemed by the end of 1166; excluding the amount held by government agencies, 9.8 million *guan* remained in circulation "among the people."[31] To inject the *huizi* bills into the economy, the court authorized proportional formulas (known as *pinda* 品搭) for payment of official salaries (60 percent silver, 40 percent *huizi*) and military stipends (50 percent silver, 30 percent coin, 20 percent *huizi*).[32] An 1161 edict expanded the zone of circulation for *huizi* to include all of the Song territories north of the Yangzi River (that is to say, the Song–Jin border areas) as well as Jiangnan. Most localities were allowed to submit their *shanggong* tax revenues half in *huizi* and half in coin; in areas poorly served by water transport, the entire *shanggong* payment could be delivered using *huizi* bills.[33] Huizi depositories (Huiziku 會子庫) were established at all major military bases to facilitate their circulation. Despite these official policies, local administrators were reluctant to accept *huizi* in tax payments. In 1165, the government reset the formula for tax remittances at 80 percent coin and 20 percent *huizi*, and the *huizi* portion was further reduced to 10 percent in the following year.[34] Moreover, although in principle the bills were convertible with coin, the state had set aside only nominal reserves to back them. As a result, *huizi* began to depreciate in private markets.

Emperor Xiaozong (r. 1162–1189), a committed revanchist but scrupulously cautious in fiscal affairs, had been skeptical about the new paper currency from the outset. After the new truce with the Jurchen was concluded in 1165, Xiaozong resisted the pleas of his fiscal officials to expand the issue of *huizi*. Instead, Xiaozong resolved to withdraw *huizi* from circulation altogether. At the close of 1166, he ordered that 2 million *liang* (75,000 kg) of silver be disbursed from the Inner Palace Treasury and the Southern Depository of the Left Treasury (Zuocang nanku 左藏南庫) – a new fiscal organ created in 1162 as a reserve for military emergencies – to redeem and retire the *huizi* bills. Officials in the Ministry of Revenue objected to Xiaozong's decision, arguing that it was impossible to withdraw all the *huizi* bills without causing disruption in the marketplace, and in the summer of

30 *RZSB* sanbi, 14.584–85; Dai Zhi, "Shuquan yuanliu," in *SP* shang, 36b. According to Qian Duanli's biography, several million *guan* were issued within the space of several months. See *SS* 385.11829.

31 *WXTK* 9.98c. Li Xinchuan recorded the same data but without mentioning his source. See *CYZJ* jiaji, 16.362.

32 *XNYL* 180.3159.

33 *XNYL* 191.3203–4.

34 *SHY* shihuo 44.9a–b.

1167 Xiaozong assented to allowing the 4.9 million *guan* of *huizi* still in circulation to continue. Four months later Xiaozong approved a new issue of 5 million *guan* to replace the worn bills.[35]

By redeeming the bills with silver, however, the state inadvertently boosted popular confidence in *huizi*, and their market value rebounded. In the summer of 1168, Xiaozong convened a court conference to discuss the viability of the *huizi* currency. The state councilor Jiang Fu, pointing to the recent success of the policy of using silver to redeem *huizi*, argued that if the value of *huizi* faltered the court could simply reprise the strategy of retiring excess bills with hard currency. Others invoked the chartalist principles of the *Guan Zi* to assure Xiaozong that the power and authority to leverage (*quan* 權) the value of the currency lay in the sovereign's hands. In the end, Xiaozong was persuaded to retain the *huizi* currency on a permanent basis.[36] Following the precedents for the Sichuan paper currencies, in the first month of 1169 the court formally declared the inauguration of issue number one (第一界) of new *huizi* bills with a total quota of 10 million *guan* to replace the *huizi* currently in use.[37] (Old bills had to be exchanged for new ones by the third month of 1169.) The new *huizi* would have a three-year term of expiry, in contrast to the two-year terms for the *qianyin* bills already circulating in Sichuan, but no longer would be convertible with coin.[38] Shortly afterward, the court decided to imitate the practice in Sichuan of having two issues circulate simultaneously and commenced printing #2 *huizi* bills,[39] bringing the total amount in circulation to 20 million *guan*.[40]

35 *CYZJ* jiaji, 16.362; *WXTK* 9.99a; *SS* 388.11901.

36 Wu Yong 吳泳, "Qian-Chun jianglun huizi wushi" 乾淳講論會子五事, *Helin ji* 鶴林集 ([hereafter *HeLJ*]; SKQS ed.), 15.27b–28a.

37 For this dating, see *CYZJ* jiaji, 16.362; Liu Zheng 留正, *Huang Song zhongxing liangchao shengzheng* 皇宋中興兩朝聖政 ([hereafter *LCSZ*]; Wanwei biecang ed.; rpt. Taipei: Wenhai chubanshe, 1967), 56.2b; Wang Yinglin 王應麟, *Yuhai* 玉海 ([hereafter *YH*]; 1883 ed., rpt. Nanchang: Jiangsu guji chubanshe, 1988), 180.40b. Other sources date the inauguration of the first issue of *huizi* to 1168: see Zhang Ruyu 章如愚, *Shantang qunshu kaosuo* 山堂群書考索 (1521 ed.; rpt. in BTZB), houji 後集 52.13a; *WXTK* 9.99a; *SS* 181.4407. Since the formal issue of *huizi* on a permanent basis surely followed the court debate in the summer of 1168 discussed at the beginning of this paragraph, I am inclined to accept the dating of the first month of 1169. Other scholars have accepted the date of 1168: see Kusano Yasushi 草野靖, "Nan-Sō gyōzai kaishi no hatten (II)" 南宋行在会子の発展 (下), *Tōyō gakuhō* 東洋学報 49.2 (1966): 193; Li and Lin, *Chubi shi xinian*, 146–48; Gao, *Huobi liutong*, p. 186. Bao Weimin notes the discrepancy but takes no position on which is correct. See Bao Weimin 包伟民, *Songshi shihuozhi buzheng* 宋史食货志补正 (Beijing: Zhonghua shuju, 2008), vol. 2, p. 484.

38 *WXTK* 9.99a; *SS* 181.4407. The new bills were stamped with a seal reading "Supervisory Office of the Huizi Depository" (Tiling cuozhi huiziku 提領措置會子庫).

39 Hereafter I will refer to the issue numbers of *huizi* using this formula: #n. For a list of all issues, see Table 6.1.

40 *CYZJ* jiaji, 16.362; *LCSZ* 56.2b.

Although the government declared that the choice of payment in private transactions should "follow the people's convenience," policymakers recognized that requiring the use of *huizi* in state payments would be crucial to maintaining their market value. Shortly after Qian Duanli inaugurated the issue of *huizi* in Hangzhou, Shi Hao – then tutor to the crown prince, the future Xiaozong, who would elevate him to the office of state councilor in 1163 – had enthusiastically endorsed *huizi* as a means of solving several problems at once, including deterring the drain of bronze coin to the Jin territories. Shi also recommended that the government accept *huizi* in state payments, encourage their use in private transactions and moneylending, and enforce an official rate of exchange with bronze coin. By requiring *huizi* in state payments, the rich would be forced to dishoard coin to obtain the bills, and bronze coin would accumulate in state treasuries.[41]

Although local officials often were reluctant to accept *huizi* in payment of twice-a-year taxes, the bills became a crucial feature of the central government's fiscal operations. In the early 1160s, amid renewed war with Jin, the Song allowed merchants to purchase salt, tea, and alum licenses using a *pinda* formula of 60 percent "light goods" (*qingji*, referring here to silver and *xianqian guanzi*/*xianqian gongju* bills) and 40 percent in coin. But in practice, according to a Ministry of Revenue report in late 1166, merchants mostly used *huizi* to purchase monopoly commodity licenses. With its coin reserves depleted, the ministry reset the *pinda* payment ratio to half in coin and half in *huizi*.[42] From this time onward, *huizi* replaced *xianqian guanzi* and *xianqian gongju* remittance bills in state payments, and the latter – which primarily had been used for "harmonious purchases" of military supplies – largely disappeared from circulation.[43] In 1168, an allocation of 1.25 million *guan* for "harmonious purchases" consisted of 56 percent "newly printed" *huizi*, 22 percent coin, and 22 percent silver.[44] In the summer of 1169, shortly after the decision to make *huizi* permanent, an edict decreed that all payments to the state must be made half in coin and half in *huizi*.[45] But in early 1171, the

[41] Shi Hao 史浩, "Linbi ciri jin neixiu bashi zhazi" 臨陛辭日進內修八事箚子, *Maofeng zhenyin manlu* 鄮峯真隱漫錄 (SKQS ed.), 9.8a.

[42] *SHY* shihuo 27.9a–b, 27.21b–22a.

[43] In 1169, the state formally ceased to accept *xianqian guanzi* bills as payment for commodity licenses, although there is evidence that merchants continued to use them into the early 1170s. Liang Gengyao 梁庚堯, *Nan Song yanque: Shiyan chanxiao yu zhengfu kongzhi* 南宋鹽榷:食鹽產銷與政府控制 (Taipei: Guoli Taiwan daxue chubanshe, 2010), pp. 127–30.

[44] *SHY* shihuo 40.47b–48a, 41.5a–b. In the following year, "several million *guan*" of *huizi* were allocated to the Huaidong, Huaixi, and Huguang general commands for "harmonious purchases." *SHY* shihuo 41.6a.

[45] Xie Shenfu 謝深甫 (ed.), *Qingyuan tiaofa shilei* 慶元條法事類 ([hereafter *QYTF*]; Seikado Library ms., rpt. Taipei: Xinwenfeng chubanshe, 1976), 47.426. Another source

portion of *huizi* in *shanggong* payments was lowered from 50 to 30 percent, and later the same year reports that local officials demanded full payment in coin prompted the court to enact harsh penalties for officials who did not abide by the 70/30 *pinda* formula.[46] The exchange rate of *huizi* – officially set at 770 *wen* – slipped to 610–620 *wen* in marketplaces, prompting the government to take a more aggressive approach to shore up their value. An imperial directive issued in 1173 restored the 50/50 coin-*huizi* formula for state payments and disbursements.[47] Subsequently, the government steadfastly maintained this 50–50 *pinda* formula, with a few exceptions.[48]

Still, Emperor Xiaozong remained dubious about the long-term viability of paper currency. At the beginning of 1175, in a private communication with Ye Heng, whom he had just appointed as chief state councilor after long service as vice-minister of revenue, Xiaozong expressed his concerns that popular confidence in their worth would not endure. Declaring that "for ten years I have not been able to sleep soundly because of *huizi*," the emperor proposed that Ye should disburse silver and coin from various sources – 9 million *guan* in the Ministry of Revenue treasuries, 5 million from the Inner Palace Treasury, and 7 million in *shanggong* revenues from Sichuan – to retire the 22 million *guan* of *huizi* then in circulation.[49] It is not clear how far Ye went to implement this plan, but less than six months later officials were reporting shortages of *huizi* for purposes such as military stipends. Mystified by this turn of events, Emperor Xiaozong sought explanation from his ministers. Ye Heng replied that while *huizi* comprised half of the Ministry of Revenue's annual revenue of 12 million *guan*, the Southern Depository had disbursed silver to redeem 4 million *guan* of *huizi*, leaving only 2 million *guan* still in circulation. Taxpayers thus were encountering difficulties obtaining the *huizi* they needed for payments. The other state councilor, Gong Maoliang, chimed in to say that merchants preferred *huizi* over coin because they were more convenient to carry, exempt from transit taxes, and no longer subjected to discounting. Although the emperor marveled at the unexpected success of the paper currency, he demurred from his state councilors' request to increase the issue of paper currency, opting for a more deliberate wait-and-see

dates this edict to the intercalary fifth month of 1170: *LCSZ*, 48.13a. The *Song shi* biography of Qiu Chong (*SS* 398.12110) suggests that Qiu, while serving as prefect of Suzhou, was the progenitor of this edict, but he did not take up that office until 1172.

46 *SHY* shihuo 35.42a–b.; *QYTF* 30.319.

47 *QYTF* 30.319.

48 For example, the government was in a stronger position to demand payment in hard currency for the lucrative commodity monopoly licenses. In 1173, the Quehuowu won approval to demand that a minimum of 40 percent of the payments for salt and tea licenses be made in silver; the rest could be paid in *huizi* or coin. *SHY* shihuo 27.42a.

49 *SS* 384.11823–24; Dai Zhi, "Shuquan yuanliu," in *SP* shang, 36b–37a.

strategy.[50] Still, a year later, in 1176, Xiaozong extended the term of expiry for #3 and #4 *huizi* for an additional three years as well as authorizing the emission of an additional 2 million *guan* of #4 *huizi* to be allocated to the Southern Depository.[51]

Amid the debates over monetary policy at the Xiaozong court, advocates of paper currency stressed two key principles: maintaining balance among different forms of money and ensuring their acceptability in state payments. During one of these conferences in 1166, Xiaozong declared that "paper currency can be implemented in certain places as long as reserves of coin are used to maintain equilibrium (*chengti* 稱提)."[52] "Maintaining equilibrium" (*chengti*) became a technical term in monetary policy for regulating the relative quantities of coin and paper money. Depreciation of paper currency was attributed to an excess supply of bills relative to the amount of coin in circulation (as opposed to the relative demands for money and goods). A variety of *chengti* strategies could be employed to reestablish equilibrium: (1) implicitly backing fiat currency with hard currency by redeeming excess bills with silver or coin; (2) replacing old issues with a smaller quantity of new issues, often discounting the old bills; (3) mandating that some portion of tax payments be made in paper currency; and (4) requiring merchants to use paper currency to purchase commodity licenses.[53] Although Song officials recognized that depreciation of paper currency induced inflation, they were preoccupied not with balancing the supply of goods with the demand for money but rather with maintaining an equilibrium between paper currency and bronze coin. Applying the old metaphor of the "mutual balance between child and mother" to the current monetary situation, coin was deemed the "mother" currency, and paper money the "child." Paper currency thus was conceived as a subordinate currency whose value ultimately derived from the stock of bronze coin. A prevalent theme in the discourse about money during the Southern Song period was the necessity for state intervention to maintain the equilibrium (expressed as "balancing," *quan* 權) between coin and paper currencies.[54]

50 *LCSZ* 54.1b–2b; Wu Yong, "Huizi wushi," *HeLJ* 15.28a–b. *Huizi* were exempted from transit duties in 1168: *QYTF* 36.375.

51 *WXTK* 9.99a; *SS* 181.4407.

52 楮幣在處可行,但須得本錢稱提乃可. *CYZJ* jiaji, 16.362.

53 Tian Liying 田黎英, "Chengti zhi shuo: Nan Song de zhibi guanli lilun" 称提之说：南宋的纸币管理理论, *Zhongguo qianbi* 中国钱币 1986.1: 51–55; Wang Shengduo 汪圣铎, "Nan Song dui huizi de liangci daguimo 'chengti'" 南宋对会子的两次大规模'称提', *Zhongguo qianbi* 中国钱币 1993.1: 15–20.

54 What passed unmentioned in the debates about paper currency, however, was the issue of specie convertibility. It was the state's willingness to accept paper bills in public payments, not the obligation to redeem paper bills with coin or bullion, that ensured popular confidence in their value. As we have seen, during Xiaozong's reign the use of silver as

Of course, the diminished supply of bronze coin and the state's inability to mint new coin in sufficient quantities compelled an alternative strategy: relying on silver to serve – implicitly, at least – as the monetary reserve backing *huizi*. During the court conference about the feasibility of the *huizi* currency held in 1170 some officials noted that in times of military or economic crisis popular confidence in the value of paper money evaporates, while the price of silver soars. They urged the court to take advantage of the current period of calm, when the price of silver was relatively low, to buy up stocks of silver as preparation against future emergencies.[55] Although the court's response to this proposal is unknown, in subsequent fiscal and monetary crises it typically disbursed silver rather than bronze coin to redeem excess paper money in circulation. As we have seen, in 1175 the Ministry of Revenue disbursed 4 million *guan* of silver and gold to remove *huizi* from circulation, and the rebound in the value of the paper currency persuaded Xiaozong to abandon his plan to withdraw *huizi*.

The implicit promise that *huizi* were backed by silver reserves succeeded in reviving popular confidence in their worth. In a memorial of 1175, Xin Qiji reported that whereas the market exchange ratio for *huizi* had dipped to 610–620 coins per *guan* a few years before, now it had recovered to well over 700 coins, and in some places the bills traded at a premium, thanks to the *chengti* measures adopted by the court. But Xin urged more action to expand their range of circulation, which was mostly limited to the capital region and the military bases. He emphasized tax policy as the mechanism for spreading *huizi* to distant provinces and rural hinterlands, proposing that the more affluent taxpayers (the top three ranks in the five-rank categorization of household wealth) should pay 70 percent of their tax obligations in *huizi*. Xin even floated the idea that the government should require that 50 percent of private land sales transactions be paid in *huizi*.[56]

Despite gnawing doubts about the wisdom of relying on paper currency, Emperor Xiaozong concluded that the *chengti* policies had worked successfully. In 1179, when the vice-minister of revenue requested suspension of the policy allowing soldiers to convert the *huizi* portion of their stipends to coin or silver, Xiaozong reluctantly agreed to a temporary halt. "We have heard that recently the people greatly esteem *huizi*, to the point that their value equals that of bronze coin," Xiaozong declared, "but if We had failed to cherish *huizi* and issued them in excessive quantities, how could We have achieved our

a notional reserve currency backing the *huizi* bills played a crucial role in supporting the value of the latter. By the 13th century, however, state treasuries lacked sufficient stocks of either silver or coin to redeem paper money, rendering moot the question of specie convertibility.

55 *SHY* shihuo 56.7b–8a; *CYZJ* jiaji, 16.362.

56 Xin Qiji 辛棄疾, "Lun xingyong huizi shu" 論行用會子疏, in *MCZY* 272.13a–14b.

present success?"[57] A year later the state councilor Zhao Xiong lauded the emperor saying, "we can now see the benefits of Your Majesty's *chengti* strategy, to the point where the value of *huizi* exceeds that of coin." In reply, Xiaozong brusquely retorted, "the benefits accrue to the Subcelestial Realm; the power to maintain balance (*quan*) resides with the court" (利在天下,權在朝廷).[58] In Xiaozong's eyes, the success of *huizi* paper currency should be credited to his own vigilant stewardship. Perhaps there was some truth to this claim. After Xiaozong abdicated in favor of his son, who reigned as Emperor Guangzong (r. 1189–1194), the prudent restraint he exercised over the issue of paper currency faded away.

5.3 Institutionalization of Multiple Currency Zones in the Southern Song

Although humbled by the failure of his offensive against the Jin in 1163–1164, Emperor Xiaozong did not abandon his revanchist ambitions. He established new treasuries, including the Southern Depository of the Left Treasury, that siphoned revenues from the operating budget of the Ministry of Revenue to build up monetary reserves in preparation for a future offensive. In 1167, Xiaozong created a new Budget Department (Guoyongsi 國用司) that in effect displaced the Ministry of Revenue in management of tax receipts and expenditures not only for the armies and the civil offices at the capital but also for the general commands. The Reserve Depository of the Left Treasury, established by Xiaozong in 1177 and supervised by palace administrators, superseded the Southern Depository and consolidated control over key revenue sources. The Reserve Depository also was the principal repository of the state's reserve *huizi* funds.[59] The new fiscal superstructure diminished the role of the Ministry of Revenue and left it dependent on regular infusions of funds from the treasuries under the thumb of the emperor and palace personnel.[60]

Xiaozong also engaged in a "currency war," withdrawing bronze coins from the border areas to prevent them from draining into Jin territories, where the value of bronze coin was significantly higher. In 1165, the government created a new iron currency zone in Huainan, the main battleground between the Song and Jin, transferring 150,000 *guan* of iron coins from Sichuan to

57 Xiaozong's language here (*bu aixi huizi* 不愛惜會子) invokes Kong Yi's hallowed metalist defense of full-bodied money (see Chapter 1).

58 Both of these dialogues were recorded in Wu Yong, "Huizi wushi," *HeLJ* 15.29a. In 1186, Xiaozong exulted that "soldiers and civilians alike prefer *huizi* to coin." But he still opposed increasing the quantity of *huizi* in circulation. See *LCSZ* 63.5a.

59 Umehara, "Naizō to sazō," pp. 161–62.

60 Christian Lamouroux and Richard von Glahn, "Public Finance, 1000–1800," in Debin Ma and Richard von Glahn (eds.), *The Cambridge Economic History of China* (Cambridge: Cambridge University Press, 2022), vol. 1, pp. 351–52.

Huainan, followed shortly afterwards by the introduction of another new paper currency, *huaijiao* 淮交, specifically limited to the Huainan region.[61] Initially, the *huaijiao* were standard *huizi* bills countermarked with an inscription confining their use to the Huainan region, but in 1166 distinctive *huaijiao* bills were printed in denominations of 200, 300, and 500 *wen* and 1 *guan* of iron coins. These actions enabled the government to withdraw bronze coin from Huainan. The *huaijiao* failed to win acceptance though, and *huizi* once again were allowed to circulate in the region. In 1170, as part of its strategy to convert Huainan to an iron currency standard, the court established iron coin mints throughout the region. In 1172, the government began to withdraw the *huaijiao* from circulation (exchanging current bills with standard *huizi*), although they did not fully disappear, and Huainan remained an iron currency zone. The court repeatedly sought to buy up bronze coin in Huainan by disbursing *huizi* in exchange, and *huizi* prevailed as the crucial means of commercial exchange in the region.[62]

Huainan's monetary system continued to experience difficulties, however. Although the region's agricultural economy had recuperated from the disruptions of the Song–Jin wars, it remained an underpopulated frontier zone that attracted few merchants. Huainan's iron currency hindered interregional trade: merchants entering Huainan were obliged to convert their bronze coin or *huizi* to iron coin, which was the region's only legal tender. In the 1180s, the output of Huainan's mints soared even as the quality of iron coin degraded, inviting rampant counterfeiting.

By the early 1190s, the problem of counterfeit iron coin reached epidemic proportions, leading to the dismissal of a raft of officials, including prefects as well as fiscal and judicial intendants, for failing to curb their use. An official named Liu Wei was appointed to a plenipotentiary office to resolve the problem. Liu's draconian actions to suppress counterfeit coin (for example, discounting private coins by 50 percent and refusing to accept them in state payments) provoked uproar among the populace and soldiers stationed in Huainan, who were accustomed to accepting iron coins without discrimination. Now all iron coins were deemed suspect, and even state-issued coins suffered steep depreciation. According to Ye Shi, then a prefect in Huainan, 300–400 out of every 1,000 coins were rejected in the marketplace.[63] In response, the government reduced mint output, delivered several million *guan* of *huizi* to Huainan to buy up iron coin, and raised the *pinda* ratio for

[61] *CYZJ* jiaji, 16.360; *WXTK* 9.100b.

[62] *LCSZ* 60.15b.

[63] Ye Shi, "Huaixi lun tieqian wushi zhuang" 淮西論鐵錢五事狀, *Shuixin wenji* 水心文集 2, in *YSJ*, 1, pp. 20–24.

state payments to two-thirds iron coin and one-third *huizi*.[64] But these measures failed to calm the markets in Huainan, and at the beginning of 1192 Liu was dismissed.[65]

Resurrecting the *huaijiao* paper currency then became the focus of the court's strategy to address the iron currency crisis in Huainan. In the summer of 1192, at the instigation of Zhao Ruyu (then minister of the civil service, but promoted to chief state councilor in 1194), the government issued 3 million *guan* of *huaijiao* (two-thirds in Huaidong, one-third in Huaixi) in denominations of 200 *wen*, 500 *wen*, and 1 *guan*. Zhao and others had become convinced that the depreciation of Huainan iron coin resulted from excess supply, in part due to counterfeiting, which could be remedied by replacing coin with paper currency. The court settled on two tactics to ensure the success of *huaijiao*. The first was to allow the bills to serve as legal tender in areas along the southern bank of the Yangzi River (the "eight prefectures along the Yangzi" 沿江八州軍), which would integrate Huainan into a larger commercial network. Taxpayers in the eight prefectures also would be allowed to substitute *huaijiao* for the *huizi* portion (50 percent) of their *shanggong* payments. The second tactic was to require that merchants use *huaijiao* to purchase licenses for salt, by far Huainan's most important commodity. The initial plan was to require payments half in *huaijiao* and half in iron coin, but this was adjusted to 30 percent each in *huizi* and iron coin and 40 percent in *huaijiao*.[66]

Officials in Huainan remained divided over the reintroduction of *huaijiao* paper currency. Wei Jing, then the Huaidong salt monopoly intendant, warmly endorsed the policy.[67] But Yang Wanli, commissioner of the Huaixi General Command, voiced vehement opposition. Yang observed that iron coin sufficed for the fiscal needs of the Huainan military bases, and the fixed allocations of silver, iron coin, and *huizi* paid as stipends to soldiers could not be easily changed. Moreover, introducing the *huaijiao* to the eight prefectures south of the Yangzi would create havoc, since the bills were incompatible with the bronze coin that circulated there. Ultimately Yang fell back on a theoretical argument: coin – whether bronze or iron – was the "mother" currency (i.e., the monetary standard), and paper money merely the "child" (subsidiary currency). To allow the *huaijiao* to circulate in bronze-coin-using

[64] In 1191, the government disbursed 2 million *guan* of *huizi* and 250,000 *shi* of rice (with a market value of 400,000 *guan*) to repurchase counterfeit iron coin in the region. Takahashi, *Genchō kahei*, p. 260.

[65] This episode is examined in detail in Wang Shengduo, *Liang Song huobi shi*, vol. 2, pp. 590–96.

[66] *CYZJ* jiaji, 16.364; Anon., *Liangchao gangmu beiyao* 兩朝綱目備要 ([hereafter *LCGM*]; SKQS ed.), 2.13a–14a; *SHY* shihuo 28.38a.

[67] Wei Jing, "Shang Liu chengxiang zhazi" 上留丞相箚子, *HLJ* 14.20b–22a; *SHY* shihuo 28.38a.

areas would be akin to having a "motherless child," which hardly would be welcomed by the local inhabitants.[68] Invited by the court to discuss the matter, Yu Chou, the vice-intendant for grain tribute in Huaidong, reported that although iron coin was deeply unpopular in Huainan, the inhabitants welcomed *huaijiao*, and he urged the court to retain the paper currency.[69] Chen Zao, a native of the region then serving as a magistrate in Ningbo, wrote a letter to Zhao Ruyu arguing that the chief monetary problem in Huainan was not a surfeit of iron coin but the overvaluation of *huizi*, and he urged the court to adopt policies to strengthen both iron coin and *huaijiao*, including expanding the iron currency zone south of the Yangzi.[70] Zhu Xi, the leading figure in the Learning of the Way (Daoxue 道學) movement within Confucian philosophical circles, endorsed using both iron coin and *huaijiao* in Huainan as buffers to prevent the drain of bronze coin across the frontier to Jin territories. But Zhu proposed that the Yangzi River should serve as a barrier between the *huaijiao* and capital *huizi* spheres of circulation, and like his fellow Daoxue adherent Yang Wanli he insisted that *huaijiao* should not be allowed to circulate in the territories south of the Yangzi.[71]

In the end, the court decided to retain the *huaijiao* paper currency (without extending their use to the eight prefectures), yet Huainan's monetary situation remained unstable. Salt merchants regarded the *huaijiao* with disfavor. To appease them, the portion of *huaijiao* required for purchasing salt licenses was reduced to 20 percent and in 1202 abolished altogether (merchants were allowed to pay half in iron coin and half in *huizi* instead).[72] But in 1212, *huaijiao* once again were to be utilized in payments merchants made to the Quehuowu; while the Quehuowu office at Zhenjiang would only accept iron coin and *huizi*, the office at Jiankang would accept *huaijiao*, *huizi*, and iron coin (in unspecified proportions), and payments at Zhenzhou would be made in *huaijiao* and *huizi*.[73] This decision followed on the heels of another attempt in 1209 to expand the iron currency zone to include the eight prefectures south of the Yangzi, which instantly caused turmoil and was quickly rescinded. Huainan's iron coin continued to depreciate: the exchange ratio of 1 *guan huizi* = 1.5 *guan* iron coin reported by Chen Zao in 1194 fell to 1:2.3 in 1212 and to 1:3.4 in the early 1220s, and at times was said to have

[68] Yang Wanli 楊萬里, "Qi ba Jiangnan zhoujun tieqian huizi zouyi" 乞罷江南州軍鐵錢會子奏議, *Chengzhai ji* 誠齋集 (SKQS ed.), 70.12b–15b.

[69] Yu Chou 虞儔, "Beizhao shangdian zhazi" 被召上殿劄子, in *MCZY* 272.2b.

[70] Chen Zao 陳造, "Shang Zhao chengxiang zhazi" 上趙丞相劄子, *Jianghu changweng wenji* 江湖長翁文集 (SKQS ed.), 27.10b–12a.

[71] Zhu Xi 朱熹, *Zhuzi yulei* 朱子語類 (Taipei: Wenhai chubanshe, 1986), 111.2722–23.

[72] *SHY* shihuo 28.49a.

[73] *SHY* shihuo 28.53b. The revenues of the Jiankang Quehuowu (12 million *guan* annually) far surpassed those of the Zhenjiang office (4 million); see *SHY* shihuo 55.28a.

exceeded 1:4.[74] By contrast, the value of *huaijiao* remained relatively robust. In lectures on affairs of state delivered to Emperor Ningzong in the early 1220s, Cheng Bi noted that soldiers in Huainan were unhappy to receive 30 percent of their pay in *huaijiao* (the rest was disbursed in *huizi*). But Cheng also reported that the market value of *huaijiao* bills was only 5–10 percent lower than *huizi*.[75] From 1218, the court adopted a policy of reducing the minting of iron coin and increasing the emission of *huaijiao*. Most of the region's iron coin mints were shuttered, while the issue of *huaijiao* rose to over 10 million *guan* from 1218 to 1225.[76] *Huaijiao* became the major currency in the region.[77]

Farther west, in the Han River highlands frontier zone, the Huguang General Command had issued a new paper currency (designated *zhibian huizi* 直便會子 but more commonly referred to as *huhui* 湖會) to facilitate payments to soldiers at the front lines since 1163. Like *huizi*, this regional paper currency began as a wartime expedient. In 1168, after the military crisis had passed, roughly half of the 7 million *guan* of *huhui* emitted by the general command were removed from circulation by redeeming them for tea licenses and capital *huizi*.[78] Despite appeals – especially from salt merchants who preferred to use the single medium of *huizi* for interregional trade – to abolish *huhui* in favor of allowing capital *huizi* to circulate in the region, the general command steadfastly supported retaining *huhui* as a regional currency. The priority for the Huguang General Command was to sustain the value of tea licenses, one of its most important sources of income. If merchants selling salt in Huguang could receive payment in *huizi*, then the demand for tea licenses would suffer, endangering the crucial source of revenues to pay soldiers' stipends. Cognizant of the precarious finances of the Huguang General Command – which was perpetually in deficit, in contrast to the relatively stable fiscal situation in Huaidong and Huaixi, and required regular infusions of funds from Sichuan – the court was persuaded to retain the separate *huhui* paper currency zone in Huguang.[79]

74 Wang Shengduo, *Liang Song huobi shi*, vol. 2, pp. 598–99.

75 Cheng Bi 程珌, "Jin gushi" 進故事, *Mingshui ji* 洺水集 (SKQS ed.), 4.16b–17a.

76 *SS* 181.4412.

77 In this respect, my conclusion is diametrically opposite to that of Wang Shen, who argues that *huizi* and iron coin remained the dominant currencies, with *huaijiao* playing only a marginal role. See Wang Shen 王申, "Huainan jiaozi yu Nan Song Lianghuai diqu de caizheng yunzuo: jian yu dongnan huizi bijiao" 淮南交子与南宋两淮地区的财政运作: 兼与东南会子比较, *Anhui shixue* 安徽史学 2021.1: 128–34.

78 *WXTK* 9.100c.

79 For studies of *huhui*, see Higuchi Yoshishige 樋口能成, "Nan-Sō Kohoku kaishi no shijō kōzō" 南宋湖北會子の市場構造, *Shiteki* 史滴 28 (2006): 86–102; Wang Shen 王申, "Hubei huizi yu Nan Song guojia caizheng geju bianqian" 湖北会子与南宋国家财政格局变迁, *Hubei shehui kexue* 湖北社会科学 2021.6: 102–10. On the regular transfer of

The circulation of *huhui* seems to have stabilized in the 1180s. New bills were issued to retire worn ones, but the practice of standardized issues with fixed (three-year) terms of expiry was adopted only in 1190, when the Huguang General Command emitted two issues of 2.7 million *guan* each (for a total of 5.4 million *guan* in circulation).[80] Although the market value of *huhui* had slipped to an exchange value of 600 *wen* by 1173, it stabilized thereafter, remaining in the range of 500–600 *wen* down to the 1220s. In 1180, iron coin was introduced to the frontier prefectures (Jingxi circuit), which became extensions of the Huainan iron coin zone. Gradually iron coin was adopted in other parts of Huguang, and mints were established there in the early 1190s.[81] The relationship between these iron coins and *huhui* (nominally denominated in bronze coins) is unclear. Cao Yanyue, while serving as the ever-normal granary intendant in Hubei in 1208, noted that the Huguang General Command collected and expended revenues in a mix of *huhui*, capital *huizi*, and coins.[82] In 1215, Huang Gan, the prefect of Hanyang, reported that the exchange ratio between *huhui* and iron coins was 1:1.7, while the ratio between *huizi* and *huhui* likewise was 1:1.7.[83] In Huang's numerous memorials regarding economic conditions in Hanyang, he consistently reported market prices and government funds in *huhui*, which suggests that *huhui* in effect had become the region's monetary standard.[84]

As mentioned in Chapter 4, the Jin invasion compelled officials in Sichuan to resort to issuing massive quantities of *qianyin* paper currency during the

funds from Sichuan to the Huguang general command beginning in the 1140s, see Higuchi Yoshishige, "Nan-Sō Sōryōjo taiseishita no Chōkō keizai: Kokō Sōryōjo to Shisen no kankei kara" 南宋総領所体制下の長江経済: 湖広総領所と四川の関係から, *Waseda daigaku daigakuin bungaku kenkyūka kiyō* 早稲田大学大学院文学研究科紀要 51 (2005): 77–86.

80 *CYZJ* jiaji, 16.363 (the dating in this text to 1174 is clearly wrong, however); *SS* 181.4412. Subsequently, the simultaneous emission of two issues was discontinued, and only one issue circulated at a time, although for longer and longer periods. Wang Shengduo, *Liang Song huobi shi*, vol. 2, p. 746.

81 Wang Shengduo, *Liang Song huobi shi*, vol. 2, pp. 603–7.

82 Cao Yanyue 曹彦约, "Hubei tiju changpingsi shenqi zhenji shangge zhuang" 湖北提举常平司申乞賑濟賞格狀, *Changgu ji* 昌谷集 (SKQS ed.), 9.2a.

83 Huang Gan 黃榦, "Shen Jing-Hu zhizhisi ban Hanyangjun dimi shi" 申京湖制置司辦漢陽軍糴米事, *Mianzhai ji* 勉齋集 (hereafter *MZJ*; SKQS ed.), 30.10a–14a.

84 Huang cited *huhui* as the money of account even for transactions that were not conducted in paper currency. For example, he reported that the normal price for one *sheng* of rice was 17–18 *wen* in *huhui*, even though the smallest *huhui* bill was 500 *wen*. See "Shen zhizhisi wei zhen mijia taigao shi" 申制置司為賑米價太高事, *MZJ* 30.16a–17b. According to Zhou Quyang, from 1165 grain prices in the region were calculated in *huhui*, but Zhou does not cite any sources. Zhou Quyang 周曲洋, "Nan Song Jing-Hu diqu junshi buji taizhi de goujian yu yunzuo: jian lun Song Yuan Xiang-Fan zhi zhan shili zhi yuanyin 南宋荆湖地区军事补给体制的构建与运作: 兼论宋元襄樊之战失利之原因, *Xueshu yanjiu* 学术研究 2016.3: 143.

1130s, with the total amount in circulation rising from 7 million *dao* in 1133 to 40 million *dao* by the armistice of 1142. During the following two decades the volume of *qianyin* in circulation remained constant. In 1161, Wang Zhiwang, commissioner of the Sichuan General Command, reported that 41.7 million *dao* of *qianyin* were in circulation, against a reserve of only 700,000 strings of iron coin. The reason that *qianyin* had gained popular conference, Wang asserted, was that the income from the liquor and salt excises and other commercial revenues "covertly acted to maintain equilibrium" (*yin wei chengti* 陰為稱提). By this, Wang meant that market confidence in *qianyin* rested on requiring their use in payments for monopoly commodities, by far the most important source of the general command's revenues (see Table 5.3). Implicitly, he rejected the argument that the chief means of *chengti* was to restrict the amount of paper currency in circulation, and indeed in this memorial Wang requested that the court authorize an additional 3 million *guan* of *qianyin* in anticipation of securing Song control over territories in Shaanxi recently (albeit briefly) seized from the Jin.[85] Although the quantity of *qianyin* in circulation rose to 45 million *guan*, it remained at that level down to 1191, and prices in Sichuan remained stable as well.[86] Debates over monetary questions at the court frequently invoked the example of Sichuan's *qianyin* currency as the positive model for managing *huizi*, as we will see in Chapter 6.

5.4 The Development of Paper Currencies Under the Jin Dynasty

The Jurchen Jin dynasty that ruled North China from 1127 to 1234 initially sought to establish bronze coin as its sole currency.[87] The new regime benefited from an enormous windfall, the capture of the stocks of coin left behind when the Song court abandoned its capital at Kaifeng.[88] The Jin used some of this coin to purchase and retire the iron coins (notably the *jiaxi* coins minted

85 *XNYL* 193.3253.

86 Gao, *Huobi liutong*, pp. 264–73; Wang Shengduo, *Liang Song huobi shi*, vol. 2, pp. 637–43. According to one estimate, *qianyin* comprised 98 percent of Sichuan's money supply in the Southern Song. See Guan Hanhui 管汉晖 and Qian Sheng 钱盛, "Songdai zhibi de yunxing jizhi: benwei, huishu, zhanzheng yu tongzhang" 论宋代纸币的运行机制: 本位，回赎，战争与通胀, *Jingji kexue* 经济科学 2016.4: 124.

87 For the details of Jin monetary history, I have drawn on Qiao Youmei 乔幼梅, "Jindai huobi zhidu de yanbian jiqi dui shehui jingji de yingxiang" 金代货币制度的演变及其对社会经济的影响, *Zhongguo shi yanjiu* 中国史研究 1983.3: 113–24; Takahashi Hiroomi 高橋弘臣, "Kindai no shihei to sono unyō seido" 金代の紙幣とその運用制度, *Shikyō* 史境 2 (1989): 25–40; Takahashi, *Genchō kahei*, pp. 54–141; Miyazawa Tomoyuki 宮澤知之, "Kindai zenki no heisei" 金代前期の幣制, *Tōyōshi kenkyū* 東洋史研究 79.2 (2020): 205–35.

88 One Southern Song historian estimated that the Northern Song imperial treasuries held 98.7 million *guan* of coin at the time of the Jin conquest: *SCBM*, 3, p. 543 (Yanxing xiazhi 炎興下帙, juan 卷 81). Ye Shi claimed that under Cai Jing the state treasuries had

under the aegis of Cai Jing) that had circulated in the northern provinces of the Northern Song. By the 1160s, all cash payments received by the Jin state were collected in bronze coin. But there were no copper mines in North China, and the Jin state issued virtually no new coin of its own. Because of the worsening shortage of coin in the north, the purchasing power of bronze coin in the Jin realm was much higher than in the Southern Song domain. Consequently, the stock of bronze coin in the south tended to flow – through clandestine trade, since export of coin was strictly forbidden – to the Jin territories (and abroad to Japan and Southeast Asia as well, as we shall see in Chapter 6).[89] A memorial on cross-border smuggling submitted by a Song official in 1160 reported that "when southern merchants cross the Huai River, they find that 1 *guan* of coins will purchase several *guan* of goods."[90] Salt smuggling along the Song–Jin border in Hubei/Henan was especially flagrant. Given that the purchasing power of Song coin was three to four times greater in the Jin territories, the populace on the Song side of the border traded for contraband salt from Xiezhou Lake (now in Jin hands) rather than settle for the far more expensive Huainan salt sold by monopoly merchants.[91] The restoration of cross-border trade following the truce enacted in 1165, while subject to close official scrutiny, brought even more opportunities for smuggling.

The Jin sought to ensure that the coin in its possession would not return to the Song by creating a coin-free buffer zone along its border with the Song. In 1154, the Jin issued its own paper currency, known as *jiaochao* 交鈔 or "exchange bills," modeled after the eponymous Sichuan *jiaozi*, with a seven-year term of expiry, and intended primarily for interregional money transfers. The official *Jin History* states that from the outset *jiaochao* were issued in both five large denominations (*dachao* 大鈔) of 1 to 10 *guan* and five small denominations (*xiaochao* 小鈔) of 100 to 700 *wen*, but Miyazawa Tomoyuki has persuasively argued that the small bills were introduced only in the late 1190s.[92] According to the eyewitness testimony of Fan Chengda, who traveled to Kaifeng in 1170 as an ambassador from the Song court, the *jiaochao* in circulation were in denominations of 1 to 3 *guan*; Fan made no mention of smaller bills.[93]

amassed "more than 50 million *guan*": Ye Shi "Cai zonglun (er)" in *Shuixin bieji* 11, *YSJ*, 3, p. 773.

89 Qiao Youmei 乔幼梅, "Song Jin maoyizhong zhengduo tongbi de douzheng" 宋金贸易中争夺铜币的斗争, *Lishi yanjiu* 历史研究 1982.4: 115–27.

90 *XNYL* 186.3117.

91 Based on a memorial from 1175 in *SHY* shihuo 28.7a–b.

92 *Jin shi* 金史 ([hereafter *JS*]; Beijing: Zhonghua shuju ed.), 48.1073; Miyazawa, "Kindai zenki heisei," pp. 220–21.

93 Fan Chengda 范成大, *Lanpei lu* 攬轡錄 (hereafter *LPL*), 2a, in Tao Zongyi 陶宗儀 (ed.), *Shuofu* 說郛 (1646 ed.), vol. 65.

The inauguration of *jiaochao* bills coincided with the restructuring of Jin political institutions under Hailing, who usurped the throne in 1150. In 1152, Hailing relocated the Jin court and government from the Supreme Capital (near modern Ha'erbin in Heilongjiang) to the newly designated Central Capital (modern Beijing) and proceeded to streamline their operations by consolidating all authority in the Department of State Affairs (Shangshusheng 尚書省). Simultaneous with the issue of *jiaochao*, the Jin government enacted state monopsonies on the sale of ten kinds of goods, including tea, iron, and liquor, but above all salt. The office that issued the *jiaochao* bills, located at the Central Capital, also printed the commodity licenses used to obtain monopoly goods. In 1160, Hailing moved the government, including the agency that issued *jiaochao* bills, to the Southern Capital (Kaifeng) in preparation for the war against Song he launched in the following year. Fan Chengda asserted that the main purpose of the bills was to remove bronze coins from the frontier regions to the capital. North of the Yellow River people used coins rather than paper currency, Fan wrote, but these coins invariably were Northern Song issues.[94] Hailing had commenced minting his own coin in 1157, but only in trifling quantities, and the populace far preferred Song coins.

The 1161–1165 war with Song utterly depleted the currency reserves in the Jin treasuries. Although the Jin, like the Song, enjoyed a summer of economic stability in the 1170s–1180s, inherent weaknesses began to fester. Neglect of dike maintenance along the Yellow River resulted in repeated flooding during these decades, culminating in the catastrophic alteration in the river's course in 1194, which ruined the richest agricultural regions in Henan and Shandong. In addition, by the 1190s bronze coin had largely disappeared from circulation, leaving the Jin little choice but to depend on *jiaochao* bills as the means of exchange and state payments.[95] In 1189, in another effort to transfer coin from the provinces to the capital (once again ensconced at the Central Capital), the Jin undertook an ambitious effort to entrench paper currency as the common

94 *LPL* 2a.

95 In contrast to Song territories, where hoards almost entirely coincide with the Jurchen and Mongol invasions, Jin coin hoards were deposited fairly evenly throughout the dynastic period (see Chapter 6, Figure 6.1). Not surprisingly, Song issues comprise 99 percent of all coins from Jin hoards. In 1180, the Jin court set the official short-string standard at 80 coins per *mo* (i.e., 800 coins per *guan*), a rate that was printed on Jin paper currencies (see Chapter 7). However, the *mo* units from excavated Jin hoards invariably consist of 50 or 40 coins (the 40-coin unit is from a later deposit), further testimony to the scarcity of coin in the Jin realm. Yang Jun 杨君, "Jinchao tongqian huobi liutong zhucang xingtai guankui: yi chutu Jinchao huobi shiwu wei zhongxin" 金朝铜钱货币流通贮藏形态管窥：以出土金朝货币实物为中心, *Zhongguo qianbi* 中国钱币 2015.6: 3–11; Miyake Toshihiko 三宅俊彦, *Chūgoku no uzumerareta senka* 中国の埋められた銭貨 (Tokyo: Dōseisha, 2005), pp. 25–29, 94–102.

money of the realm. Larger quantities of paper currency were issued, the seven-year term of expiry was annulled, and offices to exchange *jiaochao* for coin were established in the provinces.

The Jin state husbanded its own stocks of coin while relying on paper money and silver in its fiscal expenditures. But rampant growth in state spending, especially during the first Jin–Mongol war of 1195–1198, forced the government to issue large quantities of paper money. In 1197, salaries for officials and soldiers were converted to payments made half in silver and half in *jiaochao*. On the revenue side, merchants who purchased commodity licenses (primarily for salt) likewise had to make payments half in silver and half in bills, in imitation of the current Southern Song practice. In 1198, the Jin state began to issue smaller denominations (from 100 to 700 *wen*) of *jiaochao* in four circuits – the Central Capital, the Western Capital (Datong), Liaodong, and Linhuang (Lanzhou), areas in which the scarcity of bronze coin apparently was especially acute. The emission of small bills was part of a broader effort to replace bronze coin with paper currency (and also silver) in the whole range of transactions from everyday purchases to interregional trade.[96] In 1194, the Jin had adopted the novel expedient of creating a silver coin – the first ever issued in the Chinese ecumene – denominated in weights of silver (five altogether) ranging from 1 to 10 *liang* 兩 (1 *liang* = 39.6 g) and pegged to an official exchange rate of 1 *liang* = 2 *guan* of *jiaochao* (raised to 1:3 in 1198). But the Jin abruptly halted the use of silver coin in 1200, citing the problem of counterfeiting and the rebound in the value of paper money after the Mongols paused their attacks.

Around this time, it appears that the Jin court began to allow provincial authorities to issue bills, beginning with the "small bills" issued in four circuits in 1198 mentioned above, although the sources are mute about when this became a general practice. By 1202, "triple endorsement bills" (*san hetong jiaochao* 三合同交鈔) – which, similar to the Song *xianqian guanzi* bills, specified the multiple circuits in which the bills could be redeemed – were in circulation (for a later specimen of such a bill, see Figure 7.5). Most likely such bills were issued at the circuit level. The earliest confirmation for the general issue of provincial currencies dates to 1206, when small-denomination *jiaochao* bills were introduced on an empire-wide basis.[97]

Although the value of the *jiaochao* bills briefly stabilized, renewed war with the Song (1206–1207) and the Mongols (1211–1214; resulting in the Mongol occupation of more than half of the Jin territories) dealt severe shocks to the Jin fiscal and monetary systems. The principle of convertibility of paper

96 Miyazawa, "Kindai zenki heisei," pp. 220–21.

97 Miyazawa ("Kindai zenki heisei," pp. 223–26) suggests that regional currencies may have been inaugurated as early as 1189, but his evidence is highly inferential and ultimately unpersuasive.

currency, intermittently honored in the past, was suspended permanently. The Jin resorted to a series of expediencies to cope with soaring military expenditures, including allowing provincial governments to issue their own paper money in far larger denominations ranging from 20 to an astonishing 1,000 *guan* – stark evidence of the severe depreciation in the *jiaochao*'s value.[98] In 1215, reeling from the loss of much of its territory to the Mongols, the Jin court introduced a new paper money, the *zhenyou baoquan* 貞祐寶券, which initially was well-received but soon lost favor.[99] Strong regional differences in the value of the new bills encouraged speculation and arbitrage. To curb these practices, the Jin opted to restrict the circulation of paper bills to specific regions, which further eroded the bills' value.

These policies in effect demonetized bronze coin. Consequently, the flow of coin reversed: the remaining stocks of bronze coin in northern China disappeared across the frontier to the Southern Song, or overseas to Japan.[100] Since the depreciation of paper money vitiated its utility as a means of exchange, the Jin populace turned toward silver as a more trustworthy monetary standard. From 1216 onward, references to prices denominated in silver increase in frequency.[101] In 1223, the Ministry of Revenue conceded that "in private trade, the people exclusively express prices in silver."[102]

Jin officials sought to accommodate this shift to a de facto silver standard by linking the state's paper money to silver. In 1217, as war with the Song resumed, the Jin launched a new paper bill, the *zhenyou tongbao* 貞祐通寶, with an official exchange rate of 1 *liang* of silver = 4 *guan* of bills. Within five years, however, these bills were circulating at an exchange rate of 1:800, or a mere 1/200 of their official value. In 1221, the Jin tried to replace the *zhenyou tongbao* with yet another new paper currency, the *xingding baoquan* 興定寶券, proposing to redeem 400 *guan* of the old bills with 1 *guan* of the new (thus restoring the official exchange rate of 1 *liang* of silver = 2 *guan* of paper currency). This initiative seems to have died stillborn, however.

98 Takahashi, *Genchō kahei*, pp. 100–103.

99 Liu Qi 劉祁, *Guiqian zhi* 歸錢志 ([hereafter *GQZ*]; SKQS ed.), 10.2b–3b.

100 On the flow of coin out of Jin territories into the hands of Song merchants, see the eyewitness testimony of the Jin official Liu Qi: *GQZ* 10.3b. See also Qiao, "Song Jin tongbi douzheng." For export of Song coins abroad, see Chapter 6.

101 This trend also appears in the state's fiscal records. For example, the market prices for tea recorded in the official *Jin History* are given in coin units up to 1199; beginning with the next entry that mentions a price, in 1223, the prices are given in silver units. *JS* 49.1107–9.

102 *JS* 48.1089–90. On the adoption of silver as the monetary standard for expressing prices in Jin territories, see also Wang Wencheng 王文成 et al., *Song Jin Yuan Ming shiqi de shichang fazhan yu huobi liutong yanjiu* 宋金元明时期的市场发展与货币流通研究 (Beijing: Zhongguo shehui kexue chubanshe), 2021, pp. 54–59.

From 1227 onward, the Mongol armies steadily encroached on Jin territories, capturing the Central Capital in 1233. In the same year, the Jin court at Kaifeng issued the *tianxing baohui* 天興寶會, the first paper money to be denominated in silver units rather than bronze coin. These bills were issued in four denominations of 1, 2, 3, and 5 *qian* 錢 (1 *qian* = 0.1 *liang*). The adoption of silver units to denominate paper money attested to the prevalence of silver as the measure of value in private markets. Silver assumed particular importance as a store of value, a function that paper money and bronze coin no longer could perform. According to a contemporary Jin official, the new currency was designed to complement the use of silver in exchange: "At that time, the prices of goods had soared, while the currency (i.e., both paper money and bronze coin) failed to circulate. Market transactions were conducted exclusively in silver. But silver was inconvenient as fractional currency, therefore the new paper money was established to serve this purpose."[103] It is impossible to assess whether the new paper currency achieved any success. Within a year, the Mongols had vanquished the Jin and took full possession of North China.

To an even greater degree than in the Southern Song, paper money displaced coin as a medium of exchange at all levels of society in the Jin-ruled territories of North China. However, the steep depreciation of the Jin paper currencies after 1207 forced a shift to commodity monies – silver and silk – in private exchange. At the time of the final Mongol conquest of the Jin in 1234, uncoined silver had become the effective monetary standard in North China.

5.5 Conclusion

Over the course of the second half of the 12th century, the Song government created four distinct regional fiscal and monetary zones under the direction of the four general commands, each with its own paper currency linked to either bronze or iron coins (Map 5.3). The Jin territories in North China comprised yet another separate monetary zone with its own state-issued paper currencies. The Southern Song multiple currency system was designed to serve the fiscal needs of the general commands, although it surely raised transaction costs for interregional commerce. The profusion of paper currencies along with the continued importance of commodity licenses in the state's fiscal operations created ample opportunities for arbitrage and an even greater need for a secondary market of financial intermediaries to negotiate bills, coin, and silver. Not all policymakers welcomed this multiplication of currencies. In 1195, the newly appointed commissioner of the Huguang General Command, Yang Wangxiu, argued that the division of the empire into separate monetary

[103] Wang E 王鶚, *Runan yishi* 汝南遺事 (SKQS ed.), 3.8b.

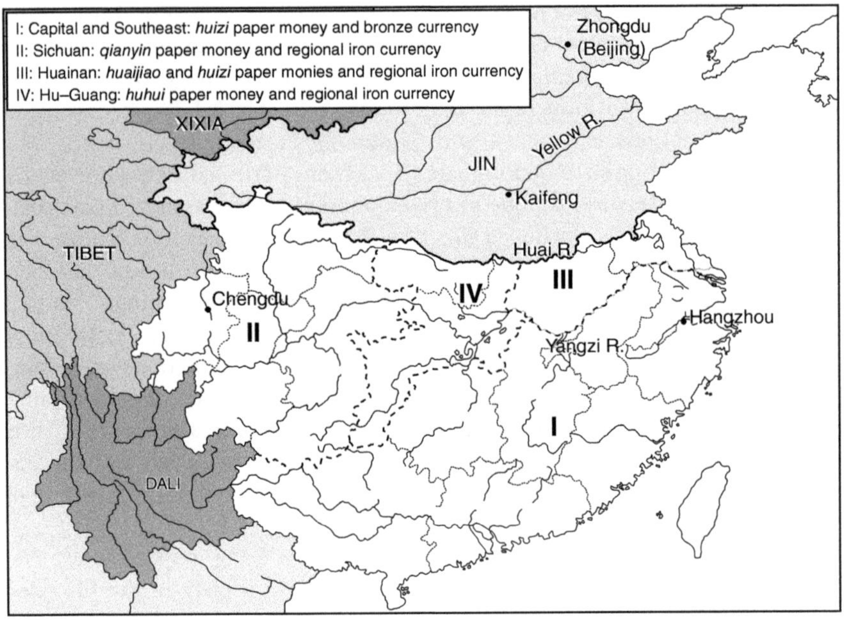

Map 5.3 Monetary regions in Southern Song China, c. 1200.
Source: von Glahn, "Origins of Paper Money in China," p. 74. Reproduced from Lamouroux and von Glahn, "Public Finance, 1000–1800," p. 358, map 9.1.

regions impeded the circulation of money and harmed interregional commerce. Yang urged the court to abolish the *huhui* and *huaijiao* currencies and allow *huizi* to circulate throughout the whole realm.[104] In the same year, the prefect of Jiangling, Peng Guinian, complained that financiers at Ezhou, the seat of the Huguang General Command, used their leverage over the market in bills to demand discounts as much as 50 percent for exchanging *huhui*, which adversely affected interregional merchants on the one hand and soldiers who received most of their pay in *huhui* on the other.[105] These appeals fell on deaf ears. However, the monetary crisis precipitated by renewed warfare in the early 13th century ultimately caused the demise of the regional paper currencies and the de facto emergence of *huizi* as the empire-wide monetary standard.

[104] Lou Yue 樓鑰, "Wenhuage daizhi Yang gong xingzhuang" 文華閣待制楊公行狀, *Gongkui ji* 攻媿集 (SKQS ed.), 91.11a–b.

[105] Peng Guinian 彭龜年, "Lun Hubei Jingxi chubi shu disizha" 論湖北京西楮幣疏第四劄, *Zhitang ji* 止堂集 ([hereafter *ZTJ*]; SKQS ed.), 6.21b–22a.

6

Emergence of a Paper Currency Monetary Standard

In the multiple currency system devised by the Southern Song leadership, each of the four monetary zones – defined by institutional structures to expedite the flow of fiscal resources to frontier armies – featured distinctive paper currencies linked to different coin standards. Maintaining stable exchange values between paper money and hard currency proved to be an intractable challenge. In lieu of specie convertibility, Song policymakers relied on two main strategies of *chengti* ("maintaining equilibrium"): (1) utilizing silver as an implicit hard currency reserve to redeem excess bills and withdraw them from circulation; and (2) requiring public payments in paper currency, usually in a ratio of half paper and half coin. The initial success of these monetary strategies stoked confidence in the viability of paper currency among statesmen and scholars. From the early 1190s, however, marked deterioration in the value of paper currencies set in. In the early decades of the 13th century, resurgent military crises – including civil war against a separatist regime in Sichuan, renewed conflict with Jin, and ultimately the Mongol invasions – intensified the burden of defense expenditures on state finances. *Chengti* strategies no longer proved effective, compelling the Song government to resort to debasing paper currencies to align them with their depressed market value. The pressure of military costs became even more acute after the Mongols vanquished Jin in 1234 and absorbed its territories into their expanding imperium, bringing them into direct confrontation with the Song. Limited in their capacity to expand fiscal resources through new forms of taxation, Song fiscal officials resorted to printing ever greater quantities of paper currency.

Yet despite fiscal woes and monetary turmoil, the *huizi* paper currency became deeply implanted in the market economy. Already in the Northern Song period, paper currencies had displaced iron coin as the monetary standard in the Sichuan region, and the importance of Sichuan's *qianyin* paper currency in private exchange as well as in state finances continued to expand during the Southern Song. The *huizi* paper currency followed a parallel course in the heartland of the Southern Song realm. At the time *huizi* were first issued in the 1160s, many contemporaries already were complaining of shortages of bronze coin. In subsequent decades, such fulminations become legion, although whether the proliferation of paper currency was the cause or the consequence of the scarcity of bronze coin requires closer scrutiny. From the early 13th century, the evidence of land sale contracts, property disputes, and anecdotal information about market trade shows that paper currency increasingly displaced coin in private commerce, most conspicuously in large-scale transactions such as land sales but also in ordinary market purchases as well. Small *huizi* bills – the smallest denomination was 200 *wen*, although there is some evidence that 50- and 100-*wen* bills were issued in the capital region in the 1240s – became widely used in market transactions. The inflationary trend in the 13th century rendered small *huizi* bills more useful for everyday exchange, and the devaluation of the #17 *huizi* in 1240 in effect transformed these bills into fractional currency. In addition, there is also evidence that *huizi* to some degree displaced coin as a store of value. By the end of the Southern Song period, paper currency – despite its manifest problems – had become the monetary standard of the Song economy.

The institution of paper currency also compelled rethinking the theory of money. Fiat currencies of course could be readily accommodated by the chartalist principles of the *Guan Zi*, still the mainstream of Chinese monetary thought. The abstract theories of Pseudo-Guanzi were given more specific grounding in monetary and fiscal practices based on the Song government's experiences with paper money and successive efforts to reform the currency. But the monetary troubles afflicting the Southern Song court also fueled dissident opinion that to varying degrees repudiated paper currency and affirmed a metallist conception of money.

6.1 The First Devaluation Crisis

The reign of Emperor Ningzong (r. 1194–1224) – a weak monarch thoroughly dominated by his chief advisers – was marked by constant political strife. Han Tuozhou, a palace official who was instrumental in installing Ningzong on the throne, manipulated his influence over the emperor to gain ascendancy at the court. Han faced concerted opposition, especially from adherents of the Learning of the Way (Daoxue), whose rigorously moralistic brand of Confucianism had emerged as the dominant force in intellectual circles within and outside of the government. Han orchestrated a campaign to expel Daoxue luminaries from influential positions at the court, accusing them of insidious partisanship. In 1197, he succeeded in branding Daoxue as "false learning" and induced Ningzong to proscribe its leaders – and other political rivals – from holding office. The success of these maneuvers left Han politically isolated, however, and by 1200 he began to backtrack, seeking to repair his frayed relationships with the bureaucratic elite by rescinding the proscription. Many targets of the "false learning" ban were restored to court office, while Han trained his energies on consolidating control over the military. The Daoxue leaders had been vociferous proponents of the revanchist cause, and Han

Tuozhou sought to curry favor with them by preparing a new assault against the Jin, whose leaders were preoccupied by domestic economic troubles and the looming threat of the Mongol armies mobilized by Chinggis Khan.[1]

Although the Jin leaders hardly desired renewed conflict on their southern border, the Song offensive launched in 1206 – what came to be known as the Kaixi War, after the current reign title – proved to be an unmitigated disaster. Wu Xi, scion of the family of generals who had controlled Sichuan on and off since the 1130s, negotiated an entente with the Jin and declared his independence from Song rule, eviscerating Song military strength. Although Wu Xi was soon assassinated by loyalist officers, he was succeeded by a warlord who refused to render aid to the Song forces. Battlefield reversals at the hands of the Jin compelled the Song to sue for peace, and in 1208 a new armistice was declared – and sealed by delivering the head of Han Tuozhou, who had been assassinated by palace guards, to the Jin. The Daoxue leaders railed against this pusillanimous conclusion to the war and pressed Ningzong and his new paladin, the chief state councilor Shi Miyuan, to resume the offensive. In the meantime, the Jin's own predicament turned dire. Chinggis launched a full-scale invasion in 1211, and by 1214 the Mongol armies had captured most Jin territories north of the Yellow River, forcing the Jin court to flee to Kaifeng, the Southern Capital. But Chinggis then turned his attention to campaigns against the Kara Khitai and Khwarazm kingdoms in Central Asia. It was only after Chinggis's death in 1227 that the Mongols once again renewed their assault against the Jin.

During this reprieve from the Mongol threat, war again erupted between the Song and Jin. While Shi Miyuan tried to focus his attention on domestic matters, including the falling value of Song paper currencies, the revanchists prodded him to halt the payment of tribute to Jin. When Shi did so in 1214, the Jin leaders regarded his action as tantamount to a declaration of war. Both sides mounted large-scale attacks against the other. Battlefield victories proved ephemeral, however, and by 1221 warfare sputtered to a halt. The fifteen years of carnage precipitated by the Kaixi War had catastrophic consequences for Song finances. Unable to tap new sources of revenue, the court turned to printing prodigious quantities of paper currency to finance its swelling military expenditures, at the cost of undermining the monetary system and endangering its solvency.

The volume of *huizi* in circulation had been steadily increasing even before the Kaixi War (Table 6.1). Although there are some gaps in our information, several sources report that by the time of Xiaozong's abdication in 1189 the volume of *huizi* had reached 45–48 million *guan*.[2] From 1186, the government

[1] On the political warfare between Han Tuozhou and the Daoxue partisans, see Richard L. Davis, "The Reigns of Guang-tsung (1189–94) and Ning-tsung (1194–1224)," in Twitchett and Smith, *Cambridge History of China*, vol. 5, pt. 1, pp. 775–812.

[2] The figure of 45 million *guan* is cited in an anonymous essay, "Chubi" 楮幣, reprinted in an encyclopedia published in 1237. See Lin Jiong 林駉 (comp), *Gujin yuanliu zhilun xuji* 古今源流至論續集 ([hereafter *GJYL*; 1427 ed.), 4.14b. The late Song encyclopedist Wang

Table 6.1 *Volume of* huizi *in circulation in Southern Song China*

Issue number	Term of circulation	Quantity of bills (millions of *guan*)	Total volume of bills in circulation at time of issue (millions of *guan*)
1	1168–1171	10	10
2	1170–1173	10	20
3	1171–1180	10	20
4	1173–1183	10	20
5	1180–1186	10	22[a]
6	1183–1189	18	28
7	1186–1195	23.23	41.2
8	1189–1198	?	[46.5][b]
9	1195–1204	30	[53.2][b]
10	1198–1204	?	[60.0][b]
11	1204–1211	36.33	83.9
12	1204–1211	47.58	83.9
13	1207–1211	55.48	139.4
14	1211–1234	112.63	232.4[c]
15	1211–1234	119.80	232.4[c]
16	1231–1240	129.25	361.6
17	1234–1264	139.86	273.4
18	1240–1276	?	?

Notes: [a] In 1176, an additional 2 million *guan* of #4 *huizi* were issued.
[b] Numbers in brackets are estimates based on the assumption that the quantity of issues #8 and #10 were the same as the previous issues, #7 and #9 respectively.
[c] Beginning with issue #14, the Song government abandoned the principle of fixed terms of expiry and instead repeatedly issued the same bills over an extended period of time. Thus the figures in this column for issues #14–#15 indicate the total volume of bills issued over their lifetime (1211–1234), not when they were first issued.
Source: Gao, *Huobi liutong*, pp. 186–201.

began to increase the quantity of bills per issue, as well as extending the term of expiry to nine years. Still, the value of *huizi* remained buoyant, around 750 *wen*, nearly equal to the official exchange rate of 770 *wen*.[3] But by 1195, following the issue of #9 *huizi*, a significant depreciation had begun to set in. In a memorial dating from the mid 1190s, Yuan Yueyou observed that while *huizi* continued to exchange for 720–730 *wen* in the capital, their value had depreciated elsewhere: 670–680 *wen* in adjacent areas such as Huzhou, Jiaxing,

Yinglin asserted that the combined #6 and #7 issues totaled 48-plus million *guan*, although he erroneously stated that the issue of these bills commenced in 1179. See *YH* 186.20b.

[3] Gao, *Huobi liutong*, p. 196.

and Shaoxing, even less than 600 *wen* in Fujian and Jiangxi.[4] Hong Mai, who applauded the success of earlier efforts to disburse silver to redeem excess bills, recounted that the market value of *huizi* had fallen from 750 *wen* in 1085 to 620 *wen* by 1196.[5]

The ill-fated Kaixi War overwhelmed the capacities of the Song fiscal system. In 1207, the government added a third issue of *huizi*, for the first time allowing three issues (#11, #12, and #13) – a total of nearly 140 million *guan* – to circulate simultaneously. This resort to wanton printing of paper money triggered steep discounting.[6] Despite efforts to enforce the official exchange rate of 770 *wen* – such as threatening to confiscate the property of those who discounted *huizi* and punishing officials who did so – the market value of the bills fell to merely half of their face value, and dealers in exchange bills offered as little as 300–400 *wen*.[7] An anonymous source from this time complained that the problem was exacerbated by local officials who failed to apply the fifty-fifty *pinda* formula in tax collection and urged the court to return to Emperor Xiaozong's policies of insisting on accepting *huizi* in tax payments and releasing the state's reserves of precious metals and silks to repurchase excess bills.[8] In 1210, with peace restored, the Song tried to revive the value of *huizi* by disbursing coin, land grants, monopoly goods, and official titles to remove 20 million *guan* (i.e., about 15 percent) of the bills in circulation.[9] The following year, the government took the more extreme step of retiring issues #11–#13 by obliging holders to exchange them for two new issues (#14 and #15) at a 50 percent discount, in essence a devaluation that reduced the value of *huizi* by half. In an act of desperation, the government went so far as to mandate that individual households hold a certain quantity of *huizi* based on their household wealth. Zhen Dexiu – one of the leading Daoxue figures of the day and an ardent advocate of aggression against the Jin – informed the court that in his native Fujian households with assets of 1,000 *guan* (which he regarded as relatively affluent) were required to hold 50 *guan* of *huizi*, forcing them to sell lands to comply with the mandate.[10] Chen Chun, then serving as registrar in Zhangzhou (Fujian), reported that rich families, pawnbrokers, and

[4] Memorial by Yuan Yueyou 袁說友 in *MCZY* 272.17b–19b; Ji Huang 嵇璜 et al. (comp), *Xu wenxian tongkao* 續文獻通考 ([hereafter *XWXTK*]; ST ed.), 7.2841a–b.

[5] *RZSB*, sanbi, 14.584–85. In 1198, the prefect of Taizhou reported that in the rice-producing areas of Liangzhe the value of *huizi* had fallen to the 620–630 *wen* range, which had pushed rice merchants to demand higher prices. *SHY* zhiguan 26.22a.

[6] Dai Zhi, "Shuquan yuanliu," in *SP* shang, 37a; *CYZJ* yiji 乙集, 16.787; *LCGM* 12.2b.

[7] Ye Shi, "Fujian yunshi zhixian moge shaoqing Zhao gong muzhiming" 福建運使直顯謨閣少卿趙公墓誌銘, *Shuixin wenji*, in *YSJ* 23.448; *SHY* shihuo 28.51b.

[8] *GJYL* 14.14b–15b.

[9] *SS* 181.4408; *CYZJ* yiji, 16.787–89; *LCGM* 12.9a–10a.

[10] Zhen Dexiu 真德秀, "Guiyou wuyue ershi'er ri zhenqian zoushi, zouzha'er" 癸酉五月二十二日真前奏事,奏箚二, *Zhen Wenzhong gong wenji* 真文忠公文集 ([hereafter *ZWZWJ*]; SKQS ed.), 2.30b–32a.

affluent households in the prefectural city were required to hold 200 *guan*, middling households 100 *guan*, and poorer households 50 *guan*.[11] Such coercive measures ignited furious protest, prompting the court to rescind the order.

A similarly steep depreciation of paper currency occurred in Sichuan. The civil war that erupted in Sichuan in 1206 incited a financial panic, causing the value of the *qianyin* paper currency to tumble. The general command responded by disbursing its funds to buy back half of the issue #90 *qianyin* bills in circulation (amounting to 13 million *guan*). Since the state had no reserves of iron coin, it used silver and ordination certificates (*dudie* 度牒) to repurchase the bills.[12] The authorities expended 1.5 million *liang* of silver (at prevailing exchange rates, worth 9.3 million *guan*); silver expenditures thus accounted for about 70 percent of the monies used to redeem the bills. Two years later, in 1210, the government embarked on a campaign to redeem issue #91 *qianyin* bills by compensating the bearers 70 percent in new bills (#93) and 30 percent in silver.[13] The ready availability of silver for this purpose was noted by the commissioner of the Huguang General Command, who in 1212 reported that although officials in Sichuan could redeem excess paper currency by selling silver because Sichuan had ample stocks of precious metals, in Hubei silver was scarce and the state instead had to exchange tea licenses for paper bills.[14]

In the wake of the severe depreciation of paper currencies that followed the outbreak of the Kaixi War, then, Song authorities applied a full range of *chengti* measures to restore their value. The success of these measures is difficult to determine. With the abrupt devaluation of *huizi* in 1211, which reduced their nominal value by half, public confidence in paper currency evaporated. Wu Yong, then in Hangzhou, described the impact of the devaluation in these terms: "When the new order was issued, public opinion reacted with shock and dismay. Sounds of bitter wailing filled the streets. The august lineages and great families went so far as piling their paper bills in the streets and setting them ablaze. Such was the extent to which the currency had lost the people's trust."[15] Initially, issues #14 and #15 were set to expire in 1219, but the court decided to extend their circulation indefinitely, apparently to reassure the populace that another devaluation of *huizi* like that of 1211 would not recur.[16] Opinion about the lasting impact of the devaluation diverged. In 1214, the Department of State Affairs (Shangshusheng 尚書省)

[11] Chen Chun 陳淳, "Shang Zhao sicheng lun chengti huizi" 上趙寺丞論稱提會子, *Beixi da quanqi* 北溪大全集 ([hereafter *BXQJ*]; SKQS ed.), 44.1b.

[12] Ordination certificates were awarded to Buddhist clerics and entailed significant tax exemptions. The Southern Song state often used these certificates as financial instruments to raise revenue. In 1206, they had a value of 1,000 *guan*. See *SS* 181.4408.

[13] *CYZJ* yiji, 16.789–91.

[14] *LCGM* 13.22a–23a.

[15] Wu Yong, "Jiao Xue Ji zengguan citou" 繳薛極贈官詞頭, *HeLJ* 21.9b.

[16] Gao, *Huobi liutong*, pp. 190–91.

pronounced that "in recent years we have been blessed with bountiful harvests, rice prices have moderated, and the balance between paper currency and coin has returned to the former level."[17] In a memorial of 1215, Wei Jing, then prefect of Fuzhou (Fujian), stressed the positive effects of the devaluation, which he believed brought the price of *huizi* in alignment with their real value. Most people, Wei wrote, did not regard the devaluation as harmful: "it was only the powerful lineages and rich families who hold stores of *huizi*" that were alarmed by the sudden loss in the value of the bills they held. Wei conceded that even "middling households" sought to sell off bills, causing a further decline in their value. He also criticized the mandate requiring households to hold savings in the form of *huizi*, objecting that it was in the nature of money to flow freely. The *chengti* measures had induced an abrupt rise in the value of *huizi* – above 800 *wen* – but as the new issues flooded the market their value had slipped back to the range of 620 *wen*. Still, Wei concluded, "the people can conduct trade using *huizi*, which can be readily exchanged for coin; this cannot be considered a case of deceiving the populace by artificially raising their value."[18] The conversion of Fujian's entire *shanggong* tax obligations to *huizi* in 1213 also was said to have contributed to the rebound in the value of *huizi*.[19]

In principle, the retirement of old bills by new ones at a 2:1 ratio reduced the quantity in circulation by half. We do not know how many of the #14 and #15 issues were emitted initially because – contrary to prevailing practice – these new bills had no terms of expiry. Over 232 million *guan* of #14 and #15 *huizi* were issued over the next twenty-three years (see Table 6.1), but presumably at a more gradual rate than the sudden infusion of 140 million *guan* of #11, #12, and #13 bills in 1204–1207. From 1215 down to the early 1230s, the market value of *huizi* held steady around 600 *wen*, and the absence of discussion about the value of *huizi* during these years suggests that depreciation of paper currency had receded as an urgent concern.[20] Despite the massive increase in the emission of *huizi* bills since Xiaozong's reign, prices remained stable until the 1230s, when new crises overwhelmed the Song state's capacity to manage its paper currency.[21]

17 *SHY* shihuo 70.108b.

18 民間通行執會,便可得錢,此非虛漲高價以事欺之謂也. Wei Jing, "Lun chubi lihai," *HLJ* 15.8a–15a.

19 *SHY* shihuo 44.16b.

20 In a lecture before the emperor in 1234, Zhen Dexiu dismissed the *chengti* measures of the 1210s as ineffective, but he also observed that the value of *huizi* in the outlying provinces in 1231–1232 was generally in the range of 600 *wen*, and no less than 500–550 *wen* anywhere. See Zhen, "Jiangyan jindu Daxue zhangju shouji" 講筵近讀大學章句手記, *ZWZWJ* 18.30a–b.

21 Guan and Qian, "Zhibi de yunxing jizhi," pp. 122–27.

6.2 Recurring Devaluation Crises

Although the Jin preoccupation with domestic turmoil and the Mongol threat provided temporary relief, the Song monetary system suffered another series of shocks in the 1230s. The great Hangzhou fire of 1231 destroyed a large swath of the capital, including (ominously) the imperial family's ancestral temple. By 1233, fiscal expenditures had reached 94 million *guan*, nearly 30 percent greater than at the end of Emperor Xiaozong's reign.[22] Plans had been drawn up to remove the long-circulating (and many now tattered) #14 and #15 *huizi* bills from circulation, but to defray the enormous costs of rebuilding the capital the court – still under the control of the chief state councilor Shi Miyuan – hastily arranged the emission of issue #16, bringing the total number of *huizi* in circulation to over 300 million *guan*.[23] The value of *huizi* plummeted, and once again the court invoked the *chengti* strategy of disbursing gold, silver, salt licenses, and other paper assets to redeem the excess supply of paper currency (Table 6.2). But this time, the massive quantity of outstanding paper currency dwarfed the hard currency reserves held in state treasuries. Wei Liaoweng, an ardent Daoxue partisan, and other critics derided Shi Miyuan for having emptied state coffers – Wei asserted that altogether 40 million *guan* of gold and silver had been expended – in exchange for worthless paper, while having only a slight effect in shoring up the value of *huizi*.[24]

The Mongol conquest of Jin in 1234, replacing one enemy with a much more formidable menace, exacerbated the fiscal distress of the Song state. During the more than twenty-five years that he had dominated the court, Shi Miyuan had hewed to a conservative defensive posture, avoiding conflict with Jin. But after Shi's death at the end of 1233, Emperor Lizong (r. 1224–1264) was persuaded to seek to capitalize on the demise of Jin and launch an offensive to recover the former Song capital of Kaifeng. The Mongols quickly annihilated the Song forces, however, and Mongol counterattacks made deep incursions into Song territories, especially in Sichuan. The Mongols overran nearly all of Sichuan, putting its main cities to the torch, before the death of

22 Dai, "Shuquan yuanliu," in *SP* shang, 37b.

23 Dai Zhi, a contemporary, estimated that the quantity of *huizi* in circulation had reached 320 million *guan*. See Dai, "Shuquan yuanliu," in *SP* shang, 38b. Table 6.1 estimates the total volume of #14, #15, and #16 bills at 361.6 million *guan*, but of course many bills already had worn out.

24 Wei Liaoweng 魏了翁, "Bei zhao chu libu shangshu neiyin zoushi" 被召除禮部尚書內因奏事, *Heshan xiansheng da quanji* 鶴山先生大全集 (SKQS ed.), 19.20b; see also Wu Qian 吳潛, "Yingzhao shangfengshi tiaochen guojia dati zhidao yaowu fan jiushi" 應詔上封事條陳國家大體治道要務凡九事, *Xu guogong zouyi* 許國公奏議 ([hereafter *XGGZY*]; CSJC ed.), 1.23. On Wei Liaoweng's deep hostility to Shi Miyuan and his policies, see Hartman, *Structures of Governance*, pp. 110–13.

Table 6.2 *Disbursements to retire current* huizi *issues, 1233*

Type of payment	Amount	Value in *guan*
Bronze coin	200,000 *guan*	200,000
Gold	91,830 *liang*	3,673,200
Silver	2,016,900 *liang*	6,450,000
Paper assets (e.g., official investitures, ordination certificates, salt licenses)	Unspecified	?

Source: Wu Yong, "Xue Ji citou," *HeLJ* 21.10a

Ögödei, Chinggis's son and successor as great khan, in 1241 triggered a succession crisis that forced the Mongols to halt their campaigns of conquest, from China to eastern Europe. Only in 1252, after the installation of Möngke – grandson of Chinggis by his son Tolui – as great khan did the Mongols resume their efforts to conquer the Southern Song.

The defeats suffered at the hands of the Mongols intensified appeals for fiscal and monetary reform. Needing another upsurge in military spending, the court decided to release a new issue of *huizi* (#17) and simultaneously retire issues #14 and #15 – without applying the 50 percent devaluation enacted in 1210 when issues #11–#13 were withdrawn.[25] But with #16 and #17 both in circulation, the supply of *huizi* surpassed that of the combined #14 and #15 issues and depreciation continued to worsen. Wu Qian, commissioner of the Huaixi General Command, reported that the introduction of the new *huizi* bills led to discounting of the old (issues #14 and #15) relative to the new ones: the market value of the old bills was a mere 300 *wen*, while the new bills traded at 429 *wen* – still well below the prevailing exchange rate before 1233. Since the government had already expended its silver reserves, Wu argued, the only way to revive the value of *huizi* was to compel merchants to purchase salt licenses using the old bills (although in principle the *pinda* formula for salt licenses required partial payment in *huizi*, according to Wu this rule was rarely enforced). Wu optimistically projected that rigorous enforcement of the *pinda* formula would enable the state to retire 90 million *guan*, or more than 80 percent, of the old bills still in circulation. The remaining 10–20 million *guan* of old bills could be removed by repurchasing them through a combination of ordination certificates and official titles (20 percent), gold and silver (20 percent) and new bills (60 percent).[26] To the best of our knowledge no action was taken on Wu's proposal, however.

[25] *SS* 181.4408. Given the number of memorials opposing a new devaluation, it appears that the idea was seriously considered before it was discarded.

[26] Wu Qian, "Guojia dati jiushi," *XGGZY* 1.23.

In stressing the urgency of the currency problem, Wu Qian warned that the Mongol conquest of Jin was a direct result of the deterioration of the Jin currency – to the point where by the end Jin paper bills were worth only 1 percent of their face value – which fatally undermined its ability to mount an effective defense.[27] An equally bleak assessment was delivered by Xu Luqing, who argued that the currency crisis was an even greater threat than the Mongols. Replacing old bills with new ones had accomplished little, Xu concluded. The value of *huizi* had fallen as low as 220 *wen* in the provinces and was scarcely higher in the capital. The only solution was to devalue the bills currently in circulation by replacing them with yet another issue of *huizi* that would be tariffed at the official exchange rate of 770 *wen*. The existing issues, #16 and #17, would be redeemed with the new bills at only one-third of their face value (i.e., slightly above their current market value). Local officials also should expend their coin reserves to buy up issues #16 and #17 at the same price (240 *wen* of coin for 1 *guan* of paper currency).[28] In 1235, the court created a new Huizi Superintendency Office (Tiling huizi suo 提領會子所), specifically charged with devising new strategies to reverse the deterioration of paper currency. Numerous *chengti* measures – collecting all taxes in *huizi*, further disbursements of silver and official titles to redeem bills, levying a land tax surcharge payable in new *huizi* – were proposed, but efforts to implement them derailed. In 1240, the court acceded to the necessity of Xu Luqing's devaluation strategy, issuing #18 *huizi* to redeem the #16 bills at a steep discount of 80 percent (i.e., 1 *guan* of #18 *huizi* would be exchanged for 5 *guan* of #16 bills). The #17 *huizi* would remain in circulation, but at the same 80 percent discount (i.e., they had an official exchange value of 154 *wen*).[29]

The devaluation that accompanied the introduction of issue #18 in 1240 proved to be a serious miscalculation. The arbitrary devaluation of #17 bills sent their market value skidding to a mere 50–80 *wen* (Table 6.3), while the new #18 bills also were steeply discounted at around 250–260 *wen*. From 1240 down to the 1260s, the exchange value of circulating bills remained at these depressed levels. In 1247, when rumors of the impending issue of #19 *huizi* sparked widespread panic over another possible devaluation, the court declared that issues #17 and #18 would circulate in perpetuity. During the 1250s, the court occasionally offered to replace worn bills with new bills, or redeemed them with ordination certificates, official titles, coin, or even rice.

27 As early as 1215, Huang Gan had asserted that the Mongol victories over the Jin directly resulted from the deterioration of the Jin currency, leaving the rulers unable to feed and supply their armies. Huang Gan, "Yu Li Jingzi sizhi shu" 與李敬子司直書, *MZJ* 5.11a–b.

28 Xu Luqing 徐鹿卿, "Lun dailu jiuchu erzhazi shang shumiyuan di'erzha" 論待虜救楮二箚子上樞密院第二箚, *Qingzheng cungao* 清正存稿 ([hereafter *QZCG*; SKQS ed.), 5.15a–18b.

29 *Songshi quanwen* 宋史全文 ([hereafter *SSQW*]; SKQS ed.), 33.25a–b.

Table 6.3 *Market values of #17* huizi

Value (*wen*)	Place	Date	Source
70	Yanzhou (Zhejiang)	1241	*Yanzhou tujing* 嚴州圖經 (SYDFZ ed.), 1.49b–50b
80 <	Taizhou (Zhejiang)	1241	Wu Yong, "Yu Ma Guangzu huzou zhuang" 與馬光祖互奏狀, *HeLJ* 23.23.6a–b
70	Ningbo (Zhejiang)	1244	[*Baoqing*] *Siming zhi* [寶慶] 四明志 (SYDFZ ed.), 5.15a
67	—	1240s	Zhang Duanyi 張端義, *Gui'er ji*貴耳集 (SKQS ed.), shang上, 6b
54, 59[a]	—	1247	Qin Jiushao 秦九韶, *Shushu shizhang* 數書十章 (1841 Yijiatang congshu ed.), 11.1a
55[b]	Ningbo (Zhejiang)	1256	[*Kaiqing*] *Siming xuzhi* [寶慶] 四明續志 (SYDFZ ed.), 4.6b
44[c]	Changsha (Hunan)	1258	Li Zengbo 李曾伯, "Huizou xuanyu" 回奏宣諭, *Kezhai zagao* 可齋雜藁 (SKQS ed.) xugaohou 續藁後, 6.36b
50	—	1264	Fang Hui 方回, "Jianbu Lügong jiazhuan" 監簿呂公家傳, 3a, in Lü Wu呂午, *Zuoshi jiancao* 左史諫草 (SKQS ed.)

Notes: [a] Values given in problems presented in a mathematics treatise.
[b] Official exchange rate for liquor franchise tax based on market value.
[c] Exchange rate calculated from relative exchange rates of #17 *huizi*, silver, and coin.

Many levies were collected entirely in paper currency.[30] We do not know how many #18 bills were issued. In the early 1240s, Yuan Fu – who had earned a reputation for his knowledge of fiscal and military affairs – asserted that 500 million *guan* of old bills remained in circulation and it would take fifty years to retire all of them.[31] Another memorial from 1246 claimed that "the old bills had exceeded 420 million *guan*, and the new ones have already reached 230 million *guan*."[32] Yet in the quarter-century after the introduction

[30] Wang Shengduo, *Liang Song huobi*, vol. 2, pp. 725–28.
[31] Yuan Fu 袁甫, "Lun huizi zhazi" 論會子箚子, *Mengzhai ji* 蒙齋集 ([hereafter *MeZJ*]; SKQS ed.), 7.18b.
[32] Sun Mengguan 孫夢觀, "Bingwu lundui zhazi" 丙午輪對箚子, *Xuechuang ji* 雪窗集 (SKQS ed.), 1.20a–b.

of #18 *huizi*, the monetary situation seems to have stabilized, and most likely the total quantity of *huizi* remained roughly constant.[33]

The issue of #18 *huizi* in 1240 was part of a comprehensive fiscal and military reorganization that concentrated control over resources in the hands of the court at the expense of military commanders and fiscal agencies (such as the general commands) in the field. The Kaixi War had exposed the marked deterioration of the standing armies as fighting forces, and the government turned instead to newly mustered armies to boost its military strength. Although the Song armies had swelled to 500,000–600,000 men by the 1230s, this dramatic increase in size was not accompanied by a commensurate improvement in military preparedness. In 1245, the state councilor Fan Zhong estimated that while the combined Song armies enrolled 700,000 soldiers, only 10 percent were deemed battle ready.[34] Nonetheless, military outlays surged. In a memorial dating from the mid 1250s, Gao Side stated that according to what he learned from an official in charge of national accounts, government expenditures exceeded 250 million *guan* annually, in contrast to revenues of only 120 million *guan*. In the face of these intractable deficits, the only response from fiscal officials was to print more money, which Gao likened to "drinking poison to slake one's thirst."[35]

In 1239, Shi Songzhi – a nephew of the late Shi Miyuan – was appointed state councilor and dispatched to the frontier to supervise military operations against the Mongols. After his recall to the capital in the third month of 1240, Shi aimed to strengthen central control over military and fiscal affairs while curbing Lizong's extravagant expenditures on the palace and imperial clan. Shi Songzhi played a key role in the decision to issue #18 *huizi*, which was enacted six months after his return to Hangzhou. At the same time, he created a new Tea and Salt Commission (Zhizhi chayansi 制置茶鹽司) that assumed authority over nearly all tea and salt revenues. Under the auspices of this new administration of state monopolies, the government once again replaced

[33] Fang Hui, writing after the Mongol conquest of Southern Song, claimed that from 1240 to 1264, "the people generally were satisfied with [the paper currency]" 民頗安之. See Fang Hui 方回, "Jianbu Lügong jiazhuan" 監簿呂公家傳, 3a, in Lü Wu 呂午, *Zuoshi jiancao* 左史諫草 ([hereafter *ZSJC*]; SKQS ed.). Honda Seiichi also underscores the relative stability of paper currency exchange values during the 1240–1264 period: Honda Seiichi 本田精一, "Nan-Sō kankaishi no ronri to jittai" 南宋官会子の論理と実態, *Kyūshū daigaku tōyōshi ronshū* 九州大学東洋史論集 25 (1997): 116.

[34] Fang Yue 方岳, "Dai Fan chengxiang" 代范丞相, *Qiuya xiansheng xiaogao* 秋崖先生小稿 (Qing ms.), 3, cited in Zhang Jinling 张金岭, *Wan Song shiqi caizheng weiji yanjiu* 晚宋时期财政危机研究 (Chengdu: Sichuan daxue chubanshe, 2001), p. 45.

[35] Gao Side 高斯得, "Lundui zouzha" 輪對奏劄, *Chitang cungao* 恥堂存稿 (SKQS ed.), 1.30b. On the state's fiscal straits in the late Southern Song, see Zhang Jinling, *Wan Song caizheng weiji*.

the salt licensing system with a state monopoly.[36] The Tea and Salt Commission, together with the Zhexi–Lianghuai Transport Agency (Zhexi Lianghuai Fayunsi 浙西兩淮發運司) established at Suzhou in 1239 at Shi's behest to supervise military provisioning, gradually wrested away the key revenue streams of the general commands.[37] Entrenched opposition from Daoxue partisans – with whom Lizong, annoyed by Shi Songzhi's efforts to rein in palace spending, was ready to comply – pushed Shi from office in 1244. Nonetheless, the centralizing policies Shi initiated only intensified in the following years. In 1246, the government reestablished the Budget Department (Guoyongsi), which had been abolished in 1207, to coordinate military expenditures from the capital. The state began to demand advanced payments of twice-a-year taxes under the name of "advance loans" (*yujie* 預借). "Harmonious purchases" (*hedi*) were transformed into compulsory tax assessments. By the early 1250s, the Tea and Salt Commission had usurped control over the tea revenues that had become the staple source of income for the Huguang General Command. In the eyes of some historians, the diversion of revenues away from the frontline armies to the capital and the court fatally compromised Song defenses after the Mongols renewed their onslaught against the Song.[38]

One consequence of these efforts to strengthen central control over fiscal administration was the displacement of regional paper monies by capital *huizi*. When the Mongol counterattacks in 1235–1236 forced the court to rush emergency funds to the armies along the Huainan/Hubei frontier, it did so mostly using *huizi*. For example, only 100,000 *guan* of the 800,000 *guan* dispatched to the crucially strategic military base at Jiangling were delivered in the form of *huhui*, the rest consisting of *huizi*. In the 1250s, the Huguang General Command's allocations for military expenses, harmonious purchases, and other fiscal expenditures were routinely made in *huizi*, not *huhui*, and *huizi* had also become the standard money of account in local government fiscal administration.[39] Similarly, by the 1240s, soldiers' stipends in Huainan were paid solely in *huizi* (20–30 percent in #18 bills, the remainder in #17

[36] Wang Shengduo 汪圣铎 and Guo Lan 郭兰, "Nan Song houqi yanzheng kaolun" 南宋后期盐政考论, *Yan wenhua yanjiu luncong* 盐文化研究论丛1 (2006): 148–55; Liang Gengyao, *Nan Song yanque*, pp. 166–79.

[37] On the displacement of the Huaidong General Command by the Zhexi–Lianghuai Transport Agency, see Kobayashi Akira 小林晃, "Nan-Sō kōki ni okeru Ryōwai bōeigun no tōsei seisaku: Sessai Ryōwai hatsu'unshi kara kōtenhō e" 南宋後期における両淮防衛軍の統制政策: 浙西両淮発運司から公田法へ, *Rekishigaku kenkyū* 歴史学研究 923 (2014): 1–17.

[38] Zhou Quyang, "Jing-Hu junshi buji taizhi."

[39] Wang Shen, "Hubei huizi." New issues of *huhui* continued to be emitted at least as late as 1254, but largely to replace worn notes.

bills) rather than *huaijiao*.[40] In 1249, Chen Qingmian, a local prefect reassigned from Guangdong to Hubei, observed that even though *huizi* were scarcely used in market trade in Guangdong, *huizi* bills traded at a higher rate of exchange in Guangdong than did the *huhui* paper currency at his new post, which he attributed to the limited range of circulation of the latter.[41]

The most dramatic change came in Sichuan, where the value of *qianyin* steeply eroded after a third concurrent issue was introduced in 1204.[42] A series of familiar *chengti* interventions – notably, winnowing the paper bills in circulation by exchanging gold, silver, and ordination certificates for them – initially stabilized the value of *qianyin*, but by 1234 it was reported that the volume of *qianyin* had reached 170 million *dao*, 50 percent greater than in the 1210s. In 1254, Sichuan officials introduced a new type of currency called "silver *huizi*" (*yinhui* 銀會), about which we have scant information.[43] The *yinhui* bills appear to have been highly overvalued, resulting in ruinous depreciation and price inflation. Li Zengbo blamed the depreciation on excessive issue of *yinhui* (totaling, in the space of two years, an amount equivalent to the previous twelve years of *qianyin* issues) by the Sichuan military commissioner, who had arrogated the right to print money. The market value of *yinhui* relative to #18 *huizi* had fallen by 80 percent (from 1:1.2 to 1:5), making them roughly equivalent to #17 *huizi* (which were officially worth only 20 percent of the value of #18 *huizi*). Observing that "Sichuan people highly esteem capital *huizi*," Li urged the court to replace the Sichuan paper currencies with capital *huizi*, which would have multiple benefits: the monetary system would be unified; the court could hold in check the amount of paper currency issued; and the value of paper currency would rise. The *yinhui* would be allowed to circulate, not only in Sichuan but beyond, at the same value as

40 Li Zengbo 李曾伯, "Chu Huaikun neiyin zouzha dierzha" 除淮閫內引奏劄第二劄, *Kezhai zagao* 可齋雜藁 ([hereafter *KZZG*]; SKQS ed.), 17.8b.

41 Chen Qingmian 陳慶勉, "Puqi hui Ye dianyuan lun qianhui shu" 蒲圻回葉殿院論錢會書, *Xin'an wenxian zhi* 新安文獻志 ([hereafter *XAWX*]; SKQS ed.), 10.3a–7a.

42 According to a local official in Sichuan, each issue amounted to 36–37 million *dao*, or roughly 110 million *dao* altogether. Du Zheng 度正, "Shang benlu zhuanyun lun fuqian zhazi" 上本路轉運論夫錢劄子, *Xingshantang ji* 性善堂集 (SKQS ed.), 7.1a–4a.

43 A brief and cryptic passage states: "The exchange value of *yinhui* was 1:100. The bills were intended as a temporary expedient to facilitate exchange and enhance the value of paper currency, yet instead the paper currency continued to depreciate." Li Zengbo, "Jiu Shuchu mizou" 救蜀楮密奏, *KZZG* xujihou 續集後, 3.44a. Previously the Sichuan General Command had occasionally issued, for short periods of time and in small quantities, "coin/silver *huizi*" (*qianyin huizi* 錢銀會子) bills denominated in silver units (1.0 and 0.5 *qian*) with a fixed exchange rate with *qianyin* (1 *qian* silver = 250 *wen* in *qianyin*). See Wang Shengduo, *Liang Song huobi*, vol. 2, pp. 763–65. Thus the official value of the new silver notes, at an exchange rate of 1:100, was two-and-a-half times greater than the older ones. But the real exchange rate of the bills relative to silver fell from 1 *liang* = 3000 *wen* in 1255 to 1:7,500 in 1256. See Li Zengbo, "Jiu Shuchu mizou."

#17 *huizi*.[44] In 1256, the court acted precisely as Li had advised, ordering the printing of Sichuan *huizi* (*chuanhui* 川會) bills that would be modeled on #18 *huizi* and circulate at par with them. *Qianyin* bills were to be withdrawn from circulation and destroyed, while *yinhui* would remain in circulation at the same value as #17 *huizi*. We know little about the extent to which this plan was put into effect, but in 1269 the court transferred the authority to issue *chuanhui* bills to the Sichuan fiscal intendant and set a quota of 5 million *guan*.[45]

In 1258, the Mongols – under the leadership of the Great Khan Möngke and his brother Khubilai – intensified their assaults on the Southern Song, although the death of Möngke while on campaign in Sichuan prompted a pause in hostilities. After vanquishing a rival claimant to the title of great khan in 1264, Khubilai quickly returned his attention to the conquest of Song. In the same year, the long-reigning Lizong died, leaving a teenage nephew to inherit the throne. Jia Sidao, to whom Lizong had entrusted full control of state affairs after making him the sole councilor of state in 1260, seized the opportunity to embark on a program of radical fiscal reform. Jia sought to raise revenue through reallocation of the tax burden, most infamously through the "public lands" (*gongtian* 公田) program inaugurated in 1263. Large landowners were required to sell most of their holdings to the state, for which they would be compensated in *huizi* bills. Although these expropriations predictably were roundly denounced by the landholding elites – including many families of government officials – the revenues they generated enabled Jia to curb the burdensome "harmonious purchase" levies imposed on a much wider swath of the population.[46]

Jia also was determined to carry out an ambitious monetary reform, once again coupled to a devaluation. In 1264, he announced the creation of a new currency called "Gold/Silver/Ready Coin Sureties" (*jinyin xianqian guanzi* 金銀見錢關子), which would replace #18 *huizi* bills at a rate of 1 *guan* of the new bills for 3 *guan* of the old (#17 *huizi* were declared defunct and irredeemable). Despite its name, the new currency was not convertible with bronze coin or precious metals, and the sudden abandonment of the *huizi* currency created havoc in the marketplace. Prices once again soared, and in the next few years the government repeatedly issued edicts forbidding the discounting of the new *guanzi* currency, to no avail.[47] The #18 *huizi* remained in circulation, although

44 Li Zengbo, "Jiu Shuchu mizou," *KZZG* 3.44a–48a.

45 *SS* 181.4410–11; *Songji sanchao zhengyao* 宋季三朝政要 ([hereafter *SCZY*]; SKQS ed.), 2.29b.

46 Sudō Yoshiyuki 周藤吉之, "Nan Sō sue no kōdenhō" 南宋末の公田法, in Sudō, *Tō Sō tochi seido shi kenkyū* 唐宋土地制度史研究 (Tokyo: Tokyo daigaku shuppankai, 1954), pp. 537–92.

47 *SCZY* 3.19a–b; *MLL* 13, in *DJMHL*, p. 238; *XWXTK* 7.2844a.

at deeply discounted value. In a diatribe against the numerous "crimes" of Jia Sidao written in 1275, Fang Hui declared that "after the change to the *guanzi* currency, 200 *guan* of #18 *huizi* could not buy a pair of straw sandals, yet that is what soldiers received as a daily allowance."[48] The hyperinflation that often spells the doom of a regime had set in. By that time, Khubilai's armies had crossed the Yangzi River and were marching on the Song capital, which fell to the Mongols in March of 1276.

6.3 Paper Currencies and Market Exchange

The paper currencies developed during the Southern Song period were integrally linked to the fiscal operations of the imperial state. The division of the empire into four distinct currency zones, each anchored by a unique paper currency, reflected the primacy of fiscal priorities in devising the architecture of the monetary system. The *pinda* formulas for public payments (taxes, sales of commodity licenses) and disbursements (officials' salaries, soldiers' stipends, *hedi* purchases) ensured the regular flow of paper currencies between state treasuries and the wider economy. Paper currencies grew increasingly prominent in this system of fiscal circulation over time, while the role of coin steadily diminished. Silver also emerged as a crucial medium of fiscal circulation in the Southern Song, but the role of silver was constrained by its limitations as a means of exchange, almost never used in private market transactions.

As we have noted previously, in the eyes of some scholars the dissemination and use of Song paper currencies, including the *huizi* bills, was driven entirely by their fiscal functions. Bronze coin remained the money of account, and some would argue that paper bills did not serve as a genuine medium of market exchange.[49] Yet, regardless of the importance of state initiative in compelling the use of paper currencies, once created they took on a life of their own and became indispensable features of the Song market economy. Indeed, by the end of the Song, the *huizi* paper currency had displaced bronze coin as the monetary standard, even though *huizi* continued to be denominated in bronze coin units. Despite the depreciation of *huizi* in the 13th century, apart from in times of war the inflationary effects of this depreciation were relatively modest before the 1240s.[50]

48 Fang Hui 方回, "Yihai qian shangshu benmo" 乙亥前上書本末, *Tongjiang ji* 桐江集 (XX SKQS ed.), 6.8b.

49 See Chapter 4. This argument has also been made for *huizi* specifically. See Wang Shen 王申, "Lun Nan Song qianqi dongnan huizi de xingzhi yu liutong zhuangkuang" 论南宋前期东南会子的性质与流通状况, *Qinghua daxue xuebao (zhexue shehui kexue ban)* 清华大学学报 (哲学社会科学版) 34.3 (2019): 106–17.

50 The gradual pace of inflation before 1240 is affirmed in Guan and Qian, "Zhibi de yunxing jizhi," 125–26; Honda, "Kankaishi no ronri to jittai," 124–27. See also Figure 4.1.

The prevalence of paper currencies in market exchange varied by region. In Sichuan, where paper currencies had been in use since the beginning of the 11th century, the *qianyin* bills had long been adopted as the monetary standard (and also as the money of account, expressed as *dao*). As we saw in Chapter 5, in 1163 Wang Zhiwang, then the commissioner of the Sichuan General Command, reported that nearly 42 million *dao* of *qianyin* were in circulation, whereas government treasuries held only 700,000 strings of iron coin. In Wang's view, the value of *qianyin* was sustained by their use in fiscal circulation, specifically for purchases of salt and tea licenses. Two years later, when the court ordered the authorities in Sichuan to transfer 1 million *guan* of iron coins to the Huainan region, the military commissioner (Zhizhishi 制置使) of Sichuan, Wang Yingchen, objected on the grounds that Sichuan "depended entirely on iron coin to maintain the equilibrium (*chengti*) in the value of *qianyin*." Wang conceded that the amount of iron coin was a mere 1–2 percent of the quantity of *qianyin* bills in circulation, yet he insisted that iron coin remained vitally important: while *qianyin* always are used in transactions of 800–900 *wen*, amounts of 400–500 *wen* must be settled in coin. Invoking the famous metaphor from the *Guan Zi*, Wang declared that "balancing the equilibrium in the values of coin and *qianyin* is the Master of Destiny in Sichuan (錢引權衡,為四川之司命)."[51] Still, like other Sichuan officials, Wang routinely reported market prices for rice in *qianyin* units.[52] A report from 1195 on the low price of ramie cloth in Sichuan noted that "the price of one bolt does not exceed 67 *wen* of *jiaozi* [sic]."[53] Expressing this price in *qianyin* (apparently the *jiaozi* label remained in vernacular use) even

[51] Wang Yingchen 汪應辰, "Qi mian jiefa tieqian fu Lianghuai shu" 乞免解發鐵錢赴兩淮書, *Wending ji* 文定集 ([hereafter *WDJ*]; SKQS ed.), 13.12b. Other officials in Sichuan at this time focused on the central importance of paper currency rather than iron coin. Li Liuqian, a Sichuan native then serving as personal secretary to the Sichuan pacification commissioner Yu Yunwen, wrote a letter to Wang Yingchen in 1167 declaring that *qianyin* currency was a deeply established institution in Sichuan, which even "sagely wisdom" could not alter. Li went on to say that oscillations in the value of *qianyin* were not the result of market forces but rather determined by whether or not the state employs paper currency. The value of *qianyin*, which was low in the early spring, rose abruptly after the tea harvest (generally in late April to early June) because the Sichuan authorities (the Tea and Horse Agency) disbursed *qianyin* at that time to purchase tea. In Li's mind, this pattern showed the power of the state to control the value of paper currency, which Sichuan's "knowledgeable and experienced elders" (老練達者) recognized as "the knack of how to induce paper currency to circulate" (*liutong zhibi zhi miao* 流通紙幣之妙). Li Liuqian 李流謙, "Yu Wang zhizhi zhazi" 與汪制置劄子, *Danzhai ji* 澹齋集 (SKQS ed.), 9.15a–17a. For the invocation of the Master of Destiny (albeit in a different sense than Wang Yingchen) in the fiscal philosophy of the *Guan Zi*, see Chapter 1.

[52] See, for example, Wang Yingchen, "Yuzha wen Shuzhong hanlian yihui zou" 御劄問蜀中旱歉一回奏, *WDJ* 4.1a–6a.

[53] *SHY* shihuo 18.22a.

though the amount was far less than the smallest *qianyin* bill of 200 *wen* testifies to the prevalence of *qianyin* as Sichuan's monetary standard.

Over time, the capital *huizi* bills became indispensable to the commercial vigor of the regions (referred to as "the southeast") in which they circulated. Xin Qiji, an enthusiastic proponent of paper money, wrote in 1175 that *huizi* circulated only in the capital region and in the vicinity of the major military bases; they were not found in villages or remote parts of the empire. Xin urged the court to take more affirmative actions to ensure the broader dissemination of *huizi*.[54] Among those who extolled the benefits of *huizi* to lubricate the wheels of commerce was the philosopher Lu Jiuyuan. In a letter (probably dating from the 1180s) urging local officials in his native county of Jinxi (Jiangxi) to replenish granary reserves by purchasing grain following a bountiful harvest using *huizi*, Lu emphasized both opportunity and means: plenty of merchants frequented Jinxi, and they preferred *huizi* rather than coin because it was more convenient to carry.[55] *Huizi* also functioned as a convenient means of remitting funds for personal as well as commercial purposes. An anecdote in Hong Mai's *Tales of the Listener* recounts that an official stationed at the Huainan frontier, wishing to send home to his mother in Jiaxing (Zhejiang) 100 *guan* he had accumulated from his salary payments, exchanged the coin for *huizi* to do so.[56] In 1191, Peng Guinian declared that "the circulation of *huizi* surpasses that of bronze coin, and both public and private derive benefit from it."[57]

With the development of regional paper currencies, by 1200 paper money was used almost everywhere except the Lingnan littoral in the far south. According to one author, who regarded paper currency as a boon to commerce, around 1210 *huizi* were circulating in Liangzhe, Jiangxi, Huainan, and Fujian.[58] The circulation of *huizi* throughout these same regions was confirmed by another contemporary essayist who marveled that it took "only a single porter to transport a thousand or ten thousand *guan* of money."[59] In 1211, the court dispatched envoys to assess the progress of the redemption

54 Xin Qiji, "Lun xingyong huizi shu," *MCZY* 272.13a–14b.

55 Lu Jiuyuan 陸九淵, "Yu Chen jiaoshou (er)" 與陳教授 (二), *Lu Xiangshan quanji* 陸象山全集 (Taipei: Shijie shuju, 1969), 8.70–71.

56 *YJZ* zhigui 支癸 3, p. 1244.

57 Peng Guinian, "Lun leixue zhi yi wei yinsheng qinyang zhi zheng shu" 論雷雪之異為陰盛侵陽之證疏, *ZTJ* 1.18a–b.

58 *GJYL* 14.14b–15a. Since this passage refers to three issues circulating simultaneously, it must date from 1207 to 1211.

59 Cited in Xie Weixin 謝維新, *Gujin hebi shilei beiyao* 古今合璧事類備要 ([hereafter *GJHB*]; SKQS ed.), waiji 外集, 66.5a. The author of the essay, Zhang Wenbo 張文伯, wrote a work of classical exegesis but otherwise we have no biographical information about him. Presumably he was active around the turn of the 13th century, as were the other writers cited by Xie in this chapter of his encyclopedia (published in 1257).

of #11–#12 *huizi* by the new #13–#14 bills at the local level. The list of thirty-one prefectures to which the envoys were sent probably indicates areas where paper currency was in widespread use (Map 6.1). It includes all of Liangzhe and Jiangxi East circuits, but only half of Jiangxi West and a single prefecture, Jianning, in Fujian. We know from other sources, however, that *huizi* also were in common circulation in the coastal regions of Fujian as well.

Despite the steep depreciation in its value in the 13th century, *huizi* currency became even more essential to both public finance and private commerce, as numerous statesmen avowed amid the debates over monetary policy in the turbulent 1230s. In his memorial submitted to the throne in 1234, Wu Qian asserted that "paper currency truly is the lifeblood (*mingmai*) of the nation."[60] Writing a year later, Xu Luqing employed the same metaphor in attributing the state's fiscal distress to the combined problems of runaway military expenditures and profligate issue of paper currency: "our lifeblood is bound to the power to open and close the levers of profit (*liquan*)."[61] As we have seen, since the time of Sang Hongyang the "levers of profit" (*quanli, liquan*) denoted the state's power to make money and generate revenues, which Xu here invoked in reference to emitting paper currency. Addressing the emperor upon being recalled to the court in 1235, Yuan Fu spoke of his recent experiences as a provincial official in Jiangxi and Fujian, concluding with the observation that "in the present day every need requires using *huizi*."[62] Xu Luqing was referring specifically to the fiscal and military predicaments confronting the empire, but Wu Qian and Yuan Fu spoke more broadly of the economy as a whole. The displacement of coin by paper money even in hinterland areas was confirmed in a memorial of 1247 from Du Fan, then prefect of Ningguo (Anhui), who complained that his district's coin had all flowed out of the region, leaving both public finance and private trade completely dependent on paper money.[63]

Although the *huaijiao* and *huhui* paper currencies were even more tightly yoked to fiscal purposes, their introduction spread paper currencies throughout the Yangzi River basin. In response to a request in 1192 to assess the viability of *huaijiao* paper currency, the vice-intendant for grain tribute in Huaidong wrote "from what I have heard and seen, there are none who do not recognize the convenience of *jiaozi* [i.e., *huaijiao*]. When people gather in the

[60] 楮者,誠國家之命脈. Wu Qian, "Guojia dati jiushi," *XGGZY* 1.25. *Guojia*, which I have translated here as "nation," encompassed both state and society but of course should be distinguished from modern notions of nationhood.

[61] 利權通塞,命脈系焉. Xu Luqing, "Jiuchu dierzha," *QZCG* 5.15a–18b.

[62] 目今百需皆要會子. Yuan Fu 袁甫, "Mishu shaojian shangdian dier zhazi" 秘書少監上殿第二劄子, *MeZJ* 4.23a.

[63] Du Fan 杜范, "Bianmin wushi zouzha" 便民五事奏劄, *Qingxian ji*清獻集 ([hereafter *QXJ*]; SKQS ed.), 8.13a.

Map 6.1 Prefectures specified for assessing redemption of old *huizi*, 1211.
Source: *SHY* zhiguan 52.18.a–b.

marketplace and trade in the hundred goods, bronze coin, iron coin, and paper currency each have their fixed values."[64] As Chen Qingmian's letter of 1249 cited earlier confirms, by that time *huaijiao* had been largely displaced by *huizi* in Hubei. By contrast, Chen wrote, bronze coin was the most

[64] Yu Chou, "Beizhao shangdian zhazi," *MCZY* 272.2b.

prevalent medium for transactions in Guangdong.[65] Surprisingly, Chen made no mention of the use of silver in Guangdong. But we know from other sources that silver was the predominant medium of public payments in Guangdong.[66]

From the 1230s down to the Mongol conquest of the Southern Song in 1276, the exchange value (in bronze coin) of *huizi* bills hovered around a mere one-third of their nominal value. Nonetheless, paper money dominated both public finance and large-scale private trade, and it became common practice to stipulate prices in paper currency. The few surviving Southern Song land sale contracts confirm this trend. All seven of these contracts, dating from 1215, 1252, 1255, 1260, 1264, 1267, and 1270, are from Huizhou (Anhui) and specify payment in *huizi* (*guanhui* 官會).[67] *The Record of Millet Dreams* and *Hangzhou in Past Times*, nostalgic memoirs commemorating life in Hangzhou in the waning days of the Song dynasty, reveal that *huizi* were deeply woven into the fabric of the capital's everyday life: used to hire boats for festival excursions on West Lake; for bonuses to soldiers and their families; as – together with silver – indispensable betrothal gifts (even families of middling means were obliged to submit "one or two sheets" of *huizi*); as prizes for champions in wrestling tournaments; and as imperial alms distributed to the poor on New Year's Day.[68] Zhou Mi, the author of *Hangzhou in Past Times*, sought to illustrate the self-indulgent lifestyle of the capital's womenfolk in his observation that during the midsummer festival honoring the city's patron deity women would spend "several tens of bills" on jasmine flowers for their headdresses that would last for only a day.[69] Evidence for the everyday use of *huizi* also appears in the section on practical advice for travel included in a daily-use encyclopedia from the late Song, whose author recommends that the amounts of "coin and bills" (*qianhui* 錢會) to be paid for porters and boats be

65 Chen Qingmian, "Lun qianhui shu," *XAWX* 10.3a–7a.

66 Richard von Glahn, "Cycles of Silver in Chinese Monetary History," in Billy K. L. So (ed.), *The Economy of Lower Yangzi Delta in Late Imperial China: Connecting Money, Markets, and Institutions* (London: Routledge, 2013), pp. 25–26.

67 See Zhang Chuanxi 张传玺 (ed.), *Zhongguo lidai qiyue huibian kaoshi* 中国历代契约会编考释 (Beijing: Beijing daxue chubanshe, 1995), vol. 1, pp. 532–42. Notably, the three contracts dating from 1264–1270 still specify *huizi* as the medium of payment, even though in principle *huizi* had been superseded by Jia Sidao's *xianqian guanzi* currency. An inscription recording tenancy contracts dating from the 1230s to the 1270s for lands owned by a Confucian school in Suzhou records that in five cases (out of several dozen) the rent was specified as payment in #18 *huizi*. See "Wuxue liangtian xuji" 吳學糧田續記, in *Jiangsu jinshi zhi* 江蘇金石志 (n.p.: Jiangsu tongzhiju, 1927), 20.5b–17a.

68 *MLL* 12, 18, 20, and 20, in *DJMHL* pp. 235, 292–93, 305, and 312 respectively; Zhou Mi 周密, *Wulin jiushi* 武林舊事 [hereafter *WLJS*], 8, in *DJMHL*, p. 483.

69 *WLJS* 3, in *DJMHL*, p. 380.

specified in written contracts; he also gives advice on carrying *huizi* (*guanhui*) for traveling expenses.[70]

Nor were *huizi* restricted to large-scale transactions. A number of price quotations from the early 13th century give prices for purchases of sundry goods in *huizi*; for example, "no more than 100 *wen* of *huizi*" for one *jin* (600 g) of cooking oil, or 200 *wen* of *huizi* for one *jin* of pork.[71] Although the actual means of payment in these cases was not specified, they demonstrate that paper currency had come to serve as the money of account even for petty transactions.

The *Enlightened Judgments*, a casebook of judicial rulings by exemplary magistrates dating from the 1210s to the 1250s, offers especially valuable insights on the use of paper money in private payments and savings. Many of the land sale contracts described in these legal proceedings specified payments in *qianhui* 錢會, a term that probably should be understood as half in coin, half in *huizi*.[72] In other cases land purchases and loans were transacted entirely in *huizi*.[73] In two cases that dealt with sales of persons – one legally (a child bride), the other not – the price was paid in *huizi*.[74] After the state began to devalue older issues, it became common practice to specify which issue of *huizi* was used in payment. In a case involving hired labor, a father signed a contract that committed his daughter to indentured labor service of seven years in return for a payment of 220 *guan* of "old *huizi*," in this instance referring to #17 *huizi*.[75] Also noteworthy was the practice of combining different types of money in single transactions, for example in a case dating

70 Chen Yuanjing 陳元靚, [*Chongbian qunshu leiyao*] *Shilin guangji* [重編群書類要]事林廣記 (1325 ed., rpt. Kyoto: Yamaoka Ichibe hankō, 1699), gengji 庚集, 2.10b–11b. Of the three extant Yuan editions of this book, this Japanese reprint appears to be the closest to the Song original (now lost), and this section on travel clearly references Song rather than Yuan paper money. For a study of the various editions of the text, see Morita Kenji 森田憲司, "'Jirin kōki' no shohanpon ni tsuite: kokunai shozō no shohon o chūshin to shite"『事林廣記』の諸版本について：国内所蔵の諸本を中心として, in Sōdaishi kenkyūkai (ed.), *Sōdai no chishikijin: shisō, seido, chiiki shakai* 宋代の知識人:思想,制度,地域社会 (Tokyo: Kyūko shoin, 1993), pp. 287–316.

71 Cited in Takahashi, *Genchō kahei*, p. 212.

72 For example, a case from 1220 specifies that the redemption of a conditional land sale in the amount of 300 *guan* was to be paid half in coin, half in *huizi*: "Yidang" 倚當, in *QMJ* 6.170–71. See also the translation in McKnight and Liu, *Enlightened Judgments*, pp. 195–98.

73 "Ludi guiguan yi xi zhengjing" 陸地歸官以息爭競, in *QMJ* 6.187–88; "Chu jizi buxiao leling guizong" 出繼子不肖勒令歸宗, in *QMJ* 7.224–25; viz. McKnight and Liu, *Enlightened Judgments*, pp. 204–5, 251–53.

74 "Dingduo zhenghun" 定奪爭婚, in *QMJ* 9.348–49; "Hunjia jie wei tiaofa" 婚嫁皆違條法, in *QMJ* 9.352; viz. McKnight and Liu, *Enlightened Judgments*, pp. 341–42, 343–44.

75 "Maiguo shenziqian" 賣過身子錢, in *QMJ* 9.357–58 (not included in McKnight and Liu, *Enlightened Judgments*). Since this official served as a circuit judicial intendant in the 1240s, "old *huizi*" surely referred to #17 *huizi*.

from 1223 concerning a loan of 5,000 *guan* paid in "gold, silver, coin, and *huizi*" (*jinyin qianhui* 金銀錢會) that was used to purchase a substantial tract of land.[76] Estates often included sums of paper money as well. In one case, the government seized the assets – described as "coin, *huizi*, silverware, and other goods" (*qianhui yinqi deng* 錢會銀器等) – of a deceased man without an heir and placed them in an escrow account to be used as the future dowry of his minor daughter.[77] In a lawsuit concerning a foster son's theft of his father's estate, the property was described as consisting of 160 ounces of silverware, six trunks of unspecified goods, silk fabrics, calligraphy and paintings, *huizi*, and clothing.[78] Interestingly, this itemization of the estate's assets did not include coin.

The discounting of paper currency had to be taken into consideration in debt repayments. For example, a loan contracted in 1231 for the amount of 100 *guan* was made half in coin (50 *guan*) and half in paper money, but the creditor delivered 65 *guan* of *huizi*, reflecting the official discount of *huizi* at 770 *wen/guan*.[79] Devaluations of old bills created a conundrum in repayment of long-term debts. One magistrate asserted that the law required that debts be discharged in the media in which they were contracted. In the case before him, involving the redemption of a conditional land sale, the land had been sold for a payment of 120 *guan* in coin, but now the original owner sought to redeem the land with a mix of 50 *guan* of coin and 65 *guan* of paper currency (once again discounting the paper currency based on the official rate of 770 *wen/guan*).[80] The buyer insisted on full payment in coin. The magistrate observed that the current market rate of "old *huizi*" (in this case, presumably #17) was a

[76] "Zhi yu chujishu zhengye" 姪與出繼叔爭業, in *QMJ* 5.135–36; viz. McKnight and Liu, *Enlightened Judgments*, pp. 163–64.

[77] "Guan wei quchu" 官為區處, in *QMJ* 7.230–31; viz. McKnight and Liu, *Enlightened Judgments*, pp. 255–57.

[78] "Yizi baobing qinzi caiwu" 義子包併親子財物, in *QMJ* 7.242–43; viz. McKnight and Liu, *Enlightened Judgments*, pp. 269–71. In another case of theft, dating from the late 1230s, the accused was charged with having stolen jewelry, silver, *huizi*, and unspecified "baskets" of goods, all of which presumably can be understood as the victim's life savings. See "Zhangzhu yu kankuren huzheng" 掌主與看庫人互爭, in *QMJ* 9.339–43 (not included in McKnight and Liu, *Enlightened Judgments*). For a dispute over an inheritance of 500 *guan* of *huizi*, see "Jia wei di mingji wei ciyu wulai qi tangdi caiwu" 假為弟命繼為詞欲誣賴其堂弟財物, in *QMJ* 13.512–14 (not included in McKnight and Liu, *Enlightened Judgments*).

[79] "Chongdie jiaoyi he jian qinei qian guihuan" 重疊交易合監契內錢歸還, in *QMJ* 5.142–43; viz. McKnight and Liu, *Enlightened Judgments*, pp. 172–74.

[80] The document is somewhat garbled on this point. It states that the seller sought to redeem the land with 50 *guan* of coin and 65 *guan* of paper money (i.e., at the 770 *wen/guan* rate), but that would yield a total of 115 *guan*, less than the 120 *guan* of the debt. The magistrate later states that 50 *guan* in coin had been paid and the outstanding balance was 70 *guan*. Presumably what was meant was that the seller sought to pay off the remaining balance of 70 *guan* at the 770 *wen/guan* rate. The lawsuit had dragged on for

mere 200 coins; thus the full value of the outstanding debt, if paid in current *huizi*, should be 350 *guan*.[81] An even more complicated case involved a conditional sale that operated as a disguised loan. Taking the land as collateral, the creditor extended a loan of 280 *guan* in *huizi* (presumably #15 *huizi*) in 1215, and in 1241 the debtor's heirs sought to invoke their right to redeem the land. Over the years, the debtor had paid the creditor 30 *guan* of *huizi* per year in what were in effect interest charges. Given the pronounced decline in the value of *huizi* during the intervening twenty-six years, the creditor demanded repayment of the balance of the loan – which he claimed was 70 *guan* – in rice rather than money. The magistrate, noting that the price of rice had soared in recent years, insisted that the payment be made in money, but decided on a compromise: 30 percent of the debt (60 *guan*) would be paid in new bills (presumably the recently issued #18 bills) to redeem the land, and 70 percent (280 *guan*) in a mix of 30 percent new bills and 70 percent old bills (presumably #17 *huizi*) to settle the debt. Since #17 bills were worth only 20 percent of #18 bills, the nominal value of settling the debt would have been 123.2 *guan* of #18 bills.[82] How the magistrate arrived at this sum is unclear, but the case certainly illustrates the complexity of trying to settle debts using paper currencies of different values. In a memorial of 1246 based on his recent experiences as prefect of Taizhou (Zhejiang), Du Fan warned the court that debtors who sought to repay loans solely in paper currency were causing uproar and much iniquitous litigation. Du urged the court to reinforce the rule that loans must be repaid in the media, whether coin or paper currency, in which they were originally contracted.[83]

The distinction between the relative values of #17 and #18 *huizi* of course also was significant for public payments. Takahashi Hiroomi has found that of the thirteen entries between 1244 and 1265 regarding awards of military bonuses recorded in the late Song chronicle *Songshi quanwen*, nine specify payment in either #17 bills (five cases) or #18 bills (four cases).[84] Itemized revenues in Ningbo recorded in the prefectural gazetteer in 1259 specify whether cash payments were collected in #17 or #18 *huizi*.[85] But the gazetteer

nine years, but the case file does not mention how much time elapsed between the original sale and when the seller sought to redeem it.

81 The document actually states 450 *guan*, but this must be a clerical error. "Dianmai tianye . . . huo xianqian huo qianhui zhongban shoushu" 典買田業··或見錢或錢會中半收贖, in *QMJ* 9.311–13; viz. McKnight and Liu, *Enlightened Judgments*, pp. 316–20. The litigation began before the issue of #18 *huizi* but continued into the 1240s, and thus the old *huizi* presumably refers to #17 *huizi*.

82 "Didang bujiao ye" 抵當不交業, in *QMJ* 6.167–68; viz. McKnight and Liu, *Enlightened Judgments*, pp. 193–95.

83 Du Fan, "Dianyuan zoushi dierzha" 殿院奏事第二劄, *QXJ* 8.6b–8a.

84 Takahashi, *Genchō kahei*, p. 237, table 3.

85 [*Kaiqing*] *Siming xuzhi* [開慶]四明續志 (SYDFZ ed.), *juan* 4, passim.

for Jiankang (Nanjing) published some years later – after Jia Sidao introduced the *xianqian guanzi* paper currency in 1264 – omits mention of #17 *huizi*. It reports that cash revenues were collected half in coin and half in *huizi*, but it specifies payment of the paper currency portion in #18 *huizi*.[86] For the commutation of the silk pongee tax into cash, however, payment could be made either in *xianqian guanzi* or #18 *huizi*, but the latter were subject to the government-mandated two-thirds discount.[87]

As many scholars have observed, 1-*guan huizi* bills, the most common denomination, were too large for the quotidian needs of petty trade.[88] Beginning in 1163, the Song government also issued smaller *huizi* bills in denominations of 200, 300, and 500 *wen*. Unfortunately, we have no information about the relative quantities of each denomination, although surely the 1-*guan* bills were the most prevalent. Nor is it clear how widely the smaller bills disseminated. Hong Mai remarked with approbation that when he passed through Wuzhou (Liangzhe) in 1185 "small notes" (*xiaotie* 小帖) were being utilized in the local markets at an exchange rate of 1:750.[89] An anonymous essay on paper currency written in the first years of the 13th century asserted that "the people greatly appreciate the convenience of *huizi* bills, ranging from 1-*guan* bills to 500-, 300-, and 200-*wen* denominations."[90] The implication of this passage surely was that the smaller bills were commonly used in market transactions. A memorial submitted in 1222 by Ge Hong describing the monetary situation in Hangzhou complained that the state hoarded coin rather than releasing it, yet officials expected shopkeepers and moneychangers (*puhu zhuopu* 鋪戶卓鋪) to exchange coin for paper bills on demand. The latter – with no stocks of coin in hand to do so – were forced to shut their doors, and itinerant merchants could find no one to accept their *huizi* bills in payment. Ge also observed that "residents of the city must use coin in market transactions of less than 200 *wen*," yet for lack of coin they were unable to conduct even such minor transactions.[91] Implicitly, however, Ge's comments suggest that *huizi* typically were used in transactions of 200 *wen* or more.

86 [*Jingding*] *Jiankang zhi* [景定]建康志 ([hereafter *JKZ*]; SYDFZ ed.), *juan* 40, passim. Although the publication of this gazetteer conventionally is dated to 1261, mention of *xianqian guanzi* (first issued in 1264) indicates that it must have been published several years later.

87 *JKZ* 40.21a–22a.

88 During the 1170s–1190s, the price of 1 *dou* of rice (9.5 liters) – enough to feed one person for a week – in the Jiangnan region fluctuated between 200 and 400 *wen*, usually at the lower end of this range. Cheng, *Songdai wujia*, pp. 117–19.

89 *RZSB* sanbi, 14.584–85.

90 Cited *GJHB* waiji, 66.5a.

91 Ge Hong 葛洪, "Lun chengti chuquan baizhazi" 論稱提楮券白劄子, *Panshi laoren wenji* 蟠室老人文集14, rpt. in Zhang Tao 张海 and Jin Chengyu 金程宇, "'*Quan Song wen*'

Many officials urged the government to issue greater quantities of small bills while lamenting that officials refused to accept them in public payments and thus constricted their utility. Chen Chun, while serving as a prefect in Fujian during the monetary crisis of 1207, advocated issuing more small bills to meet the needs of the common people (*pingmin* 平民) and to facilitate the circulation of *huizi* at all levels of trade.[92] In a pair of memorials submitted in 1238, in the wake of the devaluation of issues #15 and #16, Lü Wu reported that many local jurisdictions had turned to issuing their own paper tickets (*zhitiezi* 紙帖子) or bamboo and lacquer tokens (*zhumupai* 竹木牌) valued at 50 or 100 *wen* as temporary expedients to provide small change in local markets.[93] Since these tokens had won acceptance in various localities, Lü recommended that the court follow this precedent by redeeming worn 200- and 300-*wen* bills with new 100- and 200-*wen* bills. Not only would this measure remove dilapidated bills from circulation, but it would reduce the need for coins in everyday transactions, and thus help to revive the exchange value of paper currency generally.[94] We have no confirmation that any action was taken on Lü Wu's proposal, but there is indirect evidence that smaller bills were issued, at least in Hangzhou. Fang Dacong, in a letter written c. 1240–1241, makes mention of small bills in 50- and 100-*wen* denominations "newly printed" by the Hangzhou authorities.[95] Fang derided these bills, which he described as "only three fingers in size," as "effigies of fractional paper bills" (*lingchu zhi yong* 領楮之俑), implying that the bills were cheap simulacra of real money.[96] In any event, in contrast to Chen Chun and Lü Wu, Fang strongly opposed the

buyi (shang): yi '*Panshi laoren wenji*' wei zhongxin" '全宋文' 补遗 (上): 以'蟠室老人文集'为中心, *Gudian wenxian yanjiu* 古典文献研究11 (2008): 386.

92 Chen Chun, "Lun chengti huizi," *BXQJ* 44.1a–5a.

93 Wu Zimu's memoir, written thirty-five years later, mentions that because of the scarcity of bronze coin the Hangzhou authorities issued wax tokens (*lapai* 鑞牌) as fractional currency. *MLL* 13, in *DJMHL*, p. 238.

94 Lü Wu, "Zou wei xingqi tianxia zhi zhi zaiyu heping shidafu zhi xin" 奏為興起天下之治在於和平士大夫之心 and "Zou wei tequan zai de qi dao ji shenming cuozhi guanhui xianqian" 奏為持權在得其道及申明措置官會見錢, in *ZSJC*, 11a–15b, 16a–20a, respectively. Lü acknowledged that smaller denominations would entail higher production costs, but he suggested these costs could be minimized by "following the example of *huhui*" to make the bills "simpler" (*jianjing* 簡徑) – presumably referring to the design of the printed bills – and smaller in size.

95 Fang Dacong 方大琮, "Yu Liu langzhong shu" 與劉郎中書, *Song zhonghui tie'an Fang gong wenji* 宋忠惠鐵庵方公文集 (1521 ed.; rpt. BTCK), 15.35a.

96 "Making an effigy" (*zuoyong* 作俑) (i.e., small effigies placed in tombs) was a metaphor for creating a sham precedent. The same metaphor was employed by Fang Hui in his acerbic critique of Song monetary policy from Ningzong to the eve of the Mongol conquest in which he concluded, "today, when coin has been completely discarded and only paper money is in current circulation, have we not truly made money into an effigy?" (實為之作俑歟). Fang Hui 方回, "Fu shaofu jinqian ji jinshi zhuqian shuo" 附少府禁錢及近世鑄錢說, *Xu gujin kao* 續古今攷 (SKQS ed.), 10.12a.

issue of these small bills, claiming that they only further encouraged hoarding of coin and depreciation of paper currency.

Yet in a real sense with the issue of #18 *huizi* in 1240 the Song authorities created a fractional paper currency by retaining the #17 bills at a steep discount, setting their official exchange value at one-fifth of #18 bills.[97] Xu Luqing, then serving as the vice fiscal intendant in Jiangxi, recognized this effect. Xu proposed retaining the sound (i.e., not worn or tattered) #17 bills in circulation "to serve as small *huizi*" (*yi dang xiaohui* 以當小會).[98] From this point forward, officials began to speak of #17 *huizi* as "small bills" (*xiaojiao* 小交) and #18 *huizi* as "large bills" (*dajiao* 大交). Thus the devaluation of #17 *huizi* can be seen as a deliberate effort by the government to create small-denomination bills.[99] In 1242, a school preceptor in Yanzhou (Liangzhe) expressed alarm that the recent devaluation of #17 *huizi* by imperial edict – setting their exchange value at 154 *wen* (i.e., one-fifth of the 770 *wen* exchange rate for 1-*guan* #18 bills) – had caused a fivefold increase in the prices the prefectural school paid for chickens, pork, vegetables, and firewood. Although market prices were calculated in #18 *huizi*, the school actually purchased such items with #17 bills, now subject to steep discount. Moreover, the exchange rate with coin was even more depressed: a 200-*wen* #17 bill was worth only 14 bronze coins.[100] Huang Zhen, serving as a salt official in Huating (near modern Shanghai) in 1260, reported that the market exchange value of 1-*guan* #17 *huizi* was a mere 53 *wen*, or one-fifth that of 1-*guan* #18 bills (265 *wen*).[101] Thus, the official ratios in the valuations of the #17 and #18 bills remained in force in the marketplace, where it appears that #17 *huizi* endured as a common means of payment. This system of using separate issues of paper currency to designate the measure of value and the means of exchange anticipated the dual paper currency system eventually adopted during the Yuan period (see Chapter 8).

Revisionist scholars who argue that Song paper bills were essentially fiscal instruments ill-suited to serve as market money emphasize that paper bills could not fulfill the function of money as a store of value. Yet this argument is based more on conjecture than evidence. We have just seen from several of the inheritance disputes cited in the *Enlightened Judgments* that estates commonly included paper currency. Consider, too, Wu Yong's vivid description cited

97 As Table 6.3 indicates, #17 *huizi* remained in circulation together with #18 bills at least until the mid 1260s.

98 Xu Luqing, "Shang miaotang lun chuyan shu" 上廟堂論楮鹽書, *QZCG* 5.18b–19b.

99 On this point, see Wang Shen 王申, "Lun xiao'e dongnan huizi dui Nan Song huobi liutong de yingxiang" 论小额东南会子对南宋货币流通的影响, *Zhejiang xuekan* 浙江学刊 2020.5: 231–38.

100 *Yanzhou tujing* 嚴州圖經 (SYDFZ ed.), 1.49b–50b.

101 Huang Zhen 黃震, "Qi shen tian renhu mai yandai pucao jiaqian zhuang" 乞申添人戶賣鹽袋蒲草價錢狀, *Huangshi richao* 黃氏日抄 (SKQS ed.), 71.18b.

above of Hangzhou's wealthy residents setting their paper currency ablaze in the streets after the devaluation of 1211. This theatrical gesture revealed that paper money had come to serve as a significant form of savings for the affluent. Other contemporaries confirm this point. In 1215, the Fuzhou (Fujian) prefect Wei Jing observed that since 1170 the value of *huizi* had been tied to silver, and thus government monetary policy had aimed, with a reasonable degree of success, at maintaining a balance in the exchange values of *huizi* and silver. But the uncontrolled issue of paper currency since 1205 had upset this balance. Both the rich and households of middling property saw the value of their savings – held in the form of *huizi* – evaporate.[102] The evisceration in the value of savings held in the form of *huizi* after the 1211 devaluation also was noted in a memorial of 1217 by Yuan Xie.[103] Yet, ironically, the depreciation of paper currency also diminished the attraction of coin – tethered to paper money at a fixed exchange rate – as a store of value. In response, wealthy households possessing substantial stocks of coin found it highly profitable to export coin abroad, where it fetched a much higher price.

6.4 Export of Song Coin

The outflow of coin beyond the Song realm to no small degree was precipitated by the proliferation of paper currency. We have already seen that in the early Southern Song period the much higher value of bronze coin in the Jin territories triggered a large-scale cross-border smuggling trade. By the early 13th century, however, Jin efforts to substitute paper currencies for bronze coin caused a reversal in this flow, with coin now flowing back into the Southern Song territories. More importantly, the scale of coin exports via maritime trade grew exponentially following the introduction of paper currencies in the Southern Song territories, suggesting a causal connection.

Overseas trade with the Indian Ocean world had flourished since the late Tang period. In the 11th century, convoys from Sumatra, the Malay Peninsula, and Java arrived annually at ports in southern China. China chiefly imported exotic and luxury goods such as aromatics, ivory, hardwoods, and pepper, while porcelain wares superseded silk goods as its leading export. By the 12th century, Chinese officials were expressing concern about contraband trade in Song bronze coins. In 1133, a local official in Guangdong warned the court about the drain of bronze coin abroad from the seaports of Guangdong and Guangxi in exchange for precious metals and aromatics.[104] While serving as a prefect in Guangxi in 1171–1172, Fan Chengda reported that although the

102 Wei Jing, "Lun chubi lihai zhazi," *HLJ* 15.8b–9a.

103 Yuan Xie 袁燮, "Lun guojia yi ming zhengxing zhazi" 論國家宜明政刑箚子, *Jiezhai ji* 絜齋集 (SKQS ed.), 3.6a.

104 *XNYL* 69.1170.

Song had enacted harsh penalties on the export of coin in 1160, "countless" quantities of bronze coin were being carried away from the ports of Quanzhou, Guangzhou, and Ningbo.[105] One of the principal destinations of coin exports was Java, where Song coins came into use in domestic trade by the late 11th century.[106] A geographical survey of overseas lands compiled by the maritime customs inspector at Quanzhou in 1225 claimed that Chinese mariners routinely defied the imperial prohibition to bring Chinese coin to the Javanese kingdom of Kediri to trade for pepper and other tropical products.[107] The export of bronze coin also brought in gold and silver from overseas. In the 1250s, a revenue officer stationed at Guangzhou reported that because the value of bronze coin relative to silver was three times greater abroad than in China, foreign merchants carried silver to the ports of Guangzhou and Quanzhou to trade for Chinese coin.[108]

The real surge in coin exports beginning in the mid 12th century was destined not for Southeast Asia, however, but rather for Japan. In the 8th century, the Japanese imperial court at Heijōkyō (Nara) had begun to imitate Chinese bronze coinage, but limited copper production and the disintegration of centralized rule brought minting to a halt in the mid 10th century. By the turn of the 12th century, the quickening pace of commercial exchange – and the Japanese elites' need to transfer revenues from their far-flung estates to the capital at Heian (Kyoto) – created demand for a more convenient means of exchange than cumbersome goods like rice and cloth.[109] Archaeological evidence attests to imports of Song coin beginning in the late 11th century, but by the 1170s the trickle of imported coin swelled into a flood. The avid enthusiasm for Chinese coin was noted by a Japanese chronicler in 1179 who wrote that "recently throughout the realm everyone, high and low, has been afflicted by an ailment known as the 'coin disease' (*zeni no yamai* 錢病)"[110] We also

[105] Fan Chengda 范成大, "Lun toulou tongqian zhazi," 論透漏銅錢劄子, in *MCZY* 272.8a–b. Among the contemporaries who likewise decried the drain of bronze coin abroad was Zhu Xi, who claimed that seagoing merchants filled their holds with coin and then covered them with other trade goods to hide the real cargo. See Zhu Xi, *Zhuzi yulei*, 111.2722.

[106] Derek Heng, *Sino-Malay Trade and Diplomacy from the Tenth Through the Fourteenth Century* (Athens: Ohio University Press, 2009), pp. 161–67.

[107] Zhao Rugua 趙汝适, in Yang Bowen 楊博文 (ed.), *Zhufan zhi jiaoshi* 諸蕃志校釋 (Beijing: Zhonghua shuju, 2000), shang 上, p. 55.

[108] Bao Hui 包恢, "Jin tongqian shensheng zhuang" 禁銅錢申省狀, *Bizhou gaoluë* 敝帚稿略 (SKQS ed.), 1.20b.

[109] On the monetization of the Japanese economy in this era, see Ethan Isaac Segal, *Coins, Trade, and the State: Economic Growth in Early Medieval Japan* (Cambridge, MA: Harvard University Asia Center, 2011).

[110] *Hyakurenshō* 百錬抄, 8:98, entry for 1179/6 治承三年六月, in Kuroita Katsumi黒板勝美 (ed.), [*Shintei zōho*] *Kokushi taikei* [新訂增補] 國史大系, vol. 11 (Tokyo: Yoshikawa kōbunkan, 1929).

witness a surge in Song edicts banning export of coin via maritime trade beginning in 1171.[111] Despite its initial resistance, the Kamakura bakufu was compelled to grant Song coin official recognition as legal tender in 1226. Over the course of the 13th century, bronze coin steadily became the preferred means of both public and private transactions, and by 1300 imported Chinese coin had fully displaced rice and silk as Japan's monetary standard.[112]

Massive coin exports – which led to the establishment of Song coin as the international monetary standard of the East Asian maritime world down to the 16th century – can readily be explained in terms of the rising demand for money abroad. But the export of Song coin also must be understood in the context of supply-side factors: Why was Song coin available for export? Ōta Yukio was the first scholar to draw attention to the significance of the development of paper currencies in creating a "surplus" of bronze coin available for export. In Ōta's view, bronze coin exported to Japan mainly came from North China, and he sees the monetary policies of the Jin and Yuan states as the primary forces driving the flight of Chinese coin abroad.[113] I see the dynamics of coin exports somewhat differently, and I would argue that the main source of coins imported into Japan came from the Southern Song rather than North China.

Based on evidence from land contracts, estate payments, and hoards of Chinese coin excavated in Japan, Ōta discerned two waves in the expansion of the use of Song coin in Japan: the first peaked around the year 1215, the second around the year 1270. Ōta contended that these surges were triggered by, first, the Mongol conquest of much of the Jin territory in 1215 (and the Jin prohibition on the use of coin in the same year) and, second, the incorporation of South China into the Yuan paper money system following the Mongol conquest of the Southern Song in 1276. In both cases, Ōta sees the actions of the North China states as having the effect of devaluing bronze coin, spurring holders of coin to divest.

I would like to suggest an alternative – or perhaps complementary – explanation that links the timing of coin exports to monetary crises in the Southern Song. As we have seen, the devaluation of *huizi* currency in 1211 incited market panic. Numerous contemporaries expressed alarm that the depreciation of paper currency caused wealthy households to hoard the coin

111 Takahashi has tabulated a total of fifteen Song edicts issued between 1171 and 1265 that proscribed the export of coin via ocean-going ships: Takahashi, *Genchō kahei*, p. 232, table 2.

112 On the rising demand for coin in Japan, see Inoue Masao, *Kokusai tsūka*, pp. 162–223; von Glahn, "Ningbo–Hakata Merchant Network."

113 Ōta Yukio 大田由紀夫, "Jūni-jūgo seiki shoto Higashi Ajia ni okeru dōsen no ryufu" 十二・十五世紀初頭東アジアにおける銅銭の流布, *Shakai keizai shigaku* 社会経済史学 61.2 (1995): 156–84.

in their possession, reducing the amount of coin in circulation and contributing to a vicious cycle of paper money depreciation. The state took action to prevent the appreciation of bronze coin by reinforcing the official exchange rate for *huizi* (770 *wen*) with hefty legal penalties and strictly enforcing laws forbidding hoarding of coin or carrying coin away from the capital.[114] Despite the steep appreciation in the nominal value of bronze coin after this time, I would argue that the monetary crises of the 13th century actually discouraged savings in coin. Instead of seeing stocks of coin as a hedge against the depreciation of paper money, it is more likely that the wealthy feared that the ongoing monetary distress would further erode the value of the bronze coin they held as savings. The most expedient response would have been to dispose of their stocks of coin (and the high value that Chinese coin commanded in Japan provided a profitable outlet for doing so) in favor of holding precious metals (that is to say, silver), whose value was not subject to state regulation. The available data on coin hoards in China seems to confirm this hypothesis: the number of coin hoards dropped significantly in the first half of the 13th century (Figure 6.1). The spike in hoarding in the first quarter of the 12th century can be attributed to the Jin invasions of Song, while the equally sharp rise in hoards during 1150–1200 – more than 90 percent located in Jin territories – probably resulted from Jin efforts to replace bronze coin with paper money. Scarcely any hoards have been found in the Southern Song territories for the period between 1150 and 1250.

As Ōta has argued, the timing of the surges of exports of Song coin to Japan must be understood in the context of the spreading use of *huizi* paper currency and the sharply diminished demand for bronze coin in China, ironically creating a "surplus" of coin available for profitable investment in clandestine overseas trade. In the eyes of Song statesmen, the export of bronze coin appeared as a hemorrhaging of the empire's economic lifeblood. Yet from the perspective of modern monetary theory there is no reason to assume that the export of coin had damaging effects on the Chinese economy. On the contrary, coin exports acted as a major stimulus to a foreign trade boom.[115]

The export of bronze coin was a further expression of the disintegration of the bronze coin monetary standard during the Song period. The function of bronze coin in the Southern Song economy became fragmented into essentially discrete uses: (1) in small quantities, bronze coin served as the primary medium for petty trade; (2) in large quantities, it was held as savings; (3) among all ranks of society a certain quantity of bronze coin had to be used to pay taxes. Paper money was widely used in market exchange – universally in large-scale transactions such as land sales – as well as state

[114] Wang Shengduo, *Liang Song huobi*, vol. 2, pp. 706–9.
[115] Von Glahn, "Ningbo–Hakata Merchant Network."

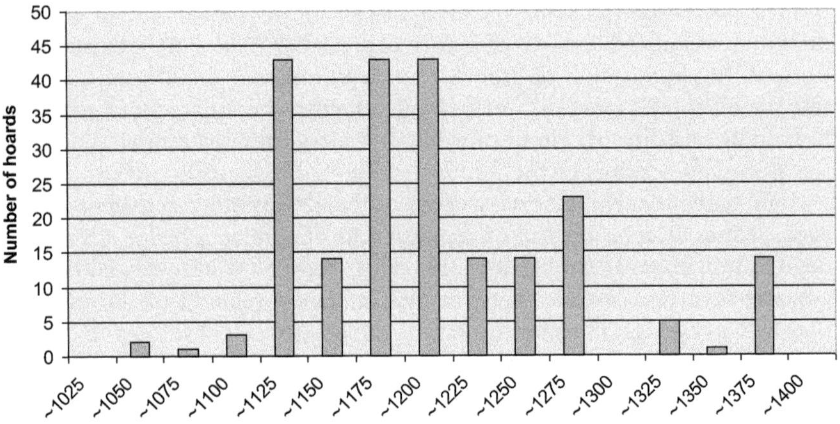

Figure 6.1 Coin hoards in China, 1000–1400.
Source: Miyake, *Uzumerareta senka*, p. 53, table 12.

payments; there is also evidence that people held savings in the form of paper money. Regardless of its nominal depreciation relative to bronze coin, paper currency had largely superseded coin as the monetary standard.

6.5 Theorizing Paper Money

The empire-wide development of paper currencies in the Southern Song prompted a reconfiguration of classical principles of monetary analysis. Although paper money evolved out of a series of expedient measures, eventually it was ratified in terms of the tenets of classical monetary theory. Of course, the principle that fiat currency derived from the sovereign's absolute authority over making money was firmly grounded in Chinese monetary analysis, especially in the chartalist tenets of the "Light and Heavy" chapters of the *Guan Zi*. Still, paper money, since it clearly lacked intrinsic value, provided the most severe test of the chartalists' faith in the power of the ruler to determine the value of money. Earlier experiments with pure fiat currencies, such as Emperor Wu's "deer-hide money" and the "thousand-cash" coin issued by Sun Quan (r. 222–252), ruler of the state of Wu in the Three Kingdoms era, ended in abysmal failure and forceful appeals for a full-bodied coin to serve as a sound currency.

Despite the proliferation of remittance bills, bills of exchange, and the paper currencies adopted in Sichuan (and briefly Shaanxi) in the Northern Song, it was only with the introduction of *huizi* paper money that the question of whether paper bills were indeed money became a pressing theoretical problem. In his memoirs, Zhou Bida, one of the leading statesmen of Xiaozong's reign, expressed bafflement at the abrupt emergence of the neologism *chubi* 楮幣 (lit., "mulberry money," alluding to the paper from which it was made), which had become the generic term for paper currency in his day. "Since the Qin and Han dynasties, money has exclusively meant coin," Zhou declared, "yet in recent years *huizi* have come into use. Now, the *jiaozi* institution in Sichuan was merely a special form of government bill (*te guanquan* 特官券). I do not know who began to call such bills *chubi*, which confers a certain kind of dignity." But subsequently the term *chubi* was widely adopted inside and outside of government, and – apparently to Zhou's dismay – it became a standard feature of political discourse: Zhou relates that *chubi* appeared in civil service examination questions as early as 1166, and it was routinely used in the compilation of the *Record of Sagacious Rule* (*Shengzheng lu* 聖政錄, completed in 1192) for Xiaozong's reign.[116] If Zhou displayed uncertainty about whether *chubi* indeed could be considered money, his contemporaries fully affirmed that – for better or worse – the fortunes of the dynasty depended on the viability of paper currency.

In keeping with Pseudo-Guanzi's chartalist principles, proponents of paper currency underscored the crucial significance of sovereign authority over money. Yang Guanqing – a poet who spent his career serving as a personal secretary to several officials – forcefully enunciated the chartalist argument for fiat currency in an essay probably dating from the 1190s: "money is neither cheap nor dear; the determination of its value rests with the sovereign" (幣無輕重,輕重在我). The same, Yang goes on to say, is true of goods. Therefore the monarch who "grasps the levers of profit (*liquan*) to rule the Subcelestial Realm fears not that the value of goods will not submit to His will" (執利權以制天下者,不患乎物之不我隨也). The proof of this, according to Yang, was the success of *jiaozi* as a fiat currency in Sichuan for more than a century and a half. Yang partly ascribed this success to the manifest advantages of bills over iron coin; unlike bronze coin, which has been hoarded by the rich households of the capital region, iron coin is too brittle to serve as a store of savings over the long term. But more importantly, Yang stressed, were the fiscal policies enacted in Sichuan, where "all tax payments submitted by the people, all payments for tea, salt, and liquor licenses, and all commercial excises and transit fees must be paid in paper currency, to the common benefit of the people." In addition, if *qianyin* began to depreciate, Sichuan officials disbursed precious metals to remove excess bills from circulation and restore public confidence in their value. The sovereign similarly can enhance the value of *huizi* by following the example of Sichuan officials and flexing his control over these same "levers of profit," namely, accepting *huizi* in state payments (which,

116 Zhou Bida 周必大, "Bian chubi erzi" 辨楮幣二字, *Erlaotang zazhi* 二老堂雜志 (CSJC ed.), 4.59–60.

Yang says, officials in the capital region were reluctant to do) and repurchasing excess bills with hard currency. Only if the state treats paper currency as the same as bronze coin will the people do likewise.[117] In his memorial of 1175, Xin Qiji had made a similar declaration: "It is commonly thought in the present day that bronze coin is valuable and paper currency is not. This simplistic view fails to recognize that neither can clothe the naked or feed the hungry. Copper coin and paper currency in truth are the same." Xin applauded the decision to collect state payments half in coin and half in *huizi*, which had revived the value of the latter.[118]

The theoretical precepts of paper money also drew from the corollary to the basic theorem of exchange values encapsulated in the formula *zimu xiangquan* (lit., "mutual balance between child and mother"), first expressed (as we saw in Chapter 1) in the Warring States era. In its original context, the formula was invoked as the principle for maintaining stable exchange values between large and small coins. During the early imperial period, when a single form of currency – the Wuzhu coin in the Han and after, and the Kaiyuan coin in the Tang – prevailed, the issue of exchange ratios between separate currencies rarely arose. In the Song, however, with its manifold currencies, the *zimu xiangquan* formula, originally applied to different weights of the same form of money, was adapted to the problem of balancing exchange values among different forms of money.

The term "mother" signified the primary or common currency, while the "child" was seen as a subsidiary currency. In the Song, the most prevalent view recognized bronze coin as the primary currency and iron coin and paper money as subsidiary currencies. As we shall see in Chapter 8, in the Yuan dynasty – whose Mongol rulers sought to eliminate coin entirely in favor of paper currency – these roles were reversed: paper money was regarded as the "mother" and coin as the "child." In addition, the "child and mother" metaphor was applied to paper currencies of different denominations. But beginning in the Yuan, too, we find silver assuming the role of "mother" and both paper currency and coin relegated to the subordinate position of subsidiary currencies. By the mid Ming period, silver had fully usurped the role of primary currency, and in the late Ming period the *zimu xiangquan* formula almost always referred to regulating the exchange ratio between silver and coin.

The problem of maintaining balance in the exchange ratios of disparate currencies was conceptualized in terms of Pseudo-Guanzi's quantity theorem.

[117] Yang Guanqing 楊冠卿, "Zhong chubi shuo" 重楮幣說, *Keting leigao* 客亭類稿 (SKQS ed.), 9.1a–4b. Most likely this essay was composed in the 1190s, when *huizi* first began to suffer significant depreciation. A similar analysis for the success of *qianyin* in contrast to *huizi* was expressed by Zhang Wenbo in a roughly contemporary essay quoted in *GJHB* waiji, 66.5a.

[118] Xin Qiji, "Lun xingyong huizi shu," *MCZY* 272.13a–14b.

Song statesmen assumed that the law of inverse proportion applied to exchange ratios between different types of money just as it did between money and commodities. The primary responsibility of the monetary authority was to ensure that a stable ratio prevailed between bronze coin and paper currency by regulating the quantity of both. Despite his full-throated endorsement of sovereign authority over money, Yang Guanqing's analysis conceded that the viability of paper currency as money also depended on "maintaining equilibrium" (*chengti*) between the values of paper money and hard currency. Chief among the means for "maintaining equilibrium" – as both Yang Guanqing and Xin Qiji underscored – was accepting public payments in paper currency. Their views echoed that of Wang Zhiwang, the commissioner of the Sichuan General Command in 1161, who claimed that the income from the liquor and salt excises and other commercial revenues "subtly acts to maintain equilibrium" (*yin wei chengti* 陰為稱提) in the value of *qianyin*.[119] The same idea was conveyed by government officials in 1220 when they allowed the commutation of the silk pongee tax (*zhejuanqian* 折絹錢) to be paid half in *huizi* and half in coin, which "secretly enables the technique of maintaining equilibrium in the value of *huizi* to operate."[120] The anonymous author of *Catalogue of Paper Currency*, commenting on the history of *qianyin* in Sichuan, wrote that there were two methods of *chengti*: one is to increase the supply of coin, and the other is to accept bills in state payments (in other words, to create sufficient demand). He continued saying, "following the outbreak of hostilities [i.e., the Song–Jin wars], the quantity of *qianyin* soared, paving the way for bills to take the place of coin. Imperial finances became wholly dependent on paper. Fortunately, the truce has been preserved, and the issue and redemption of *qianyin* have stabilized. Half of the bills are stored in government treasuries, while half circulate among the people, and their value remains intact."[121] Peng Guinian went further to underscore that in addition to accepting bills in state payments, sustaining the viability of paper currency required that "the moneychangers who exchange bills in the marketplace (市井兌便者) are sufficiently numerous." In other words, it was necessary to have a financial infrastructure in the private market that would facilitate ready convertibility between coin and bills.[122]

Yet despite strenuous efforts by the government to prop up paper currency, the value of *huizi* eroded beginning in the 1190s, raising doubts about the effectiveness of *chengti* strategies. In the mid 1190s, Yuan Yueyou wrote that

119 *XNYL* 193.3253.

120 稱提會子之術,且隱然行於其中. *SHY* shihuo 68.24b.

121 自軍興增料,鑿空為錢,天下大計,仰給於紙;猶幸守和議,引之出納有常,半藏諸司之庫,半流轉於民,維持不壞, *CBP*, in *SZGJ*, 67.711. As noted earlier (Chapter 4, n17), this text most likely was first published in 1199.

122 Peng Guinian, "Lun leixue zhi yi," *ZTJ* 1.18a–b.

for more than a decade the court and the literati had deliberated on how to "maintain equilibrium" between coin and bills, yet despite the wide range of *chengti* measures instituted by the government none succeeded for long.[123] Some critics of the state's paper currency policies blamed the depreciation of paper bills on the scarcity of coin rather than a surfeit of money. Yuan Xie, serving as the granary intendant in Jiangxi in 1211, criticized local officials for failing to abide by the fifty-fifty *pinda* formula and demanding more coin – or only coin – in public payments. But the main problem, as Yuan saw it, was the scarcity of coin, which had disappeared overseas or into the melting pot.[124] Around the same time, Chen Qiqing, a magistrate in Zhejiang, urged the court to focus on the supply of coin rather than the emission of paper currency: "Coin is the mother, and paper currency but the child. To maintain equilibrium between child and mother, one cannot dote on the child and neglect the mother" (母子所以相權也,不可重子而輕母也). Chen blamed the shortages of coin on magnate households who hoarded coin and rich merchants who exported coin abroad. But hoarding at least preserved coin within imperial territories, while exported coin was forever lost.[125]

In the early decades of the 13th century, as hard-pressed fiscal officials succumbed to the temptation to finance deficit spending by printing more paper money, concern shifted to reducing the excess supply of paper currency. Writing in aftermath of the issue of #17 *huizi* in 1234, Wu Yong expressed admiration for the prudence of Emperor Xiaozong, in contrast to the profligate issue of paper money by his successors, to the point where the volume of paper currency in circulation was "now thirteen times greater than in

[123] Yuan Yueyou, *MCZY* 272.17b–19b; *XWXTK* 7.2841a–b.

[124] Yuan Xie 袁燮, "Shang bianmin shu" 上便民疏, *MCZY* 273.4b–6a. Chinese scholars see Yuan Xie as expressing the basic idea of Gresham's Law, namely that bad money (paper) drives out good (coin), but I believe this interpretation is misleading. Certainly, in contrast to Yuan Guanqing and others, Yuan asserted that paper money differed in nature from coin: the former was "empty" (*kong* 空; i.e., had no intrinsic value), in contrast to "substantive" (*shi* 實) coin. But it was still possible to "use the empty to equilibrate the substantive" (以虛權實) by enforcing *chengti* measures, notably by redeeming excess bills with hard currency, as Emperor Xiaozong had done. Yuan does state that in places where paper currency is used coin had become scarce, whereas where coin alone circulates no such shortage occurs. He concludes that "at present, given the depreciation (*qing* 輕) of paper money, how could it compensate for the scarcity of coin?" In my view, Yuan was not saying that paper money was inherently deficient (however "empty"), but rather that the government has failed to apply *chengti* measures effectively. For the argument that Yuan formulated a version of Gresham's Law, see Hu, *Zhongguo jingji sixiang shi*, vol. 3, pp. 230–31; Zhang Jiaxiang 张家骧, Wan Anpei 万安培, and Zou Jinwen 邹进文 (eds.), *Zhongguo huobi sixiang shi* 中国货币思想史 (Wuhan: Hubei renmin chubanshe, 1981), vol. 1, pp. 361–66.

[125] Untitled memorial by Chen Qiqing 陳耆卿 in *MCZY* 273.1a–2a. Chen was a native of coastal Zhejiang and perhaps a firsthand witness to the export of coin.

Xiaozong's reign." The need to restore the mutual balance between "child and mother" in the monetary system, Wu insisted, was no different than "the mutual infusion of breath and blood" in sustaining the organic vitality of the human body.[126] Around the same time, Dai Zhi, a young scholar from Ningbo, stated forthrightly that "what we suffer from today is not a shortage of coin, but a surfeit of paper currency."[127] In contrast to his contemporaries, Dai recognized that inflation was caused by an excess in the total stock of money rather than simply an imbalance in the quantities of coin and paper currency. Dai roundly condemned what he regarded as the government's wanton abuse of fiat money, but he concluded that paper money was no different in kind than coin. Both paper notes and coin, Dai insisted, were "useless" (*wuyong* 無用) substances employed as tokens to facilitate the exchange of useful commodities. The value of paper money, like that of coin, was simply a function of its quantity relative to the supply of goods in the market. Dai dismissed the prevalent view that increasing the quantity of coin would enhance the exchange value of paper money, and instead contended that inflation could be curbed only by reducing the total quantity of money. Dai was specifically addressing what he regarded as the failure of the attempt to reduce the total quantity of bills in circulation by issuing #17 *huizi* bills in exchange for the older #14 and #15 bills. Like many others, Dai advocated a return to the prudent policies of Emperor Xiaozong's reign that maintained strict limits on the money supply.[128]

Despite the frequent failure of the state to abide by prudent monetary policies, general opinion defended the principle of fiat currency grounded in the monarch's sovereign authority to make money. But as the Southern Song state increasingly relied on the fiscal expediency of printing enormous quantities of paper currency to defray its spiraling deficits, some statesmen abandoned chartalist beliefs and embraced some form of metalism instead. In their minds, the erosion of popular confidence in paper money, as seen in the steep depreciation of the value of *huizi* relative to bronze coin, belied the presumption that currency was an artifact of imperial will. The retreat from chartalism also reflected diminished faith in the power of the state after the demise of Wang Anshi's New Policies.

126 Wu Yong, "Huizi wushi," *HeLJ* 15.30a–b.

127 We know little about Dai other than the fact that he obtained his *jinshi* degree in 1238. Based on internal evidence, his "Shuquan yuanliu" must have been composed between 1234 and 1240.

128 Dai Zhi, "Shuquan yuanliu," in *SP* shang, 39a–b. Dai thus rejected the ideas of those who focused on increasing the supply of coin. Regarding the export of coin abroad, Dai – a native of Ningbo, the most important maritime port in his day – shrugged off this concern, stating that such exports had been going on for many years and were not the source of the current monetary distress.

One example of the reorientation in monetary thought provoked by the profligate issue of paper currency can be seen in an essay recounting the history of money by the Daoxue philosopher Lü Zuqian.[129] Lü reiterated the standard narrative that the sages invented coinage to relieve the distress of the people, but he emphasized that money was a mere expedience, of no value in itself. Instead, value inheres in the direct products of consumption, such as food and cloth. The sage-kings did not collect taxes in money or distribute money in salaries and stipends. It was only with the Han Emperor Wu's deviation from former practices that making money became central to the state's fiscal regime. Still, Lü spurned the idea that it was possible to return to the pre-monetary world of the Three Dynasties. Although money lacks use value – he too invoked the refrain that money "cannot clothe the naked nor feed the hungry" – "it is indispensable because the hundred craftsmen all depend on it for their livelihood" (百工之事皆資以為生,不可缺者). It is incumbent upon the ruler to issue sound coins that – like the Han Wuzhu and Tang Kaiyuan coins – uphold a proper balance between the values of goods and money and thus makes possible the circulation of goods essential to popular welfare. Here Lü liberally drew upon Kong Yi's arguments in favor of full-bodied money.

Not surprisingly, Lü derided the fiat currencies of Emperor Wu and Wang Mang as "parasitic" (*du* 蠹) devices employed by tyrants to expropriate the wealth of the people. In his own day, he concluded, it was acceptable to use *qianyin* as a practical expedient in Sichuan, but he firmly opposed the adoption of paper currency in the rest of empire. In Sichuan, the inadequacy of iron coin as means of commercial exchange had induced the people themselves to invent the *jiaozi* paper currency (交子之法,出於民之所自為), which they subsequently "entrusted" (*tuo* 託) to the government to administer. *Huizi* paper currency, however, was a product of the fiscal crisis of the state and the narrow-minded goal of amassing revenues. Lü condoned resorting to paper money in the face of the present threats to the survival of the empire as a temporary expedient, but he firmly rejected *huizi* as a permanent institution. Most strikingly, the distinction Lü drew between *qianyin* and *huizi* implied a difference between a fiduciary currency whose utility derives from the people's faith in its value and a fiat currency that is imposed by the state.

An even more forceful repudiation of fiat currency appears in the writings of the statesman Ye Shi. Ye's writings on fiscal and monetary institutions were composed early in his career, in the 1180s, before his firsthand engagement with economic problems while serving in a series of local and provincial fiscal offices in Hubei and Huainan. From the outset, Ye vehemently condemned the

[129] Lü Zuqian 呂祖謙, *Lidai zhidu xiangshuo* 歷代制度詳說 (CSJC xubian ed.), 7.8b–10b. Lü's essay is quoted in full in *WXTK* 9.101a–102a.

adoption of paper currency, which had driven sound money out of circulation and caused ruinous inflation. Diverging from the trend that had prevailed in monetary analysis since the 2nd century BCE, Ye articulated a catallactic conception of money premised on the primacy of money as a medium of exchange: "currency arose among merchants and tradesmen who traveled and traded widely throughout the four corners of the world. Since goods themselves could not be transported over such long distances, gold and coin were carried instead."[130] Although Ye elsewhere indicated that it was the sage-kings who created money, in this instance too he emphasized the role of money as a medium of exchange: "since the people lacked a means of exchange to facilitate the flow and transfer of goods, [the sage-kings] created money and cast coin in order to balance [buying and selling]."[131] Ye envisioned the society of high antiquity as simple and contented. Quoting liberally from the description of the primitive utopia of the past found in chapter 80 of the *Dao De Jing*, Ye argued that in the age of the sage-kings the people produced all the goods they needed for their own subsistence. With the progress of time, increasing complexity of social organization engendered a division of labor and consequently a need for exchange. Money thus established itself as a measure of value as well as a means of exchange. After the emergence of money, however, other commodities were reduced to quantifiable sums of exchange value: cloth began to be measured in feet and inches, and grain in pecks and bushels. The founding of the Qin and Han empires vastly extended the horizons of trade, and coin, because of its superior utility, gradually supplanted all other media of exchange. By the end of the Former Han dynasty, jade, pearls, and even gold had been reduced to merely ornamental uses. In Ye's view, though, a sound currency system did not emerge until the Tang state began to mint its Kaiyuan coin in 621.[132]

Ye Shi's recapitulation of the history of money stood in marked contrast to the chartalist tradition of Pseudo-Guanzi. Ye believed that the failures of the paper currency system of his own day amply confirmed his metallist analysis. Both the state and wealthy individuals hoarded coin because of its intrinsic value. The more paper money was put into circulation, the more coin was withdrawn from exchange. At the same time, the uncontrollable inflation spawned by the imprudent issue of paper currency eroded incomes and hampered production. Only by abolishing the use of paper currency, what Ye called "empty money" (*kongqian* 空錢), could the court reestablish a reliable currency (i.e., coin) and regain some leverage over the ratios of exchange.[133]

130 Quoted in *WXTK* 9.102a. (Not included in Ye's collected works.)

131 為其無以阜通流轉, 則作幣鑄金以權之. Ye Shi, "Cai zonglun (yi)" 財總論 (一), *Shuixin bieji* 11, in *YSJ* 3, p. 770.

132 *WXTK* 9.102a–103a.

133 Ye Shi, "Caiji (zhong)" 財計(中), *Shuixin bieji* 2, in *YSJ* 3, pp. 660–62.

Ye's disaffection was a fairly isolated case, however. Many of his contemporaries concurred that paper money failed to fulfill one of the basic functions of money, that of serving as a store of value, a role only metallic money could perform. Yet it was generally accepted that paper currency provided a viable means of exchange provided that the state regulated its quantity. Indeed, later theorists, notably the 15th-century statecraft scholar Qiu Jun, endorsed the principle that the separate functions of money were best served by different forms of money; coin, paper money, and silver could coexist as functionally discrete parts of an integrated monetary system.[134]

The coda to the repudiation of paper currency voiced by Lü Zuqian and Ye Shi was composed in the early Yuan period by Ma Duanlin in his *Comprehensive Documentary Study of Government Institutions*, one of the monumental achievements of Chinese historical scholarship. Ma, son of a Song state councilor, withdrew from public life after the Mongol conquest and dedicated himself to writing the *Comprehensive Study*, which he completed in 1307. As an historian following in the footsteps of Du You, Sima Guang, and Ye Shi, Ma stressed the historicity of political institutions: the ideals of the golden age of antiquity can be realized in the present not by reviving (now anachronistic) classical models, but rather by developing new institutions grounded in the wisdom of the past but adapted to the unique needs of the present. Ye Shi's writings had an especially pronounced impact on Ma's conceptions of historical development and institutional change.[135] Ma's views on money as an institution can be readily anticipated by his decision to give Lü Zuqian and Ye Shi the last words in his chapters on money.

Ma Duanlin sharply distinguished paper bills from coin, which he regarded as the only genuine form of money. In the preface to the *Comprehensive Study*, Ma asserted that the sages invented money to enable exchange of the necessities of life: food and clothing. Initially the sages attempted to use jade, pearls, and gold for this purpose, but these precious substances were too rare to serve as general means of exchange. Bronze coin alone proved to be a "suitably practical device" (*shiyong zhi wu* 適用之物) for "balancing exchange values" (*quan qingzhong* 權輕重) and creating "unity between the poor and the rich" (*tong pinfu* 通貧富).[136] In Ma's view, the "flying cash" of Tang and Song

[134] *DXYYB* 27.14a–17a. For Qiu's views on money, see Chapter 9.

[135] Jaeyoon Song, "Debates on Just Taxation in Ma Duanlin's *Comprehensive Survey*," in Patricia B. Ebrey and Paul Jakov Smith (eds.), *State Power in China, 900–1325* (Seattle: University of Washington Press, 2019), pp. 244–73. See also Hok-lam Chan, "'Comprehensiveness' (*T'ung*) and 'Change' (*Pien*) in Ma Tuan-lin's Historical Thought," in Hok-lam Chan and Wm. Theodore de Bary (eds.), *Yuan Thought: Chinese Thought and Religion Under the Mongols* (New York: Columbia University Press, 1982), pp. 27–87.

[136] My translation here of *tong* – ordinarily meaning "connection" or "channel" – as "unity" is meant to capture Ma's contention (echoing Lu Zhi and Ye Shi) that in the present age,

jiaoyin bills of exchange, while useful as remittance bills, were never intended to circulate as money. When Song policymakers began to treat paper bills as money, they in effect tried to turn a "worthless substance" – what Ma calls a "flimsy foot-square piece of paper" (*fangchi fubai zhi quan* 方尺腐敗之券) – into something of genuine utility (以楮為幣,則始以無用為用矣).[137]

Given Ma Duanlin's staunchly metallist conception of money, "worthless" paper was doomed to fail as a replacement for coin. Initially, *huizi* bills, like commodity licenses, were conceived as an expedient means of facilitating military logistics, a purpose for which they were well suited. The turning point came in the wake of the Kaixi War, when the government on one hand began to print massive quantities of paper currency and on the other substituted paper bills for coin in all types of public payments. Unlike minting coin – which in Ma's view augmented the stock of wealth in proportion to the quantity produced – printing paper currency upset the balance between goods and the means of exchange. Ma also deplored the division of the empire into separate monetary zones (with multiple agencies issuing money independently), which eviscerated the emperor's sovereign authority over what should be a universal monetary standard.

In pursuit of fiscal remedies, Ma Duanlin concluded, the original purpose of money – to facilitate market exchange – was lost. Yet as much as Ma vilified paper currency, he also testified to the eclipse of coin by paper bills as the monetary standard of the Song realm: "in buying and selling, payments and disbursements, both public and private, nowhere were *huizi* not used" (會子則公私買賣支給,無往而不用). When the government began to issue small denomination bills, "clearly they were supposed to substitute for coin (是明以之代見錢矣). . . . The court initially intended to use paper currency as a temporary expedient which later would be discarded, but it did not realize that once these bills infiltrated among the people, they would be considered the same as coin. Consequently, when later the court encountered difficulties in trying to redeem paper bills it had no choice but to print more. As the quantity of bills increased, their value fell. This happened because when paper currency was first adopted its implications were not fully thought out."[138]

Elided from Ma's analysis – but clearly evident in his text – is confirmation that market exchange had come to rely on paper currency as the predominant

when private ownership ineluctably prevails, poor and rich must rely on each other to ensure the optimum (but far from equal) distribution of wealth. See Song, "Debates on Just Taxation," pp. 261–67.

137 *WXTK* preface, 4a–b.

138 朝廷初意, 欲暫用而即廢, 而不知流落民間, 便同見錢. 所以後來收換生受, 只得再造.遂愈多愈賤, 亦是立法之初, 講之未詳故也. *WXTK* 9.100c–101a.

means of exchange, and indeed the people accepted it as such. At the time Ma was writing the *Comprehensive Study*, the new Mongol rulers of China had gone farther than the Song monarchs in implementing fiat money by demonetizing bronze coin and establishing paper currency as the sole legal tender. Ma undoubtedly was appalled, but his narrative ends with the reign of the Song emperor Ningzong, and he did not address the institutional innovations of his Mongol overlords.

7

Visualizing Paper Money

The viability of any fiat currency depends on the willingness of its users to accept paper instruments as tokens of real value measurable in hard (metallic) currency. This faith in the value of paper money is conditioned by a range of variables, including the credibility of the issuing agent (whether a government or private entity), its range of utility both domestically and in international exchange, the extent to which it could be redeemed for hard currency or other assets, and its acceptability in public payments. The susceptibility of paper money to counterfeiting also was an important variable in its credibility within both the private and public economies. Just as the value of metallic money was to an important degree a function of its physical properties (size, weight, fineness, and the emblems and inscriptions stamped on it), so too the tangible features of paper money – the quality of paper and the designs imprinted on it – were essential to the calculus that determined its value. Any effort to gauge the economic impact of paper money must consider its physical properties as well.

No actual specimens of Song paper money are known to exist. The oldest extant paper money specimens are the *zhongtong jiaochao* 中統交鈔 notes issued by the Mongol khan Khubilai beginning in 1260. The Mongols modeled the design of their paper money after the bills issued by its predecessors as rulers of northern China, the Jurchen Jin dynasty. Although no specimens of Jin currency have survived either, the plates used for printing Jin bills show clear affinities with the later Mongol paper currency (and also with the *baochao* 寶鈔 paper currency issued in the early years of the Ming dynasty). To reconstruct the actual appearance of Song paper money, we must rely on documentary sources and a small number of surviving metal printing plates. The identity and authenticity of the extant printing plates has been a subject of controversy, however, and some scholars question whether any of them are genuine examples of Song paper money. This chapter reexamines both the textual and material evidence to assess the authenticity of these printing plates.[1]

[1] The most thorough study of the extant Song printing plates is Inoue Yasuya 井上泰也, "Sō no shōpan o megutte" 宋の鈔版をめぐって, *Tōhō gakuhō* 東方学報 86.2 (1993): 82–100. I have greatly benefited from the materials Inoue brought together.

In contrast to the Yuan and Ming dynasties, which issued paper money in one or a few standard forms, the Song paper money system was characterized by an enormous and ever-changing variety of distinctive types. Not until the final decade of the Southern Song did the Song court issue paper money that passed current throughout the whole empire. The circulation of the earliest form of Song paper money, the *jiaozi* currency, was (with brief exceptions) confined to Sichuan. In 1107, the court discontinued the *jiaozi* currency and replaced it with a new form of paper money known as *qianyin*, whose circulation likewise was restricted to Sichuan. Several efforts were made to introduce paper money in other parts of the empire in the late Northern Song and the first years of the Southern Song, but none of these initiatives endured before the issue of the *huizi* currency in the southeastern circuits beginning in 1161. As we have seen, separate paper money systems were subsequently established in Huainan and Huguang, resulting in four distinct paper money systems in operation for most of the remainder of the Southern Song period.

In addition to this pattern of regional diversity, a second key feature of Song paper money was the imposition of fixed terms of expiry. In order to deter counterfeiting, maintain control of the quantity of paper money in circulation, and replace bills before they became too worn, the Song government limited the circulation of any given issue to a fixed term, after which the holder of the bill had to return it to the government in exchange for a new issue. The term of Sichuan's *jiaozi* and *qianyin* currencies was set at two years until the early 13th century, when it was raised to three years. Altogether 103 issues of *jiaozi* and *qianyin* were emitted between 1024 and 1256. The regulations governing the issue of *huizi* adopted in 1168 set the term of expiry at three years, but already with the third issue the term of expiry typically was extended to ten years, and in 1211 the principle of fixed terms was abandoned entirely in practice. A total of eighteen *huizi* issues were emitted between 1168 and 1264. In addition, at least a dozen other types of paper money were issued for shorter periods of time ranging from a few months to a decade. Each issue had its own distinctive design, resulting in a vast proliferation of individual types. The main purpose behind these distinctive designs was to inhibit counterfeiting. Yet the diversity of paper money types also impeded efforts to create a single, sovereign currency.

7.1 Textual Evidence for the Design of Song Paper Currencies

As we have seen, provincial officials in Sichuan had become concerned about the proliferation of private *jiaozi* notes in Sichuan in the early 11th century – concerns that eventually culminated in the state takeover of Sichuan's paper currency in 1024. In 1005, the prefect of Chengdu imposed a set of regulations that restricted the issue of *jiaozi* currency to a consortium of sixteen firms, which were required to print standardized notes using government-issued supplies and service labor. An early Southern Song historical work by a native of Sichuan provides our most complete description of the *jiaozi* notes issued under this new regulatory regime:

> [The merchants] were required to manufacture these bills using paper of uniform color, which was imprinted with illustrations of buildings and human figures. Each merchant house affixed a seal with its own unique hidden mark, in overlapping red and black colors, as a sign of personal identification. The denomination was written on the bill by hand. There was no limit to the bills' value.[2]
>
> 同用一色紙印造,印文用屋木人物。鋪戶押字,各自隱密題號,朱墨間錯,以為私記。書填貫,不限多少。

While these regulations stipulated the type and color of paper used to manufacture *jiaozi* and it is likely that the figural designs also were standardized, issuing merchants also stamped the bills with their own identifying marks. It is unclear in what sense these marks were "hidden" (perhaps a watermark?). Nor can we determine which elements of the design were printed in which color, though based on later practice it seems likely that the merchants' personal seals were printed in red.

We are better informed about the design of the *qianyin* bills that replaced Sichuan's *jiaozi* currency in 1107.

> In the fifth month of 1107 the Jiaozi Currency Bureau was changed to the Qianyin Currency Bureau. Altogether six printing plates were cast to manufacture the new currency: one each for the authorizing imperial edict, the denomination of the note, the term of expiry, and the reverse illustration. These elements were all printed in black ink. A fifth plate for the face illustration was printed in blue, and the sixth plate, called the "red circle," was printed in crimson. All six plates were embellished with figural designs. The "red circle" and reverse illustrations depicted narrative tales.[3]
>
> 大觀元年五月, 改交子務為錢引務。所鑄印凡六, 曰 : 敕字, 大料例, 年限, 背印, 皆以黑; 曰青面, 以藍; 曰紅團, 以朱。六印皆飾以花印。紅團, 背印則以故事。

The same source also provides detailed descriptions of the ten issues of *qianyin* (#70–#79) emitted between 1161 and 1179 (see Table 7.1 for two examples, from 1161 and 1165). The six design elements of the *qianyin* notes were unique to a particular issue, with rare exceptions,[4] and all *qianyin* bills were printed using six printing blocks and three colors (red, black, and blue).

[2] *SCSS* 15.5a–b.

[3] *CBP*, in *SZGJ*, 67, p. 710.

[4] Among the ten *qianyin* issues (#70–#79) described in detail in *CBP*, there are only two exceptions to this principle: the authorizing edict illustration was repeated in #76 and #77, and the reverse illustration of the 1-*guan* note was repeated in #74 and #79.

Table 7.1 *Design of Sichuan* qianyin *bills*

Design element	Description/Text	Description/Text
Issue number 界分	Issue #70 第七十界	Issue #72 第七十二界
Date of issue 年號	Thirty-first year of Shaoxing (1161) 辛巳紹興三十一年	Inaugural year of Qiandao (1165) 乙酉乾道元年
Serial number and denomination 貼頭五行料例	Inscription: "Attaining wealth also enriches the realm" 至富財國並	Inscription: "Strengthen farming and economize on expenditure" 強本而節用
Authorizing edict figural illustration 敕字花紋印	Golden cock upholding an edict 金雞棒敕	Golden flowers upholding an edict 金花棒敕
Blue-inked obverse figural illustration 青面花紋印	Long-life wisteria 合歡萬歲藤	Mirage departs the azure sea[c] 蜃樓去滄海
Red-inked circular narrative illustration 紅團故事印	Dragon and tortoise bearing "Charts and Documents" 龍龜負圖書	Rotting grain and moldering rice[d] 朽粟紅腐
Term of expiry figural illustration 年限花紋印	Three-handled jug with dragon design 三耳卣龍文	Yao submits the menstrual flower[e] 堯階蓂莢
1-*guan* bill reverse illustration 一貫故事背印	Wu Yinzhi's poem "Drinking from the Spring of Avarice"[a] 吳隱之酌飲貪泉賦詩	Honest officials of Han are rewarded with rank and gold[f] 漢循吏增秩賜金
500-*wen* bill reverse illustration 五百故事背印	Wang Xiang's filial piety moves carp to leap and sparrows to fly[b] 王祥孝感躍鯉飛雀	Bu Shi presents a letter offering his personal property[g] 卜式書獻家財

Source: *CBP*, in *SZGJ*, 67, pp. 713, 715.

Notes: [a] The episode of Wu Yinzhi's poem is recorded in the Jin dynastic history.

[b] The story of Wang Xiang as a paragon of filial piety also appears in the Jin dynastic history.

[c] Perhaps a reference to a verse by the renowned Northern Song poet Su Shi: "A hundred-foot clamshell tower looms above the azure sea" (蜃樓百尺橫滄海). "Clamshell tower" refers to a mirage that appears to be a magnificent palace floating over the sea.

Table 7.1 (*cont.*)

[d] Metaphor for a prosperous state (whose stores of grain never need to be used).
[e] According to legend, the *mingjia* flower waxes and wanes with the cycles of the moon, putting forth a new bud each day for fourteen days, and dropping a bud each day for fourteen days. The sage-king Yao discovered this correlation and used the plant to set his calendar.
[f] Exact reference uncertain, but perhaps alluding to the "Biographies of the Honest Officials" chapter in the *Later Han History*.
[g] Bu Shi appears in Sima Qian's *Historical Records* as a paragon of both private entrepreneurship and dutiful citizenship. After making his fortune raising sheep, Bu Shi donated his wealth to the Han court to be used for the common benefit of the people.

The capital *huizi* issued at Hangzhou beginning in 1161 was the most widely circulated form of Song paper money, but descriptions of these notes are surprisingly rare. The main textual evidence for its design comes from an impeachment written by the renowned Dao Learning philosopher Zhu Xi in 1183 in which Zhu accused the prefect of Taizhou (Zhejiang) of collaborating with criminals to print counterfeit *huizi* notes. Zhu's indictment quotes extensively from legal depositions concerning the forger, a woodblock-carver by the name of Jiang Hui:[5]

> On the fourteenth day of the twelfth month of 1181, at the home of Lou Dalang in Suxi in Wuzhou prefecture, Jiang Hui together with Huang Nianwu carved six counterfeit seals in addition to copying the official signature and cutting figural designs of people and objects for illustrating *huizi* notes. They manufactured 900 copies of the bills denominated as one full *guan*.[6]
>
> 淳熙七年十二月十四日，蔣輝同黃念五，在婺州蘇溪樓大郎家，開偽印六顆，並寫官押及開會子出相人物，造得成貫會子九百道。
>
> In the second ten-day week of the twelfth month of 1182, Grandmother Jin delivered to Hui a wicker box containing 200 sheets of paper for making *huizi* and the blocks he had cut previously, together with pigments like mineral red, indigo blue, and palm-brown, and other things. Hui printed 200 bills, but he did not apply the seals at that time. ... The next day Grandmother Jin brought out master copies for the inscription

[5] For a full translation of Zhu Xi's account of the forger Jiang Hui, see Lien-sheng Yang, "The Form of the Paper Note *Hui-tzu* of the Southern Sung Dynasty," *Harvard Journal of Asiatic Studies* 16.3–4 (1953): 365–73.
[6] Zhu Xi 朱熹, "An Tang Zhongyou disizhuang" 按唐仲友第四狀, *Zhu Wengong wenji*朱文公文集 ([hereafter *ZWW*; SBCK ed.), 19.10a. The deposition mentions one specific figural illustration (接履先生), but the reference is unclear (possibly alluding to the legendary official Yi Yin 伊尹).

> "1-*guan* short-string" in seal script, the signature of the authorizing official in three graphs, and in addition a blue pattern bearing the legend "serial number." At that time Hui applied the three red seals to the bills.[7]
>
> 至十二月中旬，金婆婆將藤箱貯出會子紙二百道，並雕下會子板及土朱，靛青，棕黑等物，付與輝。印下會子二百道，了未使朱印……次日金婆婆出篆寫『一貫文省』並專典官押三字，　又青花上寫『字號』二字。輝是實[read 時]方使朱印三顆。

Although vague on some key details, these passages indicate that *huizi* notes were manufactured using a combination of printing plates and seals. The main plate on the face included a figural design (apparently a narrative scene). Separate plates were used to print the denomination, the signature of the authorizing official, and the serial number. The serial number was printed in blue, while the other elements apparently were printed in a brownish-black color. Finally, the notes were impressed with three red official seals.

Initially the capital *huizi* apparently were embossed with a single seal. An edict of 1163 (first year of the Longxing reign era) ordered that the capital *huizi* should be printed with the legend "Seal of the Officially-Printed *Huizi* Bill of the Ministry of Revenue of the Department of State Affairs in the Longxing Era" (隆興尚書戶部官印會子之印).[8] After the currency reform of 1168, which formally established *huizi* as a permanent institution, the government began to use a seal with the legend "Supervisory Office of the Huizi Depository" (提領措置會子庫).[9] It is not clear whether the use of three red seals also began at this time. The Song dynasty regulations on official seals specify four seals that were used to authenticate capital *huizi* bills:[10]

Huizi Seal of the Budget Office of the Revenue Department of the Three Ministries

三省戶房國用司會子印

Authentication Seal of the *Huizi* Depository

提領會子庫檢察印

Seal of the *Huizi* Currency Printing Workshop of the *Huizi* Depository

會子庫印造會子印

Endorsement Seal of [1-*guan*, 500-*wen*, 200-*wen*] Bill of the *Huizi* Depository

會子庫 [一貫文,五百文,二百文] 合同印

7 Zhu Xi, "An Tang Zhongyou diliuzhuang" 按唐仲友第六狀, *ZWW*, 19.25b.
8 *WXTK*, 9.98c; *SS* 181.4407.
9 *WXTK* 9.99a; *SS* 181.4407.
10 *SS* 154.3593–94.

The endorsement seal (*hetongyin* 合同印) was stamped on the reverse of the bill, while the other three seals were placed on the face. Although the text does not indicate when these seals were adopted, it seems likely that they were in use at the time of the counterfeiting activities of 1181–1182 described by Zhu Xi.

The prominence of multiple red seals on *huizi* differs strikingly from the complex figural designs apparently used to print *qianyin* bills. Like *qianyin*, however, *huizi* were produced using multiple impressions and three colors (red, black, and blue). What remains unclear is whether *huizi* were printed with figural illustrations on both sides as was clearly the case for *qianyin*.

Additional insight into the design of *huizi* can be gleaned from comments made by the Southern Song official and historian Xie Caibo about the short-lived small-denomination notes (known as Chongning [era] *xiaochao* 崇寧小鈔) issued in 1106–1107 to redeem 10-*wen* coins circulating in certain regions of North China. According to Xie, these notes were modeled after the *qianyin* issued in Sichuan at the same time:[11]

> The text and printing design, term of expiry, and statutes stipulating the prohibitions [against counterfeiting] of these notes all were modeled on the laws regulating Sichuan currency.
>
> 書押印造樣號，年限，條禁，並依川錢法。

Xie Caibo also observed that these Northern Song *xiaochao* notes were "roughly similar" in design to the *huizi* notes of his own day (the preface to his book is dated 1256, when #18 *huizi* bills would have been in circulation). His description of the design of the Chongning *xiaochao* as divided into three vertical registers thus provides important clues about the *huizi* notes as well:

> In the upper register was printed: "It is decreed: those who make counterfeit notes will be exiled 3,000 *li*; those who use counterfeit notes will be punished by beheading; no longer valid for exchange after the ninth month of the *gengyin* year (1110)."
>
> In the middle register was printed an illustration of springs and mountains.
>
> In the lower register "1-*guan*, short string" was written horizontally, and the responsible official affixed his personal seal.
>
> 上段：印『准偽造鈔已成流三千里，已行用者處斬，至庚寅九月更不用』
>
> 中段：印畫泉山
>
> 下段：平寫『一貫文省』，守倅姓押子 [read 字]

[11] Xie Caibo 謝采伯, *Mizhai biji* 密齋筆記 (SKQS ed.), 1.3a–b.

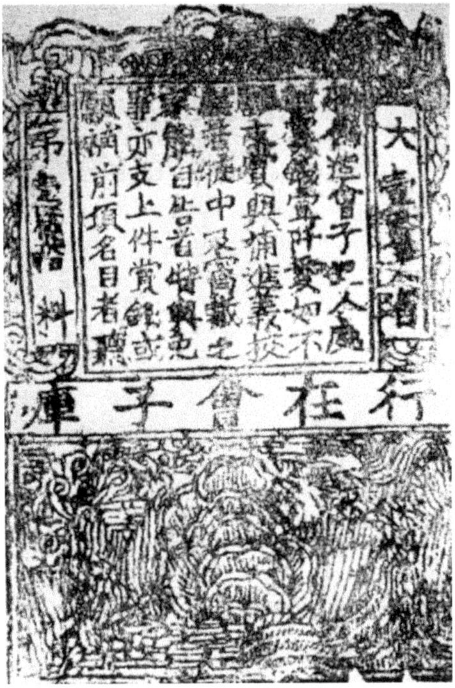

Figure 7.1 National Museum of China printing plate.
Source: Zhongguo renmin yinhang Zhongguo lidai huobi bianjizu 中国人民银行中国历代货币编辑组 (ed.), *Zhongguo lidai huobi* 中国历代货币 (Beijing: Xinhua chubanshe, 1982), p. 51, pl. 2. Dimensions: 17.4 cm x 11.8 cm.

The tripartite design of the Chongning *xiaochao* described by Xie in fact corresponds to the design of the *huizi* printing plate shown in Figure 7.1, although on the latter the denotation of the bill's denomination appears in the middle rather than at the bottom.

A final bit of textual evidence for the design of *huizi* currency comes from colloquial names for specific issues. In a discussion of the currency reform enacted by the prime minister Jia Sidao in 1264, Fang Hui stated that *huizi* issue #17 (emitted in 1234) was popularly known as the "vase bill" (*pingchu* 瓶楮), while issue #18 (emitted in 1240) was known as the "mushroom bill" (*zhichu* 芝楮). Fang commented that these names "were taken from the objects illustrated on them" (取繪物名).[12]

Fragmentary as this evidence is, it is clear that the *qianyin* and *huizi* bills, the most widely used forms of Song paper money, were printed using at least

[12] Fang Hui, "Jianbu Lügong jiazhuan," 4a, in *ZSJC*.

six printing plates and/or seals and illustrated with narrative scenes or iconic emblems. Both notes also were printed in three colors. Unfortunately, not only is the artifactual evidence limited to a few specimens, but they consist of single printing plates, which can give us only an incomplete picture of the actual bills. Moreover, the designs of the few printing plates at our disposal diverge from the textual testimony, raising questions about their authenticity.

7.2 Song-Era Printing Plate Specimens

The printing plate shown in Figure 7.1 is the specimen most commonly accepted as a genuine Song artifact. First published in facsimile in 1941, this copper plate now is in the collection of the National Museum of China. The plate is divided into upper and lower registers separated by a horizontal legend identifying the bill as issued by the Huizi Depository of the Provisional Capital (Xingzai huiziku 行在會子庫). In the upper portion, a cloud-scroll border frames a box of text that is flanked on the left by the denomination of the note (1-*guan* short string) and on the right by the serial number "110" (第壹百拾料). The central box of text stipulates the punishment for counterfeiting this bill:

> By imperial decree: criminals who counterfeit *huizi* are to be punished by beheading. The reward [for informers] shall be 1,000 *guan*. Those who do not wish to accept the monetary reward can instead receive titular appointment as Expectant Commandant in the Jinyi Guard. Accomplices of counterfeiters or any who harbor them willingly who identify the ringleaders to the authorities will be absolved of criminal liability and given the above-stipulated reward. If they wish they may instead receive the previously mentioned titular appointment.
>
> 敕偽造會子犯人處斬，賞錢壹阡貫，如不願支賞，與補進義校尉。若徒中及窩藏之家，能自告首，特與免罪，亦支上件賞錢。或願補前項名目者，聽。

This passage exactly replicates the language of the statute enacted in 1162 that specified the legal penalties for counterfeiting of *huizi* currency.[13]

The bill in Figure 7.1 is "roughly similar," to use Xie Caibo's language, to the three registers described by Xie in his discussion of the Northern Song *xiaochao* notes. The main differences are (1) the sequence of elements (according to Xie, the landscape scene appears in the middle, not the bottom), and (2) the horizontal legend, which in this case identifies the type of currency rather than its denomination. Of course, since this specimen is a single plate from what would have been a set of six, a number of elements are missing,

[13] *WXTK* 9.98c.

Figure 7.2 Auspicious mushroom.
Source: Yang Jun and Zhang, "'Qiansicang' ban 'Xingzai huiziku' ban kaobian," p. 39, fig. 6.

most importantly the issue number and the date of expiry. The scene in the lower portion of Figure 7.1 is not easily deciphered, but recently it has been identified not as a landscape but rather as a pair (male and female) of phoenixes flanking a tiered "auspicious mushroom" (*lingzhi* 靈芝), which would suggest that the plate could be the #18 "mushroom" bill described by Fang Hui (for an example of an "auspicious mushroom" artifact, see Figure 7.2).[14] This interpretation strengthens the case for identifying the Figure 7.1 specimen with the #18 *huizi* bill.

Although the Figure 7.1 plate has long been accepted as a genuine Song specimen, some scholars have voiced skepticism. Liu Sen identified a number of discrepancies between the language found on this bill and surviving documentation regarding the design of *huizi*: (1) there is no precedent for the insertion of the word "large" (*da* 大) before the denomination of the bill ("1-*guan*, short-string");[15] (2) the format for the serial number does not conform to any know forms for writing these serial numbers on paper currency or other paper instruments;[16] and (3) the name of the issuing authority ("Huizi

[14] Yang Jun 杨君 and Zhang Anhao 张安昊, "'Qiansicang' ban 'Xingzai huiziku' ban kaobian" '千斯仓' 版 '行在会子库' 版考辨, *Zhongguo qianbi* 中国钱币 2023.4: 34–42.

[15] But note that Li You refers to the denomination of the *qianyin* currency as *daliaoli* 大料例. See *SCSS* 15.5a–b.

[16] The formula 第 [numeral] 料 was used in some cases to refer to the issue number of a type of paper currency (in such cases, the meaning of *liao* 料 was equivalent to *jie* 界). But since there were only eighteen issues of *huizi*, the number 110 on this plate certainly cannot have this meaning. The phrase "record its value and assign a serial number based on the sequence of the *Thousand Word Primer*" (立料例以千字文為號) occurs in a

Depository of the Provisional Capital") prominently displayed at the center of the plate does not appear in any Song documents – although it can be read as a contraction of the full title of this agency, the Huizi Depository of the Tea Market Supervisor of the Provisional Capital (Xingzai duchachang huiziku 行在都茶場會子庫).[17]

From a different angle, Sheng Guanxi contends that the calligraphy displayed on this bill resembles the archaic "Wei monument" (魏碑) style rather than the "Song style" (宋體) found on Song bronze coins. Sheng also observes that the quality of the calligraphy is greatly inferior to that of extant Yuan specimens.[18] Sheng concludes that it is unlikely that this specimen was a product of a government workshop, though he leaves open the possibility that it might have been produced by counterfeiters. Yet since forgers were obliged to imitate the appearance of genuine state-issued currency, for our purposes it is irrelevant whether or not the printing plate is counterfeit. Despite the anomalies cited by Liu, Sheng, and others, in light of the direct evidence (especially Xie Caibo's testimony) the Figure 7.1 specimen still seems to be a genuine (even if "forged") Song artifact that we can most likely identify with the #18 *huizi* bills.

Even more problematic is the printing plate shown in Figure 7.3, which has been frequently reproduced as an example of Song paper money since its first publication in facsimile by a Japanese numismatist in 1938. Because it bears no identification, this specimen (which has become known as the Qiansicang plate) has provoked much controversy and speculation.[19] It often has been identified as an example of *jiaozi* currency despite the fact that the text clearly

number of Song official documents regarding the issue of commodity licenses, land contracts, and other legal documents, and such serial numbers are referred to as *liaoli zihao* 料例字號. Jin and Yuan bills have two handwritten serial numbers (actually graphs from the *Thousand Word Primer*, at least in the Yuan case) denoted as *liaohao* 料號 and *zihao* 字號. But the Figure 7.1 specimen only displays a numeral without a serial graph from the *Thousand Word Primer*.

17 Liu Sen, *Song Jin zhibi*, pp. 171–77.

18 Sheng Guanxi 盛观熙, "Liang Song chaoban bianxi" 兩宋鈔版辨析, *Zhongguo qianbi* 中国钱币 1994.4: 11–14. As Sheng notes, the calligraphy for Song coins often was composed by celebrated literati such as Su Shi and Sima Guang and by the reigning emperors themselves.

19 For summaries of the debate over the authenticity of this specimen, see Li Weiguo 李伟国, "Liang Song yinchao tongban wenzi kao – yi 'Qiansicang chaoban' wei zhongxin" 两宋印钞铜版文字考 – 以'千斯仓钞版'为中心, *Henan daxue xuebao (shehui kexue ban)* 河南大学学报（社会科学版）2011.2: 74–80; Gao Congming 高聡明, "'Qiansicang' Songdai chaoban bianwei" '千斯仓' 宋代钞版辨伪, *Zhongguo qianbi* 中国钱币 2023.3: 3–13. Gao also traces this printing plate back to the collection of a renowned Liulichang antiquarian shop in Beijing before it was sold to a Japanese buyer sometime after 1928.

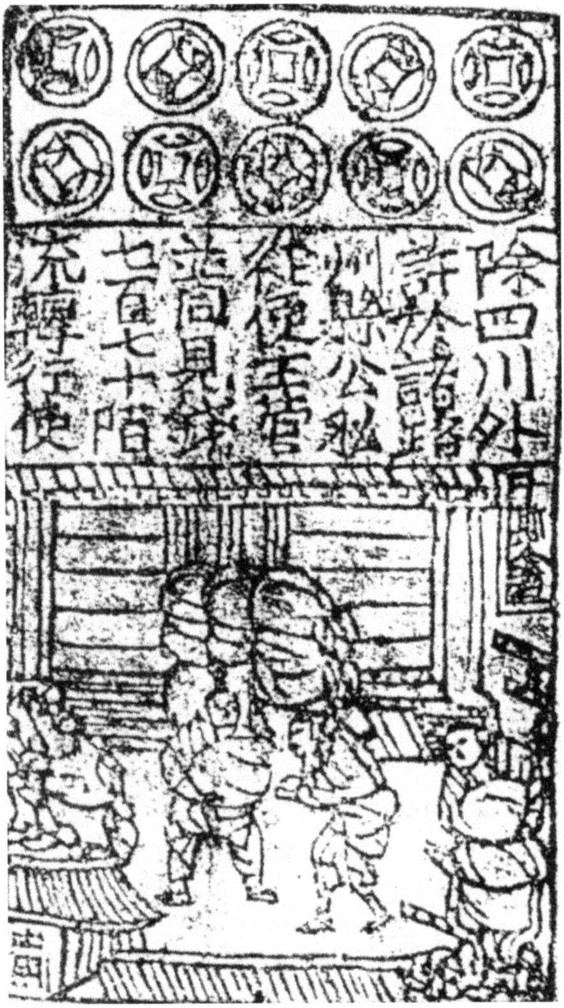

Figure 7.3 "Qiansicang" paper currency printing plate.
Source: Okuhira, *Tōa senshi*, p. 92.

states that this bill was not legal tender in Sichuan.[20] In the revised edition to his magnum opus on Chinese monetary history, Peng Xinwei suggested that it represents the Chongning *qianyin* currency that was issued briefly in North

[20] The clearly erroneous identification of this specimen as a *jiaozi* note appears prominently in what stands as the definitive history of printing in China: see Tsen-hsuin Tsien, *Paper and Printing*, in Joseph Needham (ed.), *Science and Civilisation in China* (Cambridge: Cambridge University Press, 1985), vol. 5, pt. 1, p. 97, fig. 1080.

China in 1106–1107.[21] In the definitive catalogue of Chinese paper money, however, it is simply described as a "Song paper money printing plate" (宋紙幣版) and not identified with any specific type of Song paper money.[22]

The Qiansicang plate is divided into three registers but otherwise bears little resemblance to the Figure 7.1 plate. In the top register is an illustration of ten bronze coins. The bottom register displays an illustration of two men carrying sacks of rice into a granary under the watchful supervision of a figure in official robes. At the upper right corner of the illustration is a small cartouche with the legend "May there be a thousand such granaries" (*qiansicang* 千斯倉), a quotation from a song in the *Book of Odes*. In the middle register we find the following text:

> Negotiable for public and private debts in all circuits, prefectures, and counties outside of Sichuan. Shall circulate at an exchange value equivalent to ready cash at the rate of 770 [*wen*] short-string.
>
> 除四川外，許於諸路州縣，公私從便主管。並同見錢七百七十陌，流轉行使。

Although this statement in itself does not identify the type of currency, this language hints at a link to *huizi* bills that were issued following the depreciation of #11–#13 bills issued in 1204–1207. At that time, we are told, the emperor "for the first time issued an edict to the various circuits of Jiangnan and Liangzhe requiring enforcement of the 770-*wen* exchange rate," which led to criminal punishment for violators.[23] But it is only with the issue of #18 bills that enforcement of the 770-*wen* exchange rate became a constant refrain in the policy debates about *huizi* currency, as we see in the following texts:

(1) A memorial by Yuan Fu dating from shortly after the issue of #18 *huizi* affirms that the state established the fixed exchange rate of 770-*wen* short-string for the new bills:

> The draft memorandum states, "All tax receipts that the various prefectures must relay to the capital may be paid one-half in ready cash [and one-half in paper currency], or if they wish this sum may be wholly commuted to payment in *huizi*. If payment is made in the old issues #16 and #17 *huizi* bills, they shall be valued at the prevailing market rate of exchange in each locality. If payment is made in the new #18 *huizi* bills, they shall be valued at the official tariff." . . . The newly issued *huizi* bills circulate at a fixed rate of exchange of 770-*wen* short-string. . .[24]

[21] Peng, *Zhongguo huobi shi*, pl. 58.
[22] Neimenggu jinrong yanjiusuo 内蒙古金融研究所, *Zhongguo guchao tuji* 中國古鈔圖輯 (Beijing: Zhongguo jinrong chubanshe, 1987), pp. 3–4.
[23] Dai Zhi, "Shuquan yuanliu," in *SP* shang, 37a.
[24] Yuan Fu, "Lun huizi zhazi," *MeZJ* 7.21b.

白箚子云:『諸郡應干賦稅, 一半見錢, 並許折納純會。如用十六, 十七界舊會, 則照各處民價。如用十八界新會, 則照官價』⋯⋯且新會作七百七十陌行使⋯⋯

(2) A legal ruling enforcing the principle of making payments based on the means of payment stipulated in land transaction contracts, written by a local judge named Hu Ying, reiterated the precise language (indicated by bold type) of the Qiansicang plate regarding the negotiability of *huizi* currency at par with bronze coin:[25]

> The Imperial Court's laws for maintaining a balance in the exchange value of paper currency absolutely cannot be violated. It is already stipulated that in both the collection of public revenues and in private commercial exchange paper currency **shall circulate and be negotiable at an exchange value equivalent to ready cash**. ... At the time of the original transaction, the old *huizi* bills specified their value as **negotiable at the rate of 770 *wen***. Now their value has fallen to 200 bronze coins short-string...
>
> 稱提楮幣, 朝廷之法, 固曰斷斷乎其不可違。州縣之租賦, 商賈之貿易,已既『並同見錢, 流轉行使』⋯⋯其時舊會係作『七百七十行使』, 今既減作二百文省⋯⋯

Hu's ruling mentions that "old *huizi* notes" (presumably #17 *huizi*) were imprinted with the value 770 *wen*, but at the time he was writing (in the 1240s, after the issue of #18 *huizi*) their value had fallen by nearly three-quarters (see Chapter 6). For our purposes, Hu provides confirmation that the text "negotiable at the rate of 770 *wen*" was inscribed on the #17 *huizi* bills.

(3) In a memorial of 1246 addressing the decision to retain the two #17 and #18 issues in perpetuity, Du Fan observed that based on the new policy:

> The rule that paper currency shall be negotiable at the rate of 770 *wen* will be rigorously enforced; violators, whether officials, clerks, or commoners, will be dismissed from office and stripped of their rank.
>
> 斷欲七百七十行使, 違者官吏百姓, 罷鐫黜籍。

Du objected to the decision, arguing that it would be impossible to apply criminal penalties to enforce the 770-*wen* exchange rate. When he previously served as prefect in Taizhou (Liangzhe), Du reported, the judicial intendant

[25] "Dianmai tianye ... huo xianqian huo qianhui zhongban shoushu" 典買田業⋯⋯或見錢或錢會中半收贖, in *QMJ* 9.311–12. For a translation of the full document, see McKnight and Liu, *Enlightened Judgments*, pp. 316–20.

had tried to do so, inciting popular uproar and forcing markets to close.[26] Although Du probably was not repeating verbatim the inscription on the bills, his memorial provides further evidence that the "negotiable at the rate of 770 *wen*" portion did indeed appear on them.

(4) A memorial submitted by the Sichuan native Li Zengbo in 1256 proposed replacing Sichuan's *qianyin* currency, which had suffered a devastating depreciation of its value after the renewal of the Mongol invasions, with the capital *huizi*. Li's memorial confirms that language barring their circulation in Sichuan was specifically written on the issue #18 capital *huizi* bills:

> Although capital *huizi* bear a legend specifying "Shall circulate outside of Sichuan," at the present time people in Sichuan place greater value on the capital bills [than Sichuan *qianyin* currency].[27]
>
> 雖是京會指揮，有『除四川行用』之文，見今蜀人已重京楮。

(5) Li's proposal was reiterated by censorate officials in the capital in the same year. Their memorial also mentions that the exchange rate for #18 *huizi* currently in circulation had been fixed at 770-*wen* short-string, and further specifies that this exchange rate was initially enacted sometime after the #18 issue was created in 1240:

> The censorate officials memorialized the court saying, "The defects of Sichuan's *qianyin* and silver *huizi*[28] currencies are wholly a result of allowing regional officials to print and utilize them at their own discretion. The currencies are issued by the government but not accepted in payments to the state. At the present time, the authority to print these currencies should revert to the court. We recommend that a Sichuan *huizi* currency should be issued modeled on the issue #18 capital *huizi*. In accordance with the decree of the Chunyou reign-era, the rate of exchange should be fixed at 770-*wen* short-string, and the notes will be negotiable for public and private debts in the prefectures and counties of Sichuan."[29]
>
> 臺臣奏：川引，銀會之弊，皆因自印自用，有出無收。今當拘其印造之權，歸之朝廷，倣十八界會子造四川會子，視淳祐之令，作七百七十陌，於四川州縣公私行使。

26 Du Fan, "Dianyuan zoushi dierzha," *QXJ* 8.6b–8a.

27 Li Zengbo, "Jiu Shuchu mizou" 救蜀楮密奏, *KZZG*, xugaohou 續稿後, 3.46a–b.

28 The "silver *huizi*" (*yinhui*) currency was introduced exclusively in Sichuan in 1242 in an effort to mitigate the deep erosion of the purchasing power of the greatly depreciated *qianyin* notes. See Chapter 6.

29 *SS* 181.4410–11.

The last line of this text – "negotiable for public and private debts in the prefectures and counties of Sichuan" – seems to be a deliberate alteration of the Qiansicang plate text ("negotiable for public and private debts in all circuits, prefectures, and counties *outside of* Sichuan") to extend the use of *huizi* to Sichuan. This memorial also confirms that a Chunyou-era (1241–1252) decree fixed the value of *huizi* bills at 770-*wen* short-string, as specified on the Qiansicang plate, although we have no other mention of such a decree.[30]

Moreover, the identification of the Qiansicang plate with the issue #18 *huizi* has gained credence since the discovery of a full set of printing plates for the final form of Song paper currency, the *jinyin xianqian guanzi.*

In 1983, a set of eight lead printing plates were found in a trash deposit in Dongzhi county, Anhui (Figure 7.4).[31] The printing plates are clearly labeled "Gold/Silver/Ready Cash Surety Deposit Bills of the Commodity Monopoly Bureau of the Provisional Capital" (*Xingzai quehuowu duizhuang jinyin xianqian guanzi* 行在榷貨務對樁金銀見錢關子). As we saw in Chapter 6, the *jinyin xianqian guanzi* bills were issued in 1264 by the administration of Jia Sidao and intended to replace the #17 and #18 *huizi* bills then currently in circulation. The set of plates includes two large plates for the face and reverse of the note. The face plate (Figure 7.4a) is in the form of a stone stele with a canopy-like capital and a base depicting types of money (bronze coins at left, silver ingots at right, and ten strings of coin in the center). At the center of the plate, the denomination of the note, "1-*guan* short-string," is written vertically in large graphs. The name "Gold/Silver/Ready Cash Surety Deposit Bills of the Commodity Monopoly Bureau of the Provisional Capital" is displayed vertically above the denomination cartouche, and both sides of the central cartouche are flanked by a lengthy text, no doubt a passage from the authorizing edict. The reverse plate (Figure 7.4b) has the legend "By imperial decree" in large graphs at the top, and seven itemized passages stipulating the penalties for forgery and rewards for informers.

30 Recently the distinguished Song monetary historian Gao Congming has concluded that the Figure 7.3 specimen is a modern forgery based on a highly technical argument that the word that appears on the plate's inscription for the short-string unit (*mo*) was confined to the private sector; government documents instead specified *sheng* 省. See Gao, "'Qiansicang' bianwei." But this document, along with the memorial by Yuan Fu quoted above, show that by the 1240s *mo* in fact was used precisely to designate the value of #18 bills.

31 The most thorough study of the Dongzhi plates and the circumstances of their discovery is Shi Jilong 施继龙 and Li Xiusong 李修松, *Dongzhi guanzi chaoban yanjiu* 东至关子钞版研究 (Hefei: Anhui daxue chubanshe, 2008). See also Yao Shuomin 姚朔民, "Dongzhi guanziban kaocha ji (shang, xia)" 东至关子版考察记（上·下）, *Zhongguo qianbi* 中国钱币 1994.3: 23–27, 1994.4: 5–10.

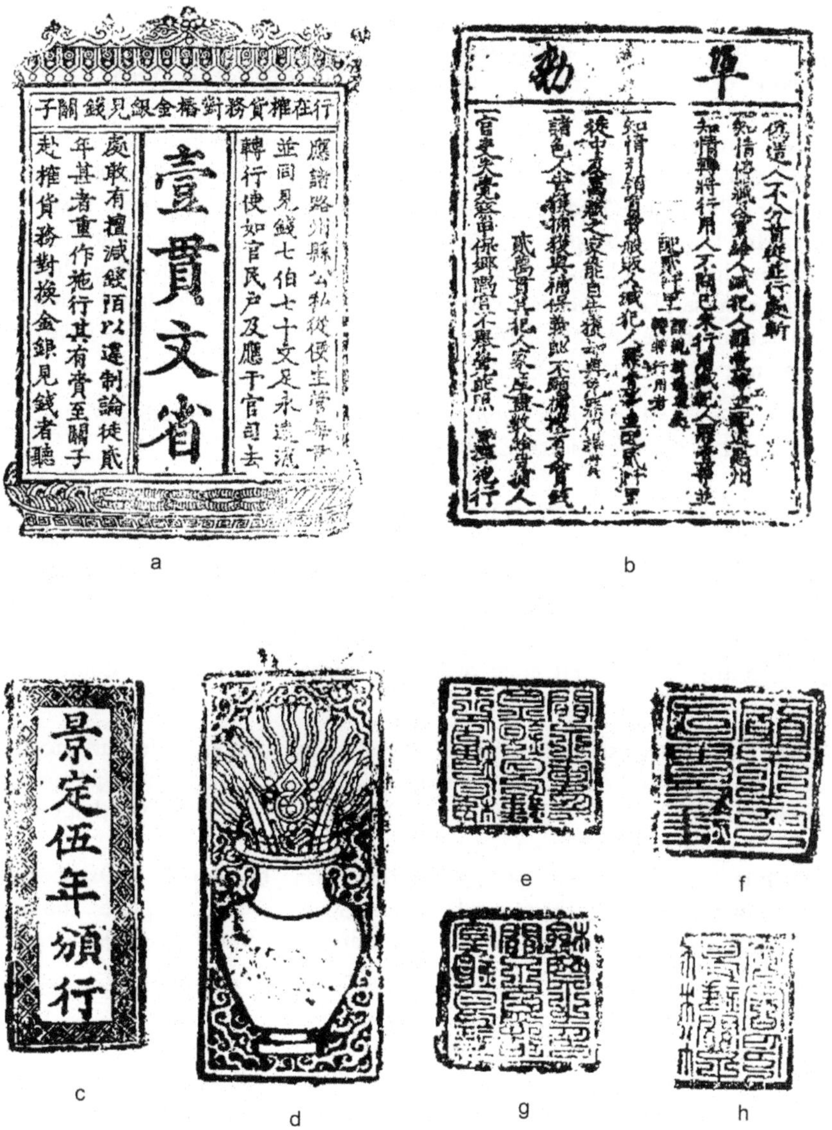

Figure 7.4 Set of eight printing plates for *jinyin xianqian guanzi* bills.
Source: Shi Jilong and Li, *Dongzhi guanzi chaoban yanjiu*, pp. 8–13, pls. 9, 12, 15, 18, 21, 24, 27, 30.

The set of plates also includes two large, vertically oriented rectangular pieces and four smaller square seals. One of the larger plates specifies the year of issue of the *jinyin xianqian guanzi* (景定伍年頒行; i.e., 1264) enclosed within a border with a geometric design (Figure 7.4c). The other depicts a vase filled with various forms of "treasure" (coins, silver ingots, jewels, and two long, tapered objects that probably represent ivory tusks) emitting glowing rays of light (Figure 7.4d). Most likely this vase is a depiction of the "treasure-gathering bowl" (*jubaopen* 聚寶盆) that served as a popular icon of material wealth. These two plates, placed side by side, are slightly smaller than the size of the reverse plate. The four seals (Figures 7.3e–h) read as follows (the first seal retains traces of black pigment, while the other three seals have red pigment):

Seal of the *Jinyin xianqian guanzi* Depository of the Commodity Monopoly Bureau of the Provisional Capital
行在榷貨務金銀見錢關子庫印 (Figure 7.4e)
Xianqian guanzi Seal of the State Budget [Office]
國用見錢關子之印 (Figure 7.4f)
Seal of the *Jinyin xianqian guanzi* Supervisory Inspector
金銀見錢關子監造檢查之印 (Figure 7.4g)
Endorsement Seal of [Commodity Monopoly Bureau?] *Xianqian guanzi* Bill
…見錢關子合同印 [left edge of seal is broken off; perhaps should read "Quehuowu" 榷貨務] (Figure 7.4h)

These four seals closely correspond (except for the differences in bureaucratic nomenclature) to the four types of seals recorded in the regulations governing *huizi* seals cited above. This set of seals thus provides us with a good approximation of the types of seals used on Southern Song *huizi* bills.

While the replacement of figural illustrations by lengthy texts sharply distinguishes the Dongzhi plates from the Figure 7.1 and 7.3 plates, the text on the face of the note displays an important affinity with the "Qiansicang" plate:

> Shall be **negotiable for public and private debts in all circuits, prefectures, and counties, and circulate** in perpetuity **at an exchange value equivalent to ready cash at the rate of 770 coins** full-**string**. If officials dare to illegally discount these notes when submitted by official or commoner households for payments to the state they shall be deemed in violation of the laws and punished by two years' exile. Those who wish to bring these bills to the Commodity Monopoly Bureau and exchange them for gold, silver, or ready cash are permitted to do so.
>
> 應諸路州縣, 公私從便主管, 並同見錢七伯七十文足, 永遠流轉行使。如官民戶及應干官司去處, 敢有擅減錢陌, 以違制論, 徒貳年, 甚者重作施行。有賫至關子赴榷貨務對換金銀見錢者, 聽。

The text in bold corresponds exactly to the text that appears on the Qiansicang plate. In fact, the entire text of the Qiansicang plate is reproduced on the face of the Dongzhi bill with two exceptions: the anachronistic "outside of Sichuan" was dropped (*jinyin xianqian guanzi* bills were intended to be a universal currency, in contrast to the earlier regionally specific forms of paper money), and the unit of account was changed from short-string to full-string coin. The insertion of the phrase "in perpetuity" also is a new feature of the *jinyin xianqian guanzi*, since *huizi* were limited to fixed terms of expiry (although this limit had been suspended for issues #17–#18 in 1247). This striking textual correlation lends further support to the argument for identifying the Qiansicang plate with the #18 *huizi* bill.

Nonetheless, the authenticity of the Dongzhi plates also has been questioned by Wang Shengduo, one of China's leading numismatists.[32] Wang has observed that a number of key features of *huizi* bills, such as narrative illustrations, serial numbers, and signature seals of the authorizing officials, are absent from any of the Dongzhi plates. Given that the *jinyin xianqian guanzi* bill was intended to replace earlier *huizi* issues entirely, though, it would not be surprising if the design of the new notes differed radically from its predecessors. Wang also noted that since these plates were made of lead rather than bronze, it is likely that they are the work of counterfeiters rather than actual plates from the government currency printing office. In this respect, too, the question of whether the plates are forgeries is irrelevant for our purposes.

The more substantial objection raised by Wang Shengduo concerns whether these plates conform to contemporary descriptions of the *jinyin xianqian guanzi* bills. Several sources dating from the early Yuan period relate that Jia Sidao – roundly denounced as a tyrannical "last bad minister" who presided over the fall of the Song to the Mongols – created a new design for the bills that was meant to resemble his own surname. Liu Yiqing, an eyewitness to the fall of Hangzhou, regarded Jia Sidao's new currency as a harbinger of the imminent demise of the Song dynasty in an essay entitled "Premonition of the Silver Surety Notes":[33]

> In 1264, when state councilor Jia was presiding over the affairs of the state, he created the Gold/Silver/Ready Cash Surety currency, what would have been the #19 *huizi* issue. One *guan* of the new bills was equivalent in value to 3 *guan* of the issue #18 *huizi* bills, while the #17 *huizi* bills no longer were to be used. The format of the *guanzi* bills was as follows: a black seal at top in the shape of the 品 graph; three red seals in the center

32 Wang Shengduo 汪圣铎, "Guanyu Dongzhi guanzi chaoban de jige yidian" 关于东至关子钞版的几个疑点, *Zhongguo qianbi* 中国钱币 1994.3: 28–30.

33 Liu Yiqing 劉一清, "Yinguan xianchen" 銀關先讖, *Qiantang yishi* 錢塘遺事 (1799 ed.; rpt. Shanghai: Shanghai guji chubanshe, 1985), 5.4a–b.

> linked together in the shape of the 目 graph; and two small elongated black seals at the bottom corners, so that the image looked exactly like the "Jia" 賈 graph [i.e., Jia's surname]. The top of the Silver Surety note was embellished with a decorative emblem in the form of a "precious canopy." These notes were called "Gilded Crest" on account of their appearance. Its logo was "In the Unicorn Hall of the present day, who will rank first in noble deeds?"[34] When the great [Mongol] army conquered Jiangnan, it seemed to be entering an uninhabited country. People regarded this paper money as a premonition of the coming calamity. Indeed it was.
>
> 景定甲子, 賈相當國, 造金銀現錢關子。時十九界矣。以一準十八界之三, 十七界不用。其關子之制: 上黑印如〈品〉字; 中紅印三,相連如〈目〉字; 下兩旁各一小長黑印, 宛然一賈字也。銀關之上, 列為寶蓋幢幡之狀。目之曰『金旛勝』。以『今代麒麟閣,何人第一功』為號。大兵下江南, 如入無人之境, 人以為讖,信然。

A similar record was preserved in a Yuan-period chronicle of the late Southern Song period:[35]

> On the *yichou* day of the twelfth month of 1264, an edict was issued saying, "The dearness of goods originates in the excess of paper money. Now we will restore the old precedents of the mid-dynastic renewal by using the Ready Cash Surety Bills. The exchange rate of the new bills will be 77-*wen* full-string per *mo*. One *guan* of the new bills will be equivalent in value to 3,000 *wen* of issue #18 [*huizi*]. . . . [Jia] Sidao requested that the paper currency be converted to the Gold/Cash/Ready Coin Surety Bills in order to maintain a balance in its exchange value. One guan of the new bills would be equivalent in value to 3 *guan* of #18 *huizi*, while the #17 *huizi* were discarded entirely and no longer used. The format of the *guanzi* bills was as follows: a black seal at top in the shape of the 西 graph; three red seals in the center linked together in the shape of the 目 graph; two small elongated black seals at the bottom corners like two feet. The image looked exactly like the "Jia" 賈 graph. When the surety bills were issued the prices of goods suddenly leaped.
>
> 景定五年十二月乙丑, 詔: 物貴原於楮多, 今以見錢關子, 復中興舊法。每百七十七足陌, 以一準十八楮三千‥‥‥似道請秤提楮幣, 改造金銀見錢關子。以一準十八界會子之三, 十七界廢不用。關子之制: 上黑印, 宛如〈西〉字; 三紅印相連如〈目〉字; 其下兩旁各一小長黑印, 如兩腳, 宛然一賈字也。關子行, 物價頓踴。

Wang Shengduo contends that the Dongzhi plates do not correspond to these descriptions of the *jinyin xianqian guanzi* bills. The three red seals, with a

[34] The Unicorn Hall was built by the Han emperor Wu to celebrate his hunting prowess, but it achieved lasting renown when Wu's successor Emperor Xuan transformed it into a grand memorial by placing statues of the leading statesmen of his day in it.

[35] *SSQW* 36.67a–b.

combined length of 17.2 cm, could easily fit in a vertical array on the face of the bill, which measures 22.7 cm from top to bottom. None of the plates resembles the image of the 品 or 西 graphs said to have appeared at the top of the bill, however. Yet we should keep in mind that these accounts, determined to fix the blame for the Mongol conquest on Jia Sidao's purported acts of lèse-majesté, are not wholly reliable. Their reading of the *jinyin xianqian guanzi* as projecting the image of the 賈 graph may well have required considerable imagination; it is certainly unlikely that the image would be blatantly apparent. The "logo" cited by Liu Yiqing – "In the Unicorn Hall of the present day, who will rank first in noble deeds?" – clearly should be understood as another reference to Jia Sidao's overweening arrogance. It is not clear, however, that this passage, which obviously does not appear on any of the Dongzhi plates, was actually printed on the *jinyin xianqian guanzi* bills; certainly it does not conform to what seems to have been the iconographic program of *huizi*, although it is reminiscent of the kinds of narrative illustrations that are said to have appeared on *qianyin* bills. On the other hand, Liu Yiqing's comment about the "precious canopy" image is fully confirmed by the face plate of the Dongzhi specimens. Moreover, these descriptions lend support to the idea that the design of the *jinyin xianqian guanzi* differed radically from the earlier *huizi* notes, and thus undermine Wang's other questions about their authenticity.

As noted above, Fang Hui recorded that the popular names of the #17 and #18 *huizi* issues were "vase bill" and "mushroom bill" respectively.[36] He followed up that observation with the statement that "the *jinyin xianqian* bills were called 'gate bills,' on account of their appearance. The populace joked that 'this is one gate through which you cannot pass.'"[37]

> 關子目曰『關楮』。民戲言『過此一關不得』。

While it seems clear that the design of the Figure 7.4a plate was intended to resemble a stone stele surmounted by a decorative canopy, we can readily imagine that it also appeared as a partially open gateway surmounted by a decorative arch as Fang's comment suggests.

In my view, despite the reservations expressed by Wang Shengduo (and others), the Dongzhi specimens genuinely represent the visual format of Jia Sidao's *jinyin xianqian guanzi* currency.[38] At the same time, it seems evident that the Dongzhi plates are the work of counterfeiters rather than genuine

[36] The vase-like "treasure-gathering bowl" (Figure 7.4d) calls to mind Fang's statement that the #17 *huizi* notes were known as "vase bills." It suggests the possibility that the vase design apparently found on #17 *huizi* may also have been a smaller if highly distinct design element like this "vase" plate in the Dongzhi specimens.

[37] Fang Hui, "Jianbu Lügong jiazhuan," in *ZSJC*, appendix, 4a.

[38] This is also the conclusion of Shi Jilong and Li, *Dongzhi guanzi*, pp. 102–6.

government printing plates. The discovery of the plates in Anhui (in an area that supplied paper to the government printing workshops) points toward this conclusion. The official *jinyin xianqian guanzi* were printed only in Hangzhou and Chengdu. The Dongzhi plates are made of lead, whereas government regulations stipulated that currency printing plates were to be made of copper. A scribal error appears in the text of the Dongzhi plates (對椿 instead of 封椿 in the title of the bill), an inconceivable defect if these were actual government printing plates.[39] Yao Shuomin has also drawn attention to the poor quality of the carving of the seals as telling evidence that these specimens were forgeries.[40] But regardless of whether or not the Dongzhi plates were made by counterfeiters, surely their design must have closely corresponded to the genuine *jinyin xianqian guanzi* bills.

The above evidence strongly suggests that the language found on the Qiansicang specimen was specific to #17–#18 *huizi* issues (circulated during 1234–1264), perhaps uniquely so. But several problems remain. First, and most puzzling, is the illustration of ten coins in the upper register. The Jin *baoquan* bills issued beginning in 1215 bore illustrations of strings of coin to indicate their value (for example, a 5-*guan* bill would display five strings of coin), a practice that became universal for Yuan and Ming paper currency (see Figures 7.5–7.9). But we have no evidence that such illustrations ever appeared on any Song paper money before the creation of the *jinyin xianqian guanzi* first issued in 1264. Moreover, although the Yuan issued bills in denominations as small as 10-*wen* (i.e., ten coins), *huizi* bills were issued in only larger denominations (the smallest being 200-*wen*; the smallest *qianyin* bill was 500-*wen*). No Song paper currencies corresponded to the value of 10-*wen* presumably represented by the illustration of ten coins on the Qiansicang plate.[41] It is possible, though, that the ten coins represent ten strings of 100 coins (also expressed as *mo* 陌) and thus a total value of 1 *guan*. Yuan and Ming bills – and also the late Song *jinyin xianqian guanzi* – invariably depict coins in *mo* units, albeit depicted as strings of coins. Yang Jun and Zhang Anhao have argued that the statement "shall circulate at an exchange value equivalent to ready cash at the rate of 770 [*wen*] short-string" inscribed on the Qiansicang plate actually denominates the bill as a 1-*guan* bill.[42] I doubt that we can make

39 In addition, we would expect to see "700" written as 七佰 instead of 七伯. But note that the Jin bronze plate specimens (e.g., Figure 7.5) typically write "hundred" as 伯.

40 Yao Shuomin, "Dongzhi guanziban (xia)," p. 9.

41 Citing the depiction of ten coins on the Qiansicang plate, Yao Shuomin proposed that this note corresponded to the Chongning *xiaochao* bills used to redeem 10-*wen* coins for a brief period in 1106–1107. But Xie Caibo's detailed description of the Chongning *xiaochao* bills cited above differs in every respect from the Qiansicang plate. See Yao Shuomin 姚朔民, "Song zhibiban de zaijiantao" 宋纸币版的再检讨, *Wenwu* 文物 2000.4.

42 Yang Jun and Zhang, "'Qiansicang' ban," p. 39.

such a deduction; surely the denomination would be clearly printed on the bill as in the case of Figure 7.1. But it remains a possibility.

Second, as noted above, Fang Hui observed that the #18 *huizi* was colloquially known as the "mushroom bill" because of the main motif of its design. While the design of Figure 7.1 can be reasonably interpreted as illustrating an "auspicious mushroom" (viz. Figure 7.2), the granary motif of the Qiansicang specimen is wholly different. Yet we should also remember that this specimen is but one of a set of plates, in effect one piece in a larger puzzle. Li Weiguo has observed that the *Book of Odes* verse "May there be a thousand such granaries" repeatedly occurs in Song poetry and other writings as a metaphor for benevolent rule epitomized by overflowing granaries to feed the populace.[43] It surely would be a fitting device for state-issued paper currency. This particular plate may well be a forgery. A memorial of 1243 informs us that the decision to manufacture #18 *huizi* solely using the coarse, heavy paper of Anhui rather than fine, thin Sichuan paper used in earlier issues prompted rampant counterfeiting on an unprecedented scale.[44] But whether state-issued or not, the bill would have to replicate the visual appearance of genuine bills.

Despite these anomalies, given the affinities between the documentary evidence cited above as well as the language of the Dongzhi plate (Figure 7.4a) on one hand and the Qiansicang plate on the other, I am inclined to believe that the latter represents some version of the #18 *huizi* bills issued after 1240 (and before 1256, when the circulation of *huizi* was extended to Sichuan), a conclusion also voiced by Li Weiguo. More speculatively, I would suggest that the Qiansicang plate perhaps was used to print the smaller *huizi* bills (such as the 200-*wen* bill), or the "small bills," such as the 50- and 100-*wen* bills reportedly issued by the Hangzhou authorities c. 1241 (see Chapter 6). The smaller size of the Qiansicang plate (about 30 percent smaller than the Figure 7.1 specimen and half the size of the largest Dongzhi plates) lends support to this hypothesis.[45]

In the last analysis, the argument that the Qiansicang plate is a modern forgery stumbles on its sheer implausibility. Forgery implies some intelligible simulacrum of an original. But a modern forger would have no specimens or models of Song paper bills on which to draw and thus would have to rely on sheer invention. (Clearly the Jin–Yuan paper currencies did not serve as

43 Li Weiguo, "Qiansicang chaoban," p. 79.

44 *SS* 181.4408.

45 Yang Jun and Zhang Anhao ("'Qiansicang' ban," 39–41) conclude that the Figure 7.1 and 7.3 specimens both are plates for #18 *huizi* bills, citing their physical similarities (the plates themselves and the calligraphy of the inscriptions), the textual evidence that connects them to #18 *huizi*, and their simultaneous appearance in the antiquities market in the 1920s. They propose that the plates perhaps were excavated together from the same site – a suggestion that certainly remains mere speculation.

models for the Qiansicang specimen.) Moreover, it would seem likely that a forgery would seek to identify itself – in the case of paper money, to indicate what type of bill it is and what its value might be, wholly absent in this case. The enigmas of the Qiansicang plate, however confounding to any effort to prove its authenticity, likewise militate – even more so, in my opinion – against the possibility of its being sheer forgery.

Much uncertainty remains concerning the provenance of each of the three extant specimens of Song paper currency printing plates, but the correlations between textual evidence and physical specimens tends to confirm that all three are probably authentic representations of Southern Song paper money. The fact that all three specimens most likely were the products of counterfeiters rather than the official currency printing workshop does not diminish their value as evidence of the design and manufacture of Song paper currency. Unfortunately, the extant specimens shed light on only a small corner of the world of Song paper currency. Even if we accept Figures 7.1 and 7.3 as examples of genuine Song *huizi* bills, these two plates are only single elements from sets of six or more printing plates that were used to manufacture *huizi*. The Dongzhi specimens provide us with a complete set of printing plates, but the *jinyin xianqian guanzi* currency circulated only briefly during the twilight years of the Southern Song, from 1264 to 1276. Moreover, the design of the *jinyin xianqian guanzi* bill appears to have differed radically from the *huizi* bills which it was intended to replace. The extant specimens also fail to enlighten us about the design of the *jiaozi* and *qianyin* currencies of Sichuan. The detailed descriptions of the textual elements and narrative illustrations that appeared on *qianyin* bills during 1161–1179 do not correlate with the principal features of *huizi* currency introduced to the southeastern provinces of the Southern Song realm in 1161. Pronounced differences in the design of paper money reflected – at least symbolically – the autonomy of the Sichuan economy during the Southern Song period.

7.3 Jin Paper Currency Specimens

We are far better informed about the visual appearance of Jin paper money even in the absence of actual specimens, partly because of the greater number of extant (and incontrovertibly authentic) printing plates and partly because Jin currencies apparently were made using a single plate, plus a series of red-inked seals. At least nine intact printing plates, plus several fragments, are known.[46] All of these plates were used by provincial authorities to print either *jiaochao* or *zhenyou baoquan* bills during the period 1212–1216, and thus are

[46] For surveys of Jin paper currency printing plates, see Zhou Xiang 周祥, *Zhongguo gudai zhichao* 中国古代 纸钞 (Shanghai: Shanghai renmin chubanshe 2004), pp. 36–56; Takahashi, "Kindai no shihei." Facsimiles of most of the Jin paper currency printing

confined to a relatively short period in the evolution of Jin paper currencies (Table 7.2). They confirm that a standardized format for the issue of paper currencies had been developed by the early 13th century.

Unfortunately, these plates cannot provide direct evidence for the visual appearance of the initial *jiaochao* bills, issued beginning in the 1150s. For that we must rely instead on the firsthand testimony of the Song envoy Fan Chengda, whose memoir of his diplomatic mission to Kaifeng in 1170 contains a detailed description of the *jiaochao* bills. Although this passage from Fan's memoir is prefaced by "the inscription on the bill reads as follows" (鈔文曰), it actually mixes the inscriptions on the bills with Fan's own commentary. In my translation I have rendered in bold type the portions that, based on the evidence of later printing plates, likely were inscribed on the bills:

> **The Southern Capital Jiaochao Office, according to the rescript of the Ministry of Revenue as endorsed by the Department of State Affairs, received authorization** of the previous memorial requesting establishment of a bureau in the Southern Capital **to print and issue *jiaochao* bills** in denominations from one to three *guan*. **The populace is allowed to submit coin and receive bills in exchange that will circulate like coin and be valid for public and private transactions in Henan circuit. If the bill is brought to the depository for exchange, it shall be immediately honored and be paid. A labor and materials fee of 15 *wen* shall be assessed for each *guan*. The bills will have a seven-year term of expiration, after which they can be redeemed in coin at the short-string rate of 70 *wen*. The punishment for forgery is beheading; those who provide information leading to the arrest of counterfeiters shall receive a reward of 300 *guan*.** Before and after [the above text] there are seals of the **Ministry of Revenue Staff Manager (Hubu goudang);**[47] **the Clerk (Lingshi); the Administrator (Gandang); and the Assistant Keeper of the Jiaochao Depository (Jiaochaoku shifu)**. Along the four borders of the bill are decorations of clouds and cranes.[48]
>
> 南京交鈔所准戶部符，尚書省批，降檢會昨奏南京置局，印造一貫至三貫例交鈔；許人納錢給鈔，河南路官私，作見錢流轉。若赴庫支取，即時給付。每貫收工墨錢十五文。七年納還，別給錢，以七十為陌。偽造者處斬，捕告者賞錢三百千。前後有戶部勾當，令史，幹當官，交鈔庫使副書押，四周畫雲鶴為飾焉。

According to the Jin dynastic history, the inscription for *jiaochao* in the lower portion of the bill read as follows:

plates included in Table 7.2 were first published in Luo Zhenyu 羅振玉, *Sichao chaobi tulu; fu kaoshi* 四朝鈔幣圖錄; 附考釋 (Shangyu: Luoshi, 1914).

47 This office had responsibility over the issue of paper currency as well as salt and other commodity licenses.

48 *LPL* 2a.

Table 7.2 *Jin dynasty paper currency bronze printing plate specimens*

Type of bill	Issuing authority	Denomination	Places of redemption	Date (dimensions)
1. Tongxing jiaochao 通行交鈔	Shandong East Circuit 山東東路	10-*guan*; 80 coins per *mo* 足陌	Yidu and Ji'nan prefectures, Southern Capital 益都府/濟南府/南京	No date
2. Tongxing jiaochao 通行交鈔	Beijing Surveillance and Finance Intendancy 北京路按察轉運司	100-*guan*; 80 coins per *mo* 足陌	Central Capital, Southern Capital, Beijing, Upper Capital, Xianping Prefecture 中都南京交鈔庫/北京/上京/咸平府省庫	1214
3.[a] Tongxing jiaochao 通行交鈔	Shaanxi East Circuit 陝西東路	10-*guan*; 80 coins per *mo* 足陌	Central Capital, Southern Capital, Jingzhao (Xi'an), Hezhong, Luzhou 中都南京交鈔庫/京兆府/河中府/潞州省庫	1213 (21.6 cm x 14.3 cm)
4. Tongxing jiaochao 通行交鈔	Pingzhou Prefecture 平州	50-*guan*; 80 coins per *mo* 足陌	Central Capital, Southern Capital, Pingzhou, Baozhou 中都南京交鈔庫/平州/保州省庫	No date (21.9 cm x 11.6 cm)
5. Tongxing jiaochao 通行交鈔	Shaanxi East Circuit 陝西東路	10-*guan*; 80 coins per *mo* 足陌; 5 endorsement seals 五合同[b]	Central Capital, Southern Capital, Jingzhao (Xi'an), Hezhong, Luzhou 中都南京交鈔庫/京兆府/河中府/潞州省庫	1215 (21 cm x 11 cm)
6. Unknown (fragment)	Shaanxi East Circuit 陝西東路	10-*guan*; 3 endorsement seals 三合同[b]	Central Capital, Southern Capital, Pingliang Prefecture 中都合同/南京合同/平涼府合同	No date
7. Tongxing jiaochao 通行交鈔	Henan Surveillance and Finance Intendancy 河南按察轉運司	500-*wen*; 80 coins per *mo* 足陌	Pingyang and Hezhong Prefectures 平陽府河中府省庫	1212–1213
8. Zhenyou baoquan 貞祐寶券	[none]	5-*guan*; 80 coins per *mo* 足陌	Jingzhao (Xi'an) and Pingliang Prefecture 京兆合同/平涼府合同	1215–1216 (34.9 cm x 21.7 cm)
9. Zhenyou baoquan 貞祐寶券	Pingyang and Taiyuan Circuits 平陽太原兩路	50-*guan*; 80 coins per *mo* 足陌	Pingyang and Taiyuan Prefectures 平陽/太原府路	1215 (29 cm x 17.5 cm)

Sources: nos. 1–6, 8–9: Zhou Xiang, *Zhongguo gudai zhichao*, pp. 36–56; no. 7: Liu Sen, "Jindai xiaochao chaoban chutan," pp. 47–49.

Notes: [a] Two identical specimens of this plate exist.

[b] The designations of three (三合同) or five (五合同) endorsement seals indicated the multiple places where the bills could be redeemed.

> The Central Capital Jiaochao Depository, in accordance with the rescript of the Department of State Affairs' Ministry of Revenue, has been authorized by the executive office of the Department of State Affairs, under the further supervision of the Ministry of Revenue. The seal with the personal name of the clerk has been affixed.
>
> The emperor has decreed that *jiaochao* bills be printed and issued by the various circuits, which can be obtained in exchange for coin at the depositories in [specified place(s)]. In addition, bills can be exchanged for coin at the depositories in [specified place(s)]. [The bills] will circulate like coin and are valid for public and private transactions.[49]
>
> 中都交鈔庫准尚書戶部符，承都堂劄付，戶部復點勘，令史姓名押字聖旨印造逐路交鈔，於某處庫納錢換鈔，更許於某處庫納鈔換錢，官私同見錢流轉。

It is unclear what time period this passage referred to, but since it mentions the issue of bills by "the various circuits" rather than the depositories in the Central and Southern Capitals, most likely it dates from the early 13th century.[50]

Consider, for comparison, the text on the earliest datable printing plate, from 1212–1213 (the text appears in the lower portion of the bill shown in Figure 7.5), held in the private collection of the Jinquan Company in Xi'an (no. 7 in Table 7.2).[51] I have divided my translation by the columns as they appear in the specimen, reading from right to left:

(A) The office of the Surveillance Commissioner and Fiscal Intendant of Hedong Circuit[52] . . . [Department of State Affairs?] further supervision of the responsible officials of the [Ministry of Revenue?]

(B) Approval has been granted to the memorial requesting that this circuit shall print and issue fractional bills of Hedong South circuit. The populace

[49] *JS* 48.1074.

[50] Miyazawa ("Kindai zenki heisei," pp. 220–21) dates this passage to 1189, since it appears between entries for 1189 and 1191. However, this text does not refer to any specific policies or time periods, and Miyazawa himself has shown that the text of *JS* is not wholly reliable in terms of dating. Miyazawa uses this passage to date the emission of regional paper currencies to 1189, although there is no concrete evidence for the issue of paper currencies by circuits before the 13th century.

[51] Liu Sen 刘森, "Jindai xiaochao chaoban chutan" 金代小钞钞版初探, *Zhongguo qianbi* 中国钱币 2006.3: 47–49; Rong Tiansong 戎畋松, "Gupin xunzong: Jindai chongqing wubai wen xiao'e tong chaoban" 孤品寻踪：金代崇庆五伯文小额铜钞版, *Shoucang* 收藏 2022.12: 9–13.

[52] The surveillance commissioner (a judicial office) and fiscal intendant were combined into a single office in 1208 and assigned responsibility for circuit-level paper currencies.

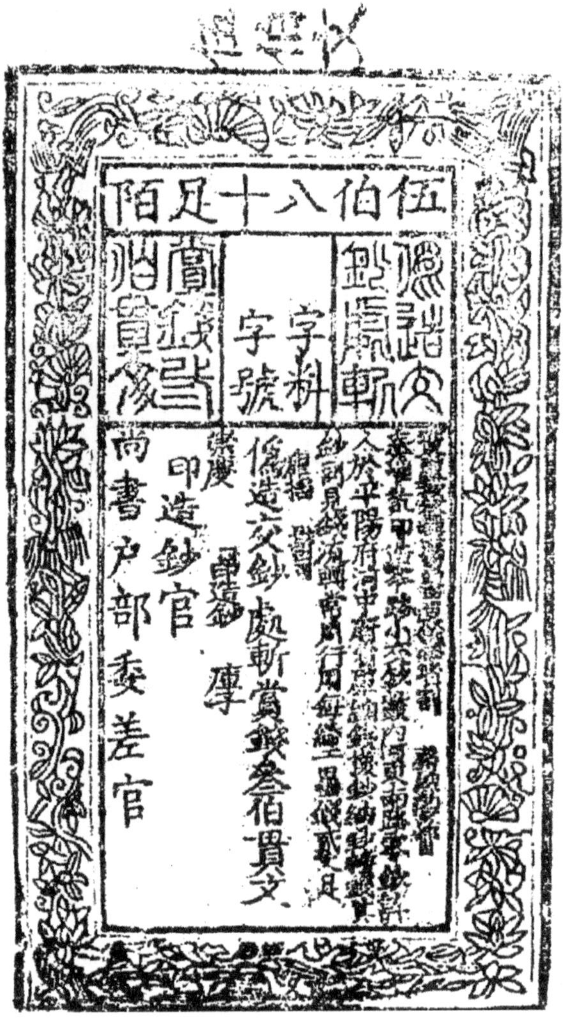

Figure 7.5 500-*wen jiaochao* bill printing plate impression.
Source: Rong, "Gupin xunzong," p. 9.

(C) is allowed to submit coin and receive bills in exchange at the depositories in Pingyang prefecture and Hezhong prefecture. If the bill is brought to the depository, it shall be redeemed in coin. These

(D) bills shall circulate the same as coin and be valid for ... public and private transactions in Henan circuit. A labor and materials fee of 2 *wen* shall be assessed for each *guan*.

(E) Storehouseman (*kuqia*) Accountant (*zansi*)
[spaces left for seals/signatures]

(F) The punishment for forgery is beheading; those who provide information leading to the arrest of counterfeiters shall receive a reward of 300 *guan*

(G) Chongqing [reign era][53] … bill printing office Depository Keeper (*kuzi*)

(H) Official in charge of printing and issuing bills

(I) Courier (*weichaiguan*) of the Department of State Affairs' Ministry of Revenue[54]

(A) 河東南路按察轉運司……省 □ 復點勘，訖都目
(B) 奏准：訖印造本路小交鈔數內，河東南路領鈔。許
(C) 人於平陽府河中府省庫，納錢換鈔，納鈔提錢。其
(D) 鈔同見錢流轉。常 □ 行用每緡工墨錢貳文足
(E) 庫掐 攢司
(F) 偽造者處斬，捕告者賞錢三百千
(G) 崇慶 □印造鈔 庫子
(H) 印造鈔官
(I) 尚書戶部委差官

According to the Jin dynastic history, the officials whose seals were applied to *jiaochao* bills included the storehouseman, accountant, the depository keeper, and a representative of the Ministry of Revenue (on some bills this would be the staff manager [also mentioned by Fan Chengda]; on others, including this specimen, the Ministry of Revenue courier). The five officials who applied their seals to this bill are essentially identical to the dynastic history's list.

The discrepancies between Fan's text and the Jinquan specimen largely reflect intervening changes in the administration of Jin paper currency: (1) the original redemption fee of 15 *wen* was lowered to 8 *wen* in 1175 and finally 2 *wen* in 1207; (2) the exchange rate was raised from the 70 *wen* mentioned by Fan to 80 *wen* in 1180; and (3) the seven-year term of expiry was abolished in 1189, and thus would not appear on subsequent bills. Most importantly, in contrast to the initial restriction of issuance of paper currency to offices in the two capitals, the Jinquan bill was issued by a regional authority, the chief fiscal officer of Henan South circuit (roughly equivalent to the southern half of modern Shanxi province), and nominally could be redeemed at the two main prefectural seats of the circuit.

53 There is a space left to enter the actual year by hand. The Chongqing reign era spanned only two years (1212–1213).

54 Since these bills were being printed at the prefectural level, the Ministry of Revenue dispatched these couriers to supervise the process.

Fan described Jin bills as having a decorative border with pictorial motifs of flowers and cranes, which is consistent with all the extant printing plates. In addition, inset in the top portion of the printing plates is a panel stating the value of the bill (in the case of the Jinquan bill, 500 *wen* at the nominal full-string exchange rate of 80 *wen* per *mo*), below which there are blank spaces in which the serial numbers of the bill would have been written by hand. This top panel is flanked by cartouches with legends in archaic script declaring the penalty for forging paper money (beheading) and the reward offered to informers (300 *guan*). In addition, outside the border at the top of the bill the value is written in large graphs, in this case oriented toward the right edge, although more commonly this inscription is oriented toward the left edge. Absent from the Jinquan bill, although found on most printing plates, are legends along the right edge specifying the "paper and ink" fees for purchasing the bill or exchanging an old bill for the new one.

The *zhenyou baoquan* bills introduced in 1215 largely replicated the format of the *jiaochao* bills, with a few changes, as can be seen in the 50-*guan* bill in Figure 7.6 (no. 9 in Table 7.2), which was issued by the two prefectures of Pingyang and Taiyuan (in modern Shanxi province). At the top of the plate, above the four large graphs identifying the bill as a *zhenyou baoquan* bill, is a cartouche depicting five sets of strings of coin, corresponding to the 50-*guan* value of the bill. This is the earliest specimen that depicts the bill's value using the visual cue of images of strings of coin, which became a standard feature of Yuan paper currency (and is also seen in the late Song *jinyin xianqian guanzi* bill, Figure 7.4a). The left border of the bill includes two partial, diagonally affixed "endorsement seals" (labeled as *hetong* 合同; known in modern Chinese as a "seam-binding seal" 騎縫印) designating the two provincial depositories (in this case, Pingyang and Taiyuan) where the bill could be redeemed. Other plates have three or even five such seals (nos. 6 and 5 in Table 7.2, respectively).

With the singular exception of the Jinquan "small bill," the denominations for all of the surviving Jin printing plates are large, ranging from 5 to 100 *guan*. As noted in Chapter 5, with the introduction of the regional paper currencies, the government increased the denominations of bills from 10 to as much as 1,000 *guan*. Although the Jin had introduced small-denomination bills in 1198 (at least in some areas), only in 1206 were small bills issued on an empire-wide basis (Table 7.3). In the same year, the government decreed that small bills would be allowed to circulate in all circuits without discrimination. But it appears that bills could be redeemed – to the extent that was even allowed in practice – only in the circuits in which they were issued. In 1214–1215, the Jin court created Regional *Jiaochao* Depository Printing Workshops (Suichu jiaochaoku chaozhifang 隨處交鈔庫抄紙坊) throughout the realm (Table 7.4). These new regional centers largely overlapped with those granted authority to issue small bills in 1206 as shown in Table 7.3, except that more of

Figure 7.6 50-*guan zhenyou baoquan* bill printing plate impression.
Source: Neimenggu jinrong yanjiusuo, *Zhongguo guchao tuji*, p. 20, pl. 2.13a.

them were located in the northeast (Manchuria), which was bearing the brunt of the Mongol attacks at that time. The creation of these paper currency printing workshops, twenty-one in all, established beyond a doubt the regionalization of paper currencies.

The Figure 7.6 plate conforms to the regional profile shown in Table 7.4. The Figure 7.6 specimen does not specify the circuit of issue, but rather the two circuit seats of Hedong South and Hedong North, Pingyang and Taiyuan, respectively. Like the other Jin plates, this specimen attests to the pronounced regionalization of Jin paper currencies by the 1210s, if not earlier. Indeed,

Table 7.3 *Locations for issuing Jin small bills, 1206*

Circuit	Issuing prefectures
Central Capital	Central Capital 中都, Baozhou 保州
Southern Capital	Southern Capital 南京, Guide 歸德, Henan 河南
Liaodong	Upper Capital 上京 (modern Ha'erbin), Xianping 咸平
Shandong East	Yidu 益都, Jinan 濟南
Shandong West	Dongping 東平, Daming 大名
Hebei East	Hejian 河間, Jizhou 冀州
Hebei West	Zhending 真定, Zhangde 彰德
Hedong North	Taiyuan 太原, Fenzhou 汾州
Hedong South	Pingyang 平陽
Western Capital	Western Capital 西京 (Lanzhou), Fuzhou 撫州

Source: *JS* 48.1079.

none of the ten specimens itemized in Table 7.2 were issued at either the Central or the Southern Capital. Three of the ten bills were issued in Shaanxi circuit, at the circuit capital of Jingzhao (modern Xi'an), which was not one of the circuits listed in Tables 7.3–7.4.[55] Although the seals of central government officials remained obligatory, the actual issuing agents were the circuit-level surveillance/finance intendants.

The size of the *jiaochao* bills appears to have been fairly standard (21–22 cm long and 11–14 cm wide), whereas the two *zhenyou baoquan* bills – although issued at the same time in adjacent circuits – are both much larger and significantly differ in size from each other. The 5-*guan* Shaanxi bill (no. 8 in Table 7.2) actually is one-third larger than the 50-*guan* Shanxi bill (no. 9 in Table 7.2), and more than twice the size of the 10-*guan jiaochao* bill issued in the same circuit two years before (no. 3 in Table 7.2). Given the severe depreciation in the value of Jin paper currency at this time – as evidenced by the issue of bills in denominations as large as 1,000 *guan* – most likely the larger dimensions of the *zhenyou baoquan* bills were intended to bolster public confidence in their value.

Based on the textual and artifactual evidence, then, Jin paper currencies appear to have been printed in a fairly standardized format from their inception down to the *zhenyou baoquan* bills issued beginning in 1215. The *zhenyou baoquan* bills essentially reprised the illustrative design of the *jiaochao* bills; the two significant differences were (1) the prominent placement of the name of the bill ("*zhenyou baoquan*") above the denomination and serial

55 At the request of the circuit military commander, the court granted Shaanxi circuit the authority to issue its own paper bills in 1215. *JS* 48.1083–84.

Table 7.4 *Regional* jiaochao *depository printing workshops, 1214–1215*

Circuit	Issuing prefectures
Upper Capital	Upper Capital 上京 (modern Ha'erbin)
Central Capital	Pingzhou 平州, Tongzhou 通州, Shunzhou 順州, Jizhou 薊州
Northern Capital	Northern Capital 北京 (near Ningcheng in modern Inner Mongolia), Guangning 廣寧, Ruizhou 瑞州
Xianping	Xianping 咸平
Western Capital	Western Capital 西京 (Lanzhou), Weizhou 蔚州
Shandong East	Yidu 益都
Shandong West	Dongping 東平
Daming	Daming 大名
Hebei East	Hejian 河間, Qingzhou 清州
Hebei West	Zhending 真定
Hedong North	Taiyuan 太原
Hedong South	Pingyang 平陽
Fengxiang	Pingliang 平涼

Source: *JS* 56.1284.

numbers and (2) (in the case of the 50-*guan* bill in Figure 7.6) the addition of the illustration of strings of coin at the very top. Border designs vary among the bills, one sign of local adaptation of a common format. In contrast to Song paper currency designs, illustrative elements were relegated to the margins of Jin bills, in which textual elements dominate. The documentary descriptions of Song *qianyin* and *huizi* bills strongly foreground their multiple illustrations, and the available printing plate specimens (Figures 7.1 and 7.3) reaffirm the prominence of the pictorial aspect of the Song paper currencies. Only on the much-later *jinyin xianqian guanzi* bills (issued in 1264, long after the demise of Jin) do textual elements dominate on Song bills, and in the case of the *jinyin xianqian guanzi* the visual appearance of the bill still radically differed from that of Jin bills. The Jin thus established a visual program for its paper currency that diverged markedly from Song precedents, but it would become the basis for the Yuan paper currencies.

7.4 Yuan Paper Currencies

When we come to the Yuan period, we are fortunate to have more than 500 extant specimens of paper currency, most of which have been recovered from tomb excavations (462 from the trove of documents unearthed at Khara-Khoto [modern Edjina Banner in Inner Mongolia] and 75 from ten other sites). Yuan paper currencies essentially consisted of two types: (1) "Inaugural

Treasure Exchange Bills of the Zhongtong Era" (*zhongtong yuanbao jiaochao* 中統元寶交鈔) – hereafter ZTC, for sake of convenience – inaugurated by Khubilai Khan in 1260; and (2) "Commonly Circulated Treasure Bills of the Zhiyuan Era" (*zhiyuan tongxing baochao* 至元通行寶鈔) – ZYC, likewise for sake of convenience – introduced in 1287.[56] Although issue of ZTC bills was suspended after 1287, the Yuan government renewed the issue of ZTC bills in smaller quantities from 1311. In 1350, with its fiscal and monetary affairs in disarray, the Yuan leadership decided to reestablish its paper money by issuing a new ZTC bill bearing a reverse stamp indicating that they were printed in the Zhizheng (1341–1367) reign era (see Figure 7.9). The vast majority of extant ZTC bills consists of these post-1350 issues. But a few rare specimens of the original issue of ZTC have survived, such as the Figure 7.7 bill, which we can date to the period 1260–1269. The paper of Yuan notes was bluish-gray in color, what contemporaries referred to as "crow-blue" (*yaqingse* 鴉青色). The term "crow-blue" became a colloquial metaphor for money during the Yuan period.

The ZTC bills essentially conform to the model of the Jin *zhenyou baoquan* bills.[57] The format of the inscriptions is virtually identical to that of the *zhenyou baoquan* bills, and the inscriptions themselves likewise follow the Jin precedents, with the necessary changes in the nomenclature of bureaucratic offices (although titles such as storehouse keeper and accountant were retained unaltered). The major change in design is that the illustration of the corresponding strings of coins is prominently displayed at the center of the bill, immediately below the denomination printed in large graphs. On the 500-*wen* bill in Figure 7.7 this central panel is flanked by two legends written in archaic script, reading "Zhongtong Inaugural Treasure" (中統元寶) on the right and "Commonly Circulates in All Circuits" (諸路通行) on the left. In 1269, Khubilai officially adopted the 'Phags-pa script for writing Mongolian, and thereafter these legends were printed either in Mongolian 'Phags-pa script (Figure 7.8) or both archaic Chinese and Mongolian scripts (Figure 7.9). The main inscription on the Figure 7.7 bill states that it was issued by the Inaugural Treasure Exchange Bill Depository (Yuanbao jiaochao ku 元寶交鈔庫) under the authority of the Provisional Secretariat (Xing Zhongshusheng 行中書省), also an indication that the bill dates from early in Khubilai's reign, before the Secretariat was established as a permanent institution. Another variation from Jin bills is that the reward for exposing counterfeiters (which, like Jin bills,

[56] A third bill, the *Zhida yinchao*, was in circulation for only slightly more than one year (1309–1310), and no specimens survive. The "Inaugural Treasure" (*yuanbao*) in the full designation of the ZTC bill alluded to the 50-*liang* silver ingot. See Chapter 8.

[57] For a general introduction to the design of Yuan paper currency, see Maeda Naonori 前田直典, *Genchō shi no kenkyū* 元朝史の研究 (Tokyo: Tokyo daigaku shuppankai, 1973), pp. 3–17.

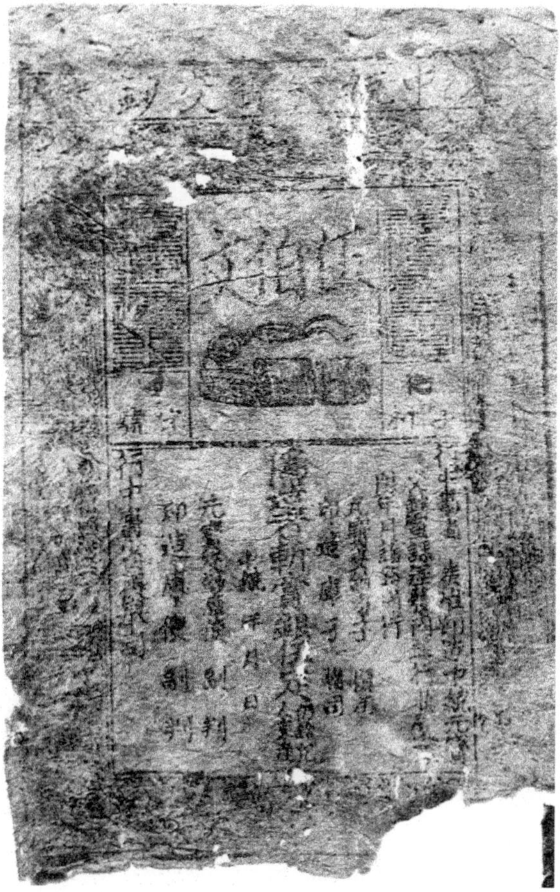

Figure 7.7 500-*wen zhongtong chao* bill.
Source: Lei Runze, Yu, and He, "Ningxia Baisikou Shuangta faxiande Dachao tongbao he zhongtong yuanbao jiaochao," rear cover illustration.

appears prominently in the center of the inscription) is stipulated in *ding* (定, an abbreviation of 錠), the paper money unit derived from silver ingots, rather than the *guan* unit that referred to coins. Finally, the decorative border around the edges of the text portions includes images of dragons as well as flora.

The 500-*wen* ZYC bill in Figure 7.8 conforms to the ZTC model in Figure 7.7, with a few changes. The inscriptions flanking the denomination of the bill at top center are written in Mongolian rather than Chinese. In addition, the ZYC bills were issued under the authority of the Department of State Affairs (Shangshusheng 尚書省) rather than the

Figure 7.8 500-*wen zhiyuan chao* bill.
Source: Neimenggu jinrong yanjiusuo, *Zhongguo guchao tuji*, p. 46, pl. 3.30.

Secretariat, as was duly inscribed on the bills, as well as the specific office of the Depository for Baochao Bills (Baochao ku 寶鈔庫). The red seals on this bill are not legible, but the red seals on other ZYC specimens read in Mongolian "Seal of the General Depository for Baochao Bills" (寶鈔總庫之印 in Chinese). The new ZTC bill issued in 1350 shown in Figure 7.9 also replicates its predecessor, the Figure 7.8 bill, with the addition of legends in Mongolian flanking the denomination and changes in nomenclature to reflect that the bill was issued by the depository for *baochao* bills under the authority of the Department of State Affairs. This bill also bears a single endorsement seal on the upper left edge. The reverse side of the bill features a stamp reading "Inaugural Treasure Exchange Bill printed in the Zhizheng era" (Zhizheng yinzao Zhongtong jiaochao 至正印造元寶交鈔) – indicating that it was

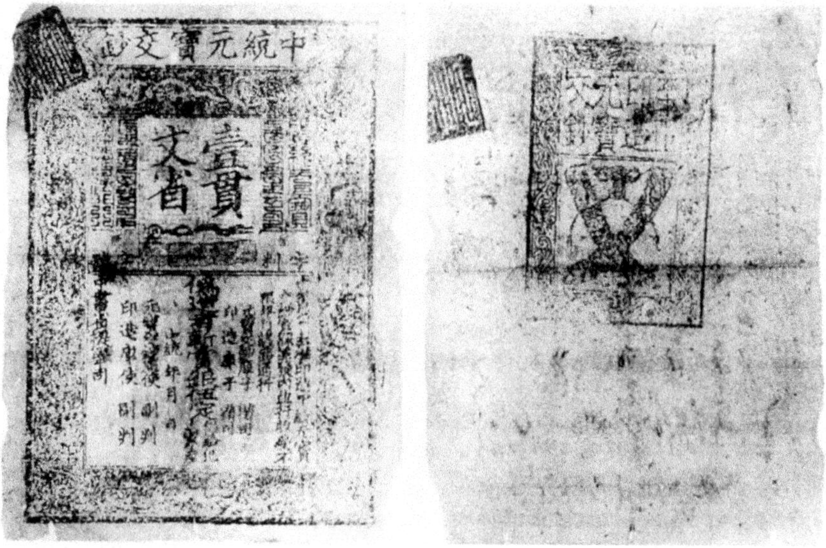

Figure 7.9 1-*guan zhizheng zhongtong chao* bill.
Source: Neimenggu jinrong yanjiusuo, *Zhongguo guchao tuji*, pp. 27–28, pl. 3.16a, 3.16b.

printed during the Zhizheng reign-period (1340–1367) – above an image of strings of coin. Despite the images of strings of coin that appear on Yuan bills, in both government fiscal accounts and private market exchange the bills were referred to using silver units of value (see Chapter 8).

It appears that Yuan paper currency was printed using a single plate for the face of the note, along with two red seals, and often a diagonally affixed endorsement seal at the upper left edge. Surviving examples of Yuan paper money have at least two seals on the reverse: a large rectangular seal bearing either the name of the type of note or its denomination and an illustration of strings of coin indicating its denomination within a floral border, and a partial, diagonally affixed endorsement seal at the upper left edge.[58] The design of Yuan paper currency largely imitated the paper currency issues of the Jin dynasty. Despite the abiding hostility of Zhu Yuanzhang, founder of the Ming dynasty, to Mongol culture and customs, the *baochao* paper currency that Zhu

[58] See the examples in Neimenggu jinrong yanjiusuo, *Zhongguo guchao tuji*, colour plates 2–6, b/w plates 3.15a–3.40; Zhang Ziying 张子英, "Cixian faxian Zhiyuan tongxing baochao tuban ji tuyin 磁县发现至元通行宝钞铜版及铜印," *Zhongguo qianbi* 中国钱币 1993.1: 36–37; Li Zhengxin 李正鑫, "Hunan Huarong chutu yuanchao 湖南华容出土元钞," *Zhongguo qianbi* 中国钱币 1994.4: 33–35.

inaugurated in 1375 was virtually identical to Yuan precedents. Like Jin and Yuan notes, Ming *baochao* prominently displayed the value of the note with an illustration of the corresponding amount of bronze coin in addition to identifying the government agency issuing the bill and the penalties for counterfeiting. While Jin, Yuan, and Ming paper currencies all shared a basically similar design, they clearly differed from Song notes. Yuan and Ming specimens thus shed little light on the design of Song paper money.

7.5 Conclusion

Despite its limitations, the evidence cited above confirms the distinctive character of Song paper currencies, especially in contrast to the separate tradition of design and illustration introduced by the Jin and continued by the Yuan and Ming courts. Song paper currencies featured complex designs, multiple impressions on both sides of the bill, and three-color printing. The Jin–Yuan–Ming notes, in contrast, were manufactured using only a single plate for the face illustration plus several seals. Song paper currencies (with the exception of the last, the *jinyin xianqian guanzi*) were issued with limited terms of expiry, and the design of the notes was modified with each issue. Jin paper money originally had a seven-year term of expiry, but late Jin and subsequent Yuan and Ming paper currencies circulated without any time limit. The distinctive features of the manufacture and design of Song paper money on one hand and the Jin–Yuan–Ming currencies on the other is an example of the marked differences in material culture between northern and southern China that evolved after the Jurchen conquest of the north in 1127.

The complex iconography of Song paper currencies and frequent changes in design undoubtedly served the intended purpose of deterring counterfeiting to some degree. Yet the strong likelihood that all of the extant specimens of Song paper money printing plates are the work of counterfeiters confirms contemporary reports of the rampant counterfeiting that plagued the Song monetary system beginning in the early 13th century. Nonetheless, the distinctive designs of each issue reinforced their unique identities. Demarcated by region and term of expiry, each issue of paper money also circulated at varying values that reflected regional economic conditions and fiscal practice (e.g., the balance between supply and demand for paper currency, its acceptability in payments to the state, and the extent of counterfeiting).

The distinctive look (and feel) of each type of currency reinforced this variation in exchange values. As the colloquial names for specific issues mentioned by Fang Hui suggest, the iconography of paper currency provided the visual keys for discerning real differences in monetary value. Any of Fang Hui's contemporaries would have known that a given denomination of "mushroom bills" was worth fives times as much as the same denomination of "vase bills." Some of the contemporaries celebrated the prodigious alchemical powers the Song imperial court flourished in transforming mere paper into gold. Others lamented the disorder engendered by the heterogeneous and competing forms of money in the absence of a unified and sovereign currency. Both were right. It is no surprise that the critics of Jia Sidao believed they could discern the failings of his character and his policies in the design of the paper money he created.

PART III

Transition to the Silver Economy

8

Yuan Paper Currencies and the Transition to the Silver Standard

The era of Mongol rule in China marked a watershed in the evolution of the Chinese monetary system. By the 1230s China's age-old bronze coin monetary standard had been largely dismantled. Silver had superseded coin as the actual means of exchange in the Jin territories in the north, while paper currencies – to some extent backed by silver – had to a significant degree eclipsed bronze coin as the monetary standard in the Southern Song realm. Under Mongol suzerainty, silver became the chief instrument of trans-Eurasian trade and the main source of revenue for the Mongol regimes in China. Yet the fiscal and monetary policies initiated by the Mongol rulers led not to the adoption of silver as the primary means of market exchange but rather to the creation of a fiat paper money system similar in many respects to that of the Jin. In contrast to the Song and Jin paper monies, however, the Mongol paper money standard was tied to a silver money of account.[1]

The evolution of Mongol fiscal and monetary practices can be broadly divided into four stages:

(1) the elaboration of the tribute system of the Mongol confederation from the time of Temüjin (reigned as Chinggis Khan, 1206–1227) to that of the Great Khan Möngke (r. 1251–1259)
(2) the creation of a unified paper money system under the Great Khan Khubilai (r. 1260–1294) and its extension to the whole of the former Song realm after the Mongol conquest of the Southern Song in 1276
(3) the failure of the initiative launched in 1309 during the reign of Khaishan (r. 1307–1311) to restore a multiple currency monetary system based on bronze coin, which resulted in a reorganization of Khubilai's paper money system

[1] For the details of Mongol–Yuan monetary history, see Takahashi, *Genchō kahei*; Maeda, *Genchō shi*, pp. 3–143; Iwamura Shinobu 岩村忍, *Mongoru shakai keizai shi no kenkyū* モンゴル社会経済史の研究 (Kyoto: Kyōto daigaku jimbun kagaku kenkyūjo, 1968), pp. 471–545; and Miyazawa, *Kahei to zaisei*, pp. 377–523. The only study in a Western language is Herbert Franke, *Geld und Wirtschaft in China unter der Mongolen-Herrschaft: Beiträge zur Wirtschaftsgeschichte der Yüan-Zeit* (Leipzig: Otto Harrassowitz, 1949).

(4) the vain effort beginning in 1350 to revert to a multiple currency system as the Mongol empire in China crumbled.

Under the aegis of Khubilai, who adopted the Chinese-style dynastic title of Yuan in 1271, the Mongol regime demonetized both bronze coin and precious metals in favor of a fiat paper currency. Despite the formidable obstacles to amalgamating the former Southern Song territories into their fiscal regime, the Mongol leaders succeeded in instituting Khubilai's paper money system in most parts of southern China. In contrast to the Song, the Yuan government issued its paper currencies in small denominations intended for use in retail trade. Khaishan's short-lived attempt to establish a new multicurrency monetary system – including bronze and silver currencies as well as paper money – proved an utter failure. Although bronze coin did not entirely disappear from circulation, paper currencies prevailed as the lifeblood of private commerce and public revenues of the Yuan empire at least until it began to disintegrate in the late 1340s. Through the instruments of Yuan paper currencies and fiscal administration, silver became established as the new monetary standard, long before silver became the common means of market exchange and revenue extraction in the 15th century, under the Ming dynasty.

8.1 The Emerging Silver Standard in the Mongol Realm

Despite the growing prevalence of silver in the Song and Jin economies, prior to the rise of the Mongols silver had mostly disappeared from China's steppe frontier. In the heyday of the Uighur state of Khara-khoja 高昌 in the 10th and 11th centuries, both Islamic silver coin and Chinese bronze coin had receded from eastern Turkestan and no longer served as media of exchange. Although some Song bronze coin may have flowed into Central Asia, the Uighurs relied on cotton and silk cloth as well as grain as media of exchange. In addition, silver plate served as treasure, that is to say, as a store of value. But contrary to the claims of some scholars, there does not seem to have been a significant trans-Eurasian circulation of silver bullion before the Mongol era. Uighur contracts from the 11th and 12th centuries almost exclusively use *quanpu* (i.e., 官布), a measure of cotton cloth, as the monetary unit.[2]

[2] Moriyasu Takao 森安孝夫, "Shiruku rōdo tōbu ni okeru senka: Kinu, seihō ginsen, kanfu kara gintei e" シルクロード東部における銭貨：絹・西方銀銭・官布から銀錠へ, in Moriyasu Takao (ed.), *Chūō Ajia shutsudo bunbutsu ronsō* 中央アジア出土文物論叢 (Kyoto: Hoyū shoten, 2004), pp. 1–40. Moriyasu convincingly repudiates the idea of a trans-Eurasian "Silver Road" prior to the Mongol epoch proposed by Otagi Matsuo 愛宕松男, "Addatsusen to sono haikei: Jūsan seiki Mongoru Genchō ni okeru gin no dōkō (II)" 斡脱銭とその背景：十三世紀モンゴル元朝における銀の動向 (二), *Tōyōshi kenkyū* 東洋史研究 32.2 (1973): 165.

According to the testimony of Chinese envoys who visited Mongol camps in the early 1230s, members of the Mongol tribes were obligated to deliver tribute in the form of a percentage of their herds to the khan. In addition, the Mongol nobility imposed levies of food, horses, equipment, cloth, and labor services on the population of their appanage. Understood as a form of personal servitude, these requisitions collectively were known as *qubchir*.[3] The *qubchir* was an extraordinary levy, collected whenever the ruler deemed necessary. The practice of *qubchir* became the basis for collection of taxes paid in silver from the former Jin territories beginning in the 1250s.

There is some evidence – from coin specimens rather than historical documentation – that the Mongols minted silver coins in places such as Ghazna and Samarqand in the 1220s that were intended to facilitate tribute payments. Mark Whaley has proposed that Sino-Khitan administrators employed by the Mongols in Afghanistan struck silver coins bearing the Chinese legend Dachao tongbao 大朝通寶 ("Circulating Treasure of the Great Court") as early as 1222.[4] These coins presumably were issued to soldiers in the Mongol armies, who were obliged to pay the *qubchir* levy when not actively engaged in military campaigns. In recent decades, nearly twenty deposits of Dachao tongbao silver coins – mostly single finds, but two caches of 214 and nearly 400 coins – have been excavated in northwestern China, nearly all in the Gansu Corridor region, the territory of the Xia kingdom before the Mongol conquest in 1217. When Chinggis's son Ögödei (r. 1229–1241) succeeded him as great khan in 1229, he awarded most of the former Xia territories as an appanage to his second son, Köden. Zhou Kelin has persuasively argued that these Dachao tongbao silver coins (and a few rare bronze and lead specimens) were issued under Köden's authority, and their circulation was largely confined to Köden's appanage and a few adjacent areas.[5] The cache of nearly 400 Dachao tongbao coins unearthed at Longxi (central Gansu) also included a few silver coins bearing Uighur and Chinese inscriptions identifying them as Xining tongbao 西寧通寶, which indicates that they were issued at Xining (capital of modern Qinghai province), most

[3] The best exposition of the Mongol tribute system remains Franz Schurmann, "Mongolian Tributary Practices of the Thirteenth Century," *Harvard Journal of Asiatic Studies* 19.3–4 (1956): 304–89; see also Thomas T. Allsen, *Mongol Imperialism: The Policies of the Grand Qan Möngke in China, Russia, and the Islamic Lands, 1251–1259* (Berkeley: University of California Press, 1987), pp. 144–88.

[4] Mark A. Whaley, "An Account of the 13th Century Qubchir of the Mongol 'Great Court,'" *Acta Orientalia Academiae Scientiarum Hungaricae* 54.1 (2001): 1–84. The *Dachao tongbao* is not mentioned in documentary sources, and thus is attested only from excavated specimens.

[5] Zhou Kelin 周克林, "Dachao tongbao qian de xingzhi zhuxingdi jiqi xiangguan wenti" 大朝通宝钱的性质, 铸行地及其相关问题, *Zhonggguo guojia bowuguan guankan* 中国国家博物馆馆刊 2018.4: 74–87.

likely also by Köden.[6] Issue of the Dachao tongbao coins probably ceased after Möngke became great khan in 1251, displacing the lineage of Ögödei, and expropriated most of its territories, including that of Köden. Although such silver coins suggest that the Mongols collected part of the *qubchir* in the form of money at an early date and they may have been used in trade as well, it is unlikely that the Dachao tongbao provided the mechanism for the monetization of the *qubchir* levy in the former Jin territories of North China, as Whaley has argued.

Under the leadership of Ögödei, the Mongol confederation began to develop formal institutions for ruling the sedentary societies that had submitted to its rule. Ögödei instituted the appanage system by awarding swaths of the former Jin territories and their inhabitants to his sons and relatives, other Mongol princes, and a number of "Han hereditary lords" (漢家世侯; i.e., local Chinese warlords who had sided with the Mongols against the Jin).[7] Slightly more than half of the former Jin population became subject to appanage holders, with the remainder under the direct rule of the khan. Within these appanages personal rule by the nobility replaced bureaucratic governance. As in other parts of the Mongol realm, the appanage holders resorted to tax-farming to extract revenues from the sedentary agricultural populations under their dominion. Tax collection privileges were granted to merchant cartels, comprised mostly of Uighurs and Muslim foreigners, known as the *ortoq*. The *ortoq* merchants also served as commercial agents for their Mongol overlords, investing the latter's booty in trade ventures and moneylending. Under the Mongol khans, the *ortoq* dominated both fiscal administration and private commerce.[8]

Yelü Chucai, one of the chief Sino-Khitan advisers to Chinggis and Ögödei (and formerly a Jin official himself), was the principal architect of the Mongol

6 V. A. Belyaev 别利亚耶夫 and S. V. Sidorovich 西多罗维奇, "Xin faxian de gongyuan 13 shiji zhongqi da menggu diguo yinbi" 新发现的公元13世纪中期大蒙古帝国银币, *Zhongguo qianbi* 中国钱币 2014.1: 9–16. Köden was the first Mongol patron of the Tibetan lama 'Phags-pa, who would later devise the Mongolian script based on Uighur. In 1252, shortly after Köden's death, Möngke's brother Khubilai demanded that 'Phags-pa be handed over to him, and the lama subsequently became Khubilai's personal spiritual adviser.

7 The authoritative study of the Mongol appanage system is Li Zhi'an 李治安, *Yuandai fenfeng zhidu yanjiu* 元代分封制度研究 (Tianjin: Tianjin guji chubanshe, 1989).

8 On the crucial role of the *ortoq* merchants in the Mongol-ruled economy, see Otagi, "Addatsusen to sono haikei (I) (II)," *Tōyōshi kenkyū* 32.1 (1973): 1–27, 32.2 (1973): 163–201; Thomas T. Allsen, "Mongol Princes and Their Merchant Partners, 1200–1260," *Asia Major*, 3rd series, 2.1 (1989): 83–126; Elizabeth Endicott-West, "Merchant Associations in Yüan China: The Ortoγ," *Asia Major*, 3rd series, 2.1 (1989): 127–54; Uno Nobuhiro 宇野伸浩, "Ogodei han to Musurimu shōnin: Orudo ni okeru kōeki to Nishi Ajiasan no shōhin" オゴデイ・ハンとムスリム商人:オルドにおける交易と西アジア産の商品, *Tōyō gakuhō* 東洋学報 70.3–4 (1989): 71–104.

administrative system established in the former Jin territories after 1234. In 1236, Yelü introduced a regular system of taxation, but he expressed skepticism about a concurrent proposal to imitate Jin practice and issue paper currency. Mindful of Yelü's caution, Ögödei agreed to issue a new *jiaochao* currency in modest quantities.[9] Little is known about these *jiaochao* bills, which probably circulated only for a brief period. Reportedly they were denominated in silver units known as *ding* 錠, equivalent to 50 *liang* of silver bullion. The *ding* (literally, "ingot") unit originated with the common practice in Song times of casting silver into standard ingots: the full-*ding* (weighing 50 *liang*), the half-*ding* (中錠; 25 *liang*), and the small *ding* (小錠; 12.5 *liang*). The actual weight of these ingots varied slightly over time, but in general the *liang* measured 40 grams, and thus the *ding* weighed 2 kilograms.[10] The *ding* silver units did not correspond to bronze currency units; thus, these ingots served as stores of value rather than as media of exchange. Although the *ding* unit was not used by the Jin state either as a unit of account or to denominate its currency, it was a common convention for denominating silver.[11]

Beginning in the early 11th century, the Song state had paid substantial annual tribute (*suibi* 歲幣) in silk and silver to its rivals along the northern frontier, the Khitan Liao and Tangut Xia kingdoms. Although much of this silver probably returned via trade to the Song territories, some of it was retained as treasure in the steppe frontier.[12] Thus eleven of the fourteen

9 *Yuan shi* 元史 ([hereafter *YS*]; Zhonghua shuju ed.), 146.3460. Despite Yelü Chucai's skepticism, his biographer asserted that "establishing paper currency" was one of the measures by which Yelü brought relief to the people. See *YS* 146.3461.

10 A survey of 347 specimens of Southern Song silver ingots published in 1988 sorted them into five weight classes with the following weight ranges: full-*ding*, 1,850–2,030 g; half-*ding*, 914–989 g; small *ding*, 418–507 g; and two smaller sizes with weight ranges of 225–245 g and 115 g (a single specimen only) equivalent to one-eighth and one-sixteenth of a full *ding*. The report does not state how many ingots were included in each weight class, but these figures indicate that the weight of the *liang* ranged from 36.8 g to 40.6 g. See Huang Cheng 黄成, "Cong kaogu faxian tan Nan Song baiyin liutong de jige wenti" 从考古发现谈南宋白银流通的几个问题, in *Song shi yanjiu jikan* 宋史研究集刊 (Hangzhou: Hangzhou daxue lishixi Songshi yanjiushi, 1988), vol. 2, pp. 213–25. Extant weight measures from the Northern Song and Jin consistently weigh 39–40 g per *liang* (there are no surviving weight measures from the Southern Song); the two extant weight measures from the Yuan, weighing 36.6 g and 39.8 g per *liang*, show greater variation. See Guojia jiliang zongju 国家计量总局 (ed.), *Zhongguo gudai duliangheng tuji* 中国古代度量衡图集 (Beijing: Wenwu chubanshe, 1981), pp. 34–35.

11 For example, in 1201 a Jin local official reported that although the official exchange rate for 1 *ding* of silver was 100,000 *wen* of paper money (i.e., 1 *liang* = 2,000 *wen*, or 2 *guan*), the market rate was only 80,000 *wen*. *JS* 48.1078.

12 Shiba Yoshinobu, following the lead of Hino Kaisaburō, has argued that the Song's favorable balance of trade with the Liao enabled it "to regain all of the silver sent to the Liao as tribute." This statement seems to overreach. See Shiba Yoshinobu, "Sung Foreign Trade: Its Scope and Organization," in Morris Rossabi (ed.), *China Among Equals: The*

Table 8.1 *Monetary units in Uighur contracts, 10th–14th centuries*

Uighur term	Translation	Number of items
Yunglalïq quanpu	"Current" official cloth (官布)	49
Quan baqïr	Bronze coin (*guan/wen* 貫文)	2
Yunglalïq tavar	"Current" goods	4
Yunglalïq böz	"Current" cotton cloth	9
Böz	Cotton cloth	26
Yunglalïq kümüš	"Current" silver	7
Kümüš	Silver	30
Yunglalïq čao	"Current" paper currency (鈔)	5
Čao	Paper currency (鈔)	7

Source: Moriyasu, "Shiruku rōdo senka," 10–15.

provenanced specimens of Northern Song silver ingots have been recovered from excavations in the vicinity of the Liao Supreme Capital (Shangdu 上都, modern Bairin Youqi in Inner Mongolia); another was unearthed at Borgedar (northwestern Xinjiang), in what was then the territory of Xia kingdom. All of the inscribed specimens are full-*ding* ingots (with two exceptions, the weights fall in a narrow range of 1,993–2,006 g) that originally had been forwarded from local authorities (in all but one case, from silver-producing regions in South China) to the Song capital at Kaifeng.[13] Presumably these ingots subsequently were delivered to the Liao and Xia as *suibi* tribute payments. Although these ingots did not circulate as currency in the steppe regions, the conquering Mongols undoubtedly obtained similar ingots as booty well before the conquest of the Jin was completed.

The emergence of silver ingots and silver-denominated paper money as the prevailing monetary media in Central Asia can be seen in Uighur contracts dating from the 10th to 14th centuries (Table 8.1). Although these contracts cannot be dated precisely, Moriyasu Takao has proposed a rough chronological order that shows a decisive shift from *quanpu* cloth (and the few instances of bronze coin) during the heyday of the Khara-khoja kings in the 10th–11th centuries to silver (*kümüš*) and paper currency (*čao*) following the onset of the Mongol era. That this shift signaled the institution of a new fiscal

Middle Kingdom and Its Neighbors, 10th–14th Centuries (Berkeley: University of California Press, 1983), p. 98; Hino Kaisaburō 日野開三郎, "Gin ken no jyūkyūjō yori mita Godai Hoku-Sō no saihei saishi" 銀絹の需給上より見た五代・北宋の歳幣・歳賜, in *Hino Kaisaburō ronshū*, vol. 10: *Hokutō Ajia kokusai kōryū shi no kenkyū (II)* 北東アジア国際交流史の研究 (下) (Tokyo: San'ichi shobō, 1983), pp. 441–500.

13 Jin Deping 金德平, "Bei Song yinding kao" 北宋银锭考, *Zhongguo qianbi* 中国钱币 2008.3: 3–14.

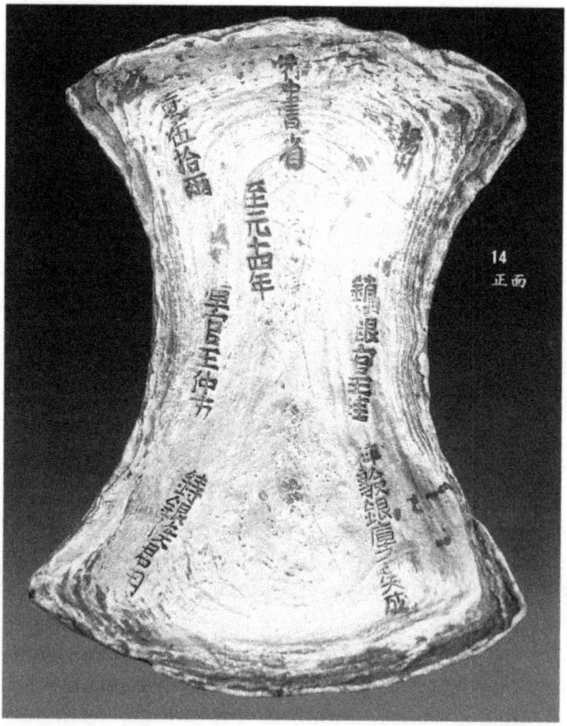

Figure 8.1 Mongol-era silver ingot (50 *liang* or 1 *ding*). This silver ingot bears inscriptions identifying it as having been deposited in the treasury of the Yuan Imperial Secretariat in 1277. The reverse is inscribed with two large graphs: *yuanbao* 元寶 ("Primordial Treasure"), designating a 1-*ding* (50-*liang*) ingot. The ingot was cast in Yangzhou, in the former Southern Song territories, which had been captured by Khubilai's army in 1276. According to the late Yuan author Tao Zongyi, after the victory at Yangzhou the Mongol commander seized the stocks of silver taken by his soldiers and had them cast into 1-*ding* ingots and sent to the imperial capital at Dadu. Khubilai distributed these ingots as gifts to family members, Mongol princes, and military commanders, but Tao notes that many of them were used in trade and thus spread among the general populace as well. Tao, *Nancun chuogenglu*, 30.377.
Source: Collection of National Museum of History, Taiwan, accession number 83-02090.

regime is evidenced by the replacement of *quanpu* (the fiscal unit established by the Uighur monarchs) by *böz* to refer to payments of cloth. Mongol-era documents also frequently mention silver ingots (*yarmaq kümüš*) denominated in *yastuq*, equivalent to 2 kilograms. The Uighur word *yastuq* means "pillow," undoubtedly an allusion to the shape of the Chinese silver *ding* (Figure 8.1), which resembles a Chinese ceramic pillow. The Mongolian term for these ingots, *süke* ("axe"), also derived from their physical appearance.[14] This nomenclature, and the fact that the Chinese *ding* was precisely 2 kilograms in weight, leaves no doubt that the Uighur and Mongol terms for silver units derived from Chinese *ding* ingots. Subsequently, the Mongol Ilkhan regime in Iran adopted the Persian word *balish* (meaning "pillow," and thus clearly borrowed semantically from the Uighur term) as the standard unit of account for its fiscal regime.[15] As a result of its prominence throughout the Central Asian trade network, the 1-*ding* silver ingot (under the names *yastuq* and *balish*) became the standard money of account across the Mongol empire from the time of Ögödei.[16]

The Mongols had begun to use the *ding* unit to reckon revenues collected in silver at least as early as 1230, when Ögödei – in imitation of the Jin practice – established tax depots to collect excise taxes on salt, liquor, and vinegar in areas north of the Yellow River. Although there is evidence to suggest that some appanages in North China already had imposed irregular *qubchir* levies collected in silver by this time, the tax system devised by Yelü Chucai in 1236 was based on a combination of land and poll taxes collected in grain and silk yarn. In 1239, the Uighur merchant ʻAbd al-Rahman, who overshadowed Yelü Chucai during the last years of Ögödei's reign, proposed establishing a *qubchir* levy collected in silver in the former Jin territories, and such a tax seems to have been enacted, probably in 1243, during the regency of Ögödei's widow Töregene. Vociferous opposition from the various Han hereditary lords soon derailed this initiative, however. Meanwhile, Mahmud Yalavach, a Khwarazmian merchant who served the Mongols as a fiscal officer, converted the *qubchir* levy in the Mongol domains of eastern Turkestan into a

14 Moriyasu, "Shiruku rōdo senka," pp. 10, 16–18, 30. The Uighur documents also use *sïtïr*, a unit 1/50 of the *yastuq*, and thus precisely equivalent to the Chinese *liang*, which was 1/50 of the *ding*. The term *sïtïr* (*sijir* in Mongolian) was an ancient one, used by Sogdian merchants to measure the weight of silver plate (Moriyasu, pp. 10).

15 The Ilkhanid historian Wassaf al-Hadrat observed that the *balish* was equivalent to 50 *sïr* and 500 *misqal* (Arabic *mithqal*); cited in Matsui Dai 松井太, "Mongoru jidai no dōryōko: Higashi Torukisutan shutsudo bunken kara no saikentō" モンゴル時代の度量衡：東トルキスタン出土文献からの再検討, *Tōhōgaku* 東方学107 (2004): 158.

16 Wang et al., *Huobi liutong yanjiu*, pp. 106–12. The Franciscan missionary William of Rubruck, who visited Möngke's court in 1254–1255, reported that the *yastuq* was equivalent to 10 silver marks (nominally speaking, roughly 2.4 kg), while the Persian historian Juvayni stated that the *balish* was equivalent to 75 gold dinars (nominally, 317.5 g). See Christopher Dawson (ed.), *The Mongol Mission: Narratives and Letters of the Franciscan Missionaries in Mongolia and China in the Thirteenth and Fourteenth Centuries* (New York: Sheed and Ward, 1955), p. 144; Ata-Malik Juvayni, *The History of the World Conqueror*, trans. John Andrew Boyle (Cambridge, MA: Harvard University Press, 1958), vol. 1, p. 23. When Khubilai's brother Hülegü captured Baghdad in 1258, he melted down the silver coins in the Abbasid caliph's treasury and recast them into *balish* ingots. See Allsen, *Mongol Imperialism*, p. 182.

tax collected in silver. Yalavach's tax system became the basis of the *baoyin* 包銀 levy, assessed in silver, imposed on the former Jin population soon after the ascension of Möngke as great khan in 1251.[17]

The *baoyin* was levied on households (rather than individual adult males, as was the common practice for the *qubchir*), initially at a standard rate of 6 *liang* per year. This rate proved unsustainable even though less affluent households generally paid only half the standard rate, and in 1255 the rate was reduced to 4 *liang*, half to be paid in silver and half in silk yarn. Even at this reduced rate, the *baoyin* levy was an onerous burden (4 *liang* of silver at this time was worth 190 liters of rice, or about one-half of the annual consumption of an adult male). Many households borrowed silver from the *ortoq* merchants, only to default on their debts, lose their land, and abscond.

The *baoyin* levy extracted enormous quantities of silver from the subject populations of the former Jin territories. ʻAbd al-Rahman reportedly promised Ögödei in 1239 that he would be able to double silver revenues from 22,000 *ding* (41.25 metric tons) to 44,000 *ding* per year. But Al-Rahman's tax measures, finally put into effect in 1243, were rescinded almost immediately. Möngke's *baoyin* levy had a far more sustained impact on the silver supply. Wang Yun, one of Khubilai's Chinese advisers, reported that in 1261 the *baoyin* levy raised 60,000 *ding* (3 million *liang*, or 112.5 metric tons) of silver each year.[18] Approximately 20 percent of this amount was retained in China to defray the administrative costs of the Mongol government. The remainder was delivered to the Mongol court at Karakorum. The Mongols in turn entrusted their silver revenues to the *ortoq* merchants to finance trading expeditions. Demand for silver in West Asia caused a steady drain of silver from China to the Islamic world and beyond.[19] One scholar has extrapolated from Wang Yun's statement to estimate the total export of silver from China to Central and West Asia during the first thirty years of Mongol rule to have been 90 million *liang* (3,375 metric tons).[20] Although this figure surely is too high,

17 My highly condensed summary of the early history of the *qubchir* levy is based on Abe Takeo 安部健夫, "Gen jidai no hōginsei no kōken" 元時代の包銀制の考研, rpt. in Abe, *Gendai shi no kenkyū* 元代史の研究 (Tokyo: Sōbunsha, 1972), pp. 75–232, and Allsen, *Mongol Imperialism*, pp. 163–171. For a different – but to my mind unpersuasive – interpretation of the origins of the *baoyin* levy, see Whaley, "13th Century Qubchir," pp. 35–46.

18 Wang Yun 王惲, "Zhongtang shiji (shang)" 中堂事記 (上), *Qiujian xiansheng daquan wenji* 秋澗先生大全文集 ([hereafter *QJWJ*]; SKQS ed.), 80.21b.

19 On the flow of silver from the Sinitic ecumene to West Asia and beyond, see Robert P. Blake, "The Circulation of Silver in the Moslem East down to the Mongol Epoch," *Harvard Journal of Asiatic Studies* 2.3–4 (1937): 291–328; Akinobu Kuroda, "The Eurasian Silver Century (1276–1359): Commensurability and Multiplicity," *Journal of Global History* 4.2 (2009): 245–69. Kuroda has linked the westward flow of silver from China to a surge in the output of silver coinage in Europe, notably in Britain.

20 Otagi, "Addatsusen to sono haikei (I)," p. 26.

by the time that Chinggis's grandson Khubilai was elected great khan in 1260, North China was suffering from severe shortages of silver.

The Dachao tongbao silver coins seem to have been minted to provide payment to soldiers, but no documentary sources mention their use in trade. However, numerous sources affirm that prior to the Mongols' adoption of paper money, silver and silk served as the principal means of commercial exchange as well as tax payments.[21] The earliest Mongol paper currencies typically were denominated in silk or silver, no doubt because they prevailed as the units of account in private trade. The growing scarcity of silver undoubtedly impelled the revival of paper currencies in imitation of Song and Jin precedents.

8.2 Reestablishing Paper Currency Under Mongol Suzerainty

The earliest evidence for paper currency issued by a Mongol authority is a recently discovered bronze plate for a *huizi* bill in the extraordinary denomination of 30,000 *guan*. It appears that this currency was issued by a Mongol general following the conquest of the Jin Central Capital (i.e., Beijing) in 1215.[22] The plate, modeled after Jin paper currency, bears the date eleventh month of 1215 according to the Jin calendar (the Mongols had not yet adopted reign titles), but it uses the Song nomenclature of *huizi* rather than that of Jin paper currencies. The inscription restricts the circulation of the bill to Tongzhou circuit (immediately east of the Central Capital) and states that it is convertible with *jiaochao*, presumably referring to the Jin *jiaochao* bills. The Mongol invasion triggered a catastrophic depreciation of Jin bills, to the point where they had sunk to one-thousandth of their face value.[23] When Yelü Chucai in 1236 warned Ögödei about the pitfalls of paper money, he observed that because the Jin had flooded the market with what he called "old bills" (*laochao* 老鈔) in massive quantities, "10,000 *guan* could purchase only a single wheatcake."[24] The Tongzhou *huizi* specimen succinctly confirms the hyperinflation that arose in the wake of the Mongol invasion.

As already mentioned, there is little evidence that the *jiaochao* associated with Yelü Chucai were put into circulation, or at least not for long. But holders of appanages in North China, both Mongol and Chinese, had already begun to issue their own paper currencies to address the problem of silver shortages. He Shi, a Han hereditary lord in Shandong, had issued *huizi* bills denominated

[21] Takahashi, *Genchō kahei*, pp. 124–26.

[22] Rong Tiansong 戎畋松, "Chaoquanban zuida mian'e xianshen: Jie Jindai 'Tongzhou xingshangshu liubu canwan guan huizi' tongchaoban lishi yunyan" 钞券版最大面额现身: 揭金代 '通州行尚书六部参萬贯会子' 铜钞版历史云烟, *Shoucang* 收藏 2022.12: 20–25.

[23] *JS* 48.1083.

[24] *YS* 146.3460.

in silk yarn beginning in 1227 that were said to have facilitated commerce in his territory.[25] The former Jin official Liu Su, appointed by Ögödei as pacification commissioner in Xingzhou (southern Hebei) in 1240, was credited with "opening iron foundries and issuing paper currency, on which both public and private transactions relied."[26] A pair of recently excavated printing plates, one intact and one broken, further attests to this proliferation of regional paper currencies. The plates, dated 1250, are entitled *Zizhou jiaohui* (淄州交會), indicating that the currency circulated in Zizhou circuit in Shandong (the plates were found in Zibo, Shandong). Between 1226 and 1260, Zizhou was under the jurisdiction of Zhang Rong, another former Jin official, appointed by Chinggis as regional governor of Shandong. This *jiaohui* currency (a conflation of Jin and Song nomenclature) was denominated in silk cloth, although the reward for exposing counterfeiters inscribed on the bill was 100 *liang* of silver.[27] According to Zhang's biography, silver was the means of market exchange at that time, but silver had become so scarce that the people of Zizhou robbed graves to obtain it, a practice that naturally Zhang took action to halt.[28]

By the early 1250s, we are told, many circuits issued paper currencies, with three-year terms of expiry. Khubilai's mother, Sorghaghtani Beki, who had ruled the appanage of Zhending (in central Hebei) since 1236, issued one such paper currency at the behest of Shi Ji, who had served her as circuit overseer of Zhending since 1242. The Zhending paper currency apparently was backed by silver.[29] Elsewhere, however, the fiat currencies had no such silver backing and merchants often refused to accept them. In 1251, Shi Ji encouraged Möngke to adopt convertibility of paper money with silver throughout the realm, although no action seems to have been taken.[30] After Möngke granted his brother Khubilai the appanage of Jingzhao (modern Shaanxi) in 1252, Khubilai issued his own paper money to pay the salaries of officials and soldiers under his command. This currency was denominated in silver, and "its value was equal to that of silver specie."[31]

25 *YS* 150.3552.
26 *YS* 160.3764. Xingzhou had been a major iron-producing center in the Northern Song.
27 Gao Congming 高聪明, "'Zizhou jiaohui' kao" 『滋州交会』考, *Zhongguo qianbi* 中国钱币 2016.1: 9–12.
28 *YS* 150.3558.
29 That would seem to be the meaning of "the method of mutually balancing silver and paper currency" (銀鈔相權法), which was how her policy was described. Wang Yun, "Da Yuan gu Zhendinglu . . . Shi gong shendaobei ming" 大元故真定路‥‥‥史公神道碑銘, *QJWJ* 54.11a. When Khubilai issued his new paper money (ZTC) in 1260, it sparked an uproar since the Zhending bills (here referred to as "silver bills" 銀鈔) were deemed invalid, but the government stepped in to exchange the new ZTC bills for the old Zhending bills. See *YS* 160.3764.
30 *YS* 147.3481.
31 價與銀埒. Yao Sui 姚燧, "Kaifuyi . . . youchengxiang Shi gong xiande bei" 開府儀‥‥‥右丞相史公先德碑, *Mu'an ji* 牧庵集 ([hereafter *MAJ*]; SKQS ed.), 26.1b.

It seems that the circulation of these paper currencies was largely confined to the appanage of the ruler who issued them. The prevalence of silver and silk yarn as measures of value in private trade led to their adoption as the principal forms of state payments as well.[32] According to a cryptic statement by the Chinese official Liu Xuan, on the eve of Khubilai's monetary reform of 1260 "the various circuits [of the Mongol domains in North China] each issued 'exchange silver' (*jiaoyin* 交銀), which in some places circulated together with negotiable bills (*xianchao* 見鈔) and in other places with silk yarn and cloth."[33] Although what Liu meant by "exchange silver" remains uncertain, his statement implied the prevalence of silver as the monetary medium.[34]

8.3 Khubilai's Currency Reforms

Immediately upon his election as great khan in 1260, Khubilai enacted a sweeping currency reform to create a unified monetary system throughout his realm. Bronze coin – already scarce – was demonetized. Khubilai based his monetary system on a new paper currency, the *Zhongtong yuanbao jiaochao* 中統元寶交鈔 (here again I will use the abbreviation ZTC). ZTC was issued in eleven denominations using bronze coin as the unit of account: 10, 20, 30, 40, 50, 100, 200, 300, and 500 *wen* and 1 and 2 *guan*. In contrast to the much larger denominations of Song and Jin paper currency, the ZTC bills were intended to replace bronze coin altogether for small-scale transactions. Khubilai's advisers also proposed to issue a separate "silver bill" (*yinchao* 銀鈔) currency (to be made of silk rather than paper) denominated in silver units (1, 2, 3, 5, and 10 *liang*) for larger transactions (the 1-*liang* "silver bill" would be equivalent in value to the largest ZTC note), but this plan was never put into effect. In 1262, Khubilai decreed that the ZTC should serve as the medium for both private exchange and state payments.

Although the plan for creating a "silver bill" was not realized, Khubilai's government sought to link the ZTC bills to silver, the primary medium of its fiscal administration (the "*yuanbao*" in the full title of the ZTC was the colloquial name for the 1-*ding* silver ingot [Figure 8.1]). The rate of exchange between the new paper currency and silver was fixed at 1 *ding* (i.e., 50 *liang*) of silver equivalent to 100 *guan* of ZTC, thus reaffirming the official rate of

32 Lu Wengui 陸文圭, "Liumin tanli yan chaofa sibi" 流民貪吏鹽鈔四弊, *Qiangdong leigao* 牆東類稿 (SKQS ed.), 4.18a.

33 Wu Cheng 吳澄, "Da Yuan gu yushi zhongcheng . . . Liu Zhongxian gong xingzhuang" 大元故御史中丞· · · · · ·劉忠憲公行狀, *Wu Wenzheng ji* 吳文正集 ([hereafter *WWZJ*]; SKQS ed.), 88.6a–b.

34 While "*jiao*" commonly was used in terms denoting various types of paper currency, it never appears on bronze coins. It is highly unlikely that Liu was referring to the Dachao tongbao coin.

exchange for Jin paper money (1 *liang* silver = 2 *guan* paper money). At the outset, a Currency Exchange Bureau (Jiaochaoku 交鈔庫) was created at the capital to handle exchanges of paper money for gold and silver. In 1264, the government set up currency exchange bureaus (renamed Pingzhunku 平準庫 or Xingyongku 行用庫) in every circuit (and also in many prefectures and counties) to facilitate the disbursal of the new bills and replace worn bills with new ones. According to Wang Yun, silver stocks were delivered to the currency exchange bureaus to provide a reserve for the ZTC bills.[35] At times the Yuan followed the Song precedent of using silver to repurchase excess paper currency and sustain public confidence in its value.[36] Following the conquest of Southern Song in 1276, the exchange bureaus were extended to nearly all of Khubilai's Chinese territories, excepting Fujian, parts of Anhui, and the whole of the Lingnan region (Map 8.1).[37] The spatial distribution of exchange bureaus largely conformed to that of commercial tax revenues, suggesting a close affinity between the circulation of paper currency and commercial networks, which were concentrated in the capital region of Dadu/Beijing, the lower Yangzi River basin, and the Grand Canal corridor (Map 8.2).

Although the ZTC bills, and later Yuan paper currencies as well, continued to bear images of strings of coin that provided visual illustration of the bills' value (see Figures 7.7–7.9), they were not convertible with bronze coin, which was wholly demonetized. From the outset, the value of the ZTC was understood in terms of its equivalent in silver.[38] The evidence from government statutes and local gazetteers shows that Yuan officials at both the central and local levels uniformly kept fiscal accounts using silver units – *ding*, *liang*, and decimal fractions of *liang*.[39] These units referred not to silver specie, however, but to ZTC bills. The drain of silver out of Khubilai's realm compelled his government to convert most of its revenues – the salt and tea excises and commercial taxes in 1261, and even the *baoyin* levy in 1263 – into payments in ZTC. After the conquest of the Southern Song, nearly all Yuan revenues, apart

35 Wang Yun, "Zhongtang shiji (shang)," *QJWJ* 80.21a.
36 Wu Cheng, "Liu Zhongxian gong xingzhuang," *WWZJ* 88.6b.
37 Maeda, *Genchō shi*, pp. 57–72. By 1287, there were 65 Pingzhunku and 79 Xingyongku. The key difference between the two types was that one could redeem bills for silver at the former, while the latter merely replaced worn bills with new ones. Chen Gaohua 陈高华 and Shi Weimin 史卫民, *Zhongguo jingji tongshi: Yuandai jingji juan* 中国经济通史:元代经济卷 (Beijing: Jingji ribao chubanshe, 1999), p. 438. Additional bureaus were created in subsequent years: for example in 1305 at the Fujian seaports of Fuzhou and Quanzhou, and subsequently in the interior prefecture of Jianning as well.
38 "When [Khubilai] first issued paper bills, their value was expressed in silver" (鈔法初行,以銀為則). Ouyang Xuan 歐陽玄, "Yuan Hanlin xueshi . . . Zhao Wenmin shendaobei" 元翰林學士……趙文敏神道碑, *Guizhai wenji* 圭齋文集 (SKQS ed.), 9.19a.
39 Miyazawa, *Kahei to zaisei*, pp. 377–414.

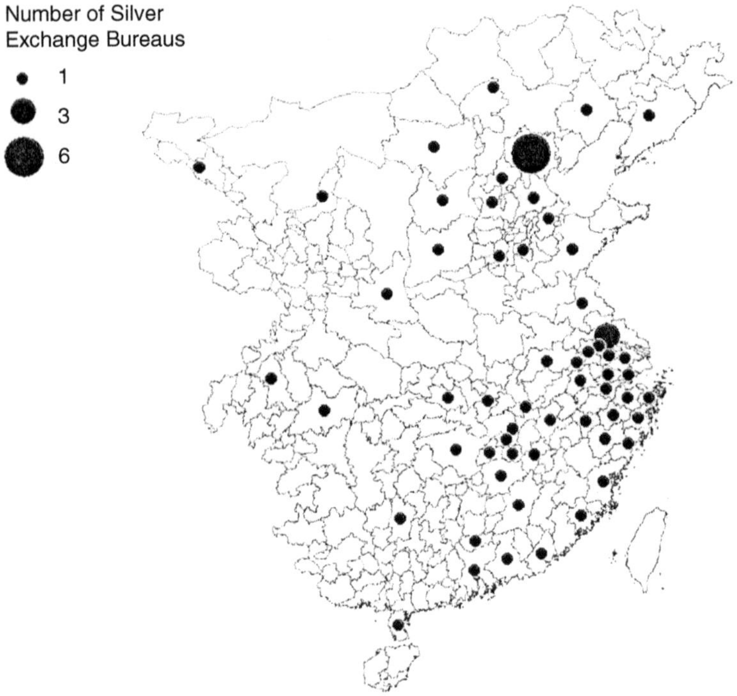

Map 8.1 Distribution of Yuan currency exchange bureaus.
Source: Guan, Palma, and Wu, "Paper Money in Yuan China," p. 1229, fig. 3.

from the tribute grain shipped from the south to the capital region, were collected in the form of paper money.

The decision by Khubilai's government to continue to display bronze coin units on its paper currency even as it demonetized actual bronze coin has confounded modern scholars. The most plausible explanation has been advanced by Takahashi Hiroomi. In Takahashi's view, Khubilai's advisers had planned to issue bronze coin at some time in the future. However, after one of the Han hereditary lords rebelled in 1263, Khubilai dismissed his principal Chinese advisers and instead turned over his fiscal administration to non-Chinese merchants whom he deemed more trustworthy – notably the notorious Ahmad, a Persian who dominated fiscal administration between 1263 and his execution (for corruption) in 1282, and the more judicious Tibetan minister Sangha, who wielded supreme influence at Khubilai's court during 1287–1291. The new cadre of ministers – accustomed to using silver as currency and indifferent to the precepts of Chinese monetary philosophy – had no interest in restoring the traditional Chinese monetary system based on

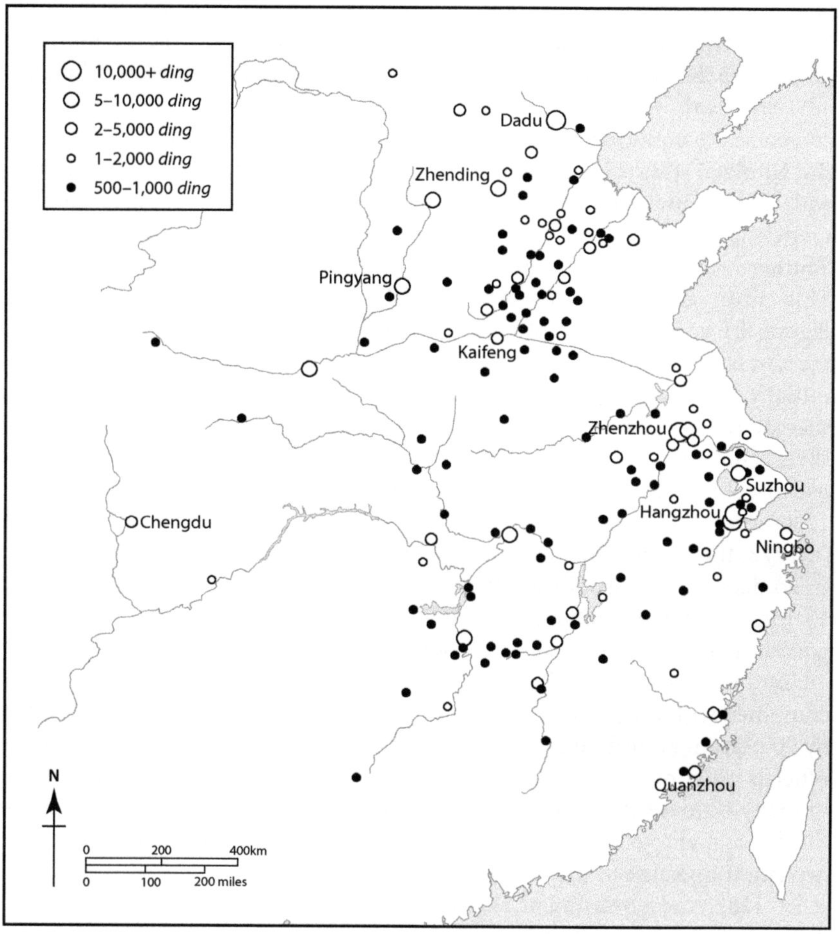

Map 8.2 Commercial tax revenues in Yuan China.
Source: Adapted from Miyazawa, *Kahei to zaisei*, p. 421.

bronze coin.[40] Despite consciously adopting the Chinese imperial model upon founding his Yuan dynasty in 1271, Khubilai continued to favor the fiscal and monetary policies of Ahmad and Sangha and largely ignored the pleas of his Chinese advisers to resume bronze coinage.

The incorporation of the Southern Song domain, with its vastly greater population and more sophisticated monetary economy, into Khubilai's empire

[40] Takahashi, *Genchō kahei*, pp. 162, 168–72.

after 1276 severely strained the capacities of the Yuan monetary system. Early in 1275, Khubilai convened a court conference to deliberate on the monetary policies to be implemented in the newly conquered territories. Khubilai's advisers, both Chinese and Mongol, urged allowing the old Song paper currencies to continue to circulate in order to minimize economic disruption. But Khubilai spurned their advice and ordered that the Song bills be redeemed with ZTC at the steep discount of 50 *guan* of Song *huizi* for 1 *guan* of ZTC, rendering the Song paper currency nearly worthless. Moreover, former Southern Song subjects were expected to purchase ZTC bills using silver. This silver then was transferred to the capital at Dadu (the ingot in Figure 8.1 is an example of such a transfer); much of it made its way into the hands of the *ortoq* merchants and thus fed the drain of silver to West Asia. Initially the Yuan allowed the use of Song coins in tax payments, although at sharply reduced value (57 percent less than their current value measured in silver). But to accelerate the adoption of ZTC, in 1277 the Yuan banned the use of coin in trade in the former Southern Song territories, and a decree of 1280 ordered the confiscation of all private stocks of coin and copper utensils. In 1278, the Yuan formally prohibited the use of Song paper currencies.[41]

To defray the costs of the conquest – as well as the invasions of Japan and Vietnam and the building of Khubilai's new capital at Dadu – the Yuan government under Ahmad's direction began to issue ZTC in vastly greater quantities (Figure 8.2). The soaring quantity of ZTC bills in circulation, combined with the growing scarcity of silver, caused a sharp fall in their value, by 90 percent according to one official.[42] Moreover, currency exchange bureau officials often refused to pay out silver in exchange for paper bills. In the eyes of many Chinese observers, the removal of silver stocks from South China and the de facto abrogation of specie convertibility were the principal causes of the deteriorating value of paper currency.[43]

In 1282, the government issued a new set of currency regulations that prohibited the use of precious metals in private trade and curtailed specie convertibility at the exchange bureaus.[44] But these actions only worsened the depreciation of paper currency and the corresponding shortfall in the real value of state revenues. Faced with mounting fiscal deficits, in early 1287 Khubilai held another court conference to discuss the monetary situation. Rejecting the entreaties of Chinese Confucian advisers who advocated a return to metallic currencies, Khubilai instead approved the proposal of

[41] Wang et al., *Huobi liutong yanjiu*, pp. 180–86.

[42] Wang Yun, "Lun chaofa" 論鈔法, *QJWJ* 90.27b–29a.

[43] For examples, see Richard von Glahn, *Fountain of Fortune: Money and Monetary Policy in China, 1000–1700* (Berkeley: University of California Press, 1996), pp. 61–63.

[44] *Da Yuan shengzheng guochao dianzhang* 大元聖政國朝典章 ([hereafter *YDZ*]; 1908 ed., rpt. Taipei: Wenhai chubanshe, 1964), 20.2a–4a.

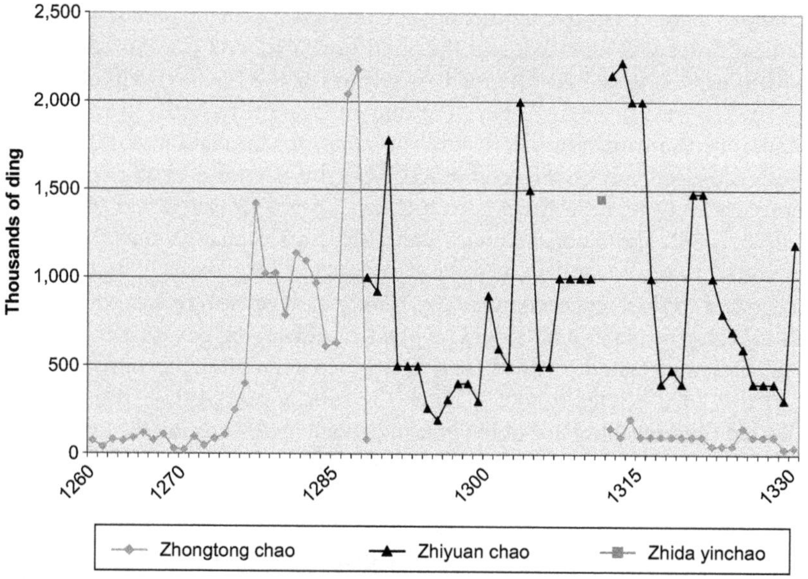

Figure 8.2 Issue of Yuan paper currencies.
Source: *YS* 94.2366–69.

Sangha, whom he appointed as chancellor, to devalue the paper currency – a return to the strategy repeatedly employed by Southern Song officials, as we have seen. One month later, Sangha introduced a new paper currency, the *Zhiyuan chao* 至元鈔 (ZYC), with an exchange value of 5 ZTC = 1 ZYC; in other words, it devalued the ZTC by 80 percent.[45]

The new paper currency was coolly received, however. In principle, ZTC would be replaced by the new ZYC, but in practice many people continued to use the ZTC bills. Although the official value of the ZYC was five times greater than the ZTC, in the private market the two types of paper money often circulated at roughly equal value; if anything, the ZYC was discounted against the ZTC, if the testimony of the Chinese official Zheng Jiefu can be believed. In a memorial written in 1303 advocating a return to bronze coinage, Zheng states in one place that the ZYC and ZTC bills circulated at par; in another passage he claimed that the value of the ZYC had fallen to only one-tenth that of the ZTC. Zheng observed that whereas Khubilai's monetary system had made silver the "mother" currency and ZTC the "child," Sangha's policy in

45 Iwamura, *Mongoru shakai keizai shi*, pp. 518–25; Wang et al., *Huobi liutong yanjiu*, pp. 197–203. The regulations governing the ZYC currency are detailed in *YDZ* 20.4a–6a.

principle made ZYC the mother to its child ZTC. Yet in practice this hierarchical order was reversed, and the child prevailed over the mother.[46]

Although Sangha had intended to remove the ZTC from circulation, he nonetheless retained the ZTC as the unit of account in Yuan fiscal administration. In the early years of Khubilai's reign, tax receipts and expenditures were recorded in both silver and ZTC, but by the time of the conquest of Southern Song in 1276 fiscal accounts had been fully converted to the ZTC unit. In 1282, the Yuan formally established an exchange rate that simply converted the *guan* unit to a "fiscal *liang*" at par (1 *guan* = 1 fiscal *liang*).[47] According to this new exchange rate, 1 *liang* of silver specie was equivalent to 2 fiscal *liang* of paper currency. The practice of keeping government accounts in ZTC denominated in fiscal *liang* continued even after the introduction of ZYC in 1287.[48] Retention of ZTC as the official accounting unit no doubt reflected the prevailing use of the bills in private trade. Among the criticisms of the government's monetary policy was the charge that it issued insufficient quantities of small bills (less than 100 *wen*).[49] After the 1287 devaluation, the ZTC bills in effect became fractional small-denomination currencies.

The sharp increase in the issue of paper currency that accompanied the introduction of ZYC eroded the value of paper currency in terms of silver, which fell 80 percent between 1285 and 1290 (Table 8.2). Subsequently, however, emission of new ZYC declined sharply and price inflation moderated. Sangha did not live to see his monetary reform bear fruit; accused of corruption, he was arrested and executed in 1291. The government of Khubilai's successor, Temür (r. 1294–1307), faced with growing fiscal deficits largely caused by spending on military campaigns against the rival Chagadai khanate, again was obliged to increase the emission of ZYC in the early years of the 14th century. According to the exchange rate prevailing in Sichuan in 1306, 1 *liang* of silver was equivalent to 20 fiscal *liang* of ZTC.[50] The sharply reduced revenues that resulted from the depreciation of the paper currency

46 Untitled 1303 memorial by Zheng Jiefu 鄭介夫 reprinted in *MCZY* 67.9a–16a. The condition of the bills also affected their value. A report from 1290 complained that in the marketplace ZTC bills in fine condition traded at a 20 percent premium over their face value, while worn and torn bills were subject to a 20 percent discount: *YDZ* 20.30a–b.

47 I use the term "fiscal *liang*" to distinguish the *liang* as a unit of account for paper currency from the *liang* unit as a weight of silver.

48 Miyazawa, *Kahei to zaisei*, pp. 385–90.

49 Complaints about the insufficiency of small bills were voiced by both advocates (Cheng Jufu) and opponents (Hu Zhiyu) of restoring bronze currency: Cheng Jufu 程鉅夫, "Jiangnan maimai weixi yi xuyong tongqian huo duozhi lingchao" 江南買賣微細宜用銅錢或多置零鈔, *Xuelou ji* 雪樓集 ([hereafter *XLJ*]; SKQS ed.), 10.4b–5b; Hu Zhiyu 胡祇遹, "Baochao fa" 寶鈔法, *Zishan daquanji* 紫山大全集 (SKQS ed.), 22.11b–12a. A report of 1294 also asserted that the shortages of small bills compelled use of tokens denominated in tea, noodles, and liquor to conduct petty trade. See *YDZ* 20.30a.

50 *YDZ* 43.13a.

Table 8.2 *ZTC:silver exchange ratios (fiscal* liang *ZTC per 1* liang *silver specie)*

Date	fiscal *liang* ZTC per 1 *liang* silver specie
1260	2
1265	2
1270	2
1275	2
1280	2
1285	2
1290	10
1295	10
1300	10
1306	20
1310	25
1315	25
1320	40
1325	—
1330	25
1335	—
1340	—
1346	30

Source: Maeda, *Genchō shi*, p. 133, table 6.

prompted the Yuan court to attempt a radical transformation of its monetary system.

8.4 The Failure of Khaishan's Currency Reform and the Return to Stability

The ascension of Khaishan (r. 1307–1311) as emperor inaugurated a surge of profligate fiscal irresponsibility on the part of the Mongol court. Lavish spending by Khaishan and the Mongol nobility exacerbated already severe fiscal deficits.[51] Saddled with soaring debts, Khaishan's government undertook an ambitious effort to restore a dual currency system by introducing a new paper money, the *Zhida yinchao* 至大銀鈔 ("Silver Bills of the Zhida Reign"; hereafter ZDYC), in

[51] For an overview of fiscal policy under Khaishan, see Ch'i-ch'ing Hsiao, "Mid-Yuan Politics," in Denis Twitchett (ed.), *The Cambridge History of China*, vol. 6: *Alien Regimes and Border States, 907–1368* (Cambridge: Cambridge University Press, 1994), pp. 508–12.

1309 and resuming the minting of bronze coin the following year. The ZTC bills were to be withdrawn from circulation, while the ZYC was devalued – just as happened with the ZTC in 1287 – by 80 percent. The official exchange rate of the ZDYC was fixed at 1 *liang* of silver and 5 *guan* of ZYC. The two new coins issued in 1310, the Zhida yuanbao 至大通寶 and Da Yuan tongbao 大元通寶, were the first bronze coins minted under Mongol rule.

A coterie of Chinese officials had long advocated the restoration of bronze currency as a means of stabilizing the value of the paper currency in circulation. Yet, as the name of the ZDYC explicitly reveals, the new paper currency was denominated in silver rather than bronze coin. Thirteen denominations of ZDYC were issued, ranging from 2 *liang* to 2 *li* 釐 (0.002 *liang*, equivalent to the smallest ZYC bill [10 *wen*]). These silver units were fiscal units; the new currencies officially became fiat currencies that could not be exchanged for precious metals. The new bronze coin was intended less as a medium of exchange for small transactions than as a means to link the ZDYC bills to a metallic currency.[52] Thus the Zhida yuanbao coins were inscribed with the value of 1 (fiscal) *li* 一釐, equivalent to 5 *wen* in ZYC. In essence, coin had become the "child" to its paper currency "mother."[53]

Khaishan's monetary reform proved an utter failure. Not only did the state issue the ZDYC in greater quantities (two sources differ on the total, one reporting 1.2 million *ding* and the other 1.45 million *ding*) than the current level of ZYC (1 million *ding*; see Figure 8.2), but in nominal terms this amount of ZDYC was equivalent to 30–36 million *ding* of ZTC. The flood of new paper currency triggered a powerful burst of inflation. Moreover, the state was able to mint only a token amount of new bronze coin, whose circulation seems to have been confined to the vicinity of the capital.[54] Shortly after Khaishan's death early in 1311, the new emperor – Ayurbawada (r. 1311–1320) – withdrew both the ZDYC and the bronze coin issued by his predecessor and restored the ZYC along with the ZTC as legal tender.

Ayurbawada's repeal of Khaishan's monetary reform did not simply restore the status quo ante. The suspension of convertibility with precious metals was retained, and the ZYC became a pure fiat currency. Khaishan's reform, having demonetized ZTC, made ZYC the new standard for government accounts. But the edict announcing the withdrawal of Khaishan's new currencies explicitly recognized that although no new ZTC bills had been issued for more than

52 On this point, see Miyazawa Tomoyuki 宮澤知之, "Gendai kōkanki no heisei to sono bōkai" 元代後半期の幣制とその崩壊, *Ōryō shigaku* 鷹陵史学 27 (2001): 58–59.

53 These metaphors were employed in the edict recommencing bronze coinage. See Yao Sui, "Xing tongqian zhao" 行銅錢詔, *MAJ* 1.4b.

54 We have no information on the amount of bronze coin minted at this time, but it was surely negligible. These issues comprise well under 1 percent of the coins found in Yuan-era coin hoards: Miyake, *Uzumerareta senka*, pp. 110–11, table 19.

Table 8.3 *Paper money units of account in private transactions*

	ZTC	ZYC	Generic paper money	Total
Before 1311	2	0	9	11
After 1311	24	2	19	45
Total	26	2	28	56

Source: Tables 8.7 and 8.8.

Table 8.4 *Units of account in Yuan land sale contracts*

	ZTC	ZYC	Generic paper money	Silver	Rice
Before 1311	2	1	1	0	0
After 1311	24	0	1	1	1
Total	26	1	2	1	1

Note: Three contracts (after 1311) are from Quanzhou (Fujian); the rest are all from Huizhou (Anhui).
Source: Zhang Chuanxi, *Qiyue huibian*, 1, pp. 543–86.

twenty years, in the private market the ZTC continued to prevail as the money of account for expressing prices.[55] The court decided to reaffirm the ZTC as the monetary standard for both public finance and private exchange, even though actual payment ordinarily was made in ZYC bills. Henceforth the Yuan recommenced issuing small quantities of ZTC in addition to ZYC bills (Figure 8.2). Evidence from private transactions, especially in land sale contracts, shows a marked tendency to specify payment in ZTC as the unit of account (Tables 8.3 and 8.4). Although prices and values almost always were expressed in ZTC units, ZYC predominated as the circulating media of exchange. Evidence from tomb excavations, while limited, supports the conclusion that ZYC prevailed as the actual circulating medium of exchange even though the ZTC was fully entrenched as the money of account (Table 8.5).

Further corroboration of the primacy of ZYC as the media of exchange can be found in the *Nogŏltae* 老乞大, a Korean primer of vernacular Chinese compiled in the 1340s. The *Nogŏltae* (the title can be translated as "The Old China-Hand") is comprised of a series of dialogues featuring a group of Korean horse traders who travel to the Yuan capital at Dadu to conduct business. The dialogues frequently involve haggling over prices and means

[55] *YDZ* 20.8b.

Table 8.5 *Paper money specimens excavated from Yuan-era sites*

	Time period	ZTC	ZYC
Huarong, Hunan[a]	Late 13th century	6	5
Khara-Khoto, Inner Mongolia[b]	1294–1371	12	132
Yuanling, Hunan[c]	c. 1305	0	7
Wuxi, Jiangsu[d]	c. 1320	0	33
Xianyang, Shaanxi[e]	After 1350	2	1

Sources: [a] Li Zhengxin, "Hunan Huarong chutu yuanchao," pp. 33–35.
[b] Li Yiyou, "Yuandai caoyuan sichou zhi lu shangde zhibi," pp. 16–23.
[c] "Yuanlingxian Shuangqiao Yuandai fufu hezangmu," p. 182.
[d] Feng Lirong, "Wuxishi bowuguan cang Zhiyuan tongxing baochao," pp. 44–45.
[e] Xianyangshi bowuguan, "Xianyang faxiande Yuandai zhibi," pp. 70–76.

of payment.[56] In a typical scene, set at an inn near Dadu, the Koreans engage in a dispute with the innkeeper over the acceptability of the paper bills they use to pay for wine and the bills they receive as change. Mention is made of bills worth 5 *qian*, 1.5 *liang*, and 2.5 *liang*.[57] The Yuan never issued paper currency bearing these face values. Instead, these statements must be understood as referring to ZYC bills in terms of their ZTC values according to the official 1:5 exchange rate. Thus the "5 *qian*" (0.5 *liang* in ZTC) bill was a ZYC bill with a face value of 100 *wen* (see Table 8.6).

The numerous discussions of prices in the *Nogŏltae* attest both to the prevalence of ZYC as means of exchange and to popular observance of the official 1:5 exchange rate between ZYC and ZTC currencies. The same relationship between ZTC as unit of account and ZYC as means of payment can be observed in an entry in a Ningbo gazetteer published in 1342 concerning the *baoyin* levy imposed on the twenty-four Muslim and other foreign merchant households residing in the port city. The statutory rate for the *baoyin* levy was 2 *liang* per household, but in Ningbo "the 2 *liang* of silver is commuted to 10 *guan* of ZYC, which is valued at 1 *ding* [i.e., 50 *guan*/fiscal *liang*] of ZTC. The total assessment [for twenty-four households] is 24 *ding*

56 For an analysis of monetary values and means of payment in this text, see Funada Yoshiyuki 船田善之, "Gendai shiryō to shite no kyūhon '*Rōkitsudai*': Chō to bukka no kisai o chūshin to shite" 元代史料としての旧本「老乞大」:鈔と物価の記載を中心として, *Tōyō gakuhō* 東洋学報83 (2001): 1–30.

57 Chŏng Kwang 鄭光 (ed.), *Yuanben Laoqida* 原本老乞大 (Beijing: Waiyu jiaoxue yu yanjiu chubanshe, 2002), p. 48. See also Kim Munkyŏng 金文京 et al. (eds.), *Rōkitsudai: Chōsen chūsei no Chūgokugo kaiwa dokuhon* 老乞大:朝鮮中世の中国語会話読本 (Tokyo: Heibonsha, 2002), p. 166.

Table 8.6 *Values of Yuan paper currency in* Nogŏltae

Stated value in text (in ZTC)	Face value (ZYC bill)
Five *qian* 五錢	100 *wen*
One-and-a-half *liang* 一兩半	300 *wen*
Two-and-a-half *liang* 二兩半	500 *wen*

Source: Chŏng Kwang, *Yuanben Laoqida*, p. 48.

[ZTC]."[58] In addition to affirming the 1:5 exchange ratio between ZYC and ZTC, this statement also reiterated the 1:25 exchange ratio between silver specie and ZTC prevailing at this time (see Table 8.2).

The *Nogŏltae* dialogues likewise confirm that the practice of rendering the ZTC money of account in terms of silver units had become fully entrenched. Although the two forms of Yuan paper money in common circulation, the ZTC and the ZYC, were still denominated in coin units (and bore images of coins), prices were routinely expressed in the fiscal *liang* unit of account.[59] As the *Nogŏltae* dialogues show, this was also true in vernacular speech. In some records, the *guan* unit (the face value of the paper currency) was combined with silver units. Thus, an inscription from 1324 recording the renovation of a Confucian temple in Shouxian (Anhui) expressed the costs of construction as "714 *ding* and 15 *guan* of ZTC."[60] In other words, the *guan* and the fiscal *liang* served as mutually interchangeable units of account (in this case, *guan* served as a fractional unit: 15 *guan* was equivalent to 0.30 *ding*). The prevalence of this practice among the population at large is attested already in Zheng Jiefu's memorial of 1303, in which Zheng reported that "paper bills denominated as '100-*wen*' nominally have a value of 100 bronze coins . . . at present when the people refer to 'one *liang*' [i.e., a fiscal *liang*] they mean that one *qian* [one-tenth of a fiscal *liang*] is worth 100 coins, and ten *qian* [one fiscal *liang*] is worth 1,000 coins."[61]

Further confirmation of the prevalence of ZTC measured in silver as the standard unit of account appears in *A Brief Gazetteer of the Foreign Isles*, a geography of maritime Southeast Asia compiled in the 1330s by the seafarer Wang Dayuan. In his accounts of the monetary systems of Vietnam, Thailand, and Burma, Wang recorded the exchange rates of foreign currencies as measured in silver *liang* of ZTC. In the marketplaces of Annam, he reported, the exchange rate for 1 silver *liang* of ZTC was 67 bronze coins (presumably

58 [*Zhizheng*] *Siming zhi* [至正] 四明志 (SYDFZ ed.), 6.24a–b.

59 See the grain price data assembled in Maeda, *Genchō shi*, pp. 126–27, tables 4 and 5.

60 "Anfenglu Kongzimiao bei" 安豐路孔子廟碑, in Liu Chang 劉昌 (ed.), *Zhongzhou mingxian wenbiao* 中州名賢文表 (SKQS ed.), 18.6a.

61 夫鈔云一伯文者，乃百銅錢......今民間稱為一兩，是一錢準為百錢，十錢準為千錢. *MCZY* 67.12a.

imported Song coins), whereas the official rate was 70 coins. In Lopburi in the Chao Phraya delta, 10,000 cowries had an exchange value of 24 silver *liang* of ZTC, while in Pegu the local silver coin had an exchange rate of 10 silver *liang* of ZTC or 11,520 cowries.[62] Wang was born in Nanchang, Jiangxi, and departed from Quanzhou on his first overseas voyage at age twenty in 1331. We cannot say for certain whether he was a merchant, but it seems likely given the close attention he paid to local products, commercial customs, and prices in each of the places he visited. His testimony suggests that the ZTC (measured in fiscal *liang*) prevailed as the standard money of account among maritime traders in the southern regions of the Yuan empire.

By the middle of the Yuan era, then, the value of paper currency was expressed in silver units of account in the private economy as well as public finance in the core commercial regions of South China, such as the lower Yangzi River basin and coastal Fujian. The shift in money use over time is vividly demonstrated in an inscription from 1343 recording the tenancy contracts for lands owned by the prefectural school of Ningbo. At the time the lands were originally leased in 1250, when the region was still ruled by the Southern Song, the rents were paid in *huizi*. Under Yuan rule (exactly when is unclear), the rents were converted to Yuan paper currency denominated in *guan*. In 1333, however, the contracts specified payment in ZTC denominated in silver units (*ding/liang*).[63]

The establishment in 1311 of a dual monetary system based on ZTC as the money of account and ZYC as the actual circulating currency ushered in a period of monetary stability that endured until the late 1340s. A surge in the issue of paper money in 1320–1321 caused a sharp fall in its value, sending the silver:ZTC exchange ratio plummeting to 1:40 (Table 8.2). But the silver:ZTC exchange ratio rebounded to the 1:25 level in the late 1320s and remained stable for the next two decades (in 1346 the value of the ZTC stood at 1:30). The estimates of the total stock of paper currency during the Yuan period compiled by Huanhui Guan and his collaborators indicate that the volume of

62 Wang Dayuan 汪大淵, in Su Jiqing 蘇繼庼 (ed.), *Daoyi zhilüe jiaoshi* 島夷志略校釋 (Beijing: Zhonghua shuju, 2000), pp. 51, 114, 376. Most likely the silver coin in Pegu mentioned by Wang was the heavy *tanka* coin minted by the Bengal sultanate, which created a dual monetary system using silver coins and cowries. See John S. Deyell, "Cowries and Coins: The Dual Monetary System of the Bengal Sultanate," *Indian Economic and Social History Review* 47.1 (2010): 63–106.

63 "Qingyuanlu ruxue tutian ji" 慶元路儒學塗田記, in Ruan Yuan 阮元 (ed.), *Liangzhe jinshi zhi* 兩浙金石志 (rpt. Hangzhou: Zhejiang shuju, 1890), 16.49a–53b. A stele dated 1348 recorded the annual rents "submitted" (*banna* 辦納) in ZTC by tenants on lands belonging to the Confucian school in Chuzhou (Anhui). This language suggests that ZTC were the means of payment, not only the unit of account. "Chuzhou xuetian ji" 滁州學田記, in Xu Naichang 徐乃昌 (ed.), *Anhui tongzhi gao jinshi guwu kao* 安徽通志稿金石古物攷 (Taipei: Dingwen shuju, 1972), 5.59a–63b.

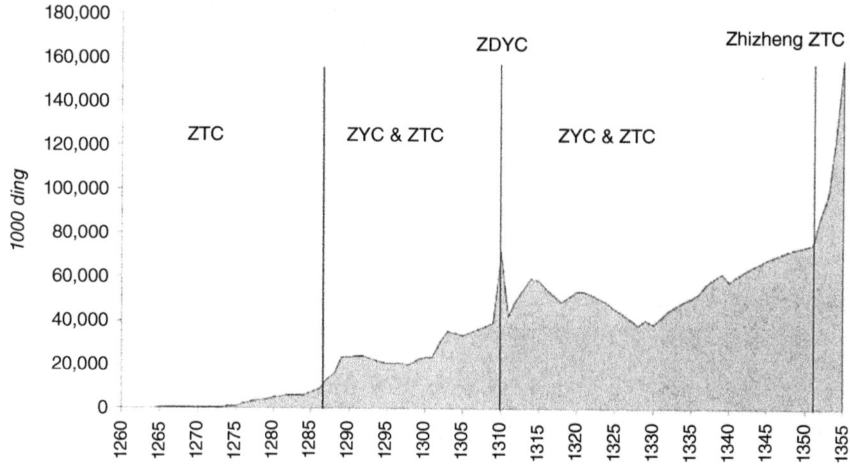

Figure 8.3 Nominal stock of paper money during the Yuan dynasty.
Source: Guan, Palma, and Wu, "Paper Money in Yuan China," p. 1233, fig. 5.

currency peaked around 1314 and subsequently declined. In the early 1330s, the stock of money again increased, surpassing the 1314 level around 1338 and continuing to grow moderately before soaring precipitously after 1350 (Figure 8.3). The available price data for this era – admittedly scarce – indicates that prices remained stable throughout the 1320s and began to rise again in the 1330s, but marked inflation occurred only after 1345.[64]

This monetary stability was abruptly disrupted by the widespread outbreak of popular revolts against Yuan rule in the late 1340s. Apart from the military costs of confronting the rebels, the central government suffered a drastic shortfall in revenue after the piratical warlord Fang Guozhen interdicted the shipment of tribute grain from the south. In addition, the devastating breach of the Yellow River dikes in 1344 required massive new spending to reestablish a stable river course by diverting its flow to the Huai River valley.[65] In 1349, the former chancellor Toghtō was recalled to take the reins of government once again. Toghtō launched a new monetary reform to raise the revenues needed to cope with these grave fiscal crises. Like Khaishan's initiative in 1309–1310, Toghtō sought both to devalue the circulating paper currency

64 Hanhui Guan, Nuno Palma, and Meng Wu, "The Rise and Fall of Paper Money in Yuan China, 1260–1368," *Economic History Review* 77.4 (2024): 1234, fig. 6. Herbert Franke likewise concluded that price inflation remained modest before the final decades of the Yuan: Franke, *Geld und Wirtschaft*, p. 158.

65 Ruth Mostern, *The Yellow River: A Natural and Unnatural History* (New Haven, CT: Yale University Press, 2021), pp. 206–7.

and to link paper money to a new issue of bronze coin.[66] The ZYC, which constituted the vast majority of the bills in circulation, was to be replaced by a new issue of ZTC, which had long been relegated to the role of money of account. In a reversal of the devaluation of ZTC in 1287, the new exchange ratio of 1 new ZTC = 2 ZYC promulgated by Toghtō devalued the ZYC by 90 percent. The new ZTC bills resembled the original ones, but were countermarked on the reverse with the legend "Inaugural Treasure Exchange Bill Printed in the Zhizheng Era" (Zhizheng yinzao Zhongtong jiaochao 至正印造元寶交鈔; see Figure 7.9). Although the government officially designated the new bills "Zhongtong exchange bills" (中統交鈔), apparently in the popular idiom they were known as "Zhizheng exchange bills" (*zhizheng jiaochao* 至正交鈔) or simply "new bills" (新鈔).[67]

The new coin, Zhizheng tongbao 至正通寶, was issued in multiple denominations (1, 2, 3, 5, and 10 *wen*) and pegged to the new ZTC at a rate of 1,000 coins = 1 *guan* ZTC. Use of old Song coins in private trade (at par with the Zhizheng tongbao) once again was permitted. Confronted with ballooning deficits, Toghtō countenanced massive emissions of new ZTC: 1.9 million *ding*, quadruple the annual volume of ZYC issued in recent years, in 1352, and 6 million *ding* in 1355. These desperate measures, like Khaishan's reforms, triggered an unprecedented surge of inflation, further eviscerating popular confidence in state-issued money. By the mid 1350s the Yuan paper currency was utterly discredited, and silver specie along with bronze coin reemerged as the actual media of exchange. Yet – in telling confirmation of how deeply embedded the ZTC monetary standard had become in popular consciousness – bronze coin itself was measured in the ZTC unit of account. Some of the coins issued in the 1350s bore the legend "equivalent to paper currency" (*quanchao* 權鈔) and were denominated in silver units of account.[68]

8.5 Regional Variation in Money Use and the Money of Account During the Yuan

However much Marco Polo was prone to exaggeration, there is little reason to doubt his claims that "paper currency is circulated in every part of the Great Khan's dominions" and "all of his subjects receive it without hesitation."[69] In town after town that Polo visited in his peregrinations across Khubilai's

[66] On the 1350 monetary reform and its consequences, see Miyazawa, "Gendai kōkanki no heisei," pp. 67–81. The court debate over the 1350 reform is recapitulated in Iwamura, *Mongoru shakai keizai shi*, pp. 534–37.

[67] *XWXTK* 9.2857b; Changgu zhenyi 長谷真逸 (pseud.), *Nongtian yuhua* 農田餘話 (Baoyantang miji ed.), 1.6a–7a.

[68] Miyazawa, *Kahei to zaisei*, pp. 487–523; Thierry, *Monnaies*, p. 379.

[69] Polo, *Travels*, pp. 160–61.

empire, he routinely attested that commerce was conducted using paper money. Despite its ubiquity within the realm of Khubilai and his successors, however, paper money failed to gain traction elsewhere. The only attempt to imitate Yuan paper currency in other parts of the Mongol ecumene was undertaken by the Ilkhanate regime in Iran and Iraq, ruled by the descendants of Khubilai's brother Hülegü. In 1294, the ilkhan Gaykhātū (r. 1291–1295), beset by mounting deficits, issued paper money (*cāv*) in denominations from one-half dirham to ten dinars. Contemporary chroniclers portrayed this paper money as a nefarious device concocted by Gaykhātū's venal advisors to sate the ilkhan's thirst for profligate spending. Within days of its issue trade was said to have come to a standstill at the Ilkhanate capital of Tabriz. The bills were soon withdrawn, but their unpopularity directly led to Gaykhātū's assassination several months later.[70]

In the Sinitic world, paper currency displaced bronze coin in quotidian trade to a far greater degree during the Yuan compared to Song times. As part of its effort to demonetize bronze coin, the Yuan state issued paper currency in denominations as small as 10 *wen*. The evidence of the *Nogŏltae* demonstrates that paper currency was routinely used in petty transactions in the capital region. Exports of bronze coin (overwhelmingly Northern Song issues) to Japan peaked at this time, suggesting that demand for bronze coin in China had reached its nadir.[71] Many other contemporary accounts attest to the retreat of coin from economic life. For example, Cheng Jufu, writing in the wake of the Khaishan monetary reform debacle, observed that the inhabitants of Jiangnan scarcely used coin, and the stock of coin held by the populace was less than one-tenth of Song times.[72] At the metropolitan civil service examination held in 1330, a candidate responded to a question on monetary policy by writing that "since 1311 [i.e., when Khaishan's coinages were withdrawn] coin has been discarded and is no longer used in trade. Most of the coin has been melted down by the people or surreptitiously carried off by ocean-going ships.

[70] Karl Jahn, "Paper Currency in Iran: A Contribution to the Cultural and Economic History of Iran in the Mongol Period," *Journal of Asian History* 4.2 (1970): 101–35; Satō Keishirō 佐藤圭四郎, "Genchō no kōshō to Iruhanchō no chō cāv: Jūsan-shi seiki ni okeru Higashi-Nishi Ajia no shihei seido" 元朝の交鈔とイルハン朝の鈔cāv：十三·四世紀における東·西アジアの紙幣制度, *Ryūgoku daigaku ronshū* 龍谷大學論集 428 (1986): 71–109. In addition to the *shahada* (the fundamental Islamic oath of devotion) and a legend stating "The Pādishāh of the World introduced this blessed paper money into the empire in the year 693 (1294); he who forges it or alters it in any way will be put to death with wife and child and his property will be confiscated by the state," both written in Persian, the bill was said to have been inscribed with the ilkhan's title in Mongolian, with "a few words in Chinese" along the border.

[71] Ōta, "Dōsen no ryufu"; Ōta Yukio 太田由紀夫, "Jūshi-jūgo seiki no toraisen ryūnyū: Chūsei Nihon no baai" 十四•十五世紀の渡来銭流入:中世日本の場合, *Rekishi no riron to kyōiku* 歴史の理論と教育 128 (2008): 3–19.

[72] Cheng Jufu, "Jiangnan maimai weixi," *XLJ* 10.4b–5b.

Only 20–30 percent of old coins [i.e., Song issues] remain. Villagers regard them with disdain."[73]

Still, this testimony suggests that bronze coin had not wholly disappeared as a monetary medium. In a 2002 article, Ichimaru Tomoko challenged the assumption that paper currency was universally used during the Yuan dynasty. In her reappraisal of this issue, Ichimaru examined three types of documentary sources: (1) mathematical treatises and encyclopedias; (2) excavated contracts at Khara-Khoto (in present-day Inner Mongolia); and (3) surviving contracts from Huizhou (Anhui).[74] A common feature in all of these types of sources is the use of *qian* 錢 ("bronze coin") to simply denote "money" (in the modern sense of the word), as in the typical formula: *qian* / number / *guan* or *ding*. But in other respects, Ichimaru argued, these sources display marked regional and temporal variations in expressing monetary values.

Sample problems in mathematical treatises vary in the ways in which they register prices. The *Primer of Mathematics* (*Suanxue qimeng* 算學啟蒙), published in Yangzhou in the late 13th century, uniformly renders prices in *guan*/*wen*, but it is not clear whether these prices refer to bronze coin or paper money. Late Yuan mathematical treatises, in contrast, exclusively use silver units (*liang*, etc.) to denominate paper currency.[75] Ichimaru concluded that the *Primer of Mathematics* provides evidence of the continued customary use of bronze coin in private transactions in the former Southern Song territories during the early period of Mongol rule.[76] In her view, the exclusive use of silver units as the money of account in late Yuan mathematical works reflect the perspective of officialdom but not necessarily the marketplace.

From the evidence of contracts, Ichimaru inferred a sharp regional disparity in units of account and by extension the types of money that prevailed in market exchange. The Khara-Khoto contracts, which date from 1294 to 1371,

73 蓋自皇慶以來, 錢廢不用, 多爲民間銷鎔, 或爲海舶竊逸, 舊錢之存十僅二三. 里閭視之不甚惜. From *Sanchang wenxuan duice, renji* 三場文選對策·壬集, 6; text reproduced in Shen Wanli 申萬里, "Yuandai shiren de zhengzhi guanhuai yu shiwu duice: Yi *Sanchang wenxuan duice renji* wei zhongxin de kaochao" 元代士人的政治關懷與時務對策: 以《三場文選對策•壬集》爲中心的考察, *Sui Tang Liao Song Jin Yuan shi luncong* 隋唐辽宋金元史论丛 7 (2017): 255. Cheng Jufu likewise had attributed the disappearance of coin to the melting pot and export overseas: Cheng, "Tongqian" 銅錢, *XLJ* 10.24b–25b.

74 Ichimaru Tomoko 市丸智子, "Gendai kahei no kan-mon, tei-ryō tan'i no betsu ni tsuite: Kurojō shutsudo oyobi Kishū keiyaku monjo o chūshin to shite" 元代貨幣の貫文•錠両単位の別について:黒城出土及び徽州契約文書を中心として, *Shakai keizai shigaku* 社会経済史学68.3 (2002): 249–70.

75 See, for example, the fragments of the anonymous *Dingju suanfa* 丁巨算法, published in 1355 (CSJC ed.).

76 However, Maeda concluded that based on gold:silver exchange ratios and price data in the *Primer* the text probably was compiled before the Mongol conquest and thus reflects the late Southern Song monetary situation. See Maeda, *Genchō shi*, pp. 80–81.

include seventy-seven documents that specify sums of money, in all cases Yuan paper currency (with the exception of a few references to ZYC, nearly all cite ZTC). All but one of these seventy-seven contracts use silver units. In contrast, of the forty-two extant Yuan contracts from Huizhou (dating from 1289 to 1367), thirty-six are denominated in paper currency (ZTC, except for a single case of ZYC) in coin units; five are denominated in paper currency in silver units, and one specifies payment in silver specie. Ichimaru suggested that the five contracts denominated in silver units all involved large sums (from 250 *liang* to 100 *ding* [5,000 *liang*]) and thus the higher-value currency unit was used.[77] However, she also noted that the three extant Yuan-era Huizhou land sale tax receipts all specify silver units. From this disparity, Ichimaru concluded that in former Southern Song territories such as Huizhou bronze coin remained the monetary standard in private transactions, whereas it was obligatory to record tax payments in the silver money of account used in government accounting.

Thus Ichimaru posited that two separate monetary regimes coexisted in Mongol-ruled China: a silver-based monetary system in North China that was tied to the silver economy of the pan-Eurasian Mongol empire and the traditional silver-using areas of West Asia and the Islamic world; and a bronze coin-based monetary system in South China that reflected the continuing use of Song coin in private exchange.

While Ichimaru's conclusion regarding the Huizhou evidence appears plausible if not conclusive, the question remains as to whether Huizhou can be regarded as representative of South China as a whole. Huizhou was located in a rugged inland area of low agricultural productivity. Despite its importance as a major producer of paper and tea, Huizhou's local economy at this time was still relatively undeveloped. Ichimaru's other evidence for the persistence of the use of coin in South China comes from a household encyclopedia published in Jianyang, Fujian, in 1324. Of the fourteen sample contracts in this work, thirteen denominate ZTC in coin units and only one in silver units. Jianyang, like Huizhou, was a modest commercial center located in the interior of South China. Significantly, the Yuan government never established a branch of its currency exchange bureaus in Huizhou, and did so in Jianyang only sometime after 1303.[78]

In a later article, Ichimaru revised her conclusions about money use during the Yuan based on the more geographically dispersed evidence from stele inscriptions.[79] An examination of inscriptions recording private payments –

77 But not all large sums were rendered in silver units. Ichimaru's data ("Gendai kahei," p. 261, table 2) shows that four of the thirty-six contracts denominated in coin are for sums of 500 or more *guan*, including one for 2,600 *guan*.

78 Maeda, *Genchō shi*, pp. 60–65, tables 1–3.

79 Ichimaru Tomoko 市丸智子, "Gendai ni okeru gin, chō, dōsen no sōgo kankei ni tsuite: Shiyō tan'i no bunseki o chūshin ni" 元代における銀・鈔・銅銭の相互関係につい

Table 8.7 *Monies of account in private payments in North China under Mongol rule*

	Silver (specie)	Paper currency (silver unit of account)	Paper currency (bronze coin unit of account)	Unspecified* (bronze coin unit of account)	Total
Period I: before 1260	2	0	0	0	2
Period II: 1260–1310	2	2	7	5	16
Period III: 1311–1349	0	6	11	10	27
Period IV: 1350–1368	0	1	1	2	4
Total	4	9	19	17	49

Note: *In most of these cases, the text refers to strings (*min* 緡) of cash (*qian* 錢), which could refer to either bronze coin or paper money denominated in bronze coin.
Sources: Ichimaru, "Gin, chō, dōsen no sōgo kankei," pp. 115–17, table 1; additional data collected from Yuan literary anthologies and stele inscriptions.

for expenditures such as temple renovations, bridge and dike construction, and other building projects; donations to temples and schools; land rent and sale records; and other price quotations – reveals a markedly different pattern than the evidence used in her earlier article. I have incorporated Ichimaru's data along with additional data from other Yuan sources in Tables 8.7 and 8.8.[80]

Among the noteworthy trends found in the North China data are the disappearance of silver payments altogether after the late 1280s and the marked propensity to denominate paper currency in bronze coin rather than silver units of account, an especially strong bias if the "unspecified" cases are regarded – as I believe they should be – as referring to paper money (Table 8.7). Ichimaru concluded that this predominance of bronze coin units

て:使用単位の分析を中心に, *Kyūshū daigaku tōyōshi ronshū* 九州大学東洋史論集36 (2008): 88–122.

80 In addition to the private transactions tabulated in Tables 8.7 and 8.8, Ichimaru also separately analyzes data regarding money use based on three additional categories: (1) the court and the nobility, (2) the military, and (3) government agencies. Not surprisingly, silver units of account predominated in all of these cases.

of account reflected the persistence of bronze coin in private exchange – the reverse of her initial postulation about North China. However, the evidence for South China, and the Jiangnan region in particular, conveys a strikingly different picture (Tables 8.8a-d).[81] Silver payments, while only a small portion of the total, occasionally recurred in Jiangnan throughout the Yuan period. More importantly, references to paper money payments in Jiangnan are divided roughly equally between silver and bronze coin units of account. By contrast, in the interior regions of South China the prevalence of bronze coin units of account resembles the pattern found in the North China data.

In Ichimaru's view, these findings show that bronze coin along with silver continued to be used as means of payment in South China.[82] It is by no means clear, however, that the use of the bronze coin unit of account is proof of the persistence of bronze coin in exchange, as Ichimaru infers. As we have already seen, by the middle of the 13th century bronze coin had largely been displaced as a means of exchange by silver in the Jin territories of North China and paper money in the Southern Song realm. Indeed, the continued use of Song paper money – doctored to resemble Yuan bills – in private exchange long after the Mongol conquest of South China is attested in a 1319 report from Zhejiang.[83] In Jiangnan cities during the mid Yuan period, the demand for fractional currency in some cases was satisfied not by bronze coin but by lacquered tokens and paper tickets privately issued by local shops, as we also saw in the late Southern Song.[84]

Even if we accept Ichimaru's assumption that expressing the value of paper money in bronze coin units of account attests to the use of bronze coin in exchange, a more nuanced delineation of the spatial and temporal range of bronze coin use is required. Direct testimony for the continued use of bronze coin in South China can be found in Zheng Jiefu's memorial of 1303. Zheng, a strong advocate of restoring the bronze coin monetary standard, claimed that Song bronze coin remained in common use throughout Fujian, and in various parts of Jiangxi, Anhui, and Hunan provinces.[85] This pattern also is consistent

81 In Yuan administrative nomenclature, "Jiangnan" encompassed all of South China south of the Yangzi River. Here I use Jiangnan in the more conventional sense of the term, designating the parts of the lower Yangzi River basin in southern Jiangsu and northern Zhejiang provinces.

82 Ichimaru does not distinguish among South China subregions as I do in Table 8.8, but rather considers all of South China as a whole.

83 *YDZ* 20.23b.

84 See the testimony cited in von Glahn, *Fountain of Fortune*, p. 67.

85 *MCZY* 67.9a–16a. For Zheng Jiefu's views on money, see von Glahn, *Fountain of Fortune*, pp. 64–65.

Table 8.8a *Monies of account in private payments in South China under Mongol rule: Period II: 1276–1310**

Period	Area	Silver (specie)	Bronze coin	Paper currency (silver unit of account)	Paper currency (bronze coin unit of account)	Unspecified (bronze coin unit of account)	Total
Period II	Jiangnan	1	0	4	1	1	7
Period II	Fujian/ Guangdong	0	1	0	0	0	1
Period II	Other South China	0	0	0	3	0	3
Total	—	1	1	4	4	1	11

Note: *South China came under Yuan rule beginning in 1276.
Sources: Ichimaru, "Gin, chō, dōsen no sōgo kankei," pp. 118–21, table 3; additional data collected from Yuan literary anthologies and stele inscriptions.

Table 8.8b *Monies of account in private payments in South China under Mongol rule: Period III: 1311–1349*

Period	Area	Silver (specie)	Bronze coin	Paper currency (silver unit of account)	Paper currency (bronze coin unit of account)	Unspecified (bronze coin unit of account)	Total
Period III	Jiangnan	3	0	18	9	16	46
Period III	Fujian/ Guangdong	0	1	2	0	1	4
Period III	Other South China	0	0	4	5	2	11
Total	—	3	1	24	14	19	61

Sources: Ichimaru, "Gin, chō, dōsen no sōgo kankei," pp. 118–21, table 3; additional data collected from Yuan literary anthologies and stele inscriptions.

Table 8.8c *Monies of account in private payments in South China under Mongol rule: Period IV: 1350–1368*

Period	Area	Silver (specie)	Bronze coin	Paper currency (silver unit of account)	Paper currency (bronze coin unit of account)	Unspecified (bronze coin unit of account)	Total
Period IV: 1350–1368	Jiangnan	1	0	3	0	3	7
Period IV	Fujian/ Guangdong	0	0	0	0	0	0
Period IV	Other South China	0	0	0	0	0	0
Total	—	1	0	3	0	3	7

Sources: Ichimaru, "Gin, chō, dōsen no sōgo kankei," pp. 118–21, table 3; additional data collected from Yuan literary anthologies and stele inscriptions.

Table 8.8d *Monies of account in private payments in South China under Mongol rule: Totals*

Period	Silver (specie)	Bronze coin	Paper currency (silver unit of account)	Paper currency (bronze coin unit of account)	Unspecified (bronze coin unit of account)	Total
Period II	1	1	4	4	1	11
Period III	3	1	24	14	19	61
Period IV	1	0	3	0	3	7
Total all	5	2	31	18	23	79

Sources: Ichimaru, "Gin, chō, dōsen no sōgo kankei," pp. 118–21, table 3; additional data collected from Yuan literary anthologies and stele inscriptions.

with the evidence in Tables 8.8a-d. Since Zheng was seeking to affirm the viability of bronze coin, we can take his statement as a delineation of the maximum range of coin use in his day.

With the exception of coastal areas of Fujian, where maritime trade thrived, the coin-using areas demarcated by Zheng were confined to the hinterland interior of South China. In more commercially developed regions such as

Jiangnan, paper money and the silver unit of account prevailed. For example, government price reports from southern Zhejiang dating from the years 1321 and 1346 copied into the *Yuan gongdu lingshi* 元公牘零拾, a handbook for composing Yuan bureaucratic correspondence, all express grain prices in fiscal *liang* units. Ichimaru contended that this evidence cannot be taken as an accurate depiction of market prices; rather, it should be seen as testimony of the use of silver units in official reports. This argument is not persuasive, however. The prices are clearly identified as "market prices" (*shijia* 市價), and it seems unlikely that the officials would have converted them from *guan*-unit prices given that the *guan* and fiscal *liang* units were identical.[86]

The adoption of silver units of account seems to have accelerated after the reestablishment of a stable paper money system in 1311. Three land sale registers from Quanzhou, the great international port in Fujian province, preserved in the genealogy of an Arab merchant family provide evidence of this trend. All three of these documents date from 1336 and denominate ZTC in silver units.[87] A paper currency exchange bureau was established in Quanzhou only in 1305, which may explain the discrepancy with Zheng Jiefu's claim that coin was used exclusively in all parts of Fujian. The only other evidence I have found for money use in Quanzhou, an inscription dated 1334 detailing expenses for a land reclamation project, likewise denominates ZTC in silver units.[88]

Ichimaru also claimed that the existence of hoards of bronze coin dated to the Yuan period confirms continued use of bronze coin. Yet the most comprehensive survey of excavated bronze coin hoards identifies only eight hoards (leaving aside one site containing only forty-eight coins and thus hardly meriting consideration as a hoard) for Yuan-era China, in contrast to 165 hoards for the Southern Song–Jin period. Furthermore, only two of the Yuan hoards were located in North China (one in Hebei and one in Liaodong); four of the rest were found in the interior region of South China identified by Zheng Jiefu as coin-using areas, and two in the vicinity of Hangzhou, probably dating from the late Yuan.[89] In my view, the available

[86] Maeda, *Genchō shi*, p. 127, table 5. Most of the other Yuan price data for South China collected by Maeda – all of which express prices in silver units – is derived from official accounts.

[87] Zhang Chuanxi, *Qiyue huibian*, vol. 1, pp. 568–70. In land sale contracts dating from 1366–1367, at a time when the Yuan regime and its paper currency were defunct, this family stipulated payment in "stamped" silver bullion (*huayin* 花銀). See Zhang Chuanxi, pp. 580–83.

[88] "Chongjian Qingyuan Chunyangdong ji" 重建清源純陽洞記, in Chen Panren 陳槃仁 (ed.), *Minzhong jinshi lüe* 閩中金石略 (1865), 12.3a.

[89] Miyake, *Uzumerareta senka*, pp. 19–31. One of the hoards near Hangzhou contained Zhizheng yuanbao coins and so must date from after 1350, when coin reemerged as the monetary standard in Jiangnan.

evidence from hoards contradicts Ichimaru's hypothesis of widespread use of coin during the Yuan period. It may be true, as Ichimaru suggested, that bronze coin continued to be used in some areas, especially in the interior of South China. But there is little doubt that the ZTC denominated in silver units had become the dominant monetary standard in the private and public spheres alike.

Bronze coin did reemerge as a means of exchange in war-torn Jiangnan in the 1350s, after paper currency suffered steep depreciation. Kong Qi, writing in Ningbo in 1360, observed that by 1356 paper currency had been displaced from exchange by bronze coin. However, the value of coin fluctuated enormously from place to place: "the official exchange rate was set at 100 coins per string,[90] but throughout Jiangnan the prevailing rate of exchange varies from 80 to 60 – or even 40 – coins, depending on the place. In Huzhou and Jiaxing the old rate of 100 coins per string prevails; but in Suzhou the rate is 54; in Hangzhou, 20 [error for 50?]; in Ningbo, 60. The people are greatly inconvenienced by the lack of a uniform standard."[91] Kong's quotations of exchange rates attest both to the extreme scarcity of coin (reflected in the premium coin enjoyed in the marketplace over the official rate of exchange) and its highly localized range of circulation. Wang Yi, writing at the same time, reported that the brief restitution of coinage in 1350 merely incited a flight from paper currency to old Song coins: "In recent times, the two types of paper money [ZTC and ZYC] have entirely fallen into disuse, and only coin is employed. The mints in the capital were closed after producing little coin. Thus the coin in use among the people consists solely of old coins from earlier dynasties." Given the shortage of coin, counterfeiters had emerged to satisfy the demand for currency. Wang recommended reopening local mints and minting gold and silver coins as well as bronze currency, stark testimony of his lack of faith in fiat currency. "Paper currency is nothing but empty script (*xuwen* 虛文)," Wang declared, "while coin is a tangible object (*shiwu* 實物)."[92] This

[90] In this case, *guan* must refer to strings of coin rather than the paper money unit of account.

[91] Kong Qi 孔齊, *Zhizheng zhiji* 至正直記 (Shanghai: Shanghai guji chubanshe, 1987), 1.25–6.

[92] Wang Yi 王褘, "Quanhuo yi" 泉貨議, in Chen Zilong 陳子龍 (ed.), *Huang Ming jingshi wenbian* 皇明經世文編 ([hereafter *HMJSWB*]; 1637; rpt. Taipei: Guofeng chubanshe, 1964), 4.14b. Wang's essay essentially reprised Ye Shi's critique of paper currency as "empty money" (*kongqian* 空錢; see Chapter 6), but it also echoed the language of Xu Heng, an ardent advocate of Dao Learning at Khubilai's court. Xu, who grew up in Mongol-ruled North China, drew on the Southern Song Dao Learning criticisms of *huizi* to denounce paper money as "empty script" (*xuquan* 虛券) in contrast to "substantive coin" *(shiqian* 實錢). Xu Heng 許衡, "Chubi zhazi" 楮幣箚子, in *Xu Wenzheng yishu* 許文正遺書 (Fujingtang ed., 1891), 7.14a–16b.

forthright pronouncement was a harbinger of a reversion to metallist doctrines that would gain ascendancy in Chinese monetary thought throughout the rest of the imperial era.

In the final years of the Yuan dynasty, we are told, trade regressed to the level of barter: "in the capital, 10 *ding* [i.e., 500 *guan*] of paper currency could not buy a kilo of grain. In the various localities, trade was conducted entirely by bartering goods. Paper currency that had accumulated in both public and private stocks became worthless. The people regarded it as nothing more than scrap paper, and consequently the state had no means to defray its expenses."[93] In this economic climate, precious metals were most treasured of all. The safety found in silver propelled the value of silver to the highest recorded levels in Chinese history.[94] Despite government efforts to restore paper currency in the early Ming dynasty, silver continued to prevail as the preferred medium of market exchange, and in the early 15th century the state acceded to this economic reality and gradually adopted silver as the means of state payments.

8.6 Conclusion

The Mongol rulers of China jettisoned the bronze coin monetary standard that had existed since the inception of the first empires and in its stead created a new monetary standard based on paper money denominated in silver units of account. In contrast to Song policymakers, for whom paper money was one component of a multiple currency system, the Mongols sought to eliminate bronze coin and silver specie entirely. Apart from a couple of short-lived, abortive trials, the Mongol rulers of China did not issue any coin, but rather relied entirely on paper currency for public and private transactions alike.

Of course, the inability of the Song and Jin states to generate sufficient coin to keep pace with the rising market demand for money was also a key cause of the shift away from bronze coin. After 1160, both the Song and Jin states increasingly relied on paper bills – denominated in bronze coin but in the case of Song backed by silver as the hard currency reserve – as their principal currency. The dearth of coin became especially severe in the Jin territories. By 1200, the Jin state had demonetized bronze coin, briefly experimented with silver coin, and established a fixed exchange rate between paper currency and silver – measures never adopted by the Southern Song government. The dire military and fiscal predicament of the Jin state compelled it to resort to printing ever-greater quantities of paper money while suspending

93 *YS* 97.2485.

94 Von Glahn, *Fountain of Fortune*, p. 61, fig. 2.

convertibility, with predictable consequences: the severe depreciation of paper bills and, from 1215 onward, the flight to bullion silver as the monetary standard for private exchange. After subjugating the Jin territories – partially in 1215 and completely in 1234 – the Mongol rulers mostly collected revenues from their North China subjects in silver. Under the great khan Ögödei, the Mongol Empire adopted the standard Song–Jin silver ingot (*ding*) as the common unit of account (known as *yastuq* in Mongolian and *balish* in Persian) across its far-flung territories. The silver exacted as tribute from the former Jin territories in North China became the commercial lifeblood of the trans-Eurasian Mongol realm.

In the 1250s, the *baoyin* levy imposed by the great khan Möngke extracted enormous quantities of silver from the former Jin territories, most of which was carried off to West Asia by *ortoq* merchants acting as financial agents for the Mongol nobility. The drain of silver to the west resulted in shortages that hobbled commerce within the Chinese ecumene. From the inception of the Mongol conquests of the Jin territories, individual Mongol rulers (including Khubilai's mother, as well as Khubilai himself) introduced paper currencies modeled on the Jin precedents (but denominated in silver or silk) within their personal appanages. By the time of Möngke's death in 1259, the scarcity of silver in North China had become an acute problem for fiscal operations as well as market exchange.

Upon his election as great khan in 1260, Khubilai undertook a broad array of measures to re-center the Mongol Empire on China and to complete the conquest of the Southern Song. To mobilize the fiscal resources needed to achieve these goals, Khubilai immediately conducted a sweeping consolidation of monetary media within his realm, issuing a new paper currency (ZTC) and barring the use of bronze coin, gold, or silver in private transactions. In contrast to the Song paper currencies, the ZTC was issued in small denominations (eleven altogether, from 10 *wen* to 2 *guan*). Although denominated in bronze coin, the ZTC actually was linked to silver units (*ding*/fiscal *liang*) that replaced the *guan* as the basis of the state's fiscal bookkeeping.

The incorporation of the far more populous Southern Song territories into the Yuan Empire (the dynastic name adopted by Khubilai in 1271) after 1276 posed formidable fiscal and monetary challenges. In response, the Yuan increased the output of ZTC more than tenfold. To conserve their stocks of silver, local officials often refused to honor the principle of convertibility with hard currency. But the swelling volume of paper currency caused the silver value of the ZTC in the marketplace to fall sharply. In 1287, the government sought to stem the depreciation of its paper currency by devaluing the ZTC by 80 percent and issuing a new paper currency (ZYC) to replace ZTC as the circulating medium of exchange. This policy followed the precedent of the Song government when it inaugurated the issue of #18 *huizi* bills in 1240 while discounting #17 *huizi* by 80 percent, in essence turning the #17 *huizi* into a fractional currency. Nonetheless, the Yuan state retained the ZTC as its fiscal unit of account.

The adoption of this dual currency system initially arrested the depreciation of paper money, but the silver value of paper currency fell sharply in the first decade of the 14th century. In 1309, under the aegis of Emperor Khaishan, the Yuan again attempted to buoy its paper currency by devaluing the ZYC, introducing yet another new bill (ZDYC, nominally denominated in silver) intended to replace ZTC as the monetary standard, and resuming bronze coinage. These policies failed utterly, however, and were rescinded following Khaishan's death in 1311. The court reestablished a dual paper currency system in which ZTC served as the unit of account in both public finance and private trade, while the great majority of the circulating currency consisted of ZYC bills. The value of paper currency rebounded and then stabilized until the collapse of effective Mongol rule beginning in the late 1340s. Although there is some evidence for the persistence of bronze coin in the hinterland regions of the former Southern Song territories, in the more commercially advanced regions both trade and public finance were conducted using the common medium of paper currency.

By the middle of the Yuan era, the practice of expressing the value of paper currency in silver units had become widely diffused. The links between paper currency and silver forged by the Southern Song state prepared the way for the emergence of a new money of account based on silver. The Yuan paper currency system was a synthesis of earlier Jin and Song precedents as well as the silver unit of account widely adopted by Mongol rulers in the initial stages of imperial expansion. The stability of the dual paper currency system created in 1311 fostered the widespread popular use of this silver unit of account to denominate paper currency. In contrast to the usual progression in monetary history, in which monies of account typically are the vestiges of a defunct circulating currency ("ghost monies," in Carlo Cipolla's memorable phrase), in the Chinese case the use of silver units of account to denominate paper currency actually preceded the widespread adoption of silver specie as the major form of market money from the 15th century onward.[95] The fiscal and monetary policies of the Mongol Yuan state thus established a silver unit of account that endured throughout China's late imperial era, when silver itself became the principal form of money.

[95] Carlo M. Cipolla, *Money, Prices, and Civilization in the Mediterranean World, Fifth to Seventeenth Century* (Princeton, NJ: Princeton University Press, 1956), pp. 38–39.

9

Triumph of the Silver Economy

The Mongol conquest subjected China's populace to predatory tributary exactions. Yet the Yuan rulers esteemed commerce as a perpetual fountain of wealth and enacted monetary policies to facilitate the circulation of traders, merchandise, and money. Although large swaths of North China and especially the Sichuan region in the west were devastated during the Mongol invasions, the commercial efflorescence of the Song era continued in South China, especially in the Yangzi Delta region, during the Yuan period.[1] But this trend abruptly reversed with the restoration of Chinese rule under the Ming dynasty. The founder of the Ming dynasty, Zhu Yuanzhang (who reigned as the Hongwu emperor, r. 1368–1398), was determined to eradicate what he regarded as the pernicious infection of Mongol customs and to restore the institutions and values enshrined in the Confucian Classics. Inspired by the Confucian ideal of an autarkic agrarian society untarnished by the profit-seeking of the marketplace, Hongwu repudiated the market economy that had developed during the preceding centuries. In pursuit of his atavistic social agenda he established a fiscal system based on in-kind payments to the state (principally grain), conscripted labor and military service, and payments to officials and soldiers in the form of goods rather than money. Hongwu's policies ultimately foundered in the face of ineluctable economic forces that rekindled private enterprise and the market economy. But the early Ming marked a crucial disjuncture in the course of China's economic development, and especially its monetary system.[2]

Hongwu's anti-mercantile convictions extended as far as banning private overseas trade, crippling one of the major engines of economic growth in the Song–Yuan era. Despite his anathema for the Mongols, Hongwu retained the

[1] Richard von Glahn, "Towns and Temples: Urban Growth and Decline in the Yangzi Delta, 1100–1400," in Paul Jakov Smith and Richard von Glahn (eds.), *The Song–Yuan–Ming Transition in Chinese History* (Cambridge, MA: Harvard University Council on East Asian Studies, 2003), pp. 176–211.

[2] Von Glahn, *Economic History of China*, pp. 285–88; Wang et al., *Huobi liutong yanjiu*, pp. 244–49.

system of hereditary occupational households that had been a key pillar of Yuan social control. Artisan households were obliged to serve in periodic rotation at government workshops and factories, diminishing the need to procure goods from the market. Military households – who comprised one-fifth of the total population in the early 15th century – supplied the manpower for garrisons broadly dispersed throughout the empire. In contrast to the paid professional soldiery of the Song era, the Ming military was expected to be self-supporting: the military household provided its own equipment, weapons, and horses, and the government allocated lands for soldiers to farm while not engaged in active campaigns. Hongwu intended to restore bronze currency as the basis of a monetary system that would provide for the minimal needs for exchange in local markets. But the insuperable costs of issuing full-bodied coin derailed this effort, compelling the Ming to issue its own paper currency. To shore up the value of this paper currency the government resorted to banning the use of precious metals and even its own bronze currency in market exchange. These extreme measures failed to sustain the Ming paper currency, however, and by the second decade of the 15th century paper money was defunct. No future imperial regime would seek to resuscitate it.

During the 15th and 16th centuries, we witness a turn from fiat paper money to metallic currencies whose value was determined in the marketplace. The Ming state proved unable to maintain not only its paper money but its bronze currency as well. Instead, over the course of the 15th century a new monetary system based on uncoined silver and privately issued ("counterfeit") bronze coin percolated up from below, from unsanctioned moneyers, and eventually was incorporated into the state's reengineered fiscal order. The dual silver/bronze coin monetary system that emerged in the mid–late Ming would persist through the remainder of the imperial era. The dominance of uncoined silver in this last phase of China's imperial monetary history testifies to the power of the marketplace in shaping monetary practices and institutions.

9.1 Restoration of Coinage and Paper Currency in the Early Ming

In 1361, seven years before he declared the inauguration of his Ming dynasty, Zhu Yuanzhang took a decisive step toward asserting his claim to sovereignty by issuing his own coin, known as Dazhong tongbao 大中通寶, at his base in Nanjing. At the time, Zhu's advisers reported that the obsolescence of Yuan paper currency had left grain as the principal medium of exchange in the marketplaces of Jiangnan. The territories under Zhu's control did not have any sources of raw copper. To produce new coins, Zhu's officials resorted to recovering copper by melting down utensils and old coins. Stymied by the meager output of his mint, Zhu cried up the value of the new coins; under his currency regulations of 1361, the standard money of account – the *guan* – contained a mere 400 coins rather than 1,000. Aware of its limited leverage over the economy, Zhu's fledgling government condoned the use of old coins and declared that the market should be allowed to determine prices.[3] Moreover, Zhu implicitly sanctioned the continued use of silver and Yuan paper currency by setting exchange values between the Dazhong tongbao and "silver" units that must have referred to Yuan paper currencies.[4] At the same time that the Dazhong tongbao coin was issued in 1361, Zhu decreed that commercial taxes would be collected in both coin and (Yuan) paper currency.[5] According to the Ming dynastic history, in the early years of the Ming "merchants and shopkeepers followed the former custom of the Yuan in using paper currency; most of them did not find it convenient to use coin."[6]

For Zhu Yuanzhang, minting coin was more a political act than an economic policy.[7] His immediate rivals among the warlords of South China, such as Zhang Shicheng, had announced their imperial ambitions by minting coin as early as 1353. As Zhu's dominion expanded in the early 1360s, he demarcated the lengthening reach of his sovereignty by founding mints in the newly subjugated territories. After the formal establishment of the Ming dynasty in 1368, Zhu cast coins bearing his new reign-title, Hongwu, in five denominations. The larger coins immediately encountered resistance in the marketplace, though, and were discontinued in 1371. Even the standard 1-*wen* coins had difficulty circulating. Most of the Hongwu coinage was disbursed to soldiers in the capital region, while the armies on campaign received emoluments in the form of silver.[8]

The emperor's advisers attributed the problems encountered by the Hongwu coin to insufficient supply, and in 1374 they proposed reducing the copper content of coin by 10 percent to boost the output of the mints. Hongwu recoiled from the notion of debasing his coin, though, and asked for other solutions. Clearly the empire's copper mines could not produce enough metal to meet the demand for an abundant and inexpensive metallic currency. Faced with the intractable problem of inadequate supplies of specie, in 1375 the court

[3] *Ming shilu* 明實錄 ([hereafter *MSL*]; rpt. Taipei: Zhongyang yanjiuyuan lishi yuyan yanjiusuo, 1962), Taizu 太祖 9.1a–b.

[4] While the *guan* – now reduced to 400 coins – was retained as the standard unit of account for Zhu's Dazhong tongbao coin, this *guan* also was subdivided into 10 *liang* and 100 *qian*, units of account expressed in silver and derived from the Yuan paper currency system. Zhu's decree also established an exchange rate of coin relative to "silver" at 40 *wen* = 1 *liang*, but this exchange rate must have referred to silver-denominated Yuan paper currency, not silver bullion. Peng, *Zhongguo huobi shi*, pp. 468–69.

[5] *XWXTK* 18.2930c.

[6] *Ming shi* 明史 ([hereafter *MS*; Beijing: Zhonghua shuju ed.), 81.1962.

[7] For an analysis of early Ming monetary policy that persuasively emphasizes this political dimension, see Danjō Hiroshi 壇上寛, "Shoki Min ōcho no tsūka seisaku" 初期明王朝の通貨政策, *Tōyōshi kenkyū* 東洋史研究 39.3 (1980): 527–56.

[8] Okuyama Norio 奥山憲夫, *Mindai gunsei shi kenkyū* 明代軍政史研究 (Tokyo: Kyūko shoin, 2003), pp. 124, 164–65.

committed itself to reviving paper currency in imitation of the Song and Yuan precedents. The new paper bills, known as the *Da Ming tongxing baochao* 大明通行寶鈔 (hereafter *baochao*), would circulate as the primary instrument of exchange and tax payments, while coin would serve as a subsidiary currency. Initially *baochao* were issued in six denominations ranging from 100 *wen* to 1 *guan*.[9] Numerous specimens of the Ming *baochao* bills survive. The bills vary somewhat in size depending on their denomination, but otherwise they were highly standardized; even after the death of the Ming founder, the bills were printed exclusively with the Hongwu reign title. When inaugurated in 1375 the *baochao* were issued in the name of the Secretariat, but in 1380 the Ministry of Revenue took over issuance of bills. In 1389, the Ming introduced small bills in denominations of 10, 20, 30, and 40 *wen*. The format of the bills closely imitated that of Yuan paper currency, including depicting the value of the bill visually with illustrations of coins or strings of coin (Figure 9.1).[10] Microscopic analysis of nine Ming *baochao* bills in the collection of the British Museum has revealed that they were made principally from mulberry bark fibers, although mixed with bamboo, rice straw, and hemp; the paper was relatively crude, rather than being finely processed.[11] The mediocre quality of the paper perhaps affected the bills' value, and certainly made counterfeiting easier.

The Ming state, like its predecessors, largely concerned itself with two functions of money: as a vehicle of revenue extraction, and as a means of maintaining an equilibrium in exchange values (i.e., keeping prices stable). In other words, the state was primarily interested in a form of money amenable to its own control; it was less concerned about the intrinsic value of money, and well might have considered the intrinsic value of money a hindrance to its own objectives. Despite the inflation and depreciation of currency that plagued the Yuan in its final years, the concept of a fiat currency by no means had been discredited. Faith in the sovereign authority of the state to determine the value of money, the fundamental tenet of theoretical chartalism, remained an abiding feature of Chinese political thought. Ye Ziqi, recounting what he deemed the sorry history of Yuan monetary policy in a tract published in 1378, proclaimed that there was nothing wrong in principle with paper money, or fiat currency generally. Ye went farther than most in trying to trace a noble pedigree for paper currency and blamed Yuan policies, not paper money itself, for the ultimate collapse of the Yuan monetary system.

9 *MSL*, Taizu 98.1a–b.

10 For a study of the design of *baochao* bills in Chinese collections, see Wang Liyan 王俪阎, "Da Ming tongxing baochao kao" 大明通行宝钞考, *Zhongguo qianbi* 中国钱币 2007.3: 58–64.

11 Caroline R. Cartwright, Christina M. Duffy, and Helen Wang, "Microscopical Examination of Fibres Used in Ming Dynasty Paper Money," *British Museum Technical Research Bulletin* 8 (2014): 105–16.

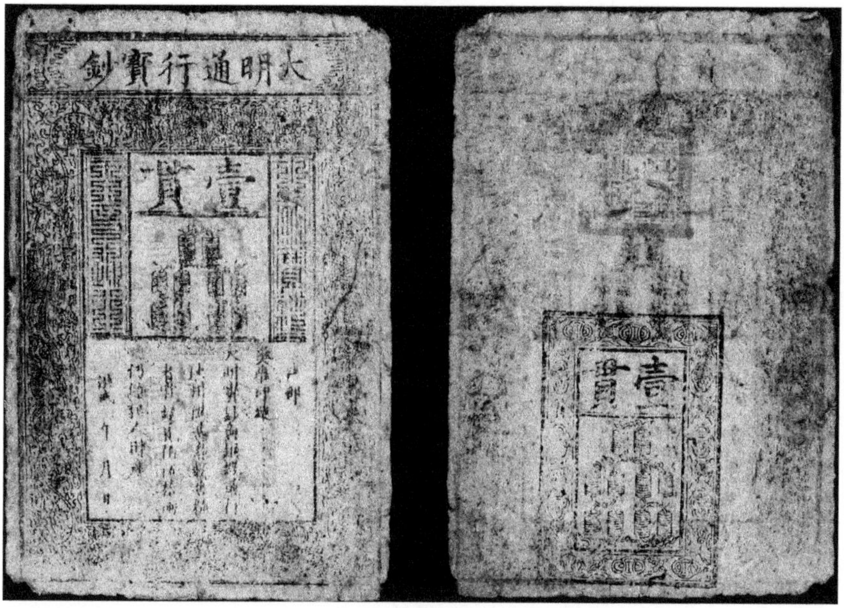

Figure 9.1 Ming 1-*guan baochao* bill.
Source: British Museum 1942,0805.1.

But Ye echoed many Yuan statesmen in stressing that paper money can succeed only if it is backed by adequate reserves of specie. He approved of the Ming state's decision to restore paper currency as long as the state ensured that it was convertible with coin.[12]

While reviving paper currency, the Ming, in contrast to the Yuan, remained determined to supplement its bills with bronze coin. Like the Yuan, though, the Ming attempted to establish its paper currency as the primary medium of exchange by banning the use of precious metals or any other commodity monies in trade.[13] But whereas the Yuan, at least initially, had backed its paper money with hard currency by making its notes convertible with silver, from the first the Ming *baochao* were inconvertible. As a result, large discrepancies emerged between the nominal value of the bills as fixed by the state and the real value they could command in the marketplace. The Ming *baochao* depreciated in value, not only in terms of precious metals but also relative to coin, causing some officials to regard the state's own coin as the nemesis of its

12 Ye Ziqi 葉子奇, *Caomuzi* 草木子 (Beijing: Zhonghua shuju, 1959), 3B, pp. 65–66.
13 *MSL*, Taizu 98.1a–b. The ban on the use of gold and silver in trade was repeatedly issued in the late Hongwu, Yongle, and early Xuande reigns, to little effect. See Wang et al., *Huobi liutong yanjiu*, pp. 275–77.

paper currency. Shortly after the state began to issue paper money in 1375, the mints were closed. The reason given for the interruption in minting was that coinage imposed too great a burden on the people in terms of requisitions for labor and materials.[14] No suggestion was made that the state intended to demonetize coin, and two years later mints were reopened in several provinces. Throughout the 1380s, the course of Ming monetary policy veered erratically between emphasizing either coin or paper currency. Issue of paper money was halted in 1384, then resumed in 1389, and discontinued once more in 1391; the mints were closed again in 1387 and reopened in 1389.[15] Despite all of this tinkering with the money supply, the downward slide of the *baochao* continued. In 1390, officials reported that in the markets of Jiangnan the 1-*guan* bill had an exchange value of only 250 *wen*, a mere one-fourth of its nominal value. Pressure on the government to devalue the *baochao* mounted, but Hongwu stood firm.[16]

The reasons for the depreciation of paper currency are not difficult to discern. As Ray Huang has shown, the Ming government spent far greater sums of paper currency than its revenues warranted. In 1390, a year in which the state received 20.4 million *guan* in paper currency income, its disbursements amounted to at least 95 million *guan* of *baochao* (the actual total was probably even greater).[17] We lack aggregate data for the quantity of *baochao* issued by the Ming government, but according to the second installment of Hongwu's *Grand Announcements* the government printed 6.94 million *ding* (34.7 million *guan*) in 1385. Ōta Yukio has conjectured that annual issue of *baochao* probably was roughly 50 million *guan*, in contrast to average annual cash revenues in the range of 20 million *guan*.[18] Clearly Hongwu's

[14] *MSL*, Taizu 98.3b–4a.

[15] *MSL*, Taizu 160.10a, 196.1b, 196.5b, 208.6a.

[16] *MSL*, Taizu 205.1b.

[17] Ray Huang, *Taxation and Governmental Finance in Sixteenth-Century Ming China* (Cambridge: Cambridge University Press, 1974), pp. 69–70. The report on state revenues in 1390 did not specify the sources of income in the form of *baochao* (see *MSL*, Taizu 206.6b), but apparently most of the *baochao* revenue derived from commercial taxes. The *Roll of Central Government Offices* (*Zhusi zhizhang* 諸司職掌), published in 1393, reported that the twice-a-year tax generated annual revenues of 29.44 million *shi* of grain (with a market value of 15 million *guan*) but only 0.23 million *guan* in *baochao* receipts. See Miyazawa, *Kahei to zaisei*, pp. 537–38. Presumably the salt monopoly was a major source of payments in *baochao*, but we have no quantitative data on salt revenues for the early Ming.

[18] Ōta Yukio 大田由紀夫, "Chūgoku ōchō ni yoru kahei hakō to ryūtsū: Min Kōbuki no shōhō ni tsuite" 中国王朝による貨幣発行と流通:明洪武期の鈔法について, in Ike Susumu 池享 (ed.), *Senka: Zenkindai Nihon no kahei to kokka* 銭貨:前近代日本の貨幣と国家 (Tokyo: Aoki shoten, 2001), pp. 171–72. Huang Aming estimates the maximum yearly output of *baochao* at 35 million *guan* in 1385–1393 and 25 million in 1393–1398.

administration injected far more paper currency into the economy than it absorbed through tax revenues.

Prodigious issue of paper currency undermined efforts to shore up its value. The Ming converted a portion of official salaries, originally paid in rice, into *baochao* in 1380, and entirely into *baochao* from 1385. But the depreciation of the paper currency forced the government to revert to paying official salaries in rice in 1387.[19] Similarly, the government had replaced stipends and emoluments for soldiers stationed in the capital originally paid in grain, cloth, salt, pepper, coin, and silver with *baochao* when the paper currency was first issued in 1375. But by 1386 payments in commodities were restored, along with allowances in *baochao*.[20] By 1394, the exchange rate of the 1-*guan baochao* had fallen to 160 bronze coins in Jiangnan. Citing the deep discounting of bills in the southern provinces of Fujian, Jiangxi, and Guangdong as well as Jiangnan, the court blamed coin for the resulting inflation of (nominal) prices. Hongwu then took the extraordinary step of prohibiting the use of even his own coin in trade. All coin in private hands had to be surrendered to the government in return for paper money.[21] *Baochao* would be the sole form of legal tender.

This drastic demonetization of bronze coin flouted economic realities. The state stipulated that coins would be redeemed at the official exchange ratio, which would have entailed serious losses of purchasing power. The result instead was to accelerate the flight to silver. Three years later, in 1397, the deepening erosion of the value of *baochao* prompted the government to reiterate its ban against the use of silver as money. Between 1378 and 1397, the value of silver, measured against paper currency, had risen tenfold; even in real terms, measured against grain, the purchasing power of silver increased by 400 percent.[22] Despite the high price silver commanded, "in Hangzhou and surrounding areas merchants and tradesmen set prices for both dear and cheap goods exclusively in terms of gold and silver, to the detriment of the paper money system."[23]

Hongwu's feckless efforts to impose *baochao* as a fiat currency probably should be understood in terms of the emperor's determination to assert his imperial prerogatives and to ensure that the power to fix the ratios of exchange would rest with him alone, as hoary chartalist tradition demanded. Danjō Hiroshi has argued that Hongwu's anti-silver policies stemmed from his

See Huang Aming 黄阿明, *Mingdai huobi baiyinhua yu guojia zhidu biange yanjiu* 明代货币白银化与国家制度变革研究 (Yangzhou: Guangling shushe, 2016), p. 49.

19 Miyazawa, *Kahei to zaisei*, pp. 536; Huang Aming, *Huobi baiyinhua*, pp. 79–80.

20 Okuyama, *Mindai gunsei shi*, pp. 170–71.

21 *MSL*, Taizu 234.2a.

22 Peng, *Zhongguo huobi shi*, p. 669.

23 *MSL*, Taizu 251.2b.

abiding hostility to the wealthy landowners of Jiangnan, who had supported his principal rival Zhang Shicheng in their struggle for suzerainty. Once installed as emperor, Hongwu carried out a ruthless campaign of expropriation against the Jiangnan elite, seizing their personal wealth and saddling the rich Yangzi Delta prefectures of Suzhou, Changzhou, Songjiang, Jiaxing, and Zhenjiang with onerous taxes, fully one-quarter of the empire's total land tax quota. Hongwu also scattered the members of these magnate families, moving many of them to his capital at Nanjing, where he could keep a watchful eye over them. Throughout his reign, Hongwu harbored grave suspicions about the loyalties of the Jiangnan elite and aggressively pursued policies to elevate himself to the empyrean dignity of an absolute monarch. Danjō suggests that silver, uncoined and largely sequestered in private hoards, enjoyed an autonomy from state control that Hongwu could not abide. Thus he sought to impose a unified currency system that would insinuate the state's authority into Jiangnan's flourishing commercial economy and vitiate the concentration of private wealth, in the form of silver, that appeared to challenge his sovereignty. Seen from this perspective, the refusal of the Ming to take the logical step of making its paper currency convertible with metallic money to instill confidence in its value becomes more readily understandable.[24]

The reign of the dynasty's third emperor, Yongle (1402–1425), witnessed an utter collapse in the value of *baochao*, and correspondingly the highest purchasing power of silver in the Ming era.[25] Yongle repeatedly reissued edicts barring the use of silver (in 1403, 1404, 1419, and 1425), to no avail. Contemporaries recognized that excessive issues of paper currency had compromised its value, but rather than curbing this practice, Yongle printed money in an even more wanton fashion than the dynastic founder. The enormous deficits incurred by Yongle's costly foreign military campaigns, the relocation of the capital from Nanjing to Beijing, and the overseas expeditions dispatched to Southeast Asia and the Indian Ocean under the command of Zheng He were abated, albeit only temporarily, by printing more money. Efforts to stimulate the use of paper currency by requiring its use in payment of new capitation taxes such as salt ration payments (*hukou shiyan chao* 戶口食鹽鈔) had little practical effect.[26]

[24] Danjō, "Shoki Min tsūka," pp. 540–44.

[25] See Peng Xinwei's tables on *baochao* exchange values and the purchasing power of silver: Peng, *Zhongguo huobi shi*, pp. 671–72, 705.

[26] R. Huang, *Taxation and Governmental Finance*, pp. 138–39. The salt ration payment was a compulsory purchase of salt assessed on the total population (similar to the "silkworm salt" tax of the Southern Tang; see Chapter 3) and paid in *baochao* or grain. Enacted in a few provinces in the early Ming, it was applied empire-wide in 1404 and collected exclusively in *baochao* as a means of promoting the use of paper currency. See *MSL*, Taizong 太宗 33.8a–b. By the 1440s, the salt ration payment had devolved into a simple capitation tax for which no salt was received in compensation. See Fujii Hiroshi 藤井宏,

Yet Yongle retreated from his father's position of basing the monetary system solely on paper money. Early in his reign (c. 1408 or 1410), Yongle issued coin under his own reign-title.[27] But it is not clear how much of this coin was released into common circulation. Most of these coins apparently were deposited in state treasuries, another indication of the way in which coin, despite its low unit value, was treated as bullion. Foreign tribute missions paying visits to the Ming court received substantial quantities of coin as gifts. Nonetheless, one late Ming historian credited Yongle for allowing "coin once again to circulate together with *baochao*," in contrast to the subsequent Xuande (1425–1435) and Zhengtong (1435–1447) courts, which returned to a policy of favoring paper money to the exclusion of coin.[28]

9.2 The Demise of Ming Paper Currency

At the time of Yongle's death in 1424, the *baochao* circulated at less than 2 percent of their face value.[29] His successors Hongxi (r. 1424–1425), who died within eight months, and Xuande undertook more determined efforts to resuscitate the beleaguered *baochao*. Xuande pursued the same anti-silver policies his predecessors had laid out. Paper currency remained a purely fiat currency, inconvertible with metallic money, while the interdiction against the use of silver was renewed.[30] Although Xuande issued coins under his own reign-title, his monetary policies primarily focused on promoting the use of *baochao*. The new departure in Xuande's monetary policy took the form of increasing the utility of *baochao* in state payments through a proliferation of duties and excises imposed on commerce. Already in 1424, two months after his enthronement, Hongxi had raised the salt ration payment for adults from 12 *guan* per year to 100–300 *guan*, depending on the region.[31] Shortly after his coronation Xuande increased the franchise fees for wholesale and retail shops (*mentanshui* 門攤稅) and mandated that these fees be paid in *baochao*.

"Mindai no kokō shokuen ni tsuite" 明代の戸口食鹽に就いて, *Shakai keizai shigaku* 社会経済史学 13.3 (1943): 1–30.

27 The exact date is a matter of dispute. According to the *Comprehensive Statutes of the Great Ming*, Yongle coins were first issued in 1408; another passage in the same work states that the coins were first issued in 1410 and additional mints were established in Zhejiang, Jiangxi, Fujian, and Guangdong in 1411. See Shen Shixing 申時行 et al. (comp), *Da Ming huidian* 大明會典 ([hereafter *DMHD*]; 1587; rpt. Taipei: Xinwenfeng chuban gongsi, 1976), 194.8b, 31.8b–9a. The late Ming historian Sun Chengze dated the initial emission of the Yongle coin to 1410: Sun Chengze 孫承澤, *Chunming mengyu lu* 春明夢餘錄 ([hereafter *MYL*]; 1883 Guxiangzhai ed., rpt., Yangzhou: Jiangsusheng guangling guji keyinshe, 1990), 47.3b–4a.

28 *MYL* 47.3b–4a.

29 *MSL*, Xuanzong 宣宗 6.15a–b.

30 *MSL*, Xuanzong 19.1a.

31 *MSL*, Renzong 仁宗 2A.2a–b.

In 1429, a wide array of new commercial fees payable in bills was enacted: the franchise fees on shops were increased fivefold in thirty-three major cities; new excises were levied on inns, warehouses, and animal-drawn carts; and toll stations collecting transit duties assessed in *baochao* were set up at six major cities along the Grand Canal.[32] The rationale for creating the inland customs stations – later known as "paper currency tolls" (*chaoguan* 鈔關) – specifically invoked the goal of promoting the use of paper currency.[33] At the same time, Xuande heeded the pleas of officials who urged him to restrict the issue of new *baochao* to ensure a balance between supply of bills and market demand.[34] In the summer of 1428, Xuande ordered a temporary halt in the issue of new *baochao*.[35]

Another strategy for stimulating the circulation of *baochao* was to use the lucrative lure of monopsony rights over the sale of salt. In 1371, the Ming had enacted a policy (similar to the Song *ruzhong* system, but renamed *kaizhong* 開中) of compensating merchants who delivered provisions to frontier garrisons with salt licenses. In 1424, the government began to allow purchases of salt licenses with payments in *baochao*. However, this plan resulted in windfall profits for merchants without reviving the exchange value of paper currency, as the Ministry of Revenue ruefully acknowledged in 1429:

> In recent years, whenever the great merchants, rich households, and persons of power and privilege engage in trade, they demand gold and silver as payment, and thus paper currency fails to circulate. In 1425, wishing to encourage its use, the court permitted officials, soldiers, and ordinary subjects to purchase salt licenses with paper money. Greedy profiteers rushed to submit worn and decrepit bills in exchange for the salt licenses. A single person would buy up licenses numbering in the thousands. But upon selling the salt thus obtained they invariably demanded payment in gold and silver. Paper currency now circulates even less successfully than before.[36]

Not only did this policy fail to revive the paper currency, it also created a glut of salt licenses. The Ministry of Revenue then took the extreme measure of compulsorily redeeming old salt licenses with paper money – in effect, the government was defaulting on its debt. Although this action dealt a serious blow to market confidence in the validity of salt licenses, it was repeated throughout the 15th century. The failure of those efforts to resuscitate the

32 Huang Aming, *Huobi baiyinhua*, pp. 68–71.

33 *MSL*, Xuanzong 55.9b–10b.

34 Xuande reportedly was deeply impressed by the argument of Fan Ji on this issue. See Fan Ji 范濟, "Yique shangshu" 詣闕上書, in *HMJSWB* 29.1a–3b; *MS* 164.4444, 4447.

35 *MSL*, Xuanzong 44.9a–10a; *XWXTK* 10.2861c. It is not clear how long this suspension lasted.

36 *MSL*, Xuanzong 55.8b.

value of salt licenses ultimately resulted in the demise of the salt monopoly as a means of financing the military.[37]

The proliferation of commercial taxes paid in *baochao* dramatically increased the state's nominal revenues in paper currency, which rose from 20 million *guan* in the 1390s to 50 million *guan* in 1410, then leapt to 188 million *guan* in 1425 and 350 million *guan* or more in 1432.[38] But the depreciation of *baochao* eviscerated the real value of this income: at the current exchange rate in 1432, 350 million *guan* of paper currency was worth only 3.5 million *guan* of coin. Still, in the summer of 1432, Xuande boasted that in the wake of adopting the new commercial taxes "the paper currency system has begun to function well."[39] Reports from the mid 1440s claimed that recent improvement in the market value of *baochao* warranted adjustments in the official exchange values of paper currency relative to rice and silver.[40] By the late 1440s, however, the value of *baochao* once again fell sharply.

To the extent that *baochao* bills circulated in the marketplace, they probably did so as a fractional currency (at this time the 1-*guan* bill was worth 2 to 10 *wen* in coin). Indeed, it appears that *baochao* and coin began to compete with each other. The proscription against coin probably had never been strictly enforced, and in late 1433 Xuande ordered the mints in Beijing and four southern provinces to manufacture 100,000 strings of coin.[41] In 1436, a prefect in Guangxi, observing that coin prevailed as the means of market exchange in the southernmost provinces, appealed to the newly enthroned Zhengtong emperor to follow the *Ming Code* as laid down by Hongwu and allow the use of coin as well as *baochao* in trade.[42] Zhengtong assented, although it is not clear whether the ban was rescinded throughout the empire or only for the southern provinces.[43] Yet under Zhengtong the Ming mints ceased operation, and for the next seventy years the Ming produced no new coin whatsoever.

Even in the absence of new infusions of coin, existing coins – mostly Song issues – persevered in retail commerce. In 1447, Zhou Jian, the governor of

37 Wing-kin Puk, *The Rise and Fall of a Public Debt Market in 16th-Century China: The Story of the Ming Salt Certificate* (Leiden: Brill, 2016), pp. 36–47.

38 Huang Aming, *Huobi baiyinhua*, p. 76.

39 近聞鈔法稍通. *MSL*, Xuanzong 77.2a.

40 Qiu Yongzhi 邱永志, "Zhanzheng, shichang, yu guojia: Zhengtong Jingtai zhi ji tonghuo liutong tizhide bianqian" 战争，市场，与国家:正统景泰之际通货流通体制的变迁, *Zhongguo jingji shi yanjiu* 中国经济史研究 2017.6: 33.

41 *MSL*, Xuanzong 106.13b; *DMHD* 194.8b.

42 *MSL*, Yingzong 英宗 12.5b.

43 Qiu Yongzhi argues that the repeal applied only to Guangdong and Guangxi. See Qiu, "Tonghuo liutong tizhi," p. 31. Yet in 1447 the governor of North Zhili requested that the use of coin should be prohibited in all regions "outside of Guangdong and Guangxi," which suggests that Zhengtong rescinded the ban on coin for the entire empire. See Zhang Xueyan 張學顏 (comp), *Wanli kuaiji lu* 萬曆會計錄 ([hereafter *KJL*; BTZB rpt. of 1587 ed.), 41.2a.

North Zhili, reported that private trade in the capital and the major commercial emporia along the Grand Canal was conducted exclusively in coin, which impeded the circulation of *baochao*. The Ministry of Revenue concurred, and the prohibition on coin was renewed.[44] But this measure had little effect; a year later the market value of 1 *guan* of *baochao* had fallen to a mere two coins, or 1/500 of their nominal value, prompting the court to increase the penalties for conducting transactions in coin.[45]

Market demand for coin clearly remained strong, and after the state mints ceased operations in 1435, private moneyers rushed in to fill the vacuum. In 1456, the Beijing constabulary reported that recently markets in the capital had become inundated with counterfeit coins manufactured in the Jiangnan cities of Suzhou and Songjiang, and the capital's artisans were beginning to copy these ersatz coins.[46] By the 1470s, these cheap privately issued "new coins" (*xinqian* 新錢) predominated in both the capital and the provinces. However, many merchants refused to accept the debased coins – a practice known as "shroffing" (*tiaojian* 挑揀, *xuanjian* 選揀) – or discounted them by as much as 70 percent. Shroffing induced a sharp spike in coin-denominated prices, bringing distress to urban consumers.[47] Since the new coins were imitations of previous Ming issues (Hongwu, Yongle, and Xuande coins), their proliferation provoked a reaction against even genuine Ming coins (referred to as "standard coins," *zhiqian* 制錢). In 1481, the Ministry of Revenue reported that Hongwu and Yongle coins now were routinely refused in the marketplace.[48] Other contemporaries confirm that the standard Hongwu and Yongle coins disappeared from circulation, to be replaced by "old coins" (i.e., Song issues). By all accounts, the bulk of circulating coin was counterfeit, and from this point forward distinct regional variations in coin use appeared throughout the Ming empire.[49]

Attempts to legislate the use of paper currency through taxation continued into the second half of the 15th century. In 1465, the Ministry of Revenue affirmed that commercial taxes of all sorts, including the salt ration levy, should be paid half in *baochao* and half in coin. But its chief concern was the deteriorating value of coin because of the spreading use of private coin.[50] As early as 1452, officials had noted that merchants often paid the transit duty

44 *KJL* 41.2a.
45 *MSL*, Yingzong 166.2a.
46 *MSL*, Yingzong 268.3b–4a.
47 In 1480, a Beijing resident reported that because of the influx of counterfeit coin and the spread of shroffing, the value of coin relative to silver had fallen by 60 percent, causing food prices to soar. See *KJL* 41.4a–b.
48 *MSL*, Xianzong 憲宗 212.3a–b.
49 On the proliferation of private coinage in the 15th and 16th centuries, see von Glahn, *Fountain of Fortune*, pp. 84–88, 97–112.
50 *MSL*, Xianzong 19.5a; *KJL* 41.3b–4a.

tolls in silver rather than *baochao*. Repeated decrees to enforce collection of the transit tolls in a combination of *baochao* and silver proved ineffective. In 1488, the government conceded to what had become common practice and officially sanctioned the conversion of the transit tolls (and also the salt ration levy) to silver payments, albeit at an exchange rate that valued *baochao* at twice the prevailing market rate.[51] By this time, the institutional framework created by Hongwu was essentially defunct, and Ming policymakers had begun – in incremental and halting fashion – to rebuild the fiscal system based on the silver monetary standard that had come to prevail in market exchange.

9.3 The Silverization of Public Finance

According to the Ming dynastic history, in 1436 the court lifted the ban on the use of silver in trade.[52] However, this assertion is not corroborated by any contemporary sources, and Momose Hiromu has persuasively argued that the *Ming History* compilers miswrite "coin" as "silver."[53] The error is understandable in retrospect, since it was during the mid 1430s that the state began to incorporate silver into its fiscal regime. Over the remainder of the 15th century, the silverization of state finances steadily progressed. Yielding to economic reality, Ming policymakers readmitted the use of silver in exchange, in practice if not in principle, and in so doing abandoned Hongwu's atavistic vision of agrarian paternalism intended to shield his subjects from the corrosive effects of the money economy.

Standard accounts of Ming fiscal history – both by late Ming scholars and modern historians – attribute the origins of the silverization of state finances to the land tax policies enacted by Zhou Chen.[54] Between 1430 and 1434, Zhou introduced wide-ranging reforms in the administration of the land tax in the Yangzi Delta, including commuting a portion of the grain tribute levy in the heavily taxed prefectures of Suzhou, Songjiang, Changzhou, and Zhenjiang to payments in silver and cotton cloth. Zhou's reorganization of land taxation in the Yangzi Delta has been seen as the decisive first step toward the eventual adoption of silver as the monetary standard for government finance under the chief grand secretary Zhang Juzheng in the 1570s. However, this transition

[51] Huang Aming, *Huobi baiyinhua*, pp. 135–40.

[52] *MS* 81.1964.

[53] Wada Sei 和田清 (ed.), *Minshi shokkashi yakuchū* 明史食貨志譯註 (Tokyo: Tōyō bunko, 1957), vol. 2, pp. 721–22. As noted above, the court did indeed lift the ban on the use of coin in trade in 1436.

[54] For influential statements, see R. Huang, *Taxation and Governmental Finance*, p. 52; Tang Wenji 唐文基, *Mingdai fuyi zhidu shi* 明代赋役制度史 (Beijing: Zhongguo shehui kexue chubanshe, 1991), pp. 130–44.

was not as straightforward as commonly depicted.[55] To gauge the precise significance of the 1430s reforms in Ming fiscal history, they need to be considered in the larger context of the fiscal challenges facing the state at that time.

As we have seen, Hongwu envisioned a new social order predicated on self-sufficient villages insulated from both the inequities of the market economy and the depredations of a venal bureaucracy. To realize his ambition, he reorganized society into administrative communities of 110 households (roughly corresponding to rural villages or urban neighborhoods) designated as *lijia* 里甲. *Lijia* headmen were chosen from among affluent members of the *lijia* community. Although they also acquired broader responsibilities for maintaining social order, including public security and judicial authority, the primary duty of the *lijia* headmen was to mobilize the able-bodied adult men of their communities for labor service duties. The *lijia* headmen also shared tax collection duties with tax captains (*liangzhang* 糧長), whose jurisdictions generally encompassed ten or more (and sometimes more than thirty) *li*. Tax captains were responsible for collecting and delivering the grain tax receipts of their districts to Nanjing and were held accountable for any losses or arrears. In principle tax captain duties were rotated every ten years, but by the 1430s they had become permanent obligations.

Over the course of the 15th century, this rigid organizational scheme succumbed to the ineluctable tides of demographic and economic change. As the prefect of Suzhou put it in 1430, "as for the taxpaying households in each locality, the wealthy of past times today are indigent; the poor and needy of the past today enjoy prosperity and affluence; inevitably their tax obligations have become unequal."[56] By that time, evasion of *lijia* headmen and tax captain services was rampant, a problem exacerbated by the state's growing demands for labor services. But perhaps the precipitating cause in the demise of the tax captain system was the move of the capital to Beijing in 1421, which greatly magnified the costs of tax delivery and pushed tax captains and taxpayers alike into insolvency. Mounting arrears in tax receipts – said to have reached 8 million *shi* of rice in Suzhou alone by 1430 – posed a grave fiscal crisis. Recognizing the need for substantial reform, Xuande and the chief grand secretary Yang Shiqi dispatched a cadre of experienced fiscal officials to six regions to address the tax collection problem. Zhou Chen was appointed to

[55] Wan Ming 万明, "Mingdai baiyin huobihua de chubu kaochao" 明代白银货币化的初步考察, *Zhongguo jingji shi yanjiu* 中国经济史研究 2003.2: 39–51; Noa Grass, "Imperial Silver Laundering: The Official Narrative on Gold Floral Silver and the Silverization of Ming State Finance," *Ming Studies* 76 (2017): 7–31.

[56] Cited in Mori Masao 森正夫, *Mindai Kōnan tochi seido no kenkyū* 明代江南土地制度の研究 (Kyoto: Dōhōsha, 1988), p. 198.

a new plenipotentiary office as Grand Coordinator (Xunfu 巡撫) of South Zhili, a position he would hold for the next twenty-one years.

The Yangzi Delta region was the main source of land tax revenues (and virtually the only source of the government's disposable income), even more so than in the past. Hongwu had confiscated much of the region's rich farmlands from the wealthy landowning elite, whom he deemed political enemies, and created a system of government landholdings (*guantian* 官田) which were rented out to cultivators. Tenants on government lands were exempt from *lijia* duties but shouldered an enormous land tax burden. In Suzhou, for example, government lands comprised 63 percent of registered arable land but were liable for 95 percent of the grain tax quota.[57] The major features of the reforms enacted by Zhou Chen consisted of: (1) reducing the tax quotas on government lands by 20–30 percent; (2) allowing taxpayers to bring their payments to local granary depots rather than having to deliver them to Beijing; (3) assessing standardized surcharge fees to cover the costs of shipping grain to the north; and (4) allowing tenants on government lands burdened with heavy quotas to pay in silver or cotton cloth instead of grain. The exchange rates for silver were highly favorable to taxpayers, in effect further reducing the real cost of their tax assessment by half while also eliminating the substantial costs of delivering grain to the tax depots. The earliest quantitative data on the extent of commutations dates from 1502: at that time, 37.2 percent of Suzhou's tax quota was commuted to silver payments, and 9.2 percent in cloth; for Songjiang (the capital of the cotton textile industry), the figures were 36.8 percent silver and 22.2 percent cloth. A late 16th-century Songjiang native asserted that Zhou's reform commuted 482,687 *shi* of rice – roughly half of the total assessment – to silver and cloth payments.[58]

In 1436, commutation of land taxes into silver and cloth payments was extended to all of South Zhili and Zhejiang. In this case, the commutation was aimed not so much at alleviating the burdens of taxpayers as rectifying another problem created by the move of the capital to Beijing. Civilian officials attached to military guards stationed in Beijing as well as the soldiers themselves continued to receive their grain stipends from state granaries in Nanjing. The cost of transferring the grain stipends to Beijing, or even selling the grain in Nanjing, eroded their net income. To remedy this situation, the Ministry of Revenue proposed to convert tribute grain payments into silver and cloth that would be delivered directly to Beijing; after being reassured that this commutation was consistent with the principles of the dynastic founder,

57 According to a memorial submitted by the prefect of Suzhou in 1430. See Mori, *Kōnan tochi seido*, p. 219.

58 For the 1430s reorganization of the Yangzi Delta land tax system, see Mori, *Kōnan tochi seido*, pp. 197–350. For the commutation figures cited here, see Mori, pp. 304–5.

the emperor gave his consent.[59] According to the *Collected Statutes of the Great Ming*, this action marked the beginning of the collection of "gold floral silver" (*jinhuayin* 金花銀), with an annual quota of 1 million taels.[60] By the time the *Collected Statutes* was compiled in 1587, "gold floral silver" had become a mainstay of Ming fiscal administration.

As Wan Ming and Noa Grass have demonstrated, however, the account of the origins of gold floral silver presented in the *Collected Statutes* is unreliable.[61] The earliest references to gold floral silver date from the 1470s–1480s, and the term became widely used only in the 16th century. The gold floral silver funds were closely linked to the growing costs of military expenditure borne by the central government. The system of self-supporting military garrisons, a signature feature of Hongwu's original political vision, gradually crumbled over the course of the 15th century, leaving many soldiers destitute. Moreover, in the wake of the catastrophic battle at Tumu in 1449, when the Ming army was routed by the Oirat Mongols (and the Ming emperor taken captive), the government greatly expanded its frontier garrison system, which required a substantial increase in cash outlays. From the 1440s, the Ministry of Revenue occasionally delivered funds in the form of silver to various garrisons along the northern frontier, more frequently after the Tumu debacle. By the early 1480s, transfers of silver to the frontier garrisons became annual allocations (known as *nianli* 年例).[62] By this time, the Taicang Treasury (太倉庫), first established in 1442, had emerged as a principal agency for military finance. In the late 1480s, the silver stocks of the Taicang Treasury reached 800,000 taels, and by 1502 the annual quota of silver revenues delivered to the Taicang Treasury was set at 1 million taels. It seems that it was at this time that the commutations of tax quotas to silver payments inaugurated by Zhou Chen became fixed assessments. During the 16th century, the importance of the Taicang Treasury in state finance steadily increased, and total silver outlays for the northern garrisons rose to over 8 million taels in 1582.[63]

59 *MSL*, Yingzong 15.10a, 21.6b; see also Huang Aming, *Huobi baiyinhua*, p. 104. Wan Ming and Noa Grass contend that this commutation was a temporary expedient that did not become a permanent policy. See Wan, "Baiyin huobihua," pp. 46–49; Grass, "Imperial Silver Laundering," pp. 20–22. But the problem it was meant to address certainly was a perennial issue.

60 *DMHD* 30.1a. Since at this time silver had become the standard unit of account, henceforward in this chapter I will translate *liang* (the unit of weight) as "tael" (the standard term for silver as a unit of account) when citing fiscal records.

61 Wan, "Baiyin huobihua"; Grass, "Imperial Silver Laundering."

62 Huang Aming, *Huobi baiyinhua*, pp. 193–213.

63 On military finance in the 16th century, see Lai Jiancheng 赖建诚, *Bianzhen liangxiang: Mingdai zhonghouqi de bianfang jingfei yu guojia caizheng weiji, 1531–1602* 边镇粮饷: 明代中后期的边防经费与国家财政危机 (Hangzhou: Zhejiang daxue chubanshe, 2010). On the Taicang Treasury, see Su Xinhong 蘇新红, *Taicangku yu Mingdai caizheng*

It was the swelling cost of frontier defense amid the collapse of the self-sustaining military farms created by the dynastic founder that propelled the silverization of Ming public finance. The emergence of the Taicang Treasury as the main agency for military finance in the 1480s was a key turning point in this shift. Silver also became a mainstay of the salt monopoly from this time. In 1492, the Ministry of Revenue formally began to allow merchants to exchange silver for salt licenses. Purchases of salt licenses in silver had become a frequent practice during the previous twenty years. Henceforth the government in effect abandoned the *kaizhong* policy of awarding salt licenses to merchants who delivered provisions to frontier garrisons, although sale of salt licenses for silver payments only became fully institutionalized in 1527.[64]

A parallel transformation of in-kind exactions to silver payments can also be observed in labor service duties. The breakdown of the *lijia* system of village governance made it increasingly difficult to impose labor service assignments. As evasion of labor service worsened, local officials responded by shifting the basis for service assignments from household registration to property ownership. This practice, which originated as the initiative of a provincial official in Jiangxi in the 1440s, was widely adopted after 1450 and culminated in the creation of an empire-wide system of "equalized service" (*junyao* 均徭) in 1488. In many places, the institutionalization of "equalized service" was accompanied by the conversion of some service duties, especially for poorer households, into silver payments, creating a distinction between those who performed labor service in person (*lichai* 力差) and those who simply made payments in silver (*yinchai* 銀差).[65]

During the 16th century, the conversion of labor services into silver payments became more and more widespread. Again at the initiative of local authorities, the various types of labor service obligations were consolidated into a single payment in silver at uniform rates. In some cases, land taxes assessed in grain also were commuted to silver payments and combined with the service duty payments. These reforms came to be known collectively as the "single-whip" policy (*yitiaobian fa* 一條鞭法). During the 1570s, the chief grand secretary Zhang Juzheng promoted the single-whip reforms as part of his broader agenda of strengthening the central bureaucracy's control over resources and revenues. Still, implementation of the single-whip model varied

zhidu yanbian yanjiu 太仓库与明代财政制度演变研究 (Beijing: Zhongguo shehui kexue chubanshe, 2021).

64 Puk, *Rise and Fall*, pp. 47–50.

65 Yukio Yamane, "Reforms in the Service Levy System in the Fifteenth and Sixteenth Centuries," in Linda Grove and Christian Daniels (eds.), *State and Society in China: Japanese Perspectives on Ming–Qing Social and Economic History* (Tokyo: University of Tokyo Press, 1984), pp. 279–310; R. Huang, *Taxation and Governmental Finance*, pp. 109–33.

from region to region. Even if the single-whip reforms did not establish a uniform tax system, their main features – the replacement of highly variable demands for labor service with fixed and uniform rates; the conversion of labor services into silver payments; assessments primarily based on property rather than persons; and entrusting administration of the tax system to county-level officials rather than *lijia* headmen – constituted a fundamental break with the original Ming fiscal regime.[66] By the time the tide of single-whip reforms crested during Zhang Juzheng's administration, a substantial portion of state revenues had been converted to silver payments. Ray Huang estimated that over 80 percent of the land tax had been converted to silver payments, and total silver revenues reached the range of 30–35 million taels.[67] However, Huang did not have access to the *Record of National Accounts of the Wanli Era*, compiled under Zhang Juzheng's direction and published in 1582. Although the figures in the *National Accounts* are incomplete, the compilers reported that the annual revenues received from commuted tax payments amounted to 14.61 million taels, while expenditures exceeded 15.31 million taels.[68] These figures fall significantly below Huang's estimates, but they confirm that silver had become the monetary standard of imperial fiscal administration.

9.4 Transition to the Silver Economy

The silverization of state finance was a gradual, piecemeal process. An important threshold was crossed in the 1480s with the pivot toward financing frontier garrisons out of the central government's silver reserves and the adoption of the "equalized service" reforms, although the real surge in commutation of taxes to silver payments occurred in the mid 16th century. In adopting silver as the monetary standard for its fiscal administration, Ming state policy was driven by the predominance of silver in market trade.[69]

Following the evisceration of the value of the *baochao* paper currency in the first quarter of the 15th century and the inadequate supply of coin, silver remained the only viable option as a means of commercial exchange. By any measure – gold, grain, paper currency, or coin – the value of silver peaked during the first seventy years of the Ming dynasty. However, Adachi Keiji has suggested that the "coin economy" that flourished during the Tang and Song dynasties still held sway over the early Ming. Adachi emphasized the high and stable value that coin commanded during the first century of the Ming while

66 Fang-chung Liang, *The Single-Whip Method of Taxation in China* (Cambridge, MA: Harvard University Press, 1956).

67 R. Huang, *Taxation and Governmental Finance*, pp. 175, 213, 263.

68 *KJL* 1.23a.

69 On this point, see also Wan, "Baiyin huobihua."

dismissing paper currency as a limited form of money, required as payment for certain taxes but worthless as a medium of exchange, at least after its rapid depreciation in the 1390s. In his view, silver did not fully assume the functions traditionally performed by coin until the turn of the 16th century.[70]

Given the limits of the available evidence it is difficult to determine the relative prevalence of the various types of money as instruments of market exchange in the early Ming. Adachi points out that the 1397 edict banning the use of precious metals in trade merely states that the populace had used silver as a measure of value without specifying the actual means of payment. It does not follow from this, however, that coin was used in this capacity. Other documents, though still cryptically worded, suggest that in fact silver and paper currency were the most common forms of commercial exchange, as in this excerpt from a report of 1404: "among the people both silver and bills are in use, but the exchange value of silver is high, while that of paper currency is low."[71] "Use" here almost certainly refers to market transactions. It is likely that the author of this memorial was referring to large-scale trade rather than petty commerce, and coin undoubtedly still figured significantly in local markets. But only in the provinces of the southern littoral – Fujian, Guangdong, and Guangxi – does coin seem to have prevailed as the dominant medium of exchange.[72] Over the course of Yongle's reign, as the value of *baochao* plummeted, paper currency ceased to be used in private trade. In 1425, fiscal officials conceded that market transactions were conducted solely using silver, silk, and cotton cloth as means of exchange.[73] The authors of the Ming dynastic history would later write that by the time of Zhengtong's enthronement in 1435 "as a rule, in the capital and the countryside, everyone used silver, although petty trade was conducted in coin."[74]

The relative importance of the various monies circulating in early Ming China can be given some quantitative measurement by examining the corpus

70 Adachi Keiji 足立啓二, "Min Shin jidai ni okeru senkeizai no hatten" 明清時代における銭経済の発展, in Chūgokushi kenkyūkai (ed.), *Chūgoku sensei kokka to shakai tōgō* 中国専制国家と社会統合 (Kyoto: Bunrikaku, 1990), p. 393.

71 *MSL*, Taizong 29.2b.

72 Maeda, who strongly emphasized the primacy of Yuan paper currency as a medium of exchange, acknowledged that paper bills failed to establish a foothold in Fujian, Guangdong, and Guangxi; see Maeda, *Genchō shi*, p. 76. A 1436 memorial stated that coin was the primary medium of exchange in Guangdong and Guangxi: see *MSL*, Yingzong 12.5b. Another report from 1432 testified that both coin and silver circulated together in Guangdong, Guangxi, and Fujian; see "Guoshi sharen jiaozui. . ." 過失殺人絞罪 . . ., in Dai Jin 戴金 (ed.), *Huang Ming tiaofa shilei zuan* 皇明條法事類纂 ([hereafter *TFSL*]; undated ms.; rpt. Taipei: Wenhai chubanshe, 1985), 1, p. 6. Qiu Jun, writing in the late 15th century, asserted that the only provinces in which coin prevailed in the early Ming were Fujian, Guangdong, and Guangxi; see *DXYYB* 27.16a.

73 *MSL*, Renzong 6B.6a.

74 *MS* 81.1964.

Table 9.1 *Means of payment in Huizhou land sale contracts prior to 1500 (I)*

Reign period	*Baochao*	Grain	Cloth	Silver	Total
Hongwu 1368–1398	37	6	—	5	48
Jianwen 1399–1402	7	11	—	4	22
Yongle 1403–1425	84	14	3	1	102
Hongxi 1425	4	1	1	—	6
Xuande 1426–1436	9	9	21	1	40
Zhengtong 1436–1450	—	7	12	35	54
Jingtai 1450–1457	—	1	2	27	30
Tianshun 1457–1464	—	2	—	31	33
Chenghua 1465–1480	—	—	—	90	90
Total, 1368–1480	141	51	39	194	425

Source: Wan Ming, "Mingdai baiyin huobihuade chubu kaochao," 40–1.

of land sale contracts from Huizhou prefecture (Anhui), one of the most commercially developed areas in the empire. Li Ruoyu has vividly demonstrated the extent of silver's dominance in the Chinese economy after 1450: in every one of the 836 Huizhou contracts dating from 1456 to 1644 the sale price was denominated and paid in silver.[75] Moreover, the 425 contracts that antedate 1480, tabulated by Wan Ming (Table 9.1), offer valuable insight into the shifting preferences among different currencies in the early Ming period. Wan Ming aggregated her data by reign period, an arbitrary unit that obscures some of the correlations between the trends that emerge from the contracts and new departures in monetary policy. I have used the published collection of documents drawn from the archives examined by Wan to present the data in decennial aggregates in Table 9.2. However, because the published collection contains only two-fifths of the contracts Wan tabulates, I have also provided her cruder aggregates in Table 9.1.

From the time the Ming began to issue *baochao* in 1375 down to the end of Yongle's reign (1424), the great majority of the Huizhou land sales were contracted in paper currency. During the years 1396–1405, a period in which paper currency suffered ruinous depreciation, *baochao* were displaced by a commodity money, grain, as the favored means of payment. However, in one-third of the contracts from this decade that specified grain as the means of payment the sale price was given in *baochao*, implying that the paper currency served as the measure of value. Conversely, in half of the six cases in which silver was used as the means of payment the price of the land was fixed in grain

[75] Li Ruoyu 李若愚, "Cong Mingdaide qiyue kan Mingdai de bizhi" 从明代的契约看明代的币制, *Zhongguo jingji shi yanjiu* 中国经济史研究 1988.4: 39–43.

Table 9.2 *Means of payment in Huizhou land sale contracts prior to 1500 (II)*

Period	*Baochao*	Grain	Cloth	Silver	Total
1368–1375	—	—	—	2	2
1376–1385	5	—	—	—	5
1386–1395	9	—	—	—	9
1396–1405	8	15	—	6	29
1406–1415	9	—	1	—	10
1416–1425	11	2	2	—	15
1426–1435	1	5	11	1	18
1436–1445	—	3	1	8	12
1446–1455	—	3	2	12	17
1456–1500	—	1	—	51	52
Total, 1368–1500	43	29	17	80	169

Source: Anhuisheng bowuguan, *Ming Qing Huizhou shehui jingji ziliao congbian*, vol. 1.

and then converted to a silver equivalent for payment. While *baochao* rebounded somewhat in the first quarter of the 15th century, confidence in paper currency clearly evaporated after 1425, and people turned to commodities like grain and silk as both measures of value and means of payment. Once the state indicated its de facto acceptance of silver for some tax payments in the mid 1430s, silver quickly displaced all other currencies, and by 1450 the silver monetary standard was firmly entrenched.

The most striking finding that emerges from these documents is the utter absence of coin: none of the land contracts refer to coin as either a measure of value or a means of payment. Of course, we must keep in mind that very substantial quantities of coin would be needed for large transactions such as land purchases, and the absence of coin in these contracts does not preclude the likely probability that coin was commonly used in petty commerce.[76] It is also interesting to note that land prices were still calculated in *baochao* even after the drastic depreciation of paper currency had reduced its market value

[76] To be sure, the bulk and low unit value of bronze coins, while hindrances for the purposes of long-distance trade, were by no means obstacles to their use in land transactions. In the 18th century, when coin was both abundant and rising in value relative to silver, there was a decisive shift toward transacting land sales in coin in the highly commercialized Jiangnan region. The coin presumably was on deposit in local banks, and thus these sales were essentially giro paper transactions between bank accounts. See Kishimoto Mio 岸本美緒, *Shindai Chūgoku no bukka to keizai hendō* 清代中国の物価と経済変動 (Tokyo: Kembun shuppan, 1997), pp. 353–63; Kuroda Akinobu 黒田明伸, "Kenryū no senki" 乾隆の銭貴, *Tōyōshi kenkyū* 東洋史研究 45.5 (1987): 692–723.

to a mere fraction of its nominal value; 80 percent of the contracts from 1405 to 1425 were denominated in paper money. Since these contracts were subject to public scrutiny, it is conceivable that the parties involved felt obliged to employ paper currency values to remain on the right side of the law. The disappearance of silver from land contracts between 1375, when the ban on the use of silver was first enacted, and 1435 may reflect mere legal subterfuge, and perhaps many sales actually were paid for in silver. (Tellingly, the two contracts that antedated the anti-silver legislation of 1375 were both denominated in silver.) But for these contracts to have any binding power, paper currency at least had to serve as a money of account and measure of value. It appears that in the early Ming paper currency – however depreciated in value – continued to serve as a monetary standard. But, from the 1430s, silver displaced the *baochao* paper currency from land transactions, no doubt a reflection of more general trends in market exchange.

In 1436, the minister of revenue, Huang Fu, offered a strategy for resuscitating paper currency that ignored the anti-silver legislation still in force and conceded the necessity of using silver as a reserve to maintain the value of paper money:

> Originally paper bills and bronze coins jointly served as currency. In the Hongwu period [1368–1398], 1 *liang* of silver was equivalent to 3–5 *guan* of paper money, yet today 1 *liang* of silver is worth more than 1,000 *guan*. The paper currency system has utterly failed. I recommend dispatching officials bearing silver from the state treasuries to the two capitals and to the entrepôts in the various prefectural seats to buy up the old bills at prevailing market rates. At the close of the year, the old bills will be transmitted to the capital. Then, when the old bills have disappeared from circulation, we can issue new bills in appropriate quantities and exchange them for silver, which will be remitted to the capital.[77]

Although Huang was careful to emphasize that the state would recover its stocks of silver after the new bills were put in circulation, he admitted the need to establish specie convertibility to inspire confidence in paper currency. No action was taken on his proposal, but the expression of such views from a fiscal adviser of Huang's stature signaled a significant concession to the primacy of silver as the standard of value.

Primarily concerned with the failure of paper money as a means of exchange, writers on political economy paid scant attention to the fact that *baochao* proved even more disastrous as a store of value. This myopia is evident in the views of Liu Dingzhi, who addressed the failings of the Ming monetary system in a collection of examination essays on statecraft he composed in 1434, two years before Liu achieved third place in the *jinshi*

[77] *MSL*, Yingzong 15.9b–10a.

examination and embarked on his official career. Liu departed from the standard premise of theoretical chartalism that money lacks intrinsic value by asserting that money indeed has a utility value, which in turn is a function of its physical characteristics and relative scarcity. Thus Liu observed that different monies have different values. Liu championed the use of paper currency, stressing that it does not suffer from the physical limitations of coin and commodity monies, whose utility is circumscribed by the inconvenience of transporting them. He advocated the restoration of a prudent monetary policy that restricted the quantity of paper currency and once again made paper bills convertible with silver. Liu's prescription for reviving paper currency largely focused on the need to collect revenues in *baochao*. In a revealing passage, he states that at present paper bills "accumulate in the houses of great merchants, immune from taxation," while "poor folk are forced to sell their lands and pawn their wives and children, and then pay the state [presumably Liu was speaking of the salt ration payments and/or the stamp tax on deeds and contracts] in paper currency." Liu here simply intended to underscore his point that only a few sundry taxes were collected in paper currency, and the burden of these taxes fell on those who could least afford to pay. Yet his statement also implies that the rich possessed substantial savings in the form of paper currency. All other evidence indicates otherwise. The depreciation of paper currency in fact resulted from the inadequacy of paper bills as a store of value. Wealthy individuals instead preferred to hold silver, coin, or commodities such as grain and silk that retained value over time. Liu erred in thinking that the state could maintain control over the exchange values of different forms of money simply by regulating their quantities.[78]

A similar oversight is evident in the writings of Qiu Jun, whose 1487 work, *Supplement to the Extended Meanings of the Great Learning*, had a profound impact on statecraft thought in the latter half of the Ming era. In his essays on money, Qiu Jun only considered money as a store of value in the limited sense of its imperishability: whereas commodities like grain are subject to the vicissitudes of harvests, money endures through flood or drought and, alone among commodities, its quantity can be regulated directly by the state. Qiu began his treatise with a study of the origins of money in which he reiterated the claim found in the *Guan Zi* that the sages invented money specifically to provide a means whereby the ruler can secure the welfare of his subjects in times of dearth. He extolled the fluid quality of money and its ability to draw goods to the places where they are most needed without the intervention of the state. Qiu subscribed to the chartalist view that money lacks intrinsic value; like Liu Dingzhi, he assumed that the value of money can be modulated by

[78] Liu Dingzhi 劉定之, *Liu wenan gong daizhai xiansheng celüe* 劉文安公呆齋先生策略 (1594 ed., rpt. in Siku quanshu cunmu congshu), 6.17a–22a; 10.1a–4b; the quoted passage appears on 10.4a. See also Peng, *Zhongguo huobi shi*, pp. 729–31.

regulating its quantity. Although writing at a time when the *baochao* had disappeared from the marketplace, Qiu insisted that paper currency remained a viable medium of exchange. Echoing Liu Dingzhi's warnings against attempting to create a purely fiat money, he insisted that bills can function effectively as long as they are backed by and convertible with reserves of bullion.[79]

Qiu Jun concluded his treatise by proposing a tripartite currency system in which silver would serve as the "superior currency" (*shangbi* 上幣) and yet be relegated to the largely ceremonial role of providing a standard of value. Qiu envisioned that silver would be permitted as a means of payment only in transactions of no less than 10 *liang*, an amount greater than the average farming household's annual income. Paper bills and coin would circulate as the media of exchange for large and small transactions respectively. This proposal reveals Qiu's belief, shared with Liu Dingzhi, that the value of a given currency can be regulated simply by controlling its quantity. By manipulating the ratios of exchange and ensuring that the paper currency in circulation is backed by reserves of coin and silver, the government could fix and, if necessary, adjust the value of each form of money: "If the quantity of silver, coin, and bills used in trade is fixed and maintained in perpetuity, [these monies] will circulate for a hundred generations and permeate every corner of the world. If this can be done, the state's revenue base can be secured, and the abuse of misappropriation of revenue can be avoided. The will of the people will not be thwarted, and . . . sojourning merchants and local shopkeepers alike can avoid losses due to moneychanging."[80] Qiu Jun considered bronze coin to be the most perfect money, in part because of its fungibility, but primarily because the ruler could, within certain limits, control its quantity. The stock of gold and silver, by contrast, was determined by Heaven (i.e., nature) and could not be augmented by human devices.[81] Despite his repeated emphasis on the ruler's supreme authority as the arbiter of exchange values, Qiu implied that there is a natural equilibrium in the relative values of the different forms of money. He proposed the following formula: 1 *liang* of silver equals 1,000 coins or 100 *guan* of paper money.[82] While Qiu's formula retained the presumed natural correspondence of 1:1000 between the values of silver and coin, he capitulated to the market's low esteem of paper money. Even so, his proposed devaluation of paper currency, to 1 percent of its nominal value, still would have cried up paper bills to ten times their current market value.[83]

79 *DXYYB*, chapters 26 and 27.
80 *DXYYB* 27.17a.
81 *DXYYB* 26.11b.
82 *DXYYB* 27.16b.
83 Peng, *Zhongguo huobi shi*, p. 671.

Qiu described his plan for monetary reform as a strategy to ensure "sufficient [revenue] for the state and convenience for the people (*zuguo bianmin* 足國便民)."[84] It is clear from the whole of his treatise that he understood "convenience for the people" in terms of satisfying the needs of consumers and petty trade. While Qiu Jun's tripartite currency system displayed an awareness of the different functions of money, Qiu remained in the mainstream of monetary thought, attending to the exchange functions of money while largely ignoring its crucial significance as a store of value. Qiu's formula also shows that he accepted the long-standing assumptions about currency as an instrument of state finance and specifically as a means of facilitating the collection of revenue. Since Qiu addressed his work to the policymakers of his day, for whom stabilizing and augmenting the state's revenue was a paramount concern, it is hardly surprising that he sought to reassure his audience that currency reform, in addition to lubricating the wheels of private commerce, would benefit the state by increasing revenues.

Qiu Jun's tripartite currency system was intended to resuscitate the moribund *baochao* and restore coin as a fractional currency. Yet what is most notable in Qiu's analysis is the central role of silver as a measure of value. Instead of leading to a rejuvenation of paper currency, his work attested to the dominance of silver and heralded the onset of the silver economy. The statesmen and theorists who succeeded Qiu abandoned paper money altogether. Instead, they sought to reassert the ruler's prerogatives in the economic sphere by restoring coin to its former role as the foundation of the monetary system.

Despite his faith in the utility of paper currency in market exchange, Qiu Jun conceded that "since the Tianshun era [1457–1464] the use of *baochao* has steadily diminished."[85] The monetary situation of Qiu's time can be glimpsed in the memoirs of a contemporary, the Suzhou native Lu Rong (1436–1494), who attested to silver's eclipse of both coin and paper currency. Lu observed that Hongwu coins had completely disappeared from circulation. He had seen some of them in his youth, Lu wrote, but they were long gone, presumably melted down to make copper utensils (or, more likely, recast as private coin). As for *baochao*, "nowadays only government offices utilize them. One *guan* of *baochao* is worth only 1 *li* [i.e., 0.001 *liang*] of silver, or two bronze coins. If ordinary people happen to obtain a paper bill, they toss it away as worthless."[86] The Beijing constabulary reported in 1465 that in recent years "generally speaking in buying and selling and purchases of firewood and rice, tradesmen and shopkeepers will only accept silver in exchange; because of

84 *DXYYB* 27.16b.
85 *DXYYB* 27.16a.
86 Lu Rong 陸容, *Shuyuan zaji* 菽園雜記 (Beijing: Zhonghua shuju, 1985), 10.123.

this, both coin and bills stagnate and fail to circulate."[87] With the *baochao* steeply discounted and the quality of bronze coin deteriorating, silver remained the only viable means of exchange and payment.

The adoption of silver as the means of exchange and payment in both the private and public sectors was constrained by the limited supply of domestic silver. Much of the silver that had circulated in China during the Song dynasty had drained off to western Asia during the Mongol epoch, and Ming mines produced only meager amounts of new ore. Fortuitously, however, the global silver supply increased dramatically during the 16th century. In Japan, discovery of the rich silver lode at Iwami in the 1520s sparked a surge in mining, with most of the silver exported to satisfy the ravenous demand for money in China. Discovery of the world's richest silver deposit at Potosí in the highlands of Peru by Spanish conquistadors in 1545 triggered an even greater silver boom, and silver mining quickly became the mainstay of Spain's colonial empire. Some Peruvian silver began to reach China as early as the 1550s, carried by Portuguese ships traversing the Indian Ocean from Europe. The lucrative profits garnered by shipping silver to China was the main motive for the founding of Spain's colony at Manila in the Philippines in 1571. Subsequently Spanish galleons embarking from Mexico carried silver destined for the Chinese market across the Pacific Ocean to Manila, creating the world's first truly global trade network.[88]

According to my conservative estimate, China imported nearly fifty tons of foreign silver a year during the second half of the 16th century. In the first half of the 17th century, silver imports – roughly equally divided between Japanese and Spanish American sources – rose to an annual average of nearly 120 tons, twenty times greater than the production of domestic mines.[89] The massive infusion of silver lubricated the wheels of commerce, spurring an unprecedented monetization of the Chinese economy and fostering prodigious growth of commercial cities and market towns. Production for the market – notably

87 *TFSL*, 1, p. 343.

88 This is a well-known story, which I will only briefly summarize here. For details, see Dennis O. Flynn and Arturo Giráldez, "Born with a 'Silver Spoon': The Origin of World Trade in 1571," *Journal of World History* 6.2 (1995): 201–21; von Glahn, *Fountain of Fortune*, pp. 113–41; Dennis O. Flynn and Arturo Giráldez, *China and the Birth of Globalization in the Sixteenth Century* (Aldershot, UK: Ashgate Variorum, 2010); von Glahn, "Cycles of Silver"; Arturo Giráldez, *The Age of Trade: The Manila Galleons and the Dawn of the Global Economy* (Lanham, MD: Rowman and Littlefield, 2015); Kris Lane, *Potosí: The Silver City That Changed the World* (Berkeley: University of California Press, 2019).

89 Von Glahn, *Fountain of Fortune*, p. 140, table 13. Other estimates generally are higher. See von Glahn, "Cycles of Silver," p. 32, table 2.6.

cotton and silk textiles – also transformed the rural economy, drawing many villagers into regional and national networks of exchange.[90]

The changes wrought by the silver-fueled commercial expansion of the late Ming period were vividly epitomized in an essay entitled "The Changing Times," composed in 1610 by Xu Dunqiu (b. 1541), a native of the market town of Yuanhua on the north shore of Hangzhou Bay. Although Xu's philippic fulminates against the decay of social customs, it also captures the manifold ways in which silver had infiltrated the Jiangnan economy:

> In my youth, around 1555 or 1556, there was only a single pawnshop in the town, owned by Zheng Zidong from [the nearby town of] Wangdian. Around that time the "Japanese pirate" troubles flared up, and then even Zheng moved away. Now there are fourteen or fifteen pawnshops in the town. The pawnshops collectively take in some 20,000 silver *liang* per month, all of which comes from the purses of households within ten *li* [5.6 km] of the town....
>
> In those days, there were five or six families whose landholdings amounted to 1,000 *mu* [172 acres]. Today, only a single family owns as much as 300 *mu*. I estimate that eight or nine out of ten households have descended from affluence to destitution within my lifetime, and only one or two out of ten have emerged from poverty to taste prosperity....
>
> In comparing the present with the past, nothing is more remarkable than the spread of mulberries and silkworms. Originally, Yuanhua had few mulberry trees; perhaps one or two in ten households raised them, and even those had no more than one or two *mu*. Now the entire landscape is covered with mulberries, and tenant farmers even plant several dozen trees on the dikes separating the rice paddies. Each spring they earn two or three silver *liang*, enough to cover the costs of seeding and transplanting rice....
>
> In the past, the dye-shops would allow customers to have several dozen pieces dyed before settling accounts and charging them. Moreover, you could pay them with rice, wheat, soybeans, chickens, or other fowl. Now, when you have your cloth dyed you receive a bill, which must be paid with silver borrowed from a pawnshop. The dye-shop will return your silk or cotton cloth only if you pay them in *qiaosi* [敲絲, literally "hammered threads," a slang term for the highest-grade silver].[91]

[90] For synopses of commercial growth in the late Ming period, see von Glahn, *Economic History of China*, pp. 295–312; Timothy Brook, *The Confusions of Pleasure: Commerce and Culture in Ming China* (Berkeley: University of California Press, 1998).

[91] Xu Dunqiu 許敦俅, "Ji shibian" 紀世變, in *Jingsuo biji* 敬所筆記, unpublished ms. transcribed in Chen Xuewen 陈学文, "'Jingsuo biji' xiaoxu," '敬所筆記' 小序, *Minsu yanjiu* 民俗研究 1989.4: 62–64.

Wedded to the notion that landholding was the only true measure of wealth, Xu repeatedly conjoined commercial vitality, and the ostentatious consumption it fostered, with latent penury. He also testified to a significant shift in investment: away from arable land and toward intensive cash-crop cultivation, moneylending, and processing industries. The ubiquity of silver in every aspect of rural families' livelihood to which Xu bore witness bespoke a crucial transformation of the Chinese economy.

9.5 The Demise of Chartalist Monetary Theory

Most contemporaries would heartily agree with Xu Dunqiu's dire predictions of the poverty portended by the growth of the silver economy. Many statesmen warned that the supply of silver, given its foreign origins, was unstable and called for a return to a sound bronze currency as the monetary standard. Persuaded by this argument, Zhang Juzheng undertook a vigorous campaign to resuscitate coinage even as his regime institutionalized silver as the money of account in state finances. In 1576, Zhang reopened the state mints to produce high-quality coins in the name of the Wanli emperor (r. 1572–1620). But Zhang's monetary offensive stalled when cheap private imitations flooded the market. Repeated efforts to revive coinage during the remainder of the Ming dynasty failed to dislodge either silver or private coin from their dominance in the marketplace.[92]

The continuing erosion of the quality of coin prompted consideration of ever more desperate remedies, including the return to paper currency. In 1629, the head of the Nanjing Ministry of Revenue, Lü Weiqi, assailed the growing dependence on silver and advocated enactment of Qiu Jun's tripartite currency system. Yet even though Lü denounced the prevalence of silver, he anticipated that paper money would make only modest inroads on silver's dominion. He merely proposed that paper bills replace silver in large transactions of more than 2.5 *liang*, and even then only 20 percent of the payment would be required in bills, with the rest paid in silver. Moreover, Lü indirectly acknowledged the supremacy of silver as the standard of value by recommending that the new paper notes be denominated in *liang* (i.e., the silver unit) rather than in *guan* (the unit for coin), as the *baochao* were.[93]

Lü's proposal was ignored, and most late Ming statecraft writers opposed reviving paper currency. Zhang Sui began his treatise on money, published in 1633, with a peremptory dismissal of paper currency, citing the ruinous experiments of the Yuan and early Ming as sufficient proof that paper

92 On the efforts by Zhang and others to reestablish a full-bodied bronze currency, see von Glahn, *Fountain of Fortune*, pp. 142–72.

93 "Tiaoyi chaofa jie" 條議鈔法揭, in Lü Weiqi 呂維祺, *Lü mingde xiansheng shendutang ji* 呂明德先生慎獨堂集 (1652), 2.9b–12b.

currency was fundamentally worthless. Zhang, an avowed metallist, vehemently proclaimed the viability of full-bodied coin.[94] A somewhat different approach, but one that also spurned paper money in favor of revitalizing coinage, was adumbrated in a series of essays written in the mid 1630s by another statecraft scholar, Zhang Shichun. Zhang agreed with the consensus opinion that the inelastic supply of silver rendered it unsuitable as the principal form of currency. In Zhang's view, the "scarcity" of silver had caused a doubling of prices denominated in silver over "the past ten-odd years," while the value of coin had depreciated by an additional 30 percent. Yet Zhang also blamed inflation on stagnating production, which resulted in a scarcity of goods. He argued that inflation could be eased only by increasing grain output and relying more extensively on coin in state finances. The chief virtue of silver, to Zhang's way of thinking, was its utility as a means of remittance, and he recommended issuing silver coins in denominations of 100 and 1,000 *wen* to facilitate long-distance transfers of funds. But Zhang adamantly opposed a reversion to paper money.[95]

An intermediate position on monetary policy began to emerge in the 1630s that rejected the prevailing obsession with the problem of silver. According to what we might call the "physiocratic school," best exemplified by the polymath statesman Xu Guangqi, contemporary political economy erred in confusing silver, or money in any form, with wealth. In his *Omnibus of Husbandry*, published posthumously in 1640, Xu argued that the only true forms of wealth were goods that satisfied the elemental needs of food, clothing, and shelter:

> If one wishes to discuss wealth, it is first necessary to distinguish what we mean by "wealth." In the Tang and Song dynasties, the meaning of "wealth" was restricted to bronze coin. In the present age, by contrast, "wealth" is presumed to mean nothing but silver. But neither coin nor silver are wealth; rather, they are merely levers of wealth [*cai zhi quan* 財之權]. When the ancient sage-kings spoke of wealth, they meant grain for feeding the people and cloth for clothing them. Thus it is said, "The Great Way of generating wealth lies in multiplying those who produce it."[96] Now if silver and coin constitute wealth, will increasing the quantity of silver and coin result in prosperity? In the case of a single family, the

94 "Qianfa kao" 錢法攷, "Qianfa geyan" 錢法格言, and "Qianfa biyu sizhu" 錢法弊於私鑄, in Zhang Sui 張燧, *Jingshi qieyao* 經世挈要 (BTZB rpt. of 1633 Fuchangchen ed.), 20.29a–30a, 30a–31a, 35b–36a.

95 "Zhong qianfa yi zu caiyong" 重錢法以足財用 and "Qianbo" 錢帛, in Zhang Shichun 章世純, *Zhiping yaolüe xu* 治平要略續 ([Chongzhen] Zhangshi sizhong ed.), shang 上, 50a–56a, 57a–59a.

96 Xu here paraphrased the *Great Learning*, one of the foundational texts of Neo-Confucian ideology: "There is a Great Way of creating wealth: let its producers be numerous and its consumers few" (生財有大道,生之者眾,食之者寡). See "Daxue" 大學, in *Liji zhengyi* 禮記正義 60, in *SSJZS*, 2, p. 1675b.

> answer to this question is yes; but if we consider the entire empire, then nothing could be further from the truth. The greater the quantity of silver and coin, the more expensive grain and cloth become, and the more severe is the dearth that ensues. Therefore, in earlier ages rulers feared that future generations would want not for lack of silver and coin but rather for lack of grain and cloth.[97]

Xu maintained that the quantity of money was irrelevant as an index of wealth, but he also recognized that changes in the quantity of money could have serious economic repercussions. The real problem was not a scarcity of money but a scarcity of goods. Xu attributed the rapid inflation of his day to both depreciation of money and demographic pressure on the land: "When times of peace endure for a lengthy period, the population grows and multiplies. If the numbers of people increase and yet they are unable to produce more grain, the reason must lie in the fact that the potential of the land has not been fully utilized." In Xu's view, demographic pressure could be alleviated by shifting the surplus population to underdeveloped areas. While the southern provinces of South Zhili, Zhejiang, and Fujian suffered from acute overpopulation, the lands of the arid north and west lay fallow for want of sufficient labor to build irrigation works. The most urgent priority, then, was to invest in irrigation systems to reclaim potentially productive lands and thereby augment the wealth of the empire.

A similar challenge to contemporaries' focus on the presumed scarcity of silver was raised by Song Yingxing, the author of the renowned encyclopedia of technology, *Exploitation of the Works of Nature*. In an essay published in 1636, Song, like Xu Guangxi, denied that money could be equated with wealth:

> Wealth in principle refers to the various and sundry goods. By no means should wealth be regarded as exclusively referring to money. How can it be that today in the empire there is a scarcity of silver! Rather, we suffer from shortages of fields cultivated with the five grains, mountain forests thick with timber, hillocks of mulberry, and ponds brimming with fish. If the empire abounds in these things, then silver and gold can be summoned in an instant; merchants carrying satchels and money-belts bulging with bullion will trample each other in their rush to come and trade.

Song thus echoed Xu's view that goods, not precious metals, constitute wealth. Money can serve as a substitute for wealth, but generating more money does not produce wealth. Instead, Song invoked a labor theory of value, one that was central to his conception of technology: while wealth is created by Heaven, it is only through human effort that the raw wealth existing in nature can be

[97] Xu Guangqi 徐光啟, Shi Shenghan 石聲漢 (ed.), *Nongzheng quanshu jiaozhu* 農政全書校注, ([hereafter *NZQS*]; Shanghai: Shanghai guji chubanshe, 1979), 16.399.

put to productive use. Like Xu, too, Song viewed overpopulation as the chief cause of poverty. But in tracing the causes of economic distress, he placed even more emphasis on moral failings, most notably the temptation of credit. Song castigated the wealthy for exploiting the toiling masses through usury, but he was equally harsh in his condemnation of the money economy for corrupting popular mores. Because of the ready availability of credit, farming folk succumbed to the temptation to borrow, indulging themselves with meat and wine while neglecting their tasks. Falling ever deeper in debt, farmers began to realize that hard work brought only greater misery, and they abandoned farming altogether. Song's labor theory of value led him to the conclusion that the putative decline in agricultural output resulted from a diminution in the intensity of labor. Song thus failed to capitalize on his insights into the nature of money and the problem of demographic pressure, instead lapsing into a conventional diatribe against the pernicious effects of the money economy.[98]

In a series of essays written in the 1630s and 1640s, the statecraft activist and prosperous landowner Chen Longzheng reiterated Xu Guangqi's thesis that the economic challenge confronting the Ming was not a dearth of silver but a crisis of production. Chen, like Xu, chastised his contemporaries for "misunderstanding the concept of wealth" and "confusing silver with prosperity": "If the whole empire devotes itself to husbandry, the quantity of grain will increase, and the demand for money will abate. What need is there to increase the supply of money? If the whole empire devotes itself to mulberry cultivation and silk weaving, then the quantity of cloth will increase, and silver produced in foreign lands will flow into China through trade. How can the supply of money not increase?" Chen warned against the veiled dangers of a silver economy. The utility of silver resided in its convenience as a store of value, the ease with which it could be converted from savings to consumption and vice versa, and its imperishability. But in Chen's view, these qualities in fact were vices. In essence, Chen argued that the superiority of silver as a store of value impeded its utility as a means of exchange. Use of silver inevitably invited hoarding, resulting in shortages of circulating media and disruption of commerce. Thus while the supply of silver was irrelevant to the question of generating wealth, the use of silver as money had deleterious consequences.[99]

Nonetheless, the persistent deterioration of coin, both standard and private, prompted some scholars to reconsider controversial measures like paper money to remedy the ailing currency system. Among them was Chen

[98] "Mincai yi" 民財議, in Song Yingxing 宋應星, *Yeyi* 野議 (1636), rpt. in Song, *Yeyi, Lunqi, Tantian, Silianshi* 野議, 論氣, 談天, 思憐詩 (Shanghai: Shanghai renmin chubanshe, 1976), pp. 9–11.

[99] Chen Longzheng 陳龍正, *Jiting quanshu* 幾亭全書 (1665), 12.8a–9a; 13.21b–22a; 51.21a–22a.

Zilong, who invoked Xu Guangqi's notion that money is merely a measure of value to argue in favor of reinstituting paper currency. In his 1640 introduction to Xu's *Omnibus of Husbandry*, which Chen himself edited for publication, Chen wrote:

> Precious metals and coin are means of measuring wealth [*suoyi hengcai* 所以衡財], but they should not be confused with wealth itself. At the present time, our most dire worry is that people solely concern themselves with the daily pursuit of silver and coin while neglecting the cultivation of the five grains, and consequently poverty steadily worsens.[100]

Elsewhere, Chen adopted the view that money does have a utility value independent of its role as a measure of value. Several years earlier, in a vehement polemic written in opposition to a proposal to expand mining, Chen warned that taking silver as the measure of value caused real hardship:

> If we value ever more abundant goods in terms of ever more scarce silver, how can the people not suffer want? How can the state not grow poorer? . . . What we lack at present is cloth and grain, because the people fail to diligently apply themselves to the fundamental occupation [of agriculture], the fields are left uncultivated, ancient customs and frugal habits decay, and strict accounting of needs and expenditures is not maintained.[101]

Silver, Chen argued, was a mere token, not wealth itself, but the scarcity of silver meant that it could not fulfill the essential function of money as a means of exchange. Chen claimed that, the earlier Ming experience with paper currency notwithstanding, paper bills could serve as viable instruments of exchange even though they possessed no intrinsic value. "Paper script is not money," Chen wrote, "but it can be used as a substitute for specie in order to transmit large sums over considerable distances without incurring significant costs." Chen contrasted the Ming *baochao*, which he faulted for not being convertible with metallic specie and therefore uncreditworthy, with the private paper instruments (both promissory notes and bills of exchange) issued by commercial establishments in his own day. He attributed the success of the latter to the fact that they were not money at all; rather, they were token substitutes for money which could be redeemed for hard currency, and thus were deemed entirely valid instruments of exchange. Paper currency, Chen pointed out, also had originated as tokens. The *jiaozi* bills of the Northern Song period were intended simply as a means of transferring funds in lieu of the extremely bulky iron coins then used in Sichuan and other border regions.

100 Chen Zilong 陳子龍, "Fanli" 凡例, in *NZQS*, p. 1.

101 Chen Zilong 陳子龍, "Caijin yi" 採金議, *Chen Zhongyu quanji* 陳忠裕全集 (1805 Ganshao caotang ed.), 22.16b.

From the Southern Song onward, successive governments tried to transform these notes, initially fully convertible with coin, into fiat currency. These efforts were doomed, though, because the same governments also embarked on ruinous courses of deficit spending and monetary inflation that exposed their paper currencies as worthless. The flaws of the Ming paper currency system lay in monetary and fiscal policies rather than in the principle of paper money itself.[102]

Chen Zilong's chartalist endorsement of fiat money thus was tempered with practical metallism. He insisted that specie convertibility was indispensable to a sound system of paper currency. A fully convertible system of paper bills would not augment the supply of money, but at least it could deflate the demand for hard currency, especially silver, and thus rein in the runaway inflation of recent years.

Although Chen and others advocated returning to a paper currency system, no concrete steps were taken until the Ming reached the point of desperation. In the winter of 1643, with both domestic rebels and the Manchu invaders menacing the capital, the Chongzhen emperor (r. 1628–1644) abruptly decided to reissue paper money.[103] But before this plan could be implemented the capital was overrun by peasant rebels, with Chongzhen taking his own life to escape capture.

9.6 Epilogue: Wang Liu's Campaign to Revive Paper Currency

Under the Manchu-ruled Qing dynasty, silver became even more deeply entrenched as the monetary standard of state finance and wholesale and interregional trade. Most Qing statesmen acknowledged that silver was indispensable to the smooth functioning of the economy and that silver imports stimulated domestic trade and industry. Confident that the wealth of China and the industry of its inhabitants ensured a favorable balance of trade, they upheld open borders and a constant influx of silver to maintain the necessary stock of money. A dissenting conception of political economy was expressed by political theorists who abhorred the autocratic rule of the Ming and Qing emperors and advocated political decentralization and economic autarky for local communities. These writers, who remained far removed from the corridors of power, repudiated the silver economy, chiefly because they saw silver as an all too efficient means for the state to extract wealth from the people. They endorsed a return to bronze coin as the monetary standard, hailing the low value and viscosity of base metal currency as virtues that would inhibit

102 Chen Zilong, "Chaobi lun" 鈔幣論, in Wang Liu 王瑬 (ed.), *Qianbi chuyan* 錢幣芻言 ([hereafter *QBCY*]; 1837), 28a–30b.

103 For this abortive plan to reintroduce paper money, see von Glahn, *Fountain of Fortune*, pp. 203–6.

depredations both by the state and by the merchants, moneylenders, and landowners who dominated the market economy.[104]

Common to these critics of imperial autocracy was a deep-seated hostility to the tenets of chartalist monetary theory that regarded money as a means for the ruler to regulate the economy and enhance state power. Unsurprisingly, they took a dim view of paper currency on principle, not just because of its practical limitations. Subsequent generations of writers on political economy ignored paper currency altogether. The monetary policies of the Qing government aimed, with reasonable success before the 1820s, at maintaining a stable dual currency system incorporating both silver and copper (now a brass alloy) coin. Exploiting the new copper mines of Yunnan, the Qing authorities minted prodigious quantities of coin between the 1730s and 1800, and the value of coin surpassed the government's target exchange ratio of 1,000 coins = 1 *liang* of silver during this time.[105] As William Rowe has noted, apart from a couple of items from the early Qing period none of the other fifty-one essays on monetary policy included in the *Compendium of Statecraft Writings from the Reigning Dynasty* (*Huangchao jingshi wenbian* 皇朝經世文編), published in 1826, endorsed fiat money, whether paper bills or fiat copper currency.[106]

Revival of paper currency became a renewed subject of debate among statecraft theorists amid the fiscal and monetary crises of 1830s. The era of the Daoguang Depression (named after the reign period of the Daoguang emperor, r. 1820–1850) witnessed contracting domestic trade, an outflow of silver, prolonged deflation, and a sharp depreciation of coin relative to silver.[107] Another feature of this period was the rise of opium imports, and many contemporary statesmen blamed what they dubbed "the silver famine" on the invidious opium trade. Calls for monetary reform resurrected the anti-silver rhetoric of the 17th century.[108]

[104] On early Qing monetary thought, see von Glahn, *Fountain of Fortune*, pp. 215–24.

[105] Hans Ulrich Vogel, "Chinese Central Monetary Policy, 1644–1800," *Late Imperial China* 8.2 (1987): 1–52; Kuroda, "Kenryū no senki."

[106] William T. Rowe, "Money, Economy, and Polity in the Daoguang-Era Paper Currency Debates," *Late Imperial China* 31.2 (2010): 82–83.

[107] On the Daoguang Depression, see von Glahn, *Economic History of China*, pp. 361–74; Richard von Glahn, "Economic Depression and the Silver Question in Nineteenth Century China," in Manuel Pérez García and Lucio de Sousa (eds.), *Global History and New Polycentric Approaches: Europe, Asia, and the Americas in a World Network System (XVI–XIXth Centuries)* (London: Palgrave Macmillan, 2018), pp. 81–117.

[108] On debates in statecraft circles about silver and opium, see Richard von Glahn, "Foreign Silver Coins in the Market Culture of Nineteenth Century China," *International Journal of Asian Studies* 4.1 (2007): 51–78; William T. Rowe, *Speaking of Profit: Bao Shichen and Reform in Nineteenth-Century China* (Cambridge, MA: Harvard University Asia Center, 2018); less reliable, in my opinion, is Man-houng Lin, "Two Social Theories Revealed: Statecraft Controversies over China's Monetary Crisis, 1808–1854," *Late Imperial China* 12.2 (1991): 1–35.

The chief proponent of restoring paper currency in lieu of silver was Wang Liu, a private scholar who from 1828 began to circulate draft proposals for monetary reform among influential scholars and statesmen. In Wang's view, the erosion of the purchasing power of coin resulted not just from the market preference for silver but also because of the circulation of Spanish pesos minted in Mexico as current coin (rather than being melted down and recast as ingots) and the proliferation of private banknotes (denominated in either coin or silver).[109] Both of these trends drove down the value of standard copper coin. Wang claimed that paper money is superior to uncoined silver because it reduced transaction costs (standard denominations, easier to transport, did not require assaying). If the government offered paper currency at a premium in exchange for silver, buyers would willingly take the bargain, and silver would "naturally cease" (*zizhi* 自止) to circulate in the market without the need for a formal ban on its use. In true chartalist fashion, Wang extolled the power of the state to create as much paper money as it needs, in contrast to the finite supply of silver. On one hand, Wang suggested that the state can print money in lieu of taxing the wealth of the people (the state of course must accept paper currency in tax payments), but on the other hand he duly recognized the need to limit the quantity of bills in circulation to market demand. Wang's critics of course seized on the logical contradiction between these two assertions. Although Wang expected the state to remove the stock of silver from private hands, his paper currency would be a pure fiat money, inconvertible with silver. Wang pointed to the growing utility of private banknotes as proof that the state too could adopt a fiat currency, and he intended to use private banks as intermediaries to inject government bills into the marketplace (while simultaneously prohibiting private banknotes). Wang also proposed that the state would issue fiat copper currency in denominations of 10- and 100-*wen* to substitute for the Spanish peso coins.[110]

Wang Liu's proposals elicited vigorous debate, and when he printed his treatise in 1837 Wang included correspondence with various interlocutors as well as writings from Song and Ming scholars and statesmen, both interspersed with Wang's copious commentary. Among those who received Wang's ideas favorably, if critically, was Bao Shichen, who despite having

[109] On the rapidly growing popularity of Spanish pesos (and later Mexican Republican dollars) in market exchange in 19th-century China, see von Glahn, "Foreign Silver Coins." For the types of private banknotes that circulated in the Qing, see Liu Qiugen 刘秋根 and Liu Na 刘娜, "Qingdai qianqi qianpu yinhao yinqian piao" 清代前期钱铺银号银钱票, *Zhongguo qianbi* 中国钱币 2019.1: 3–14; Cao Shuji 曹树基 and Yang Qiming 杨启明, "Qingdai dongnan difang xiaoshichang de pingpiao yu xinyong" 清代东南地方小市场中的凭票与信用, *Zhonggguo jingji shi yanjiu* 中国经济史研究 2020.6: 102–17.

[110] *QBCY* 1a–18b. Wang's proposals are summarized in Rowe, "Money, Economy, and Polity."

failed the civil service exams and never serving in government office was one of the leading public intellectuals of the day. While Bao applauded Wang's general plan for a fiat paper currency, he deemed it unrealistic to expect silver to disappear "naturally." Bao's most forceful rebuttal questioned Wang's confidence that paper currency could serve as an inexhaustible source of wealth. Instead, Bao insisted that the quantity of bills must be tightly restricted; he proposed setting an initial ceiling equal to one-half of annual land tax revenues. Bao envisioned a tripartite currency system, similar to Qiu Jun's earlier scheme, in which paper currency, silver, and full-bodied copper coin (not the fiat coins Wang proposed) would each fulfill different monetary needs, with paper currency crucially important as the means of state payments.[111]

Although many leading statecraft scholars of the day – for example, Wei Yuan and Lin Zexu – weighed in on Wang's proposals for a new paper currency, it seems that no one in government seriously considered enacting them. Instead, Wang's treatise marks the denouement of the chartalist tradition that laid the conceptual foundations for fiat currency. In addition, as Rowe observes, Wang Liu added a novel nationalist twist to the already prevalent anti-silver rhetoric. Wang excoriated the "despoilation" (*haoshi* 耗蝕) of China's wealth caused by increasingly frequent use of Spanish pesos in commercial transactions, and he framed his arguments against silver in terms of how dependence on foreign silver entailed loss of control over the "levers of profit" (*liquan*).[112] As we saw in Chapter 1, *liquan* was central to the chartalist theories of Pseudo-Guanzi and Sang Hongyang that rooted the ruler's sovereign power in his monopoly over money and strategic resources, which enabled him to control the terms of trade both at home and abroad. Rowe sees in Wang's particular iteration of *liquan* the germ of ideas of national sovereignty and economic independence that were only just beginning to coalesce on the eve of the Opium War and China's fateful confrontation with the West. Indeed, Wang abjured mention of the Qing dynasty in his writings, preferring to speak of "the nation" (*guojia* 國家), and affirmed that the adoption of "Chinese paper money" (*Zhongguo zhi chao* 中國之鈔) would secure the "integrity of the nation" (*guojia zhi titong* 國家之體統) – language that Rowe suggests is imbued with the basic, if still inchoate, idea of "national sovereignty."[113]

111 "Da Wang Liang sheng shu" 答王亮生書 and "Zaida Wang Liang sheng shu" 再答王亮生書, in Bao Shichen 包世臣, *An Wu sizhong* 安吳四種 (1888 rpt. of 1872 ed.) 26.8a–14b; *QBCY* 38a–b, 42a–43a. On Bao's ideas on money, see Rowe, "Money, Economy, and Polity"; Rowe, *Speaking of Profit*, pp. 150–76.

112 *QBCY* 2b, 1a–b.

113 Rowe, "Money, Economy, and Polity," pp. 87–88; Rowe, *Speaking of Profit*, pp. 172–74.

Creation of a national currency would indeed become a key objective of nationalist economic rhetoric in the late 19th century. For example, Zheng Guanying, a longtime employee in British trading companies who took up the cause of nationalist reform in the face of what he described as the looming specter of "commercial warfare" (*shangzhan* 商戰) between China and the West, argued for the need for a national currency in a treatise published in 1880. But Zheng made no mention of paper money; instead, he advocated for the creation of China's own silver currency in order to wrest *liquan* (in this case, the translation of "economic sovereignty" is surely apt) from the foreign powers.[114] In 1889, the governor of Guangdong built a mint using imported machinery to produce what became China's first state-issued silver coins (albeit issued in the name of the provincial government, not the imperial court) as well as new fractional copper coins. Monetary reform would remain focused on creating a new silver dollar standard rather than paper currency even after the fall of the Qing dynasty in 1911.[115]

9.7 Conclusion

The abrupt collapse of the Ming *baochao* paper currency stands in marked contrast to the long-term viability of paper monies during the Song and Yuan eras. Although the Ming founder, Hongwu, initially endeavored to reestablish bronze coin, he ultimately chose to rely on a fiat paper currency as the sole form of legal tender, both public and private, as had the Yuan rulers. The profligate issue of *baochao*, far beyond the demand for it in the private economy, triggered ruinous depreciation that undermined efforts to reestablish a paper currency monetary standard. Hongwu's fiscal policies aimed at minimizing the role of the market and paid little heed to the needs of private trade. These policies succeeded in arresting the commercial vigor of the Song-Yuan era. By the 15th century, market trade had slowly begun to recover, yet the catastrophic depreciation of the *baochao* paper currency induced a flight to silver as the medium of commercial exchange.

The evidence of Huizhou land contracts suggests that *baochao* prevailed as the primary instrument of large-scale transactions throughout the remainder of Hongwu's reign, even as the bills suffered serious erosion in their exchange value to a far greater degree than the Song and Yuan paper currencies. The sudden swerve toward using grain (and to a lesser extent silver) as the means of payment in Huizhou land sales during the brief reign of the Jianwen

114 Zheng Guanying 鄭觀應, "Lun zhuyin" 論鑄銀, in *Yiyan* 易言, rpt. in Xia Dongyuan 夏东元 (ed.), *Zheng Guanying ji* 鄭觀應集 (Shanghai: Shanghai renmin chubanshe, 1982), 1, pp. 95–96.

115 Austin Dean, *China and the End of Global Silver, 1873–1937* (Ithaca, NY: Cornell University Press, 2020).

emperor (r. 1398–1402) vividly signaled flagging popular confidence in *baochao*. Yongle's repeated efforts to ban the use of silver in market transactions attest to the reality that merchants increasingly resorted to silver as the preferred means of exchange. Although *baochao* once again became the standard currency of Huizhou land sales during the Yongle reign, their exchange value, relative to either silver or coin, plummeted to 2 percent of their face value at the time of Yongle's death in 1424.

Subsequent efforts to resuscitate paper currency – such as creating or increasing commercial taxes payable in *baochao* – "utterly failed," in the words of the minister of revenue Huang Fu in 1436. The sharp fall in the exchange value of *baochao* bills reduced them to a fractional currency, and thus put them in competition with coin as the medium of retail trade. The Ming court once again shuttered its mints and banned the use of coin in exchange, as Hongwu had done earlier, but these actions only created more incentive for private coinage. The proliferation of private coin from the 1450s further contributed to the disappearance of *baochao* from market trade. Silverization of public finance proceeded incrementally beginning with ad hoc conversions of the grain tribute from the southern provinces to silver payments in the 1430s. In the 1480s, a crucial threshold was crossed, with the creation of annual allocations of silver to provision the frontier garrisons and the conversion of a substantial portion of labor services and commercial taxes to silver payments. By the early 16th century, 90 percent of official salaries were paid in silver and 10 percent in coin.[116] The adoption of silver as the monetary standard of fiscal accounts also accelerated the monetization of taxation. By the end of the 16th century, most government revenues were collected in silver, a complete reversal of the Ming founder's original conception of a system of in-kind payments that would insulate the population from market intercourse.

The silverization of government finance was driven by the spreading use of silver as the monetary standard of the market economy. To be sure, bronze coin played an indispensable role as the medium of everyday retail trade, but by the 16th century most of this coin was supplied by private moneyers (in addition to the existing and not inconsiderable stock of Song coins) rather than Ming mints. As the conversion of taxes to payments in silver progressed, the state's motivation to mint new coin – especially given the high costs of standard coin – ebbed. The dynamic market expansion of the 16th century and after thus was stoked by the infusion of private rather than state-issued media of exchange. The influx of foreign silver after the 1520s should be understood not simply as the fortuitous effect of new sources of supply, but also as a response to intensified market demand. The rich profits gained from

[116] Peng, *Zhongguo huobi shi*, p. 721.

selling silver to the Chinese market stimulated silver production in Japan and Peru, fostered the formation of global networks of exchange, and made fortunes around the world.

The dual currency system combining uncoined silver and copper coins that emerged in the mid Ming period persisted under the Qing dynasty and was reinforced in the 18th century by the surge in minting of standard coin and a new swelling of silver imports. Growing penetration of the market into local economies stimulated the demand for money but did not lead to monetary unification. On the contrary, the needs of rural inhabitants who engaged in small-scale, seasonal, and proximate transactions generated demand for large stocks of locally available, small value currencies (copper coin and local banknotes), while the growing elaboration of regional and national commercial networks benefited from high value and highly fungible currencies suitable for deferred payments (silver, bills of exchange, and universally recognized banknotes). The viscosity of coin, with much of the money stock idle for most of the year, reflected the episodic nature of local exchange, while the liquidity of silver facilitated rapid adjustment of money supply to money demand.[117] Given these divergent needs, shortages of one currency could not be easily compensated by increasing the supply of the other. Commercialization thus bolstered complementary use of multiple currencies and the growing heterogeneity of local monetary systems in China, a pattern that persisted well into the 20th century. This dual currency system, and above all the triumph of the silver economy, attested to the power of the marketplace to determine the value and utility of money, turning the chartalist principles of Chinese monetary theory on their head.

117 Kuroda, *Global History of Money*.

Conclusion

Making money was integral to imperial governance in China. The sovereign's responsibility to provide for the economic welfare of his subjects laid the foundation for the fiscal constitution of the Chinese empire. Philosophers and statesmen conceived of money as the crucial tool by which the ruler ensures economic prosperity. The canon of Chinese monetary theory, which coalesced already at the inception of the first empires, leaned heavily toward chartalist ideas that invested sole authority to make money in the state. Power over money – sanctioned since Han times as the monarch's rightful command of "the levers of profit" (*quanli*) – entailed control over the ratios of exchange between money and goods. Whereas the supply of goods – determined by productive forces, market institutions, and (for the most important necessity of life, grain) the unpredictable vicissitudes of weather and harvests – remained beyond the ruler's reach, the supply of money was amenable to the state's monetary and fiscal policies.

But control over the money supply, the ability to issue and withdraw money at will, rested on the premise that making money incurred minimal cost. Gold and silver were far too scarce and precious to enable the ruler to adjust the money supply as needed. In contrast, the supply of bronze coin, manufactured from cheaper and more abundant metals, was in theory unlimited. Bronze currency implicitly was a fiat money, yet its value was determined not simply by the ruler's decree but rather through careful management of the money supply relative to the demands for money and goods. To exercise such command over the money supply, the ruler was obliged to hold substantial stocks of coin in his treasury. The common form of moneymaking in medieval Europe, in which individuals at their own initiative brought gold and silver to the moneyer to be struck into the prince's coin ("free minting"), surrendered sovereign power to private agents in ways wholly antithetical to Chinese monetary theory and practice.[1]

[1] In England, free minting was inaugurated by Henry II in 1154. Desan, *Making Money*, p. 70.

Of course, the prerogative to create money faced formidable technical, political, and economic obstacles. Bronze coin was by no means cost free; on the contrary, the low unit value of bronze coin meant that the state typically lost money minting it rather than reaping seigniorage income. Nor were the supplies of copper as limitless as theory presumed. Even the most successful full-bodied early imperial coinages, the Han Wuzhu and Tang Kaiyuan coins, could not be produced in sufficient quantities to meet the demand for means of public and private payments. During the Northern Song period, fiscal policymakers dramatically increased the output of state mints, far beyond the peak levels of preceding dynasties, yet coinage was unable to keep pace with demand, resulting in what contemporaries described as "coin famines." Still, by this time, money had become one of the principal institutions mediating the relationship between the imperial state and its subjects. Monetization of taxation, especially during the New Policies era, reshaped the political economy by deepening the populace's indebtedness to the state. The New Policies agenda was focused not so much on nurturing the growth of the market as strengthening the interdependence between the state and its subjects. Indeed, the particular form of the "mercantilist state" that took shape under the New Policies regime (in many ways harking back to the fiscal strategies of Emperor Wu of the Han) aimed at shielding the populace from the pernicious effects of the market. Economic justice would be achieved by substituting public-minded state agents in place of profiteering private merchants. As monetization of obligations to the state advanced, control over the money supply once again leapt to the forefront of the state's fiscal priorities.[2]

The economic agenda of the New Policies has served as the template for Miyazawa Tomoyuki's concept of "fiscal circulation," in which the state retains the bulk of the money supply in its treasuries and directly or indirectly organizes the circulation of goods on an empire-wide scale through its procurement policies, especially military expenditures. In Song times, Miyazawa argues, money was used principally for payments to the state rather than in market exchange. He concludes that the expanding use of money did not betoken the growth of a market economy; instead, within the long arc of imperial history, the Song marked the zenith of the state's autocratic control over society and economy.[3] In Miyazawa's view, the Song also witnessed the maturation of a unified "fiscal currency" in the form of bronze coin. In contrast to Peng Xinwei, who argued that the multiplicity of currencies in the Song engendered the most fragmented monetary system in Chinese history, one that inhibited political centralization, Miyazawa contends that the Song state successfully utilized its bronze currency standard to unify the

[2] On the "mercantilist state" in Chinese fiscal history, see von Glahn, "Modalities of the Fiscal State," pp. 14–17.

[3] Miyazawa, *Kokka to keizai*, pp. 21–26.

national economy.[4] Consequently, state procurement exerted a powerful influence on commodity prices. Miyazawa emphasizes that prices displayed long-term stability throughout the Song, excepting the inflationary spikes triggered by war and invasion in the Qingli War of the 1040s, the Jurchen conquest of the north in the 1120s–1130s, the Kaixi War in the early 13th century, and after the onset of the Mongol invasions in 1234. Administered prices set through state procurement systems determined market prices at the national level, although local markets, isolated from the fiscal circulation system, displayed a high degree of seasonal and annual volatility.[5]

Miyazawa is certainly correct to stress the important influence of the Song fiscal administration and its logistical requirements on the Song economy. Yet his analysis is limited by his focus on particular fiscal institutions and practices, notably the New Policies, in isolation from larger economic trends. The case studies he cites as examples of fiscal circulation, such as Wang Anshi's State Trade Agency and *mianhangqian* 免行錢 levy (a money tax levied on merchants and artisans in lieu of requisitions of goods), were short-lived experiments that, contrary to Miyazawa's argument, betrayed the limitations of the fiscal powers of the Song state even in its most activist mode. Miyazawa's version of the "state theory of money" – borrowed from G. F. Knapp by way of Max Weber – surely exaggerates the extent of the Song state's sovereign control of money and the dominance of fiscal circulation within the money economy as a whole.[6]

Still, the prominent role of fiscal circulation within the distinctive fiscal constitution and institutional infrastructure of the Song state gave a distinctive cast to its moneymaking. The turn toward monetization of taxation had begun in the wake of the An Lushan rebellion in the mid 8th century. Yang Yan's twice-a-year tax system, introduced in 780, reestablished the principle of direct taxation, but it was premised on private ownership of land and the disparities of wealth among taxpayers. Already in 792, the state councilor Lu Zhi condemned the twice-a-year tax system for abetting the corrosive effects of the

4 Miyazawa, *Kahei to zaisei*, pp. 45–55. In arguing for a unified currency system in the Song, Miyazawa emphasizes that cloth lost the monetary functions it performed in the early empires and that silver remained a special form of state finance, not a general purpose money. In his view, paper money was a mere substitute for coin and should be seen as an extension of the unified fiscal currency system. For Peng Xinwei's emphasis on the fragmentation of the Song monetary system, see Peng, *Zhongguo huobi shi*, p. 398.

5 Miyazawa, *Kokka to keizai*, pp. 481–82.

6 Miyazawa, *Kokka to keizai*, p. 16. Miyazawa draws on the Weberian distinction between administrative and market monies delineated by Adachi Keiji, a fellow member of the Chūgokushi kenkyūkai circle of Chinese historical studies in Japan. See Adachi, "Sensei kokka to zaisei kahei," pp. 117–46, esp. pp. 124–27. For Weber's formulation, see Max Weber, *Economy and Society* (Berkeley: University of California Press, 1978), vol. 1, pp. 75–79.

market economy. Since antiquity, Lu avowed, taxation had been based on the labor power of adult males. Rulers enacted uniform levies in the form of labor services and taxation of the goods – grain and cloth – directly produced by household labor. The *zu-yong-diao* tax system instituted by the founders of the Tang dynasty had abided by these principles. The twice-a-year tax, levied on household wealth (measured as an abstract sum of money) and collected (partly) in coin, violated the principle of uniform taxation and engendered profound inequities, not least by exposing farming families to the marketplace by forcing them to sell their produce to earn coin.[7] Although some Song scholars (notably of the Dao Learning persuasion) reiterated Lu's critique of the twice-a-year tax as a perversion of classical institutions, as a practical matter Song statesmen, including even Ye Shi, endorsed it as a pragmatic adaptation to the irreversible privatization of landownership since the late Tang era.[8]

An even more significant change was the shift from direct taxation of land and people to commercial and consumption taxes inaugurated with the salt monopoly established by Liu Yan in 760. This trend intensified during the post-Tang period of disunion and under Song imperial dominion. The adoption of indirect taxation as the main source of state revenues was not explicitly theorized, but it revealed a radically different conception of taxation that aroused vehement opposition among many Confucian literati. Pseudo-Guanzi had in fact advocated this shift on the pragmatic grounds that indirect taxation disguised the tax itself (consumers paid these taxes through higher prices, not payments directly to the state, and thus they would not resent the ruler), but few Song statesmen dared to cite *Guan Zi* as an authority.[9] Proponents of the New Policies from Wang Anshi to Cai Jing aimed at enhancing the fiscal capacity of the state through monetization of direct taxation, greater reliance on indirect taxes, and the displacement of private merchants by state agents. Southern Song policymakers withdrew from the kind of direct control of commercial exchange enacted under the New Policies. But, faced with the urgent need to raise revenues to meet intractable military costs, they largely acquiesced to even greater reliance on indirect taxation.

Fiscal governance assumed an unusually prominent place in the Song as the cornerstone of what Charles Hartman has defined as the "technocratic state."

7 Lu Zhi 陸贄, "Junjie fushui xu baixing liutiao" 均節賦稅恤百姓六條, in *Lu Xuangong ji* 陸宣公集 (Hangzhou: Zhejiang guji chubanshe, 1988), pp. 243–61. See also Li Zhixian, *Yang Yan*, pp. 327–79.

8 For a brief survey of Song debates over the twice-a-year tax, see Song, "Debates on Just Taxation," pp. 261–67.

9 For Pseudo-Guanzi's arguments for the wisdom of indirect rather than direct taxation, see chapter 78, "Kuidu"; chapter 80, "Qingzhong (jia)"; chapter 81, "Qingzhong (yi)," in *GZ*, 3, pp. 1379, 1412–13, and 1450–51, respectively.

Hartman observes that the standard narrative of Song history from the 12th century down to modern times has depicted the Song as the epitome of civil bureaucratic governance, consolidated by the resurgence of Confucianism (in its Neo-Confucian forms) as the core of Chinese intellectual and cultural values. This narrative, constructed by literati historians themselves, has trained attention on Confucian literati and enlightened emperors as the positive forces for the installation of moral rulership.[10] But this narrative obscures crucial features of Song political culture, marginalizing the fiscal operations of the state (typically depicted in Neo-Confucian writings as predatory and malignant) and erasing the participation of major stakeholders in governance, including the imperial clan, eunuchs, palace women, military-grade officials, merchants, and the landholding elite. These groups, deeply deplored by literati officials, influenced governance not through success in the civil service examinations and bureaucratic office but rather through their roles in the operation of a "technocratic state" centered in the inner court, the emperor and his palace administration. In contrast to the career bureaucrats, esteemed for their classical education and generalized knowledge of government affairs, the technocratic elite developed expertise in finance, accounting, engineering, and military technology that made them invaluable subalterns in service to imperial will. Hartman re-centers Song political culture on the abiding tension between the technocratic state administered from the inner court and the "bureaucratic institutionalism" espoused by activist literati committed to Neo-Confucian moral precepts. The ideological triumph of the latter – which prevailed throughout the late imperial era – must not overshadow the reality of the predominance of the technocratic state within Song governance, however.[11]

Fiscal expertise had become a crucial feature of imperial governance since the late Tang period. The fiscal reforms enacted by Liu Yan and Yang Yan were accompanied by the compilation of treatises on "national accounts" (*guoji* 國計) to provide policymakers with comprehensive data on the empire's fiscal resources. The Song created an Accounting Bureau (Kuaijisi 會計司) to compile statistical digests on a regular basis.[12] Originally subordinate to the Finance Commission, in 1005 the Accounting Bureau was transferred to the Supervisory Office for Capital Agency Treasuries and Storehouses (Tiju zaijing

[10] Charles Hartman, *The Making of Song Dynasty History: Sources and Narratives, 960–1279 CE* (Cambridge: Cambridge University Press, 2021).

[11] Hartman, *Structures of Governance*, passim.

[12] The *Song Dynastic History* is the only official dynastic history to include a chapter on national accounts (*kuaiji* 會計), which appears prominently at the head of the chapters devoted to state finance. See Christian Lamouroux, *Fiscalité, comptes publics et politiques financières dans la Chine des Song: le chapitre 179 du* Songshi (Paris: Collège de France, Institut des Hautes Études Chinoises, 2003).

zhusi kuwu si 提舉在京諸司庫務司), a new agency attached to the inner court. Along with the expanding role of the Inner Palace Treasury (Neicangku) in state finances, this agency – headed by eunuchs and military-grade officials – ensured that the emperor and his staff would have a monopoly on the most comprehensive information regarding state finances.[13] In the New Policies era, the functions of the Supervisory Office for Capital Agency Treasuries and Storehouses were transferred to the State Trade Agency, part of Wang Anshi's plan to wrest control over fiscal affairs from the inner court.[14] The inauguration of the New Policies marked the beginning of systematic use of fiscal accounting to guide budget planning.[15]

The finance commissioners likewise consisted of technocrats with long experience in fiscal matters, at least up until the Qingli War, which marked the onset of the ascendancy of Confucian literati within the Song bureaucracy.[16] Both Wang Anshi and Cai Jing created ad hoc agencies staffed by relatively low-ranking officials who were given freedom from regular civil service protocols and broad discretion to devise strategies to raise revenues. This mechanism for mobilizing fiscal expertise – which Paul Smith, in reference to Wang Anshi's personnel strategy, has dubbed "bureaucratic entrepreneurship" – was routinely practiced throughout the Southern Song as well.[17] As we have seen, a notable feature of Song fiscal governance was the regular consultation with merchants as legitimate stakeholders in fiscal decision-making, for example in the ad hoc commissions created to deliberate on tea and salt policies. Certainly, such consultations were controversial, and literati officials often complained that merchants had too much influence in crafting policies that were unduly favorable to their interests. Implicit in the operation of fiscal administration throughout the Song – with the notable exception of Wang Anshi's brand of mercantilism – was an acceptance of the market economy and the crucial role of merchants in facilitating exchange. As I have suggested elsewhere, the Song manifested what might be described

13 Hartman, *Structures of Governance*, pp. 204–6.

14 Li Weiguo 李伟国, "Lun Bei Song de tiju zhusi kuwu si" 论北宋的提举诸司库务司, in Li, *Songdai caizheng he wenxian kaolun* 宋代财政和文献考论 (Shanghai: Shanghai guji chubanshe, 2007), pp. 43–61.

15 Lamouroux, *Fiscalité*, pp. 57–62.

16 Based on examination of the bureaucratic careers of Northern Song officials, Robert Hartwell found a pattern of repeated service in fiscal offices, in essence a separate career track for officials who developed fiscal expertise. See Robert M. Hartwell, "Financial Expertise, Public Policy, and the Formation of Economic Policy in Northern Sung China," *Journal of Asian Studies* 30.2 (1971): 281–314. Hartman has determined that this pattern only held up until 1040. See Hartman, *Structures of Governance*, pp. 125–29.

17 P. J. Smith, *Taxing Heaven's Storehouse*, pp. 111–18. Hartman counts at least six instances of the creation of such ad hoc fiscal agencies in the Southern Song. See Hartman, *Structures of Governance*, p. 209.

as a "synergistic fiscal state" predicated on cooperative rather than antagonistic relationships with merchant groups. Song policymakers sought to harness market forces, rather than arrest or subvert them, to achieve their fiscal and economic goals.[18]

The crucial position of fiscal policymaking within Song governance elevated the importance of making money. The massive increase in mint output during the Northern Song facilitated both fiscal circulation and market expansion, but demand for money continued to outrace supply. Moreover, the viscosity of low-value bronze and iron coins inhibited their utility as means of fiscal circulation as well as long-distance trade. Already at the time of the fiscal reforms of the late 8th century, the Tang state had begun to issue "flying cash" bills to enable long-distance remittance transfers, a practice renewed during the Song under the rubric of "convenient cash." A long history of paper contracts and debt instruments in common use among ordinary farm families as well as merchant firms buttressed the general validity of paper documents as promises of payment. Provisioning armies on the empire's northern frontiers, the preeminent fiscal concern of the Song state, fostered innovation in the form of bills of exchange. Revenues from the tea and salt monopolies, mediated through paper bills, became a principal means of inducing merchants to supply provisions to the frontier garrisons through the *ruzhong* system. Making the commodity bills of exchange negotiable and transferable enhanced their attractiveness to merchants. To be sure, the functioning of commodity bills of exchange was by no means smooth, principally because the state had difficulty balancing their supply and demand; the urgent need for military supplies led to overissue of licenses, depressing their market value and prolonging the time to redeem them. *Jiaoyinpu* exchange bill dealers provided a secondary market that sustained the circulation of these bills. Denunciations of *jiaoyinpu* – voiced by merchants and fiscal policymakers alike – for the "stranglehold" they exerted over one of the crucial elements in state finance only underscored their importance as an indispensable link between state and market. The adoption of Fan Xiang's salt license system in 1048, which decoupled the salt monopoly from frontier provisioning, struck a more sustainable balance. Salt licenses themselves became monetary instruments, held by the rich as savings, according to the testimony of the finance commissioner Shen Gua in 1077.

Recognizing the constraints of bronze coin as the primary form of money, Shen Gua also advocated making greater use of silver to augment the money supply. Shen did not go so far as to propose coining silver, but he implicitly acknowledged the rising importance of silver as a monetary instrument. The state already had come to rely on silver as the means for transferring revenues

[18] Von Glahn, "Modalities of the Fiscal State," pp. 17–22.

from the distant southern provinces to the capital, and silver was the principal conduit for conducting trade between Sichuan, an iron coin monetary region, and both the frontiers and the metropolitan regions of the empire. Silver was not used in ordinary market transactions, but it had become a preferred store of value and was widely held as savings. In the Southern Song period, silver would become an integral part of state finance as the hard currency reserve backing the issue of paper money.

The invention of paper money was a logical corollary of the ruler's supreme authority to make money. Yet the first bills to circulate as means of exchange, the *jiaozi* currency, emerged from the private sector. The immediate circumstances surrounding the birth of *jiaozi* in the 990s – created by private firms in Sichuan, whose robust commercial economy was handicapped by its designation as an iron currency zone and the outbreak of a rebellion that shut down the iron coin mints – were unique. Sichuan officials were quick to recognize the utility of *jiaozi* even as lack of regulation resulted in reckless issuance and insolvencies. State interventions to impose discipline on the market for private *jiaozi* bills failed. But *jiaozi* had become vitally important to the Sichuan economy, and rather than abolishing them in 1023 the state itself took over the issue of paper bills as state-authorized money. Although fiscal policymakers soon moved to incorporate *jiaozi* into the *ruzhong* procurement system, the paper bills also displaced iron coins as the principal market money in Sichuan (and also in the frontier zone of neighboring Shaanxi). Fiscal exigencies and monetary turbulence under Cai Jing's regime in the early 12th century led to profligate overissue of *jiaozi*, causing their value to collapse. The government devalued the paper currency by replacing *jiaozi* with a new paper money, *qianyin*, at a steep discount. Nevertheless, the introduction of *qianyin* proved a success. The Sichuan monetary system stabilized with *qianyin* as the monetary standard and iron coin reduced to a subsidiary currency. During the Southern Song period, the success of Sichuan's *qianyin* currency was repeatedly invoked as the model for the adoption of paper money in other parts of the empire.

In contrast to the history of the Sichuan paper currencies, the creation of *huizi* bills in the metropolitan region of southeastern China in 1161 from the outset was designed to facilitate fiscal circulation, specifically to cope with the surge in expenditures triggered by renewed war with Jin. Initially intended as a temporary wartime expedient, the *huizi* paper currency quickly achieved broad acceptance in the marketplace. When the government began to withdraw *huizi* bills from circulation by redeeming them with silver, merchants clamored to retain the *huizi*. In 1168, the court decided to institutionalize *huizi* on a permanent basis, following the model of the *qianyin* currency in Sichuan. During the Song–Jin war of the early 1160s, the court also approved the issue of paper currencies in the war zone borderlands of Huainan and Jing–Hu. These two paper currencies (*huaijiao* in Huainan and *huhui* in Jing–Hu) likewise were used to provision and pay the frontier troops, but they also served as a buffer zone of low-value currencies (both paper currencies were linked to regionally specific iron coins) to stem the outflow of bronze coin into the Jin territories. Although *huaijiao* and *huhui* were less favored by long-distance merchants because they were denominated in iron currencies and not directly exchangeable with the bronze coin-denominated *huizi*, they prevailed as the monetary standards in their respective regions until well into the 13th century. Rather than a unified monetary regime, the Southern Song empire was divided into four separate monetary regions, each with its own distinct paper money and link-coins. The Jin, too, imitated Song practice and created its own paper currency.

Huizi bills, like *qianyin*, were an inconvertible fiat currency. What sustained their value were the strategies employed by the state to "maintain equilibrium" (*chengti*): (1) implicitly backing paper bills with hard currency by redeeming excess bills with silver (bronze coin being in short supply); (2) mandating that some portion (typically half) of tax payments be made in paper currency; and (3) requiring merchants to use paper currency to purchase commodity licenses. For the first three decades after *huizi* were established as a permanent institution, these strategies worked well and the bills enjoyed favor in the marketplace, maintaining their value at or close to par. The value of *huizi* began to slip in the 1190s, and the military crises of the early 13th century burgeoned into monetary crises as the state vastly increased its issue of paper currency, causing sharp depreciation. Devaluations that accompanied new issues of *huizi* in 1211 and 1234 helped to stabilize the currency, but at significant cost to those holding old bills, and popular confidence in paper money faltered. Yet despite the steep depreciation in the value of *huizi* relative to bronze coin, *huizi* superseded coin as the monetary standard in both state payments and market exchange, so much so that substantial quantities of coin began to drain off to overseas markets. Fiscal circulation was crucially important to the transition to the paper money standard, but so too was the use of paper currency in private transactions.

The powerful Mongol military juggernaut assembled by Chinggis Khan invaded and occupied a large portion of the Jin realm in 1215 and completed the conquest of Jin in 1234 under the leadership of Chinggis's successor Ögödei. Already by 1215, silver had superseded both coin and paper currency in market exchange within the Jin territories, and under Mongol suzerainty silver became the chief instrument of trans-Eurasian trade and the main source of revenue for the Mongol regimes in China. Yet the fiscal and monetary policies initiated by Khubilai after his election as great khan in 1260 led not to the adoption of silver as the primary means of market exchange but rather to the creation of a fiat paper money that displaced metallic money altogether. The rulers of the appanages established by the Mongols in the former Jin territories – including Khubilai himself – had devised their own paper currencies modeled after Jin precedents, using silver or silk as their units of account. Khubilai introduced a new paper currency as the sole form of legal tender within his empire while demonetizing both bronze coin and precious metals. In contrast to the Song and Jin paper monies, however, Mongol paper money was tied to a silver money of account that served as the basis for government fiscal accounting. In the wake of the Mongol conquest of Southern Song in 1276, Khubilai's paper currency system was extended to South China as well. For the next seventy years, Mongol paper currencies linked to a silver unit of account prevailed as the monetary standard throughout the Chinese ecumene and became the chief means of exchange even in everyday market transactions.

But the implosion of Mongol rule in the face of popular rebellions in the 1340s quickly ramified into fiscal and monetary crises. Desperate efforts to revive paper currency by linking it to a fresh issue of bronze coin only further undermined popular faith in its value. Hongwu, founder of the Ming dynasty that supplanted Mongol rule in 1368, was no more successful in restoring a bronze coin monetary standard. Hongwu, born a peasant but schooled in Neo-Confucian morality, nurtured an abiding hostility to the flourishing market economy of the Song–Yuan era and sought to shelter his subjects from what he perceived as the corrupting influences of markets and money. The fiscal system instituted by Hongwu returned to direct in-kind taxation of agricultural produce and corvée labor services instead of the indirect taxation of commerce and consumption that had been the foundation of state finance since the late Tang. Hongwu also resorted to imitating Khubilai's example by creating a paper currency as the exclusive form of legal tender, even going so far as to demonetize the bronze coin he had issued in the early years of his reign. Rampant overissue of the Ming *baochao* paper currency without mechanisms for reabsorbing paper money through state payments deeply eroded its value, however. Efforts by Hongwu's successors to revive the *baochao* currency proved fruitless. With the demise of *baochao* as a viable currency and in the absence of new state-issued coin, market exchange was principally conducted using uncoined silver and "private" (i.e., counterfeit) coin. Despite Hongwu's anti-market policies, commercial activity gradually revived over the course of the 15th century. The flood of foreign silver that poured into China from the mid 16th century onward lifted market expansion even beyond Song levels.

The institutional infrastructure of Hongwu's command economy, including fiat paper currency, already was in shambles by the mid 15th century. The late Ming leadership reconciled itself to the rise of the silver monetary standard and withdrew from activist management of the economy. By the 18th century, writers on political economy both within and outside the government to an unprecedented degree conceded to the autonomy of the market and the efficiency of market prices in adjusting the circulation of goods. In the words of William Rowe, "the Qing imperial administration as a whole was remarkably committed to relying on what we would call 'market mechanisms' to achieve its economic ends."[19] Helen Dunstan suggests that the mid 18th century witnessed a swerve toward a kind of "economic liberalism" that eschewed state intervention in favor of "allowing [market forces] to follow their own course" (*ting qi ziran* 聽其自然), even if it did not pose a radical challenge to paternalist and ethical precepts of Confucian governance.[20] In my own formulation, the late imperial fiscal regime can be characterized as a "providential state" in which steadfast commitment to the welfare of the agrarian populace guided fiscal policies. The providential state was premised on a low level of taxation levied on landholding, with minimal taxation of commerce, industry, or consumption.[21] Despite (or perhaps because of) the general principle of noninterference in the workings of the market economy, the merchant class was placed at an even farther remove from political power.

With the rise of the silver economy, the monetary order envisioned in the classical tradition of monetary thought tracing back to the *Guan Zi* had been inverted. Metallist convictions overturned chartalist theory. Private monies, not state-issued currencies, provided the essential liquidity markets needed to function. During the 18th century, the revival of bronze coinage restored some flexibility to the money supply and sustained a relatively stable bimetallic currency system encompassing coin as the medium of local and proximate transactions complemented by silver as the high-value currency for commercial exchange and state payments. But faith in the sovereign power of the state to make money had evaporated. The early Ming *baochao* debacle utterly discredited paper money. In reaction to the reversal of bullion flows and the drain of silver abroad in the second quarter of the 19th century, a few intrepid voices embraced the cause of reviving paper currency. Yet fiscal policymakers remained resolutely opposed to fiat money.

By the end of the 19th century, the imperial state began to issue its own silver coin in imitation of the Mexican Republican dollars that had already become a significant part of the domestic money supply.[22] Still, on the eve of the fall of the empire in 1911, China's money supply remained a heterogeneous mix of uncoined (sycee) silver (including a multitude of tael standards), foreign and domestic silver coins (abiding to a relatively uniform *yuan*

[19] William T. Rowe, "State and Market in Mid-Qing Economic Thought: The Case of Chen Hongmou (1696–1771)," *Études Chinoises* 12.1 (1993): 7–40.

[20] Dunstan is careful to distinguish this form of economic liberalism from "laissez-faire" liberalism. Helen Dunstan, *Conflicting Counsels to Confuse the Age: A Documentary Study of Political Economy in Qing China, 1644–1840* (Ann Arbor: University of Michigan Center for Chinese Studies, 1996), pp. 327–33; Helen Dunstan, "A Different Trajectory: Market-Consciousness in Chinese Political Economy, 800–1800," *Journal of Chinese History* 4.1 (2020): 55–83.

[21] Von Glahn, "Modalities of the Fiscal State," pp. 22–29.

[22] Von Glahn, "Foreign Silver Coins."

monetary standard derived from the Mexican dollar), new and old copper coins, and a variety of paper bills (denominated in both copper coin and silver) issued by private firms and foreign banks that had highly circumscribed spheres of circulation.[23] Only in 1935, when the Guomindang Republican government nationalized the banking sector and issued a new fiat paper currency (*fabi* 法幣), did China abandon the silver standard.[24]

The invention of paper money in China was rooted in the basic principles of Chinese monetary theory, the fiduciary nature of the bronze coin standard, and the specific forms of the fiscal state that characterized Song political economy rather than simply being an outgrowth of market expansion. The demise of paper money in the early Ming dynasty likewise stemmed from radical changes in the fiscal constitution of the imperial state. Not surprisingly, then, the course of Chinese monetary history diverged markedly from the path leading to the adoption of paper money in Western Europe. To clarify this divergence, it is worth considering the long-term trends in moneymaking in Europe and the distinctive forms of paper money that arose there in the early modern era.

In early medieval Europe, even as coins receded from market exchange, they remained potent symbols and instruments of political power, their iconography encoding the legitimacy of sovereign authority.[25] As in China, the quality of coin was believed to personify the moral integrity of the ruler, perhaps even more so as lordship fragmented among a broad spectrum of landed elites and ecclesiastic institutions. Charlemagne's restoration of the royal bust on his coins harked back not only to Roman practice but to the Roman idea of emperorship, even if Carolingian claims to universal dominion proved fleeting. The geography of coinage mirrored the distribution of political power, not the contours of commercial networks. Demanding payment in money tightened the grip of lords over peasants. Yet elite demand for coin fostered its wider circulation among the populace and its use in local market exchange. The intensity of monetization varied unevenly across and within regions, often flowing and ebbing in temporal cycles. Moreover, although the proliferation of coin as a medium of exchange altered the modes of peasant-based agricultural production and the social and political dominance of the elites, it did not fundamentally transform them.[26]

23 For an overview of the monetary landscape in late 19th-century China, see Niv Horesh, *Chinese Money in Global Context: Historic Junctures Between 600 BCE and 2012* (Stanford, CA: Stanford University Press, 2014), chapters 4 and 5.

24 On the creation of the *fabi* currency, see Tomoko Shiroyama, *China During the Great Depression: Market, State, and the World Economy, 1927–1937* (Cambridge, MA: Harvard University Asia Center, 2008); Dean, *End of Global Silver*.

25 This paragraph draws on Naismith, *Making Money in the Early Middle Ages*.

26 For a trenchant but contestable argument for the fundamental stability of agrarian modes of production throughout Eurasia during the Middle Ages, see Chris Wickham, "How

The principle that the king exercised sovereign authority over the making of money remained inviolable. Aquinas, seeking to settle the inconsistencies in Aristotle's declarations about money, affirmed the right of the prince to make or unmake money and, through the instrument of law, to establish his coin as the exclusive means of public and private payments.[27] Still, given the vagaries of the supplies of gold and silver, European monarchs only had limited flexibility to coin money as they desired. Bills of exchange were highly encumbered and had no validity as means of public payments. Instead, when strapped for cash for its current expenditures, the English Crown resorted to issuing wooden tallies (claims on future revenues) that were denominated in the official units of account (pounds and shillings), convertible with silver coin, and transferable to third parties. These tokens, precursors of bonds as a form of public debt, constituted as large a share of the English money supply in the late 14th and 15th centuries as did coin. The proliferation of tallies testified to the power of the English monarchy to make money on the strength of sovereign authority.[28]

Yet sovereign power over money became increasingly contested in the late medieval and early modern eras, when European rulers constantly resorted to depreciation, debasement, recoinage, and legislation to steady the value of their coin, with decidedly mixed results. The onset of the Hundred Years' War with the English invasion of Flanders in 1337 forced the French king Philip VI to resort to radical debasement, reducing the silver content of his coin by half, which provoked strident reaction among the landed aristocracy. An even more vehement uproar greeted Edward III's debasement of English coinage in 1351, compelling him to surrender crucial fiscal powers to Parliament and to pledge never to seek recourse to debasement in the future. Guillaume le Soterel, treasurer general of Navarre, cogently observed c. 1340 that those who live off rents favored strong money (full-bodied coin that retained its value over time); the laboring classes desired "weak" money (cheap and plentiful coin for conducting immediate transactions); merchants favored "a middle sort of money," neither too cheap nor too dear; while princes debased their coin in times of war to pay their armies.[29] Writing two decades later, Nicole Oresme denounced debasement as a royal tax on the wealth of the people. Oresme's famous declaration that money belongs to the community, not the prince, won widespread endorsement in no small part because it defended the interests of the rentier landowners, the lay and clerical elites. In the context of the general debasement of silver currencies across Europe during the 14th and 15th

Did the Feudal Economy Work? The Economic Logic of Medieval Societies," *Past and Present* 251 (2021): 3–40.

27 Lapidus, "Metal, Money, and the Prince," pp. 25–27.

28 Desan, *Making Money*, pp. 171–89.

29 Cited in Spufford, *Money in Medieval Europe*, pp. 305–6.

centuries (excepting England and Aragon, whose kings could more readily levy taxes to raise revenues), Oresme's views became enshrined as the new orthodoxy intended to constrain the ruler's arbitrary manipulation of the money he coined.[30] In this intellectual and political milieu, credibility would not be readily granted to fiat money of any sort.

Not surprisingly, then, the earliest form of paper money to appear in Europe was the invention not of sovereign authorities but rather private agents. In Naples in the early 1570s, bills known as *fedi di credito* (literally, "statements of trust") issued by deposit branches of lay charitable foundations began to circulate as means of payment. Only later did the Neapolitan government charter these institutions as public banks and authorize them to issue such bills. *Fedi di credito* originated as receipts for deposits; endorsed by the issuing institution, they could be transferred to third parties and were payable to the bearer on sight. *Fedi* were liabilities against the assets of the bank, not the depositor, and enjoyed public confidence because of the reputation of the charities' powerful benefactors and the aura of piety evoked by their religious mission. In principle, *fedi* could only be issued to depositors, in amounts equal to the coin they deposited, and thus were fully backed by cash assets. But behind the shield of their patrons, the banks circumvented the rules by issuing overdrafts and credits well beyond their cash reserves (precipitating a crisis, if not a mortal blow, when Neapolitan coin was devalued in 1622). These banks continued to issue *fedi* bills for centuries, until they were merged into the Banco Nazionale di Napoli in 1794. The *fedi* bills were fiduciary money, not backed by any state authority, although their circulation was largely limited to Naples – but, it should be noted, Naples was one of early modern Europe's most important financial centers.[31]

The Neapolitan *fedi* were not widely imitated, however.[32] Nor did they challenge the principle of sovereign authority over money. (The Kingdom of Naples was, after all, a distant appendage of the Habsburg monarchy in Spain.)

30 Spufford, *Money in Medieval Europe*, pp. 289–318.

31 Lilia Costabile and Eduardo Nappi, "The Public Banks of Naples Between Financial Innovation and Crisis," in Lilia Costabile and Larry Neal (eds.), *Financial Innovation and Resilience: A Comparative Perspective on the Public Banks of Naples (1462–1608)* (Cham, Switzerland: Springer International, 2018), pp. 17–53.

32 In 1661, the royally chartered Bank of Stockholm began to issue banknotes as a substitute for Sweden's cumbersome copper currency, but overissue of notes led to insolvency and dissolution of the bank two years later. The French royal mint inaugurated the issue of paper *billets de monnaie* in 1701 as a wartime expedient; these bills later were superseded by those issued by John Law's ill-fated Banque Générale, which failed spectacularly in 1720. The Bank of England established the first viable paper currency in Europe. See François R. Velde, "Experiments with Paper Money," in Stefano Battilossi, Youssef Cassis, and Kazuhiko Yago (eds.), *Handbook of the History of Money and Currency* (Singapore: Springer Nature Singapore, 2020).

Ultimately, it was the political and economic turmoil of the 17th-century English civil wars that eroded long-standing convictions about sovereign authority to make money and set its value by decree. The transformation of public finance during the civil wars, the restoration, and the onset of the Hanoverian monarchy engendered a constitutional shift in economic as well as political theory. The creation of public debt under parliamentary sanction not only remade state finance and radically increased the scale of taxation but also reinvented the concept of money. Paper money, understood as a loan by the state to the public that would be acceptable for payment of taxes and other obligations, emerged as an alternative to short-term tax levies for purposes such as waging war. The creation of the Bank of England in 1694 joined the private interests of investors to the public interest in promoting fiscal stability at home and foreign commerce abroad. The bank issued both bonds and "cash notes," which could be redeemed in specie on demand. Through a series of legislative actions – allowing them to be assigned to third parties, accepting them in public payments, and granting the Bank of England a monopoly on the issue of such bills – these banknotes gradually began to circulate as general currency. Over the course of the 18th century, the Bank of England's banknotes – denominated in a new unit of account (the gold guinea, in place of the silver penny) and supplemented by notes issued by country banks – largely replaced specie in the marketplace, enabling the government to increase the money supply without minting new gold and silver coins.[33] Yet banknotes remained a creature of the British state; their validity rested on the state's obligation to honor its commitments to its creditors.

At the same time the theoretical foundations of money were transformed. With the advent of paper currency, the value of money depended not on its intrinsic metallic content but rather on the obligation of the government to accept it in payment of public debts. Moreover, political theorists – beginning most famously with John Locke – repudiated the sovereign's arbitrary authority over money. Although Locke remained wedded to the idea that silver was the true form of wealth (with the mercantilist corollary that increasing the domestic stock of silver increased the nation's wealth), he enunciated the principle that the purpose of money was to enable trade among private individuals. Like Davanzati (see the Introduction of this book), Locke restricted the role of the sovereign to guaranteeing the quality of coin in circulation, sternly rejecting any political intervention to change its value (i.e., through debasement or devaluation).[34] Locke's full-throated commitment

[33] Desan, *Making Money*, pp. 231–329.

[34] Desan, *Making Money*, pp. 345–59. The English translation of Davanzati's treatise published in 1696 figured significantly in debates over money in the wake of England's Great Debasement of 1694; the translation itself was undertaken to support Locke's position. See Stefano Adamo, "Recovering Unnoticed Ideas: On the English Translation

to metallism was catalyzed by the dynamic growth of international trade in his day and the ready outflow of bullion in the wake of debasements that it facilitated.[35] The proliferation of banknotes in the 18th century contradicted Locke's identification of money with silver but vindicated his larger point that money served private, not sovereign, interests. Understood as a substitute for specie, not a form of credit, banknotes enjoyed full confidence among merchants and landed elites. The financial revolution of 18th-century England was rooted, as Christine Desan has put it, in this "credibility of money."[36] The credibility of banknotes also enabled the practice of fractional lending, expanding the role of banks in trade and investment. At the same time, the government's future revenues secured the Bank of England's nominal promise to redeem its banknotes with specie without requiring it to dispense gold and silver coin. Nonetheless, the government's role in making money was veiled by the idea (later the theoretical foundation of the gold standard) that it is the private economy which creates and validates money. The emergence of exclusive national fiat currencies in the 19th century coincided with rising ideas of popular sovereignty asserting that money belonged to and served the interests of the people.[37]

In Britain as in China, the acceptability of paper money in state payments was crucial to its credibility in the eyes of the people. The conceptualization of money in 18th-century Europe veered in different directions than the chartalist tradition that prevailed in China down to the Ming era, but in both cases public finance was the underlying foundation of fiat currency. During the Song–Yuan era, the state's commitment to accepting its paper money in public payments sustained its viability, even when fiscal exigencies compelled excessive issue of bills that weakened their exchange value. Under Ming rule, however, the circular flow of paper money between state and society was sundered, fatally compromising its credibility. Sovereign money receded from market exchange, its place usurped by uncoined silver. The massive infusions of foreign silver from the 16th century onward cemented the primacy of silver in both private and public payments.

Desan has noted that medieval and early modern European writers frequently spoke of money using metaphors of blood and bodily fluids to define money as a substance essential to the vitality and organic unity of the polity. As we have seen, Davanzati invoked this metaphor when he alluded to money as the "second blood," which by analogy with the blood of the human body

of Bernardo Davanzati's 'Lezione delle monete,'" in Lidia de Michelis, Lia Guerra, and Frank O'Gorman (eds.), *Entangled Histories: Politics and Culture in 18th-Century Anglo-Italian Encounters* (Newcastle-upon-Tyne: Cambridge Scholars Publishing, 2019), pp. 47–75.

35 Andrew Sartori, "Silver and the Social in Locke's Monetary Thought," *Journal of Modern History* 93.3 (2021): 501–32.

36 Desan, *Making Money*, p. 386.

37 Eric Helleiner, *The Making of National Money: Territorial Currencies in Historical Perspective* (Ithaca, NY: Cornell University Press, 2003).

"preserves alive the civil body of the commonwealth."[38] The blood metaphor and the assertion that monetary circulation animated the national economy found favor among both mercantilists in the 17th century and physiocrats in the 18th century. But in the liberal economic philosophy that arose in 18th-century England, the blood metaphor was eclipsed by the new metaphor of water, as in David Hume's formulation that money, like water, seeks equilibrium: money will flow from nation to nation, following the gravitational pull of price-setting demand, overriding the artificial barriers that states erect to restrict its movement. The analogy to water as a natural and irresistible force beyond human capacity for control complemented the newly ascendant idea that the circulation of money responded to the autonomous workings of the private market rather than the arbitrary will of the sovereign.[39]

We also find the metaphors of blood and water widely applied to money and trade in Chinese political economy. Strikingly, the analogy to blood was most prominently invoked in the context of paper money, for example by the Southern Song statesmen Wu Yong, Wu Qian, and Xu Luqing, who spoke of *huizi* as the "blood" or "lifeblood" (*mingmai*) of state and society.[40] The metaphor of money as water had a more ancient lineage in China, applied to the circulation (*liutong* 流通) of both money and commodities. The word "circulation" itself referred to the flow (*liu*) of water, but not its free dispersal. Instead, *tong* denoted conduits whereby water is channeled to its proper place. Indeed, early references to the circulation of money and goods evoked the crucial intervention of the sage-ruler who creates the channels by which money and trade can nourish the economic welfare of the people.[41] It is hardly surprising that in China, where control of water for irrigation was essential to agricultural livelihood, water would be understood not simply as a free-flowing natural resource but one whose benefits can be realized only through wise human intervention. The analogies to bodily fluids and water often fused together, since Chinese medicine defined the healthy body as one in which vital energies flowed unimpeded. But here, too, proper circulation required vigilance and human remedy. We see this in the *Salt and Iron Debates*, for example, where Sang Hongyang declares that when Emperor Wu charged him with overseeing the state's fiscal policies "it was to use moxibustion and acupuncture to treat the stagnant humors, to open the hundred arteries of

[38] See Introduction.

[39] Desan, *Making Money*, pp. 422–27.

[40] See Chapter 6.

[41] For example, Xun Zi wrote that the enlightened ruler "regulates the flow of goods and opens up their fount, pouring forth from it only at the proper times" (節其流，開其源，而時斟酌焉), followed up by the statement that the sage-kings Yu (immortalized as the conqueror of the primeval flood by digging river channels) and Tang (who along with Yu was credited with creating money) "understood the primary and the secondary [sources of wealth], the fount and flow of goods" (知本末源流之謂也). See chapter 10, "Fuguo" 富國, in *XZ*, p. 220.

profit and thereby stimulate the circulation (*liutong*) of the myriad goods and fill the coffers of the state."[42] Borrowing metaphors ubiquitously employed in Chinese medicine, in Chinese political economy it is the sovereign who ensures the proper circulation necessary to the health of the body politic.

In the opinion of William Rowe, the concept of *liutong* "achieved a new legitimacy and urgency" in the mid Qing period "when it became a central goal of imperial economic policy."[43] But *liutong* was no longer orchestrated by the state. Instead, statesmen and writers on political economy championed the unfettered circulation of goods – notably grain and other foodstuffs – through private market exchange as the most efficient way to relieve scarcities and modulate prices. Merchants were recognized for their positive contributions to public welfare, and commerce was seen not merely as enabling the circulation of necessities but also as generating wealth in its own right. By contrast, state actors – misguided officials and predatory clerks – often were vilified for impeding the free circulation of goods. The political economy of the 18th century not only endorsed the idea that commercial exchange should "follow its own course" (*ziran*) but validated the pursuit of private profit as a proper incentive for engaging in commercial activities that benefited the state (through enhanced revenues) as well as "the livelihood of the people" (*minsheng* 民生).[44] In the monetary sphere, as we have seen, the tide turned decisively in a metallist direction that abjured the chartalist doctrines underpinning the issue of paper money in earlier times. Wei Yuan, one of the most influential statecraft scholars in the first half of the 19th century, embraced this metallist conception of money, which he defined as "treasure created naturally by Heaven and Earth" (*tiandi ziran zhi zhen* 天地自然之珍).[45] In his vehement rejection of Wang Liu's proposal to revive paper currency, Wei reiterated the failures of paper money in the past, concluding – in an unwitting echo of Hume – that imposing fiat currencies would only cause sound metallic money to flow abroad, as was happening with silver in the present day. Wei devoted most of his treatise on provisioning the military (written on the eve of the Opium War) to strategies for increasing the domestic supply of silver and thereby "open up the benefits of the fount of money" (*kai huoyuan zhi li* 開貨源之利).[46] Following the triumph of the silver economy, historical memory consigned the paper money of the Song–Yuan era to the dustbin.

42 灸刺稽滯，開利百脈，是以萬物流通，而縣官富實. Chapter 14, "Qingzhong," in *YTL*, 1, p. 180.

43 William T. Rowe, *Saving the World: Chen Hongmou and Elite Consciousness in Eighteenth-Century China* (Stanford, CA: Stanford University Press, 2001), p. 198.

44 Rowe, *Saving the World*, pp. 197–214. Rowe emphasizes, however, that Chinese political economy always envisioned that governance required moral leadership and never countenanced the sanctity of the individual at the core of Lockean and subsequent liberal thought in the West. On *ziran*, see above.

45 Wei Yuan 魏源, "Junchu pian (san)" 軍儲篇 (三), in *Wei Yuan ji* 魏源集 ([hereafter *WYJ*]; Beijing: Zhonghua shuju, 1976), 2, p. 484.

46 "Junchu pian," in *WYJ*, 2, pp. 468–89. The quoted phrase appears on p. 471.

BIBLIOGRAPHY

Abbreviations for Collectanea

BTZB	*Beijing tushuguan guji zhenben congshu* 北京圖書館古籍珍本叢書. Beijing: Shumu wenxian chubanshe, 1987–1999.
CSJC	*Congshu jicheng* 叢書集成. Shanghai: Shangwu yinshuguan, 1935–1939.
DJMHL	*Dongjing menghua lu wai sizhong* 東京夢華錄外四種. Beijing: Zhonghua shuju, 1962.
SBCK	*Sibu congkan* 四部叢刊. Shanghai: Shangwu yinshuguan, 1929.
SKQS	*Wenyuange Siku quanshu*文淵閣四庫全書. Taipei: Taiwan shangwu yinshuguan, 1983.
SSJZS	Ruan Yuan 阮元 (comp.). *Shisanjing zhushu* 十三經注疏. Rpt., Beijing: Zhonghua shuju, 1980.
ST	Wang Yunwu 王雲五 (ed.). *Shitong* 十通. Shanghai: Shangwu yinshuguan, 1935.
SYDFZ	*Song Yuan difangzhi congshu* 宋元地方志叢書. Taipei: Dahua shuju, 1970.
XX SKQS	*Xuxiu Siku quanshu* 續修四庫全書. Shanghai: Shanghai guji chubanshe, 1995.

Primary Sources in Chinese

An Wu sizhong 安吳四種. Bao Shichen 包世臣. 1888 rpt. of 1872 ed.

Anhui tongzhi gao jinshi guwu kao 安徽通志稿金石古物攷. Ed. Xu Naichang 徐乃昌. Taipei: Dingwen shuju, 1972.

Bao Xiaosu zouyi ji 包孝肅奏議集. Bao Zheng 包拯. SKQS ed.

Beixi da quanqi 北溪大全集. Chen Chun 陳淳. SKQS ed.

Bizhou gaoluë 敝帚稿略. Bao Hui 包恢. SKQS ed.

Caomuzi 草木子. Ye Ziqi 葉子奇. Beijing: Zhonghua shuju, 1959.

Cefu yuangui 冊府元龜. Wang Qinruo 王欽若 et al. (comp.). Rpt. Beijing: Zhonghua shuju, 1960.

Changgu ji 昌谷集. Cao Yanyue 曹彥约. SKQS ed.

Chen Zhongyu quanji 陳忠裕全集. Chen Zilong 陳子龍. 1805 Ganshao caotang ed.

Chengzhai ji 誠齋集. Yang Wanli 楊萬里. SKQS ed.

Chitang cungao 恥堂存稿. Gao Side 高斯得. SKQS ed.
Chunming mengyu lu 春明夢餘錄. Sun Chengze 孫承澤. 1883 Guxiangzhai ed., rpt. Yangzhou: Jiangsusheng guangling guji keyinshe, 1990.
Da Ming huidian 大明會典. Shen Shixing 申時行 et al. (comp). 1587 ed.; rpt. Taipei: Xinwenfeng chuban gongsi, 1976.
Da Yuan shengzheng guochao dianzhang 大元聖政國朝典章. 1908 ed., rpt. Taipei: Wenhai chubanshe, 1964.
Danzhai ji 澹齋集. Li Liuqian 李流謙. SKQS ed.
Daoyi zhilüe jiaoshi 島夷志略校釋. Wang Dayuan 汪大淵. Ed. Su Jiqing 蘇繼廎. Beijing: Zhonghua shuju, 2000.
Daxue yanyi bu 大學衍義補. Qiu Jun 邱濬. SKQS ed.
Dingju suanfa 丁巨算法. CSJC ed.
Dongjing menghua lu 東京夢華錄. Meng Yuanlao 孟元老. DJMHL ed.
Ducheng jisheng 都城記勝. DJMHL ed.
Erlaotang zazhi 二老堂雜志. Zhou Bida 周必大. CSJC ed.
Gongkui ji 攻媿集. Lou Yue 樓鑰. SKQS ed.
Guan Zi jiaozhu 管子校注. Ed. Li Xiangfeng 黎翔鳳. Beijing: Zhonghua shuju, 2004.
Gui'er ji 貴耳集. Zhang Duanyi 張端義. SKQS ed.
Guiqian zhi 歸錢志. Liu Qi 劉祁. SKQS ed.
Guizhai wenji 圭齋文集. Ouyang Xuan 歐陽玄. SKQS ed.
Gujin hebi shilei beiyao 古今合璧事類備要. Xie Weixin 謝維新. SKQS ed.
Gujin yuanliu zhilun xuji 古今源流至論續集. Lin Jiong 林駉 (comp.). 1427 ed.
Guoyu zhijie 国语直解. Ed. Lai Kehong 来可泓. Shanghai: Fudan daxue chubanshe, 2000.
Han shu 漢書. Ban Gu 班固. Beijing: Zhonghua shuju ed.
Helin ji 鶴林集. Wu Yong 吳泳. SKQS ed.
Heshan xiansheng da quanji 鶴山先生大全集. Wei Liaoweng 魏了翁. SKQS ed.
Hou Han shu 後漢書. Beijing: Zhonghua shuju ed.
Houle ji 後樂集. Wei Jing 衛涇. SKQS ed.
Huainan honglie jishi 淮南鴻烈集釋. Ed. Liu Wendian 劉文典. Beijing: Zhonghua shuju, 1989.
Huaman lu 畫墁錄. Zhang Shunmin 張舜民. In Tao Zongyi 陶宗儀 (ed.), *Shuofu* 說郛. 1646 ed.
Huang Ming jingshi wenbian 皇明經世文編. Ed. Chen Zilong 陳子龍. 1637 ed.; rpt. Taipei: Guofeng chubanshe, 1964.
Huang Ming tiaofa shilei zuan 皇明條法事類纂. Ed. Dai Jin 戴金. Rpt. Taipei: Wenhai chubanshe, 1985.
Huang Song zhongxing liangchao shengzheng 皇宋中興兩朝聖政. Liu Zheng 留正. Wanwei biecang ed.; rpt. Taipei: Wenhai chubanshe, 1967.
Huangchao biannian gangmu beiyao 皇朝編年綱目備要. Chen Jun 陳均. Rpt. Taipei: Chengwen chubanshe, 1966.
Huangshi richao 黃氏日抄. Huang Zhen 黃震. SKQS ed.

Hyakurenshō 百錬抄. In Kuroita Katsumi 黑板勝美 (ed.), [*Shintei zōho*] *Kokushi taikei* [新訂增補] 國史大系, vol. 11. Tokyo: Yoshikawa kōbunkan, 1929.
Jianghu changweng wenji 江湖長翁文集. Chen Zao 陳造. SKQS ed.
Jiangsu jinshi zhi 江蘇金石志. N.p.: Jiangsu tongzhiju, 1927.
[*Jingding*] *Jiankang zhi* [景定] 建康志. SYDFZ ed.
Jianyan yilai chaoye zaji 建炎以來朝野雜記. Li Xinchuan 李心傳. Beijing: Zhonghua shuju, 2006.
Jianyan yilai xinian yaolu 建炎以來繫年要錄. Li Xinchuan 李心傳. Beijing: Zhonghua shuju, 1988.
Jiezhai ji 潔齋集. Yuan Xie 袁燮. SKQS ed.
Jin shi 金史. Beijing: Zhonghua shuju ed.
Jingshi qieyao 經世挈要. Zhang Sui 張燧. 1633 Fuchangchen ed., rpt. BJZB.
Jingsuo biji 敬所筆記. Xu Dunqiu 許敦俅. Unpublished ms. transcribed in Chen Xuewen 陈学文, "'Jingsuo biji' xiaoxu" '敬所筆記' 小序, *Minsu yanjiu* 民俗研究 1989.4: 62–64.
Jiting quanshu 幾亭全書. Chen Longzheng 陳龍正. 1665.
Jiu Tang shu 舊唐書. Beijing: Zhonghua shuju ed.
Keting leigao 客亭類稿. Yang Guanqing 楊冠卿. SKQS ed.
Kezhai zagao 可齋雜藁. Li Zengbo 李曾伯. SKQS ed.
Lanpei lu 攬轡錄. Fan Chengda 范成大. In Tao Zongyi 陶宗儀 (ed.), *Shuofu* 說郛, vol. 65. 1646 ed.
Lao Zi jiaoshi 老子校釋. Zhu Qianzhi 朱謙之. Beijing: Zhonghua shuju, 1984.
Li Gou ji 李覯集. Li Gou 李覯. Beijing: Zhonghua shuju, 2011.
Liangchao gangmu beiyao 兩朝綱目備要. Anon. SKQS ed.
Liangzhe jinshi zhi 兩浙金石志. Ed. Ruan Yuan 阮元. Rpt. Hangzhou: Zhejiang shuju, 1890.
Lidai mingchen zouyi 歷代名臣奏議. Ed. Yang Shiqi 楊士奇. 1416 ed.
Lidai zhidu xiangshuo 歷代制度詳說. Lü Zuqian 呂祖謙. CSJC xubian ed.
Liji zhengyi 禮記正義. SSJZS ed.
Lingyan ji 靈巖集. Tang Shichi 唐士耻. SKQS ed.
Longquan lüezhi 龍川略志. Su Che 蘇徹. Beijing: Zhonghua shuju, 1982.
Liu Wenan gong daizhai xiansheng celüe 劉文安公呆齋先生策略. Liu Dingzhi 劉定之. 1594 ed., rpt. in Siku quanshu cunmu congshu.
Lü Mingde xiansheng shendutang ji 呂明德先生慎獨堂集. Lü Weiqi 呂維祺. 1652 ed.
Lu Xiangshan quanji 陸象山全集. Lu Jiuyuan 陸九淵. Taipei: Shijie shuju, 1969.
Lu Xuangong ji 陸宣公集. Lu Zhi 陸贄. Hangzhou: Zhejiang guji chubanshe, 1988.
Luancheng ji 欒城集. Su Che 蘇轍. SBCK ed.
Lüshi chunqiu jiaoshi 呂氏春秋校釋. Ed. Chen Qiyou 陳奇猷. Shanghai: Xuelin chubanshe, 1994.
Maofeng zhenyin manlu 鄮峯真隱漫錄. Shi Hao 史浩. SKQS ed.
Mencius. Mengzi 孟子. SSJZS ed.

Meng liang lu 夢梁錄. Wu Zimu 吳自牧. DJMHL ed.
[*Xin jiaozheng*] *Mengxi bitan* [新校正]夢溪筆談. Shen Gua 沈括. Ed. Hu Daojing 胡道靜. Beijing: Zhonghua shuju, 1957.
Mengzhai ji 蒙齋集. Yuan Fu 袁甫. SKQS ed.
Mianzhai ji 勉齋集. Huang Gan 黃幹. SKQS ed.
Ming Qing Huizhou shehui jingji ziliao congbian 明清徽州社会经济资料丛编. Ed. Anhuisheng bowuguan 安徽省博物馆. N.p.: Zhongguo shehui kexue chubanshe, 1988.
Ming shi 明史. Beijing: Zhonghua shuju ed.
Ming shilu 明實錄. Rpt. Taipei: Zhongyang yanjiuyuan lishi yuyan yanjiusuo, 1962.
Minggong shupan Qingming ji 名公書判清明集. Beijing: Zhonghua shuju, 1987.
Mingshui ji 洺水集. Cheng Bi 程珌. SKQS ed.
Minzhong jinshi lüe 閩中金石略. Ed. Chen Panren 陳棨仁. 1865.
Mizhai biji 密齋筆記. Xie Caibo 謝采伯. SKQS ed.
Mo Zi jiaozhu 墨子校注. Ed. Wu Yujiang 吳毓江. Beijing: Zhonghua shuju, 1993.
Mu'an ji 牧庵集 , Yao Sui 姚燧. SKQS ed.
Nan Qi shu 南齊書. Xiao Zixian 蕭子顯 et al. Zhonghua shuju ed.
Nancun chuogenglu 南村輟耕錄. Tao Zongyi 陶宗儀. Beijing: Zhonghua shuju, 1959.
Nongtian yuhua 農田餘話. Changgu zhenyi 長谷真逸 (pseud.). Baoyantang miji ed.
Nongzheng quanshu jiaozhu 農政全書校注. Xu Guangqi 徐光啟. Ed. Shi Shenghan 石聲漢. Shanghai: Shanghai guji chubanshe, 1979.
Ouyang Xiu quanji 歐陽脩全集. Ouyang Xiu 歐陽脩. Taipei: Shijie shuju, 1971.
Panzhou wenji 盤洲文集. Hong Kuo 洪适. SBCK ed.
Qianbi chuyan 錢幣芻言. Wang Liu 王瑬. 1837.
Qiangdong leigao 牆東類稿. Lu Wengui 陸文圭. SKQS ed.
Qiantang yishi 錢塘遺事. Liu Yiqing 劉一清. 1799 ed.; rpt. Shanghai: Shanghai guji chubanshe, 1985.
Qingyuan tiaofa shilei 慶元條法事類. Ed. Xie Shenfu 謝深甫. Seikado Library ms., rpt. Taipei: Xinwenfeng chubanshe, 1976.
Qingxian ji 清獻集. Du Fan 杜范. SKQS ed.
Qingzheng cungao 清正存稿. Xu Luqing 徐鹿卿. SKQS ed.
Qintang yusu bian 琴堂諭俗編. Ying Jun 應俊. SKQS ed.
Qiujian xiansheng daquan wenji 秋澗先生大全文集. Wang Yun 王惲. SKQS ed.
Qiuya xiansheng xiaogao 秋崖先生小稿. Fang Yue 方岳. Qing ms.
Quan Tang wen 全唐文. Beijing: Zhonghua shuju, 1983.
Quanzhi 泉志. Hong Zun 洪遵. Rpt. in Ren Renren 任仁仁 (ed.), *Quanzhi wai sanzhong* 泉志外三種. Shanghai: Shanghai shudian chubanshe, 2018.
Rongzhai suibi 容齋隨筆. Hong Mai 洪邁. Shanghai: Shanghai guji chubanshe, 1978.
Runan yishi 汝南遺事. Wang E 王鶚. SKQS ed.
Sanchao beimeng huibian 三朝北盟會編. Xu Mengxin 徐夢莘. 1939 ed.; rpt. Taipei: Dahua shuju, 1977.

Shang shu 尚書. SSJZS ed.
Shantang qunshu kaosuo 山堂群書考索. Zhang Ruyu 章如愚. 1521 ed.; rpt. in BTZB.
Shi ji 史記. Sima Qian 司馬遷. Zhonghua shuju ed.
[*Chongbian qunshu leiyao*] *Shilin guangji* [重編群書類要]事林廣記. Chen Yuanjing 陳元靚. 1325 ed., rpt. Kyoto: Yamaoka Ichibe hankō, 1699.
Shuowen jiezi zhu 說文解字注. Ed. Duan Yucai 段玉裁. Shanghai: Shanghai guji chubanshe, 1981.
Shuoyuan 說苑. Liu Xiang 劉向. Taipei: Guoli Taiwan shifan daxue chuban zhongxin, 2012.
Shupu 鼠璞. Dai Zhi 戴埴. SKQS ed.
Shushu shizhang 數書十章. Qin Jiushao 秦九韶. 1841 Yijiatang congshu ed.
Shuyuan zaji 菽園雜記. Lu Rong 陸容. Beijing: Zhonghua shuju, 1985.
Shuzhong guangji 蜀中廣記. Cao Xuequan 曹學佺. Shanghai: Shanghai guji chubanshe, 2020.
[*Kaiqing*] *Siming xuzhi* [開慶] 四明續志. SYDFZ ed.
[*Baoqing*] *Siming zhi* [寶慶] 四明志. SYDFZ ed.
[*Zhizheng*] *Siming zhi* [至正] 四明志. SYDFZ ed.
Song Duanmingdian xueshi Cai Zhonghui gong wenji 宋端明殿學士蔡忠惠公文集. Cai Xiang 蔡襄. 1740 Xunminzhai ed.
Song huiyao jigao 宋會要輯稿. Ed. Xu Song 徐松. Rpt. Taipei: Xinwenfeng chuban gongsi, 1976.
Song shi 宋史. Beijing: Zhonghua shuju ed.
Song xing tong 宋刑統. Beijing: Zhonghua shuju, 1984.
Song zhonghui tie'an Fang gong wenji 宋忠惠鐵庵方公文集. Fang Dacong 方大琮. 1521 ed.; rpt. in BTZB.
Songchao shishi 宋朝事實. Li You 李攸. Wuyingdian zhenban ed.; rpt. Taipei: Wenhai chubanshe, 1967.
Songji sanchao zhengyao 宋季三朝政要. SKQS ed.
Songshi quanwen 宋史全文. SKQS ed.
Su Dongpo quanji 蘇東坡全集. Su Shi 蘇軾. Taipei: Shijie shuju, 1982.
Taiping zhiji tonglei 太平治蹟統類. Peng Baichuan 彭百川. SKQS ed.
Tang hui yao 唐會要. Wang Pu 王溥. Shanghai: Shanghai guji chubanshe, 1981.
Tongdian 通典. Du You 杜佑. ST ed.
Tongjiang ji 桐江集. Fang Hui 方回. XX SKQS ed.
Wang Linchuan quanji 王臨川全集. Wang Anshi 王安石. Taipei: Shijie shuju, 1966.
Wanli kuaiji lu 萬曆會計錄. Zhang Xueyan 張學顏 (comp.). 1587 ed., rpt. in BTZB.
Wei Yuan ji 魏源集. Wei Yuan 魏源. Beijing: Zhonghua shuju, 1976.
Wen Lugong ji 文潞公集. Wen Yanbo 文彥博. SKQS ed.
Wending ji 文定集. Wang Yingchen 汪應辰. SKQS ed.
Wenxian tongkao 文獻通考. Ma Duanlin 馬端臨. ST ed.
Wu Wenzheng ji 吳文正集. Wu Cheng 吳澄. SKQS ed.

Wudai huiyao 五代會要. Wang Pu 王溥. Shanghai: Shanghai guji chubanshe, 1978.
Wulin jiushi 武林舊事. Zhou Mi 周密. DJMHL ed.
Xiangshan yelu 湘山野錄. Wen Ying 文瑩. Xuehai leibian ed.
Xuelou ji 雪樓集. Cheng Jufu 程鉅夫. SKQS ed.
Xin'an wenxian zhi 新安文獻志. SKQS ed.
Xingshantang ji 性善堂集. Du Zheng 度正. SKQS ed.
Xinshu jiaozhu 新書校注. Jia Yi 賈誼. Ed. Yan Zhenyi 閻振益 and Zhong Xia 鐘夏. Beijing: Zhonghua shuju, 2000.
Xu gujin kao 續古今攷. Fang Hui 方回. SKQS ed.
Xu guogong zouyi 許國公奏議. Wu Qian 吳潛. CSJC ed.
Xu wenxian tongkao 續文獻通考. Ji Huang 嵇璜 et al. (comp.). ST ed.
Xu wenzheng yishu 許文正遺書. Xu Heng 許衡. Fujingtang ed., 1891.
Xu zizhi tongjian changbian 續資治通鑒長編. Li Tao 李燾. Beijing: Zhonghua shuju, 2004.
Xu zizhi tongjian changbian shibu 續資治通鑑長編拾補. Ed. Qin Xiangye 秦緗業 and Huang Yizhou 黃以周. 1882 ed., rpt. Shanghai: Shanghai guji chubanshe, 2006.
Xuechuang ji 雪窗集. Sun Mengguan 孫夢觀. SKQS ed.
Xun Zi jishi 荀子集釋. Ed. Li Disheng 李滌生. Taipei: Xuesheng shuju, 1979.
Yan Zi Chunqiu 晏子春秋. Ed. Zhang Jingxian 张景贤. Zhengzhou: Zhongzhou guji chubanshe, 2010.
Yantie lun jiaozhu 鹽鐵論校注. Huan Kuan 桓寬. Ed. Wang Liqi 王利器. Beijing: Zhonghua shuju, 1992.
Yanzhou tujing 嚴州圖經. SYDFZ ed.
Ye Shi ji 葉適集. Ye Shi 葉適. Beijing: Zhonghua shuju, 1961.
Yeyi, Lunqi, Tantian, Silianshi 野議, 論氣, 談天, 思憐詩. Song Yingxing 宋應星. Shanghai: Shanghai renmin chubanshe, 1976.
Yi Zhou shu huijiao jizhu 逸周書彙校集注. Ed. Huang Huaixin 黃懷信 et al. Shanghai: Shanghai guji chubanshe, 2007.
Yijian zhi 夷堅志. Hong Mai 洪邁. Beijing: Zhonghua shuju, 1981.
Yinhua lu 因話錄. Zhao Lin 趙璘. SKQS ed.
Yuan shi 元史. Beijing: Zhonghua shuju ed.
Yuhai 玉海. Wang Yinglin 王應麟. 1883 ed., rpt. Nanchang: Jiangsu guji chubanshe, 1988.
Zhang Fangping ji 張方平集. Zhang Fangping 張方平. Zhengzhou: Zhongzhou guji chubanshe, 1992.
Zhanguo ce jizhu 戰國策集注. Ed. Cheng Zhuchang 程朱昌 and Cheng Yuquan 程育全. Shanghai: Shanghai guji chubanshe, 2013.
Zhen Wenzhong gong wenji 真文忠公文集. Zhen Dexiu 真德秀. SKQS ed.
Zheng Guanying ji 鄭觀應集. Zheng Guanying 鄭觀應. Ed. Xia Dongyuan 夏东元. Shanghai: Shanghai renmin chubanshe, 1982.
Zhiping yaolüe xu 治平要略續. Zhang Shichun 章世純. Zhangshi sizhong ed.
Zhitang ji 止堂集. Peng Guinian 彭龜年. SKQS ed.

Zhizheng zhiji 至正直記. Kong Qi 孔齊. Shanghai: Shanghai guji chubanshe, 1987.
Zhongzhou mingxian wenbiao 中州名賢文表. Ed. Liu Chang 劉昌. SKQS ed.
Zhou yi 周易. SSJZS ed.
Zhouli zhushu 周禮注疏. SSJZS ed.
Zhu wengong wenji 朱文公文集. Zhu Xi 朱熹. SBCK ed.
Zhufan zhi jiaoshi 諸蕃志校釋. Zhao Rugua 趙汝适. Ed. Yang Bowen 楊博文. Beijing: Zhonghua shuju, 2000.
Zhuzi yulei 朱子語類. Zhu Xi 朱熹. Taipei: Wenhai chubanshe, 1986.
Zishan daquanji 紫山大全集. Hu Zhiyu 胡祗遹. SKQS ed.
Zizhi tongjian 資治通鑑. Sima Guang 司馬光. Beijing: Zhonghua shuju, 1956.
Zizhi tongjian changbian jishi benmo 資治通鑒長編紀事本末. Yang Zhongliang 楊仲良 (comp.). Rpt. Guangya shuju, 1893.
Zuoshi jiancao 左史諫草. Lü Wu 呂午. SKQS ed.
Zuozhuan 左傳. SSJZS ed.

OTHER WORKS CITED

Abe Takeo 安部健夫. "Gen jidai no hōginsei no kōken" 元時代の包銀制の考研. Rpt. in Abe, *Gendai shi no kenkyū* 元代史の研究. Tokyo: Sōbunsha, 1972, pp. 75–232.
Adachi Keiji 足立啓二. "Min Shin jidai ni okeru senkeizai no hatten" 明清時代における銭経済の発展. In *Chūgoku sensei kokka*, pp. 387–412.
"Sensei kokka to zaisei kahei" 専制国家と財政貨幣, in Chūgokushi kenkyūkai (ed.), *Chūgoku sensei kokka to shakai tōgō* 中国専制国家と社会統合. Tokyo: Bunrikaku, 1990, pp. 117–46.
Adamo, Stefano. "Recovering Unnoticed Ideas: On the English Translation of Bernardo Davanzati's 'Lezione delle monete.'" In Lidia de Michelis, Lia Guerra, and Frank O'Gorman (eds.), *Entangled Histories: Politics and Culture in 18th-Century Anglo-Italian Encounters*. Newcastle-upon-Tyne: Cambridge Scholars Publishing, 2019, pp. 47–75.
Aglietta, Michel. *Money: 5,000 Years of Debt and Power*. London: Verso Press, 2016.
Allsen, Thomas T. *Mongol Imperialism: The Policies of the Grand Qan Möngke in China, Russia, and the Islamic Lands, 1251–1259*. Berkeley: University of California Press, 1987.
"Mongol Princes and Their Merchant Partners, 1200–1260." *Asia Major*, 3rd series, 2.1 (1989): 83–126.
Aoki Atsushi 青木敦. "Kaihatsu, chika, minjiteki hōki: 'Seimeishū' ni mieru jakkan tochi tenbai kankeihō o megutte" 開発, 地価, 民事的法規：「清明集」に見える若干土地典売関係法をめぐって. *Machikaneyama ronshū (shigaku hen)* 待兼山論集 (史学篇) 40 (2006): 1–47.
"Sōdai teitōhō no suii to 'nōdenchoku': yōso shijō ni okeru shihō to shūkan" 宋代抵当法の推移と「農田勅」：要素市場における司法と習慣. In Furuta Kazuko 古田和子 (ed.), *Chūgoku no shijō chitsujo: jūnana seiki kara nijū*

seiki zenhan o chūshin ni 中国の市場秩序: 十七世紀から二十世紀前半を中心に. Tokyo: Keio daigaku shuppankai, 2013, pp. 19–47.

Aristotle. *Ethics*. In Jonathan Barnes (ed.), *The Complete Works of Aristotle: The Revised Oxford Translation*. Princeton, NJ: Princeton University Press, 1995.

Politics. In *Complete Works of Aristotle*.

Rhetoric. In *Complete Works of Aristotle*.

Balazs, Étienne. "A Forerunner of Wang An-shih." In Balazs, *Chinese Civilization and Bureaucracy*. New Haven, CT: Yale University Press, 1964.

Bao Weimin 包伟民. "Shilun Songdai zhibi de xingzhi jiqi lishi diwei" 试论宋代纸币的性质及 其历史地位. In Qi Xia 漆侠and Hu Zhaoxi 胡昭曦 (eds.), *Songdai yanjiu lunwenji* 宋代研究论文集. Baoding: Hebei daxue chubanshe, 1994, pp. 135–52.

Songshi shihuozhi buzheng 宋史食货志补正. 2 vols. Beijing: Zhonghua shuju, 2008.

Barbieri-Low, Anthony, and Robin D. S. Yates. *Law, State, and Society in Early Imperial China: A Study with Critical Edition and Translation of the Zhangjiashan Legal Texts from Zhangjiashan Tomb no. 247*. 2 vols. Leiden: Brill, 2015.

Belyaev, V. A. 别利亚耶夫 and S. V. Sidorovich 西多罗维奇. "Xin faxian de gongyuan 13 shiji zhongqi da menggu diguo yinbi" 新发现的公元13世纪中期大蒙古帝国银币. *Zhongguo qianbi* 中国钱币2014.1: 9–16.

Blake, Robert P. "The Circulation of Silver in the Moslem East down to the Mongol Epoch." *Harvard Journal of Asiatic Studies* 2.3–4 (1937): 291–328.

Blanc, Jérôme, and Ludovic Desmedt. "Debating Sound Money in Early Modern Europe: From Dualist to Metallic Monetary Systems." In Renate Pieper, Claudia de Lozanne Jefferies, and Markus Denzel (eds.), *Mining, Money and Markets in the Early Modern Atlantic: Digital Approaches and New Perspectives*. Cham, Switzerland: Springer Nature, 2019, pp. 29–61.

Bonney, Richard, and W. M. Ormrod. "Introduction: Crises, Revolutions and Self Sustained Growth: Towards a Conceptual Model of Change in Fiscal History." In W. M. Ormrod, Margaret Bonney, and Richard Bonney (eds.), *Crises, Revolutions, and Self-Sustained Growth: Essays in European Fiscal History*. Stamford, UK: Shaun Tyas, 1999, pp. 1–21.

Boyer-Xambeu, Marie-Thérèse, Ghislain Deleplace, and Lucien Gillard. *Private Money and Public Currencies: The Sixteenth Century Challenge*. London: Taylor & Francis, 1994.

Bresson, Alain. *The Making of the Ancient Greek Economy: Institutions, Markets, and Growth in the City States*. Princeton, NJ: Princeton University Press, 2016.

Brook, Timothy. *The Confusions of Pleasure: Commerce and Culture in Ming China*. Berkeley: University of California Press, 1998.

Cao Shuji 曹树基 and Yang Qiming 杨启明. "Qingdai dongnan difang xiaoshichang de pingpiao yu xinyong" 清代东南地方小市场中的凭票与信用. *Zhonggguo jingji shi yanjiu* 中国经济史研究 2020.6: 102–17.

Cartwright, Caroline R., Christina M. Duffy, and Helen Wang. "Microscopical Examination of Fibres Used in Ming Dynasty Paper Money." *British Museum Technical Research Bulletin* 8 (2014): 105–16.

Chaffee, John W. "Huizong, Cai Jing, and the Politics of Reform." In Ebrey and Bickford, *Emperor Huizong*, pp. 31–77.

Chan, Hok-lam. "'Comprehensiveness' (*T'ung*) and 'Change' (*Pien*) in Ma Tuan-lin's Historical Thought." In Hok-lam Chan and Wm. Theodore de Bary (eds.), *Yuan Thought: Chinese Thought and Religion Under the Mongols*. New York: Columbia University Press, 1982, pp. 27–87.

Chen Gaohua 陈高华 and Shi Weimin 史卫民. *Zhongguo jingji tongshi: Yuandai jingji juan* 中国经济通史:元代经济卷. Beijing: Jingji ribao chubanshe, 1999.

Chen Hongbin 陳鴻彬 (ed.). *Shuyintang shoucang yuanbao qianzhong tulu* 樹蔭堂收藏元寶千種圖錄. Taipei: N.p., 1988.

Chen Mingguang 陈明光 and Mao Lei 毛蕾. "Tang Song yilai de yaren yu tianzhai diandang maimai" 唐宋以来的牙人与田宅典当买卖. *Zhongguo shi yanjiu* 中国史研究2000.4: 63–72.

Cheng Mingsheng 程民生. *Songdai wujia yanjiu* 宋代物价研究. Revised ed., Nanchang: Jiangxi renmin chubanshe, 2021.

Chin, Tamara. *Savage Exchange: Han Imperialism, Chinese Literary Style, and the Economic Imagination*. Cambridge, MA: Harvard University Asia Center, 2014.

Chŏng Kwang 鄭光 (ed.). *Yuanben Laoqida* 原本老乞大. Beijing: Waiyu jiaoxue yu yanjiu chubanshe, 2002.

Cipolla, Carlo M. *Money, Prices, and Civilization in the Mediterranean World, Fifth to Seventeenth Century*. Princeton, NJ: Princeton University Press, 1956.

Clark, Hugh D. "The Southern Kingdoms Between the T'ang and the Sung, 907–979." In Twitchett and Smith, *Cambridge History of China*, vol. 5, pt. 1, pp. 133–205.

Costabile, Lilia, and Eduardo Nappi. "The Public Banks of Naples Between Financial Innovation and Crisis." In Lilia Costabile and Larry Neal (eds.), *Financial Innovation and Resilience: A Comparative Perspective on the Public Banks of Naples (1462–1608)*. Cham, Switzerland: Springer International, 2018, pp. 17–53.

Cullen, Christopher. *The Suàn shù shū* 筭數書 *'Writings on Reckoning': A Translation of a Chinese Mathematical Collection of the Second Century BC, with Explanatory Commentary*. Cambridge: Needham Research Institute, Cambridge University, 2004.

Dai Jianguo 戴建国. "Songdai de mintian dianmai yu 'yitian liangzhu zhi'" 宋代的民田典卖与「一田两主制」. *Lishi yanjiu* 历史研究 2011.6: 99–117.

"Songdai de tianzhai jiaoyi toushui pingyou he guanyin tianzhai qishu" 宋代的田宅交易投税凭由和官印田宅契书. *Zhongguo shi yanjiu* 中国史研究 2001.3: 97–111.

Tang Song biange shiqi de falü yu shehui 唐宋变革时期的法律与社会. Shanghai: Shanghai guji chubanshe, 2010.

Dai Yixuan 戴裔煊. *Songdai chaoyan zhidu yanjiu* 宋代鈔鹽制度研究. Rev. ed., Taipei: Huashi chubanshe, 1982.

Dai Zhiqiang 戴志强, Zhou Weirong 周卫荣, Li Yanxiang 李延祥, and Liu Wei 刘伟. "'Jiaxiqian' wenti zaiyanjiu" '夹锡钱'问题再研究. *Zhongguo qianbi* 中国钱币 1991.1: 4–9.

Danjō Hiroshi 壇上寛. "Shoki Min ōcho no tsūka seisaku" 初期明王朝の通貨政策. *Tōyōshi kenkyū* 東洋史研究 39.3 (1980): 527–56.

Davanzati, Bernardo. *A Discourse upon Coins*. Trans. John Toland. London: Awnsham and John Churchil, 1696.

Davis, Richard L. "The Reigns of Guang-tsung (1189–94) and Ning-tsung (1194–1224)." In Twitchett and Smith, *Cambridge History of China*, vol. 5, pt. 1, pp. 775–812.

Dawson, Christopher (ed.). *The Mongol Mission: Narratives and Letters of the Franciscan Missionaries in Mongolia and China in the Thirteenth and Fourteenth Centuries*. New York: Sheed and Ward, 1955.

de Roover, Raymond. *L'Évolution de la lettre de change, xiv[e]xviii[e] siècles*. Paris: Libraire Armond Colin, 1953.

Dean, Austin. *China and the End of Global Silver, 1873–1937*. Ithaca, NY: Cornell University Press, 2020.

Desan, Christine. *Making Money: Coin, Currency, and the Coming of Capitalism*. New York: Oxford University Press, 2014.

Deyell, John S. "Cowries and Coins: The Dual Monetary System of the Bengal Sultanate." *Indian Economic and Social History Review* 47.1 (2010): 63–106.

Dunstan, Helen. *Conflicting Counsels to Confuse the Age: A Documentary Study of Political Economy in Qing China, 1644–1840*. Ann Arbor: University of Michigan Center for Chinese Studies, 1996.

"A Different Trajectory: Market-Consciousness in Chinese Political Economy, 800–1800." *Journal of Chinese History* 4.1 (2020): 55–83.

Ebrey, Patricia B., and Maggie Bickford (eds.). *Emperor Huizong and Late Northern Song China: The Politics of Culture and the Culture of Politics*. Cambridge, MA: Harvard University Asia Center, 2006.

Elvin, Mark. *The Pattern of the Chinese Past*. Stanford, CA: Stanford University Press, 1973.

Emura Haruki 江村治樹. *Shunshū Sengoku jidai seidō kahei no seisei to tenkai* 春秋戦国時代青銅貨幣の生成と展開. Tokyo: Kyūko shoin, 2011.

Endicott-West, Elizabeth. "Merchant Associations in Yüan China: The Ortoγ." *Asia Major*, 3rd series, 2.1 (1989): 127–54.

Feng Lirong 冯丽蓉. "Wuxishi bowuguan cang Zhiyuan tongxing baochao" 无锡市博物馆藏至元通行宝钞. *Zhongguo qianbi* 中国钱币1989.3: 44–45.

Feng Zhuohui 冯卓慧. *Handai minshi jingji falü zhidu yanjiu: Hanjian ji wenxian suojian* 汉代民事经济法律制度研究: 汉简及文献所见. Beijing: Shangwu yinshuguan, 2014.

Figueira, Thomas. *The Power of Money: Coinage and Politics in the Athenian Empire*. Philadelphia: University of Pennsylvania Press, 1998.

Flynn, Dennis O., and Arturo Giráldez. "Born with a 'Silver Spoon': The Origin of World Trade in 1571." *Journal of World History* 6.2 (1995): 201–21.

China and the Birth of Globalization in the Sixteenth Century. Aldershot, UK: Ashgate Variorum, 2010.

Franke, Herbert. *Geld und Wirtschaft in China unter der Mongolen-Herrschaft: Beiträge zur Wirtschaftsgeschichte der Yüan-Zeit*. Leipzig: Otto Harrassowitz, 1949.

Fujii Hiroshi 藤井宏. "Mindai no kokō shokuen ni tsuite" 明代の戸口食鹽に就いて. *Shakai keizai shigaku* 社会経済史学 13.3 (1943): 1–30.

Funada Yoshiyuki 船田善之. "Gendai shiryō to shite no kyūhon '*Rōkitsudai*': Chō to bukka no kisai o chūshin to shite" 元代史料としての旧本「老乞大」：鈔と物価の記載を中心として. *Tōyō gakuhō* 東洋学報 83 (2001): 1–30.

Funakoshi Taiji 舟越泰次. *Tōdai ryōzeihō kenkyū* 唐代兩稅法研究. Tokyo: Kyūko shoin, 1996.

Gao Congming 高聪明. *Songdai huobi yu huobi liutong yanjiu* 宋代货币与货币流通研究. Baoding: Hebei daxue chubanshe, 1999.

"'Qiansicang' Songdai chaoban bianwei" '千斯仓' 宋代钞版辨伪. *Zhongguo qianbi* 中国钱币2023.3: 3–13.

"'Zizhou jiaohui' kao"『滋州交会』考, *Zhongguo qianbi* 中国钱币 2016.1: 9–12.

Giráldez, Arturo. *The Age of Trade: The Manila Galleons and the Dawn of the Global Economy*. Lanham, MD: Rowman and Littlefield, 2015.

Goetzmann, William N. *Money Changes Everything: How Finance Made Civilization Possible*. Princeton, NJ: Princeton University Press, 2016.

Goetzmann, William N., and K. Geert Rouwenhorst (eds.). *Origins of Value: The Financial Innovations That Created Modern Capital Markets*. New York: Oxford University Press, 2005.

Gotō Hisakatsu 後藤久勝. "Hoku-Sō jidai Kahoku ryōsō no ryūtsū to kōinho no honin ni tsuite" 北宋時代河北糧草の流通と交引舗の保任について. *Kyūshū daigaku tōyōshi ronshū* 九州大学東洋史論集 26 (1998): 29–48.

Graeber, David. *Debt: The First 5,000 Years*. Revised ed. Brooklyn, NY: Melville House, 2014.

Grass, Noa. "Imperial Silver Laundering: The Official Narrative on Gold Floral Silver and the Silverization of Ming State Finance." *Ming Studies* 76 (2017): 7–31.

Green, Roy. *Classical Theories of Money, Output, and Inflation: A Study in "Historical Economics."* Houndmills, UK: Macmillan Press, 1992.

Grierson, Philip. "The Origins of Money." *Research in Economic Anthropology* 1 (1978): 1–35.

Guan Hanhui 管汉晖 and Qian Sheng 钱盛. "Songdai zhibi de yunxing jizhi: benwei, huishu, zhanzheng yu tongzhang" 论宋代纸币的运行机制: 本位，回赎，战争与通胀. *Jingji kexue* 经济科学 2016. 4: 114–28.

Guan, Hanhui, Nuno Palma, and Meng Wu. "The Rise and Fall of Paper Money in Yuan China, 1260–1368." *Economic History Review* 77.4 (2024): 1222–50.

Guo Dongxu 郭东旭. "Songdai maimai qiyue zhidu de fazhan" 宋代买卖契约制度的发展. *Hebei daxue xuebao (zhexue shehui kexue ban)* 河北大学学报(哲学社会科学版) 1997.3: 28–36.

Guo Zhengzhong 郭正忠. "Nan Song zhongyang caizheng huboi suishou kaobian" 南宋中央财政货币岁收考辨, pp. 168–91. In Zhongguo kexueyuan Song Liao Jin Yuan shi yanjiushi (ed.), *Song Liao Jin shi luncong* 宋辽金史论丛. Beijing: Zhonghua shuju, 1985.

Songdai yanye jingji shi 宋代盐业经济史. Beijing: Renmin chubanshe, 1990.

Guojia jiliang zongju 国家计量总局 (ed.). *Zhongguo gudai duliangheng tuji* 中国古代度量衡图集. Beijing: Wenwu chubanshe, 1981.

Hansen, Valerie. *Negotiating Daily Life in Traditional China: How Ordinary People Used Contracts, 600–1400*. New Haven, CT: Yale University Press, 1995.

Hartman, Charles. *The Making of Song Dynasty History: Sources and Narratives, 960–1279 CE*. Cambridge: Cambridge University Press, 2021.

Structures of Governance in Song Dynasty China, 960–1270 CE. Cambridge: Cambridge University Press, 2023.

"A Textual History of Cai Jing's Biography in the *Song shi*." In Ebrey and Bickford, *Emperor Huizong*, pp. 517–64.

Hartwell, Robert M. "Classical Chinese Monetary Analysis and Economic Policy in T'ang-Northern Sung China." *Transactions of the International Conference of Orientalists in Japan* 13 (1968): 70–81.

"The Evolution of the Early Northern Sung Monetary System, A.D. 960–1025." *Journal of the American Oriental Society* 87.3 (1967): 280–89.

"Financial Expertise, Public Policy, and the Formation of Economic Policy in Northern Sung China." *Journal of Asian Studies* 30.2 (1971): 281–314.

"The Imperial Treasuries: Finance and Power in Song China." *Bulletin of Sung-Yuan Studies* 20 (1988): 18–89.

He Ping 何平 and Lin Lin 林琳. "Zhongguo gudai tongzhubi liutong lingyu 'duanmo' xianxiang de qiyuan jiqi xingzhi yanjiu" 中国古代铜铸币流通领域'短陌'现象的起源及其性质研究. *Zhongguo jingji shi yanjiu* 中国经济史研究 2013.1: 10–22.

Heidemann, Stefan. "Numismatics." In Chase F. Robinson (ed.), *The New Cambridge History of Islam*, vol. 1: *The Formation of the Islamic World, Sixth to Eleventh Centuries*. Cambridge: Cambridge University Press, 2010, pp. 648–63.

Helleiner, Eric. *The Making of National Money: Territorial Currencies in Historical Perspective*. Ithaca, NY: Cornell University Press, 2003.

Heng, Derek. *Sino-Malay Trade and Diplomacy from the Tenth Through the Fourteenth Century*. Athens: Ohio University Press, 2009.

Herbert, Penelope. "A Debate in T'ang China on the State Monopoly on Casting Coin." *T'oung Pao* 62.4–5 (1977): 254–92.

Hicks, John. *A Theory of Economic History*. Oxford: Clarendon Press, 1969.

Higashi Ichio 東一夫. *Ō Anseki shinpō no kenkyū* 王安石新法の研究. Tokyo: Kazama shobō, 1970.

Higuchi Yoshishige 樋口能成. "Nan-Sō Kohoku kaishi no shijō kōzō" 南宋湖北會子の市場構造. *Shiteki* 史滴 28 (2006): 86–102.

"Nan-Sō Sōryōjo taiseishita no Chōkō keizai: Kokō Sōryōjo to Shisen no kankei kara" 南宋総領所体制下の長江経済: 湖広総領所と四川の関係から. *Waseda daigaku daigakuin bungaku kenkyūka kiyō* 早稲田大学大学院文学研究科紀要 51 (2005): 77–86.

Hino Kaisaburō 日野開三郎. "Gin ken no jyūkyūjō yori mita Godai Hoku-Sō no saihei saishi" 銀絹の需給上より見た五代・北宋の歳幣・歳賜, in *Hino Kaisaburō ronshū*, vol. 10: *Hokutō Ajia kokusai kōryū shi no kenkyū (II)* 北東アジア国際交流史の研究 (下). Tokyo: San'ichi shobō, 1983, pp. 441–500.

"Godai shi gaisetsu" 五代史概説. In *Hino Kaisaburō Tōyō shigaku ronshū* 日野開三郎東洋史学論集, vol. 2: *Godai shi no kichō* 五代史の基調. Tokyo: San'ichi shobō, 1982, pp. 87–124.

"Hoku-Sō jidai no enshō ni tsuite – fu: kōinho" 北宋時代の塩鈔について—附: 交引舗. In *Hino Kaisaburō ronshū*, vol. 6: *Sōdai no kahei to kin'yū (I)* 宋代の貨幣と金融 (上). Tokyo: San'ichi shobō, 1983, pp. 19–244.

"Hoku-Sō jidai no tegata 'Gensen kōin' o ronjite shihei 'Sen'in' no kigen ni oyobu" 北宋時代の手形 '見銭交引' を論じて紙幣 '銭引' の起源に及ぶ. In *Hino Kaisaburō ronshū*, vol. 7: *Sōdai no kahei to kin'yū (II)*. Tokyo: San'ichi shobō, 1983, pp. 69–133.

"Nan-Sō no shihei 'Gensen kōkyo' oyobi 'Gensen kanshi' no kigen ni tsuite" 南宋の紙幣'見銭公據'及び'見銭關子'の起源について. In *Hino Kaisaburō ronshū*, vol. 7: *Sōdai no kahei to kin'yū (II)* 宋代の貨幣と金融 (下) . Tokyo, San'ichi shobō, 1983, pp. 19–68.

"Nan-Sō Rin'anfu no shika kaishi ni tsuite" 南宋臨安府の私下會子について, in *Hino Kaisaburō ronshū*, vol. 7: *Sōdai no kahei to kin'yū (II)*. Tokyo: San'ichi shobō, 1983, pp. 177–211.

"So no Ba In no tsūka seisaku to Godai jidai no kin'yūgyōsha" 楚の馬殷の通貨政策と五代時代の金融業者. In *Hino Kaisaburō ronshū*, vol. 5: *Tō Godai no kahei to kin'yū*. Tokyo: San'ichi shobō, 1982, pp. 417–84.

"Tōdai no kifuho to kibō: Tōto Chōan no kin'yūgyōsha" 唐代の寄附鋪と櫃坊: 唐都長安の金融業者. In *Hino Kaisaburō ronshū*, vol. 5: *Tō Godai no kahei to kin'yū* 唐五代の貨幣と金融. Tokyo: San'ichi shobō, 1982, pp. 159–202.

Honda Seiichi 本田精一. "Nan-Sō kankaishi no ronri to jittai" 南宋官会子の論理と実態. *Kyūshū daigaku tōyōshi ronshū* 九州大学東洋史論集 25 (1997): 101–29.

Horesh, Niv. *Chinese Money in Global Context: Historic Junctures Between 600 BCE and 2012*. Stanford, CA: Stanford University Press, 2014.

Hsiao, Ch'i-ch'ing. "Mid-Yuan Politics." In Denis Twitchett (ed.), *The Cambridge History of China*, vol. 6: *Alien Regimes and Border States, 907–1368*. Cambridge: Cambridge University Press, 1994, pp. 490–560.

Hu Jichuang 胡寄窗. *Zhongguo jingji sixiang shi* 中國經濟思想史. 3 vols. Shanghai: Shanghai renmin chubanshe, 1962–1981.

Huang Aming 黄阿明. *Mingdai huobi baiyinhua yu guojia zhidu biange yanjiu* 明代货币白银化与国家制度变革研究. Yangzhou: Guangling shushe, 2016.

Huang Cheng 黄成. "Cong kaogu faxian tan Nan Song baiyin liutong de jige wenti" 从考古发现谈南宋白银流通的几个问题. In *Song shi yanjiu jikan* 宋史研究集刊, vol. 2. Hangzhou: Hangzhou daxue lishixi Songshi yanjiushi, 1988, pp. 213–25.

Huang, Ray. *Taxation and Governmental Finance in Sixteenth-Century Ming China*. Cambridge: Cambridge University Press, 1974.

Huang Xiquan 黄锡全. *Xian Qin huobi tonglun* 先秦货币通论. Beijing: Zijincheng chubanshe, 2001.

Hudson, Michael. "The Archaeology of Money: Debt Versus Barter Theories of Money's Origins." In L. Randall Wray (ed.), *Credit and State Theories of Money: The Contribution of A. Mitchell Innes*. Cheltenham, UK: Edward Elgar, 2004, pp. 93–116.

"Reconstructing the Origins of Interest-Bearing Debt and the Logic of Clean Slates." In Michael Hudson and Marc van de Mieroop (eds.), *Debt and Economic Renewal in the Ancient Near East*. Bethesda, MD: CDL Press, 2002, pp. 7–58.

Ichimaru Tomoko 市丸智子. "Gendai kahei no kan-mon, tei-ryō tan'i no betsu ni tsuite: Kurojō shutsudo oyobi Kishū keiyaku monjo o chūshin to shite" 元代貨幣の貫文•錠両単位の別について:黒城出土及び徽州契約文書を中心として. *Shakai keizai shigaku* 社会経済史学 68.3 (2002): 249–70.

"Gendai ni okeru gin, chō, dōsen no sōgo kankei ni tsuite: Shiyō tan'i no bunseki o chūshin ni" 元代における銀・鈔・銅銭の相互関係について:使用単位の分析を中心に. *Kyūshū daigaku tōyōshi ronshū* 九州大学東洋史論集 36 (2008): 88–122.

Inaba Ichirō 稲葉一郎. "Kandai no kazoku keitai to keizai hendō" 漢代の家族形態と経済変動. *Tōyōshi kenkyū* 東洋史研究 43.1 (1984): 88–117.

Ingham, Geoffrey. *The Nature of Money*. Cambridge: Polity Press, 2004.

Inoue Masao 井上正夫. *Higashi Ajia kokusai tsūka to chūsei Nihon: Sōsen to kawase kara mita keizai shi* 東アジア国際通貨と中世日本：宋銭と為替からみた経済史. Nagoya: Nagoya daigaku shuppankai, 2022.

"Hoku-Sō Shisen ni okeru kōshi no hassei katei ni tsuite" 北宋四川における交子の発生過程について. *Matsuyama daigaku ronshū* 松山大学論集 32 (*kinengo* 記念号) (2020): 5–32.

Inoue Yasuya 井上泰也. "Sō no shōpan o megutte" 宋の鈔版をめぐって. *Tōhō gakuhō* 東方学報 86.2 (1993): 82–100.

Iwamura Shinobu 岩村忍. *Mongoru shakai keizai shi no kenkyū* モンゴル社会経済史の研究. Kyoto: Kyōto daigaku jimbun kagaku kenkyūjo, 1968.

Jahn, Karl. "Paper Currency in Iran: A Contribution to the Cultural and Economic History of Iran in the Mongol Period." *Journal of Asian History* 4.2 (1970): 101–35.

Jia Daquan 贾大泉. "Songdai fushui jiegou chutan" 宋代赋税结构初探. *Shehui kexue yanjiu* 社会科学研究 1981.3: 51–58.

Jin Deping 金德平. "Bei Song yinding kao" 北宋银锭考. *Zhongguo qianbi* 中国钱币2008.3: 3–14.

Jura, Michael, and Juan Carlos Moreno Garcia. "Ancient Near East and Egypt." In Andrew Monson and Walter Scheidel (eds.), *Fiscal Regimes and the Political Economy of Premodern States*. Cambridge: Cambridge University Press, 2015, pp. 115–65.

Juvayni, Ata-Malik. *The History of the World Conqueror*. 2 vols. Trans. John Andrew Boyle. Cambridge, MA: Harvard University Press, 1958.

Kan, Lao. "The Early Use of the Tally in China." In David T. Roy and Tsuen-hsuin Tsien (eds.), *Ancient China: Studies in Early Civilization*. Hong Kong: Chinese University of Hong Kong Press, 1978, pp. 91–98.

Kanaya Osamu 金谷治. *Kanshi no kenkyū* 管子の研究. Tokyo: Iwanami shoten, 1987.

Kaneko Yasuharu 金子泰晴, "Nan-Sō shoki no Kokō Sōryōjo to sangōdō kanshi" 南宋初期の湖廣総領所と三合同関子. *Shikan* 史観 123 (1990): 34–46.

Katō Shigeshi 加藤繁. "Sōdai no shōshūkan 'sha' ni tsuite" 宋代の商習慣'賒'に就いて. In Katō, *Shina keizai shi kōshō* 支那経済史考證. Tokyo: Tōyō bunko, 1952, vol. 1, pp. 222–34.

Katsari, Constantina. *The Roman Monetary System: The Eastern Provinces from the First to the Third Century AD*. Cambridge: Cambridge University Press, 2011.

Kaye, Joel. *Economy and Nature in the Fourteenth Century: Money, Market Exchange, and the Emergence of Scientific Thought*. Cambridge: Cambridge University Press, 1998.

Kim Munkyŏng 金文京 et al. (eds.). *Rōkitsudai: Chōsen chūsei no Chūgokugo kaiwa dokuhon* 老乞大: 朝鮮中世の中国語会話読本. Tokyo: Heibonsha, 2002.

Kishimoto Mio 岸本美緒. *Shindai Chūgoku no bukka to keizai hendō* 清代中国の物価と経済変動. Tokyo: Kembun shuppan, 1997.

Knapp, George Friedrich. *The State Theory of Money*. London: Macmillan, 1924.

Kobayashi Akira 小林晃. "Nan-Sō kōki ni okeru Ryōwai bōeigun no tōsei seisaku: Sessai Ryōwai hatsu'unshi kara kōtenhō e" 南宋後期における両淮防衛軍の統制政策: 浙西両淮発運司から公田法へ. *Rekishigaku kenkyū* 歴史学研究 923 (2014): 1–17.

Korolkov, Maxim. "Between Command and Market: Credit, Labour, and Accounting in the Qin Empire (221–207 BCE)." In Sabattini and Schwermann, *Between Command and Market*, pp. 162–243.

Kurke, Leslie. *Coins, Bodies, Games, and Gold: The Politics of Meaning in Archaic Greece*. Princeton, NJ: Princeton University Press, 1999.

Kuroda Akinobu 黒田明伸. "Concurrent but Non-Integrable Currency Circuits: Complementary Relationships Among Monies in Modern China and Other Regions." *Financial History Review* 15.1 (2008): 17–36.

"The Eurasian Silver Century (1276–1359): Commensurability and Multiplicity." *Journal of Global History* 4.2 (2009): 245–69.

A Global History of Money. London: Routledge, 2020.

Kahei shisutemu no sekaishi: "Hitaishōsei" o yomu 貨幣システムの世界史:《非対称性》をよむ. Tokyo: Iwanami shoten, 2003.

"Kenryū no senki" 乾隆の銭貴. *Tōyōshi kenkyū* 東洋史研究 45.5 (1987): 692–723.

Kuroita Katsumi 黑板勝美 (ed.). *[Shintei zōho] Kokushi taikei* [新訂增補] 國史大系. Tokyo: Yoshikawa kōbunkan, 1929.

Kusano Yasushi 草野靖. "Nan-Sō gyōzai kaishi no hatten (I) (II)" 南宋行在会子の発展 (上· 下). *Tōyō gakuhō* 東洋学報 49.1 (1966): 1–41; 49.2 (1966): 169–205.

"Sōdai de yōirareta tegata no meishō to sono keishiki" 宋代で用いられた手形の名称とその形式. In *Nakajima Satoshi sensei koki kinen ronshū* 中嶋敏先生古稀記念論集. Tokyo: Kyūko shoin, 1981, vol. 1, pp. 351–83.

Lai Jiancheng 赖建诚. *Bianzhen liangxiang: Mingdai zhonghouqi de bianfang jingfei yu guojia caizheng weiji, 1531–1602* 边镇粮饷:明代中后期的边防经费与国家财政危机. Hangzhou: Zhejiang daxue chubanshe, 2010.

Lamouroux, Christian. "Bureaucratie et monnaie dans la Chine du XIe siècle: les désordres monétaires au Shaanxi." In Bruno Théret (ed.), *La Monnaie dévoilée par ses crises*. Paris: Éditions de l'École des Hautes Études en Sciences Sociales, 2007, vol. 1, pp. 171–204.

"Endettement public, trésor impérial, et monnaie dans la Chine des xe et xie siècles." In Jean Andréau, Gérard Béaur, and Jean-Yves Garnier (eds.), *La Dette publique dans l'histoire*. Paris: Institut de la gestion publique et du développement economique, 2006, pp. 129–74.

Fiscalité, comptes publics et politiques financières dans la Chine des Song: le chapitre 179 du Songshi. Paris: Collège de France, Institut des Hautes Études Chinoises, 2003.

"Fragmentation and Financial Recentralization: The Emergence of the Four General Commands (1127–1165)." In Franz-Julius Morche and Hilde de Weerdt (eds.), *Political Communication in Chinese and European History, 800–1600*. Amsterdam: Amsterdam University Press, 2021, pp. 105–41.

La dynastie des Song: Histoire générale de la China (960–1279). Paris: Les Belles Lettres, 2022.

"Organisation territorial et monopole du thé dans la Chine des Song (960–1059)." *Annales: Économies, Sociétés, Civilisations* 46.5 (1991): 977–1008.

Lamouroux, Christian, and Richard von Glahn. "Public Finance, 1000–1800." In Debin Ma and Richard von Glahn (eds.), *The Cambridge Economic History of China*. Cambridge: Cambridge University Press, 2022, vol. 1, pp. 340–80.

Lane, Kris. *Potosí: The Silver City That Changed the World*. Berkeley: University of California Press, 2019.

Lapidus, André. "Metal, Money, and the Prince: John Buridan and Nicholas Oresme After Thomas Aquinas." *History of Political Economy* 29.1 (1997): 21–53.

Lei Jiasheng 雷家聖. *Julian mouguo: Nan Song Zonglingsuo yanjiu* 聚斂謀國: 南宋總領所研究. Taipei: Wanjuanlou tushu gongsi, 2013.

Lei Runze 雷润泽, Yu Cunhai 于存海, He Jiying 何继英. "Ningxia Baisikou Shuangta faxiande Dachao tongbao he zhongtong yuanbao jiaochao" 宁夏拜寺口双塔发现的大朝通宝和中统元宝交钞. *Zhongguo qianbi* 中国钱币 1989.4: 28–31.

Levi, Jean (trans). *La Dispute sur le sel et le fer*. Paris: Belles Lettres, 2010.

Levine, Ari Daniel. "The Reigns of Hui-tsung (1100–1126) and Ch'in-tsung (1126–1127) and the Fall of the Northern Sung." In Twitchett and Smith, *Cambridge History of China*, vol. 5, pt. 1, pp. 556–643.

Lewis, Mark Edward. *Sanctioned Violence in Early China*. Albany: State University of New York Press, 1990.

Li Ruoyu 李若愚. "Cong Mingdaide qiyue kan Mingdai de bizhi" 从明代的契约看明代的币制. *Zhongguo jingji shi yanjiu* 中国经济史研究 1988.4: 39–43.

Li Shan 李埏 and Lin Wenxun 林文勛. *Song Jin chubi shi xinian* 宋金楮币史系年. Kunming: Yunnan minzu chubanshe, 1996.

Li Weiguo 李伟国. "Liang Song yinchao tongban wenzi kao: yi 'Qiansicang chaoban' wei zhongxin" 两宋印钞铜版文字考: 以'千斯仓钞版'为中心. *Henan daxue xuebao (shehui kexue ban)* 河南大学学报 (社会科学版) 2011.2: 74–80.

"Lun Bei Song de tiju zhusi kuwu si" 论北宋的提举诸司库务司. In Li, *Songdai caizheng he wenxian kaolun* 宋代财政和文献考论. Shanghai: Shanghai guji chubanshe, 2007, pp. 43–61.

"Songdai jingji shenghuo zhong de shikuai" 宋代经济生活中的市侩." In Li, *Songdai caizheng he wenxian kaolun*. Shanghai: Shanghai guji chubanshe, 2007, pp. 123–47.

Li Xiaoping 李小萍. "Nan Song jinyin yanchao jiaoyinpu yanjiu" 南宋金银盐钞交引铺研究. *Zhongguo qianbi* 中国钱币2010.2: 24–30.

Li Yiyou 李逸友. "Yuandai caoyuan sichou zhi lu shangde zhibi: Neimenggu Ejinaqi Heicheng chutude Yuanchao ji piaoquan" 元代草原丝绸之路上的纸币: 内蒙古额济纳旗黑城出土的元钞及票券. *Zhongguo qianbi* 中国钱币1991.4: 16–23.

Li Zhengxin 李正鑫. "Hunan Huarong chutu yuanchao" 湖南华容出土元钞. *Zhongguo qianbi* 中国钱币1994.4: 33–35.

Li Zhi'an 李治安. *Yuandai fenfeng zhidu yanjiu* 元代分封制度研究. Tianjin: Tianjin guji chubanshe, 1989.

Li Zhixian 李志贤. *Yang Yan jiqi liangshuifa yanjiu* 杨炎及其两税法研究. Beijing: Zhongguo shehui kexue chubanshe, 2002.

Liang, Fang-chung. *The Single-Whip Method of Taxation in China*. Cambridge, MA: Harvard University Press, 1956.

Liang Gengyao 梁庚堯. *Nan Song yanque: Shiyan chanxiao yu zhengfu kongzhi* 南宋鹽榷:食鹽產銷與政府控制. Taipei: Guoli Taiwan daxue chubanshe, 2010.

"Shiyifa shu" 市易法述. In Liang, *Songdai shehui jingji shi lunji* 宋代社會經濟史論集. Taipei: Yunchen wenhua shiye gongsi, 1997, pp. 104–260.

Lin, Man-houng. “Two Social Theories Revealed: Statecraft Controversies over China’s Monetary Crisis, 1808–1854.” *Late Imperial China* 12.2 (1991): 1–35.

Liu Qiugen 刘秋根 and Liu Na 刘娜. “Qingdai qianqi qianpu yinhao yinqian piao” 清代前期钱铺银号银钱票. *Zhongguo qianbi* 中国钱币 2019.1: 3–14.

Liu Sen 刘森. “Jindai xiaochao chaoban chutan” 金代小钞钞版初探. *Zhongguo qianbi* 中国钱币 2006.3: 47–49.

Song Jin zhibi shi 宋金纸币史. Beijing: Zhongguo jinrong chubanshe, 1993.

Lopez, Robert S. “The Dollar of the Middle Ages.” *Journal of Economic History* 11.3 (1951): 209–34.

Lorge, Peter. *The Reunification of China: Peace Through War Under the Song Dynasty*. Cambridge: Cambridge University Press, 2015.

Luo Zhenyu 羅振玉. *Sichao chaobi tulu; fu kaoshi* 四朝鈔幣圖錄；附考釋. Shangyu: Luoshi, 1914.

Maeda Naonori 前田直典. *Genchō shi no kenkyū* 元朝史の研究. Tokyo: Tokyo daigaku shuppankai, 1973.

Matsui Dai 松井太. “Mongoru jidai no dōryōko: Higashi Torukisutan shutsudo bunken kara no saikentō” モンゴル時代の度量衡: 東トルキスタン出土文献からの再検討. *Tōhōgaku* 東方学 107 (2004): 153–66.

McKnight, Brian E., and James T. C. Liu (eds.). *Enlightened Judgments, Ch’ing-ming Chi: The Sung Dynasty Collection*. Albany: State University of New York Press, 1998.

Meikle, Scott. *Aristotle’s Economic Thought*. Oxford: Clarendon Press, 1995.

Meyer, Andrew. “Feng Buys Rightness, Gongyi Xiu Expels His Wife: Economic Exemplars in the Warring States and Early Han.” In Sabattini and Schwermann, *Between Command and Market*, pp. 145–61.

Mitchell-Innes, A. “The Credit Theory of Money.” *Banking Law Journal* 31 (1914): 151–68.

Miu Kunhe 繆坤和. *Songdai xinyong piaoju yanjiu* 宋代信用票據研究. Kunming: Yunnan daxue chubanshe, 2002.

Miyake Toshihiko 三宅俊彦. *Chūgoku no uzumerareta senka* 中国の埋められた銭貨. Tokyo: Dōseisha, 2005.

Miyazaki Ichisada 宮崎市定. *Godai Sōsho no tsūka mondai* 五代宋初の通貨問題. Kyoto: Hoshino shoten, 1943.

Miyazawa Tomoyuki 宮澤知之. *Chūgoku dōsen no sekai* 中國銅銭の世界. Kyoto: Shibunkaku shuppan, 2007.

Chūgoku zenkindai no kahei to zaisei 中国前近代の貨幣と財政. Kyoto: Kyoto daigaku gakujutsu shuppankai, 2023.

“Gendai kōkanki no heisei to sono bōkai” 元代後半期の幣制とその崩壊. *Ōryō shigaku* 鷹陵史学 27 (2001): 53–92.

“Godai Jūkoku jidai no tsūka jōkyō” 五代十国時代の通貨状況. *Ōryō shigaku* 鷹陵史学 34 (2008): 1–35.

“Hoku-Sō kōshi ron” 北宋交子論. In Miki Satoshi 三木聰 (ed.), *Sō-Shindai no seiji to shakai* 宋—清代の政治と社会. Tokyo: Kyūko shoin, 2017, pp. 3–41.

"Kindai zenki no heisei" 金代前期の幣制. *Tōyōshi kenkyū* 東洋史研究 79.2 (2020): 205–35.

Sōdai Chūgoku no kokka to keizai 宋代中國の国家と経済. Tokyo: Sōbunsha, 1998.

Mori Masao 森正夫. *Mindai Kōnan tochi seido no kenkyū* 明代江南土地制度の研究. Kyoto: Dōhōsha, 1988.

Morita Kenji 森田憲司. "'Jirin kōki' no shohanpon ni tsuite: kokunai shozō no shohon o chūshin to shite"『事林廣記』の諸版本について：国内所蔵の諸本を中心として. In Sōdaishi kenkyūkai (ed.), *Sōdai no chishikijin: shisō, seido, chiiki shakai* 宋代の知識人:思想,制度,地域社会. Tokyo: Kyūko shoin, 1993, pp. 287–316.

Moriyasu Takao 森安孝夫. "Shiruku rōdo tōbu ni okeru senka: Kinu, seihō ginsen, kanfu kara gintei e" シルクロード東部における銭貨：絹・西方銀銭・官布から銀錠へ. In Moriyasu Takao (ed.), *Chūō Ajia shutsudo bunbutsu ronsō* 中央アジア出土文物論叢. Kyoto: Hoyū shoten, 2004, pp. 1–40.

Mostern, Ruth. *"Dividing the Realm in Order to Govern": The Spatial Organization of the Song State (960–1276 CE)*. Cambridge, MA: Harvard University Asia Center, 2011.

The Yellow River: A Natural and Unnatural History. New Haven, CT: Yale University Press, 2021.

Nagai Chiaki 長井千秋. "Waitō Sōryōjo no zaisei un'ei" 淮東総領所の財政運営. *Shigaku zasshi* 史学雑誌 101.7 (1992): 1235–66.

Naismith, Rory. *Making Money in the Early Middle Ages*. Princeton, NJ: Princeton University Press.

Nakajima Satoshi 中嶋敏 (ed.). *Sōshi shokkashi yakuchū* 宋史食貨志譯註. 6 vols. Tokyo: Tokyo bunko, 1960–2006.

Neimenggu jinrong yanjiusuo 内蒙古金融研究所 (ed.). *Zhongguo guchao tuji* 中國古鈔圖輯. Beijing: Zhongguo jinrong chubanshe, 1987.

Niida Noboru 仁井田隆. "Kan Gi Rikuchō no shichi seido" 漢魏六朝の質制度. In Niida, *Chūgoku hōsei shi kenkyū: tochi hō, torihiki hō* 中國法制史研究: 土地法,取引法. Tokyo: Tokyo daigaku shuppankai, 1960, pp. 477–89.

Nylan, Michael. "Assets Accumulating: Sima Qian's Perspectives on Moneymaking, Virtue, and History." In Hans van Ess, Olga Lomová, and Dorothee Schaab-Hanke (eds.), *Views from Within, Views from Beyond: Approaches to the Shiji as an Early Work of Historiography*. Wiesbaden: Harrassowitz, 2015, pp. 131–68.

Ogura Yoshihiko 小倉芳彦. "Chūgoku kodai no shichi: sono kinō no henka o chūshin to shite" 中国古代の質: その機能の変化を中心として. *Rekishigaku kenkyū* 歴史学研究 266 (1962): 1–15.

Okada Isao 岡田功. "Shunshū sengoku Shin Kan jidai no taishaku kankei o meguru ichikōsatsu" 春秋戦国秦漢時代の貸借関係をめぐる一考察. *Sundai shigaku* 駿台史学 78 (1990): 69–73.

Okuhira Masakō 奥平昌洪 (ed.). *Tōa senshi* 東亜銭志. Tokyo: Iwanami, 1938.

Okuyama Norio 奥山憲夫. *Mindai gunsei shi kenkyū* 明代軍政史研究. Tokyo: Kyūko shoin, 2003.

Ordonnance du Roy, sur le faict & Reglement de ses Monnoyes. Paris: Veufve Jehan Dallier, 1578.

Ormrod, W. M., and Janos Barta. "The Feudal Structure and the Beginnings of State Finance." In Richard Bonney (ed.), *Economic Systems and State Finance.* Oxford: Oxford University Press, 1995, pp. 53–79.

Ōta Yukio 大田由紀夫. "Chūgoku ōchō ni yoru kahei hakō to ryūtsū: Min Kōbuki no shōhō ni tsuite" 中国王朝による貨幣発行と流通:明洪武期の鈔法について. In Ike Susumu 池享 (ed.), *Senka: Zenkindai Nihon no kahei to kokka* 銭貨:前近代日本の貨幣と国家, pp. 163–85. Tokyo: Aoki shoten, 2001.

"Jūni-jūgo seiki shoto Higashi Ajia ni okeru dōsen no ryufu" 十二・十五世紀初頭東アジアにおける銅銭の流布. *Shakai keizai shigaku* 社会経済史学 61.2 (1995): 156–84.

"Jūshi-jūgo seiki no toraisen ryūnyū: Chūsei Nihon no baai" 十四•十五世紀の渡来銭流入:中世日本の場合. *Rekishi no riron to kyōiku* 歴史の理論と教育 128 (2008): 3–19.

Otagi Matsuo 愛宕松男. "Addatsusen to sono haikei: Jūsan seiki Mongoru Genchō ni okeru gin no dōkō (I, II)" 斡脱銭とその背景：十三世紀モンゴル元朝における銀の動向（一,二). *Tōyōshi kenkyū* 東洋史研究 32.1 (1973), 1–27; 32.2 (1973): 163–201.

Parsons, Jotham. *Making Money in Sixteenth-Century France: Currency, Culture, and the State.* Ithaca, NY: Cornell University Press, 2014.

"Money and Sovereignty in Early Modern France." *Journal of the History of Ideas* 62.1 (2001): 59–79.

Peerenboom, R. P. *Law and Morality in Ancient China: The Silk Manuscripts of Huang-Lao.* Albany: State University of New York Press, 1993.

Peng Xinwei 彭信威. *A Monetary History of China.* Trans. Edward H. Kaplan. Bellingham: Western Washington State University Press, 1994.

Zhongguo huobi shi 中國貨幣史. 2nd ed. Shanghai: Shanghai renmin chubanshe, 1965.

Polo, Marco. *The Travels of Marco Polo [The Venetian].* New York: Liveright, 1926.

Puk, Wing-kin. *The Rise and Fall of a Public Debt Market in 16th-Century China: The Story of the Ming Salt Certificate.* Leiden: Brill, 2016.

Qi Xia 漆侠. *Wang Anshi bianfa* 王安石变法. Shanghai: Shanghai renmin chubanshe, 1979.

Qian, Sheng, and Lemin Wu. "Who Defended Monetary Stability in a Specie Regime? Evidence from Chinese History." *Frontiers of Economics in China* 13.3 (2018): 397–435.

Qiao Youmei 乔幼梅. "Jindai huobi zhidu de yanbian jiqi dui shehui jingji de yingxiang" 金代货币制的演变及其对社会经济的影响. *Zhongguo shi yanjiu* 中国史研究 1983.3: 113–24.

"Song Jin maoyizhong zhengduo tongbi de douzheng" 宋金贸易中争夺铜币的斗争. *Lishi yanjiu* 历史研究 1982.4: 115–27.

Qiu Yongzhi 邱永志. "Zhanzheng, shichang, yu guojia: Zhengtong Jingtai zhi ji tonghuo liutong tizhi de bianqian" 战争,市场,与国家:正统景泰之际通货

流通体制的变迁. *Zhongguo jingji shi yanjiu* 中国经济史研究 2017.6: 30–41.

Reddy, Deme Raja. “The Emergence and Spread of Coins in Ancient India.” In Peter Bernholz and Roland Vaubel (eds.), *Explaining Monetary and Financial Innovation: A Historical Analysis*. Cham, Switzerland: Springer International, 2014, pp. 53–77.

Rong Tiansong 戎畋松. “Chaoquanban zuida mian’e xianshen: Jie Jindai ‘Tonghou xingshangshu liubu canwan guan huizi’ tongchaoban lishi yunyan” 钞券版最大面额现身: 揭金代‘通州行尚书六部参萬贯会子’铜钞版历史云烟. *Shoucang* 收藏 2022.12: 20–25.

“Gupin xunzong: Jindai chongqing wubai wen xiao’e tong chaoban” 孤品寻踪：金代崇庆五伯文小额铜钞版. *Shoucang* 收藏 2022.12: 9–13.

Rosenswig, Robert M. “Money, Currency, and Heterodox Economics for Archaeology.” *Current Anthropology* 65.2 (2024): 235–66.

Rowe, William T. “Money, Economy, and Polity in the Daoguang-Era Paper Currency Debates.” *Late Imperial China* 31.2 (2010): 69–96.

Saving the World: Chen Hongmou and Elite Consciousness in Eighteenth-Century China. Stanford, CA: Stanford University Press, 2001.

Speaking of Profit: Bao Shichen and Reform in Nineteenth-Century China. Cambridge, MA: Harvard University Asia Center, 2018.

“State and Market in Mid-Qing Economic Thought: The Case of Chen Hongmou (1696–1771).” *Études Chinoises* 12.1 (1993): 7–40.

Sabattini, Elisa Levi. “To Ban or Not to Ban: Jia Yi on Copper Distribution and Minting Coins.” In Sabattini and Schwermann, *Between Command and Market*, pp. 318–57.

Sabattini, Elisa Levi, and Christian Schwermann (eds.). *Between Command and Market: Economic Thought and Practice in Early China*. Leiden: Brill, 2022.

Saeki Tomi 佐伯富. “Sōdai Ninsōchō ni okeru chahō ni tsuite” 宋代仁宗朝における茶法について. In Saeki, *Chūgoku shi kenkyū* 中国史研究. Kyoto: Kyoto daigaku bungakubu Tōyōshi kenkyūkai, 1971, vol. 2, pp. 131–69.

“Sōdai Rin Toku no chahō kaikaku ni tsuite” 宋代林特の茶法改革について. In Saeki, *Chūgoku shi kenkyū*, vol. 2, pp. 105–30.

Sartori, Andrew. “Silver and the Social in Locke’s Monetary Thought.” *Journal of Modern History* 93.3 (2021): 501–32.

Satō Keishirō 佐藤圭四郎. “Genchō no kōshō to Iruhanchō no chō cāv: Jūsan-shi seiki ni okeru Higashi Nishi Ajia no shihei seido” 元朝の交鈔とイルハン朝の鈔cāv：十三·四世紀における東·西アジアの紙幣制度. *Ryūgoku daigaku ronshū* 龍谷大學論集 428 (1986): 71–109.

Schaps, David M. *The Invention of Coinage and the Monetization of Ancient Greece*. Ann Arbor: University of Michigan Press, 2003.

Scheidel, Walter. “The Monetary Systems of the Han and Roman Empires.” In Walter Scheidel (ed.), *Rome and China: Comparative Perspectives on Ancient Empires*. New York: Oxford University Press, 2009, pp. 137–207.

Schifferli, Christoph. “Le Système monétaire au Sichuan vers la fin du xe siècle.” *T'oung Pao* 72.2 (1986): 269–90.

Schumpeter, Joseph A. “The Crisis of the Tax State.” Rpt. in Joseph A. Schumpeter, *The Economics and Sociology of Capitalism*. Princeton, NJ: Princeton University Press, 1991, pp. 99–140.

History of Economic Analysis. New York: Oxford University Press, 1954.

Schurmann, Franz. “Mongolian Tributary Practices of the Thirteenth Century.” *Harvard Journal of Asiatic Studies* 19.3–4 (1956): 304–89.

Scogin, Hugh. “Between Heaven and Man: Contract and the State in Han Dynasty China.” *Southern California Law Review* 63.5 (1990): 1325–1404.

Segal, Ethan Isaac. *Coins, Trade, and the State: Economic Growth in Early Medieval Japan*. Cambridge, MA: Harvard University Asia Center, 2011.

Shen Wanli 申萬里. “Yuandai shiren de zhengzhi guanhuai yu shiwu duice: Yi *Sanchang wenxuan duice renji* wei zhongxin de kaochao” 元代士人的政治關懷與時務對策: 以《三場文選對策·壬集》爲中心的考察. *Sui Tang Liao Song Jin Yuan shi luncong* 隋唐辽宋金元史论丛 7 (2017): 231–71.

Sheng Guanxi 盛观熙. “Liang Song chaoban bianxi” 兩宋鈔版辨析. *Zhongguo qianbi* 中国钱币 1994.4: 11–14.

Shi Jilong 施继龙 and Li Xiusong 李修松. *Dongzhi guanzi chaoban yanjiu* 东至关子钞版研究. Hefei: Anhui daxue chubanshe, 2008.

Shi Yang 石洋. “Liang Han Sanguo shiqi ‘yong’ qunti de lishi yanbian: yi minjian guyong wei zhongxin” 两汉三国时期‘佣’群体的历史演变: 以民间雇佣為中心. *Zhongguo shi yanjiu* 中国史研究 2014.3: 51–77.

Shiba Yoshinobu 斯波義信. *Commerce and Society in Sung China*. Ann Arbor: University of Michigan Center for Chinese Studies, 1970.

Sōdai shōgyō shi kenkyū 宋代商業史研究. Tokyo: Kazama shobō, 1968.

“Sōto Kōshū no toshi seitai” 宋都杭州の都市生態. In Shiba, *Sōdai Kōnan keizai shi no kenkyū* 宋代江南経済史の研究. Tokyo: Tokyo daigaku shuppankai, 1988, pp. 340–63.

“Sung Foreign Trade: Its Scope and Organization.” In Morris Rossabi (ed.), *China Among Equals: The Middle Kingdom and Its Neighbors, 10th–14th Centuries*. Berkeley: University of California Press, 1983, pp. 89–115.

Shimasue Kazuyasu 島居一康. *Sōdai zeisei shi kenkyū* 宋代税政史研究. Tokyo: Kyūko shoin, 1993.

Shiroyama, Tomoko. *China During the Great Depression: Market, State, and the World Economy, 1927–1937*. Cambridge, MA: Harvard University Asia Center, 2008.

Sima, Qian. *Records of the Grand Historian: Han Dynasty II*. Trans. Burton Watson. New York: Columbia University Press, 1993.

Smith, Adam. *The Wealth of Nations*. New York: Modern Library, 1937.

Smith, Paul Jakov. “The Fragility of Peace: Song China's Northwestern Frontier and Erosion of the Chanyuan Paradigm in the Mid-Eleventh Century.” *Journal of Chinese History* 9.1 (2023): 1–29.

"Irredentism as Political Capital: The New Policies and the Annexation of Tibetan Domains in Hehuang (the Qinghai–Gansu Highlands) under Shenzong and His Sons, 1068–1126." In Ebrey and Bickford, *Emperor Huizong*, pp. 78–130.

"Shen-Tsung's Reign and the New Policies of Wang An-shih." In Twitchett and Smith, *Cambridge History of China*, vol. 5, pt. 1, pp. 347–483.

Taxing Heaven's Storehouse: Horses, Bureaucrats, and the Destruction of the Sichuan Tea Industry, 1074–1224. Cambridge, MA: Harvard University Council on East Asian Studies, 1992.

Sogabe Shizuo 曽我部静雄. "Sōdai no zaisei ippan" 宋代の財政一般. In Sogabe, *Sōdai zaisei shi* 宋代財政史. Tokyo: Seikatsusha, 1941.

Song, Jaeyoon. "Debates on Just Taxation in Ma Duanlin's *Comprehensive Survey*." In Patricia B. Ebrey and Paul Jakov Smith (eds.), *State Power in China, 900–1325*. Seattle: University of Washington Press, 2019, pp. 244–73.

Traces of Grand Peace: Classics and State Activism in Imperial China. Cambridge, MA: Harvard University Asia Center, 2015.

Soudek, Josef. "Aristotle's Theory of Exchange: An Inquiry into the Origins of Economic Analysis." *Proceedings of the American Philosophical Society* 96.1 (1952): 45–75.

Spufford, Peter. *Money and Its Use in Medieval Europe*. Cambridge: Cambridge University Press, 1988.

Su Xinhong 蘇新红. *Taicangku yu Mingdai caizheng zhidu yanbian yanjiu* 太仓库与明代财政制度演变研究. Beijing: Zhongguo shehui kexue chubanshe, 2021.

Sudō Yoshiyuki 周藤吉之. "Nan Sō sue no kōdenhō" 南宋末の公田法. In Sudō, *Tō Sō tochi seido shi kenkyū* 唐宋土地制度史研究. Tokyo: Tokyo daigaku shuppankai, 1954.

Swann, Nancy Lee. *Food and Money in Ancient China: The Earliest Economic History of China to A.D. 25*. Princeton, NJ: Princeton University Press, 1950.

Takahashi Hiroomi 高橋弘臣. *Genchō kahei seisaku seiritsu katei no kenkyū* 元朝貨幣政策成立過程の研究. Tokyo: Tōyō shoin, 2000.

"Kindai no shihei to sono unyō seido" 金代の紙幣とその運用制度. *Shikyō* 史境 2 (1989): 25–40.

Tan, Mei Ah. "Monetary Policy as the Key to State Authority and Income in Tang China." *Journal of Chinese Studies* 64 (2017): 35–109.

Tang Wenji 唐文基. *Mingdai fuyi zhidu shi* 明代赋役制度史. Beijing: Zhongguo shehui kexue chubanshe, 1991.

Tao, Jing-shen. "The Move to the South and the Reign of Kao-tsung (1127–1162)." In Twitchett and Smith, *Cambridge History of China*, vol. 5, pt. 1, pp. 644–709.

Thierry, François. *Les Monnaies de la Chine ancienne: des origines à la fin de l'empire*. Paris: Belles Lettres, 2017.

Tian Liying 田黎英. "Chengti zhi shuo: Nan Song de zhibi guanli lilun" 称提之说:南宋的纸币管理理论. *Zhongguo qianbi* 中国钱币 1986.1: 51–55.

Trombert, Éric. *Le Crédit à Dunhuang: vie matérielle et société en Chine medieval*. Paris: Collège de France Institut des Hautes Études Chinoises, 1995.

Tsien, Tsen-hsuin. *Paper and Printing*. In Joseph Needham (ed.), *Science and Civilisation in China*, vol. 5, pt. 1. Cambridge: Cambridge University Press, 1985.

Twitchett, Denis. *Financial Administration Under the T'ang Dynasty*. Cambridge: Cambridge University Press, 1963.

"The Salt Commissioners After An Lu-shan's Rebellion." *Asia Major*, new series, 4.1 (1954): 60–89.

Twitchett, Denis, and Paul Jakov Smith (eds.). *The Cambridge History of China*, vol. 5, pt. 1: *The Sung Dynasty and Its Precursors, 907–1279*. Cambridge: Cambridge University Press, 2009.

Umehara Kaoru 梅原郁. "Sōdai no naizō to sazō: kunshu dokusaisei no zaiko" 宋代の内蔵と左蔵: 君主独裁制の財庫. *Tōhō gakuhō* 東方学報 41.1 (1971): 127–75.

Uno Nobuhiro 宇野伸浩. "Ogodei han to Musurimu shōnin: Orudo ni okeru kōeki to Nishi Ajiasan no shōhin" オゴデイ・ハンとムスリム商人:オルドにおける交易と西アジア産の商品. *Tōyō gakuhō* 東洋学報 70.3–4 (1989): 71–104.

Van De Mieroop, Marc. "The Invention of Interest: Sumerian Loans." In Goetzmann and Rouwenhorst, *Origins of Value*, pp. 17–42.

Veenhoff, Klaas R. "Assur: The City, Its Traders, and Its Commercial Network." *Journal of the Economic and Social History of the Orient* 53.1 (2010): 39–82.

Velde, François R. "Experiments with Paper Money." In Stefano Battilossi, Youssef Cassis, and Kazuhiko Yago (eds.), *Handbook of the History of Money and Currency*. Singapore: Springer Nature Singapore, 2020, pp. 1–17 (online pagination).

Vogel, Hans Ulrich. "Chinese Central Monetary Policy, 1644–1800." *Late Imperial China* 8.2 (1987): 1–52.

von Glahn, Richard. "Chinese Coin and Changes in Monetary Preferences in Maritime East Asia in the 15th–16th Centuries." *Journal of the Economic and Social History of the Orient* 57.5 (2014): 629–68.

"Cycles of Silver in Chinese Monetary History." In Billy K. L. So (ed.), *The Economy of Lower Yangzi Delta in Late Imperial China: Connecting Money, Markets, and Institutions*. London: Routledge, 2013, pp. 17–71.

"Economic Depression and the Silver Question in Nineteenth Century China." In Manuel Pérez García and Lucio de Sousa (eds.), *Global History and New Polycentric Approaches: Europe, Asia, and the Americas in a World Network System (XVI–XIXth Centuries)*. London: Palgrave Macmillan, 2018, pp. 81–117.

The Economic History of China from Antiquity to the Nineteenth Century. Cambridge: Cambridge University Press, 2016.

"Foreign Silver Coins in the Market Culture of Nineteenth Century China." *International Journal of Asian Studies* 4.1 (2007): 51–78.

Fountain of Fortune: Money and Monetary Policy in China, 1000–1700. Berkeley: University of California Press, 1996.

"Household Registration, Property Rights, and Social Obligations in Imperial China: Principles and Practices." In Keith Breckenridge and Simon Szreter (eds.), *Registration and Recognition: Documenting the Person in World History*. Oxford: Oxford University Press, 2012, pp. 39–66.

"Modalities of the Fiscal State in Imperial China." *Journal of Chinese History* 4.1 (2020): 1–29.

"The Ningbo–Hakata Merchant Network and the Reorientation of East Asian Maritime Trade, 1150–1300." *Harvard Journal of Asiatic Studies* 74.2 (2014): 251–81.

"The Origins of Paper Money in China." In Goetzmann and Rouwenhorst, *Origins of Value*, pp. 65–89.

"Towns and Temples: Urban Growth and Decline in the Yangzi Delta, 1100–1400." In Paul Jakov Smith and Richard von Glahn (eds.), *The Song–Yuan–Ming Transition in Chinese History*. Cambridge, MA: Harvard University Council on East Asian Studies, 2003, pp. 176–211.

von Reden, Sitta. *Money in Classical Antiquity*. Cambridge: Cambridge University Press, 2010.

Wada Sei 和田清 (ed.). *Minshi shokkashi yakuchū* 明史食貨志譯註. 2 vols. Tokyo: Tōyō bunko, 1957.

Wan Ming 万明. "Mingdai baiyin huobihua de chubu kaochao" 明代白银货币化的初步考察. *Zhongguo jingji shi yanjiu* 中国经济史研究 2003.2: 39–51.

Wang, Helen. *Money on the Silk Road: The Evidence from Eastern Central Asia to c. AD 800*. London: British Museum Press, 2004.

Wang Lianlong 王连龙. *Yi Zhou shu yanjiu* 逸周书研究. Beijing: Shehui kexue wenxian chubanshe, 2010.

Wang Lingling 王菱菱. *Songdai kuangyeye yanjiu* 宋代矿冶业研究. Baoding: Hebei daxue chubanshe, 2005.

Wang Liyan 王俪阎. "Da Ming tongxing baochao kao" 大明通行宝钞考. *Zhongguo qianbi* 中国钱币2007.3: 58–64.

Wang Shen 王申. "Cong bianqian dao zhibi: lun Shaoxing shiqi xianqian guanzi zhi dongnan huizi de yanjin guocheng" 从便钱到纸币: 论绍兴时期见钱关子至东南会子的演进过程. *Zhongguo shehui jingji shi yanjiu* 中国社会经济史研究 2019.3: 11–19.

"Huainan jiaozi yu Nan Song Lianghuai diqu de caizheng yunzuo: jian yu dongnan huizi bijiao" 淮南交子与南宋两淮地区的财政运作: 兼与东南会子比较. *Anhui shixue* 安徽史学 2021.1: 128–34.

"Hubei huizi yu Nan Song guojia caizheng geju bianqian" 湖北会子与南宋国家财政格局变迁. *Hubei shehui kexue* 湖北社会科学 2021.6: 102–10.

"Lun Nan Song qianqi dongnan huizi de xingzhi yu liutong zhuangkuang" 论南宋前期东南会子的性质与流通状况. *Qinghua daxue xuebao (zhexue shehui kexue ban)* 清华大学学报 (哲学社会科学版) 34.3 (2019): 106–17.

"Lun xiao'e dongnan huizi dui Nan Song huobi liutong de yingxiang" 论小额东南会子对南宋货币流通的影响. *Zhejiang xuekan* 浙江学刊 2020.5: 231–38.

"Zhidu, liutong yu guojia caizheng: Nan Song zhibi shi yanjiu shuping" 制度，流通与国家财政：南宋纸币史研究述评. *Tang Song lishi pinglun* 唐宋历史评论 5.1 (2019): 203–21.

Wang Shengduo 汪圣铎. "Guanyu Dongzhi guanzi chaoban de jige yidian" 关于东至关子钞版的几个疑点. *Zhongguo qianbi* 中国钱币 1994.3: 28–30.

Liang Song caizheng shi 两宋财政史. 2 vols. Beijing: Zhonghua shuju, 1995.

Liang Song huobi shi 两宋货币史. 2 vols. Beijing: Shehui kexue wenxian chubanshe, 2003.

"Nan Song dui huizi de liangci daguimo 'chengti'" 南宋对会子的两次大规模'称提.' *Zhongguo qianbi* 中国钱币 1993.1: 15–20.

Wang Shengduo 汪圣铎 and Guo Lan 郭兰. "Nan Song houqi yanzheng kaolun" 南宋后期盐政考论. *Yan wenhua yanjiu luncong* 盐文化研究论丛1 (2006): 148–55.

Wang, Tseng-yu. "A History of the Song Military." In John W. Chafee and Denis Twitchett (eds.), *The Cambridge History of China*, vol. 5, pt. 2: *Sung China (960–1279)*. Cambridge: Cambridge University Press, 2015, pp. 214–49.

Wang Wencheng 王文成. *Songdai baiyin huobihua yanjiu* 宋代白银货币化研究. Kunming: Yunnan daxue chubanshe, 2001.

Wang Wencheng 王文成, Zhao Xiaoping 赵小平, Liu Xin 刘欣, and Ding Qiong 丁琼. *Song Jin Yuan Ming shiqi de shichang fazhan yu huobi liutong yanjiu* 宋金元明时期的市场发展与货币流通研究. Beijing: Zhongguo shehui kexue chubanshe, 2021.

Wang Ying 王颖. "Cong Baoshan Chujian kan Zhanguo zhongwanqi Chuguo de shehui jingji" 从包山楚简看战国中晚期楚国的社会经济. *Zhongguo shehui jingji shi* 中国社会经济史 2004.3: 14–17.

Weber, Max. *Economy and Society*. 2 vols. Berkeley: University of California Press, 1978.

Wennerlind, Carl. *Casualties of Credit: The English Financial Revolution, 1620–1720*. Cambridge, MA: Harvard University Press, 2011.

Whaley, Mark A. "An Account of the 13th Century Qubchir of the Mongol 'Great Court.'" *Acta Orientalia Academiae Scientiarum Hungaricae* 54.1 (2001): 1–84.

Wickham, Chris. "How Did the Feudal Economy Work? The Economic Logic of Medieval Societies." *Past and Present* 251 (2021): 3–40.

Woodhouse, Adam. "'Who Owns the Money?' Currency, Property, and Popular Sovereignty in Nicole Oresme's *De moneta*." *Speculum* 92.1 (2017): 85–116.

Wray, L. Randall. *Modern Money Theory: A Primer on Macroeconomics for Sovereign Monetary Systems*. 2nd ed. Houndmills, UK: Palgrave Macmillan, 2015.

Wu Liyu 吴丽娱. "Shiyan de huobi zuoyong yu zhebozhi de fazhan: jian lun chaoyin zhidu de qiyuan" 食鹽的貨幣作用與折博制的發展: 兼论钞引制度的起源. *Zhongguo jingji shi yanjiu* 中国经济史研究 1994.4: 94–102.

Wu Songdi 吴松弟. *Nan Song renkou shi* 南宋人口史. Shanghai: Shanghai guji chubanshe, 2008.

Xianyangshi bowuguan 咸阳市博物馆. "Xianyang faxiande Yuandai zhibi" 咸阳发现的元代纸币. *Kaogu yu wenwu* 考古与文物1980.3: 70–76.

Xie Yuanlu 谢元鲁. "Dui 'Chubi pu' he 'Qianbi pu' zuozhe ji xiezuo shidai de zairenshi" 对 «楮币谱» 和 «钱币谱» 作者及写作时代的再认识. *Zhongguo qianbi* 中国钱币 1996.1: 3–6.

"Songdai Sichuan zaozhi yinshua jishu de fazhan yu jiaozi de chansheng" 宋代四川造纸印刷技术的发展与交子的产生. *Zhongguo qianbi* 中国钱币 1996.3: 21–25.

Yamada Katsuyoshi 山田勝芳. *Kahei no Chūgoku kodaishi* 貨幣の中国古代史. Tokyo: Asahi shinbunsha, 2000.

"Ō Mō dai no zaisei" 王莽代の財政. *Tōyōshi kenkyū* 東洋史研究 33.1 (1975): 63–85.

Yamane, Yukio. "Reforms in the Service Levy System in the Fifteenth and Sixteenth Centuries." In Linda Grove and Christian Daniels (eds.), *State and Society in China: Japanese Perspectives on Ming–Qing Social and Economic History*. Tokyo: University of Tokyo Press, 1984, pp. 279–310.

Yang Jun 杨君. "Jinchao tongqian huobi liutong zhucang xingtai guankui: yi chutu Jinchao huobi shiwu wei zhongxin" 金朝铜钱货币流通贮藏形态管窥: 以出土金朝货币实物为中心. *Zhongguo qianbi* 中国钱币 2015.6: 3–11.

Yang Jun 杨君 and Zhang Anhao 张安昊. "'Qiansicang' ban 'Xingzai huiziku' ban kaobian" '千斯仓'版'行在会子库'版考辨. *Zhongguo qianbi* 中国钱币 2023.4: 34–42.

Yang, Lien-sheng. "The Form of the Paper Note *Hui-tzu* of the Southern Sung Dynasty." *Harvard Journal of Asiatic Studies* 16.3–4 (1953): 365–73.

Yao Shuomin 姚朔民, "Dongzhi guanziban kaocha ji (shang, xia)" 东至关子版考察记 (上·下). *Zhongguo qianbi* 中国钱币1994.3: 23–27, 1994.4: 5–10.

"Song zhibiban de zaijiantao" 宋纸币版的再检讨. *Wenwu* 文物2000.4.

Yates, Robin D. S. "The Economic Activities of a Qin Local Administration: Qianling County, Modern Liye, Hunan Province, 222–209 BCE." In Sabattini and Schwermann, *Between Command and Market*, pp. 247–317.

"Yuanlingxian Shuangqiao Yuandai fufu hezangmu" 沅陵县双桥元代夫妇合葬墓. In *Zhongguo kaoguxue nianjian* 中国考古学年鉴. Beijing: Wenwu chubanshe, 1986, p. 182.

Zhang Chuanxi 张传玺. "Zhongguo gudai qiyue xingshide yuan he liu" 中国古代契约形式的源和流. In Zhang, *Qin Han wenti yanjiu* 秦汉问题研究. Revised ed., Beijing: Beijing daxue chubanshe, 1995, pp. 167–86.

(ed.). *Zhongguo lidai qiyue huibian kaoshi* 中国历代契约会编考释. 2 vols. Beijing: Beijing daxue chubanshe, 1995.

Zhang Jiaxiang 张家骧, Wan Anpei 万安培, and Zou Jinwen 邹进文 (eds.). *Zhongguo huobi sixiang shi* 中国货币思想史. 2 vols. Wuhan: Hubei renmin chubanshe, 1981.

Zhang Jinling 张金岭. *Wan Song shiqi caizheng weiji yanjiu* 晚宋时期财政危机研究. Chengdu: Sichuan daxue chubanshe, 2001.

Zhang Tao 张淘 and Jin Chengyu 金程宇. "'*Quan Song wen*' buyi (shang): yi '*Panshi laoren wenji*' wei zhongxin" '全宋文' 补遗 (上): 以'蟠室老人文集'为中心. *Gudian wenxian yanjiu* 古典文献研究 11 (2008): 374–405.

Zhang Zexian 张泽咸. *Tang Wudai fuyi zhidu shicao* 唐五代赋役制度史草. Beijing: Zhonghua shuju, 1986.

Zhang Ziying 张子英. "Cixian faxian Zhiyuan tongxing baochao tongban ji tongyin" 磁县发现至元通行宝钞铜版及铜印. *Zhongguo qianbi* 中国钱币 1993.1: 36–37.

Zhao, Hao, Xiangping Gao, Yuchao Jiang, Yi Lin, Jin Zhu, Sicong Ding, Lijun Deng, and Ji Zhang. "Radio-Carbon Dating an Early Minting Site: The Emergence of Standardised Coinage in China." *Antiquity* 383 (2021): 1161–78.

Zhongguo renmin yinhang Zhongguo lidai huobi bianjizu 中国人民银行中国历代货币编辑组 (ed.). *Zhongguo lidai huobi* 中国历代货币. Beijing: Xinhua chubanshe, 1982.

Zhou Kelin 周克林. "Dachao tongbao qian de xingzhi zhuxingdi jiqi xiangguan wenti" 大朝通宝钱的性质,铸行地及其相关问题. *Zhonggguo guojia bowuguan guankan* 中国国家博物馆馆刊 2018.4: 74–87.

Zhou Quyang 周曲洋. "Nan Song Jing-Hu diqu junshi buji tizhi de goujian yu yunzuo: jian lun Song Yuan Xiang-Fan zhi zhan shili zhi yuanyin 南宋荆湖地区军事补给体制的构建与运作: 兼论宋元襄樊之战失利之原因. *Xueshu yanjiu* 学术研究 2016.3: 139–47.

Zhou Xiang 周祥. *Zhongguo gudai zhichao* 中国古代纸钞. Shanghai: Shanghai renmin chubanshe, 2004.

Zhu Zhongsheng 朱重聖. *Bei Song cha zhi shengchan yu jingying* 北宋茶之生產與經營. Taipei: Xuesheng shuju, 1985.

INDEX

For EU product safety concerns, contact us at Calle de José Abascal, 56–1°,
28003 Madrid, Spain or eugpsr@cambridge.org.

www.ingramcontent.com/pod-product-compliance
Ingram Content Group UK Ltd.
Pitfield, Milton Keynes, MK11 3LW, UK
UKHW022048220926
475880UK00012B/1303

* 9 7 8 1 0 0 9 6 9 9 4 5 7 *